ON THE POWER OF GOD

ON THE POWER OF GOD

(QUÆSTIONES DISPUTATÆ DE POTENTIA DEI)

BY
SAINT THOMAS AQUINAS

(*Three Books in One*)

FIRST BOOK
(QUESTIONS I–III)

LITERALLY TRANSLATED BY THE
ENGLISH DOMINICAN FATHERS

Wipf & Stock
PUBLISHERS
Eugene, Oregon

NIHIL OBSTAT :
GEORGIUS D. SMITH, Ph.D., S.T.D.,
Censor deputatus.

IMPRIMATUR :
✠ JOSEPH BUTT,
Vicarius generalis.

WESTMONASTERII,
die 22a Februarii, 1932.

APPROBATIO ORDINIS

NIHIL OBSTAT :
AUGUSTINUS BARKER, O.P., S.T.B.
THOMAS GILBEY, O.P., S.T.L., Ph.D.

IMPRIMATUR :
BEDA JARRETT, O.P., S.T.L., M.A.,
Prior Provincialis Angliæ.

LONDINI

Wipf and Stock Publishers
199 West 8th Avenue, Suite 3
Eugene, Oregon 97401

On the Power of God
By Aquinas, Thomas
ISBN: 1-59244-721-X
Publication date 6/11/2004
Previously published by The Newman Press, 1932

INTRODUCTION

In the thirteenth century, the public disputation was not only a sort of ecclesiastical tournament arranged for an exceptional and solemn occasion, but also an integral part of a philosophical and theological course of studies. What are now called 'public circles' still take an important place in the curriculum of a Dominican house of studies; they are held every week, while the ordinary 'class circles' are even more frequent.

A Master of Theology in the University of Paris was enjoined to provide public disputations frequently during the year. They were held more or less intermittently by other masters, but by St. Thomas with great frequency and regularity, and particularly during the three years of his first professorship at Paris, when he held them twice a week during term.

With the exception of three or four, these ordinary disputations of St. Thomas were not isolated discussions, but formed a systematic series on the subject-matter of his teaching. It is necessary to notice the difference between these *disputationes ordinariæ* which are edited in the *Quæstiones Disputatæ* and the *disputationes generales* which are edited in the *Quæstiones Quodlibetales*. For in addition to the regular disputations of the teaching course, two solemn disputations were held every year, in Advent and Lent, at which questions of current interest were freely raised by the audience and resolved by the master. They were debates, to use the words of the Blessed Humbert of Romans, *de quolibet ad voluntatem cujuslibet*. The *Quæstiones Quodlibetales* are the record of these twice-a-year disputations held by St. Thomas. They are grouped into questions, but their order is superficial. Arising out of haphazard questions, the subjects debated are scattered, and the more defined unity of theme of the *Quæstiones Disputatæ* is lacking.

Two mornings were normally set apart for a public disputation, and during them lectures in the faculty were suspended. On the first morning, a thesis, picked by the master and announced in advance, was attacked by an audience of masters, bachelors, students and interested visitors, and defended by the bachelor under the direction of the master. The master, strictly speaking, did not dispute, but controlled the discussion and magisterially resolved it. For on the next free morning, he himself reduced to order the difficulties that had been raised, countered them with brief arguments from reason and authority, and then embarked on a detailed exposition and proof of his thesis, afterwards meeting the objections that had been advanced against it.

This *magistralis determinatio* was put into writing by a reporter or the master. The *Quæstiones Disputatæ* record, then, the ordinary debates which constituted such an important part of St. Thomas's course of teaching, not indeed as a Hansard report, but in the form in which he afterwards edited them.[1] Each article represents a disputation. For the sake of convenience the articles in the four longest series of disputations have been grouped into questions.

The *Quæstiones Disputatæ* fall into seven series, arranged in chronological order as follows: on Truth (two hundred and fifty-three disputations in all); on the Power of God (eighty-three disputations); on Evil (one hundred and one disputations); on the Incarnate Word (only five disputations, the course being interrupted by the assigning of St. Thomas from his attendance on the Papal curia at Viterbo to the University of Paris); on Spiritual Creatures (eleven disputations); and on the Virtues (thirty-six disputations).

---

[1] The class atmosphere is suggested by remarks made here and there. For instance, in his course on God's Knowledge (*Quæstiones Disputatæ de Veritate*, Q. II). St. Thomas introduces a discussion of a problem that had apparently cropped up in class: *quæritur et fuit quæsitum incidenter utrum Deus possit facere infinita* (II *de Veritate*, 10).

INTRODUCTION

The disputations on Truth belong to the period of St. Thomas's first professorship at Paris, whence he was sent in 1259 to the papal court as theological lecturer and adviser, residing until 1269 in turn at Anagni, Orvieto, Rome and Viterbo. The two series of disputations on the Power of God and on Evil were written at this time, when he was about his fortieth year and at the full height of his powers. The discussions seem to have been held once a fortnight. According to Mandonnet,[1] the thirty-two disputations in this volume would date from his stay at Anagni (1259–61); according to Grabmann,[2] they would belong to his time at Rome as regent of studies at the Priory of Santa Sabina on the Aventine (1265–67).

The disputations are not linked together with the same logical concatenation as are the articles of the *Summa Theologica*, which was written as a systematic summary of theology for the use of students. They contain an ampler and more leisurely treatment and furnish the material from which St. Thomas constructed great parts of his later synthesis. They are at once untidier and richer. A comparison of the treatment of the same question in the *Summa Theologica* and in the *Quæstiones Disputatæ* will be illustrative; for instance, the problem whether the power or act of creating can be communicated to a creature. In the former (Ia. xlv, 5) there are three objections, a counter-affirmation, an exposition and proof, and the replies to the objections. In the latter (III *de Potentia*, 4) there are sixteen objections, five counter-affirmations, a lengthy exposition leading to a fivefold proof, and the replies to the sixteen objections.

St. Thomas is his own best commentator, and not the least value of this translation is the help it should afford in the study of the *Summa Theologica*.

The translation has been made by Father Lawrence Shapcote, O.P., S.T.L., now residing in South Africa, who has also been the sole translator of the whole of the *Summa Theologica*, and of the *Summa Contra Gentiles*.

THOMAS GILBEY, O.P.

---

[1] *Quæstiones Disputatæ. Introduction.* Paris 1925.
[2] *Einführung in die Summa Theologiæ des heiligen Thomas von Aquin.* Freiburg-im-Breisgau. 1928.

CONTENTS

Question I. On the Power of God

ARTICLE	PAGE
I. Is there power in God?	1
II. Is God's power infinite?	9
III. Are those things possible to God which are impossible to nature?	14
IV. Should we judge a thing to be possible or impossible with reference to lower or to higher causes?	22
V. Can God do what he does not?	26
VI. Can God do what others can do?	34
VII. Is God almighty?	38

Question II. Of God's Generating Power

I. Is there a generative power in God?	42
II. Is generation attributed to God essentially or notionally?	51
III. In the act of generation does the generative power come into action at the command of the will?	55
IV. Can there be several sons in God?	63
V. Is the generative power included in omnipotence?	70
VI. Are the generative and creative powers the same?	74

Question III. Of Creation

I. Can God create a thing from nothing?	78
II. Is creation a change?	88
III. Is creation something real in the creature, and if so, what is it?	91
IV. Is the creative power or act communicable to a creature?	96
V. Can there be anything that is not created by God?	108
VI. Is there but one principle of creation?	111
VII. Does God work in operations of nature?	123

CONTENTS

ARTICLE	PAGE
VIII. DOES GOD WORK IN NATURE BY CREATING?	136
IX. IS THE RATIONAL SOUL BROUGHT INTO BEING BY CREATION OR IS IT TRANSMITTED THROUGH THE SEMEN?	145
X. IS THE RATIONAL SOUL CREATED IN THE BODY?	161
XI. IS THE SENSIBLE AND VEGETAL SOUL CREATED OR IS IT TRANSMITTED THROUGH THE SEMEN?	170
XII. IS THE SENSIBLE OR VEGETAL SOUL IN THE SEMEN FROM THE BEGINNING OF THE LATTER'S SEPARATION?	180
XIII. CAN THAT WHICH PROCEEDS FROM ANOTHER BE ETERNAL?	185
XIV. IS IT POSSIBLE FOR THAT WHICH DIFFERS FROM GOD ESSENTIALLY TO HAVE ALWAYS EXISTED?	188
XV. DID THINGS PROCEED FROM GOD OF NATURAL NECESSITY OR BY THE DECREE OF HIS WILL?	196
XVI. CAN A MULTITUDE OF THINGS PROCEED FROM ONE FIRST THING?	205
XVII. HAS THE WORLD ALWAYS EXISTED?	219
XVIII. WERE THE ANGELS CREATED BEFORE THE VISIBLE WORLD?	235
XIX. WAS IT POSSIBLE FOR THE ANGELS TO EXIST BEFORE THE VISIBLE WORLD?	246

ON THE POWER OF GOD

QUESTION I

ON THE POWER OF GOD

THERE are seven points of inquiry: (1) Is there power in God? (2) Is God's power infinite? (3) Can God do what nature cannot do? (4) Is a thing to be judged possible or impossible in reference to lower or to higher causes? (5) Can God do what he does not, or leave undone what he does? (6) Can God do whatever others do, for instance, can he sin, walk, etc.? (7) Is God all-powerful?

ARTICLE I

IS THERE POWER IN GOD?
Sum. Th. I, Q. xxv, A. 1: *C.G.* I, 16; II, 7

THE question before us concerns God's power: the first point of inquiry is whether there is power in God. And it would seem that the reply should be in the negative.

1. Power is a principle of operation. Now God's operation, which is his essence, has no principle, since neither is it begotten nor does it proceed. Therefore power is not in God.

2. Whatever is most perfect should be ascribed to God, according to Anselm (*Monolog.* xiv). Hence that which implies a relation to something more perfect should not be ascribed to God. But all power bears a relation to something more perfect, namely a passive form and an active operation. Therefore we should not ascribe power to God.

3. Power according to the Philosopher (*Metaph.* v, 12), denotes a principle of transmutation terminating in another thing as such. Now a principle indicates relationship: and power is the relation of God to his creatures, significative of his ability to create or move them. But no such relation is really in God, but only in our way of thinking. Therefore power is not really in God.

4. Habit is more perfect than power, since it is closer to operation. But there are no habits in God. Neither, therefore, is there power in him.

5. No expression should be employed that is derogatory to God's primacy or simplicity. Now God by virtue of his simplicity, and considered as first agent, acts by his essence. Therefore we should not speak of him as acting by his power, which at least in its manner of signifying connotes something added to his essence.

6. According to the Philosopher (*Phys.* iii, 4), in everlasting things there is no difference between actual being and possible being: and much more must this be the case in God. Now where two things are identical, they should have one name taken from the more dignified. But essence is more dignified than power, because power is an addition to essence. Therefore we should speak only of God's essence and not of his power.

7. As primary matter is pure potentiality (*potentia*), so is God pure act. Now primary matter considered in its essence is entirely void of act. Therefore God considered in his essence is void of all power (*potentia*).

8. Any power apart from its act is imperfect, so that as no imperfection may be ascribed to God, such a power cannot be in him. If then there is power in God, it must needs be always united to its act, and consequently the power to create will always be united to the act of creation: so that it will follow that God created things from eternity: which is heretical.

9. When one thing suffices for a certain action, it is superfluous to add another. But God's essence suffices for God to act through it. Therefore it is superfluous to say that he has power whereby to act.

10. To this you may reply that God's power differs from his essence, not really but only in our way of thinking.—On the contrary, a concept to which there is no corresponding reality is void and senseless.

11. Substance is the most excellent of the predicaments; and yet, as Augustine asserts, it is not ascribed to God (*De Trin.* vii, 6). Much less, therefore, is the predicament of quality. Now power is assigned to the second species of quality. Therefore it should not be ascribed to God.

12. You will say, perhaps, that power as attributed to God is not a quality, but the very essence of God, differing therefrom but logically.—On the contrary, either there is something real corresponding to this logical distinction, or there is nothing. If nothing, the objection fails. If something, then it follows that in God power is in addition to his essence, even as the notion of power is distinct from the notion of essence.

13. According to the Philosopher (*Topic.* iv, 5) all power or energy is for the sake of some eligible end. But nothing of this kind can be said of God, since he is not for the sake of something else. Therefore power is unbecoming to God.

14. According to Dionysius (*De Cœl. Hier.* xi) energy is a medium between substance and work. But God does not work through a medium. Therefore he does not work by energy, nor consequently by power: and thus it follows that power is not in God.

15. According to the Philosopher (*Metaph.* v, 12; ix, 1) active power, which alone can be ascribed to God, is a principle of transmutation terminating in another thing as such. But God acts without transmutation: for instance, in the creation. Therefore active power cannot be attributed to God.

16. The Philosopher says (*ibid.*) that active and passive power are in the same subject. But passive power is unbecoming to God. Therefore active power is also.

17. The Philosopher says (*ibid.*) that a contrary privation attaches to an active power. Now it is in the nature of contraries to have the same subject. Since then there can nowise be privation in God, neither can power be in him.

18. The Master says (II *D*. i.) that action is not properly speaking attributable to God. But where action is not, there can be no power, active or passive. Therefore no kind of power is in God.

On the contrary, it is written (Ps. lxxxviii, 9) : *Thou art mighty, O Lord, and thy truth is round about thee.*

Again it is written (Matt. iii, 9) : *God is able of these stones to raise up children to Abraham.*

Moreover, all operation proceeds from power. Now operation is supremely attributable to God. Therefore power is most becoming to God.

I answer that to make the point at issue clear we must observe that we speak of power in relation to act. Now act is twofold ; the first act which is a form, and the second act which is operation. Seemingly the word ' act ' was first universally employed in the sense of operation, and then, secondly, transferred to indicate the form, inasmuch as the form is the principle and end of operation. Wherefore in like manner power is twofold : active power corresponding to that act which is operation—and seemingly it was in this sense that the word ' power ' was first employed :—and passive power, corresponding to the first act or the form,—to which seemingly the name of power was subsequently given.

Now, just as nothing suffers save by reason of a passive power, so nothing acts except by reason of the first act, namely the form. For it has been stated that this first act is so called from action. Now God is act both pure and primary, wherefore it is most befitting to him to act and communicate his likeness to other things : and consequently active power is most becoming to him : since power is called active forasmuch as it is a principle of action. We must also observe that our mind strives to describe God as a most perfect being. And seeing that it is unable to get at him save by likening him to his effects, while it fails to find any creature so supremely perfect as to be wholly devoid of imperfection, consequently it endeavours to describe him as possessing the various perfections it discovers in creatures, although each of those perfections is in some way at fault, yet so as to remove from God whatever imperfection is connected with them. For instance, *being* denotes something complete and simple, yet non-subsistent: *substance* denotes something subsistent, yet the subject of something. Accordingly we ascribe being and substance to God; but substance by reason of subsistence not of substanding; and being by reason of simplicity and completeness, not of inherence whereby it inheres to something. In like manner we ascribe to God operation by reason of its being the ultimate perfection, not by reason of that into which operation passes. And we attribute power to God by reason of that which is permanent and is the principle of power, and not by reason of that which is made complete by operation.

Reply to the First Objection. Power is a principle not only of the operation but also of the effect. Hence it does not follow if power be in God as the principle of his effect, that it is a principle of God's essence which is his operation.—Another and a better reply is that there is a twofold relation in God. One is real, that namely, by which the persons are mutually distinct, for instance, paternity and filiation; otherwise the divine persons would be distinct not really but logically, as Sabellius maintained. The other kind of relation is logical, and is indicated when we say that the divine operation comes from the divine essence, or that God works by his essence: for prepositions indicate some kind of relationship. This is because when we attribute to God operation considered as requiring a principle, we attribute to him also the relationship of that which derives its existence from a principle, wherefore such relation is only logical. Now operation involves a principle, whereas essence does not: hence, although the divine essence has no principle, neither really nor logically, yet the divine operation has a principle in our way of thinking.

Reply to the Second Objection. Although all that is most perfect should be attributed to God, it does not follow that whatsoever is attributed to him is most perfect, but that it is suitable to designate that which is most perfect. The reason is that to a most perfect thing something may be attributed, so far as it is itself perfect, which however admits of something else more perfect still, though lacking the perfection which the other has.

Reply to the Third Objection. Power is said to be a principle, not as though it were the very relation signified by the name principle, but because it is identical with the principle.

Reply to the Fourth Objection. Habit is never in an active power, but only in a passive power, and is more perfect than it : such a power, however, is not attributed to God.

Reply to the Fifth Objection. It is absurd to say that though God works by his essence there is no power in God. Because that which is a principle of action is a power : wherefore the mere fact that God works by his essence implies that there is power in God. Hence the notion of power in God does not derogate from his simplicity or his primacy, since it does not indicate something in addition to his essence.

Reply to the Sixth Objection. The statement that in everlasting things there is no difference between actual being and possible being, refers to passive power : consequently it has no bearing on the point at issue, because no such power is in God. Nevertheless, since it is true that active power in God is identical with his essence, we must reply that although the divine essence and power are the same in reality, yet seeing that power by its manner of signification indicates something in addition, it requires a special name : for names correspond to ideas, as the Philosopher says (*Periherm.* i).

Reply to the Seventh Objection. This argument proves that there is no passive power in God : and this we grant.

Reply to the Eighth Objection. God's power is always united to act, i.e. to operation (for operation is the divine essence) : but the effects follow according as his will commands and his wisdom ordains. Consequently it does not follow that his power is always united to its effect, or that creatures have existed from eternity.

Reply to the Ninth Objection. God's essence suffices for

him to act thereby : and yet his power is not superfluous : because it is understood not as a thing in addition to his essence, but as connoting in our way of thinking the sole relation of a principle : for from the mere fact that the essence is the principle of action it follows that it has the formality of power.

Reply to the Tenth Objection. The reality corresponds to the concept in two ways. First, immediately, that is to say, when the intellect conceives the idea of a thing existing outside the mind, for instance, a man or a stone. Secondly, mediately, when, namely, something follows the act of the intellect, and the intellect considers it by reflecting on itself. So that the reality corresponds to that consideration of the intellect mediately, that is to say, through the medium of the intellect's concept of the thing. For instance, the intellect understands animal nature in a man, a horse, and many other species : and consequently it understands that nature as a genus : to this act, however, whereby the intellect understands a genus, there does not correspond immediately outside the mind a thing that is a genus ; and yet there is something that corresponds to the thought that is the foundation of this mental process. It is the same with the relation of principle that power adds to essence : since something corresponds to it in reality, not however immediately, but mediately. For our mind conceives the creature as bearing a relation to and dependent on its Creator : and for this very reason, being unable to conceive one thing related to another, without on the other hand conceiving that relation to be reciprocal, it conceives in God a certain relation of principle, consequent to its mode of understanding, which relation is referred to the thing mediately.

Reply to the Eleventh Objection. The power that is assigned to the second species of quality is not ascribed to God : it belongs to creatures who do not act immediately through their essential forms, but through the medium of accidental forms, whereas God acts immediately by his essence.

Reply to the Twelfth Objection. Something does indeed

correspond in the divine reality to our various concepts of the divine attributes, but that something is one and the same. Because our mind is compelled to represent by means of various forms, that most simple being which is God, by reason of his incomprehensibility : so that these various forms which our mind conceives about God, are indeed in God as the cause of truth, in so far as the thing which is God can be represented by all these forms : nevertheless they are in our mind as their subject.

Reply to the Thirteenth Objection. The saying of the Philosopher applies to active and effective powers and the like, as applied to the productions of art and human activity : since not even in the physical order is it always true that an active power is for the sake of its effects. Thus it were absurd to say that the power of the sun is for the sake of the worms produced by its power : and much less is the divine power for the sake of its effects.

Reply to the Fourteenth Objection. God's power is not a medium in reality, since it differs not from his essence except logically : which suffices for our speaking of it as though it were a medium. But God does not work through a medium that is really distinct from himself : wherefore the argument fails.

Reply to the Fifteenth Objection. Action is twofold. One is accompanied by transmutation of matter ; the other presupposes no matter, for instance, creation : and God can act either way, as we shall see further on. Hence active power may rightly be ascribed to God, although he does not always act by causing a change in something.

Reply to the Sixteenth Objection. The Philosopher's statement is not general but particular, and applies to a thing which, like an animal, causes its own movement. When, however, one thing is moved by another, passive and active power do not coincide.

Reply to the Seventeenth Objection. The privation that is contrary to power is impotence. But we must not speak of contraries in connection with God, because nothing in God has a contrary, since he is not in a genus.

Reply to the Eighteenth Objection. We do not remove

action as such from God, but that kind of action which belongs to nature, where things are at the same time active and passive.

ARTICLE II

IS GOD'S POWER INFINITE?
Sum. Th. I, Q. xxv, A. 2: *C.G.* I, 43

THE second point of inquiry is whether God's power is infinite: and it would seem that it is not.

1. It is stated in *Metaph.* ix, 1, that in nature any active power that has no corresponding passive power is fruitless. But no passive power in nature corresponds to an infinite power in God. Therefore an infinite power in God would be fruitless.

2. The Philosopher proves (*Phys.* viii, 10) that a thing of finite magnitude has not infinite power: since if it had it would act in no time. Because the greater power acts in less time: wherefore the greater the power the less the time. But there is no proportion between an infinite and a finite power. Neither, therefore, is there proportion between the time taken by the action of an infinite power, and that taken by the action of a finite power. Yet between any time and any other time there is proportion. Therefore since a finite power takes time to move, an infinite power will move in no time. For the same reason if God's power is infinite, it will always act without time: but this is false.

3. To this you may reply that God's will determines in how much time he will bring his effects to completion. —On the contrary, God's will cannot change his omnipotence. But it is natural to an infinite power to act without time. Therefore this cannot be changed by God's will.

4. A power is made known by its effect. But God cannot produce an infinite effect. Therefore his power is not infinite.

5. Power is proportionate to operation. But God's operation is simple. Therefore his power is simple also

But the simple and the infinite are mutually incompatible. Therefore the same conclusion follows.

6. Infinity is an attribute of quantity according to the Philosopher (*Phys.* i, 1). But in God there is neither quantity nor magnitude. Therefore his power cannot be infinite.

7. Whatever is distinct is finite. But God's power is distinct from other things. Therefore it is finite.

8. The infinite denotes something endless. Now end is threefold: the end of a magnitude, as a point; the end of perfection, as a form; and the end of intention, as a final cause. But the last two since they belong to perfection must not be removed from God. Therefore the divine power is not infinite.

9. If God's power be infinite, this can only be because it is concerned with infinite effects. But there are many other things which have effects potentially infinite; thus the intellect can understand an infinite number of things potentially, and the sun can produce an infinite number of things. If, then, God's power be infinite, for the same **reason** many other powers will be infinite: which is impossible.

10. Finish is something excellent: and all that is excellent should be ascribed to God. Therefore God's power should be described as finite.

11. According to the Philosopher (*Phys.* iii, 6) infinity implies parts and **matter**: which imply imperfection and are unbecoming to God. Therefore there is no infinity in God's power.

12. According to the Philosopher (*Phys.* i, 6) a term is neither finite nor infinite. But God's power is the term of all things. Therefore it is not infinite.

13. God works with his whole power. If then his power be infinite, his effect will be always infinite: and this is impossible.

On the contrary, Damascene says that the infinite is that which neither time nor place nor mind can grasp. Now this is becoming to the divine power. Therefore God's power is infinite.

Further, Hilary says (*De Trin.* viii) that *God's power is immeasurable; he is the living mighty One, ever present, never failing.* Now that which is immeasurable is infinite. Therefore God's power is infinite.

I answer that a thing is said to be infinite in two ways. First, by way of privation; thus a thing is said to be infinite, when it is in its nature to have an end, and yet it has none: but such infinity is found only in quantities. Secondly, by way of negation, when it has no end. Infinity cannot be ascribed to God in the former sense, both because in him there is not quantity, and because all privation denotes imperfection, which is far removed from God. On the other hand infinity in the second sense is ascribed to God and to all that is in him, because he himself, his essence, his wisdom, his power, his goodness are all without limit, wherefore in him all is infinite.

With special regard to the infinity of his power it must be observed that whereas active power answers to act, the quantity of a power depends on the quantity of the act: since the more actual a thing is the more it abounds in active power. Now God is infinite act: for act can be finite in two ways only. First, on the part of the agent: thus an architect by his will sets definite bounds to the beauty of a house. Secondly, on the part of the recipient: thus the heat of a furnace is limited by and its intensity depends upon the disposition of the fuel. Now God's action is not limited by any agent, because it proceeds from no other but himself: nor is it limited by any recipient, because since there is no passive potency in him, he is pure self-subsistent act. Wherefore it is clear that God is infinite: and this can be made evident as follows: The being of man is limited to the species of man, because it is received into the nature of the human species: the same applies to the being of a horse, or of any other creature. But the being of God, since it is not received into anything, but is pure being, is not limited to any particular mode of a perfection of being, but contains all being within itself: and thus as being taken in its widest sense can extend to an infinity of things, so the divine being is infinite: and hence it is clear that his might or active power is infinite. But we must note that, although his power is infinite by reason of his essence, nevertheless from the very fact that we refer it to the things whereof it is the source, it has a certain mode of infinity which the essence has not.

For in the objects of power there is a certain multitude, in action also there is a certain intensity—according to its efficiency, so that a certain infinity may be ascribed to active power after the manner of the infinity of quantity, whether continuous or discrete. Of discrete quantity, forasmuch as the quantity of a power is measured by many or few objects,—and this is called extensive quantity: of continuous quantity, forasmuch as the quantity of a power is measured by the intensity or slackness of its action, —and this is called intensive quantity. The former quantity is ascribed to power in respect of its objects, the latter in respect of its action: and active power is the principle of both. In both ways the divine power is infinite: since never does it produce so many effects that it cannot produce more; nor does it ever act with such intensity, that it cannot act more intensely. But in the divine operation intensity is not measured according as operation is in the operator, for then it is always infinite, since God's operation is his essence, but according as it attains its effect, for thus some things are moved by God more efficaciously, some less.

Reply to the First Objection. Nothing in God can be called fruitless: for a fruitless thing is one that is directed to an end which it cannot attain: whereas God and all that is in him, are not directed to an end, but are the end. Or we may reply that the Philosopher is speaking of a natural active power. For there is co-ordination in the things of nature, and in all created things: whereas God is outside that order, since to him as an extrinsic good is the whole of it directed, as the army to the commander-in-chief, as the Philosopher says (*Metaph.* xii, 10). Consequently there is no need in creatures for a power corresponding to God's power.

Reply to the Second Objection. According to the commentator (*Phys.* viii, com. 79) this argument drawn from the proportion between time and the mover's power means that a magnitude's infinite power is proportionate to an infinity of time, since they both belong to one definite genus, i.e. continuous quantity; but it does not hold with regard to an infinity apart from magnitude, that is not proportionate to an infinity of time, since it is of another kind. It may also be replied, as hinted in the objection, that since God acts by his will, he adapts the movement of whatever he moves, according as he wills.

Reply to the Third Objection. Although God's will cannot change his power, it can limit its effect: because the will is the motive force of power.

Reply to the Fourth Objection. The very notion of being made or created is incompatible with the infinite. The very fact that it is made out of nothing, argues its imperfection and potentiality, and shows that it is not pure act: and consequently it cannot be equalled to the infinite, as though it also were infinite.

Reply to the Fifth Objection. Privative infinity is an attribute of quantity and is repugnant to simplicity; whereas negative infinity is not.

Reply to the Sixth Objection. This argument applies to infinity taken as a privation.

Reply to the Seventh Objection. A thing may be distinct in two ways. First, by some kind of adjunct; thus man is distinct from an ass by the difference of reason: and a distinct thing of this kind must needs be finite, because the adjunct defines it as a particular thing. Secondly, by itself; and thus God is distinct from other things: and this for the simple reason that it is impossible to add anything to him: hence it does not follow that he is finite, either in himself or as regards anything that is attributed to him.

Reply to the Eighth Objection. Since end implies perfection, it is ascribed to God in the highest possible way; namely, that he is essentially the end, and not denominatively finite.

Reply to the Ninth Objection. As in quantities we may consider infinity in regard to one dimension, and not in regard to another, or again in regard to all dimensions; even so may we consider infinity in effects. Thus it is possible for a creature considered in itself to be able to produce an infinity of effects in some particular respect, for instance, as regards number in one species ; and then the nature of all those effects is finite, being confined to one particular species—for instance, an infinite number of men or asses. But it is impossible for a creature to be able to produce an infinity of effects in every way, in point of number, species and genera : this belongs to God alone, wherefore his power alone is simply infinite.

The reply to the Tenth Objection is the same as to the Eighth.

Reply to the Eleventh Objection. This argument takes infinity as a privation : and the same answer applies to the Twelfth Objection.

Reply to the Thirteenth Objection. God always works with the whole of his power. But his effect is limited according to the determination of his will and the order of reason.

ARTICLE III

ARE THOSE THINGS POSSIBLE TO GOD WHICH ARE IMPOSSIBLE TO NATURE ?

THE third point of inquiry is whether God can do what nature cannot : and the reply seemingly should be in the negative.

1. The (ordinary) gloss on Romans xi, 24 says that since God is the author of nature he cannot do what is contrary to nature. Now things that nature cannot do are contrary to nature. Therefore God cannot do them.

2. As all that is necessary in nature can be demonstrated, so whatsoever is impossible in nature can be disproved by demonstration. Now every conclusion of a demonstration involves the principles of that demonstration : and all principles of demonstration imply the principle that yes and no cannot be both true at the same time. Therefore this principle is involved whenever a thing is impossible to

nature. But according to the respondent God cannot make yes or no to be both true at the same time. Therefore he cannot do what is naturally impossible.

3. There are two principles under God, reason and nature. Now God cannot do what is impossible to reason, for instance, that a genus be not predicated of its species. Neither therefore can he do what is impossible to nature.

4. As false and true are in relation to knowledge, so are possible and impossible to operation. Now God cannot know what is false in nature; therefore he cannot do what is impossible in nature.

5. So far as there is uniformity among a number of things, what is proved of one is taken to be proved of all: thus if it be proved of one triangle that the three angles equal two right angles, we take this to be proved of all triangles. Now all impossible things apparently agree in the point of their being possible or impossible to God: both in relation to the doer, since God's power is infinite, and in relation to the thing done, since everything has an obediential potentiality to God. Therefore, if there be anything naturally impossible that God cannot do, seemingly he cannot do anything that is impossible.

6. It is written (2 Tim. ii, 13) that God is *faithful, he cannot deny himself.* But he would deny himself, says the (interlinear) gloss, if he fulfilled not his promise. Now, as God's promise comes from God, so is all truth from God: because (according to a gloss of Ambrose[1] on 1 Corinthians xii, 3, *No man can say, the Lord Jesus, but by the Holy Ghost*) all truth, by whomsoever uttered, is from the Holy Ghost. Therefore God cannot act counter to the truth. He would, however, were he to do what is impossible. Therefore he cannot do what is naturally impossible.

7. Anselm says (*Cur Deus homo*, i, 24) that God cannot do what is in the least way unbecoming. Now it would be unbecoming for yes and no to be true at the same time, because the mind would be in a fix. Therefore God cannot do this; and consequently he cannot do whatever is impossible to nature.

[1] Ambrosiaster.

8. No artist can work counter to his art, since this is the very principle of his work. But God would be working against his art, were he to do what is impossible in nature, because the order of nature, in relation to which that thing is impossible, is a reflection of the divine art. Therefore God cannot do what is naturally impossible.

9. That which is impossible in itself is more impossible than what is impossible accidentally. Now God cannot do what is accidentally impossible, for instance, that what has been should not have been; thus Jerome says (Ep. 22, *Ad Eustoch., de cust. virg.*) that God, whereas he can do other things, cannot make a virgin of one who is not a virgin. See also Augustine (*Contra Faust.* xxvi, 5) and the Philosopher (*Ethic.* vi, 2). Therefore God cannot do what is in itself naturally impossible.

1. *On the contrary,* it is written (Luke i, 37): *No word shall be impossible with God.*

2. Any power that can do one thing, but not another, is limited. If, then, God can do what is possible to nature, but not that which is impossible, or some that are impossible and not others, it would seem that his is a limited power, which is contrary to what we have proved above. Therefore, etc.

3. That which is uncircumscribed by anything in existence, cannot be hindered by anything in existence. Now God is uncircumscribed by anything in existence. Therefore nothing in existence can be a hindrance to him: so that the truth of the principle of contradiction cannot be a hindrance to God's action. The same applies to all other principles.

4. Privation is not susceptive of degrees. Now the impossible connotes privation of power. Therefore if God can do one impossible thing, for instance restore sight to the blind, it would seem that he can do all.

5. All resistance is by reason of opposition. But nothing can oppose God's power, as shown above. Therefore nothing can resist it: and so he can do all things impossible.

6. As blindness is opposed to sight, so is virginity opposed to birth-giving. Now God made a virgin to give birth and

yet remain a virgin. Therefore he can equally make a blind man to see while remaining blind, and he can make yes and no to be true at the same time, and consequently all impossible things.

7. It is more difficult to unite diverse substantial forms, than diverse accidental forms. Now God united together the most diverse substantial forms, namely the divine and human natures, which differ as uncreated and created. Much more, therefore, can he unite two accidental forms, so that the same thing be black and white: and thus the same conclusion follows.

8. If we deny of the thing defined part of its definition, it will follow that contrary statements are true at the same time; for instance, if we were to say that a man is not a rational being. Now it is part of the definition of a straight line that its extremities are points. Therefore if anyone were to deny this of a straight line, it would follow that two contrary statements are simultaneously true. Now God did this when he came in to his disciples, the doors being closed: since two bodies were then in the same place, so that two lines would have terminated in two points only, and each of them also in two points. Consequently God can make yes and no to be true at the same time, and therefore he can do all things impossible.

I answer that according to the Philosopher (*Metaph.* v, 12) a thing is said to be possible or impossible in three ways. First, in respect of a power active or passive: thus it is possible for a man to walk in respect of his ability to walk, whereas it is impossible for him to fly. Secondly, not in respect of a power but in itself: thus we say that a thing is possible if it be not impossible, and that a thing is impossible which of necessity is not. Thirdly, a thing is said to be possible in respect of mathematical power, as we say in geometry; thus a certain line is potentially measurable, because its square is measurable. Omitting this last kind of possibility, let us consider the other two. It must be noted that a thing is said to be impossible, not in respect of any power, but in itself, by reason of the mutual exclusion of terms. Now all such mutual exclusion corresponds to some opposition : and every opposition connotes affirmation and negation, as is proved in *Metaph.* x, 4, so that all impossibilities of this kind imply the mutual exclusion of an affirmation and a negation. That this cannot be ascribed to any active power is proved as follows. All active power is consequent upon the actuality and entity of the thing to which it belongs. Now every agent has a natural tendency to produce its like : wherefore every act of an active power terminates in being. For although at times non-being is the result of an action, such as, for instance, corruption, this is simply because the being of one thing is incompatible with the being of another ; thus the being of a hot thing is incompatible with the being of a cold thing : wherefore the chief purpose of heat is to generate heat, but that it destroys cold is by way of consequence. Now, for yes and no to be true at the same time cannot have the nature of being, nor even of non-being, since being removes non-being, and non-being removes being : and consequently it can be neither the principal nor the secondary term of action of an active power.

On the other hand a thing is said to be impossible in respect of a power in two ways. First, on account of an inherent defect in the power, in that the effect is beyond its reach, as when a natural agent cannot transform a certain matter. Secondly, when the impossibility arises from without, as in the case of a power that is hindered or tied. Accordingly there are three ways in which it is said to be impossible for a thing to be done. First, by reason of a defect in the active power, whether in transforming matter, or in any other way. Secondly, by reason of a resistant or an obstacle. Thirdly, because that which is said to be impossible cannot be the term of an action. Those things, then, which are impossible to nature in the first or second way are possible to God : because, since his power is infinite, it is subject to no defect, nor is there any matter that he cannot transform at will, since his power is irresistible. On the other hand those things which involve the third kind of impossibility God cannot do, since he is supreme act and **sovereign being** : wherefore his action cannot terminate otherwise than principally in being, and secondarily in non-being. Consequently he cannot make yes and no to be true at the same time, nor any of those things which involve such an impossibility. Nor is he said to be unable to do these things through lack of power, but through lack of possibility, such things being intrinsically impossible : and this is what is meant by those who say that ' God can do it, but it cannot be done.'

Reply to the First Objection. Augustine's words quoted in the gloss mean, not that God is unable to do otherwise than nature does, since his works are often contrary to the wonted course of nature ; but that whatever he does in things is not contrary to nature, but is nature in them, forasmuch as he is the author and controller of nature. Thus in the physical order we observe that when an inferior body is moved by a higher, the movement is natural to it, although it may not seem in keeping with the movement which it has by reason of its own nature : thus the tidal movement of the sea is caused by the moon ; and this movement is natural to it as the Commentator observes (*De cœlo et mundo*, iii, comm. 20), although water of itself has naturally a downward movement. Thus in all creatures, what God does in them is quasi-natural to them. Wherefore we distinguish in them a twofold potentiality : a natural potentiality in respect of their proper operations and movements, and another, which we call obediential, in respect of what is done in them by God.

Reply to the Second Objection. Every impossibility involves the incompatibility of affirmation and negation as such. Those things, however, that are impossible by reason of a lack of the natural power, such as that a blind man can be made to see, and the like, since they are not intrinsically impossible, do not involve such an impossibility in themselves, but only in relation to the natural power to which they are impossible. Thus were we to say that nature can make a blind man to see, the statement would involve an impossibility of this kind, because nature's power is confined to definite effects, beyond which is the effect we would ascribe to it.

Reply to the Third Objection. Philosophical reasoning regards impossibilities not in relation to a power, but in themselves: because it does not consider things in their application to matter or to any natural power.

Reply to the Fourth Objection. That which is naturally false is false simply; hence there is no comparison.

Reply to the Fifth Objection. Impossibilities are not all in the same ratio: since some things are impossible in themselves, and some with respect to a power, as above stated. Nor does the fact that they bear different relations to the divine power militate against the infinity of that power, or the obedience of the creature thereto.

Reply to the Sixth Objection. God does not destroy what is already true: because he does not make that which was true not to have been: but he does make that which otherwise had been true, not to be true. Thus when he raises the dead to life, he makes it to be untrue that he is dead, which would have been true otherwise.—Or we may reply, that there is no comparison, since were God not to keep his promise, it would follow that he is untruthful: whereas this does not follow if he undoes what he has done: because he has not decreed that whatever he does should always remain so, as he has ordained to keep his promise.

Reply to the Seventh Objection. God cannot make yes and no to be true at the same time, not because it is unbecoming, but for the reason stated above.

Reply to the Eighth Objection. God's art extends not only to the things made but to many others also. Hence when he changes the course of nature in anything, he does not therefore act against his art.

Reply to the Ninth Objection. It is accidentally impossible for Socrates not to have run, if he did run: since that Socrates runs or runs not, considered in itself, is a contingency: yet since it would imply that what has been has not been, it becomes impossible in itself. Hence it is said to be impossible accidentally, that is through some adventitious circumstance: which circumstance is impossible in itself, and clearly involves a contradiction: since to say that a thing has been, and that it has not been are contradictory statements : which would be the case if the past were made not to have been.

Reply to the First Objection on the other side. A word is not only uttered by the lips but is also conceived in the mind. Now the mind cannot conceive yes and no as being true at the same time (*Metaph.* iv, 3), and therefore it cannot conceive anything in which this is involved. For otherwise since, according to the Philosopher, contrary opinions involve contrary statements, it would follow that the same person would have contrary opinions at the same time. Wherefore it is not contrary to the angel's statement to say that God cannot do the above-mentioned kind of impossibility.

Reply to the Second Objection. God cannot do this kind of impossibility because it is outside the range of possibility : wherefore God's power is not said to be limited, although he cannot do it.

Reply to the Third Objection. God is said to be unable to do this, not as though he were prevented by the free-will, as stated above, but because this cannot be the term of action of an active power.

Reply to the Fourth Objection. Privation as such is not susceptive of degrees, but it can be in respect of its cause : thus a man who has lost an eye is more blind than one who is prevented from seeing by some disease of the eye. In like manner that which is impossible in itself may be said to be more impossible than a thing which is impossible simply.

Reply to the Fifth Objection. As stated above, God is said to be unable to do this, not because something prevents him, but for the reasons given.

Reply to the Sixth Objection. Virginity is not opposed to child-bearing as blindness to sight : it is opposed to copulation without which nature cannot cause a child to be born, whereas God can.

Reply to the Seventh Objection. The created and uncreated, though disparate, were not in Christ in the same respect, but in respect of the different natures : hence it does not follow that God can make opposite things to be in the same subject and in the same respect.

Reply to the Eighth Objection. When Christ entered, the doors being closed, and two bodies were in the same place, nothing occurred contrary to the principles of geometry. For then not one but two lines terminated in two points of different bodies on the one side. Although two mathematical lines are not distinguishable except by their position, so that one cannot conceive two such lines to be in the same place : nevertheless two natural lines are distinguishable by their subjects, so that, granted that two bodies occupy the same place, it follows that two lines coincide, as well as two points, and two surfaces.

ARTICLE IV

SHOULD WE JUDGE A THING TO BE POSSIBLE OR IMPOSSIBLE WITH REFERENCE TO LOWER OR TO HIGHER CAUSES ?

THE fourth point of inquiry is whether we ought to judge of a thing's possibility or impossibility in reference to its lower or its higher causes. And it would seem that we should consider its higher causes.

1. The (interlinear) gloss on 1 Corinthians i says that the folly of the wise men of the world consisted in their judging of possibility and impossibility by observing nature. Therefore we should judge a thing to be possible or impossible by considering not its lower but its higher causes.

2. According to the Philosopher (*Metaph*. x, 1), that which is first in any genus is the measure of whatsoever is included in that genus. Now God's power is the first power. Therefore a thing should be deemed possible or impossible in reference to it.

3. The more a cause penetrates its effect, the better it serves as a guide to our judgement of the effect. Now the First Cause reaches further into the effect than do secondary causes. Therefore we should rather judge of an effect by referring to the First Cause : and consequently we should deem a thing possible or impossible in relation to the higher causes.

4. To give sight to a blind man is impossible with respect to the lower causes: and yet it is possible, since sometimes it is done. Therefore we should judge of a thing's impossibility not according to the lower but according to the higher causes.

5. Before the world existed it was possible that it would exist. But this possibility did not rest on lower causes. Therefore the same conclusion follows.

1. *On the contrary* an effect should be adjudged possible in reference to the cause on which its possibility is based. Now an effect derives its possibility, contingency or even necessity from its proximate and not from its remote cause: thus merit is a contingent effect by reason of the free-will, its proximate cause, and not a necessary effect by reason of its remote cause which is divine predestination. Therefore one should judge of a thing's possibility or impossibility by referring to its lower or proximate causes.

2. What is possible in regard to lower causes is also possible in regard to higher causes, and therefore in every way possible. Now that which is possible in every way is possible simply. Therefore in order to judge whether a thing be simply possible, we must refer to the lower causes.

3. The higher causes are necessary. If, then, we are to consider effects in the light of higher causes, all effects will be necessary: and this is impossible.

4. All things are possible to God. Therefore if we must judge of a thing's possibility or impossibility in reference to him, nothing will be impossible: and this is absurd.

5. In the employment of terms we should follow the common use. Now we are wont in referring to power, to speak of power, disposition, necessity and action as being related to one another. But these are to be found in the lower and not the higher causes. Therefore we should judge of the possibility or impossibility of a thing in reference to the lower and not the higher causes.

I reply that judgement as to the possibility or impossibility of a thing may be considered in two ways; with reference to the one who judges, and with reference to the thing in question.

As regards the first it must be observed that if there are two sciences, one of which considers the higher causes, and the other the less high, judgement in each must not be formed in the same way, but in reference to those causes which both sciences consider. Take, for instance, the physician and the astrologer, of whom the latter considers the highest causes and the former the proximate causes: the physician will form his judgement about a man's illness or death according to the proximate causes, namely the forces of nature and the gravity of the disease : whereas the astrologer will judge according to the remote causes, namely the position of the stars. It is thus with the point at issue. For wisdom is twofold : mundane wisdom called philosophy, which considers the lower causes, causes namely that are themselves caused, and bases its judgements on them : and divine wisdom or theology, which considers the higher, that is the divine, causes and judges according to them. Now the higher causes are the divine attributes, such as the wisdom, goodness, will of God, and the like. It must be noted, however, that there is no point in referring this question to those effects which belong exclusively to the higher causes, and which God alone can produce ; since it were senseless to say that they are possible or impossible in relation to lower causes. The point in question is about effects produced by lower causes : since such effects may be produced by both lower and higher causes, and it is about them that a doubt may occur. Again the question at issue does not concern things that are possible or impossible not with respect to a power, but in themselves. Accordingly these effects of second causes with which this question is concerned are judged by the theologian to be possible or impossible with regard to the higher causes, and by the philosopher, with regard to the lower causes. If, however, this judgement be formed with respect to the nature of the thing in question, it is clear that the effects must be judged to be possible or impossible with respect to their proximate causes, since the action of their remote causes is determined according to their proximate causes, to which those effects are especially likened : and with respect to which, therefore, any judgement about the effects should be formed. This may be made evident by comparison with passive power. For properly speaking matter is not said to be potentially this or that when the matter is remote, as earth with respect to becoming a goblet: but when the matter is proximate and potentially receptive of actuality by one agent, as the Philosopher says (*Metaph.* ix, 1, 7): thus gold is potentially a goblet, since it receives that form by art alone. In like manner an effect, so far as its nature is concerned, is said to be possible or impossible in respect of its proximate causes alone.

Reply to the First Objection. The wise men of the world are said to be foolish because they judged things that are impossible with regard to lower causes, to be absolutely and simply impossible even to God.

Reply to the Second Objection. The possible is compared to power not as the thing measured is compared to its measure, but as object to power. And yet the divine power is the measure of all powers.

Reply to the Third Objection. Although the first cause has the greatest influence on the effect, its influence, nevertheless, is determined and specified by the proximate cause, whose likeness therefore the effect bears.

Reply to the Fourth Objection. Although to make the blind see is possible to God, it cannot be said to be possible in every way.

Reply to the Fifth Objection. That the world would exist was possible with respect to the higher causes; hence this does not concern the question at issue. Wherefore the statement that the world will exist, was possible not only as regards the divine power, but also in itself, because the terms do not contradict each other.

Reply to the First Objection on the other side. This argument considers the nature of the effect that is in question.

Reply to the Second Objection. Although what is possible with respect to inferior causes is also possible with respect to higher causes, this does not apply to the impossible, rather is it the other way about. Consequently we must not form a universal decision on the matter, or judge that a thing is possible or impossible in every case with respect to lower causes.

Reply to the Third Objection. We do not judge a thing to be possible or impossible to this or that cause through some likeness in point of possibility or impossibility between that cause and some other cause, but because it is possible or impossible to that cause.

Reply to the Fourth Objection. The theologian would say that whatever is not impossible in itself is possible to God; according to Mark ix, 22, *All things are possible to him that believeth*, and Luke i, 37, *No word shall be impossible with God*.

Reply to the Fifth Objection. Though all these things are not to be found in the higher causes, they are subject to them: hence this argument considers passive and not active power of which we are speaking now.

ARTICLE V

CAN GOD DO WHAT HE DOES NOT?
Sum. Th. I, Q. xxv, A. 5: *C.G.* II, 23–30

THE fifth point of inquiry is whether God can do what he does not, and leave undone what he does? It would seem that the reply should be in the negative.

1. God cannot do otherwise than what he foresees that he will do. Now he does not foresee that he will do otherwise than what he does. Therefore God cannot do otherwise than he does.

2. But, say you, that argument considers power in its relation to prescience, and not absolutely.—On the contrary, the things of God are more unchangeable than the things of man. Now with us it is impossible for what has been not to have been. Much less then is it possible that God did not foresee what he foresaw: and so long as his foreknowledge stands, he cannot act otherwise. Therefore absolutely speaking God cannot do otherwise than he does.

3. God's wisdom is unchangeable even as his nature. Now those who said that God acts by natural necessity, said that he cannot do otherwise than he does. Therefore we too must say so, who say that God acts according to the order of his wisdom.

4. But it may be said that the foregoing argument considers power as controlled by wisdom and not absolutely. —On the contrary, that which is impossible in the order of wisdom is said without qualification to be impossible to the man Christ : although it was possible to him absolutely. Thus it is said (Jo. viii, 55) : *If I shall say that I know him not, I shall be like to you, a liar.* For Christ could say those words, but since it was against the order of wisdom, it is said without any qualification that he could not lie. Much more therefore must we say absolutely that God cannot do what is contrary to the order of wisdom.

5. Two things that are in mutual contradiction cannot be in God. Now the absolute and the conditional are in mutual contradiction, since the absolute is that which is considered in itself, while the conditional depends on something else. Therefore we should not place in God an absolute and a conditional power.

6. God's power and wisdom are equal : wherefore one does not extend beyond the other. Therefore his power cannot be separated from his wisdom, and consequently is always regulated by it.

7. What God has done is just. But he cannot act but justly. Therefore he cannot do otherwise than he has done or will do.

8. It becomes God's goodness not only to communicate itself, but to do so in most orderly fashion ; hence what God does is done in an orderly way. Now God cannot act without order. Therefore he cannot do otherwise than he has done.

9. God cannot do but what he wills to do : because in voluntary agents the power follows the will as commanded by it. Now he wills not save what he does. Therefore he cannot do save what he does.

10. Since God is a most wise operator, he does nothing

without an idea. Now the ideas[1] on which God acts are, according to Dionysius (*Div. Nom.* v), productive of the things that exist : and the things that exist are the things that are : wherefore God has no other things in his mind save those that are. Therefore he cannot do otherwise than he does.

11. According to the philosophers, the things of nature are in the first mover, thàt is God, as in the craftsman are the things that he makes : wherefore God works like a craftsman. Now a craftsman does not work without having the form or idea of his work : for according to the Philosopher (*De Gener. Anim.* ii, 1) the material house comes from the house that is in the builder's mind. But God has ideas of those things only that he has done, or does, or will do. Therefore God cannot do anything else.

12. Augustine (*De Symbolo* i) says : *God is unable to do that alone which he does not wish to do.* Now he does not wish to do save what he does. Therefore he cannot do but what he does.

13. God cannot change. Therefore he cannot be indifferent to either of two contraries : so that his power is fixed on one thing. Therefore he cannot do otherwise than he does.

14. Whatever God does or omits to do, he does or omits for the best reason. Now God cannot do or omit to do save for the best reason. Therefore he cannot do or omit except what he does or omits to do.

15. According to Plato the best produces the best : and so God who is supremely good, does whatever is best. Now the best, being superlative, is only one. Therefore God cannot do otherwise or other things than he has done.

1. *On the contrary* Christ, God and man, said (Matt. xxvi, 53) : *Cannot I ask my Father?* Therefore Christ could do what he did not.

2. It is said (Ephes. iii, 20) : *To him who is able to do all things more abundantly than we desire or understand.* But he does not do all things. Therefore he can do things that he does not.

3. God's power is infinite. But it would not be were it

[1] *Sum. Theol.* I, Q. xiv, A. 8 : Q. xv.

confined to the things that he does. Therefore he can do other things besides.

4. Hugh of St. Victor says that God's works are not equal to his power. Therefore his power surpasses his work: and consequently he can do more than he does.

5. God's power is an endless act, since nothing can put an end to it. Now this would not be the case if it were limited to what it does. Therefore the same conclusion follows.

I reply that the error of those who say that God cannot do otherwise than he does is connected with two schools of thought. Certain philosophers maintained that God acts from natural necessity: in which case since nature is confined to one effect, the divine power could not extend to other things besides what it actually does. Then there have been certain theologians who maintained that God cannot act beside the order of divine justice and wisdom according to which he works, and thus they came to say that God cannot do otherwise than he does. This error is ascribed to Peter Almalar.

Let us now inquire into the truth or falsity of these opinions. To begin with the first, it is evident that God does not act from natural necessity. Every agent acts for an end, since all things seek the good. Now for the agent's action to be suited to the end, it must be adapted and proportionate to it, and this cannot be done save by an intellect that is cognisant both of the end and of its nature as end, and again of the proportion between the end and the means: otherwise the suitability of the action to the end would be fortuitous. But this intellect ordering the means to the end is sometimes united to the agent or mover; such is man in his actions: sometimes it is separate, as in the case of the arrow whose flight in a definite direction is effected by an intellect united not to it but to the archer. Now that which acts of natural necessity cannot determine its end: because in the latter case the agent acts of itself, and when a thing acts or is in motion of itself, there is in it to act or not to act, to be in motion or not to be in motion, which cannot apply to that which is moved of necessity, since it is confined to one effect. Hence everything that acts of natural necessity must have its end determined by an intelligent agent. For this reason philosophers say that the work of nature is the work of an intelligence. Therefore whenever a natural body is united to an intellect, as in man, as regards those actions whereby that intellect determines the end, nature obeys the will, as when a man walks: whereas as regards those actions by which the intellect does not fix the end, nature does not obey, as in the process of nourishment and growth. Accordingly we conclude that a thing which acts from natural necessity cannot be a principle of action, since its end is determined by another. Hence it is impossible that God act from natural necessity, and so the foundation of the first opinion is false.

It remains for us to examine the second opinion. Observe then that there are two senses in which one is said to be unable to do a thing. First, absolutely: when, namely, one of the principles necessary for an action does not extend to that action; thus if his foot be fractured a man cannot walk. Secondly, by supposition, for if we suppose the opposite of an action, that action cannot be done, thus so long as I sit I cannot walk. Now since God is an intellectual and voluntary agent, as we have proved, we must consider in him three principles of action: first, the intellect, secondly, the will, thirdly, the power of nature.

Accordingly the intellect directs the will, and the will commands the executive power. The intellect, however, does not move except by proposing to the will its appetible object, so that the entire movement of the intellect is in the will. Now God is said in two ways to be unable to do a thing. In one way when his power does not extend to it; thus we say that God cannot make yes and no to be true at the same time, as we have shown above. In this way it cannot be said that God cannot do but what he does, for it is evident that his power can extend to many other things. In another way, when God's will cannot extend to it. For every will must needs have an end which it wills naturally, the contrary of which it cannot will: thus man naturally desires to be happy and cannot wish to be unhappy. Moreover the will, besides having of necessity a desire for its natural end, desires also of necessity those things without which it cannot obtain that end, if they be known : such things are those that are proportionate to the end : thus if I wish to live I wish for food : whereas it does not of necessity desire these things without which the end can be obtained. Now the natural end of the divine will is the divine goodness, which it is unable not to will. Creatures, however, are not proportionate to this end, as though without them the divine goodness could not be made manifest, which manifestation was God's intention in creating. For even as the divine goodness is made manifest through these things that are and through this order of things, so could it be made manifest through other creatures and another order : wherefore God's will without prejudice to his goodness, justice and wisdom, can extend to other things besides those which he has made. And this is where they erred : for they thought that the created order was commensurate and necessary to the divine goodness. It is clear then that God absolutely can do otherwise than he has done. Since, however, he cannot make contradictories to be true at the same time, it can be said *ex hypothesi* that God cannot make other things besides those he has made : for if we suppose that he does not wish to do otherwise, or that he foresaw that he would not do otherwise, as long as the supposition stands, he cannot do otherwise, though apart from that supposition he can.

Reply to the First Objection. When you say that God is not able to do except what he has foreseen that he would do, the statement admits of a twofold construction : because the negative may refer either to the power signified in the word *able*, or to the act signified in the word *do*. In the former case the statement is false : since God is able to do other things besides those that he foresees he will do, and it is in this sense that the objection runs. In the latter case the statement is true, the sense being that it is impossible for God to do anything that was not foreknown by him. In this sense the statement is not to the point.

Reply to the Second Objection. In God nothing is past or future : in him everything is in the eternal present. And when we speak of him in a past or future tense, it is not he but we who are past or future: wherefore the objection by referring to the necessity of the past misses the mark. We must also observe that the objection is not to the point, since God's foreknowledge of what he will do is not commensurate with his power to do (which is the object of our present inquiry) but only with what he actually does, as already stated.

Reply to the Third Objection. Those who maintained that God acts from natural necessity, held the opinion we are discussing, not only on account of the unchangeableness of nature, but also because nature is confined to one process of action. But divine wisdom is not confined to one manner of action, and its knowledge extends to many things. Hence the comparison fails.

Reply to the Fourth Objection. Christ could not wish to say those words absolutely, without prejudice to his goodness, since they would be untrue. This does not apply to the question at issue, as we have already indicated; hence the conclusion does not follow.

Reply to the Fifth Objection. The absolute and the conditional are ascribed to the divine power solely from our point of view. To this power considered in itself and which we describe as God's absolute power, we ascribe something that we do not ascribe to it when we compare it with his ordered wisdom.

Reply to the Sixth Objection. Wherever God's power works his wisdom is present; nevertheless we consider his power without reference to his wisdom.

Reply to the Seventh Objection. God has done whatever is actually just, not whatever is just potentially: since he is able to do that which at present is not just through not being in existence; yet if it were, what he does would be just.

Reply to the Eighth Objection. The divine goodness is able to communicate itself in orderly fashion, not only in the way in which things are actually set in order, but in many other ways.

Reply to the Ninth Objection. Though God does not wish to do save what he does, he can nevertheless wish to do other things: wherefore absolutely speaking he can do other things.

Reply to the Tenth Objection. When Dionysius speaks of the divine ideas as being productive of things, he is speaking absolutely without implying that those things actually exist at present.

Reply to the Eleventh Objection. The question is whether there is in God an idea of those things that neither exist, nor will exist, nor have existed, and that nevertheless God is able to make. Seemingly the reply should be, if we take an idea in its complete signification, namely as signifying the art-form, not only as conceived by the intellect, but also as directed to execution by the will, then of such things God has no idea. On the other hand if we take an idea in its incomplete state, as the mere mental conception of the worker, then God has an idea of those things. For it is clear that the created craftsman conceives works that he has no intention of executing. Now whatever God knows is in him as something thought out, since in him actual and habitual knowledge do not differ: for he knows his whole power and whatsoever he is able to do: hence in him are, thought out as it were, the ideas of whatsoever things he is able to make.

Reply to the Twelfth Objection. This means that God is unable to do what he does not wish to be able to do; hence it is not to the point.

Reply to the Thirteenth Objection. Though God is unchangeable, his will is not confined to one issue as regards things to be done: hence he has free-will.

Reply to the Fourteenth Objection. The best reason for which God does everything, is his goodness and wisdom, which would remain even though he made other things or acted otherwise.

Reply to the Fifteenth Objection. What God does is the best in reference to his goodness: hence whatsoever else can be referred to his goodness, according to the order of his wisdom, is still the best.

ARTICLE VI

CAN GOD DO WHAT OTHERS CAN DO?

THE sixth point of inquiry is whether God can do things that are possible to others, for instance, can he sin, walk and so forth? And seemingly the reply should be in the affirmative.

1. Augustine says (*Enchir.* cv) that it is a better nature that can sin than that which cannot. Now whatsoever is best should be ascribed to God. Therefore God can sin.

2. We should not withhold from God anything that is praiseworthy. Now it is said in praise of a man (Ecclus. xxxi, 10) that he *could have transgressed and hath not transgressed*. Therefore the power to sin and not to sin should be ascribed to God.

3. The Philosopher says (*Topic.* iv, 5) that evil deeds are possible to a god or a wise man. Therefore God can sin.

4. To consent to a mortal sin is to sin mortally: and he who commands the commission of a mortal sin, is a consenting party, in fact sometimes he is the principal. Since then God commanded Abraham to commit a mortal sin, namely to slay his innocent son, and Osee to take a wife of fornication, and have of her children of fornication, and Semei to curse David (2 Kings xvi), although he sinned by so doing since we find that he was punished for the deed (3 Kings ii); it would seem that he sinned mortally.

5. It is a mortal sin to co-operate with one who sins mortally. Now God co-operates with him who commits a mortal sin: since he operates in every deed, and consequently in every man who commits a mortal sin. Therefore God sins.

6. Augustine (*De Gratia et Lib. Arb.* xxi, cf. Gloss on Rom. i) says that God operates in the hearts of men, by inclining their will whithersoever he will, be it to good or to evil. Now it is a sin to incline a man's will to evil. Therefore God sins.

7. Man was made to God's image (Gen. i). Now whatsoever is in the image must needs be in the original: and

man's will is indifferent to this or that. Therefore God's will is also : and consequently he can sin and not sin.

8. Whatsoever a lower power can do, a higher power can do also. Now man whose power is inferior to God's power is able to walk, to sin and so forth. Therefore God also can do these things.

9. To omit is not to do the good one is able to do. But God is able to do many good things that he does not. Therefore he omits them and consequently sins.

10. Apparently he sins who can prevent the commission of sin, and prevents it not. Now God can prevent all sins being committed. Since then he does not do so it would seem that he sins.

11. It is written (Amos iii, 6) : *Shall there be evil in a city, which the Lord hath not done?* But this cannot refer to penal evil, since it is written (Wis. i, 13) : *God made not death.* Therefore it must refer to the evil of sin : so that God is the author of the evil of sin.

On the contrary it is said (1 Jo. i, 5) : *God is light, and in him there is no darkness.* Now sin is spiritual darkness. Therefore in God there can be no sin.

Moreover, a sovereign is not bound by his own laws. And every sin is contrary to the divine law as Augustine says (*Contra Faust.* xxii, 27). Therefore God cannot be subject to sin.

I answer that, as already stated (A. 5) there are two ways in which God may be said to be unable to do a thing, in respect of his will and in respect of his power. On the part of his will God cannot do what he cannot will. And since no will can consent to the contrary of what it naturally desires,—thus a man's will cannot desire unhappiness,—it is clear that God's will cannot will what is contrary to his goodness, since he wills this naturally. Now sin is a lapse from divine goodness : wherefore God cannot will to sin. Therefore we must grant absolutely that God cannot sin. On the part of his power God is said in two ways to be unable to do a thing, in respect of his power and in respect of the thing. His power considered in itself, since it is infinite, lacks nothing that appertains to power. There are certain things, however, which in name denote power whereas in reality they are wanting in power. Such are many negations that are expressed affirmatively: as when we say that so and so can fail, the terms would seem to imply some sort of power, whereas it is rather a lack of power that is signified. For this reason, according to the Philosopher (*Metaph.* v, 12) a power is said to be perfect when it is unable to do such things: because while such affirmations are in reality negations, the corresponding negations have an affirmative force. Hence we say that God cannot fail, and consequently that he cannot be moved (since movement and failing imply imperfection), and therefore that he cannot walk nor perform any other bodily actions, since these are inseparable from movement. On the part of the thing, God is said to be unable to do a thing when it implies a contradiction, as stated above (A. 5): and in this way we say that God cannot make another God equal to himself: since a contradiction is implied in that what is made must needs be somewhat in potentiality, seeing that it receives its being from another, and consequently cannot be pure act which is proper to God.

Reply to the First Objection. This comparison must not be taken universally, but only as between man and dumb animals.

Reply to the Second Objection. That which is said in praise of man is not always becoming to the praise of God; it might even be a blasphemy, as if I were to say that God repents and the like. Because, as Dionysius says (*De Div. Nom.* iv) what is praised in a lower nature is blamed in a higher.

Reply to the Third Objection. The saying of the Philosopher must be understood as conditional to the will. This conditional statement is true: God can do wicked things if he will, although both antecedent and consequence are impossible; thus it is clear that if a man flies he has wings.

Reply to the Fourth Objection. Nothing prevents an act that is in itself a mortal sin from becoming virtuous through the addition of a circumstance. Thus absolutely speaking it is a mortal sin to kill a man : yet it is not a mortal sin but an act of justice for the judge's minister to put a man to death for justice' sake in pursuance of the judge's sentence. Now, even as the civil authority has the disposal of men in matters of life and death, and all that touches the end of its government, namely justice, so God has all things at his disposal to direct them to the end of his government, which end is his goodness. Wherefore though it may be in itself a mortal sin to slay an innocent son, yet if this be done at God's command for an end foreseen and preordained by God, though unknown to the slayer, it is not a sin but a meritorious act. The same applies to the fornication of Osee, for it is clear that God orders all human procreation. Some, however, assert that this did not happen in reality, but only in a prophetic vision. As to the command given to Semei we must give a different reply. God is said in two ways to command. In one way by speaking either interiorly or outwardly through a created substance : and thus he commanded Abraham and the Prophets. In another way by inclination : thus it is related that he commanded (Vulg., *prepared*) a worm to consume the ivy (Jonas iv, 7). In this way he commanded Semei to curse David, by inclining his heart, and this in the manner we shall explain in the Reply to the Sixth Objection.

Reply to the Fifth Objection. The sinful act, forasmuch as it has entity and actuality, is to be referred to God as its cause ; but in so far as it has the deformity of sin, it must be referred to the free-will and not to God : thus all that there is of movement in limping comes from the power to walk, whereas the defect is owing to a misshapen leg.

Reply to the Sixth Objection. God is said to incline man's will to evil, not as though he infused malice into it, or urged it to wickedness, but by permitting and directing the evil, for instance he directs the exercise of cruelty to the punishment of those whom he deems deserving of it.

Reply to the Seventh Objection. Although man is made in God's image, it does not follow that whatever is in man is also in God. Nevertheless, as to the point raised, God's will is indifferent to this or that, since it is not fixed to one object. For he is able either to do a thing or not to do it, to do this or to do that: yet it does not follow that in either case he can do ill, which is to sin.

Reply to the Eighth Objection. This argument applies to those things which refer to the perfection of power but not to those which refer to the lack of power.

Reply to the Ninth Objection. Though God is able to do many good things which he does not, he does not omit them, since he is not bound to do them, which is a necessary condition of an omission.

Reply to the Tenth Objection. The same answer applies here, since a man is not guilty of a sin through failing to prevent it, unless he be bound to do so.

Reply to the Eleventh Objection. The words of Amos refer to penal evil. And the words of the Book of Wisdom, *God hath not made death*, refer to the cause of death, as the wages of sin; or to the original formation of human nature when man was made by nature immortal.

ARTICLE VII

IS GOD ALMIGHTY?

Sum. Th. I, Q. xxv, A. 3 : III, Q. xiii, A. 1 : *C.G.* ii, 22, 25

THE seventh point of inquiry is: Why is God called almighty?

1. It would seem that the reason is because he can simply do all things. For he is called almighty in the same way as he is called omniscient. Now he is called omniscient because he simply knows all things. Therefore he is called almighty because he can simply do all things.

2. If the reason for calling him almighty is not because he can simply do all things, then the implication that he can do all things is not absolutely true but only in an accommodated sense: in which case the predication would not be universal but particular, and consequently the divine power would be confined to certain effects and therefore finite.— On the contrary, as stated above (AA. 3, 5) God cannot

make yes and no to be true at the same time : neither can he sin or die. Yet these things would be included in the above predication were it to be taken absolutely. Therefore it must not be taken absolutely : and consequently the reason why God is called almighty is not because he can absolutely do all things.

3. It would seem that he is called almighty because he can do whatsoever he wills. For Augustine says (*Enchir.* xcvi) : *He is called almighty for no other reason but that he can do whatsoever he wills.*—On the contrary. The blessed can do whatsoever they will, otherwise their will would not be perfect. And yet they are not called almighty. Therefore the fact that God can do whatsoever he wills is not sufficient reason for calling him almighty. Further, a wise man does not will the impossible, wherefore no wise man desires to do except what he is able to do. And yet not all the wise are almighty. Therefore the same conclusion follows.

4. It would seem that he is called almighty because he can do whatsoever is possible. For he is called omniscient because he knows all things knowable. Therefore there is equal reason for calling him almighty because he can do all things possible.—On the contrary, if he be called almighty because he can do all things possible, this is either because he can do all things possible to him, or because he can do all things possible to nature. In the latter case his power would not surpass that of nature, which is absurd : in the former case, everyone would be called almighty, since everyone can do what is possible to himself. Moreover such an explanation is by way of circumlocution, which is inept.

5. If God is called almighty and all-knowing, why is he not also called all-willing ?

I answer that in an attempt to assign a reason for God's omnipotence some have sought it in things that are not the reason but rather the cause of omnipotence, or which appertain to the perfection of his omnipotence, or to the nature of his power, or to the way in which he has power. Thus some have said that God is almighty because his power is infinite : these assigned not the reason but the cause of omnipotence: for instance, a rational soul is the cause not the definition of a man. Some said that God is almighty because he is impassible and indefectible, and nothing can act on him, and so on, all of which appertain to the perfection of his power. And some said that he is called almighty because he can do whatsoever he wills, and this by nature and essentially; but this regards the way in which he has power. Now all these reasons are insufficient in that they fail to account for the relation between operation and its object, which relation is implied in omnipotence. Wherefore we reply that we must take one of the explanations indicated in the objections which take into account this relationship to objects.—Accordingly, as stated above (A. 5) God's power, considered in itself, extends to all such objects as do not imply a contradiction. Nor does the objection stand that refers to things which imply a defect or bodily movement, since the very possibility of such things involves their impossibility to God. And as regards things that imply a contradiction, they are impossible to God as being impossible in themselves. Consequently God's power extends to things that are possible in themselves: and such are the things that do not involve a contradiction. Therefore it is evident that God is called almighty because he can do all things that are possible in themselves.

Reply to the First Objection. God is called omniscient because he knows all things knowable. Now the false are not knowable and therefore he knows them not: and things impossible in themselves are compared to power as the false are compared to knowledge.

Reply to the Second Objection. This argument would stand if the universality were confined within the genus of things possible so as not to extend to all things possible.

To the second reason suggested for calling God almighty we have to say that to be able to do whatsoever he wills is not a sufficient reason, though it is a sufficient sign: it is in this sense that we must take the works of Augustine. To the argument advanced for the third reason, we reply that God is called almighty because he is able to do all things that are absolutely possible: hence it is not to the point where the objection distinguishes between things possible to God and those which are possible to nature.

To the last question we reply that in voluntary actions, power and knowledge (as stated in *Metaph.* ix, 2, 5) are brought into action by the will: wherefore in God power and knowledge are described in universal terms as being without limit, as when we say that God is all-knowing and almighty: whereas the will, seeing that it is the determining force, cannot cover all things, but only those to which it determines power and knowledge: hence God cannot be called all-willing.

QUESTION II

OF GOD'S GENERATING POWER

THERE are six points of inquiry : (1) Is there a generating power in God ? (2) Whether the power to generate is applied to God essentially or notionally ? (3) Whether the power to generate is brought into act by a command of the will ? (4) Whether there can be more than one Son in God ? (5) Whether the generating power is included in omnipotence ? (6) Whether the generating power is the same as the creative power ?

ARTICLE I

IS THERE A GENERATIVE POWER IN GOD ?

Sum. Th. I, Q. xli, A. 4

WE are inquiring about God's generative power, and the first point of inquiry is whether in God there is the power to beget. The reply seemingly should be in the negative.

1. All power is either active or passive. Now there can be no passive power in God : nor in him can a generative power be active, because then the Son would be the result of an action and would be made, which is against the faith. Therefore there is no generative power in God.

2. According to the Philosopher (*De Somn. et Vig.* i), action belongs to that which has power. Now in God there is no begetting : and consequently there is no generative power. The middle proposition is proved thus. Wherever there is a begetting there is communication and reception of nature. But since reception involves matter and a passive power, which are not in God, reception is inadmissible in God : and therefore there can be no begetting in God.

3. The begetter must needs be distinct from the begotten.

Not, however, in that which the begetter communicates to the begotten, since rather are they the same in that regard. Consequently in the begotten there must needs be something besides that which he receives by generation from the begetter : so that seemingly whatsoever is begotten must be composite. But in God there is no composition. Therefore there cannot be a begotten God, and consequently there can be no begetting in God, and the same conclusion follows.

4. No imperfection should be ascribed to God. Now every power, active or passive, in comparison with its act is imperfect. Therefore we should not attribute a generative power to God.

5. But, you will say, this applies to a power that is not united to its act.—On the contrary, whatsoever is perfected by another is less perfect than that by which it is perfected. Now the power that is united to its act is perfected by that act. Therefore that act is more perfect than the power : so that even a power that is united to its act is imperfect in comparison with its act.

6. The divine nature is more effective in acting than created nature. Now there is among creatures a nature that works not through the medium of a power, but by itself : thus the sun enlightens the air, and the soul quickens the body. Consequently there is much stronger reason why the divine nature should be by itself the generative principle and not through a power. Therefore there is no generative power in God.

7. Generative power is a sign either of perfection or of imperfection. It is not, however, a sign of perfection because if it were it would be found in the higher ranks of creatures rather than in the lower, in the angels and heavenly bodies more or rather than in animals and plants. Therefore it is a sign of imperfection, and consequently should not be ascribed to God.

8. A twofold generative power is to be found in things here below. It is complete in those things where generation is effected by sexual intercourse : it is incomplete when generation takes place without mingling of sexes ; in plants, for instance. Since then we cannot ascribe the complete

power to God in whom there cannot be an intercourse of sexes, it would seem that generative power cannot in any sense be ascribed to God.

9. The object of power can only be something possible: since power (*potentia*) is so called from its relationship to the possible (*possibilis*). Now the existence of generation in God is not a possible or a contingent thing, since it is eternal. Therefore we cannot ascribe to God a power in respect of generation, and consequently the power to generate is not in him.

10. The power of God, being infinite, is not terminated either by its act or by its object. Now if in God there be a generative power, its act will be generation, and its effect will be a Son. Therefore the Father's power will not be confined to the begetting of one Son but will extend to many; which is absurd.

11. According to Avicenna, when a thing has a certain quality entirely from without, to that thing considered in itself we attribute the opposite quality: thus the air which has no light except from without, is dark considered in itself. In this way since all creatures derive being, truth, and necessity from without, considered in themselves they are non-existent, untrue, and impossible. But nothing of the kind is possible in God. Consequently in God there cannot be one who has being entirely from another, nor can there be one that is begotten, nor generation and generative power.

12. In the Godhead the Son has nothing but what he receives from the Father, else it would follow that there is composition in him. Now he receives his essence from the Father: and consequently there is nothing in him but the essence. Hence if there be generation in God, or if the Son be begotten, it will follow that the essence is begotten: and this is false, since then there would be a distinction in the divine essence.

13. If, in God, the Father begets, this must belong to him in respect of his nature. But the nature is the same in Father, Son, and Holy Ghost. For the same reason, then, both Son and Holy Ghost will beget; which is contrary to the teaching of faith.

14. A nature that exists perpetually and perfectly in one supposit, is not communicated to another supposit. Now the divine nature exists perfectly in the Father, and again perpetually since it is incorruptible. Therefore it is not communicated to another supposit: and consequently there is no generation there.

15. Generation is a kind of change. But there is no change in God. Neither therefore is there generation or generative power.

On the contrary, according to the Philosopher a thing is perfect when it is able to produce its like. Now God the Father is perfect. Therefore he can produce his like, and beget a Son.

Moreover Augustine says (*Cont. Maxim.* iii, 7) that if the Father could not beget, it follows that he lacked the power. But there is no lack of power in God. Therefore he was able to beget, and in him is the generative power.

I answer that it is in the nature of every act to communicate itself as far as possible. Wherefore every agent acts forasmuch as it is in act: while to act is nothing else than to communicate as far as possible that whereby the agent is in act. Now the divine nature is supreme and most pure act: wherefore it communicates itself as far as possible. It communicates itself to creatures by likeness only: this is clear to anyone, since every creature is a being according to its likeness to it. The Catholic Faith, moreover, asserts another mode of communication of the divine nature, in that it is communicated by a quasi-natural communication: so that as one to whom the human nature is communicated is a man, so one to whom the Godhead is communicated is not merely like God, but is truly God. But here we must observe that there is a twofold difference between the divine nature and material forms. In the first place material forms are not subsistent, so that the human nature in a man is not the same thing as the man who subsists: whereas the Godhead is the same thing as God, so that the divine nature itself is subsistent. Secondly, no created form or nature is its own being: whereas God's very being is his nature and quiddity; so that the name proper to him is: *He who is* (Exod. iii, 14), because thereby he is named as if from his proper form. Consequently since forms here below are not self-subsistent, there must needs be in the subject to which a form is communicated, besides the form, something whereby the form or nature receives subsistence: this is matter, which underlies material forms and natures. And seeing that a material form or nature is not its own being, it receives being through its reception into something else: wherefore according as it is received into a diversity of subjects it has a diversity of being: thus human nature in respect of being is not one in Socrates and Plato, although the essential notion of humanity is the same in both. On the other hand since the divine nature is self-subsistent, in the communication thereof there is no need of anything material for subsistence: and consequently it is not received into a subject by way of matter, so that he who is begotten be composed of matter and form. And because again the divine essence is its own being, it does not receive being from the supposit in which it is: so that by virtue of one and the same being it is in both the communicator and the one to whom it is communicated, thus remaining identically the same in both.

We have an example of this communication, and that most becomingly, in the intellect: for the divine nature is spiritual, wherefore it is manifested better by means of spiritual examples. Thus when our intellect conceives the quiddity of a thing that is self-subsistent and outside the mind, there is a kind of communication of this self-subsistent thing, inasmuch as our intellect receives in a way from the exterior thing the form of the latter: and this intelligible form having its existence in our intellect proceeds in a way from that exterior thing. Since, however, the exterior thing differs in nature from the understanding intellect, the form understood by the intellect and the form of the self-subsistent object differ in their respective beings. But when our intellect understands its own quiddity, both conditions stand, since in its process of formation the form understood proceeds after a fashion from the intellect understanding it into the intellect receiving it, and besides a certain unity is maintained between the conceived form which proceeds and the thing whence it proceeds, since both have intelligible being, seeing that one is the intellect, while the other is the intelligible form which is called the word of the intellect. Since, however, our intellect is not by its essence established in the perfect act of intellectuality, nor is the human intellect identical with human nature, it follows that although the aforesaid word is in the intellect and somewhat conformed to it, yet it is not identified with the essence of the intellect, but it expresses its likeness. Again, in the conception of this intelligible form the human nature is not communicated, wherefore it cannot properly be called a begetting which implies a communication of nature.

Now even as when our intellect understands itself there is in it a word proceeding and bearing a likeness to that from which it proceeds, so, too, in God there is a word bearing the likeness of him from whom it proceeds. The procession of this word transcends in two ways the procession of our word. First, because our word differs from the essence of the intellect, as already stated, whereas the divine intellect being by its very essence in the perfect act of intellectuality, cannot be the recipient of an intelligible form that is not its essence: consequently its word is essentially one with it. Secondly, the divine nature itself is its intellectuality, wherefore a communication that takes place in an intellectual manner, is also a communication by way of nature, so that it can be called a begetting, and thus again the divine word surpasses the procession of our word, and Augustine (*De Trin.* i) assigns this mode of generation. Since, however, we are treating of divine things according to our mode whereby our intellect proceeds from its knowledge of things here below, therefore as in these latter wherever we find action we find an active principle which we call power, so do we also in matters concerning God, although in him power and action are not distinct as in creatures. For this reason, given that in God there is generation, a term that is significative of action, it follows that we must grant him the power to beget, or a generative power.

Reply to the First Objection. The power which we attribute to God is neither active properly speaking nor passive, seeing that the predicaments of action and passion are not in him, and his action is his very substance : but the power which is in him is designated by us after the manner of an active power. Nor does it follow that the Son is the result of action or making, even as neither does it follow that in God there is properly speaking action or passion.

Reply to the Second Objection. While the term and end of receiving is having, there are two ways of receiving and two ways of having. In one way matter has its form, and a subject an accident, or in fact anything that is possessed besides the essence : in another way the supposit has a nature, for instance, a man has human nature : for the nature is not beside the essence of the haver, indeed it is his essence : thus Socrates is truly that which is a man. Accordingly the begotten one even in mankind receives the form of his begetter, not as matter receives form, or subject accident, but as a supposit or hypostasis has the specific nature : and it is thus in God. Hence in God begotten there is no need of matter or of a subject of the divine nature : but it follows that he is the subsistent Son having the nature of God.

Reply to the Third Objection. God begotten is not distinct from the begetting God by an added essence, since, as stated above, there is no need for matter as a recipient of the Godhead : they are distinct, however, by the relation implied in receiving one's nature from another : so that in the Son the relation of sonship takes the place of all the individualising principles in things created (for which reason it is called a personal property), while the divine nature takes the place of the specific nature. Yet since this same relation is not really distinct from the divine nature, it does not involve any composition therein, whereas with us a certain composition results from the specific and individualising principles.

Reply to the Fourth Objection. This argument avails when power and act, whether united or not, are distinct from each other : but this is not the case in God.

Wherefore the Reply to the Fifth Objection is clear.

Reply to the Sixth Objection. Anything that is a principle whereby an action is done is of the nature of a power, whether it be an essence, or an accidental medium such as a quality standing between essence and action. In corporeal creatures, however, seldom or never do we find a subsistent nature in action without an intervening accident; thus the sun illumines by means of the light in it. But that the soul quickens the body, is by means of the soul's essence: yet though the word quickening expresses action, it is not in the genus of action, since it is first act rather than second.

Reply to the Seventh Objection. In creatures generation is impossible without a distinction of essence or nature in point of existence, since their nature is not their existence. Consequently generation among creatures suggests imperfection: wherefore it is unbecoming to the higher creatures. But in God generation is possible without this or any other imperfection: and so nothing forbids us to ascribe it to God.

Reply to the Eighth Objection. This argument considers generation in the material world, and therefore it is not to the point.

Reply to the Ninth Objection. It is true that the object of an active or passive power must be possible and contingent, when the action or passion in question is accompanied by movement (since all movable things are possible and contingent). Such, however, is not the generative power in God, as stated above, wherefore the argument does not prove.

Reply to the Tenth Objection. The Son of God is not the effect of the generative power, for we confess our belief that he is begotten, not made. If, however, he were the effect, the power of the Begetter would not terminate in him, although he cannot beget another Son, because the Begetter is infinite. The reason why there cannot be another Son in God is because Sonship is a personal property and thereby the Son is, so to say, individualised. And the principles of individuality of each individual thing belong to that thing alone: otherwise it would follow that a person or an individual thing would be logically communicable.

Reply to the Eleventh Objection. The saying of Avicenna is true when that which is received is not identically the same in recipient and giver, as is the case in creatures in relation to God. Hence whatsoever is received by a creature is as vanity in comparison with the being of God, since a creature cannot receive being in that perfection with which it is in God. On the other hand in God the Son receives the same identical nature as that which the Father has: hence the argument fails.

Reply to the Twelfth Objection. The Son has nothing that is really distinct from the essence which he receives from the Father: but from the very fact that he receives from the Father it follows that in him is a relation by which he is referred to and distinct from the Father. And yet this relation is not distinct from his essence.

Reply to the Thirteenth Objection. Though the same nature is in Father and Son, it is in each by a different mode of existence, that is to say with a different relation. Consequently that which belongs to the Father in respect of his nature does not of necessity belong to the Son.

Reply to the Fourteenth Objection. Creatures become like God by participating in their specific nature; hence the fact that a particular created supposit subsists in a created nature, is directed to something else as its end. Consequently if the end be sufficiently attained by one individual by a perfect and proper participation in the specific nature, there is no need for another individual participating in that nature. On the other hand God's nature is the end and is not for the sake of an end: and it is meet that the end should be communicated in every possible way. Hence though in God it is found perfectly and properly in one supposit, nothing forbids its being in another.

Reply to the Fifteenth Objection. Generation is a kind of change in so far as by means of generation the common nature is received in some matter which is the subject of change. This is not the case in the divine generation, and so the conclusion does not follow.

ARTICLE II

IS GENERATION ATTRIBUTED TO GOD ESSENTIALLY OR NOTIONALLY?[1]

THE second point of inquiry is whether generation is attributed to God essentially or notionally. And it would seem that it is only attributed notionally.

1. Power is a kind of principle, as appears from the definition in *Metaph.* v, 12. Now when we use the term principle in reference to a divine person the term is used notionally. Since then the generative power implies a principle in this sense, it would seem that it is attributed to God notionally.

2. Should it be said that it denotes both the essence and a notion,—on the contrary, according to Boethius (*De Trin.*) there are two predicaments in God,—substance to which the essence belongs, and relation, to which the notional acts belong. But a thing cannot be in two predicaments, since a white man is not one thing save accidentally (*Metaph.* v, 7). Therefore the generative power cannot include both, substance namely and notional act.

3. In God the principle is distinct from that which proceeds therefrom. But there should be no distinction in his essence. Consequently the idea of principle is incompatible with the essence: so that power which involves the idea of a principle does not denote the essence in God.

4. In God property is relative and notional: while that which is common is essential and absolute. Now the generative power is not common to Father and Son, but is proper to the Father. Therefore it is attributed as a notion or relation, and not essentially nor absolutely.

5. The principle of a thing's proper action is its proper form and not the common form: thus man understands by his intellect, because this action is proper to him in relation to other animals, even as the form of rationality or intellectuality. Now generation is the proper operation of the

[1] i.e. as a property or note of a divine person. See *Sum. Theol.* I, Q. xxxii, A. 2.

Father as Father. Therefore its principle is Paternity which is the Father's proper form, and not the Godhead which is the common form. But Paternity is a relative term. Therefore the generative power not only viewed as a principle, but also as to the thing which is a principle, denotes a relation.

6. As the generative power does not really differ from the essence, so neither does paternity. But this does not prevent paternity from being a purely relative term. Therefore neither does it oblige us to say that the generative power denotes the essence together with a relation.

7. In God three things have the nature of a principle, power, knowledge and will, and these are ascribed to God essentially. Now knowledge and will in God do not each signify at the same time some relation or notion. For equal reason, therefore, neither does power: and so it cannot be said that the generative power signifies at the same time the essence on the part of the power, and a notion on the part of generation: but seemingly it signifies nothing but the notion for reasons already given.

On the contrary the Master says (I.D.vii) that the generative power in the Father is the very essence of God.

Further, Hilary says (*De Synod.*) that the Father begets by virtue of the Godhead. Therefore the Godhead is the principle of generation, and is in the nature of a power.

Further, Damascene says (*De Fide Orth.* ii, 27) that generation is the work of nature; and thus the same conclusion follows.

Further, there is but one power in God. Now the creative power is attributed to the essence. Therefore the generative power should be also.

I answer that there are several opinions on this point. Some maintained that the generative power is not ascribed to God otherwise than relatively: and they were moved by the following argument. Power is essentially a principle of a kind: and a principle signifies a relation and a property if attributed to the divine power and not to creatures. But in arguing thus they were at fault in two ways. First, although power is rightly described as a kind of principle which comes under the generic head of relation, nevertheless the thing which is a principle of action or passion is not a relation but an absolute form, namely the essence of the power. Wherefore the Philosopher places power like science in the genus, not of relation but of quality, although a relation is incidental to both. Secondly, when speaking of God, terms that signify a principle in respect of operation are not employed relatively as denoting properties but only those that signify a principle in respect of the term of operations. Because when we speak of a principle as a property in God we refer to the subsistent person : whereas the term operation does not involve subsistence : and consequently it does not follow that terms which denote a principle of operation are employed to signify a property, otherwise will, knowledge, intellect and all like terms would be employed as indicating properties. Power, however, although it is a principle sometimes both of action and of the product of action, yet the latter is incidental to it while the former is essential to it : because active power by its action does not always produce something that is the term of that action, since, according to the Philosopher (*Ethic.* i, 1 ; *Metaph.* ix, 6), there are many operations that have no product : whereas power is always a principle of action or operation. Consequently it does not follow that because power implies the relation of a principle, it is therefore predicated of God relatively.

Moreover this opinion appears to be in conflict with the truth. If the thing that is a power is the same as the principle of action, it follows that the divine nature is the thing that is a principle in God : for since every agent as such produces its like, that thing in the begetter is the principle of his begetting, in respect of which the begotten is likened to the begetter : thus a man by virtue of his human nature begets a son who is like him in that nature. Now God begotten is like God the Father in the divine nature : hence the divine nature is the generating principle whereby the Father begets, as Hilary says (*l.c.*).

For this reason others said that the generative power signifies the essence alone. But this opinion again appears to be at fault. An action done by virtue of the common nature, by an individual included in that nature, takes on a certain mode from its proper principles: thus an action due to a man's animal nature is produced in him in accordance with the principles of the human species, wherefore a man on account of his rational nature enjoys a more perfect act of the imagination than other animals. Again actions peculiar to man are performed by this or that individual in accordance with the individualising principles of this or that man; the result being that one man understands better than another. Consequently if the common nature be the principle of an operation that belongs to the Father alone, it follows that it is the principle in accordance with the personal property of the Father. And for this reason the idea of power includes, after a fashion, paternity even in respect of that which is the principle of generation.

For these reasons we must say with others that the generative power denotes at the same time the essence and the property.

Reply to the First Objection. Power conveys the idea of a principle in relation to operation which, as already stated, is not ascribed to God as a notional act.

Reply to the Second Objection. Among creatures one predicament is accidental to another, wherefore one thing cannot result from two, except what is one accidentally; whereas in God relation is in reality the very essence; and thus there is no comparison.

Reply to the Third Objection. Among creatures the principle of generation is twofold, namely the generator and that whereby he generates. The generator, however, is distinct from the thing generated by virtue of the generation, since nothing generates itself: whereas that whereby the generation takes place is not distinct but is common to both, as stated above. Consequently it does not follow that there is a distinction in the divine nature, as the generative power, since power is the principle whereby the effect is produced.

Reply to the Fourth Objection. By reason of the implied relation the generative power is not common but proper.

Reply to the Fifth Objection. In every generation the generating principle in chief is not an individual form but the form proper to the specific nature. Again there is no need for the thing generated to be like the generator in regard to individual conditions, but in regard to the specific nature. Now fatherhood is not in the Father as the form of a species, as human nature is in man, for then the divine nature is in him; but it is in him, so to speak, as the principle of his individuality, since it is a personal property. Consequently it does not follow that in him it is the generating principle in chief, but that it is understood along with it, so to speak, as we have already explained: otherwise it would follow that the Father by begetting would communicate not only his Godhead but also his Fatherhood: which is inadmissible.

Reply to the Sixth Objection. The generative power is really identical with the divine nature, so that the nature is essentially included in it: it is not the same with the Paternity, wherefore the comparison fails.

Reply to the Seventh Objection. Knowledge or will are not the principle of generation, since generation belongs to the nature which as a principle of action may be considered as a power. Hence it is that in God power is cosignified with relation, which does not apply to knowledge or will.

The replies to the arguments on the other side may be easily gathered from what has been said.

ARTICLE III

IN THE ACT OF GENERATION DOES THE GENERATIVE POWER COME INTO ACTION AT THE COMMAND OF THE WILL?

Sum. Th. I, Q. xli, A. 2

THE third point of inquiry is whether in the act of generation the generative power comes into action at the command of the will. It would seem that the reply should be in the affirmative.

1. Hilary (*De Synod.*) says that *not by natural necessity was the Father led to beget the Son*. Now if he did not beget of his will he begot of natural necessity, since an agent is either voluntary or natural. Therefore the Father begot the Son by his will: and thus the generative power proceeded to generate through the command of the will.

2. But, you will say, the Father begot the Son by an act of his will, neither preceding nor following but accompanying the act of generation.—On the contrary this argument is seemingly inadequate. For since everything in God is eternal, nothing in him can precede in point of time anything that is in him: and yet we find in him one thing having to another the relation of a principle, for instance, his will in relation to his election of the just, from the mere fact that it proceeds from his intellect. Therefore though the will to beget did not precede the begetting of the Son, nevertheless it would seem that we may consider it to be the principle of the Son's generation, for the reason that it proceeds from the intellect.

3. The Son proceeds through an act of the intellect since he proceeds as the Word: because there is no intellectual word except when thinking of a thing we understand it, according to Augustine (*De Trin.* ix, 4). Now the will is the principle of the intellectual operation: for it commands the act of the intellect, even as those of the other powers, as Anselm says (*De Simil.* ii): thus I understand because I wish to do so, just as I walk because I wish to walk. Therefore the will is the principle of the Son's generation.

4. But, say you, it is true of man that the will commands the act of the intelligence, but not of God.—On the contrary predestination is, in a way, an act of the intelligence: for we say that God predestined Peter because he willed, according to Romans ix, 18 : *He hath mercy on whom he will, and whom he will he hardeneth*. Therefore not only in man but also in God does the will command the act of the intelligence.

5. According to the Philosopher (*Phys.* viii, 5) that

which causes its own movement can be either in motion or not : and for the same reason that which is cause of its own act, can act or not act. But nature cannot act or not act, since it is determined to one action. Therefore it is not the cause of its own action, but acts as moved by another. Now this cannot be the case in God. Therefore in God no action is from nature, and consequently neither is generation. Therefore generation is from his will, since all agents are reduced to nature or will as stated in *Phys.* ii, 4.

6. If the action of nature precede that of the will, this leads to an absurdity, for the will would be rendered void. Because since nature is determined to one course of action, if it moved the will, it would move it to one thing alone, and this is contrary to the essence of the will which, as such, is free. On the other hand if the will move nature, neither nature nor will is abrogated, since that which is indifferent to many things is not debarred from moving towards one. Therefore the action of the will reasonably precedes the action of nature, rather than vice versa. Now the generation of the Son is pure action or operation. Therefore it comes from the will.

7. It is written (Ps. cxlviii, 5) : *He spake and they were made*, which words Augustine expounds as follows (*Gen. ad lit.* ii, 6, 7) : *He begat the Word in whom they were that they might be made*. Accordingly the procession of the Word from the Father is the reason of the creature's production. Wherefore if the Son proceeds not from the Father by the command of the Father's will, it would seem that all creatures proceed from the Father naturally and not only by his will : which is erroneous.

8. Hilary says (*De Synod.*) : *If anyone say that the Son was born of the Father without the concurrence of the Father's will, let him be anathema*. Therefore the Father did not beget the Son involuntarily ; and so the same conclusion follows.

9. It is written (Jo. iii, 35) : *The Father loveth the Son, and he hath given all things into his hand*, which words a gloss expounds of the giving of the eternal generation. Therefore the love of the Father for the Son is the reason rather than

the sign of the eternal generation. Now love is from the will. Therefore the will is the principle of the Son's generation.

10. Dionysius (*De Div. Nom.* iv) says that *God's love does not allow him to be without offspring.* Hence again it would seem to follow that love is the reason of generation.

11. Any opinion about God that does not involve absurdity or error can be maintained. Now if we suppose that the Father begat the Son voluntarily, no absurdity follows, since neither does it follow apparently that the Son is not eternal, nor that he is not consubstantial with or equal to the Father, since the Holy Ghost who proceeds as an act of the will, is co-eternal, co-equal and consubstantial with the Father and Son. Therefore seemingly it is not erroneous to assert that the Father begat the Son by his will.

12. No will can fail to will its last end. Now the end of God's will is to communicate his goodness, and this is especially effected by generation. Therefore the Father's will cannot but will the generation of the Son. Therefore by his will he begat the Son.

13. Human generation is drawn from the divine according to Ephesians iii, 15 : *Of whom all paternity is named in heaven and on earth.* Now human generation is subject to the command of the will, else there could be no sin in the act of generation. Therefore the divine generation is also, and so the same conclusion follows.

14. Every action proceeding from an unchangeable nature is necessary. Now the divine nature is utterly unchangeable. Wherefore if the (divine) generation be the operation of the nature and not of the will, it follows that it is necessary, so that the Father begat the Son of necessity : and this is contrary to the teaching of Augustine (*Ad Oros.* iii).

15. Augustine (*De Trin.* xv, xx) says that the Son is *Counsel of counsel, and will of will.* Now the preposition *of* (*de*) indicates a principle. Therefore the will is the principle of the Son's generation, and so the same conclusion follows.

On the contrary Augustine (*Ad Oros.* iii) says : *The Father begot the Son neither by his will nor of necessity.*

Again, the supreme effusion of the will is through the channel of love. But the Son proceeds not by way of love, rather is it the Holy Ghost who proceeds thus. Therefore the will is not the principle of the Son's generation.

Further, the Son proceeds from the Father as brightness from light according to Hebrews i, 3 : *Who being the brightness of his glory, and the figure of his substance.* Now brightness does not proceed from light by the will. Neither therefore does the Son proceed thus from the Father.

I answer that the generation of the Father may be referred to the will as the object of the will : since the Father both willed the Son and the generation of the Son from eternity : but by no means can the will be the principle of the divine generation. This is made evident as follows. The will as such being free is indifferent to either of the alternatives : for it can act or not act, do thus or do otherwise, will and not will. And if this does not apply to the will with regard to a certain thing, this will be true of the will not as will, but on account of the natural inclination it has for a certain thing, as for the last end which it is unable not to will : thus the human will is unable not to will happiness, and cannot will unhappiness. Wherefore it is clear that whenever a thing has the will for its principle, it is possible for it to be or not to be, to be such or otherwise, to be now or then. Now everything of this description is a creature ; since in an uncreated being there is no possibility of being or not being, but the essential necessity of being, as Avicenna proves (*Metaph.* viii, 4). Wherefore if we suppose the Son to be begotten by the will, it must needs follow that he is a creature. For this reason the Arians who held the Son to be a creature, said that he was begotten by the will : whereas Catholics say that he was begotten not by will but by the nature. For nature is determined to one effect : and accordingly since the Son is begotten of the Father by nature, it follows that it is impossible for him not to be begotten, or to be otherwise than he is, or not consubstantial with the Father : since that which proceeds naturally, proceeds in likeness to that from which it proceeds. This is the teaching of Hilary (*De Syn.*) : *God's will gave every creature its nature, whereas a perfect nativity gave the Son his nature.* Hence everything is such as God willed it to be, while the Son is such as God is. Now, as already stated, although the will is indifferent to some things, it has a natural inclination in regard to the last end: and in like manner the intellect has a certain natural movement in respect of its knowledge of first principles. Moreover, the principle of the divine knowledge is God himself, who is the end of his will; wherefore that which proceeds in God by his act of self-knowledge, proceeds naturally, and likewise that which proceeds by his act of self-love. And for this reason, since the Son proceeds as the Word by an act of the divine intellect inasmuch as the Father knows himself, and the Holy Ghost by an act of the will inasmuch as the Father loves the Son: it follows that both Son and Holy Ghost proceed naturally, and further, that they are consubstantial, coequal and coeternal with the Father and with each other.

Reply to the First Objection. Hilary is speaking of the necessity that denotes violence: this is evident from the words that follow: *Not led by natural necessity, since he willed[1] to beget the Son.*

Reply to the Second Objection. There is not an antecedent will in God in respect of anything whatsoever; because everything that God ever wills, he has willed from eternity. But his will is concomitant with every good that is in him and creatures: for he wills himself to be and the creature to be. It is, however, precedent or antecedent in point of time with reference to creatures alone who have not existed from eternity. His intellect is precedent as regards those eternal acts which are denominated as terminating in creatures, such as government, predestination and the like. But the generation of the Son is neither a creature nor does it signify an act terminating in a creature. Therefore with regard to it God's will is not antecedent either in time or in our way of thinking, but only concomitant.

Reply to the Third Objection. Just as the act of the

---

[1] *Vellet.* The text of Hilary has *nollet* followed by a comma—not led by natural necessity against his will.

intellect seems to follow the act of the will, in so far as it is commanded by the will, so on the other hand the act of the will seems to follow the act of the intellect, in so far as the will's object, namely the good understood, is offered to it by the intellect. Hence we should go on indefinitely unless we come to a stop either in the act of the intellect or in the act of the will. But we cannot come to a stop in an act of the will whose object is presupposed to its act. Therefore we must come to a stop in an act of the intellect, and an act which proceeds from the intellect naturally, so as not to be commanded by the will. It is in this way that the Son of God proceeds as the Word, by an act of the divine intellect, as we have already stated.

Reply to the Fourth Objection. The act of the divine intellect is natural, in so far as it terminates in God himself who is the principle of his intellect: but in so far as it is described as terminating in creatures, its relation to whom is somewhat like the relation of our intellect to its conclusions, it proceeds not naturally but voluntarily. Consequently some of the acts of the divine intellect are designated as being commanded by the divine will.

Reply to the Fifth Objection. With regard to those things to which it can extend by virtue of its essential principles, nature does not need to be determined by another, but only with regard to those things for which its own principles do not suffice. Consequently philosophers in saying that the work of nature is the work of an intelligence, were not led by observing the effects of heat and cold considered in themselves, since even those who said that natural effects were necessitated by matter referred all the works of nature to the agency of heat and cold. But they were led by observing those effects which were beyond the power of these qualities of heat and cold: such as the arrangement of members in the body of an animal in suchwise that nature is safeguarded. Since this generation is the work of the divine nature considered in itself, there is no need for it to be determined to such an action by the will.—It may also be replied that nature is determined by something for some particular end. But a nature which is itself the end and not directed to an end does not require determination from without.

Reply to the Sixth Objection. The action of the will precedes the action of nature if we take them in separate subjects. Wherefore the action of the entire inferior nature is dependent on the will of its Governor. But in the same subject the action of nature must needs precede the act of the will. For nature is logically prior to will, since nature in the logical order comes the first in a thing's subsistence, while the will comes last as directing that thing to its end. Yet it does not follow that the will is rendered void. For although the will follows the natural inclination in being determined to that one thing which is the last end to which nature inclines, it nevertheless remains undetermined with regard to other things. Take man, for instance, who desires happiness naturally and of necessity, but not other things. Accordingly in God the action of nature precedes the act of the will both naturally and logically: for the generation of the Son is the prototype of all the productions that proceed from the divine will, that is to say of all creatures.

Reply to the Seventh Objection. Though all creatures were made by the Word of God begotten of the Father, it does not follow that if the Word proceeded naturally, creatures also proceed naturally: thus although our intellect knows first principles naturally, it does not follow that it knows naturally the conclusions deduced from them. For the will makes use of our natural gifts for this or that purpose.

Reply to the Eighth Objection. The Father begot voluntarily, but this indicates nothing else than his concomitant will.

Reply to the Ninth Objection. If these words are made to refer to the eternal generation, the Father's love for the Son is not to be taken as the reason but as the sign of that giving whereby the Father from all eternity gave all things to the Son. For likeness is the reason of love.

Reply to the Tenth Objection. Dionysius is speaking of the formation of creatures, not of the generation of the Son.

Reply to the Eleventh Objection. The Holy Ghost is said

to proceed by way of the will, because he proceeds by an act which is naturally an act of the will, namely the mutual love of the Father and the Son. For the Holy Ghost is love even as the Son is the Father's Word expressive of himself.

Reply to the Twelfth Objection. Again this argument proves only that the Father wills the generation of the Son: and this denotes a concomitant will that regards the generation as its object, not as something whereof it is the principle.

Reply to the Thirteenth Objection. Human generation is effected by a natural force, namely the generative power, through the medium of the motive power which is subject to the command of the will, whereas the generative power is not. This does not apply to God, and so the comparison fails.

Reply to the Fourteenth Objection. Augustine does not mean to deny the necessity attaching to immutability as the argument suggests, but the necessity induced by force.

Reply to the Fifteenth Objection. When it is said that the Son is ' will of will ' the sense is ' will of the Father ' who is will. Hence this preposition ' of ' denotes the generative principle that is the begetter, and not the principle whereby generation is effected, which is the point of our inquiry.

ARTICLE IV

CAN THERE BE SEVERAL SONS IN GOD?

THE fourth point of inquiry is whether there can be several Sons in God. It would seem that the reply should be in the affirmative.

1. A natural operation that is becoming to one individual is becoming to every individual of the same nature. Now according to Damascene (*De Fide Orth.* ii, 27) generation is an operation of nature, and it is becoming to the Father. Therefore it is becoming also to the Son and Holy Ghost who are supposits of the same nature. But the Son does not

beget himself since, according to Augustine, nothing can generate itself. Therefore he begets another Son, so that in God there can be several Sons.

2. The Father communicated all his might to the Son. Now the generative power belongs to the Father's might. Therefore the Son has this power from the Father; and the same conclusion follows.

3. The Son is the perfect image of the Father, and this demands perfect likeness. But this would not be the case if the Son did not imitate the Father in all respects. Therefore as the Father begets a Son, so also does the Son; and the same conclusion follows.

4. According to Dionysius (*Cœl. Hier.* iii) likeness to God is more perfect in respect of conformity in action than in respect of conformity in some form: thus that which both shines and illuminates is more like the sun than that which shines only. Now the Son is most perfectly like the Father. Therefore he is conformed to him not only in the power but also in the act of generation. Thus we have the same conclusion as before.

5. The reason why God after making one creature is able to make another is because his power is neither exhausted nor diminished in creating. Now in like manner the Father's power is neither exhausted nor diminished through begetting the Son. Therefore by begetting the Son he is not disabled from begetting another: and so there can be several Sons in God.

6. But, say you, the reason why he does not beget another Son is that the result would be unbecoming, as Augustine points out, namely that there would be an infinite number of divine generations, if the Father were to beget many sons, or the Son to beget grandsons to the Father, and so on.—On the contrary nothing in God is potential but what is also actual, else he were imperfect. Therefore if it is potential that the Father beget several sons, and nothing arise to prevent it, there will be several Sons in God.

7. It belongs to the nature of that which is generated to proceed in likeness to the generator. Now as the Son is like the Father, so also is the Holy Ghost: so that the Holy

Ghost is likewise a Son : and thus there are several Sons in God.

8. According to Anselm (*Monolog.* xxxii) for the Father to beget the Son is nothing else but for the Father to speak himself. Now, as the Father can speak himself,[1] so also can the Son and the Holy Ghost. Therefore Father, Son and Holy Ghost can beget Sons, and the same conclusion follows.

9. The Father is said to beget the Son, because he conceives intellectually his own likeness. But the Son and Holy Ghost can do the same : and thus we come to the same conclusion.

10. Power comes between essence and operation. Now the essence of the Father and the Son is one, and theirs is one power. Therefore it becomes the Son to beget : and we conclude as before.

11. Goodness is the principle of diffusion. Now even as there is infinite goodness in the Father and the Son so is there in the Holy Ghost. Therefore even as the Father by begetting the Son bestows on him his nature by an infinite communication, so likewise does the Holy Ghost by producing a divine person, since the divine goodness is not bestowed in an infinite degree on a creature. Wherefore it would seem that there can be several Sons in God.

12. No good can be possessed happily unless it be shared with another. Now Sonship is a good possessed by the Son. Therefore seemingly his perfect happiness demands that he should beget a Son.

13. The Son proceeds from the Father as brightness from light, according to Hebrews i, 3 : *Who being the brightness of his glory and the figure of his substance.* Now one splendour can produce another, and this one a third, and this one yet another. And thus it would seem to be in the procession of the divine persons, so that the Son can beget another Son ; and hence the same conclusion follows.

14. Paternity belongs to the Father's dignity. But the same dignity is both Father's and Son's. Therefore paternity is becoming to the Son : and consequently the Son begets.

---

[1] *Himself* here is the objective case.

15. Where the power is there is the act. But the Son has the power to beget. Therefore he begets.

On the contrary those creatures are most perfect which contain their entire matter, each one by itself alone forming a single species. Now as material creatures are individualised by their matter, so the person of the Son is constituted by Sonship. Therefore, as the Son of God is a perfect Son, in God seemingly Sonship is in him alone.

Further, Augustine says (*Contra Maxim.* ii, 7, 18, 23) that if the Father being able to beget did not beget he would be envious. But the Son is not envious. Therefore seeing that he does not beget, he cannot do so. Consequently there cannot be several Sons in God. Again, what has been said perfectly should not be said over again. Now the Son is the perfect Word lacking nothing (Augustine, *De Trin.* vi, 10 ; vii, 2). Therefore there ought not to be several Words in God, nor several Sons.

I answer that there cannot be several Sons in God : this is proved as follows. The divine persons in all things absolute are identical, and essentially coincident with one another : and between them there can be no other distinction but that founded on the relations, and on no other relationship but that of origin. The reason of this is that of other relations, some presuppose distinction, such as equality and likeness, while some imply inequality, such as master and servant, and so on. On the other hand relations of origin by their very nature denote conformity : because that which takes its origin from another, as such bears the likeness thereof. In God, therefore, there is nothing whereby the Son can be distinguished from the other persons, except the relation of Sonship, which is his personal property, and by virtue of which he is not only the Son but also this supposit or this person. Now it is impossible for that whereby this particular supposit is individualised to be found in anything else : otherwise the supposit itself would be communicable, which is incompatible with the very nature of an individual, supposit or person. Consequently it is utterly impossible that in God there be more Sons than one. For it cannot be said that one Sonship makes one Son, and another Sonship another Son : because as sonships do not differ logically, it would follow that if they differed in matter or supposit, there would be matter in God, or some principle of distinction other than relation.

Besides the above, another special reason may be given why the Father can beget but one Son. Nature is determined to one effect : and therefore, since the Father begets the Son by nature, there can be but one Son begotten of the Father. Nor can it be said that there are several in the one species, as is the case with us ; since in God there is no matter which is the principle of numerical distinction within the one species.

Reply to the First Objection. Although in the Father generation is an operation of the divine nature, nevertheless it belongs thereto with reference at the same time to the personal property of the Father, as stated above (A. 2) : wherefore it does not follow that it belongs to the Son, who has the divine nature without that property.

Reply to the Second Objection. The Father communicates to the Son all that divine might which goes with the divine nature absolutely. But the generative power goes with the divine nature in conjunction with the personal property of the Father, as stated.

Reply to the Third Objection. An image is like the original in point of species, not of relation. For though the image is produced by someone it does not follow that the original is also produced by someone : because neither is likeness properly considered with regard to relation but with regard to form.

Reply to the Fourth Objection. Even as the Son is like the Father in the divine nature and not in a personal property, so too is he like him in an action that goes with the nature provided it does not go with a personal property. Such, however, is not generation : wherefore the argument fails.

Reply to the Fifth Objection. Although the Father's generative power is not exhausted nor diminished by his begetting the Son : yet the Son equals the infinity of that power, for he is infinite intelligence, and not a finite creature. Hence the comparison fails.

Reply to the Sixth Objection. In a *reductio ad absurdum*, the avoiding of the absurdity is not necessarily the only reason for denying the statement from which the absurdity follows, but there are also the reasons for which the absurdity is made manifest. Hence it is not only because an infinity of generations in God would be the result, that there are not more than one Son in God.

Reply to the Seventh Objection. The Holy Ghost proceeds after the manner of love. Now *love* does not denote something that is stamped and specified with the likeness of the lover or of the beloved, whereas the *word* expresses the idea of the speaker and the thing to which that idea corresponds. Consequently, as the Son proceeds as Word, by the very nature of his procession it belongs to him to proceed in likeness to his Begetter, and therefore he is his Son, and his procession is called a generation. On the other hand this belongs to the Holy Ghost not by reason of his procession, but rather from a property of the divine nature; because in God there can be nothing that is not God: so that the divine love itself is God, precisely because it is divine, not because it is love.

Reply to the Eighth Objection. *To speak* may be taken in two senses, strictly and broadly. To speak, in a strict sense, is to utter a word, and then it denotes a notional act and is proper to the Father. Augustine employs the term in this sense when he says (*Trin.* vii, 1) that the Father alone *speaks himself.* Secondly, *to speak* may be taken broadly in so far as a person may be said to speak when he understands, and then it is an essential act. In this sense Anselm writes (*Monolog.* lx) when he says that the Father, Son and Holy Ghost *speak themselves.*[1]

Reply to the Ninth Objection. Even as *to beget* in God belongs to the Father alone, so also does *to conceive*: wherefore the Father alone conceives his own likeness intellectually, although the Son and the Holy Ghost understand it: because **no** relation is indicated in the word *understand*, except

---

[1] Himself. . . . Themselves . . . objective case.

perhaps only in our way of thinking: whereas *begetting* and *conceiving* imply real origin.

Reply to the Tenth Objection. This argument holds in regard to an action that proceeds from the nature absolutely without any relation to a property. Such, however, is not generation, wherefore the argument fails.

Reply to the Eleventh Objection. In God there can be no other than spiritual procession, and this is only by way of intellect and will. Consequently another divine person cannot proceed from the Holy Ghost, because he proceeds by way of the will as love, and the Son by way of the intellect as Word.

Reply to the Twelfth Objection. A personal property must needs be incommunicable, as stated above : wherefore happiness does not demand that it should be shared with another.

Reply to the Thirteenth Objection. This comparison does not necessarily apply in every respect.

Reply to the Fourteenth Objection. Even as paternity in the Father and filiation in the Son are one essence, so too their dignity and goodness are one.

Reply to the Fifteenth Objection. When we speak of the *potestas generandi* the gerund *generandi* may be taken in three ways. First, as the gerund of the active voice, and thus the *potestas generandi* (power of generating) is in him who has the power to generate. Secondly, as the gerundive of the passive voice, and thus the *potestas generandi* (power to be generated) belongs to one who has the power to be generated. Thirdly, as the gerund of an impersonal verb, and then the *potestas generandi* belongs to one who has the power whereby he is actually generated by another.[1] In the first sense the *potentia generandi* is not in the Son, but it is in the second and third sense : wherefore the argument does not prove.

[1] *Sum. Theol.* P. I, Q. xli, art. 6, ad 1.

ARTICLE V

IS THE GENERATIVE POWER INCLUDED IN OMNIPOTENCE?

THE fifth point of inquiry is whether the generative power is included in omnipotence. And seemingly the reply should be in the negative.

1. Omnipotence is becoming to the Son according to the words of the Creed : *The Father is almighty, the Son is almighty, the Holy Ghost is almighty.* But the generative power is not becoming to him. Therefore it is not included in omnipotence.

2. Augustine (*Enchir.* xcvi) says that God is almighty because he is able to do whatsoever he wills : so that it would seem to follow that omnipotence includes any power that is at the command of the will. Now such is not the generative power : since the Father did not beget the Son by his will, as we have shown above (A. 3). Therefore the generative power does not belong to omnipotence.

3. Omnipotence is attributed to God in the sense that it extends to all those things that are in themselves possible. But the generation of the Son or the Son himself comes within the range not of things possible, but of things necessary. Therefore the generative power is not included in omnipotence.

4. That which belongs to several things in common belongs to them in respect of something that is common to all of them. Thus in every triangle the three angles are together equal to two right angles, and this applies to all triangles inasmuch as they are triangular figures. Consequently that which belongs to one thing alone, belongs to it in respect of that which is proper to it. Now omnipotence is not proper to the Father. Since then the generative power in God belongs to the Father alone, it does not belong to him as omnipotent, and consequently is not included in omnipotence.

5. Even as there is one essence of Father and Son, so is there one omnipotence. Now it does not pertain to the

Son's omnipotence that he be able to beget. Neither, then, does it belong to the omnipotence of the Father: and consequently by no means does the generative power belong to omnipotence.

6. Things differing in kind do not come under the same heading: thus when I say '*all dogs*' I do not include both the dog that barks and the constellation. Now the generation of the Son and the formation of the other things that are the subject-matter of omnipotence are not of the same kind. Therefore when I say: 'God is almighty' I do not include his power of generating.

7. The subject-matter of omnipotence is anything to which omnipotence extends. Now in God there is no subject-matter according to Jerome.[1] Therefore neither the Son's generation nor the Son himself is the subject-matter of omnipotence: and the same conclusion follows as before.

8. According to the Philosopher (*Phys.* v, 1) a relation cannot be the direct term of a movement, nor consequently of an action: and therefore it cannot be the object of a power, since power connotes direction to an action. Now generation and Son imply relation in God. Therefore God's power does not extend to them: and consequently omnipotence does not include the power to beget.

On the contrary Augustine says (*Contra Maxim.* ii, 7, 18, 23): *If the Father is unable to beget a Son equal to him, where is his omnipotence?* Therefore omnipotence includes begetting.

Further, omnipotence is attributed to God in respect not only of external acts, such as creation, government and the like, which are expressed as terminating extrinsically in their effects, but also of interior acts, such as intelligence and will. For if anyone were to say that God cannot understand, he would take away from his omnipotence. Now the Son proceeds as Word by an act of intelligence. Therefore God's omnipotence is understood to include the begetting of the Son.

Again, it is a greater thing to beget the Son than to

[1] Damascene, *De Fide Orthod.* iii, 21; iv, 19.

create heaven and earth. But the power to create heaven and earth belongs to omnipotence. Much more, then, does the power to beget the Son.

Moreover, in every genus there is a principle to which all that belong to that genus are reduced. Now in the genus of powers the principle is omnipotence. Therefore all power is reduced to omnipotence; and consequently the generative power is either included in omnipotence, or there will be two principles in the genus of power, which is impossible.

I answer that the power to beget belongs to the omnipotence of the Father, but not to omnipotence simply. This may be proved as follows.

Since power is considered as being rooted in the essence and is the principle of action, we must judge of the power and action as of the essence. Now in the divine essence we must note that, by reason of its supreme simplicity, whatever is in God is his essence: wherefore the very relations by which the persons are distinct one from another, are in reality the divine essence. And though one and the same essence is common to the three persons, nevertheless the relation of one person is not common to the three, on account of the opposition in which these relations stand to one another. Thus paternity is the divine essence, yet paternity is not in the Son, because paternity is opposed to sonship. Hence we may say that paternity is the divine essence forasmuch as this is in the Father, not as in the Son: because the divine essence is not in the same way in the Father as in the Son: it is in the Son as received from another: but not in the Father. And although the Father has paternity which the Son has not, it does not follow that the Father has something that the Son has not: because the relation, by reason of its generic nature as such, is not a thing (*aliquid*), but is purely relative (*ad aliquid*). That it is something real is due to the fact that it is in a subject, which is either identical with it as in God, or is its cause, as in creatures. Wherefore since that which is absolute is common to Father and Son they are distinct not by something absolute but by something relative: and therefore we must not say that the Father has something that the Son has not, but that something belongs to the Father in one respect, to the Son in another. The same then applies to action and power. Generation denotes action with a certain respect, and the generative power denotes power with a certain respect: so that generation is God's action, but only as it is in the Father: likewise the generative power is the divine omnipotence, but only as this is in the Father. Yet it does not follow that the Father is able to do what the Son cannot do: but whatsoever the Father can do, the Son can do likewise, although he cannot beget, because to beget implies a relation.

Reply to the First Objection. Omnipotence includes the power to beget, but not as it is in the Son, as stated above.

Reply to the Second Objection. In these words Augustine does not intend to explain the whole meaning of omnipotence, but to indicate a sign of omnipotence. Nor is he speaking of omnipotence except in reference to creatures.

Reply to the Third Objection. The possible things to which omnipotence extends must not be confined to those that are contingent, since even necessary things were brought into being by the divine power. Hence there is no reason why the begetting of the Son should not be included among the things possible to the divine power.

Reply to the Fourth Objection. Though omnipotence absolutely considered is not proper to the Father, nevertheless as considered together with its particular mode of existence, or definite relation, it becomes proper to the Father. In the same way the expression *God the Father* is proper to the Father, although *God* is common to the three persons.

Reply to the Fifth Objection. Just as the three persons have one and the same essence, it is not in each under the same relation, or with the same mode of existence: and the same applies to omnipotence.

Reply to the Sixth Objection. The generation of the Son and the formation of creatures are of the same kind not univocally indeed, but only by analogy. Thus Basil (*Hom. de Fide* xv) says that the Son receives in common with all creatures. In this sense he is called the *First-born of every creature* (Colos. i, 15), and for the same reason his generation may be placed under one common head with the production of creatures.

Reply to the Seventh Objection. The generation of the Son is the subject-matter of omnipotence; not, however, so as to imply that being subject denotes inferiority, but so as subject-matter indicates the object of power.

Reply to the Eighth Objection. The generation of the Son signifies the relation by way of action, and the Son signifies the relation as a subsistent hypostasis: and thus there is no reason why we should not refer omnipotence to these things.

The arguments on the other side merely prove that the omnipotence of the Father includes the power to beget.

ARTICLE VI

ARE THE GENERATIVE AND CREATIVE POWERS THE SAME?

THE sixth point of inquiry is whether the power to beget is the same as the power to create : and the answer, seemingly, should be in the negative.

1. According to Damascene (*De Fide Orthod.* ii, 27) generation is the operation or work of nature: whereas according to Hilary (*De Synod.*) creation is a work of the will. Now will and nature are not one and the same principle, but are opposite members of a division, as stated in *Phys.* ii, 4, 5. Therefore the generative and creative powers are not the same.

2. Powers are distinguished by their acts (*De Anima* ii, 4). Now generation and creation are very different acts. Therefore the generative and creative powers are also distinct.

3. There is less unity among things that admit of a same common predication, than among those that have the same being. Now in no respect do the generative and creative powers admit of a same common predication, as neither do the acts of generating and creating, nor the Son and a creature. Therefore the generative and creative powers are not the same in being.

4. There is no order among things that are identical. Now the creative power logically precedes the generative power, even as the essential precedes the notional. Therefore these powers are not the same.

On the contrary in God power and essence are not distinct. But there is only one divine essence. Therefore there is only one divine power. Therefore the powers in question are not distinct.

Again, God does not do by several means what he is able to do by one. Now God is able both to generate and to create by one power, and all the more seeing that the generation of the Son is the prototype of the production of creatures, as Augustine expounds the words, *He spake, and they were made (Gen. ad lit.* ii, 6, 7) : *That is to say He begot the Word in whom they existed as things to be made.* Therefore the generative and creative powers are but one power.

I answer that, as stated above (A. 5), in speaking of the divine power we must take as our guide those things that apply to the divine essence. Now in God though one relation is really distinct from another on account of the mutual opposition between the relations which are real in God, nevertheless the relation and the divine essence are distinct not really, but only logically, since there is no opposition between them. Consequently we cannot grant that there are several absolute things in God, as some have asserted who maintained that there is a twofold being in God, an essential being and a personal being. The reason is that all being in God is essential, and the very persons are constituted by virtue of that essential being. Now when we consider the divine power we find besides the power a certain relation to what is subject to that power.

Accordingly if we take power in its relation to an essential act, such as intelligence or creation, and power in its relation to a notional act such as generation, and compare them together as power, we find that they are one and the same power, even as nature and person have but one being. And yet we understand at the same time that each power has its peculiar relationship to its respective act to which it is directed. Therefore the generative and creative powers are one and the same power, if we consider them as powers, but they differ in their respective relationships to different acts.

Reply to the First Objection. Although in creatures nature and will are distinct, in God they are one and the same.—Or we may reply that the creative power does not denote the purpose or will, but the power as directed by the will: whereas the generative power acts as inclined by nature. But this does not necessitate a distinction of powers, since there is nothing to prevent the same power from being directed to one act by the will and inclined to another by nature. Thus our intellect is urged by the will to believe, and is led by nature to understand first principles.

Reply to the Second Objection. The higher the power the wider its scope: so that a diversity of objects does not require that it should be divided: thus the imagination is one power covering all objects of sense, for the perception of which distinct senses are appropriated. Now the divine power is raised above all others: wherefore a difference of acts requires no distinction therein, if we consider it as power; but God by his one power is able to do all things.

Reply to the Third Objection. The generative and creative powers, considered as to their substance, so to speak, do not merely admit of a same common predication, but they are one and the same thing: the analogy comes in through this relationship to their respective acts.

Reply to the Fourth Objection. There is no order of first and second between these powers, except in respect of their being distinct : so that such an order is only in reference to their acts. Hence it is clear that the generative power precedes the creative power, as generation preceded creation. But in relation to the essence they are identical and there is no order between them.

QUESTION III

OF CREATION

THERE are nineteen points of inquiry : (1) Can God create ? (2) Is creation a kind of change ? (3) Is creation something real in the creature ? (4) Can the creative power be communicated to a creature ? (5) Is it possible for anything to be that is not created by God ? (6) Is there but one principle of creation ? (7) Does God operate in every operation of nature ? (8) Does creation take part in the works of nature ? (9) Is the soul created ? (10) Is the soul created in the body, or outside the body ? (11) Do the sensitive and vegetative souls come into being by creation ? (12) Are those souls in the seed at the time of impregnation ? (13) Can that which derives its being from another be eternal ? (14) Can anything that is essentially distinct from God be eternal ? (15) Did things proceed from God by natural necessity ? (16) Is it possible for many things to proceed from one ? (17) Has the world always existed ? (18) Were the angels created before the material world ? (19) Could angels have existed before the material world ?

ARTICLE I

CAN GOD CREATE A THING FROM NOTHING ?

Sum. Th. I, Q. xlv, A. 2

WE now inquire about the creation, which is the first effect of the divine power ; and the first point of inquiry is whether God can create anything out of nothing. Seemingly the reply should be in the negative.

1. God cannot act counter to first principles ; for instance,

he cannot make a whole not greater than its part. Now according to Aristotle (*Phys.* i, 8) philosophers declare it is a commonly received axiom that out of nothing nothing comes. Therefore God cannot make a thing out of nothing.

2. Whatever is made was possible before it was made : for if it could not be, it could not be made, since the impossible cannot be the term of a change. Now the potentiality by virtue of which a thing is possible, cannot be otherwise than in a subject, unless it be itself a subject : because an accident cannot exist but in a subject. Therefore whatever is made, is produced from matter or a subject. Therefore nothing can be made out of nothing.

3. Infinite distance cannot be crossed. Now there is an infinite distance between absolute non-being and being : because the less a potentiality is disposed to actuality the further is it removed from act, so that if there be no potentiality at all, the distance will be infinite. Therefore it is impossible for a thing to come into being from absolute non-being.

4. The Philosopher says (*De Gen.* i, 7) that things utterly dissimilar do not act on one another : because there must be common genus and matter in agent and patient. Now absolute non-entity and God are utterly dissimilar. Therefore God cannot act on absolute non-entity : and consequently he cannot make a thing out of nothing.

5. Should it be said that the foregoing argument applies to an agent whose action is distinct from its substance, and presupposes a subject into which it is received ?—On the contrary, Avicenna says (*Metaph.* ix, 2) that if heat were separated from matter it would act of itself without its matter : and yet its action would not be its substance. Therefore the fact that God's action is his substance is no reason for his not needing matter.

6. From no premises we can draw no conclusion, which is a process of reason. Now logical being is consequent to natural being. Therefore neither can anything in nature be made from nothing.

7. If a thing is made from nothing, this preposition *from* connotes either cause or order. And apparently if it

connotes a cause it will be either the efficient or the material cause. But *nothing* cannot be the efficient cause of being, nor can it be the material cause, so that as regards the point at issue ' from ' does not denote a cause. Nor can it denote order, because as Boëthius says there is no order between non-being and being. Therefore in no sense can a thing be made from nothing.

8. According to the Philosopher (*Metaph.* v, 12) active power is the cause whereby one thing is changed into another, as such. Now there is no power in God save that which is active. Therefore it requires a thing which is the subject of change and consequently cannot make a thing out of nothing.

9. Things differ from one another in that one is more perfect than another. Now the cause of this difference is not on the part of God, since he is one and simple. Therefore we must assign matter as the cause thereof: and consequently we must hold that things were made from matter and not from nothing.

10. That which is made from nothing has being after non-being. Consequently it is possible to conceive an instant which is the last of its non-being, and when it ceases not to be; and another instant which is the first of its being and from which it begins to be. Now these instants are either one and the same, or distinct. If they coincide it follows that two contradictory statements are true at the same instant: if they are distinct, then since there is an intervening time between the two instants, it follows that there is a mean between affirmation and negation: for it cannot be said that it is not after the last instant of its non-existence, nor that it is before the first instant of its existence. But both these things are impossible, namely that contradictory statements be true simultaneously, and that they have a mean. Therefore a thing cannot be made from nothing.

11. That which is made of necessity at some time was becoming: and what is created was at some time being created. Hence that which is created was becoming and was made either simultaneously or not simultaneously. Now it cannot be said that it was not simultaneously, since the

creature, before it is made, is not : and if its becoming precedes its having been made, there must have been a subject of the making, and this is contrary to the definition of creation. On the other hand if its becoming and its having been made are simultaneous, it follows that at the same time it is being made and not being made, since in things that are not purely transient, that which has been made is : whereas that which is being made, is not. But this is impossible. Therefore it is impossible for a thing to be made from nothing or to be created.

12. Every agent produces its like : and every agent acts forasmuch as it is actual. Therefore nothing is made but what is actual. Now primal matter is not actual. Therefore it cannot be made, especially by God who is pure act. Hence whatsoever things are made, are made from pre-existing matter, and not from nothing.

13. Whatsoever God makes he fashions according to his idea, even as an artist produces art-works according to art-forms. Now there is no idea of primal matter in God, because an idea is a form and the likeness of that which it represents : whereas primal matter, since it is conceived to be essentially formless, cannot be represented by a form. Therefore primal matter cannot be made by God ; and thus the same conclusion follows.

14. The same thing cannot be a principle both of perfection and of imperfection. Now things are said to be imperfect when they are inferior to others, and this can only be the case when their inferiority is due to their being imperfect. Since then God is the principle of perfection, we must needs ascribe imperfection to some other principle : and this can only be matter. Therefore things must needs have been made from matter of some kind, and not from nothing.

15. If a thing is made from nothing, it is made therefrom either as from a subject, as a statue made of bronze ; or as from its opposite, as a shape from something shapeless : or as from these two combined, as a statue from shapeless bronze. Now a thing cannot be made from nothing as subject, since non-being cannot be the matter of being. Nor as a composite, since then non-being would be trans-

formed into being, as shapeless bronze is transformed into shapely bronze ; so that there would have to be something common to being and non-being ; which is impossible. Nor again as from its opposite, since absolute non-being differs more from being than two beings of the same genus, and yet one of the latter cannot be changed into another ; for instance, shape is not changed into colour, except perhaps accidentally. Therefore by no means can a thing be made from nothing.

16. Whatsoever accidentally is originates in that which is essential. From that which is opposite a thing is made accidentally, and from a subject a thing is made essentially : thus a statue is made accidentally from that which is shapeless, but from bronze essentially, since shapelessness is accidental to the bronze. If, then, a thing is made from nothing, this will be accidentally : and thus it follows that it will need to be made from a subject, and therefore not from nothing.

17. The maker gives being to that which is made. If then God makes a thing out of nothing, he gives being to that thing. Hence either there is something that receives being, or there is nothing. If nothing, then nothing receives being by that action of God's, and thus nothing is made thereby. And if there is something that receives being, this something will be distinct from that which is from God, since recipient is distinct from that which is received. Therefore God makes a thing from something already existing, and not from nothing.

On the contrary, on Genesis i, 1, *In the beginning God created heaven and earth,* a gloss taken from Bede says that *to create is to make a thing from nothing.* Therefore God can make a thing from nothing.

Again, Avicenna (*Metaph.* vii, 2) says that an agent who acts by virtue of an accident requires matter to act upon. But God does not act by virtue of an accident, indeed his action is his very substance. Therefore he requires no matter to act upon, and consequently can make a thing from nothing.

Again, God's power is greater than that of nature. Now

the power of nature makes things from that in which previously they were in potentiality. Therefore God's power does something more, and makes things out of nothing.

I answer that we must hold firmly that God can and does make things from nothing.

In order to make this evident we must observe that every agent acts forasmuch as it is in act : wherefore action must needs be attributed to an agent according to the measure of its actuality. Now a particular thing is actual in a particular manner, and this in two ways. First by comparison with itself, because its substance is not wholly act, since such things are composed of matter and form : for which reason a natural thing acts not in respect of its totality, but in respect of its form whereby it is in act. Secondly, in comparison with things that are in act : because no natural thing comprises the acts and perfections of all the things that are in act : but each one has an act confined to one genus and one species, so that none has an activity extending to being as such, but only to this or that being as such, and confined to this or that species : for an agent produces its like. Wherefore a natural agent produces a being not simply, but determines a pre-existent being to this or that species, of fire, for example, or of whiteness and so forth. Wherefore the natural agent acts by moving something, and consequently requires matter as a subject of change or movement, and thus it cannot make a thing out of nothing.

On the other hand God is all act,—both in comparison with himself, since he is pure act without any admixture of potentiality,—and in comparison with the things that are in act, because in him is the source of all things, wherefore by his action he produces the whole subsistent being, without anything having existed before (since he is the source of all being), and in respect of his totality. For this reason he can make a thing from nothing, and this action of his is called creation. Wherefore it is stated in *De Causis* (prop. xviii) that being is by creation, whereas life and the like are by information : for all causation of absolute being is traced to the first universal cause, while the causation of all that is in addition to being, or specific of being, belongs to second causes which act by information, on the presupposition as it were of the effect of the first cause. Hence no thing gives being except in so far as it partakes of the divine power. For this reason it is said again in *De Causis* (prop. iii) that the soul, by giving us being, has a divine operation.

Reply to the First Objection. The Philosopher says that it is a common axiom or opinion of the physicists that from nothing nothing is made, because the natural agent, which was the object of their researches, does not act except by movement. Consequently there must needs be a subject of movement or change which, as we have stated, is not required for a supernatural agent.

Reply to the Second Objection. Before the world was, it was possible for the world to be : but it does not follow that there was need of matter as the base of that possibility. For it is stated in *Metaph.* v, 12, that sometimes a thing is said to be possible, not in respect of some potentiality, but because it involves no contradiction of terms, in which sense the possible is opposed to the impossible. Accordingly it is said that before the world was it was possible for the world to be made, because the statement involved no contradiction between subject and predicate. We may also reply that it was possible by reason of the active power of the agent, but not on account of any passive power of matter. The Philosopher uses this argument (*Metaph.* vii, 13) in treating of natural generation against the Platonists who maintained that separate forms are the principles of natural generation.

Reply to the Third Objection. Between being and absolute non-being there is an infinite distance in a certain sense, and that always, but not in the same way. Sometimes it is infinite on both sides, as when we compare non-being with the divine being which is infinite : thus we might compare infinite whiteness with infinite blackness. Sometimes it is finite on one side only, as when we compare absolute non-being with created being which is finite :

thus we might compare infinite blackness with finite whiteness. Accordingly then from non-being it is impossible to pass to the being that is infinite : but it is possible to pass to the being that is finite, inasmuch as the distance from non-being to that kind of being is determinate on the one side, although there is no passage properly speaking : for thus it is in continuous movements through which one part passes after another. But there is no such passage for that which is infinite.

Reply to the Fourth Objection. When a thing is made from nothing, non-being or nothing does not hold the position of patient, save accidentally, but rather that of the opposite to the thing made by the action. Nor again is the opposite in the position of patient in the action of nature, except accidentally ; but the subject is this.

Reply to the Fifth Objection. If heat were separated from matter, it would act indeed without matter as a requisite for the agent, but not without that matter that is required on the part of the patient.

Reply to the Sixth Objection. In the acts of the reason to come to a conclusion is like being moved in the processes of nature, because in reaching a conclusion the reason discourses from one thing to another: wherefore as all natural movement is from a starting-point, so also is every conclusion of the reason. And as the understanding of first principles, which is the starting-point whence the conclusion is derived, does not proceed as a conclusion from something else, even so creation which is the principle of all movement, is not from something else.

Reply to the Seventh Objection. When a thing is said to be made from nothing, the sense is twofold, as Anselm says (*Monolog.* v, viii). The negative implied in the word ' nothing ' may bear directly on the preposition ' from,' or it may be included in that preposition. If it bears directly on the preposition, again a twofold sense is possible. It may bear on the whole so that the negative extends not only to the preposition but also to the verb ; in this sense we might say that a thing is made from nothing because it is not made : thus it could be said of a silent man that he speaks of nothing. In this sense we may say of God that he is made from nothing, because he is utterly not made : but this manner of speaking is not customary. In another sense the verb remains affirmed, and the negative bears on the preposition only : and then we say that a thing is made from nothing, because it is made indeed, but there is no pre-existing thing from which it is made : thus we say that so-and-so grieves for nothing, because he has no cause for grieving : it is in this sense that a thing is said to be made from nothing by creation. If, however, the preposition includes the negation, then again the sense is twofold, one true, one false. It is false if the preposition connotes causality (since in no way can non-being be the cause of being) : it is true if it implies mere order, so that to make a thing from nothing, is to make a thing whereas before there was nothing, and this is true of creation. The statement of Boëthius that there is no order between non-being and being, refers to the order of definite proportion, or of real relation ; such order, says Avicenna (*Metaph.* iii) cannot be between being and non-being.

Reply to the Eighth Objection. This definition applies to a natural active power.

Reply to the Ninth Objection. God produces things not of natural necessity but according to the order of his wisdom. Hence it does not follow that diversity among things arises from their matter but from the ordering of divine wisdom, which established diverse natures for the adornment of the universe.

Reply to the Tenth Objection. When a thing is made from nothing, its being begins in an instant, and its non-being is not in that instant, nor is it in any real but only in an imaginary instant. For as outside the universe there is no real but only an imaginary dimension, in respect of which we may say that God is able to make a thing outside the universe at this or that distance from the universe ; even so before the beginning of the world there was no real but an imaginary time, wherein it is possible to conceive an instant which was the last instant of non-being. Nor does it follow that there must have been a time between those two instants, since real time is not a continuation of imaginary time.

Reply to the Eleventh Objection. That which is made from nothing becomes and is already made simultaneously : and the same applies to all instantaneous changes ; thus the air is being illuminated and is actually illuminated at the same time. For in such things to become and to be already made are synonymous, in so far as a thing already is in the first instant of its making.

It may also be replied that a thing which is made from nothing is said to be in course of making when it is already made, not in respect of movement, which is from one term to another, but in respect of the outflow of the agent into the thing made. For these two are to be found in natural generation, namely transition from one term to another, and outflow of agent into the thing made, but the latter alone has a place in creation.

Reply to the Twelfth Objection. Properly speaking neither matter, nor form, nor accident are said to be made : but that which is made is the thing that subsists. For since to be made terminates in being, it belongs properly to that to which it belongs *per se* to be, namely to a subsistent thing : wherefore neither matter, nor form, nor accident are said properly speaking to be created, but to be concreated : whereas a subsistent thing, whatsoever it may be, is properly said to be created. Without, however, laying stress on this, we may reply that primal matter has a likeness to God in so far as it has a share of being. For even as a stone, as a being, is like God, although it has no intelligence as God has, so primal matter in so far as it has being and yet not actual being, is like God. Because being is, so to say, common to potentiality and act.

The reply to the Thirteenth Objection follows from this : because properly speaking there is no idea of matter but of the composite, since the idea is the form whereby something is made. Yet we may say that there is an idea of matter in so far as matter in a sense reflects the divine essence.

Reply to the Fourteenth Objection. If one of two creatures be inferior to the other, it does not follow that it is imperfect, because imperfection denotes the lack of something which is natural or due to a thing. Hence in heaven though one saint is above another, none will be imperfect. And if there be imperfection in creatures, it need not be ascribed to God or to matter, but to the fact that the creature is made from nothing.

Reply to the Fifteenth Objection. A thing is said to be made from nothing as from an opposite, in the sense explained above. Yet it does not thereby follow that a being of one kind can be made from one of another kind, for instance, shape from colour : because being and non-being cannot possibly co-exist, whereas colour and shape can. On the other hand that wherefrom a thing is made must needs be in contact with the thing made, yet they are not simultaneous.

Reply to the Sixteenth Objection. If *from* connotes causality, a thing is not made from its opposite except accidentally, that is by reason of the subject. If however it connotes order, a thing is made from its opposite even *per se :* hence privation is said to be the principle of a thing's becoming but not of its being. It is in this sense, as stated above, that a thing is said to be made from nothing.

Reply to the Seventeenth Objection. God at the same time gives being and produces that which receives being, so that it does not follow that his action requires something already in existence.

ARTICLE II

IS CREATION A CHANGE ?
Sum. Th. I, Q. xlv, A. 2, *ad* 2

THE second point of inquiry is whether creation is a change : and seemingly the reply should be in the affirmative.

1. Change denotes the succession of one being after another, as stated in *Phys.* v, 1 : and this is true of creation, which is the production of being after non-being. Therefore creation is a change.

2. Whatever is made, in a sense is made from non-being :

since what is, is not being made. Consequently as generation (whereby a thing is made as to a part of its substance) is to the privation of the form (which privation is non-being in a certain respect), so is creation (whereby a thing is made as to its entire substance) to absolute non-being. Now properly speaking, privation is the term from which generation begins. Therefore properly speaking absolute non-being is the term from which creation begins; so that creation properly speaking is a change.

3. The greater the distance between the terms, the greater the change. Thus a change from white to black is greater than a change from white to pale. Now absolute non-being is more distant from being than one contrary from another, or than relative non-being from being. Therefore since transition from contrary to contrary, or from relative non-being to being is a change, much more is creation a change, since it is the transition of absolute non-being into being.

4. That which is in a condition now otherwise than before is changed or moved. Now the creature is conditioned now otherwise than before: since formerly it was absolute non-being, and afterwards became a being. Therefore that which is created is changed or moved.

5. That which passes from potency to act is changed. Now the creature passes from potency to act: since before it was created it was only in the potency of the maker, and now it actually is. Hence that which is created is moved or changed, and consequently creation is a change.

On the contrary, according to the Philosopher (*Categ.* 14) in his work on the Categories, there are six kinds of movement or change: but none of them is creation, as one may see by taking them one by one. Therefore creation is not a change.

I answer that in every change there needs to be something common to either term thereof: because if the opposite terms of a change had nothing in common, it could not be defined as a transition from one thing to another. For change and transition signify that one same thing is otherwise now than before. Moreover the very terms of a change are not incompatible except in so far as they are referred to one same thing: because two contraries if referred to different subjects can exist simultaneously. Accordingly there is sometimes one actually existent common subject of both terms of a change, and then we have movement properly so called, an example of which we have in alteration, increase and decrease, and local movement. In all such movements the one subject while actually remaining the same is changed from one contrary to another. Sometimes again we find the one subject common to either term, yet it is not an actual but only a potential being, as is the case in simple generation and corruption. For the subject of the substantial form and of the privation thereof is primal matter which is not an actual being: wherefore neither generation nor corruption are movements properly so called, but a kind of change. And sometimes there is no common subject actually or potentially existent: but there is the one continuous time, in the first part of which we find the one contrary, and in the second part the other: as when we say that this thing is made from that, namely after that, for instance, from the morning comes noon. This, however, is a change not properly but metaphorically speaking, forasmuch as we imagine time as being the subject of those things that take place in time. Now in creation there is nothing common in the ways above mentioned: for there is no common subject actually or potentially existent. Again there is no continuous time, if we refer to the creation of the universe, since there was no time when there was no world. And yet we may find a common but purely imaginary subject, in so far as we imagine one common time when there was no world and afterwards when the world had been brought into being. For even as outside the universe there is no real magnitude, we can nevertheless picture one to ourselves: so before the beginning of the world there was no time and yet we can imagine one. Accordingly creation is not in truth a change, but only in imagination, and not properly speaking but metaphorically.

Reply to the First Objection. As stated above, the word change denotes the existence of one thing after another in connection with one same subject : but this is not the case in creation.

Reply to the Second Objection. In generation whereby a thing is made in respect of part of its substance, there is a common subject of privation and form, that is not actually existent : wherefore, just as in generation we find a term properly speaking, so also properly speaking do we find transition : but it is not so with creation, as stated above.

Reply to the Third Objection. It is true that the greater the distance the greater the change, provided that the subject is identical.

Reply to the Fourth Objection. That which is otherwise now than it was before is changed, provided the subject remains : else absolute non-being would be changed, because it is neither the same as nor otherwise than it was before. And in order that there be a change, one same thing must be otherwise than it was before.

Reply to the Fifth Objection. Passive and not active power is the subject of change : hence that which proceeds from passive power into act is changed, but not that which proceeds from an active power : and so the objection proves nothing.

ARTICLE III

IS CREATION SOMETHING REAL IN THE CREATURE, AND IF SO, WHAT IS IT ?

Sum. Th. I, Q. xlv, A. 3

THE third point of inquiry is whether creation be anything real in the creature, and if so what is it ? Seemingly it is not anything real in the creature.

1. As stated in *De Causis* (prop. x) whatever is received into a thing is therein according to the mode of the recipient. Now the creative action of God is received in absolute non-being, since in creating God makes a thing from nothing. Therefore creation places nothing real in the creature.

2. All that is real is either God or a creature. Now creation is not the Creator, else it would be eternal : nor is it

a creature, since then it would need to be created by another creative act: and this creature again would need to be created by yet another creative act, and so on indefinitely. Therefore creation is not a real thing.

3. Whatever is is either substance or accident. But creation is not a substance, for it is neither matter nor form nor composite, as can easily be proved. Nor is it an accident, for an accident is subsequent to its subject, whereas creation is naturally prior to its subject, since it presupposes no subject. Therefore creation is nothing real in things.

4. As generation is to the thing generated, so is creation to the thing created. But the subject of generation is not the thing generated, but its term; its subject is primal matter (*De Generat. et Corrupt.* 1, 1). Neither therefore is the thing created the subject of creation. Nor can it be said that its subject is some matter, since the creature is not created from any matter. Therefore creation has no subject, and hence it is not an accident: and it is clear that it is not a substance. Therefore it is nothing real in things.

5. If creation be something real in a thing, since it is not a change, as proved above, it would seem most likely that it is a relation. But it is not a relation, since it cannot belong to any of the species of relation: because absolute being is neither subject nor equal to absolute non-being whence such relation would proceed. Therefore creation is nothing real in a thing.

6. If creation implies a relation of the creature to God from whom it has its being: since such relation remains ever in the creature, not only when the latter begins to be, but as long as it exists, something would be continually created; which would seem absurd. Hence creation is not a relation, and the same conclusion follows as before.

7. Every relation that exists really in things derives from something distinct from that relation, for instance, equality results from quantity, and likeness from quality. If then creation be a relation really existing in the creature, it must needs be distinct from the source whence it flows. Yet this is that which is received through creation. But it would follow that creation is not received by the creative act, and

consequently that it is something uncreated: which is impossible.

8. Every change is reduced to the genus which is its term, for instance, alteration is referred to quality, increase to quantity: and for this reason it is stated in *Phys.* iii, 1, that there are as many kinds of movement as there are of being. Now creation terminates in substance, and yet cannot be said to belong to the genus of substance, as was proved above (*Obj.* 3). Therefore seemingly it is nothing real.

On the contrary, if creation is nothing real, nothing is really created. Now this is clearly false. Therefore creation is something real.

Again, God is Lord of the creature because he brought it into being by creating it. Now dominion implies a real relation in the creature. Much more therefore does creation.

I answer that some have said that creation is something real between the Creator and the creature. And since the mean is neither of the extremes, it would follow that creation is neither the Creator nor the creature. But the Masters judged this to savour of error, since everything that in any way exists has its existence not otherwise than from God, and consequently is a creature.

Wherefore others said that creation itself does not posit anything real on the part of the creature. But this would also seem unreasonable. Because in all those things that are referred the one to the other, the one depending on the other but not conversely, there is a real relation in the one that is dependent, and in the other there is a logical relation, as in the case of knowledge and the thing known, according to the teaching of the Philosopher (*Metaph.* v, 15). Now the creature by its very name is referred to the Creator: and depends on the Creator who does not depend on it. Wherefore the relation whereby the creature is referred to the Creator must be a real relation, while in God it is only a logical relation. The Master says this expressly (I., D. 30).

We must accordingly say that creation may be taken actively or passively. Taken actively it denotes the act of God, which is his essence, together with a relation to the creature: and this is not a real but only a logical relation. But taken passively, since, as we have already said, it is not properly speaking a change, it must be said to belong, not to the genus of passion, but to that of relation. This is proved as follows. In every real change and movement there is a twofold process. One is from one term of movement to the other, for instance from whiteness to blackness: the other is from the agent to the patient, for instance from the maker to the thing made. These processes however differ from each other while the movement is in progress, and when the term has been reached. While the movement is in progress, the thing moved is receding from one term and approaching the other: which does not apply when the term has been reached: as may be seen in that which is moved from whiteness to blackness, for at the term of the movement it no longer approaches to blackness, but begins to be black. Likewise while it is in movement the patient or the thing made is being changed by the agent: but when it is at the term of the movement, it is no longer being changed by the agent, but acquires a certain relation to the agent, inasmuch as it has its being therefrom, and is in some way like unto it: thus at the term of human generation the offspring acquires sonship. Now creation, as stated above (A. 2), cannot be taken for a movement of the creature previous to its reaching the term of movement, but denotes the accomplished fact. Wherefore creation does not denote an approach to being, nor a change effected by the Creator, but merely a beginning of existence, and a relation to the Creator from whom the creature receives its being. Consequently creation is really nothing but a relation of the creature to the Creator together with a beginning of existence.

Reply to the First Objection. In creation the recipient of the divine action is not non-being but that which is created, as stated above.

Reply to the Second Objection. Creation taken actively denotes the divine action to which the mind attaches a certain relation, and thus it is uncreated: but taken passively, as stated above, it is a real relation signified after the manner of a change on account of the newness or beginning that it implies. Now this relation is a kind of creature, taking creature in a broad sense for anything that comes from God. Nor is it necessary to proceed to infinity, since the relation of creation is not referred to God by another real relation but by itself : because no relation is related by another relation, as Avicenna says (*Metaph*. iii, 10). If, however, we take creature in a stricter sense for that only which subsists (which properly speaking is made and created, even as properly speaking it has being), then the aforesaid relation is not a created thing, but is concreated ; even as properly speaking it is not a being, but something inherent. The same applies to all accidents.

Reply to the Third Objection. This relation is an accident, and considered in its being, inasmuch as it adheres to a subject, is subsequent to the thing created : even so an accident both logically and naturally is subsequent to its subject : although it is not an accident such as is caused by the principles of its subject. If, however, we consider it from the point of view of its arising from the action of the agent, then the aforesaid relation is after a fashion prior to its subject, because like the divine act itself it is the proximate cause thereof.

Reply to the Fourth Objection. In generation there is both change and a relation whereby the thing generated is referred to the generator. Considered from the point of view of change its subject is not the thing generated but the matter thereof : but considered as implying a relation its subject is the thing generated. On the other hand in creation there is a relation, but there is not a change properly speaking, as already stated : hence the comparison fails.

Reply to the Fifth Objection. This relation is not to be taken as existing between being and non-being, for such a relation cannot be real, as Avicenna says (*Metaph*. iii.), but as between a being and its Creator : wherefore it is clear that it is a relation of subjection.

Reply to the Sixth Objection. Creation denotes this relation together with inception of existence : hence it does not follow that a thing, whenever it may be, is being created, although its relation to God ever remains. Yet even as the air as long as it is light is illuminated by the sun, so may we say with Augustine (*Gen. ad lit.* viii, 12) that the creature, as long as it is in being, is made by God. But this is only a distinction of words, inasmuch as creation may be understood with newness of existence or without.

Reply to the Seventh Objection. That from which the creative relation derives chiefly is the subsistent being, from which that relation, itself a creature, differs, not principally but secondarily as it were, as something concreated.

Reply to the Eighth Objection. Movement is reduced to the genus of its term, in so far as there is a process from potency to act; since during the movement the term thereof is potential, and potency and act belong to the same genus. But in creation there is no process from potency to act; wherefore the comparison fails.

ARTICLE IV

IS THE CREATIVE POWER OR ACT COMMUNICABLE TO A CREATURE ?

Sum. Th. I, Q. xl, A. 5

THE fourth point of inquiry is whether the creative power or act be communicable to a creature. And seemingly it is.

1. The same manner and order in which things flow from their first principle is observed in their direction to their last end, since their first principle is the same as their last end. Now the lower creatures are directed to God as their end by means of the higher creatures, because as Dionysius says (*Cœl. Hier.* v. 1) it is a rule of the Godhead to draw to himself the last things through the first. Therefore the lower creatures also flow from their first principle through creation by means of the higher creatures, so that the creative act is communicated to the creature.

2. Whatsoever can be communicated to a creature without taking it outside the bounds of a creature is communicable to a creature by the power of the Creator, who

is able to create even new kinds of creatures. Now the power to create if communicated to a creature would not place the creature outside its bounds. Therefore the creative power is communicable to a creature. The minor is proved as follows. To place a creature outside its bounds is to attribute something that is incompatible with the notion of being created. Now it is not incompatible with the notion of being created that a creature be able to create, unless because it would seem to need an infinite power in order to create. But it would not need such a power, as it seems: since a thing is as distant from one of two opposites as it shares in the nature of the other: thus the further a thing is from being black the more white it is. Now the creature has a finite share in the nature of being: wherefore its distance from absolute non-being is also finite. And the bringing of a thing into being from a finite distance is not a proof of infinite power; wherefore the creative act can proceed from a finite power, and consequently the creative power is not incompatible with the notion of being created, nor does it place the creature beyond its bounds.

3. Regarding the statement just made that a thing is as distant from one opposite as it shares in the nature of the other, it might be remarked that this is true when both opposites are natures, such as contraries are, but not when one is a nature and the other not, as privation and habit, affirmation and negation.—On the contrary, the opposition in question is between contraries in the point of their being distant from each other, and this belongs to them inasmuch as they are opposites. Now the cause and root of opposition in contraries is the opposition of affirmation and negation (*Metaph.* iv, 6). Therefore the above statement is especially true of the opposition of affirmation and negation.

4. According to Augustine (*Gen. ad lit.* ii, 8) things are said to be made in three ways: in the Word, in the angelic intelligence, in their own nature. Wherefore it is said (Gen. i): *He said: Be . . . made, and it was made.* Now the manner in which things were made in the angelic intelligence comes between the other two ways. Therefore

seemingly creatures come into being in their own nature from the Word of the Creator through the medium of the angelic knowledge : so that they could be created by means of the angels.

5. Nothing and something are more distant than something and being, since nothing and something have nought in common, whereas something is a part of being. Now God by creating makes that which was nothing to become something, and consequently that there be power where before there was no power. Much more then can he make a limited power such as that of a creature to have omnipotence whereby things are created. Therefore he can communicate to a creature the act of creation.

6. Spiritual light is more excellent and more powerful than material light. Now material light multiplies itself. Therefore an angel who is spiritual light according to Augustine (*Gen. ad lit.* iv, 22) is able to multiply himself. But he cannot do this except by creating. Therefore an angel can create.

7. Substantial forms are not generated, since the composite alone is generated as the Philosopher proves (*Metaph.* vii, 8, 9), wherefore they cannot be brought into being except by creation. Now created nature disposes matter for its form. Therefore it co-operates in creation ministerially; and consequently a creature can receive the power to help in the work of creation.

8. The work of justification ranks higher than the work of creation, forasmuch as grace surpasses nature. Hence Augustine says (*Tract.* lxxii, 3, *in Joan.*) that the justification of a sinner is a greater work than the creation of heaven and earth. Now the creature renders service in the justification of a sinner : since the priest is said to justify or forgive sins ministerially. Much more therefore can a creature administer in the act of creation.

9. Every made thing must be like the agent, as is proved in *Metaph.* vii, 8. Now the corporeal creature is not like God either specifically or generically. Therefore it cannot come from God by creation except by means of a creature like unto it at least in genus : and consequently it would seem

that corporeal creatures are created by God by means of the higher creatures.

10. It is stated in *De Causis* (prop. xix) that the second intelligence does not receive of the higher goods which come from the first cause, save through the medium of the higher intelligence. Now being is one of the higher goods. Therefore the second intelligence does not receive its being from God except through the first intelligence : so that seemingly God communicates the creative act to a creature.

11. In the same work (prop. viii) it is stated that an intelligence knows what is beneath it after the manner of its substance inasmuch as it is its cause. Now one intelligence understands another that is beneath it : therefore it is its cause. But an intelligence, since it is not composite, is not caused otherwise than by creation. Therefore an intelligence can create.

12. Augustine says (*De immortal. anim.* xvi) that the spiritual creature gives species and being to the corporeal creature : and so it would seem that corporeal creatures are created by means of the spiritual.

13. Knowledge is twofold, that from which things derive (*ad rem*) and that which is derived from things (*a rebus*). Now an angel's knowledge of corporeal things is not derived from things, since he has no sensitive faculties which are the channels through which the intellect derives its knowledge of sensible objects. Hence he knows things by knowledge from which things derive, which is like God's. Therefore as God is the cause of things by his knowledge, so seemingly the angelic knowledge is the cause of things.

14. Things come into being in two ways ; first through issuing from absolute non-being into being by creation ; secondly through issuing from potency into act. Now the material forces of nature can produce things in the second way, namely by drawing them out of potency into act. Therefore an immaterial force which is more powerful, such as that of an angel, can bring a thing into being in the first way which belongs to the greater power, namely by producing it from absolute non-being, which is to create : and so it would seem that an angel can create.

15. Nothing surpasses the infinite. Now it requires an infinite power to produce a thing out of nothing, otherwise there would be no reason why creatures should not create. Wherefore no other power can surpass it : so that to produce a creature out of nothing and give it the power to create is no more than to create. Now God can do the latter : wherefore he can also do the former.

16. The greater the resistance offered by the patient to the agent, the greater the difficulty encountered by the agent. Now a contrary offers more resistance than a non-being : since a non-being cannot act as a contrary can. Since then a creature is able to make a thing from its contrary, much more seemingly should it be able to make something out of nothing, which is to create. Therefore a creature can create.

On the contrary being and non-being are infinitely apart. Now an infinite power is required to operate at an infinite distance. Therefore an infinite power is required to create : so that the creative power cannot be communicated to a creature.

Again, according to Dionysius (*Cœlest. Hier.* xi) the higher creatures such as the angels are divided into essence, power and operation : whence we may conclude that no creature's power is its essence : so that no creature acts of its whole self, since that by which a thing acts is its power. Now the production of the effect corresponds to the act of the agent. Therefore no creature is able to produce an effect in its entirety, and consequently it cannot create, but always presupposes matter for its action.

Moreover, Augustine (*De Trin.* iii, 8, 9) says that angels cannot create anything, be they good or bad. Now of all creatures the angels rank highest : much less then can any other creature create.

Again, it belongs to the same power to create and to preserve creatures in being. Now creatures cannot be preserved in being save by the divine power, since if it withdrew from things they would at once cease to be, as Augustine says (*Gen. ad lit.* iv, 12). Therefore things cannot be created except by the divine power.

OF CREATION

Again, that which belongs strictly to one thing cannot be appropriate to another. Now it is generally agreed that to create belongs to God. Therefore to create cannot be appropriate to a creature.

I answer that, certain philosophers held that God created the lower creatures through the instrumentality of the higher (*De Causis,* prop. x ; Avicenna, *Metaph.* ix, 4 ; Algazel). They were led to this conclusion through supposing that from one simple being only one being can be produced, and that through the instrumentality of the latter a multitude of things were produced by the first being. They spoke thus as though God acted from natural necessity ; for thus from one simple thing only one can proceed. We, on the other hand, hold that things proceed from God by way of knowledge and intelligence, in which way there is nothing to prevent a multitude of things from proceeding immediately from the one first and simple being God, inasmuch as his wisdom contains all things. Hence according to the Catholic Faith we hold that God immediately created all spiritual substances and corporeal matter, and deem it heresy to say that anything was created by an angel or by any creature. Wherefore Damascene (*De Orth. Fid.* ii, 2) declares : *Whosoever shall say that an angel created anything, let him be anathema.* Certain Catholic writers, however, have maintained that, although no creature can create, it could be granted to a creature that God should create a thing through its instrumentality. The Master favours this opinion (IV., D. 5). Some on the other hand hold that the creative act cannot in any sense be communicated to a creature : and this is the more common opinion.

In order to make this point clear, we must observe that creation denotes an active power whereby things are brought into being, wherefore it requires no pre-existing matter or previous agency : for these are the only causes that are pre-requisite for action. The reason of this is that the form of the thing generated is the term of the generator's action, and is likewise the end of generation which as to its being does not precede but follows the action. Now it is clear from its definition that creation does not presuppose matter :

since to create is to make a thing from nothing. That it does not presuppose a previous active cause is clear from the teaching of Augustine who (*De Trin.* iii, 8) proves that the angels cannot create, because they work by means of nature's implanted seeds, namely the active forces of nature. Accordingly if we take creation thus strictly, it is evident that the first agent alone is competent to create, since a second cause does not act save through the influx of the first : so that every action of a second cause is dependent on a pre-existing active cause. Nor did the philosophers maintain that angels or intelligences create, except through a divine power communicated to them : in the sense that the second cause could have a twofold action, one proceeding from its own nature, the other from the power of a pre-existing cause. For it is not possible that a second cause by its own power be the principle of being as such : this belongs to the first cause, since the order of effects follows the order of causes. Now the first of all effects is being, which is presupposed to all other effects, and does not presuppose any other effect : wherefore to give being as such must be the effect of the first cause alone by its own power : and whatever other cause gives being does this in so far as it is the recipient of the divine power and operation, and not by its own power. Thus an instrument performs an instrumental operation not by the power of its own nature, but by the power of the person who handles it : and thus the natural heat engenders living flesh by the power of the soul, while by the power of its nature it merely causes heat and dissolution. In this sense then certain philosophers held the first intelligences to create the second in giving them being by the power of the first cause communicated to them. For being is by creation, while goodness, life and so forth are by information as stated in *De Causis*. This was the foundation of idolatry, in that divine worship was accorded to created substances as though they were the creators of others.

The Master, however (*l.c.*), holds that it is possible for a creature to receive the power to create not as by its own power, or authority as it were, but ministerially as an instrument. But if we look into the question carefully, it will be clear that this is impossible. The action of any thing, even though it be performed instrumentally, must proceed from that thing's power. And since the power of every creature is finite, no creature can possibly act, even as an instrument, to the effect of creating something: since creation demands infinite energy in the power whence it proceeds. This is made clear by the five following arguments.

The first is based on the fact that the power of a maker is proportionate to the distance between the thing made and the opposite thing from which it is made: thus the colder a thing is, and therefore the further removed it is from being hot, the greater will be the heat-power required to make that cold thing hot. Now absolute non-being is infinitely distant from being: because non-being is further removed from any particular being than any other particular being however distant these may be: and consequently none but an infinite power can produce being from non-being.

The second reason is that in the making of a thing the manner of the making depends on the action of the maker. Now the agent acts forasmuch as it is in act: wherefore that alone acts by its whole self, which is wholly in act, and this belongs to none but the infinite act who is the first act: and consequently none but an infinite power can make a thing as to its whole substance.

The third reason is that since an accident must needs be in a subject, and the subject of an action is the recipient of that action, that agent alone whose action is not an accident but its very substance requires no recipient matter when it makes a thing; and such an agent is none but God, who therefore alone can create.

The fourth reason is that as all second causes derive their action from the first cause, as is proved in *De Causis*, prop. xix, xx, it follows that all second agents receive their mode and order from the first agent, who receives neither mode nor order from any other. Now, since the mode of an action depends on the matter that is the recipient of the agent's action, the first agent alone will be competent to act without presupposing matter from another agent, and to provide matter for all second agents.

The fifth argument is a reduction to absurdity. In so far as they reduce a thing from potentiality to act powers are proportionate to one another according to the distance of the potentiality from the act, since the further the potentiality is removed from the act, the greater is the power required. Hence if there be a finite power productive of something without any presupposed potentiality, there must be some proportion between it and a power that educes a thing from potentiality to act : so that there will be proportion between no potentiality and some potentiality : which is impossible : for there is no proportion between non-being and being. We conclude then that no power of a creature can create, neither by its own virtue, nor as the instrument of another.

Reply to the First Objection. In the bringing of things to their end, the means to that end are already in existence : wherefore it is not impossible for a creature to co-operate with God in the direction of things to their last end : whereas in the general bringing of things into being nothing existed as yet : hence the comparison fails.

Reply to the Second Objection. Nothing prevents our imagining a distance on the one part infinite and on the other finite. We imagine a distance infinite on either part, when either opposite extreme is infinite, for instance, infinite heat and infinite cold : but the imagined distance will be finite on the one hand, when one of the opposite extremes is finite ; for instance, infinite heat and finite cold. Accordingly infinite being is infinitely removed on both hands from absolute non-being : whereas finite being from absolute non-being is removed infinitely on the one hand only ; yet it requires an infinite active power.

The Third Objection we grant, since it makes no difference to the point at issue whether both opposite extremes be a nature, or one only.

Reply to the Fourth Objection. Things are said to be made in our intelligence in respect of knowledge only, and by reason of an operative power : wherefore things are

OF CREATION

brought into being not with the co-operation of the angels, but with their knowledge.

Reply to the Fifth Objection. A thing is said to be impossible to someone not only on account of the distance between the extremes, but also because it is altogether impossible to be done : for instance, we might say that God cannot be made from a body, because it is altogether impossible for God to be made. Accordingly we reply that omnipotence cannot be made from a power, not only on account of the distance between them, but also because omnipotence is utterly unmakable. For whatever is made cannot be pure act, since from the very fact that it has its being from another, it is proved to have potentiality, and consequently cannot have infinite power.

Reply to the Sixth Objection. Material light multiplies itself not by creating a new light, but by shedding itself over matter. This cannot be said of the angels since they are self-subsistent substances.

Reply to the Seventh Objection. A form may be considered in two ways. First, in so far as it is in potentiality : and thus God concreates it with matter, without any concurrent action of nature for the disposition of the matter. Secondly, in so far as it is in act, and thus it is not created, but is educed by natural agency from the potentiality of matter : wherefore there is no need of dispositive action on the part of nature in order that a thing be created. Seeing, however, that there is a natural form, namely the rational soul, which is brought into being by creation, and whose matter is disposed by nature, we must observe that since the creative act is independent of matter, there are two senses in which a thing is said to be created. Some things are created without any presupposed matter, and produced neither from matter nor in matter, for instance, the angels and the heavenly bodies : and for the creation of such nature can do nothing dispositively. On the other hand some things are created, without any matter presupposed from which they be made, but on the presupposition of matter in which they may be : such are human souls. So far then as they have matter in which to be, nature can act dispositively : yet not so that the action of nature extend to the substance of that which is created.

Reply to the Eighth Objection. In the work of justification man does something, but only as a minister by employing the sacraments : so that as the sacraments are said to justify instrumentally and dispositively, the solution comes to the same as the preceding one.

Reply to the Ninth Objection. Although between God and the creature there cannot be a generic or specific likeness, there can nevertheless be a certain likeness of analogy, as between potentiality and act, substance and accident. This is true in one way forasmuch as creatures reproduce, in their own way, the idea of the divine mind, as the work of a craftsman is a reproduction of the form in his mind. In another way it is true in that creatures are somewhat likened to the very nature of God, forasmuch as they derive their being from the first being, their goodness from the sovereign good, and so on. However this objection is not to the point : for even granted that creatures proceed from God through the instrumentality of some created power, the same difficulty remains, namely how this first nature can be created by God and yet not be like God.

Reply to the Tenth Objection. This error is contained explicitly in *De Causis* (prop. x) whose author holds that the lower creatures were created by God by means of the higher : wherefore in this matter the authority of this book is not to be accepted.

The same is to be said of the Eleventh Objection.

Reply to the Twelfth Objection. Augustine is speaking there of the soul which gives being and species to a corporeal thing not as creating but as informing it.

Reply to the Thirteenth Objection. Although an angel's knowledge of things is not derived from them, it does not follow that his knowledge of them is their cause. His knowledge is a mean between the two kinds of knowledge mentioned. For he knows things by a natural knowledge by means of ideas implanted in his mind from the divine intellect : so that his knowledge is not directed to things as their cause, but is a likeness of the divine intellect which is their cause.

Reply to the Fourteenth Objection. In the eduction of things from potentiality to act many degrees may be observed, inasmuch as a thing may be educed from more or less remote potentiality to act, and again more or less easily. Hence although the angel's power surpasses that of material nature it does not follow that he is able to make a thing from absolute non-being because nature is able to educe a thing from potentiality to act : but that he can do this much more easily than nature. Thus Augustine (*De Trin.* iii, 8, 9) says that demons are able to apply the forces of nature more secretly and efficaciously than we are aware.

Reply to the Fifteenth Objection. No power is greater than the power to create : nor does this prove that the creative power must include the bestowal on a creature of the power to create, since it is utterly incommunicable to a creature. That a thing be impossible may be due not only to one's inability to do it, but also sometimes to the fact that the thing itself cannot be done : thus God cannot make God, not through a defect of power, but because God cannot be made by anyone. In like manner the creative power cannot be finite, nor can it be communicated to a creature, because it is infinite.

Reply to the Sixteenth Objection. A thing is difficult to do in two ways. First, because the patient resists the agent. This does not apply in every case, but only when there is action and reaction, and the agent is subject to the reaction of the patient : thus the heavenly bodies, whose action meets with no opposition on the part of another agent, suffer no difficulty in their action through the patient's counteraction : and much less does God. Secondly, and this applies to all cases, because the patient is far removed from the action : since the further the potentiality is removed from act, the greater is the difficulty encountered by the action of the agent. Wherefore, since absolute non-being is further removed from act than matter subject to any contrary whatsoever, however intense the other contrary may be : it is evident that it requires a greater power to produce a thing from nothing, than one contrary from another.

ARTICLE V

CAN THERE BE ANYTHING THAT IS NOT CREATED BY GOD ?
Sum. Th. I, Q. xliv, A. 1

THE fifth point of inquiry is whether there can be anything that is not created by God. Seemingly this is possible.

1. Since the cause is more powerful than its effect, that which is possible to our intellect which takes its knowledge from things would seem yet more possible to nature. Now our intellect can understand a thing apart from understanding that it is from God, because its efficient cause is not part of a thing's nature, so that the thing can be understood without it. Much more therefore can there be a real thing that is not from God.

2. All things made by God are called his creatures. Now creation terminates at being : for the first of created things is being (*De Causis*, prop. iv). Since then the quiddity of a thing is in addition to its being, it would seem that the quiddity of a thing is not from God.

3. Every action terminates in an act, even as it proceeds from an act : because every agent acts in so far as it is in act, and every agent produces its like in nature. But primal matter is pure potentiality. Therefore the creative act cannot terminate therein : so that not all things are created by God.

On the contrary it is said (Rom. xi, 36) : *From him and by him and in him are all things.*

I answer that the ancients in their investigations of nature proceeded in accordance with the order of human knowledge. Wherefore as human knowledge reaches the intellect by beginning with the senses, the early philosophers were intent on the domain of the senses, and thence by degrees reached the realm of the intellect. And seeing that accidental forms are in themselves objects of sense, whereas substantial forms are not, the early philosophers said that all forms are accidental, and that matter alone is a substance. And because substance suffices to cause accidents that result from the substantial elements, the early philosophers held that there is no other cause besides matter, and that matter is the cause of whatever we observe in the sensible world : and consequently they were forced to state that matter itself has no cause, and to deny absolutely the existence of an efficient cause. The later philosophers, however, began to take some notice of substantial forms : yet they did not attain to the knowledge of universals, and they were wholly intent on the observation of special forms ; and so they posited indeed certain active causes, not such as give being to things in their universality, but which transmute matter to this or that form : these causes they called intelligence, attraction and repulsion, which they held responsible for adhesion and separation. Wherefore according to them not all beings came from an efficient cause, and matter was in existence before any efficient cause came into action. Subsequent to these the philosophers as Plato, Aristotle and their disciples, attained to the study of universal being : and hence they alone posited a universal cause of things, from which all others came into being, as Augustine states (*De Civ. Dei* viii, 4). This is in agreement with the Catholic Faith ; and may be proved by the three arguments that follow.

First, if in a number of things we find something that is common to all, we must conclude that this something was the effect of some one cause : for it is not possible that to each one by reason of itself this common something belong, since each one by itself is different from the others : and diversity of causes produces a diversity of effects. Seeing then that being is found to be common to all things, which are by themselves distinct from one another, it follows of necessity that they must come into being not by themselves, but by the action of some cause. Seemingly this is Plato's argument, since he required every multitude to be preceded by unity not only as regards number but also in reality. The second argument is that whenever something is found to be in several things by participation in various degrees, it must be derived by those in which it exists imperfectly from that one in which it exists most perfectly : because where there are positive degrees of a thing so that we ascribe it to this one more and to that one less, this is in reference to one thing to which they approach, one nearer than another : for if each one were of itself competent to have it, there would be no reason why one should have it more than another. Thus fire, which is the extreme of heat, is the cause of heat in all things hot. Now there is one being most perfect and most true : which follows from the fact that there is a mover altogether immovable and absolutely perfect, as philosophers have proved. Consequently all other less perfect beings must needs derive being therefrom. This is the argument of the Philosopher (*Metaph.* ii, 1).

The third argument is based on the principle that whatsoever is through another is to be reduced to that which is of itself. Wherefore if there were a *per se* heat, it would be the cause of all hot things, that have heat by way of participation. Now there is a being that is its own being : and this follows from the fact that there must needs be a being that is pure act and wherein there is no composition. Hence from that one being all other beings that are not their own being, but have being by participation, must needs proceed. This is the argument of Avicenna (*in Metaph.* viii, 6 ; ix, 8). Thus reason proves and faith holds that all things are created by God.

Reply to the First Objection. Although the first cause that is God does not enter into the essence of creatures, yet being which is in creatures cannot be understood except as derived from the divine being : even as a proper effect cannot be understood save as produced by its proper cause.

Reply to the Second Objection. From the very fact that being is ascribed to a quiddity, not only is the quiddity said to be but also to be created : since before it had being it was nothing, except perhaps in the intellect of the creator, where it is not a creature but the creating essence.

Reply to the Third Objection. This argument proves that primal matter is not created *per se:* but it does not follow that it is not created under a form: for it is thus that it has actual being.

ARTICLE VI

IS THERE BUT ONE PRINCIPLE OF CREATION?
Sum. Th. I, Q. xlix

THE sixth point of inquiry is whether there be but one principle of creation : and seemingly the reply should be in the negative.

1. Dionysius says (*De Div. Nom.* iv) : *The cause of evil is not a good.* Now there is evil in the world. Either, then, it is produced by a cause which is not a good, or it is not caused at all, but is a first cause : and in either case we must posit more than one principle of creation : since it is clear that the first cause of good things must be a good.

2. But someone may say that a good is the cause of evil, not *per se* but accidentally.—On the contrary every effect that flows from a cause accidentally, flows from some other cause *per se:* since everything accidental can be traced to something *per se.* Hence if evil be the effect of good accidentally, it will be the *per se* effect of something else, so that the same conclusion follows as before.

3. An effect that is produced accidentally happens beside the intention of the cause and is not a thing made. If, then, a good be the accidental cause of evil, it follows that evil is not something made. Now nothing is uncreated save the principle of creation, as we have shown above (A. 1). Therefore evil is a principle of creation.

4. No vice occurs in the effect beside the intention of the cause, except either by reason of ignorance on the part of the cause through lack of foresight, or by reason of impotence that could not be avoided. But in God the Creator of all good there is neither impotence nor ignorance. Therefore

evil, which is vicious, cannot occur in God's effects beside his intention; for Augustine says (*Enchir.* ii) that the reason why a thing is evil is because it is vicious.

5. That which occurs accidentally happens in the minority of cases (*Phys.* ii, 5). But evil occurs in the majority of cases (*Top.* ii, 6). Therefore evil is not due to an accidental cause.

6. According to Augustine (*De Civ. Dei* xii, 7) the cause of evil is not effective but defective. But an accidental cause is effective. Therefore a good is not the accidental cause of evil.

7. That which is not has no cause: since what is not is neither cause nor caused. Now evil, according to Augustine (*Tract.* i, 13, *in Joann*), is not a thing. Consequently evil has no cause, neither *per se* nor accidental. Therefore there is no truth in the statement that a good is the accidental cause of evil.

8. According to the Philosopher (*Metaph.* ii, 1) that in which a thing is first is the cause of whatsoever contains that thing subsequently: thus fire causes heat in whatsoever is hot. Now malice was first in the devil. Therefore he is the cause of malice in all the wicked: and consequently there is one principle of all the wicked as there is of all the good.

9. According to Dionysius (*Div. Nom.* iv) good is in one way, but evil in many ways. Consequently evil is nearer to being than good is. Therefore if good is a nature needing a creator, evil also will need a creator: and so the same conclusion follows.

10. That which is not can be neither genus nor species. Now evil is taken to be a genus. For it is stated *Categ.*, 10) that good and evil are not in a genus but are themselves genera. Evil, therefore, is a being and consequently needs a creator. Therefore since it is not created by a good, we must apparently admit that there is an evil principle of creation.

11. Both of two contraries is a positive nature, since contraries are in the same genus. Now what is not cannot be in a genus. But good and evil are contrary to each other.

Therefore evil is a nature: and we come to the same conclusion.

12. The difference that makes a species signifies a nature; wherefore nature, in one way, is that which gives a thing its specific difference, according to Boëthius (*De Duab. Nat.*). Now evil is a difference constituting a species: for good and evil differentiate habits. Therefore evil is a nature: and thus the same conclusion follows.

13. *Good is set against evil, and life against death: so also is the sinner against a just man* (Ecclus. xxxiii, 15). If, therefore, good is one principle of creation, there must be set against it an evil principle.

14. Intensity and remission connote relation to some term. Now one thing is worse than another. Hence there must be something supremely bad that is the term of all evil: and this must be the principle of all evil things, even as the supreme good is the principle of all good things.

15. *A good tree cannot bring forth evil fruit* (Mat. vii, 18). Now evil exists in the world. Therefore it cannot be a fruit, otherwise an effect, of a good cause which is denoted by a good tree: and consequently some first evil must be the cause of all evils.

16. We are told (Gen. i, 2) that when things were first created *darkness was on the face of the* earth. But the good by its very nature is enlightening and therefore cannot be the creation of darkness. Consequently the creation described there originates not from a good but from an evil principle.

17. The effect bears witness to its cause as being similar thereto. But evil nowise bears witness to God, nor is it in any way like him. Therefore it cannot come from him but must be from another principle.

18. Every effect exists potentially in its cause. But evil is not in God, either actually or potentially. Therefore it comes not from God; and the same conclusion follows.

19. Just as generation is a natural movement so also is corruption. Now the end of corruption is privation, just as the end of generation is the form. Hence just as the intention of nature is the induction of the form, so also does nature intend privation: and consequently evil being a

privation must be produced, even as the form, by a *per se* active cause.

20. Every agent acts on the presupposition of the first agent. Now the free-will, in sinning, does not act on the presupposition of the divine action : for there are sins like fornication and adultery which are inseparable from their deformity which cannot come from God. Therefore the free-will must either be a first agent or be reducible to a first agent other than God.

21. It will be said perhaps that the substance, and not the deformity of the act, comes from God.—On the contrary the Commentator (*in Metaph.* vii, 8) says : *It is impossible for the matter to result from the action of one agent while the form results from the action of another.* Now deformity is the form as it were of the sinful act. Wherefore the deformity of sin cannot be ascribed to one cause, and its substance to another.

22. From one simple cause only a simple effect can proceed. Now God is utterly simple. Therefore suchlike composite things are not from him but from some other cause.

23. The stain of sin is something in the soul : for were it nothing besides the privation of grace, a man by committing one mortal sin would be guilty of all. Now the stain of sin is not from God, for God is not the author of that which he punishes, as Fulgentius says (*Ad Monim.* i) : and since it is not from eternity it must have a cause. Therefore it must be ascribed to some cause other than God.

24. It is written (Ecclus. iii, 14) : *I have learned that all the works which God hath made, continue for ever.* Now corruptible things do not continue for ever. Therefore they are not the work of God, and they must be referred to another principle.

25. Every agent produces its like. But corruptible bodies are not like God, for *God is a spirit* (Jo. iv, 24). Therefore corruptible bodies are not from God : and the same conclusion follows.

26. Nature always does what is best, according to the Philosopher (*De Cœlo* ii, 5) : and this is due to the good-

ness of nature. But God's goodness surpasses nature's. Consequently God makes things as good as he can. Now spiritual things are better than things corporeal. Therefore the latter are not from God, since had he made them he would have given them spiritual goodness. It follows then that we must admit several principles of creation.

On the contrary it is written (Isa. xlv, 6, 7) : *I am the Lord, and there is none else. I form the light and create darkness, I make peace and create evil ; I the Lord do all these things.*

Again, evil has no other root but the nature of good, as Dionysius shows (*Div. Nom.* iv). But this would not be true if the creative principle of evil were distinct from that of good : else the principle of evil things would be more powerful than that of good things since it would produce its own effect even in good things. Therefore evil is not from a creative principle other than that of good.

Again, the Philosopher shows (*Phys.* viii, 6) that there is but one principle of movement. But this would not be true, if there were divers first creative principles : because one principle would not govern or move the creatures of another contrary principle. Therefore there is but one principle of creation.

I answer that, as we have already stated, the ancient philosophers, through taking note only of the material principles of nature, when they considered material things fell into the error of holding that all natural things are not created. Hence from holding matter and contrariety to be the the principles of nature they came to conceive of two first principles of things : and this was owing to a threefold fault in their consideration of contraries. The first was that they considered contraries only in the point of their specific diversity, and disregarded their generic unity and the fact that contraries are in the same genus. Consequently they ascribed to them a cause not in respect of what they have in common but in respect of that wherein they differ. Hence, as stated (*Phys.* i, 4), they referred all contraries to two first contraries as two first principles. Among them **Empedocles** made the first contraries to be the first active principles, to wit attraction and repulsion : and it is stated (*Metaph.* i, 4) that he was the first to uphold two principles, good and evil. The second fault was that they judged both contraries equally, whereas one of them must always imply privation of the other, and consequently be perfect while the latter is imperfect, the former good and the latter less good (*Phys.* i, 2). In consequence they held both good and evil to be distinct natures, because they seemed to them the most generic contraries. For this reason Pythagoras said that things were divided into two genera, good and evil; in the genus of good things he placed all perfect things, such as light, males, rest and the like, while in the genus of evil things he placed darkness, females and the like. The third fault was that they considered things in reference to the things themselves, or in the mutual relationships between one individual thing and another, but not as bearing upon the order of the universe. Hence when they found one thing harmful to another, or imperfect in comparison with perfect things, they pronounced it to be simply evil in its nature and not to owe its origin to the cause of good. Wherefore Pythagoras placed women, as being imperfect, in the genus of evil. This again was at the root of the Manichean statement that corruptible things being imperfect in comparison with things incorruptible are the work not of the good God but of a contrary principle, and likewise the visible in comparison with the invisible, and the Old Testament in comparison with the New; an opinion that was confirmed by their observing that certain good creatures, man for instance, suffer harm from certain visible and corruptible creatures. Now this error is utterly impossible : since all things must be traced to one first principle which is good. For the nonce this may be proved by three arguments.

First argument. Whenever different things have one thing in common, they must be referred to one cause in respect of that common thing : since either one is the cause of the other, or they both proceed from a common cause : seeing that it is impossible for that which they have in common to be derived from the properties in which they differ ; as we proved before (A. 5). Now all contraries and things differing from one another, that exist in the world, have some one thing in common, either the specific or the generic nature, or at least the common ratio of being : and consequently they must all have one principle which is the cause of being in all of them. Now being, as such, is a good : which is evidenced by the fact that everything desires to be ; and the good is defined as that which is desirable. Hence above all various causes we must place one first cause, even as above these contrary agents in nature the natural philosophers placed one primal agent, namely the heaven, as the cause of all movement here below. Since, however, in this heaven there is variety of position, to which variety is to be traced the contrariety of inferior bodies, it is necessary to have recourse to a first mover that is not moved either *per se* or accidentally.

Second argument. Every agent acts forasmuch as it is in act, and consequently forasmuch as it is in some way perfect. Now forasmuch as a thing is evil it is not in act, since a thing is said to be evil through being in a state of potentiality, and deprived of its proper and due act. But forasmuch as a thing is in act, it is good ; because in this respect it has perfection and entity, and it is in this that the good essentially consists. Therefore nothing acts forasmuch as it is evil, but everything acts inasmuch as it is good. Consequently there cannot be an active principle of things other than a good. And since every agent produces its like, nothing is produced except forasmuch as it is in act, and for this reason, forasmuch as it is good. On both sides therefore the position is shown to be untenable which holds evil to be the creative principle of evils. This argument agrees with the words of Dionysius (*Divin. Nom.* iv) who states that evil acts not save by virtue of a good, and that evil is outside the scope of intention and generation.

Third argument. If diverse beings were to be traced exclusively to contrary principles without these being traced to one supreme principle, they could not possibly come together into one order except accidentally : because co-ordination of many things cannot result but from one co-ordinator, except by chance. Now we observe corruptible and incorruptible things, spiritual and corporal, perfect and imperfect coming together into one order. Thus the spiritual move the corporal: which is evident at least in man. Again things corruptible are controlled by incorruptible: as may be observed in the alterations of elements by heavenly bodies. Nor may it be said that such occurrences are fortuitous: for they would not happen always or for the most part, but only in the minority of cases. Consequently all these various things must be traced to one first principle whereby they are co-ordinated: and for this reason the Philosopher concludes (*Metaph.* xii, 10) that there is one ruler over all.

Reply to the First Objection. As we have shown above, evil is not a being but a lack of being, and consequently cannot be a *per se* effect. In this sense Dionysius says that good is not the cause of evil, and not as though evil were to be made a first cause.

Reply to the Second Objection. This argument is true of an effect that can have a cause *per se*. Such is not evil: which therefore cannot properly speaking be described as an effect.

Reply to the Third Objection. Evil is incidental to an effect, but it is not an effect properly speaking: this follows from the fact that it is not intended. And yet it does not follow that it is a first principle, unless it be added that evil is a nature. For just as evil, since it is not a being but a privation of being, lacks the essential condition of an effect, so and much more indeed does it lack the necessary condition of a cause, as we have shown.

Reply to the Fourth Objection. According to Augustine (*Enchir.* xcvi): *God is so good that never would he allow evil to exist, unless he were so powerful as to be able to draw good from evil.* Hence it is due to neither impotence nor ignorance on God's part that evils occur in the world, but it is owing to the order of his wisdom and to the greatness of his goodness, whence come the many and divers grades of goodness in things, many of which would be lacking were he to allow no evil to exist. Thus there would be no good of patience without the evil of persecution, nor the good of the preservation of its life in a lion, without the evil of the destruction of the animals on which it lives.

Reply to the Fifth Objection. Evil occurs in the minority of cases if we compare effects with their proper causes. This is clear in the process of nature : because there is no fault or evil in the action of nature, except when the active cause is affected by some impediment : and this is only in the minority of cases, as when nature produces monsters and the like. On the other hand in the domain of the will evil would seem to be of more frequent occurrence in things done than in things made, forasmuch as art through imitating nature fails only in the minority of cases. Whereas in actions which are affected by vice and virtue there is a twofold appetite moving man to action, to wit the rational and the sensual : and that which is good in relation to the one appetite is evil in relation to the other : thus the pursuit of pleasure is good with reference to the sensual appetite, which we call sensuality, whereas it is evil with reference to the appetite of reason. And seeing that the majority follow their senses rather than their reason, consequently bad men are more numerous than good. On the other hand he who follows his rational appetite behaves well more often than ill.

Reply to the Sixth Objection. The accidental cause is twofold. The one does something towards the effect, but is said to cause it accidentally, because the effect that ensues is not intended by it : such is the man who finds a treasure while digging a grave. The other does nothing towards the effect, but is called accidental because it is accidental to the active cause : thus white may be said to be the cause of the house, because it is an accident of the builder. Likewise the accidental effect is twofold. The one could be the term of the cause's action, but occurs beside the cause's intention, as, for instance, the finding of the treasure : such an effect, though accidental with regard to that cause, can be the *per se* effect of another cause. In this sense evil has no accidental cause, because as already stated it cannot be the term of an action. The other kind of accidental effect is one which is not the term of an agent's action, but it is called an accidental effect because it is accidental to an effect: thus white that is accidental to a house may be said to be an accidental effect of the builder. In this sense nothing prevents evil from having an accidental cause.

Reply to the Seventh Objection. Evil, though it is not as nature, is not a pure negation but a privation: and this according to the Philosopher (*Metaph.* iv, 2) is a negation adhering to a subject, for privation is negation in a subject, so that inasmuch as it is accidental to something, it can have an accidental cause in the sense already explained.

Reply to the Eighth Objection. Evil was in the devil before others in point of time; but not in point of nature, as though wickedness were his essence or an accident deriving from the principles of his nature. Nor does it matter that he be worse than others, since this is not on account of any connaturality of wickedness to him, but is accidental through his having sinned more grievously. Now a thing is said to be a principle in relation to other things with regard to that which is said of it *per se* and not accidentally.

Reply to the Ninth Objection. It is owing to its perfection that good happens in but one way: because a thing cannot be perfect unless all those conditions are fulfilled which combine together to make it perfect. If any of these be lacking the thing is imperfect and therefore evil: and consequently the imperfection of evil is the reason why evil is so manifold: and thus evil is less a being than good is.

Reply to the Tenth Objection. The statement of the Philosopher refers to the opinion of Pythagoras who maintained that good and evil are genera, as we have said above. This opinion, however, has some truth in it. For, since, as we have observed, good indicates something positive whereas evil indicates a privation; just as every form is a good, so is every privation an evil, wherefore good and evil are in a sense convertible with being and privation of being. Now it is shown in *Metaph.* x, 4, that in all contraries there is an implication of privation and habit, so that always the contrary that is the more perfect is reducible to a good, while the other which is less perfect is reducible to an evil.

Hence the Philosopher (*Phys.* i, 9) says that one of two contraries is harmful: and in this sense good and evil may be described as contrary generically.

Reply to the Eleventh Objection. The evil that is contrary to a good indicates not only a privation of that good, but a habit to which that privation is annexed: which habit is evil not by reason of its entity, but because it has annexed to it the privation of a due perfection.

Reply to the Twelfth Objection. Evil differentiates the vicious habit, not merely as a privation, but with the addition of the intention of an undue end, which intention does not include the notion of evil except in so far as the end in question is inconsistent with a due end: thus the end of carnal pleasure is inconsistent with the good dictated by reason. The reason why good and evil are assigned as specifying the habits of the soul is that moral acts, and consequently habits, are specified by the end, which is so to say the form of the will, the proper principle of evil deeds: and good and evil denote relation to the end.

Reply to the Thirteenth Objection. The meaning is not that *good is set against evil* as one first principle against another first principle, but that they both derive from one first principle, the one *per se*, the other accidentally: this is clear from what follows: *And so look upon all the works of the Most High*, etc.

Reply to the Fourteenth Objection. Evil is not intensified by approach to a term, but by recession from a term: for as a thing is said to be good as participating of goodness, so is it said to be evil as lacking in goodness.

Reply to the Fifteenth Objection. By the good tree our Lord means a cause of good, not the first cause but the second cause in relation to some particular effect: the same applies to the evil tree. Hence by the evil tree he indicates heretics who are known by their works, as a tree by its fruit. This is clear if we consider the comparison: for the first cause of the fruit is not the tree but the root. If, however, we take the tree to signify any cause, as Dionysius apparently does, then we reply as in the answer to the First Objection, that good is not the *per se* cause of evil.

Reply to the Sixteenth Objection. The darkness mentioned as existing at the beginning of the creation was not a creature, but simply the absence of light in the atmosphere. It was not however an evil, since absence of good is an evil only when that good can and ought to be present. Thus it is not an evil in a stone that it cannot sense, nor is it an evil in a newly born child that it cannot walk. Nor was it owing to imperfection in the active cause that the air was created without light, but through its wisdom that so orders things that they are brought from imperfection to perfection.

Reply to the Seventeenth Objection. This argument supposes that evil has a cause *per se* : and we have shown this to be false.

The Eighteenth Objection is met with the same reply.

Reply to the Nineteenth Objection. Nature stands in relation to generation otherwise than to corruption. The form that is the term of generation is directly intended by nature both universal and particular, whereas privation of a form is beside the intention of a particular nature, although it is intended by universal nature, not indeed directly but as necessary for the introduction of another form. Hence generation is natural in every way, whereas corruption is sometimes against nature, if we refer it to a nature in particular.

Reply to the Twentieth Objection. Whatever there is of entity or action in a sinful act is referred to God as first cause : while the element of deformity is referred to the free will as cause. Thus when a man limps his walking is due to the motive power as first cause, but that he walks awry is due to a deformity in his leg.

Reply to the Twenty-first Objection. This argument applies to two agents entirely unrelated, but not when one of them operates in the other : for then one effect can proceed from both. Now God operates in every nature and in every will : hence the argument does not prove.

Reply to the Twenty-second Objection. This argument refers to an agent that acts of natural necessity : and one such agent is confined to one effect. Nor does it follow that an effect must be simple because its cause is simple : because an effect need not equal its cause either in universality or in simplicity. But God does not act of natural necessity, but of his own will : wherefore he is able to make both simple things and composite things, things mutable and things immutable.

Reply to the Twenty-third Objection. The stain of sin does not impose a nature on the soul, but only the privation of grace : which privation is referred to the preceding sinful act, that caused or might have caused it. Consequently it does not follow that one who has not committed the act of a particular sin, has the stain of that sin.

Reply to the Twenty-fourth Objection. God's works continue for ever not in number but in species or genus ; in their substance, but not in their mode of being, *for the fashion of this world passeth away* (1 Cor. vii, 31).

Reply to the Twenty-fifth Objection. Although God is a spirit his wisdom contains the ideas of bodies ; and bodies are made like them in the same way as a craftsman's work is like him in respect of his art. However, bodies are like God in respect of his nature, in so far as they have being, goodness and a certain unity.

Reply to the Twenty-sixth Objection. Nature always does what is best, not with regard to the part but with regard to the whole : otherwise it would make a man's body all eye or all heart : for it would be better for the part but not for the whole. In like manner, although it would be better for this or that thing to be placed in a higher order, it would not be better for the universe, which would remain imperfect if all creatures were of one order.

ARTICLE VII

DOES GOD WORK IN OPERATIONS OF NATURE ?
Sum. Th. I, Q. cv, A. 5 : *C.G.* III. lxvii

THE seventh point of inquiry is whether God works in the operations of nature : and apparently the answer should be in the negative.

1. Nature neither fails in necessary things nor abounds in the superfluous. Now the action of nature requires nothing more than an active force in the agent, and passivity in the recipient. Therefore there is no need for the divine power to operate in things.

2. It may be replied that the active force of nature depends in its operation on the operation of God.—On the contrary as the operation of created nature depends on the divine operation, so the operation of an elemental body depends on the operation of a heavenly body : because the heavenly body stands in relation to the elemental body, as a first to a second cause. Now no one maintains that the heavenly body operates in every action of an elemental body. Therefore we must not say that God operates in every operation of nature.

3. If God operates in every operation of nature God's operation and nature's are either one and the same operation or they are distinct. They are not one and the same : since unity of operation proves unity of nature : wherefore as in Christ there are two natures, so also are there two operations : and it is clear that God's nature and man's are not the same. Nor can they be two distinct operations : because distinct operations cannot seemingly terminate in one and the same product, since movements and operations are diversified by their terms. Therefore it is altogether impossible that God operate in nature.

4. It will be replied that two operations can have the same term, if one is subordinate to the other.—On the contrary, when several things are immediately related to some one thing, one is not subordinate to the other. Now both God and nature produce the natural effect immediately. Therefore of God's operation and nature's one is not subordinate to the other.

5. Whenever God fashions a nature, by that very fact he gives it all that belongs essentially to that nature : thus by the very fact that he makes a man he gives him a rational soul. Now strength is essentially a principle of action, since it is the perfection of power, and power is a principle of acting on another which is distinct (*Metaph.* v, 12). There-

fore by implanting natural forces in things, he enabled them to perform their natural operations. Hence there is no need for him also to operate in nature.

6. It might be replied that natural forces like other beings cannot last unless they be upheld by the divine power.—On the contrary, to operate on a thing is not the same as to operate in it. Now the operation whereby God either produces or preserves the forces of nature, has its effect on those forces by producing or preserving them. Therefore this does not prove that God works in the operations of nature.

7. If God works in the operations of nature, it follows that by so doing he imparts something to the natural agent : since every agent by acting makes something to be actual. Either then this something suffices for nature to be able to operate by itself, or it does not suffice. If it suffices, then since God also gave nature its natural forces, for the same reason we may say that the natural forces were sufficient for nature to act : and there will be no further need for God to do anything towards nature's operation besides giving nature the natural forces. If on the other hand it does not suffice, he will need to do something more, and if this is not sufficient, more still and so on indefinitely, which is impossible : because one effect cannot depend on an infinite number of actions, for, since it is not possible to pass through an infinite number of things, it would never materialise. Therefore we must accept the alternative, namely that the forces of nature suffice for the action of nature without God operating therein.

8. Further, given a cause that acts of natural necessity, its action follows unless it be hindered accidentally, because nature is confined to one effect. If, then, the heat of fire acts of natural necessity, given heat, the action of heating follows, and there is no need of a higher power to work in the heat.

9. Things that are altogether disparate can be separate from each other. Now God's action and nature's are altogether disparate, since God acts by his will and nature by necessity. Therefore God's action can be separated from

the action of nature, and consequently he need not operate in the action of nature.

10. A creature, considered as such, is like God inasmuch as it actually exists and acts : and in this respect it participates of the divine goodness. But this would not be so if its own forces were not sufficient for it to act. Therefore a creature is sufficiently equipped for action without God's operation therein.

11. Two angels cannot be in the same place, according to some, lest confusion of action should result : because an angel is where he operates. Now God is more distant from nature than one angel from another. Therefore God cannot operate in the same action with nature.

12. Moreover, it is written (Ecclus. xv, 14) that *God made man and left him in the hand of his own counsel.* But he would not have so left him, if he always operated in man's will. Therefore he does not operate in the operation of the will.

13. The will is master of its own action. But this would not be the case, if it were unable to act without God operating in it, for our will is not master of the divine operation. Therefore God does not operate in the operation of the will.

14. To be free is to be the cause of one's own action (*Metaph.* i, 2). Consequently that which cannot act without receiving the action of another cause is not free to act : now man's will is free to act. Therefore it can act without any other cause operating in it : and the same conclusion follows.

15. A first cause enters more into the effect than does a second cause. If, then, God operates in will and nature as a first in a second cause, it follows that the defects that occur in voluntary and natural actions are to be ascribed to God rather than to nature or will : and this is absurd.

16. Given a cause whose action suffices, it is superfluous to require the action of another cause. Now it is clear that if God operates in nature and will, his action is sufficient, since *God's works are perfect* (Deut. xxii, 4). Therefore all action of nature and will would be superfluous. But nothing

in nature is superfluous, and consequently neither nature nor will would do anything, and God alone would act. This, however, is absurd : therefore it is also absurd to state that God operates in nature and will.

On the contrary it is written (Isa. xxvi, 12) : *Lord, thou hast wrought all our works in us.*

Moreover, even as art presupposes nature, so does nature presuppose God. Now nature operates in the operations of art : since art does not work without the concurrence of nature: thus fire softens the iron so as to render it malleable under the stroke of the smith. Therefore God also operates in the operation of nature.

Again, according to the Philosopher (*Phys.* ii, 2) man and the sun generate man. Now just as the generative act in man depends on the action of the sun, so and much more does the action of nature depend on the action of God. Therefore in every action of nature God operates also.

Further, nothing can act except what exists. Now nature cannot exist except through God's action, for it would fall into nothingness were it not preserved in being by the action of the divine power, as Augustine states (*Gen. ad lit.*). Therefore nature cannot act unless God act also.

Again, God's power is in every natural thing, since he is in all things by his essence, his presence and his power. Now it cannot be admitted that God's power forasmuch as it is in things is not operative : and consequently it operates as being in nature. And it cannot be said to operate something besides what nature operates, since evidently there is but one operation. Therefore God works in every operation of nature.

I answer that we must admit without any qualification that God operates in the operations of nature and will. Some, however, through failing to understand this aright fell into error, and ascribed to God every operation of nature in the sense that nature does nothing at all by its own power. They were led to hold this opinion by various arguments. Thus according to Rabbi Moses some of the sages in the Moorish books of law asserted that all these natural forms are accidents, and since an accident cannot pass from one subject to another, they deemed it impossible for a natural agent by its form to produce in any way a similar form in another subject, and consequently they said that fire does not heat but God creates heat in that which is made hot. And if it were objected to them, that a thing becomes hot whenever it is placed near the fire, unless some obstacle be in the way, which shows that fire is the *per se* cause of heat; they replied that God established the order to be observed according to which he would never cause heat except at the presence of fire: and that the fire itself would have no part in the action of heating. This opinion is manifestly opposed to the nature of sensation: for since the senses do not perceive unless they are acted upon by the sensible object—which is clearly true in regard to touch and the other senses except sight, since some maintain that this is effected by the visual organ projecting itself on to the object—it would follow that a man does not feel the fire's heat, if the action of the fire does not produce in the sensorial organ a likeness of the heat that is in the fire. In fact if this heat-species be produced in the organ by another agent, although the touch would sense the heat, it would not sense the heat of the fire, nor would it perceive that the fire is hot, and yet the sense judges this to be the case, and the senses do not err about their proper object.

It is also opposed to reason which convinces us that nothing in nature is void of purpose. Now unless natural things had an action of their own the forms and forces with which they are endowed would be to no purpose; thus if a knife does not cut, its sharpness is useless. It would also be useless to set fire to the coal, if God ignites the coal without fire.

It is also opposed to God's goodness which is self-communicative: the result being that things were made like God not only in being but also in acting.

The argument which they put forward is altogether frivolous. When we say that an accident does not pass from one subject to another, this refers to the same identical accident, and we do not deny that an accident subjected in a natural thing can produce an accident of like species in another subject : indeed this happens of necessity in every natural action. Moreover, they suppose that all forms are accidents, and this is not true : because then in natural things there would be no substantial being, the principle of which cannot be an accidental but only a substantial form. Moreover, this would make an end of generation and corruption : and many other absurdities would follow.

Avicebron (*Fons Vitæ*) says that no corporeal substance acts, but that a spiritual energy penetrating all bodies acts in them, and that the measure of a body's activity is according to the measure of its purity and subtlety, whereby it is rendered amenable to the influence of a spiritual force. He supports his statement by three arguments. His first argument is that every agent after God requires subject-matter on which to act : and no corporeal agent has matter subject to it, wherefore seemingly it cannot act. His second argument is that quantity hinders action and movement : in proof of which he points out that a bulky body is slow of movement and heavy : wherefore a corporeal substance being inseparable from quantity cannot act. His third argument is that the corporeal substance is furthest removed from the first agent, which is purely active and nowise passive, while the intermediate substances are both active and passive : and therefore corporeal substances which come last, must needs be passive only and not active.

Now all this is manifestly fallacious in that he takes all corporeal substances as one single substance ; and as though they differed from one another only in accidental and not in their substantial being. If the various corporeal substances be taken as substantially distinct, every one will not occupy the last place and the furthest removed from the first agent, but one will be higher than another and nearer to the first agent, so that one will be able to act on another.— Again in the foregoing arguments the corporeal substance is considered only in respect of its matter and not in respect of its form, whereas it is composed of both. It is true that the corporeal substance belongs to the lowest grade of beings, and has no subject beneath it, but this is by reason of its matter, not of its form : because in respect of its form a corporeal substance has an inferior subject in any other substance whose matter has potentially that form which the corporeal substance in question has actually. Hence it follows that there is mutual action in corporeal substances, since in the matter of one there is potentially the form of another, and vice versa. And if this form does not suffice to act, for the same reason neither does the energy of a spiritual substance, which the corporeal substance must needs receive according to its mode.—Nor does quantity hinder movement and action, since nothing is moved but that which has quantity (*Phys.* vi, 10). Nor is it true that quantity causes weight. This is disproved in *De Cælo* iv, 2. In fact, quantity increases the speed of natural movement, thus a weighty body, the greater it is, the greater the velocity of its downward movement, and in like manner that of a light body in its movement upwards. And although quantity in itself is not a principle of action, no reason can be given why it should hinder action, seeing that rather is it the instrument of an active quality; except in so far as active forms in quantitative matter receive a certain limited being that is confined to that particular matter, so that their action does not extend to an extraneous matter. But though they receive individual being in matter, they retain their specific nature, by reason whereof they can produce their like in species, and yet are unable themselves to be in another subject. Hence we are to understand that God works in every natural thing not as though the natural thing were altogether inert, but because God works in both nature and will when they work. How this may be we must now explain.

It must be observed that one thing may be the cause of another's action in several ways. First, by giving it the power to act: thus it is said that the generator moves heavy and light bodies, inasmuch as it gives them the power from which that movement results. In this way God causes all the actions of nature, because he gave natural things the forces whereby they are able to act, not only as the generator gives power to heavy and light bodies yet does not preserve it, but also as upholding its very being, forasmuch as he is the cause of the power bestowed, not only like the generator in its becoming, but also in its being; and thus God may be said to be the cause of an action by both causing and upholding the natural power in its being. For secondly, the preserver of a power is said to cause the action; thus a remedy that preserves the sight is said to make a man see. But since nothing moves or acts of itself unless it be an unmoved mover; thirdly, a thing is said to cause another's action by moving it to act: whereby we do not mean that it causes or preserves the active power, but that it applies the power to action, even as a man causes the knife's cutting by the very fact that he applies the sharpness of the knife to cutting by moving it to cut. And since the lower nature in acting does not act except through being moved, because these lower bodies are both subject to and cause alteration: whereas the heavenly body causes alteration without being subject to it, and yet it does not cause movement unless it be itself moved, so that we must eventually trace its movement to God, it follows of necessity that God causes the action of every natural thing by moving and applying its power to action. Furthermore we find that the order of effects follows the order of causes, and this must needs be so on account of the likeness of the effect to its cause. Nor can the second cause by its own power have any influence on the effect of the first cause, although it is the instrument of the first cause in regard to that effect: because an instrument is in a manner the cause of the principal cause's effect, not by its own form or power, but in so far as it participates somewhat in the power of the principal cause through being moved thereby: thus the axe is the cause of the craftsman's handiwork not by its own form or power, but by the power of the craftsman who moves it so that it participates in his power. Hence, fourthly, one thing causes the action of another, as a principal agent causes the action of its instrument: and in this way again we must say that God causes every action of natural things. For the higher the cause the greater its scope and efficacity: and the more efficacious the cause, the more deeply does it penetrate into its effect, and the more remote the potentiality from which it brings that effect into act. Now in every natural thing we find that it is a being, a natural thing, and of this or that nature. The first is common to all beings, the second to all natural things, the third to all the members of a species, while a fourth, if we take accidents into account, is proper to this or that individual. Accordingly this or that individual thing cannot by its action produce another individual of the same species except as the instrument of that cause which includes in its scope the whole species and, besides, the whole being of the inferior creature. Wherefore no action in these lower bodies attains to the production of a species except through the power of the heavenly body, nor does anything produce being except by the power of God. For being is the most common first effect and more intimate than all other effects: wherefore it is an effect which it belongs to God alone to produce by his own power: and for this reason (*De Causis*, prop. ix) an intelligence does not give being, except the divine power be therein. Therefore God is the cause of every action, inasmuch as every agent is an instrument of the divine power operating.

If, then, we consider the subsistent agent, every particular agent is immediate to its effect: but if we consider the power whereby the action is done, then the power of the higher cause is more immediate to the effect than the power of the lower cause; since the power of the lower cause is not coupled with its effect save by the power of the higher cause: wherefore it is said in *De Causis* (prop. i) that the power of the first cause takes the first place in the production of the effect and enters more deeply therein. Accordingly the divine power must needs be present to every acting thing, even as the power of the heavenly body must needs be present to every acting elemental body. Yet there is a difference in that wherever the power of God is there is his essence: whereas the essence of the heavenly body is not wherever its power is: and again God is his own power, whereas the heavenly body is not its own power. Consequently we may say that God works in everything forasmuch as everything needs his power in order that it may act: whereas it cannot properly be said that the heaven always works in an elemental body, although the latter acts by its power. Therefore God is the cause of everything's action inasmuch as he gives everything the power to act, and preserves it in being and applies it to action, and inasmuch as by his power every other power acts. And if we add to this that God is his own power, and that he is in all things not as part of their essence but as upholding them in their being, we shall conclude that he acts in every agent immediately, without prejudice to the action of the will and of nature.

Reply to the First Objection. The active and passive powers of a natural thing suffice for action in their own order: yet the divine power is required for the reason given above.

Reply to the Second Objection. Although the action of the forces of nature may be said to depend on God in the same way as that of an elemental body depends on the heavenly body, the comparison does not apply in every respect.

Reply to the Third Objection. In that operation whereby God operates by moving nature, nature itself does not operate: and even the operation of nature is also the operation of the divine power, just as the operation of an instrument is effected by the power of the principal agent. Nor does this prevent nature and God from operating to the same effect, on account of the order between God and nature.

Reply to the Fourth Objection. Both God and nature operate immediately, although as already stated there is order between them of priority and posteriority.

Reply to the Fifth Objection. It belongs to the lower power to be a principle of operation in a certain way and in its own order, namely as instrument of a higher power: wherefore, apart from the latter it has no operation.

Reply to the Sixth Objection. God is the cause of nature's operation not only as upholding the forces of nature in their being, but in other ways also, as stated above.

Reply to the Seventh Objection. The natural forces implanted in natural things at their formation are in them by way of fixed and constant forms in nature. But that which God does in a natural thing to make it operate actually, is a mere intention,[1] incomplete in being, as colours in the air and the power of the craftsman in his instrument. Hence even as art can give the axe its sharpness as a permanent form, but not the power of the art as a permanent form, unless it were endowed with intelligence, so it is possible for a natural thing to be given its own proper power as a permanent form within it, but not the power to act so as to cause being as the instrument of the first cause, unless it were given to be the universal principle of being. Nor could it be given to a natural power to cause its own movement, or to preserve its own being. Consequently just as it clearly cannot be given to the craftsman's instrument to work unless it be moved by him, so neither can it be given to a natural thing to operate without the divine operation.

Reply to the Eighth Objection. The natural necessity whereby heat acts is the result of the order of all the preceding causes: wherefore the power of the first cause is not excluded.

Reply to the Ninth Objection. Although nature and will are disparate in themselves, there is a certain order between them as regards their respective actions. For just as the action of nature precedes the act of our will, so that operations of art which proceed from the will presuppose the operation of nature: even so the will of God which is the origin of all natural movement precedes the operation of nature, so that its operation is presupposed in every operation of nature.

Reply to the Tenth Objection. The creature has a certain likeness to God by sharing in his goodness, in so far as it exists and acts, but not so that it can become equal to him through that likeness being perfected: wherefore as the imperfect needs the perfect, so the forces of nature in acting need the action of God.

---

[1] i.e. not a permanent quality but something flowing 'like colours in the air, or the energy of a craftsman in his tools,' as St. Thomas explains elsewhere.

Reply to the Eleventh Objection. One angel is less distant from another in the degree of nature than God from created nature; and yet in the order of cause and effect God and the creature come together, whereas two angels do not: wherefore God operates in nature, but one angel does not operate in another.

Reply to the Twelfth Objection. God is said to have left man in the hand of his counsel not as though he did not operate in the will: but because he gave man's will dominion over its act, so that it is not bound to this or that alternative: which dominion he did not bestow on nature since by its form it is confined to one determinate effect.

Reply to the Thirteenth Objection. The will is said to have dominion over its own act not to the exclusion of the first cause, but inasmuch as the first cause does not act in the will so as to determine it of necessity to one thing as it determines nature;[1] wherefore the determination of the act remains in the power of the reason and will.

Reply to the Fourteenth Objection. Not every cause excludes liberty, but only that which compels: and it is not thus that God causes our operations.

Reply to the Fifteenth Objection. Forasmuch as the first cause has more influence in the effect than the second cause, whatever there is of perfection in the effect is to be referred chiefly to the first cause: while all defects must be referred to the second cause which does not act as efficaciously as the first cause.

Reply to the Sixteenth Objection. God acts perfectly as first cause: but the operation of nature as second cause is also necessary. Nevertheless God can produce the natural effect even without nature: but he wishes to act by means of nature in order to preserve order in things.

---

[1] *Sum. Theol.* I-II, Q. x, art. 4.

ARTICLE VIII

DOES GOD WORK IN NATURE BY CREATING?
Sum. Theol. I, Q. xlv, A. 8.

THE eighth point of inquiry is whether God works in nature by creating; and this is to ask whether creation is mingled in the works of nature: and seemingly the reply should be in the affirmative.

1. Augustine says (*De Trin.* iii, 8): *The apostle Paul considering the secret works of God in the creation and formation of things, and the outward works of creatures, takes a comparison from agriculture when he says: 'I have planted, Apollo watered, but God gave the increase.'*

2. To this it may be answered that creation here stands for any kind of making.—On the contrary Augustine (*ibid.*) intends there to draw from the Apostle's words the distinction between the creature's operation and that of God. Now this distinction is not based upon creation taken in a general sense for any kind of making, because thus even nature creates, since it does make something as we have shown above, but not by creation in the strict sense. Therefore the words quoted must be taken as referring to creation properly so called.

3. Augustine adds (*ibid.*): *Just as in our life none but God can inform the soul with righteousness, whereas even men can outwardly preach the Gospel, so God inwardly creates the visible world, while he applies to nature in which he creates all things the various external operations of good or bad angels or men or any animals whatsoever; thus to the soil he applies husbandry.* Now he informs the soul with righteousness by creating in the strict sense of the word: since grace is effected by creation. Therefore he creates the forms of things in the strict sense of the term.

4. You may say, however, that natural forms have a cause in their subject, whereas grace has not: and this is why grace is created in the proper sense of the word, while natural forms are not.—On the contrary according to a gloss on Genesis i, 1, *to create is to make a thing out of* (ex) *nothing.*

Now this preposition *ex* sometimes connotes efficient causality as in 1 Corinthians viii, 6, *Of* (ex) *whom are all things, . . . by whom are all things:* and sometimes it connotes material causality, as in Tobit xiii, 21, *all the walls thereof round about of* (ex) *precious stones.* Hence when a thing is said to be made out of nothing, it is not the relation of an efficient cause that is denied (since then God would not be the efficient cause of creatures), but that of a material cause. But natural forms have efficient causes in their subjects, and in this they differ from grace : they also have matter in which they are, and this is also competent to grace. Consequently grace is not more capable of being created than natural forms are, since it also has a cause in its subject.

5. Art-forms have no cause in their subject but are entirely effected from without. If, then, grace is said to be created because it has no cause in its subject, for the same reason accidental art-forms must be the result of creation.

6. That which has no matter as a constituent part cannot be made of matter. Now forms have no matter as a constituent part : because form is contradistinguished both from matter and from composite things (*De Anima* ii, 1). Since, then, forms are made since they have a beginning of existence, it would seem that they are not made out of matter ; and consequently are made out of nothing and therefore are created.

7. But it might be said that although natural forms have no matter as a constituent part, they have matter as a subject, and as such are not created.—On the contrary the rational soul is a form in matter like other natural forms. But it is admitted that the rational soul is created. Therefore we must say the same of other natural forms.

8. If you say that the rational soul is not as other natural forms educed from matter.—On the contrary nothing is educed from that in which it is not. Now before generation is complete the form which is the term of generation is not in the matter ; otherwise contrary forms would be in matter at the same time. Therefore natural forms are not educed from matter.

9. The form which is the term of generation does not

make its appearance before generation is complete. If then it was there it was latent: and the result would be that all kinds of forms are latent in all kinds of matter, an opinion upheld by Anaxagoras and disproved by Aristotle (*Phys.* i, 4).

10. You will say perhaps that the natural form does not exist completely as Anaxagoras maintained before generation is complete, but incompletely.—On the contrary if the form is in any way at all in matter before generation is complete, it is there as to some part of itself: and if it be not there completely as to some part of itself, it does not pre-exist at all. Hence the form will have several parts, and consequently is not simple: which is contrary to what is laid down at the beginning of the *Six Principles*.[1]

11. If the form does not pre-exist completely in matter and is made complete subsequently, this complement must be the result of generation. Now this complement does not pre-exist in matter, because in that case the form would be already complete. Therefore this complement at least would be created.

12. It will be said perhaps that this complement pre-existed in matter incompletely, not in respect of a part, but because it existed at first in one way and afterwards in another way: since at first it was potential and afterwards actual.—On the contrary, when a thing is in one way at first and afterwards in another way it is altered and not generated. Hence if the work of nature consists in nothing more than that a form which was previously in potentiality becomes afterwards actual, it follows that nature's operation does not produce generation but only alteration.

13. In the lower nature there is no active principle that is not an accident: thus fire acts by heat which is an accident, and so on. Now an accident cannot be the active cause of a substantial form, since nothing acts beyond its own species: and an effect cannot transcend its cause, whereas a substantial form transcends an accident. Therefore a substantial form is not produced by the action of a lower nature, and consequently it is the result of creation.

[1] *Liber Sex Principiorum*, by Gilbert de la Porrée.

14. The imperfect cannot be the cause of the perfect. Now the soul's power is not in the semen of the dumb animal except imperfectly. Therefore the soul of a dumb animal is not produced by the natural action of the seminal force : and thus it must needs be produced by creation, and likewise all other natural forms.

15. That which is neither animate nor living cannot be the cause of an animate and living being. Now animals engendered from putrid matter are living animated beings : and there are not to be found in nature any living beings from which they receive life. Therefore their souls must be produced by creation by the first living being, and for like reason so also must other natural forms.

16. Again, nature does not produce other than its like. But we find certain natural things of which there is no previous likeness in their generator : thus a mule is not like in species either a horse or an ass. Therefore the form of the mule is not the result of nature's action but of creation : and thus the same conclusion follows.

17. Again, Augustine says (*De Vera Relig.* iii ; *De Lib. Arb.* ii, 17) that natural things would not be informed by their forms, unless there were some first being whereby they are informed. But this is God. Therefore all forms are created by God.

18. Again, Boëthius says (*De Trin.*) that forms which exist in matter are produced by forms which exist without matter. Now a form that exists without matter, so far as the present question is concerned, can only be an idea of a thing, which idea exists in the divine mind : because the angels who may be described as forms existing without matter are not the causes of material forms, according to Augustine (*De Trin.* iii, 8, 9). Therefore natural forms are not produced by the action of nature but are bestowed by creation.

19. Being is caused by creation (*De Causis*, prop. xviii). Now this would not be true unless forms were created, since the form is the principle of being. Therefore forms are made by creation, and God produces something in nature by creation, namely forms.

20. That which is self-subsistent is the cause of that which is not self-subsistent. Now the forms of natural things are not self-subsistent but subsist in matter. Therefore their cause is a self-subsistent form : and consequently must be created by an extrinsic agent. Hence it would seem that God works in nature by creating forms.

On the contrary the work of creation is distinct from the work of government and that of propagation. Now that which is done by the action of nature belongs to the works of government and propagation. Therefore creation is not mingled with the work of nature.

Moreover, God alone can create. Hence if forms are created, they will be the work of God alone, so that all nature's work, the purpose of which is the form, will be useless.

Moreover, just as matter is not a part of the substantial form so neither is it a part of the accidental form. Hence if the reason why substantial forms must be produced by creation is because they have no matter, the same argument will apply to accidental forms. Now as the thing generated is perfected by the substantial form, so does it receive a certain disposition from the accidental form : and consequently nature would take no part in generating, neither as perfecting nor as disposing, and all natural action would be useless.

Further, nature produces like from like. Now the thing generated is like its generator in species and form. Therefore the form is produced by the action of the generator and not by creation.

Further, the actions of diverse agents do not terminate in one same effect. But matter and form combine to produce that which is one simply. Therefore there cannot be one agent to dispose the matter and another to induce the form. Now it is the natural agent that disposes the matter : therefore it also induces the form. Consequently forms are not produced by creation, and creation is not mingled with the works of nature.

I answer that there have been different opinions on this point, and they all arose seemingly from this one principle that nature cannot make a thing out of nothing. Whence some concluded that nothing is made except in the sense that it is drawn out of another wherein it was latent. The Philosopher (*Phys.* i, 4) imputes this opinion to Anaxagoras who apparently was deceived through failing to distinguish potentiality from act : for he thought that whatever is generated must already have been in actual existence : whereas it must have pre-existed potentially and not actually. For if it pre-existed potentially it would become out of nothing : while if it pre-existed actually it would not become at all, since what is does not become.

Since, however, the thing generated is in potentiality through its matter, and in act through its form, others maintained that a thing becomes as regards its form while its matter was already in existence. And seeing that nature cannot operate on nothing, and therefore presupposes something to act on, according to them nature's operation is confined to disposing matter for its form. While the form which must needs become and cannot be presupposed, must be produced by an agent who does not presuppose anything and can make something out of nothing : and such is the supernatural agent which Plato held to be the giver of forms. Avicenna held this to be the lowest intelligence among separate substances : while more recent followers of this opinion say that it is God.

Now seemingly this is unreasonable. Since everything has a natural tendency to produce its like (because a thing acts forasmuch as it is actual, namely by making actual that which previously was potential) there would be no need of likeness in the substantial form in the natural agent, unless the substantial form of the thing generated were produced by the action of the agent. For which reason that which is to be acquired in the thing generated is found to be actually in the natural generator, and each one acts inasmuch as it is in act : wherefore seemingly there is no reason to seek another generator and pass over this one.

It must be observed, then, that these opinions arose from ignorance of the nature of form, just as the first-mentioned opinions arose from ignorance of the nature of matter. For being is not predicated univocally of the form and the thing generated. A generated natural thing is said to be *per se* and *properly*, as having being and subsisting in that being: whereas the form is not thus said to be, for it does not subsist, nor has it being *per se;* and it is said to exist or be, because something is by it: thus accidents are described as beings, because by them a substance is qualified or quantified, but not as though by them it is simply, as it is by its substantial form. Hence it is more correct to say that an accident is of something rather than that it is something (*Metaph.* vii, 2). Now that which is made is said to become according to the way in which it is: because its being is the term of its making: so that properly speaking it is the composite that is made *per se*. Whereas the form properly speaking is not made but is that whereby a thing is made, that is to say it is by acquiring the form that a thing is said to be made.

Accordingly the fact that nature makes nothing out of nothing does not prevent our asserting that substantial forms acquire being through the action of nature: since that which is made is not the form but the composite, which is made from matter and not out of nothing. And it is made from matter, in so far as matter is potentially the composite through having the form potentially.

Consequently it is not correct to say that the form is made in matter, rather should we say that it is educed from the potentiality of matter. And from this principle that the composite and not the form is made the Philosopher (*Metaph.* vii, 8) proves that forms result from natural agents. Because since the thing made must needs be like its maker, and that which is made is the composite, it follows that the maker must be composite and not a self-subsistent form, as Plato maintained: so that as the thing made is composite, and that by which it is made is a form in matter made actual, so the generator is composite and not a mere form, while the form is that whereby it generates, a form to wit existing in that particular matter such as that flesh, those bones and so forth.

Reply to the First Objection. In these words Augustine

ascribes creation to God in the works of nature by reason of nature's forces which at the beginning God implanted in matter by the work of creation, not as though something were created in every work of nature.

Reply to the Second Objection. In these words of Augustine creation is to be taken in its proper sense, but it is not to be referred to natural effects but to the forces by which nature works; which forces were planted in nature by the work of creation.

Reply to the Third Objection. Since grace is not a subsistent form it cannot properly be said to be or to be made, and consequently properly speaking it is not created in the same way as self-subsistent substances are. Nevertheless the infusion of grace approaches somewhat to the nature of creation in so far as grace has not a cause in its subject;—neither an efficient cause nor a material cause wherein it pre-exists potentially in such a way that it can like other natural forms be educed into act by a natural agent.

Hence the reply to the Fourth Objection is clear: because when we say that a thing is made out of nothing we deny that it has a material cause: and it somewhat savours of absence of matter that a form cannot be educed from the natural potentiality of matter.

Reply to the Fifth Objection. Although nature contains no effective principle with regard to art-forms, such forms do not surpass the order of nature, as grace does: in fact they are beneath that order, because nature is above art.

Reply to the Sixth Objection. That a form has no matter as part thereof would prove that it is competent to be created, if like a self-subsistent thing it could be made properly speaking.

Reply to the Seventh Objection. Although the rational soul has matter for its subject, it is not educed from the potentiality of matter, since its nature is raised above the entire material order, as is evidenced by its intellectual operation. Moreover, this form is a self-subsistent thing that remains when the body dies.

Reply to the Eighth Objection. The form which is the term of generation was in matter before generation was complete, not actually but potentially : and there is nothing to prevent two contraries being together in the same subject, one actually and the other potentially.

The reply to the Ninth Objection is thus made clear : since Anaxagoras held that forms pre-exist in matter not actually but in a latent state.

Reply to the Tenth Objection. The form pre-exists in matter imperfectly, not as though a part of it were actually there and another part not, but because it is wholly there in potentiality, and is afterwards educed wholly into actuality.

Whence we may gather the reply to the Eleventh Objection, since the form is not perfected by adding to the matter something extraneous that was not already in the matter potentially.

Reply to the Twelfth Objection. Actuality and potentiality are not different accidental modes of being, such as go to make alteration : they are substantial modes of being. For even substance is divided by potentiality and act, like any other genus.

Reply to the Thirteenth Objection. An accidental form acts by virtue of the substantial form whose instrument it is : thus heat is said to be the instrument of the nutritive power (*De Anima* ii, 4) : wherefore it is not unreasonable if the action of an accidental form terminate in a substantial form.

Reply to the Fourteenth Objection. Again the heat in the semen acts as the instrument of the soul's power which is in the semen : and though this power has an imperfect being it results from the action of a perfect soul, because the semen derives it from the soul of the generator. Moreover, it acts by virtue of a heavenly body whose instrument it is after a fashion. Hence we do not say that the semen begets, but the soul and the sun.

Reply to the Fifteenth Objection. Animals engendered from putrid matter are less perfect than other animals : hence in engendering them the power of the heavenly body by acting on inferior matter has the same effect as it has in conjunction with the power of the semen in engendering the bodies of more perfect animals.

Reply to the Sixteenth Objection. Although a mule is unlike a horse or ass in species, it is like them in the proximate genus : by reason of which likeness one species, a mean species as it were, is engendered from different species.

Reply to the Seventeenth Objection. Just as the divine power, the first agent to wit, does not exclude the action of the natural forces, so neither does the prototypal form which is God exclude the derivation of forms from other lower forms whose action terminates in like forms.

Hence we gather the reply to the Eighteenth Objection ; for Boëthius means to say that forms which are in matter derive from forms which are without matter not as from proximate causes but as from the prototypes.

Reply to the Nineteenth Objection. Being is said to be the result of creation in so far as every second cause when it gives being does so forasmuch as it acts by the power of the first creating cause : since being is the first effect and presupposes nothing else.

Reply to the Twentieth Objection. A natural form that is in matter cannot be produced by a self-subsistent form of the same species because matter is essential to a natural form : yet it is produced by a self-subsistent form, as we have stated.

ARTICLE IX

IS THE RATIONAL SOUL BROUGHT INTO BEING BY CREATION OR IS IT TRANSMITTED THROUGH THE SEMEN ?

Sum. Th. I, Q. cxviii

THE ninth point of inquiry is whether the soul be brought into being by creation or by transmission through the semen : and it would seem that it is transmitted through the semen.

1. It is written (Gen. xlvi, 26) : *All the souls that went*

with Jacob into Egypt and that came out of his thigh, besides his sons' wives, sixty-six. Now nothing comes from a father's thigh but what is transmitted through the semen. Therefore the rational soul is transmitted with the semen.

2. It may be replied that the part is taken for the whole, namely the soul for the man.—On the contrary, a man is composed of soul and body, and therefore if the whole man comes out of his father's thigh, it follows as above that not the body only but also the soul is transmitted with the semen.

3. An accident cannot be transmitted unless its subject be transmitted, since an accident does not pass from one subject to another. Now the rational soul is the subject of original sin. Therefore seeing that original sin is transmitted from parent to child it would seem that the child's rational soul is transmitted from its parent.

4. It may be said that although original sin is in the soul as its subject, it is in the flesh as its cause: and consequently is transmitted by the transmission of the flesh.—On the contrary it is written (Rom. v, 12): *By one man sin entered into this world, and by sin death; and so death passed upon all men in whom all have sinned.* The words '*in quo*'[1] are expounded by a gloss of Augustine (*De Pecc. Mer. et Rem.* i, 10) as meaning '*in which sinner*' or '*in which sin.*' Now all would not have sinned in that sin, unless that same sin had been transmitted to all. Therefore the same sin that was in Adam is transmitted to all men; and consequently the soul that was the subject of that sin.

5. Every agent produces its like. Also every agent acts by virtue of its form. Therefore that which it produces is a form. Now the begetter is an agent. Therefore the form of the begetter is produced by the action of the begetter. Since then a man begets a man, and the rational soul is the form of a man, it would seem that the rational soul is produced by generation and not by creation.

6. According to the Philosopher (*Phys.* ii, 7) the efficient cause produces its own species in its effect. Now man takes his species from his rational soul. Therefore

---

[1] Douay, '*in whom*,' but may also be rendered '*in which.*'

seemingly the rational soul is caused by the begetter in the begotten.

7. Children are like their parents because they are begotten by their parents. And they are like their parents not only in dispositions of the body but also in those of the soul. Therefore as bodies derive from bodies, so do souls derive from souls.

8. Moses says (Levit. xvii, 14) : *The soul*[1] *of all flesh is in the blood.* Now blood is transmitted with the semen, especially as the seed of the male is merely blood depurated by heat. Therefore the soul is transmitted with the semen.

9. Moreover, the embryo before it is perfected with the rational soul, has certain animate actions, namely growth, nourishment and sensation : and where there is animate action there is life : consequently it lives. Now the soul is the principle of life in a body : consequently it has a soul. But it cannot be said that it receives yet another soul : because then there would be two souls in one body. Therefore the soul which was from the beginning transmitted in the semen is the rational soul.

10. Souls differing in species constitute animals of different species. If, then, before the rational soul there was in the semen a soul that was not rational, there was an animal of a different species from man : which consequently could not become a man since animals do not pass from one species to another.

11. You will say that these actions belong to the embryo not through the soul, but by some power of the soul known as the formative power.—On the contrary, power is rooted in substance ; hence it occupies a place between substance and operation according to Dionysius (*Cœl. Hier.* xi). Consequently if the soul's power is there, its substance is there also.

12. The Philosopher says (*De Gener. Anim.* ii, 3) that the embryo is a living being before it is an animal, and an animal before it is a human being. Now every animal has a soul. Therefore it has a soul before it has a rational soul whereby it is a human being.

[1] Douay,—*life.*

13. According to the Philosopher (*De Anima* ii, 1) a soul is *the act of a living body as such*. Now if the embryo is a living being and has vital functions by means of this formative power, this very power will be its act in so far as it is a living thing. Therefore it will be a soul.

14. According to *De Anima* i, 2, life comes into all living things by the vegetal soul. Now it is clear that the embryo lives before the infusion of the rational soul, since it gives signs of exercising vital functions. Therefore the vegetal soul is in it before the rational soul.

15. The Philosopher (*De Anima* ii, 4) disproves the assertion that growth is not the effect of fire as principal agent, but of the vegetal soul. Now the embryo grows before the advent of the rational soul. Therefore it has a vegetal soul.

16. If before the advent of the rational soul there is not a vegetal soul but a formative power, at the advent of the soul this power will be inoperative, since the function it exercised in the embryo will subsequently be sufficiently fulfilled in the animal by the soul. Consequently it would remain superfluous : and this would seem to be unreasonable since nothing is superfluous in nature.

17. You will say perhaps that this power ceases at the advent of the rational soul.—On the contrary, dispositions do not cease at the advent of the form, but remain, and after a fashion maintain the form in matter. Now this power was a kind of disposition to the soul. Therefore at the advent of the latter, it does not cease.

18. By its action this power conduces to the infusion of the soul. If, then, at the soul's advent this power is destroyed, seemingly the soul has something to do with its destruction : and this is impossible.

19. A man is a human being by his rational soul. Therefore if the soul is not brought into being by generation, it will not be true that a man is generated : which is clearly false.

20. Further, the human body comes into being by the action of its begetter. If, then, the soul is not brought into being by the begetter, there will be a twofold being in man ; corporeal being derived from the begetter, and animate

being derived from another source : and consequently soul and body will not form one being simply, since each has its own being.

21. Moreover, it is impossible that the matter be the term of action of one agent, and the form the term of action of another agent : otherwise form and matter would not together make one thing simply, for one thing is made by one action. Now the action of nature in generating terminates in the body. Therefore it terminates in the soul also, which is the form of the body.

22. Moreover, according to the Philosopher (*De Gen. Anim.* ii, 3) principles whose actions are not performed independently of the body are produced together with the body. Now the action of the rational soul is not performed independently of the body : since most of all would understanding be independent of the body, and this is clearly not the case, because we cannot understand without images (*De Anima* iii, 8) : and there cannot be images without a body. Therefore the rational soul is transmitted with the body.

23. To this it may be replied that the rational soul when it understands requires images for the acquisition of intelligible species but not after it has acquired them.—On the contrary, after a man has acquired knowledge, his act of intelligence is hindered if the organ of imagination be injured. And this would not be the case if the intellect after acquiring knowledge were no longer in need of images. Consequently it needs them not only in acquiring knowledge but also in applying the knowledge it has acquired.

24. And if it be replied that the impediment to the act of intelligence arising from an injury to the organ of imagination arises not from the fact that the intellect needs images in using the knowledge it has acquired, but from the imagination and intellect being both seated in the one essence of the soul, so that the intellect is hindered accidentally through the imagination being hindered.—On the contrary the conjunction of powers in the one essence of the soul is the reason why if the act of one power be intense the act of the other is remiss : thus a person who

is intent on seeing is less intent on hearing. It is also the reason why one power acts with greater strength when another is deprived of its act : thus the blind are often sharp of hearing. Therefore this conjunction of powers is not a reason for the action of the intellect being hindered through an impediment to the imagination, in fact it should rather be strengthened.

25. He who gives the work its final complement is the worker's chief co-operator. Now if all human souls are created by God and by him infused into bodies, he gives the final complement to a generation that comes of adultery. Therefore he co-operates in adultery : and this is absurd.

26. According to the Philosopher (*Meteor.* iv, 12 ; *De Anima* ii, 4) a perfect thing is one that can make its like : and consequently the more perfect a thing is, the more is it able to make its like. Now the rational soul is more perfect than the material forms of the elements which produce other forms like themselves. Therefore the rational soul has the power by way of generation to produce another rational soul.

27. The rational soul is situated between God and corporeal things : wherefore (*De Causis*, prop. ii) it is asserted that it is created on the horizon between eternity and time. Now in God there is generation and also in corporeal things. Therefore the soul which is situated between them is produced by generation.

28. The Philosopher (*De Gener. Anim.* ii, 3) says that the spirit that comes forth with the seed of the male, is a force emanating from the soul, and is a divine thing. Now such a thing is the intellect. Therefore the intellect seemingly is transmitted with the seed.

29. The Philosopher (*ibid.* 4) says that in generation the female provides the body, and that the soul proceeds from the male : so that seemingly the soul is procreated and not created.

On the contrary it is written (Isa. lvii, 16) : *Every breathing I have made,*[1] and by breathing we are to under-

---

[1] The full text is : ' *The spirit shall go forth from my face, and breathings I will make.*'

stand the soul. Therefore seemingly the soul is created by God.

Again, it is written (Ps. xxxii, 15): *He maketh the heart of each one of them.* Therefore one soul is not engendered by another, but all are created separately by God.

I answer that in times past this question has been answered in various ways by different people.[1] Some said that the soul of the child is procreated from the soul of the parent, even as its body is from the body of the parent. Others said that all souls were created apart from bodies: but they held that they were all created together without bodies, and afterwards each one was united to a body when this was begotten, either by an act of its will according to some, or by God's command and operation according to others. Others held that souls are created and at the same time infused into bodies. Although formerly these opinions were held and it was doubtful which of them came nearest to the truth, as may be gathered from Augustine (*Gen. ad lit.* x, 21, 22; *De anima et ejus orig.*), afterwards, however, the first two were condemned by the Church and the third approved.[2] Hence we read in *De Eccles. Dogm.* (xiv): *We do not believe in the fiction of Origen that human souls were created at the beginning with other intellectual natures, nor that they are procreated together with their bodies by coition, as the Luciferians with Cyril, and certain Latin writers have presumed to maintain. But we affirm that the body alone is begotten by sexual procreation, and that after the formation of the body the soul is created and infused.*

A careful examination will make it clear that the opinion now under consideration was rightly condemned which held the rational soul to be transmitted with the semen. Three arguments will make this sufficiently evident for the present.

First argument. The rational soul differs from other forms, in that the latter have a being not wherein they

---

[1] *Sum. Theol.* I, Q. cxviii, A. 3.
[2] Pope Vigilius, *Can.* i, *contra Originem*; Council of Braga, *Anathem.* vi, *contra haeret.* Pope Anastasius II, *Epist. ad episc. Galliae.*

subsist but whereby the things informed by them subsist: whereas the rational soul has being in suchwise as to subsist therein: and this is made clear by their respective modes of action. For seeing that only that which exists can act, a thing is referred to operation or action as it is referred to being: so that since the body must of necessity take part in the action of other forms, but not in the action of the rational soul, which is to understand and will: it follows of necessity that being must be ascribed to the rational soul as subsisting, but not to other forms. For this reason the rational soul is the only form that can exist separate from the body. Hence it is clear that the rational soul is brought into being not as other forms are, which properly speaking are not made but are said to be made in the making of this or that thing. That which is made is made properly speaking and *per se*. And that which is made, is made either of matter or out of nothing. Now that which is made from matter, must needs be made from matter subject to contrariety: since generation is from contraries according to the Philosopher (*De Gen. Anim.* i, 18). Wherefore since a soul has either no matter at all or at least none that is subject to contrariety it cannot be made out of something. Hence it follows that it comes into being by creation as being made out of nothing. Now to maintain that the soul is made by the generation of the body, is to say that it is not subsistent and consequently that it ceases with the body.

Second argument. It is impossible for the action of a material force to rise to the production of a force that is wholly spiritual and immaterial: because nothing acts beyond its species, in fact the agent must needs be more perfect than the patient as Augustine asserts (*Gen. ad lit.* xii, 16). Now the begetting of a man is effected by the generative power which is exercised through organs of the body: moreover, the seminal force acts only by means of heat (*De Gen. Anim.* ii, 3): wherefore since the rational soul is a wholly spiritual form, neither dependent on the body nor exercising its action in common with the body, it can by no means be produced through the procreation of the body, nor be brought into being by an energy residing in the seed.

Third argument. Every form that comes into being by generation or the forces of nature is educed from the potentiality of matter (*Metaph.* vii, 7). Now the rational soul cannot be educed from the potentiality of matter: because a form whose operation is independent of matter cannot be produced from corporeal matter. It follows, then, that the rational soul is not evolved by the generative power. This argument is given by Aristotle (*De Gen. Animal.* ii, 3).

Reply to the First Objection. In the passage quoted the part stands for the whole, namely the soul for the whole man, by the figure of synecdoche: and this because the soul is the chief part of man, and a whole is considered as though it were identified with its most important part: so that the soul or intellect is considered as constituting to whole man (*Ethic.* ix, 4).

Reply to the Second Objection. The whole man comes from the thigh of the begetter,—in so far as the force in the semen coming from the thigh conduces to the union of soul and body, by giving the matter its ultimate disposition which calls for the introduction of the form: by reason of which union man is a man:—but not as though each part of man were caused by that seminal force.

Reply to the Third Objection. Original sin is said to be the sin of the entire nature just as actual sin is said to be the sin of the individual: wherefore the comparison between actual sin and the one individual person is the same as that between original sin and the entire human nature transmitted by our first parent in whom was the beginning of sin and by whose voluntary act original sin is imputed as voluntary to all men. Hence original sin is in the soul in so far as it is the sin of human nature. Now human nature is transmitted from parent to child by procreation of the flesh into which subsequently the soul is infused: and the soul contracts the infection because together with the transmitted flesh it forms one nature: for were it not united thereto so as to form one nature it would not contract the infection, as neither does an angel by assuming a human body.

Reply to the Fourth Objection. As in Adam's nature the nature of us all originated, so original sin which is in us originated in that original sin: because nature, as already stated, is the direct recipient of original sin, while the soul is its consequent recipient.

Reply to the Fifth Objection. A man begets his like in species by virtue of his form, namely his rational soul: not that this is the immediate active principle in human generation, but because the generative force and the active principles of the semen do not dispose the matter so as to make it a body fit to be perfected by a rational soul, except in so far as they act as instruments of a rational soul. Nevertheless this action does not go so far as to produce a rational soul, for the reasons already given.

Reply to the Sixth Objection. The generator begets his like in species in so far as the begotten is produced by the action of the generator in order that it may share in his species: and this comes to pass by the begotten receiving a form like that of the generator. If, then, that form be non-subsistent, and its being consist merely in that it is united to its subject, it will be necessary for the generator to be cause of that form; as is the case with all material forms. If on the other hand it be a subsistent form, so that its being is not entirely dependent on its union with matter, as in the case of the rational soul, then it suffices that the generator be the cause of the union of such a form with matter by merely disposing the matter for the form: nor need it be the cause of the form.

Reply to the Seventh Objection. The disposition of the rational soul is in keeping with the disposition of the body: both because it receives something from the body, and because forms are diversified according to the diversity of their matter. Hence it is that children are like their parents even in things pertaining to the soul, and not because one soul is evolved from another.

Reply to the Eighth Objection. Because properly speaking a soul is the act of a living body, and life is conditional upon heat and humidity which are preserved in an animal by means of its blood: therefore it is stated that the soul is in the blood, thus indicating the proper disposition of the body as matter perfected by the soul.

Reply to the Ninth Objection. There are several opinions about the life of the embryo. According to some in human generation the soul, like the human body, is subject to stages of progression, so that as the human body is virtually in the semen, yet has not actually the perfection of a human body by having distinct members, but gradually reaches this perfection through the force of the semen, so at the beginning of the generation the soul is there having virtually all the perfection which subsequently is to be seen in the perfect human being, yet it has not this perfection actually, since there is no sign of the soul's activity, but attains thereto by degrees: so that at first there are indications of the action of the vegetal soul, then of the sensitive soul, and lastly of the rational soul. Gregory of Nyssa mentions this opinion (*De Homine*): but it cannot be admitted. It means either that the soul in its species is in the semen from the very outset, deprived however of its perfect activity through lack of organs, or that from the beginning there is in the semen some energy or form not having as yet the species of a soul (just as the semen has not as yet the appearance of a human body) but by the action of nature gradually transformed into a soul at first vegetal, then sensitive and lastly rational. The former alternative is rebutted first by the authority of the Philosopher. He says, in fact (*De Anima* ii, 1), that when we say that the soul is the act of a physico-organic body which has life potentially we do not exclude the soul, as we exclude it from the semen and the fruit. Hence we gather that the semen is animated potentially in that the soul is not therein. Secondly, because as the semen has no definite likeness to the members of the human body (else its resolution would be a kind of corruption) but is the residue of the final digestion (*De Gener. Anim.* i, 19), it was not yet while in the body of the begetter perfected by the soul, so that in the first instant of its separation it could not have a soul. Thirdly, granted that it was animated when it was separated, this cannot refer to the rational soul: because since it is not the act of a particular part of the body, it cannot be sundered when the body is sundered.

The second alternative is also clearly false. For seeing that a substantial form is brought into act not continuously or by degrees but instantaneously (else movement would needs be in the genus of substance just as it is in that of quality) the force which from the outset is in the semen cannot by degrees advance to the various degrees of soul. Thus the form of fire is not produced in the air so as gradually to advance from imperfection to perfection, since no substantial form is subject to increase and decrease: but it is the matter alone that is changed by the previous alteration so as to be more or less disposed to receive the form: and the form does not begin to be in the matter until the last instant of this alteration.

Others say that in the semen there is at first the vegetal soul and that afterwards while this remains the sensitive soul is introduced by the power of the generator, and that lastly the rational soul is introduced by creation. So that they posit in man three essentially different souls. Against this, however, is the authority of the book *De Ecclesiasticis Dogmatibus* (xv): *Nor do we say that there are two souls in one man as James and other Syrians write; one, animal, by which the body is animated and which is mingled with the blood, the other spiritual, which obeys the reason.* Moreover, it is impossible for one and the same thing to have several substantial forms: because, since the substantial form makes a thing to be, not in this or that way, but simply, and establishes this or that thing in the genus of substance; if the first form does this, the second form at its advent will find the subject already established with substantial being and consequently will accrue to it accidentally: and thus it would follow that the sensitive and rational souls in man would be united accidentally to the body, Nor can it be said that the vegetal soul which is the substantial form in a plant is not the substantial form in a man, but a mere disposition to the form, since that which is in the genus of substance cannot be an accident of anything.

Hence others say that the vegetative soul is potentially sensitive and that the sensitive soul is its act: so that the vegetative soul which at first is in the semen is raised to the perfection of the sensitive soul by the action of nature; and further that the rational soul is the act and perfection of the sensitive soul, so that the sensitive soul is brought to its perfection consisting in the rational soul, not by the action of the generator but by that of the Creator. Hence they hold that the rational soul is in man partly from within, namely as regards its intellectual nature, and partly from without as regards its vegetative and sensitive nature. Now this is altogether impossible, because either it means that the intellectual nature is distinct from the vegetal and sensitive souls, and thus we return to the second opinion, or it means that these three natures constitute the substance of the soul wherein the intellectual nature will be the form as it were, and the sensitive and vegetative natures, matter. From this it would follow, as the sensitive and vegetative natures are corruptible through being educed from matter, that the substance of the rational soul would not be immortal. Moreover, this opinion is involved in the same impossibility as we have shown to be implicated in the first opinion, namely that a substantial form be brought into act by degrees.

Others say that there is no soul in the embryo until it is perfected by the rational soul, and that the vital functions to be observed therein proceed from the soul of the mother. But this also is impossible: because living and non-living things differ in that living things are self-moving in respect of vital functions, whereas non-living things are not. Wherefore nutrition and growth which are the functions proper to a living being cannot result in the embryo from an extrinsic principle such as the mother's soul. Moreover, the mother's nutritive power would assimilate food to the mother's body and not to the body of the embryo: since nutrition serves the individual just as generation serves the species. Further, sensation cannot be caused in the embryo by the mother's soul. Wherefore others say that there is no soul in the embryo before the infusion of the rational soul, but that there is a formative force that exercises these vital functions in the embryo. This again is impossible, because before the embryo attains to its ultimate complement it shows signs of various vital functions; and these cannot be exercised by one power: so that there must needs be a soul there having various powers.

We must therefore say differently that from the moment of its severance the semen contains not a soul but a soul-power:[1] and this power is based on the spirit contained in the semen which by nature is spumy and consequently contains corporeal spirit. Now this spirit acts by disposing matter and forming it for the reception of the soul. And we must observe a difference between the process of generation in men and animals and in air or water. The generation of air is simple, since therein only two substantial forms appear, one that is voided and one that is induced, and all this takes place together in one instant, so that the form of water remains during the whole period preceding the induction of the form of air; without any previous dispositions to the form of air. On the other hand in the generation of an animal various substantial forms appear: first the semen, then blood and so on until we find the form of an animal or of a man. Consequently this kind of generation is not simple, but consists of a series of generations and corruptions: for it is not possible, as we have proved above, that one and the same substantial form be educed into act by degrees. Thus, then, by the formative force that is in the semen from the beginning, the form of the semen is set aside and another form induced, and when this has been set aside yet another comes on the scene, and thus the vegetal form makes its first appearance: and this being set aside, a soul both vegetal and sensitive is induced; and this being set aside a soul at once vegetal, sensitive and rational is induced, not by the aforesaid force but by the Creator. According to this opinion the embryo before having a rational soul is a

---

[1] See below Reply to the Eleventh Objection. Cf. also *Sum. Theol.* I, Q. cxix, art. 2. 'The semen is not something separated from what was before the actual whole: rather is it the whole, though potentially, having the power, derived from the soul of the begetter, to produce the whole body.'

living being having a soul, which being set aside, a rational soul is induced : so that it does not follow that two souls are together in the same body, nor that the rational soul is transmitted together with the body.

Reply to the Tenth Objection. Before the advent of the rational soul the embryo is not a perfect being but is on the way to perfection : and therefore it is not in a genus or species save by reduction, just as the incomplete is reduced to the genus or species of the complete.

Reply to the Eleventh Objection. Although the soul is not in the semen from the beginning, the soul-force is there, as stated above, which force is based on the spirit contained in the semen ; and is called a soul-force because it comes from the soul of the generator.

Reply to the Twelfth Objection. Before the advent of the rational soul the semen is a living and animate being, as stated above ; wherefore we grant this argument.

The same answer applies to the Thirteenth, Fourteenth and Fifteenth Objections.

Reply to the Sixteenth Objection. The formative force that is from the outset in the semen remains even after the advent of the rational soul ; just as the animal spirits remain into which nearly the whole substance of the semen is changed. This force, which at first served to form the body, afterwards regulates the body. Thus heat which at first disposes matter to the form of fire remains after the advent of the form of fire as an instrument of the latter's activity.

This answer applies to the Seventeenth and Eighteenth Objections.

Reply to the Nineteenth Objection. Although the rational soul is not evolved from the generator, its union with the body is in a manner from the generator, as stated above. Consequently we say that a man is begotten.

Reply to the Twentieth Objection. There is not a twofold being in man for the simple reason that when it is said that man's body is from his begetter and his soul from his Creator we are not to understand that the being acquired by the body from its begetter is distinct from that which the soul acquires from its Creator, but that the Creator gives being to the soul in the body, while the begetter disposes the body to participate in this being through the soul united to it.

Reply to the Twenty-first Objection. Two agents that are altogether disparate cannot combine so that the one's action terminate in the matter and the other's in the form, but this is possible in the case of two co-ordinate agents one of which is the instrument of the other : because the action of the principal agent sometimes extends to something that is beyond the range of the instrument. Now nature is a kind of instrument of the divine power as we have shown above (A. 8, rep. 14 ; A. 7). Hence it is not impossible that the divine power alone produce the rational soul, while the action of nature extends no further than to giving the body the requisite disposition.

Reply to the Twenty-second Objection. An intelligence existing in a body, in order to understand, needs nothing corporeal as a co-principle of intellectual action, in the same way as the sight in order to see : for the principle of vision is not the sense of sight only, but the eye consisting of pupil and the faculty of seeing. But it needs a body objectively, as the sight needs the wall on which is the colour : because images are compared to the intellect as colours to sight (*De Anima* iii, 5). This is why the intellect is prevented from understanding when the organ of the imagination is injured : since so long as it is in the body it needs images, not only as receiving from the images when it is acquiring knowledge, but also as referring the intelligible species to the images when it applies knowledge already acquired. For this reason science makes use of examples.

From this we gather how to reply to the Twenty-third and Twenty-fourth Objections.

Reply to the Twenty-fifth Objection. This was the argument of Apollinaris according to Gregory of Nyssa (*De Homine* vi). He was deceived, however, in failing to distinguish the action of nature which is the procreation of the child, to which action God gives the complement, from the deliberate act of adultery wherein the sin consists.

Reply to the Twenty-sixth Objection. The soul being

more perfect than material forms would be able to produce its like if a rational soul could be produced otherwise than by creation, which is impossible. And this is owing to its perfection as may be gathered from what has been said.

Reply to the Twenty-seventh Objection. In God alone can there be one nature in several supposits, wherefore in him alone can there be generation without the imperfection of change and division. Hence the higher creatures which are indivisible and unchangeable in substance such as the rational soul and the angels are not generated : whereas the lower creatures are, being divisible and corruptible.

Reply to the Twenty-eighth Objection. The force that is in the semen is called intellect by the Philosopher according to the Commentator (*in Metaph.* vii, 9) on account of a certain likeness : inasmuch as like the intellect its action is exercised without an organ.

Reply to the Twenty-ninth Objection. This saying of the Philosopher refers to the sensitive but not the rational soul.

ARTICLE X

IS THE RATIONAL SOUL CREATED IN THE BODY ?
Sum. Th. I, Q. xc, A. 4.

THE tenth point of inquiry is whether the rational soul be created in or apart from the body. Seemingly it is created apart from the body.

1. Things belonging to the same species come into being in the same way. Now our souls belong to the same species as Adam's : and Adam's soul was created apart from his body and at the same time as the angels, according to Augustine (*Gen. ad lit.* vii, 25, 27). Therefore other human souls are also created apart from their bodies.

2. A whole is imperfect if it lacks one of the parts required for its perfection. Now rational souls belong to the perfection of the universe more than corporeal substances, since an intellectual substance excels a corporeal substance. If, then, rational souls were not all created from the beginning, but

created day by day when their bodies are begotten, it follows that the universe is imperfect through lacking its most excellent parts: and this seemingly is unreasonable. Therefore rational souls were created from the beginning apart from their bodies.

3. It savours of a theatrical display that the universe should be destroyed when it attains to its ultimate perfection. Now the world will come to an end when the begetting of men ceases, and then the universe will have reached the utmost height of its perfection, if souls are created at the same time as their bodies are begotten: wherefore in that case the divine government will be like a play: which is surely absurd.

4. You will say perhaps that there is no reason why the perfection of the universe should not lack something in point of numbers, seeing that it is complete in respect of all its species.—On the contrary, as the species of things considered in themselves enjoy a certain perpetuity, they belong to the essential perfection of the universe, in that they are *per se* intended by the Author of the universe. Individuals, however, which have not perpetuity belong to a certain accidental perfection of the universe, in that they are intended not *per se* but for the conservation of the species. Now rational souls not only in their species but also in each individual enjoy perpetuity. Therefore if rational souls were all lacking at the beginning, the universe was imperfect even as it would have been had some of the species of the universe been wanting.

5. Macrobius (*Super Somn. Scip.* i) assigned two gates to heaven, one for the gods, and one for souls, in Cancer namely and in Capricorn, through one of which souls came down to earth. But it would not be so unless souls were created in heaven apart from their bodies. Therefore souls were created independently of bodies.

6. An efficient cause precedes its effect in point of time. Now the soul is the efficient cause of the body (*De Anima* ii, 4). Therefore it exists before the body and is not created in the body.

7. It is stated in *De Spiritu et Anima* (xiii) that before its

union with the body the soul has the irascible and concupiscible appetite. But these cannot be in the soul before it exists. Therefore the soul exists before its union with the body, and consequently is not created in the body.

8. The substance of the rational soul is not measured by time, since it is above time (*De Causis* ii) : nor is it measured by eternity, because this belongs to God alone. Again it is stated (*De Causis*, l.c.) that the soul is beneath eternity, therefore like the angels it is measured by eviternity, so that the duration of angels and souls has the same unit of measurement. Consequently as the angels were created at the beginning of the world, seemingly souls were created then also and not in their respective bodies.

9. In eviternity there is no before and after, else it would not differ from time, as some think. Now if angels were created before souls, or one soul before another, there would be before and after in eviternity, since this is the measurement of the soul's duration, as stated above. Therefore souls must all have been created together with the angels.

10. Unity of place indicates unity of nature : wherefore different places are assigned to bodies differing in nature. But angels and souls agree in nature, since they are spiritual and intellectual substances. Therefore souls like the angels were created in the empyrean and not in bodies.

11. The more subtle a substance is the higher place it requires : thus the place of fire is higher than that of air or water. Now the soul is a much more subtle substance than a body. Therefore seemingly it was created above all bodies and not in the body.

12. A thing reaches its ultimate perfection forasmuch as it occupies its proper place, for it cannot be outside its proper place except through violence. Now the ultimate perfection of the soul is a heavenly home. Therefore this is the place befitting its nature, and so it would seem that it was created there.

13. It is written (Gen. ii, 2) : *God rested on the seventh day from all the work which he had done :* whereby we are given to understand that God ceased then from creating

anything new. Therefore souls are not created in their respective bodies, but were created independently at the beginning.

14. The work of creation preceded the work of increase. But this would not be, if souls be created as bodies increase in number. Therefore they were created before bodies.

15. God does all things according to justice. Now justice requires that diverse and unequal awards should not be made save to those who are found to be unequal in merit. Now we find that men from their birth are subject to many inequalities of soul: in some cases the body to which a soul is united is well adapted to the soul's actions, in others the body is ill-adapted to them: some are born of unbelievers, others are born of believers and are saved through receiving the sacraments. Therefore it would seem that there preceded in souls an inequality of merits, and consequently that souls were created before bodies.

16. Things that are united in their beginning would seem to depend on each other as to their being. But the soul is independent of the body as to its being: which is shown by the fact that it remains when the body has ceased to be. Therefore it does not begin to exist together with the body.

17. Things that hinder each other are not naturally united. Now the soul is hindered in its action by the body, for *the corruptible body is a load upon the soul* (Wis. ix, 15). Therefore the soul is not naturally united to the body, and thus it would seem that before its union with the body it existed apart therefrom.

On the contrary it is stated (*Eccles. Dogm.* xiv) that souls were not created together with other intellectual creatures.

Further, Gregory of Nyssa says (*De Creat. Hom.* xxix) that it is reprehensible to *hold either opinion, whether of those who foolishly assert a previous existence of souls in a certain state and order becoming to them, or of those who maintain that our souls are created after our bodies.*

Further, Jerome says (*Symb. Fid.*[1]): *We condemn the error of those who hold that souls sinned or lived in heaven before being united to bodies.*

---
[1] Pelagius, *Expositio Fidei ad Damasum.*

Further, the proper act is evolved in its proper matter. Now the soul is the proper act of the body. Therefore it is created in the body.

I answer that as we have stated (A. 9) some held the opinion that our souls were all created together apart from our bodies : and that this is false we shall now proceed to show by four arguments.

First argument. Things when created by God were in a state of natural perfection : for the perfect naturally precedes the imperfect according to the Philosopher (*De Cælo* i, 2) : and Boëthius says (*De Consol.* x, pros. 10) that nature originates in perfect things. Now the soul apart from the body has not the perfection of its nature, because by itself it is not the complete species of a nature, but a part of human nature : otherwise soul and body would not together form one thing save accidentally. Hence the human soul was not created before its body. Now all those who held that souls exist outside bodies before being united to them, supposed them to be perfect natures, and that the natural perfection of the soul is not that it be united to its body, and that it is united to it accidentally as a man to his clothes : thus Plato said that a man is not made of soul and body, but is a soul making use of a body. Wherefore all those who held souls to be created apart from bodies, believed in the transmigration of souls, namely that a soul after casting off one body is united to another body, even as a man changes from one suit of clothes to another.

The second argument is given by Avicenna. Seeing that the soul is not composed of matter and form—for it is distinct both from matter and from the composite (*De Anima* ii, 1)—there could be no distinction between one soul and another except that which arises from a difference of forms, supposing that souls differ from one another by themselves. Now difference of form implies difference of species. And numerical distinction within the same species arises from distinction of matter : and this cannot apply to the soul as regards the matter of which a thing is made but only as regards the matter in which the soul comes into being. Consequently there cannot be many human souls of the same species and distinct individually unless from their very beginning they be united to bodies, so that their mutual distinction arises from their union to bodies, as from a material principle in a manner of speaking, although that distinction comes from God as their efficient cause. Now if souls were created apart from their bodies, as there would have been no material principle to distinguish them they would have differed in species like all separate substances which according to the philosophers differ specifically.

Third argument. We have already shown that man's rational soul is not in substance distinct from the sensible and vegetal soul : moreover the vegetal and sensible soul cannot originate except from the body since they are acts of certain parts of the body. Wherefore neither can the rational soul, so far as is becoming to its nature, be created apart from the body; without prejudice, however, to the divine power.

Fourth argument. If the rational soul were created apart from the body, and in that state were possessed of the perfection of its natural being, no reasonable cause can be assigned for its union with the body. It cannot be said that it united itself to a body of its own accord, for clearly it is not in the soul's power to abandon the body, which it could do were it united to the body by its own choice. Moreover, if souls were created wholly apart from bodies, it cannot be explained why the soul thus separated desired to be united to a body. Nor can it be said that after an interval of years the soul acquired a natural desire for union with a body, and that nature brought about this union : because things that happen at certain intervals of time, are referred to the celestial movement as their cause, since that movement is the measure of the spaces of time : and souls separate from bodies cannot be subject to the movements of heavenly bodies. Again it cannot be said that they were united to bodies by God, if they were previously created by him without bodies. For if it be alleged that he did so to perfect them, why did he create them at first without bodies ? On the other hand if he did this to punish them for their sins so that the soul was thrust into a body as into a prison, as

Origen asserted, it would follow that the formation of natures composed of spiritual and corporal substances was accidental and not according to God's original intention : and this is contrary to the statement of Genesis i, 31 : *God saw all the things that he had made and they were very good,* whence we gather that it was through God's goodness and not on account of the wickedness of any creature whatsoever that those good works were done.

Reply to the First Objection. Augustine in *De Genesi ad literam* and especially in his work *De Origine Animæ* speaks as inquiring rather than asserting, as he himself declares.[1]

Reply to the Second Objection. The universe in its beginning was perfect as regards the species of things, but not as regards all individuals : or as regards nature's causes from which afterwards other things could be propagated, but not as regards all their effects. And though rational souls are not evolved by natural causes, the bodies into which as being connatural to them they are infused by God are produced by the action of nature.

Reply to the Third Objection. The object of the play is the play itself. But in the movement whereby God moves corporeal creatures the object in view is something beside the movement, namely the complete number of the elect, and when that is reached the movement, but not the substance, of the world will cease.

Reply to the Fourth Objection. The multitude of souls belongs to the ultimate, not the initial essential perfection of the universe, since the entire transformation of mundane bodies is ordered somewhat to the multiplication of souls, which requires a multiplication of bodies as we have proved above.

Reply to the Fifth Objection. The Platonists maintained that the soul's nature is complete in itself, and that the soul is united to the body accidentally, wherefore they affirmed the transmigration of souls from one body to another. Especially were they led to hold this opinion because they held that souls are immortal and that generation never fails. Hence in order to avoid an infinite number of souls

[1] Cf. *Sum. Th.* I, Q. xc, A. 4.

they imagined a kind of circle so that a soul after leaving a body was subsequently reunited to it. Macrobius expresses himself in accordance with this opinion which is false : and consequently on this point his authority cannot be admitted.

Reply to the Sixth Objection. The Philosopher (*De Anima* ii, l.c.) does not state that the soul is the efficient cause of the body, but as he explains (*ibid.*) the cause whence the body's movements originate, in so far as it is the principle of locomotion, growth and other like movements in the body.

Reply to the Seventh Objection. The meaning of the authority quoted is that the irascible and concupiscible appetite is in the soul before its union with the body by a priority of nature, not of time : because the soul does not derive it from the body, but rather the body from the soul.

Reply to the Eighth Objection. The soul is measured by time in so far as it has being in union with the body : although considered as a spiritual substance it is measured by eviternity. But it does not follow that it began together with the angels to be measured by eviternity.

Reply to the Ninth Objection. Although there is no before and after in eviternity as regards the things it measures, nothing forbids one thing from having before another a part in eviternity.

Reply to the Tenth Objection. Although the angel and the soul agree in intellectual nature, they differ in that the angel is a nature complete in itself, so that he could be created in himself : whereas the soul through having the perfection of its nature by union with the body, required to be created, not in heaven but in that body whose perfection it is.

Reply to the Eleventh Objection. Although the soul is in itself more simple than any body, it is nevertheless the form and perfection of a body composed of elements, and to which a middle place is due : and together with this body it must needs be created here below.

Reply to the Twelfth Objection. The initial perfection of

the soul regards its natural being, and consists in the soul's union with the body : wherefore in its beginning it required to be created in the place occupied by the body. But its ultimate perfection regards that which it has in common with other intellectual substances, and this it will receive in heaven.

Reply to the Thirteenth Objection. Souls that are created now are new creatures indeed in point of number, but are old in point of species : since they already existed in the works of the six days, in those who were like them in species, namely in the souls of our first parents.

Reply to the Fourteenth Objection. It behoved the work of creation whereby the principles of nature were established to precede the work of propagation : but the creation of souls is not a work of that kind.

Reply to the Fifteenth Objection. It belongs to justice to render what is due ; wherefore it is contrary to justice to treat equal persons unequally if they are being paid what is due to them, but not if they are receiving gratis, as when souls are created. We may also reply that this diversity does not arise from a diversity of merit in souls, but from a diversity of dispositions in bodies : wherefore Plato said (*Dial. de Legibus*) that forms are infused according to the deserts of matter.

Reply to the Sixteenth Objection. Although the soul depends on the body for its beginning, in order to begin its existence in the perfection of its nature, nevertheless it does not depend on the body for its end, because it exists in the body as a subsistent being, so that when the body ceases to exist the soul remains in its own being, though not in the perfection of its nature that it receives from its union with the body.

Reply to the Seventeenth Objection. It is not the nature of the body but its corruption that is a load upon the soul, as the text itself declares.

ARTICLE XI

IS THE SENSIBLE AND VEGETAL SOUL CREATED OR IS IT TRANSMITTED THROUGH THE SEMEN ?

Sum. Th. I, Q. cxviii, A. I.

THE eleventh point of inquiry is whether the sensible soul be created or transmitted through the semen : and it would seem that it is created.

1. Things of the same kind come into being in the same manner. Now the sensible and vegetal soul in man is of the same species or kind as in dumb animals and plants : and in man it is created since it is substantially one with the rational soul, which is created, as proved above (A. 9). Therefore the sensitive and vegetal souls in animals and plants are created.

2. It might be said that the sensible and vegetal souls in animals and plants are perfections, whereas in man they are dispositions.—On the contrary the more excellent a thing is the more excellent is the manner of its coming into being. Now it is more excellent to be a form and perfection than to be a disposition : and consequently if the sensible and vegetal souls in man, in whom they are mere dispositions, come into being by creation which is the most excellent way of coming into being, since the highest creatures originate in this manner, seemingly a fortiori are they created in plants and animals.

3. The Philosopher says (*Phys.* i, 3) : *That which really exists, substance to wit, is not accidental to anything.* If, then, the sensible and vegetal souls are substantial forms in animals and plants, they cannot be accidental dispositions in man.

4. In living things the generative power is effective through the force residing in the semen. Now the sensible and vegetal souls are not actually in the semen. Since then nothing acts except inasmuch as it is in act, seemingly the sensible and vegetal souls cannot be produced by the force in the semen, and thus they are produced not by generation but by creation.

5. You will say perhaps that though the force in the semen is not actually the sensitive soul, yet it acts by virtue of the sensitive soul of the father from whom it issues.—On the contrary, that which acts by virtue of another acts as its instrument. Now an instrument moves not unless it be moved : while mover and moved must be together (*Phys.* vii, 2). Since then the force that is in the semen is not in contact with the sensible soul of the generator, seemingly it cannot act as its instrument or by virtue thereof.

6. An instrument is compared to the principal agent as a moved and commanded power to a moving and commanding power which is an appetitive and moving force. Now a power that is commanded and moved does not move anything if it be severed from the power that moves and commands it, as may be seen in the severed limbs of an animal. Neither then can the force in the separated semen act by virtue of the generator.

7. When an effect falls short of the perfection of its cause it cannot compass the action proper to that cause : since diversity of action argues diversity of nature. Now the force in the semen although an effect of the sensible soul of the generator falls short of its perfection. Therefore it cannot accomplish the action that belongs properly to the sensible soul, namely the production of another soul like to it in species.

8. Corruption of their subject leads to corruption of form and power. Now in the process of generation the semen, according to Avicenna, is corrupted and receives another form. Therefore the power that was in the semen is also corrupted, and consequently a sensible soul cannot be produced by it.

9. Lower natures function only by means of heat and other active and passive qualities. Now heat cannot give being to the sensible soul, because nothing acts outside its own species : nor can the effect surpass its cause. Therefore the sensible or vegetal soul cannot be brought into being by a natural agent, and consequently it is created.

10. A natural agent acts not by informing but by transmuting matter. Now transmutation of matter can only

lead to an accidental form. Therefore a natural agent cannot produce a sensible and vegetal soul which is a substantial form.

11. Sensible and vegetal souls have a certain quiddity, and this quiddity is brought into being by something else: moreover it did not exist before being evolved except in so far as it was possible for matter to have it. Hence it must needs be produced by an agent that produces something out of no matter: and this is no other but God creating.

12. Animals produced from seed rank higher than those engendered from corrupt matter, for they are more perfect and reproduce their like. Now the souls of animals engendered from corrupt matter are created, since no agent of like species can be assigned by which they can be produced. Therefore it would seem that there is much more reason for the souls of animals produced from seed to be created.

13. But you will say that the souls of animals engendered from corrupt matter are produced by the power of a heavenly body, just as they are produced in other an mals by the formative force in the semen —On the contrary, according to Augustine (*De Vera Relig.* lv), a living substance surpasses all inanimate substances. Now a heavenly body is not a living substance, for it is inanimate. Therefore a sensible soul being a principle of life cannot be produced by its power.

14. But you will say that a heavenly body can be the cause of a sensible soul, inasmuch as it acts by virtue of an intellectual substance that moves it.—On the contrary that which is received into another, is received according to the mode of the recipient, and not according to its own mode. Wherefore if the power of an intellectual substance is received by an inanimate heavenly body, it will not be there as a vital force that can be a principle of life.

15. An intellectual substance is not only a living but also an intelligent being. If, then, by its power a heavenly body can be so moved by it as to give life it will be able likewise to give intelligence, so that the rational soul will be produced by the begetter: which is false.

16. If the sensible soul is produced by a natural agent

and not by creation, it must be produced either by the body or by the soul. It is not produced by the body, because then a body would act beyond its species. Nor is it produced by the soul, because then either the whole soul of the father would be transmitted to his child, and thus the father would remain without a soul; or part of it would be transmitted, and thus the whole soul would not remain in the father: and either alternative is false. Therefore the sensible soul is not produced by the begetter but by the Creator.

17. The Commentator (*De Anima* iii) says that no cognitive power is evolved by the action of mixed elements. Now the sensible soul is a cognitive power. Therefore it is not evolved by the elements, and consequently not by the action of nature, inasmuch as here below no action of nature is independent of the action of the elements.

18. No form except it be subsistent can cause movement: wherefore according to the Philosopher (*Phys.* viii, 4) movement is not caused by the forms of elements but only by the generator and that which removes an obstacle. But the sensible soul is a cause of movement, since every animal is moved by its soul. Therefore the sensible soul is not a mere form but a self-subsistent substance. It is also clear that it is not composed of matter and form. Now all such substances are brought into being by creation and not otherwise. Therefore the sensible soul comes into being by creation.

19. You will say, perhaps, that the sensible soul does not by itself move the body, but that the animated body moves itself.—On the contrary the Philosopher proves (*Phys.* viii, 5) that in everything which puts itself in motion there must be one part that is mover only, and another that is moved. Now the body cannot be mover only, because no body moves except it be moved. Wherefore the soul is mover only, so that the sensible soul will have a function in which the body has no share, and consequently will be a subsistent substance.

20. But you will say that the sensible soul moves according to the command of the appetitive power, whose act is shared by both soul and body.—On the contrary in an animal

there is not only a power commanding but also a power executing movement : and the function of this latter power cannot for the reasons already given be shared by both soul and body : and consequently the sensible soul must operate by itself, and therefore is a self-subsistent substance, and is brought into being by creation and not by natural generation.

On the contrary it is written (Gen. i, 20) : *Let the waters bring forth the creeping creature having a living soul ;* so that seemingly the sensible souls of reptiles and of other animals are produced by the action of corporal elements.

Further, as the father's body is in relation to his soul, so is the son's body in relation to his soul. Therefore reciprocally as the son's body is to his father's, so is the son's soul to his father's. Now the son's body is evolved from his father's. Therefore the son's soul is evolved from his father's.

I answer that philosophers are divided in their opinions about the production of substantial forms. Some maintain that the natural agent only disposes the matter and that the form which is the ultimate perfection is produced by supernatural agency. This opinion is shown to be false chiefly on two counts. First, because seeing that the being of natural and corporal forms consists solely in their union with matter, it would seem that it belongs to the same agent to produce them and to transmute matter. Secondly, inasmuch as these forms do not surpass the power, order and faculty of the active principles of nature, there would seem to be no need to refer their origin to higher principles : wherefore the Philosopher (*Metaph.* vii, 8) says that flesh and bone are engendered by the form that is in this or that flesh and bone : and in his opinion the natural agent not only disposes the matter, but educes the form into act, which is contrary to the above opinion.

Nevertheless we must exclude the rational soul from this generality of forms : because it is a subsistent substance, wherefore its being does not consist solely in its union with the body. Otherwise it could not exist apart from the body : the possibility of which is shown by its operation, which belongs to the soul in entire independence of the body. And the mode of its operation indicates the mode of its coming into existence : since that which is not *per se* does not operate *per se*. Again the intellectual nature transcends the entire order and faculty of material and corporal principles, since by its act of intelligence the intellect is able to rise above all corporal nature, which would not be the case if its nature were confined within the limits of corporal nature.

Now neither of these things can be said of the sensible and vegetal souls. That the being of these souls cannot consist otherwise than in union with the body is shown by their functions, which cannot be exercised without a bodily organ, wherefore absolutely speaking they have no being independently of the body. For this reason they cannot exist apart from the body, nor be brought into being except in so far as the body is brought into being. Consequently these souls, like the body, are produced by the natural agency of the generator. To maintain that they are created separately would appear to be in agreement with the opinion of those who held that these souls survived their bodies, whereas both these opinions are condemned in *De Eccl. Dogmat.* Again these souls do not transcend the order of natural causes. This will be made evident if we consider their operations. The order of actions follows the order of natures. Now we find some forms whose scope of action does not go further than what can be done by material principles : thus the forms of elements and of mixed bodies do not go beyond the action of heat and cold : wherefore they are wholly immersed in matter. On the other hand although the vegetal soul does not function except by means of the qualities aforesaid, its action attains to something that is beyond the scope of these qualities, to the production, namely, of flesh and bone, to the fixation of the term of growth and the like, so that it remains within the order of material principles ; though not so much as the forms in question. But the sensible soul does not of necessity function by means of heat and cold, as evidenced by the functions of the sight, imagination and so forth : yet for the exercise of these functions, the organs require to be equipped with a certain degree of heat and cold, without which the aforesaid actions cannot be performed. Hence the sensible soul does not wholly transcend the order of material principles, although it is not lowered to their level as much as the above-mentioned forms. The rational soul, however, also exercises a function that surpasses that of heat and cold, nor does it exercise it by means of heat and cold, nor by means of a bodily organ : wherefore it alone transcends the order of natural principles, whereas the sensible soul in dumb animals and the vegetal soul in plants do not.

Reply to the First Objection. Although the sensible soul in man and dumb animals is of the same genus it does not belong to the same species : thus a man and a dumb animal are not of the same species : consequently the functions of the sensible soul are far more excellent in man than in dumb animals, as evidenced by the touch and the interior powers of apprehension. Nor is it true that things generically but not specifically the same must needs come into being in the same manner, as evidenced in the case of animals engendered from seed and from corrupt matter : since these agree in genus but not in species.

Reply to the Second Objection. In man the sensible soul is said to be a disposition, not as though it differed in substance from the rational soul, and were a disposition thereto, but because the sensitive faculty in man is not distinct from the rational, save as one power from another. On the other hand in dumb animals the sensible soul differs from the rational soul in man as one substantial form from another. Nevertheless as the sensitive and vegetal powers in man flow from the essence of the soul, so do they in dumb animals and plants : but with this difference that in plants there flow only vegetal forces from the essence of the soul, in dumb animals not only vegetal but also sensitive powers whence their soul is denominated, while in man besides the above the intellectual powers flow whence he is denominated.

Reply to the Third Objection. The substance whence the sensitive faculty flows both in dumb animals and in man is the substantial form : while in both cases the power is an accident.

Reply to the Fourth Objection. The sensible soul is not actually in the semen as to its own species but as in an active force : thus a house is actually in the mind of the builder as in an active force ; and thus are bodily forms in the heavenly powers.

Reply to the Fifth Objection. An instrument is understood to be moved by the principal agent so long as it retains the power communicated to it by the principal agent ; thus the arrow is moved by the archer as long as it retains the force wherewith it was shot by him. Thus in heavy and light things that which is generated is moved by the generator as long as it retains the form transmitted thereby : so that the semen also is understood to be moved by the soul of the begetter, as long as it retains the force communicated by that soul, although it is in body separated from it. And the mover and the thing moved must be together at the commencement of but not throughout the whole movement, as is evident in the case of projectiles.

Reply to the Sixth Objection. The soul's appetitive power has no command except on the body united to it, wherefore the separated part does not obey the behest of the soul's appetitive faculty. Nor is the semen moved by the begetter's soul through being commanded but through the transfusion of a kind of energy which remains in the semen even after its separation.

Reply to the Seventh Objection. The sensible and vegetal souls are evolved from the potentiality of matter like other material forms for the production of which a power is needed that transforms matter. Now the force that is in the semen has this power although it falls short of the other functions of the soul. For just as by the function of the nutritive force the soul transforms matter so as to change it into the whole body, so by the aforesaid force in the semen matter is transformed so as to result in conception. Consequently nothing hinders this same force from accomplishing the action of the sensitive soul and by virtue thereof.

Reply to the Eighth Objection. This same force has its root in the animal spirit enclosed within the semen as its subject. Now according to Avicenna nearly all the semen is changed into animal spirit. Hence although the corpulent matter whence the embryo is formed undergoes many changes in the process of generation, the subject of that force is not destroyed.

Reply to the Ninth Objection. As heat acts as the instrument of the substantial form of fire, so there is nothing to prevent it from acting as the instrument of the sensible soul in bringing a sensible soul into being, though it does not do so by its own power.

Reply to the Tenth Objection. Matter is transmuted not only by an accidental but also by a substantial change: for both forms pre-exist in the potentiality of matter. Hence a natural agent which transmutes matter is the cause not only of the accidental but also of the substantial form.

Reply to the Eleventh Objection. The sensible soul since it is not subsistent is not a quiddity, as neither are other material forms, but is part of a quiddity; and its being consists in its forming one substance together with matter: wherefore to say that the sensible soul is produced means nothing more than that the matter is transmuted from potentiality to act.

Reply to the Twelfth Objection. The more imperfect a thing is the fewer the requisites for its making. Wherefore since animals engendered from corrupt matter are more imperfect than those engendered from seed, in the former the sole power of a heavenly body is sufficient, which power is operative also in the semen, although it does not suffice without the power of the soul for the production of animals from seed. For the power of a heavenly body remains in the lower bodies in so far as they are transmuted by it as by the first cause of alteration. For this reason the Philosopher says (*De Animal.*) that all these lower bodies are full of a soul's energy. But the heaven, though not alike in species to the animals engendered from corrupt matter, is like them in so far as an effect virtually persists in its efficient cause.

Reply to the Thirteenth Objection. Although the heavenly body is not a living thing, it acts by virtue of a living substance by whom it is moved, whether this be an angel or God. In the opinion of the Philosopher, however, heavenly bodies are animate and living.

Reply to the Fourteenth Objection. The power of the heavenly body which causes movement remains in the heavenly body and its movement, not as a form having complete natural being, but after the manner of an intention, as power is in the craftsman's tool.

Reply to the Fifteenth Objection. As stated above, the rational soul surpasses the entire order of corporal principles, wherefore no body can act even instrumentally in its production.

Reply to the Sixteenth Objection. The sensible soul is produced in the embryo neither by the action of the body, nor by a transmission of the soul, but by the action of the formative energy that is in the semen from the soul of the begetter, as stated above.

Reply to the Seventeenth Objection. It is denied that a cognitive faculty can be produced by the action of the elements forasmuch as the forces contained in the elements are unable to produce such a power in the same way as they suffice to cause hardness or softness. But it is not denied that they may be competent to co-operate in some way instrumentally.

Reply to the Eighteenth Objection. The sensible soul causes movement by its appetite. Now the function of the sensitive appetite is seated not in the soul alone but in the composite; hence this power has a fixed organ. Therefore we cannot conclude that the sensible soul has an operation independent of the body.

Reply to the Nineteenth Objection. A body can cause a movement without being itself moved with the same kind of movement as that which it causes: thus the heavenly body which is moved locally causes alteration without itself being altered: and in like manner the organ of the appetitive power causes local movement, whereas itself is not moved but only altered somewhat locally. For the sensitive appetite does not function without alteration in the body, as evidenced in cases of anger and like passions.

Reply to the Twentieth Objection. The motive force that executes a movement does not of itself cause movement, but is rather a disposition of the thing movable whereby it has a natural aptness to be moved by this or that mover.

ARTICLE XII

IS THE SENSIBLE OR VEGETAL SOUL IN THE SEMEN FROM THE BEGINNING OF THE LATTER'S SEPARATION?

Sum. Th. I, Q. cxix

THE twelfth point of inquiry is whether the sensible or vegetal soul be in the semen as soon as this is separated: and seemingly the reply should be in the affirmative.

1. Gregory of Nyssa (*De Creat. Hom.* xxvi) says that *it is reprehensible to hold either opinion, whether of those who foolishly assert a previous existence of souls in a certain state and order becoming to them, or of those who maintain that our souls are created after our bodies.* Now if the soul was not in the semen from the beginning it must be created after the body. Therefore it was in the semen from the beginning.

2. If the sensitive like the rational soul was not in the semen from the beginning, the same rule will apply to the one as to the other. Now the rational soul comes by creation. Therefore the sensible soul is also created: whereas we have proved the contrary to be the case.

3. The Philosopher says (*De Gener. Animal.* ii, 4) that the force residing in the semen is like the son going forth from his father's house. Now the son is of the same species as his father. Therefore the force in the semen is of the same species as the sensible soul whence it derives.

4. The Philosopher says (*ibid.*) that this same force is like art which, were it in matter, would perfect the work of the craftsman. Now the species of the work done is in the art. Therefore the species of the sensible soul produced through the semen is in the seminal force.

5. The sundering of the semen is natural, whereas the sundering of an annulose animal is unnatural. Now according to the Philosopher the soul is in the sundered part of an annulose animal. Much more then is it in the sundered semen.

6. The Philosopher says (*ibid.*) that in the generation of an animal the male provides the soul. Now nothing issues from the father except the semen. Therefore the soul is in the semen.

7. An accident is not transmitted unless its subject be transmitted. Now certain diseases are transmitted from parents to their children, such as leprosy, gout and so on. Consequently the subject of these diseases is transmitted: which subject cannot be soulless. Therefore the soul is in the semen from the beginning.

8. Hippocrates says that generation is prevented by the excision of a vein in the neighbourhood of the ear. Now this would not be, unless the semen as already actually existing were taken from the whole body. Since then the soul is in whatever is actually part of an animal, it would seem that the soul is in the semen from the beginning.

9. He also says that a certain horse on account of too frequent coition was found to have no brains. But this would not be unless the semen were taken from that which is an actual part of the body. Therefore the same conclusion follows.

10. The superfluous is not part of the substance of a thing. Accordingly if the semen is superfluous it will not belong to the substance of the generator: and thus the child that results from the semen will not be of his father's substance: which is unreasonable. Therefore the semen is part of the generator's substance, and consequently the soul is therein actually.

11. That which has no soul is inanimate. If, then, the semen has no soul it will be inanimate. Consequently an inanimate body will be transformed and become animate: and this would seem absurd. Therefore the soul is in the semen from the beginning.

On the contrary the Philosopher says (*De Anim.* ii, 1) that the semen and the fruit are potentially animate but actually inanimate.

Again, it would seem impossible for the semen to be animate from the first except in two ways, either by the transmission of the generator's entire soul into the semen, or by the transmission of part thereof. Now, apparently either of these alternatives is impossible, since from the former it would follow that the soul does not remain in the father, and from the latter, that not the entire soul remains. Therefore the soul is not in the semen from the beginning.

I answer that some held the opinion that the soul is in the semen from the moment of its separation, so that they would have the soul procreated by the soul at the same time as the body (of the semen) is cut off from the body, and the part severed from the body would at once become animate. But this opinion is apparently false: because as the Philosopher proves (*De Gener. Anim.* i, 18, 19) the semen is not severed from what was an actual part, but from the surplus remaining after the final digestion,[1] and not definitely assimilated. Now no part of the body is actually perfected by the soul, unless it be finally assimilated; wherefore the semen before being separated was not perfected by the soul so as to be informed by it: but there was in the semen a certain energy in respect of which by the action of the soul it was altered and brought to the final disposition required for definite assimilation: so that after separation it was not animate but contained a certain energy derived from the soul. For this reason the Philosopher (*De Gener. Animal.* ii, 3) says that in the semen there is a power that emanates from the soul. Moreover if the soul were in the semen from the beginning, it would be either there in its species as a soul actually; or not, but as a kind of energy to be transformed afterwards into a soul. The former is impossible, because since the soul is the act of an organic body, the body cannot receive the soul before it is in any way whatever provided with organs. Moreover it would follow that all that the soul does in the semen, is to dispose the matter, so that consequently there would be no generation, since

[1] See *Sum. Th.* I, Q. cxix, A. 2.

generation does not follow but precedes the substantial form :
—unless one were to say that besides the soul there is another substantial form in the body, the result being that the soul would not be substantially united to the body, seeing that it would be added to the body after the latter had already become an individual thing by reason of this other form. It would follow moreover that the generation of a living being would not be generation but a kind of separation, just as timber cut off from timber is actually timber.

The second alternative is also impossible, since in that case it would follow that the substantial form is not at once but by degrees acquired by matter, so that there would be movement in substance as there is in quantity and quality, which is contrary to the teaching of the Philosopher (*Phys.* v, 2). It would also follow that substantial forms are subject to increase and decrease, which is impossible. It follows then that there is not a soul in the semen, but a certain energy derived from the soul, which prepares the way for the soul's advent.

Reply to the First Objection. Before the advent of the soul and the force that prepares the way for the soul, the body of a living being, e.g. a lion or an olive, is not animate but is merely the seed of a body : for the seed is related to this force as the body is to the soul.

Reply to the Second Objection. There is this difference between the rational and other souls, that the rational soul is not evolved from the energy in the seed as the other souls are ; although no soul is in the seed from the beginning.

Reply to the Third Objection. This force is likened to a son going forth from his father's house not in the point of specific completion, but with regard to the acquisition of some particular complement that is lacking. For a first perfection often takes on the likeness of a second perfection.

Reply to the Fourth Objection. The likeness between this force and art consists in this that as the thing made by the craftsman pre-exists in his art as in an active force, so before it is generated a living being pre-exists in the formative energy.

Reply to the Fifth Objection. The reason why the dissection of an annulose animal is violent and unnatural is that the severed part was actually a part of the animal and perfected by its soul : so that by the dissection of the matter the soul remains in either part, which soul was actually one in the whole body, and potentially several. This is because in animals of this kind the whole body is composed of almost homogeneous parts, and their souls being of a lower degree of perfection than others, require but little diversity of organs. Hence it is that when a part is severed it can be a subject of the soul, as having sufficient organs for the purpose : as happens in the case of other like bodies such as wood, stone, water and air. The Philosopher proves (*De Gener. Animal.* i, 18) that the semen was not actually a part before its separation, for the reason that its separation would not have been natural, but a kind of corruption : wherefore it does not follow that the soul remains in the semen after its separation.

Reply to the Sixth Objection. The male is said to provide the soul inasmuch as the seed of the male contains a force that prepares the way for the soul.

Reply to the Seventh Objection. The diseases mentioned in the objection are not transmitted together with the semen as though they were actually in the semen, but because their germs are in the semen, thus causing a certain indisposition therein.

Reply to the Eighth Objection. Seeing that the semen is a surplus, it has certain outlets like other superfluities : and if these outlets be cut off, generation is prevented, and not because something of what was an actual part of the body has been destroyed.

Reply to the Ninth Objection. It is the same with the immoderate emission of the semen as with the immoderate discharge of other superfluities which destroys that which has already been converted into bodily tissue, a destruction that is violent and unnatural. But things that happen contrary to nature, must not be ascribed to the action of nature.

Reply to the Tenth Objection. The semen is a surplus in the sense that although it is not actually a part of the father's substance, it is potentially the whole thereof ; and for this reason the child is said to be of his father's substance.

Reply to the Eleventh Objection. Although the semen is not actually animate it is so virtually, whereupon it is not simply inanimate.

ARTICLE XIII
CAN THAT WHICH PROCEEDS FROM ANOTHER BE ETERNAL ?

THE thirteenth point of inquiry is whether that which is from another can be eternal : and seemingly it cannot.

1. Nothing that always is needs something that it may be. Therefore nothing that is from another is always.

2. Nothing receives what it has already. Now that which always is always has being ; and hence that which is always does not receive being. But that which is from another receives its being from that whence it is. Therefore nothing that is from another is always.

3. That which is already is not generated or made or in a way brought into being. Because whatsoever is in a state of becoming is not yet. Consequently whatsoever is generated, made or brought into being must at one time not have been. Now such is whatsoever is from another. Therefore whatsoever is from another at some time is not. But that which at some time is not, is not always. Therefore nothing that is from another is eternal.

4. That which has not being save from another, considered in itself is not : and such a thing must needs not be at some time or other. Therefore whatsoever is from another must needs at some time have not been : and thus it is not eternal.

5. Every effect is posterior to its cause. Now that which is from another is the effect of that from which it is. Therefore it is posterior to that from which it is, and thus it cannot be eternal.

On the contrary according to Hilary (*De Trin.* xii) that which was born of the eternal Father has eternal being from his birth. Now the Son of God was born of the eternal

Father. Therefore he has eternal being from his birth; and consequently he is eternal.

I answer that since we affirm that the Son of God proceeds from the Father naturally, it follows that he must proceed from the Father in suchwise as to be co-eternal with him. This may be made clear as follows.

There is this difference between will and nature, that nature is determined to one thing both as regards what is produced by the power of nature and as regards producing or not producing: whereas the will is not determined in either respect. Thus a man is enabled by his will to do this or that, for instance a carpenter can make a bench or a box; and again make, and cease from making them: whereas fire cannot but heat if the subject-matter of its action be present: nor can it produce in matter any effect other than its like. Consequently although it may be said of creatures which proceed from God by his will, that he could make a creature of this or that fashion, and at this or that time, this cannot be said of the Son who proceeds naturally. For the Son proceeding naturally could not be of a fashion different from the nature of the Father. Nor could the Son be sooner or later in relation to the Father's nature. For it cannot be said that the divine nature was ever lacking in natural perfection, on the advent of which by virtue of the nature God's Son was begotten: since the divine nature is simple and unchangeable. Nor can it be said that this begetting was delayed through lack or indisposition of matter, seeing that it is altogether void of change. It follows then that since the Father's nature is eternal, that the Son was begotten of the Father from eternity and that he is co-eternal with the Father.

The Arians through holding that the Son does not proceed naturally from the Father, said that like other things that proceed from God according to the decree of his will he was neither co-equal nor co-eternal with the Father. The difficulty of regarding the begetting of the Son as co-eternal with the Father arose from the fact that in our human observation of nature's works one thing proceeds from another by movement: and a thing brought into being by movement begins to be at the beginning sooner than at the end of the movement. And since the beginning of a movement must needs in point of time precede the end on account of movement implying succession, and again since movement cannot have a beginning without a moving cause to produce it : it follows that the moving cause in the production of anything must precede in point of duration that which it produces. Consequently that which proceeds from another without movement is in point of duration co-existent with that whence it proceeds : such is the flash of the fire or the sun, because the flash of light proceeds from the body of light suddenly and not gradually, for illumination is not a movement but the term of a movement. It follows then that in God in whom there is absolutely no movement, the proceeding one is co-existent with him from whom he proceeds : and thus since the Father is eternal, the Son and the Holy Ghost who proceed from him are co-eternal with him.

Reply to the First Objection. If need denotes a defect or lack of what is needed, then that which is always, needs not another in order that it may exist. But if it denotes nothing more than the order of origin in reference to that whence a thing is, nothing hinders a thing that always is from needing another in order that it may exist, in so far as it has being not from itself but from another.

Reply to the Second Objection. Before receiving it the recipient has not what he receives, but he has it when he has received it : consequently if he received it from eternity he had it from eternity.

Reply to the Third Objection. This argument applies to generation in which there is movement, since that which is being moved to existence does not exist yet : which is true in the sense that what is being generated is not, whereas what has been generated, is. Consequently where there is no distinction between being generated and having been generated, it does not follow that what is generated is from another.

Reply to the Fourth Objection. It is true that what has its being from another is nothing considered in itself, if it be distinct from the being that it receives from another :

but if it be the very same being that it receives from another, then considered in itself it cannot be nothing: for it is not possible to consider non-being in being itself, although it is possible to consider something besides being in that which is. Because that which is may have a mixed being: but being itself cannot, according to Boëthius (*De Hebdom.*). The first part of this distinction applies to creatures, the second to the Son of God.

Reply to the Fifth Objection. The Son of God cannot be called an effect, because he is not made but begotten: since that is said to be made whose being is distinct from its maker. Wherefore neither can the Father be called the cause of the Son properly speaking, but his principle. Nor is it necessary for every cause to precede its effect in point of duration, but only by priority of nature, as in the case of the sun and its shining.

ARTICLE XIV

IS IT POSSIBLE FOR THAT WHICH DIFFERS FROM GOD ESSENTIALLY TO HAVE ALWAYS EXISTED?

THE fourteenth point of inquiry is whether it is possible for that which differs essentially from God to have existed always: and it would seem possible.

1. The cause that produces the whole substance of a thing has not less power over its effect than the cause which produces the form alone. Now if the cause which produces the form alone be eternal it can produce it from eternity: thus the light produced and diffused by fire is co-existent with it and would be co-eternal if the fire were eternal, according to Augustine (*De Trin.*). Much more reason then is there why God who produces the whole substance of a thing, should be able to produce a co-eternal effect.

2. It will be said perhaps that this is impossible because it leads to the false position of equalling a creature to God in point of duration.—On the contrary, a duration that is not wholly simultaneous but successive cannot be equalled to

one that is wholly simultaneous. Now if the world had always been, its duration would not have been wholly simultaneous, since it would have been measured by time according to Boëthius (*De Consol.* v). Therefore a creature would not be equalled to God in point of duration.

3. As a divine person proceeds from God without movement, so does a creature. Now a divine person can be co-eternal with God from whom he proceeds. Therefore a creature can be likewise.

4. That which is unchangeable in its being can always do the same thing. Now God is unchangeable from eternity. Therefore from eternity he can do the same thing: and consequently if he produced a creature at any time he could do so from eternity.

5. You will say perhaps that the above argument applies to a natural but not to a voluntary agent.—On the contrary, God's power is not nullified by his will. Now if he did not work by his will it would follow that he produced the creature from eternity. Therefore even given that he works by his will, it does not remove the possibility of his having created from eternity.

6. If God produced a creature at a certain time or instant, and if his power does not increase, he could have produced the creature at a previous time or instant, and for the same reason, before that, and so on indefinitely. Therefore he could have produced it from eternity.

7. God can do more than the human intellect can understand, wherefore it is said (Luke i, 37): *No word shall be impossible with God.* Now the Platonists understood God to have made something that had always existed. Thus Augustine says (*De Civ. Dei* x, 31): *Plato writing about the world and of the gods made by God in the world, asserts most explicitly that they came into existence and had a beginning; yet they will not have an end, and he states that through the all-powerful will of their maker they will live for ever. In explaining, however, what he meant by beginning, the Platonists affirm that he meant the beginning not of time but of their formation. For, say they, even as, if a foot had pressed on the dust from eternity, there would always have been the footprint*

underneath, which no one would doubt to have been made by the walker, so the world always existed and he who made it always existed, and yet it was made. Therefore God could make something that always was.

8. God can do in the creature whatever is not inconsistent with the notion of a created thing : else he were not omnipotent. Now it is not inconsistent with the notion of a created thing, considered as made, that it should always have existed, otherwise to say that creatures always existed would be the same as to say that they were not made, which is clearly false. For Augustine (*De Civ. Dei* xi, 4 ; x, 31) distinguishes two opinions, one asserting that the world always existed in suchwise that it was not made by God ; the other stating that the world always was and that nevertheless God made it. Therefore God can do this so that something made by him should always have been.

9. Just as nature can produce its effect in an instant, so also can a voluntary agent if unhindered. Now God is a voluntary agent that cannot be hindered. Therefore the creatures brought into being by his will, could be produced from eternity, even as the Son who proceeds from the Father naturally.

1. *On the contrary*, Augustine says (*Gen. ad lit.* viii, 23) : *Seeing that the nature of the Trinity is altogether uncommunicable, it is so exclusively eternal that nothing can be co-eternal with it.*

2. Damascene says (*De Fide Orthod.* i) : *That which is brought into being from nothingness by its very nature is incapable of being co-eternal with one who has no beginning and is eternal.* Now the creature is brought from nothingness into being. Therefore it cannot have been always.

3. Whatsoever is eternal is unchangeable. But a creature cannot be unchangeable, because were it left to itself it would fall back into nothingness. Therefore it cannot be eternal.

4. Nothing that depends on another is necessary, nor consequently eternal : since all that is eternal is necessary. Now that which is made depends on another. Therefore nothing made can be eternal.

5. If God could make a creature from eternity, he did; because according to the Philosopher (*Phys.* iii, 4) in eternal things there is no difference between what can be and what is. Now it is against faith to say that creatures were made from eternity. Therefore it is also against faith to say that they could be.

6. A wise man's will does not delay to do what he intends except for some reason. But no reason can be given why God made the world then and not before or from eternity, if it could be made from eternity. Therefore seemingly it could not.

7. If creatures were made, they were made either from nothing or from something. They were not made from something: since this would either be part of the divine essence, which is impossible, or it would be something else, and if this were not made, there would be something besides God not made by him, and this has been proved to be false: and if it were made from something else, we should either go on indefinitely, which is impossible, or we should come to something made from nothing. Now it is impossible for that which is made from nothing to have always been. Therefore it is impossible for a creature to have been always.

8. It is essential to the eternal not to have a beginning, whereas it is essential to the notion of a creature to have a beginning. Therefore no creature can be eternal.

9. A creature is measured either by time or by eviternity. But time and eviternity differ from eternity. Therefore a creature cannot be eternal.

10. If a thing be created it must be possible to assign an instant wherein it was created. Now before that instant it did not exist. Therefore we must conclude that creatures were not always.

I answer that according to the Philosopher (*Metaph.* v, 12) a thing is said to be possible, sometimes in reference to a power, sometimes in reference to no power. If in reference to a power, this power may be active or passive. In reference to an active power, as when we say that to a builder it is possible to build; in reference to a passive power, as when we say that it is possible for the wood to burn. Sometimes, however, a thing is said to be possible, not in reference to a power, but either figuratively, as in geometry a line is said to be potentially rational—this we may pass over for the present; or absolutely, that is when the terms of a proposition are in no way mutually contradictory: whereas we have the impossible when they exclude each other. Thus it is said to be impossible for a thing to be and not to be at the same time, not in reference to an agent or patient, but because it is impossible in itself, as being self-contradictory. If, then, we consider the statement that something substantially distinct from God has always existed, it cannot be described as impossible in itself as though it contained a contradiction in the terms: because to be from another is not inconsistent with being from eternity, as we have proved above; except when the one proceeds from the other by movement, of which there can be no question in the procession of things from God. And when we add 'substantially distinct' this again involves no contradiction absolutely speaking with the fact of having always been.

If we refer the possibility to an active power, then God does not lack the power to produce from eternity an essence distinct from himself.

On the other hand if we refer the possibility to a passive power, then given the truth of the Catholic faith, it cannot be said that something substantially distinct from God can proceed from him and yet have always existed. For the Catholic faith supposes that all things other than God at some time existed not. Now as it is impossible for a thing never to have existed, if it be granted that at some time it has been, so is it impossible for a thing to have been always, if it be granted that at some time it did not exist. Wherefore some say that this is possible on the part of God creating, but not on the part of an essence proceeding from God because our faith teaches the contrary.

Reply to the First Objection. This argument considers the question from the point of view of the power of the maker, but not of the thing made. which is supposed not to have existed at some time.

Reply to the Second Objection. Even if creatures had always existed they would not be equalled to God simply but in so far as they imitate him. There is nothing unreasonable in this, and so the objection has but little force.

Reply to the Third Objection. In the divine person there is nothing that is supposed not to have existed at some time, as there is in every essence other than God.

Reply to the Fourth Objection. This argument considers the power of the maker, which indeed is not diminished by his will, except in so far as it was by the decree of the divine will that creatures did not always exist.

This suffices for the reply to the Fifth Objection.

Reply to the Sixth Objection. If it be stated that creatures existed before any given time, the position of faith is safeguarded because it is stated that nothing except God existed always : but it is not safeguarded if we say that creatures have always existed : hence the comparison fails. It must also be noted that the argument is lacking in form. For God is able to make any creature better, yet he cannot make a creature of infinite goodness : because infinite goodness is incompatible with the notion of being created, whereas determinate goodness is not, however great it be.

It must also be observed that when we say that God could have made the world sooner than he did, if this priority be referred to the power of the maker, the statement is undoubtedly true, because he had from eternity the power to do this ; and eternity precedes the time of the creation. If, however, it be referred to the being of the thing made, as though before the instant wherein the world was created there were a real time wherein the world could have been made, it is evident that then the statement is false, since before the world there was no movement and consequently no time. Yet it is possible to imagine a time anterior to the world, just as we can imagine altitudes and dimensions outside the heavens : and forasmuch we can say that God could make the heavens higher, and that he could have created them sooner, since he could have made time longer and altitude higher.

Reply to the Seventh Objection. It is true that the

Platonists understood this : but they were not guided by faith, since it was unknown to them.

Reply to the Eighth Objection. This argument proves nothing more than that to be made and to be always are not incompatible considered in themselves : so that it considers that which is possible absolutely.

Reply to the Ninth Objection. This argument considers possibility in reference to an active power.

Whereas the arguments on the contrary side would seem to conclude that it is impossible from every point of view, we must now proceed to answer them.

Solution of the First Argument. According to Boëthius (*De Consol.* v), even if the world had always existed it would not be co-eternal with God, because its duration would not be wholly simultaneous, which is essential to eternity. For eternity is the *perfect possession of endless life without succession* (*ibid.*). Now the succession of time results from movement according to the Philosopher (*Phys.* iv, 11). Hence whatsoever is subject to change, even if it be always, cannot be eternal : wherefore Augustine says (*Gen. ad lit.* viii, 23) that no creature can be co-eternal with the unchangeable nature of the Trinity.

Solution of the Second Argument. Damascene speaks on the supposition of the Catholic faith : this is clear from his saying : *That which is brought into being from nothingness, etc.*

Solution of the Third Argument. Changeableness by its very nature excludes eternity but not indefinite duration.

Solution of the Fourth Argument. It is true that what depends on another can never exist unless it be upheld by that whence it proceeds : yet if the latter always existed the former also existed always.

Solution of the Fifth Argument. From the fact that God was able to do a thing it does not follow that he did it, because he acts by his will and not by natural necessity. And where it is said that in eternal things there is no difference between what can be and what is, this refers to passive and not to active power : because a passive power that is not perfected by its act is a principle of corruption and therefore repugnant to eternity : whereas it casts no reflection on an active power that its effect be not actually in existence, especially if the active power be a voluntary cause : because the effect is not the perfection of an active power in the same way as the form is of a passive power.

Solution of the Sixth Argument. Our intelligence is unable to fathom the production of the first creatures, because it cannot grasp that Art which is the sole reason why the creatures in question were such as they were. Hence just as no man can explain why the heavens are so great and not greater, so neither can we tell why the world was not made sooner, although both came within the scope of the divine power.

Solution of the Seventh Argument. The first creatures were produced not from something but from nothing. Not, however, from the mode of their production but from the teaching of faith do we gather that they were non-existent before they were brought into being. For the statement that a creature is made from nothing may mean according to Anselm (*Monolog.* viii) that it is not made from something, so that the negation includes the preposition and is not included by it, and thus denies the order implied by the preposition ; while the preposition itself does not imply order to nothing.[1] If on the other hand order to nothing is affirmed, and the preposition includes the negation, it still does not follow that at some time the creature was non-existent. For one might say with Avicenna that non-existence preceded the existence of a thing not by duration but by nature : since, to wit, were it left to itself it would have no existence, and it has existence solely from another : because that which a thing is competent to have of itself is naturally prior to that which it is not adapted to have save from another.

Solution of the Eighth Argument. It belongs to the notion of eternity to have no beginning of duration : while it belongs to the notion of a created thing to have a beginning of its origin but not of duration : unless we take creation according to the teaching of faith.

[1] Cf. *Sum. Th.* I, Q. xlv, A. 1 *ad* 3.

Solution of the Ninth Argument. Eviternity and time differ from eternity, not only in the point of a principle of duration but also in the point of succession. Time in itself implies succession ; while succession is annexed to eviternity, inasmuch as eviternal substances are in a way changeable, though they are unchangeable as measured by eviternity. On the other hand eternity has no succession nor is succession annexed to it.

Solution of the Tenth Argument. God's work whereby he brings things into being must not be taken as the work of a craftsman who makes a box and then leaves it : because God continues to give being, as Augustine says (*Gen. ad lit.* iv, 12 ; viii, 12). Hence it does not follow that we must assign an instant wherein things were brought into being, before which they existed not, except on account of the teaching of faith.

ARTICLE XV

DID THINGS PROCEED FROM GOD OF NATURAL NECESSITY OR BY THE DECREE OF HIS WILL ?
Sum. Th. I, Q. xix, A. 4

THE fifteenth point of inquiry is whether things proceeded from God of natural necessity or by a decree of his will : and it would seem that they proceeded of natural necessity.

1. Dionysius (*De Div. Nom.* iv) says : *As our sun neither by reason nor by pre-election, but by its very being enlightens all things that can participate its light, so the divine good by its very essence pours the rays of its goodness upon all things according to their capacity.* Seeing then that the sun enlightens without reason or pre-election, it does so of natural necessity. Therefore God also produces creatures by communicating his goodness to them of natural necessity.

2. Every perfection of a lower nature derives from the perfection of the divine nature. Now it belongs to the perfection of a lower nature by its own power to produce its like in some effect. A fortiori therefore God naturally and

not voluntarily communicates the likeness of his goodness to creatures.

3. Every agent produces its like ; wherefore the effect proceeds from its active cause in so far as it bears a likeness thereto. Now the creature bears a likeness to God as regards those things which belong to God by nature, namely being, goodness, unity and so forth ; and not as regards things willed or understood, as the product of his art bears a likeness to the craftsman as regards the art-given form and not as regards his nature, for which reason he produces it voluntarily and not naturally. Therefore things proceed from God by virtue of his nature and not by his will.

4. It may be replied that the divine will communicates the likeness of the natural attributes.—On the contrary, a likeness of nature cannot be communicated otherwise than by the power of nature. Now the power of nature is nowhere subject to the will : wherefore in God, since the Father begets the Son naturally he does not beget him by his will : and in man the forces of the vegetal soul which are called natural forces are not subject to his will. Therefore it is not possible for a likeness of the divine attributes to be communicated to creatures by the divine will.

5. Augustine says (*De Doct. Christ.* i, 32) that *we exist because God is good*, so that seemingly God's goodness is the cause of the production of creatures. Now goodness is natural to God. Therefore the emanation of things from God is natural.

6. In God nature and will are the same : and consequently if he produces things willingly it would seem that he produces them naturally.

7. Natural necessity results from the fact that nature invariably acts in the same way, unless prevented. Now God is more unchangeable than the lower nature. Therefore God produces his effects more of necessity than the lower nature.

8. God's operation is his essence : and his essence is natural to him. Therefore whatever he does he does naturally.

9. Again, according to the Philosopher (*Ethic.* iii, 2) the

end is what is willed, the means are what we choose. But God has no end since he is infinite. Therefore he acts not willingly but rather of natural necessity.

10. God operates inasmuch as he is good, according to Augustine (*De Doct. Christ.* i, 32). Now he is the necessary good. Therefore he works of necessity.

11. Whatsoever exists is either contingent or necessary. Now a thing is necessary in three ways, by coercion, by supposition and absolutely. It cannot be said that in God anything is potential or contingent: since this argues mutability according to the Philosopher (*Metaph.* xi, 5), because what is contingent may happen not to be. Again, nothing in God is necessary by coercion because in him nothing is violent or contrary to nature (*Metaph.* v, 5). Nor is there anything necessary by supposition, because this depends on certain things being presupposed, and God is not dependent on anything. It remains then that all in God is absolutely necessary, and it would seem consequently that he produced things necessarily.

12. It is written (2 Tim. ii, 13) that God *continueth faithful, he cannot deny himself.* Now seeing that he is his own goodness he would deny himself were he to deny his own goodness. But he would deny his own goodness were he not to pour it out by communicating it to others, for this is proper to goodness. Consequently God cannot but produce creatures by communicating his own goodness to them: and therefore he produces them of necessity: because that which cannot but be is convertible with that which is necessary (*Perihermen.* ii, 3).

13. According to Augustine the Father in begetting the Son expressed himself by his word. Now Anselm says (*Monolog.* lii) that by the same word the Father expresses himself and the creature. Seeing then that the Father begot the Son naturally and not by the command of his will, it would seem that thus also did he produce creatures, since in God to speak and to make do not differ according to the words of Scripture (Ps. xxxi, 1, 9): *He spake and they were made.*

14. Every voluntary agent wills of necessity his ultimate

end ; thus man of necessity wills to be happy. Now the ultimate end of the divine will is the communication of his goodness : since to this end did he make creatures that he might communicate his goodness to them. Therefore God wills this of necessity, and thus of necessity does he produce them.

15. Just as God is good by his essence so is he necessary by his essence. Now because God is good by his essence there is nothing in God but what is good. Therefore in like manner there is nothing in him but what is necessary : and consequently he produces things necessarily.

16. God's will is determined to one thing, namely the good. Now nature through being determined to one works necessarily. Therefore God's will produces creatures necessarily.

17. The Father by virtue of his nature is the principle of the Son and the Holy Ghost, as Hilary says (*De Synod.*). Now the same nature that is in the Father and Son is also in the Holy Ghost. Therefore likewise the Holy Ghost is a principle by his nature. But he is not a principle except of creatures. Therefore creatures proceed from God naturally.

18. The effect proceeds from its cause in action : wherefore a cause is not related to its effect except as related to its action or operation. Now the relation of God's action or operation to himself is natural, since God's action is his essence. Therefore the relation of God to his effect is also natural so that he produces it naturally.

19. By that which is essentially good nothing is made but what is good and well made. Therefore by that which is essentially necessary, nothing is made but what is necessary and necessarily made. Now such is God. Therefore all things proceed from him of necessity.

20. Since what exists of itself is prior to that which exists by another, it follows that the first agent acts by his essence. Now his essence and his nature are the same. Therefore he acts by his nature : and thus creatures proceed from him naturally.

On the contrary Hilary says (*De Synod.*) : *The will*

of God gave all things their substance: and (*ibid.*): *Such are creatures as God willed them to be.* Therefore God produced creatures by his will and not by natural necessity.

Moreover Augustine addressing God says (*Confess.* xii, 7): *Lord, thou didst make two things, one nigh to thyself,* the angel, to wit, *the other nigh to nothing,* namely matter. *Yet neither is of thy nature, since neither is what thou art.* Now the Son proceeds from the Father naturally inasmuch as he has the same nature as the Father, as Augustine says (*De Trin.* xv, 14). Therefore the creature does not proceed naturally from God.

I answer that without any doubt we must hold that God by the decree of his will and by no natural necessity brought creatures into being. This may for the present be made clear by four arguments.

First argument. The universe must needs be directed to an end, otherwise all things in the universe would befall by chance. Unless one were to say that the first creatures were not directed to an end but produced by natural necessity; and that subsequent creatures are directed to an end. This was the opinion of Democritus who maintained that the heavenly bodies were produced by chance, but lower bodies by determinate causes; and is refuted (*Phys.* ii, 4) for the reason that more exalted beings cannot be less ordinate than those of lower dignity. We must therefore hold that in producing creatures God had some end in view. Now both will and nature act for an end, but not in the same way. Nature has no knowledge of the purpose for which it acts, nor does it view it in the light of an end, nor is it aware of the connection between the means and the end; so that it cannot propose an end to itself, nor move order or direct itself towards the end, whereas this is within the competency of a voluntary agent that can understand the end and all those other things. Wherefore the voluntary agent acts for the end in suchwise that he proposes the end to himself, and to a certain extent moves himself towards the end by directing his actions thereto. On the other hand nature tends to its end as a thing that is moved and directed by an intelligent and voluntary agent, even as an arrow flies towards a certain mark through the aim of the archer: and in this sense philosophers say that the work of nature is the work of an intelligence. Now that which is by another is always preceded by that which is of itself. Consequently the first director to an end must direct by his will: and thus God brought creatures into being by his will and not naturally. Nor may it be objected that the Son was naturally begotten by the Father, and yet his birth preceded creation: because the Son proceeds not as one ordained to an end, but as the end of all.

Second argument. Nature is determined to one thing: and since every agent produces its like, it follows that nature must tend to produce a likeness that is determinately in one subject. Now seeing that equality is caused by unity, whereas inequality is caused by multitude which is manifold (wherefore equality exists between things in only one way, but inequality in many various degrees), nature always produces its equal unless it be hindered by a defect either in the active force or in the recipient or patient. But God is not hindered by a defect in the patient, since he needs not matter: nor is his power defective, but infinite. Wherefore nothing proceeds from him naturally but what is his equal, namely the Son. On the other hand creatures, being unequal, are produced not naturally but voluntarily, for there are many degrees of inequality. Nor may it be said that the divine power is determined to one only, seeing that it is infinite. Wherefore since the power of God extends to the production of various degrees of inequality among creatures, it was by the decree of his will and not of natural necessity that he fashioned this or that creature in this or that particular degree.

Third argument. Since every agent in some way produces its like, the effect must in some way pre-exist in its cause. Now whatsoever is contained in another is therein according to the mode of the container: wherefore as God himself is intelligence it follows that creatures pre-exist in him intelligibly, in which sense it is written (Jo. i, 3): *That which was made was life in him.* But that which is in an intelligence does not proceed therefrom except by means of the will: for the will is the executor of the intellect, and the intelligible moves the will. Consequently creatures must have proceeded from God by his will.

Fourth argument. According to the Philosopher (*Metaph.* ix, text 16) action is twofold: one that remains in the agent, of which it is the perfection and act; such as to understand, to will and the like: the other issues from the agent into an extrinsic patient which it perfects and actuates, such as to heat, to move and the like. Now God's action cannot be taken as belonging to this latter kind of action, because his action is his very essence, and consequently does not issue outside him. Hence it must be taken as belonging to the former kind of action which is only to be found in one possessed of intelligence and will, or also of the faculty of sense, which latter again does not apply to God, because sensation, though it does not issue into an external object, is caused by the action of an external object. Therefore whatsoever God does outside himself he does it as understanding and willing it. Nor does this argument belie the naturalness of the Son's begetting, the term of which was not something outside the divine essence. We must therefore hold that all creatures proceeded from God by his will and not of natural necessity.

Reply to the First Objection. The comparison of Dionysius must be understood to refer to the universality of diffusion: as the sun sheds its rays on all bodies without differentiating one from another, so likewise is it with God's goodness: but it does not apply to the absence of will.

Reply to the Second Objection. It is owing to the perfection of the divine nature that by virtue thereof its likeness is communicated to creatures: yet this communication was made not of natural necessity but voluntarily.

This suffices for the reply to the Third Objection.

Reply to the Fourth Objection. Nature is not subject to will from within: but in externals nothing prevents nature from being subject to the will. Thus in the local movements of animals nature in their muscles and sinews is subject to the command of their appetite. Consequently it is not unreasonable if by virtue of the divine nature creatures be brought into existence according to the behest of the divine will.

Reply to the Fifth Objection. The good is the proper object of the will : hence the goodness of God as willed and loved by him is the cause of things through his will.

Reply to the Sixth Objection. Although will and nature are identically the same in God, they differ logically, in so far as they express respect to creatures in different ways : thus nature denotes a respect to some one thing determinately, whereas will does not.

Reply to the Seventh Objection. It is owing not merely to the unchangeableness of nature that it produces a particular effect of necessity, but to its being determined to one : this does not apply to the divine will although it is supremely unchangeable.

Reply to the Eighth Objection. Although God's operation belongs to him naturally seeing that it is his very nature or essence, the created effect follows the operation of his nature which, in our way of understanding, is considered as the principle of his will, even as the effect that is heating follows according to the mode of the heat.

Reply to the Ninth Objection. Although God is infinite he is the end of all things. He is not infinite as though he were deprived of finiteness in the same way as there may be an infinite in quantity, although quantity by nature is finite, for in this way an end is neither finite nor infinite. But he is infinite in a negative sense, because he is altogether without an end.

Reply to the Tenth Objection. It is true that God operates inasmuch as he is good, and that goodness is in him of necessity, but it does not follow that he works of necessity. Because his goodness works through his will in so far as it is the object or end of his will. Now the will is not inclined of necessity to the means, although it is necessitated in respect of the last end.

Reply to the Eleventh Objection. As regards the things which are in God himself, nothing can be described as potential : all is naturally and absolutely necessary. But in respect of creatures we can call certain things potential not in regard to passive potentiality, but in regard to an active power which is not limited to one effect.

Reply to the Twelfth Objection. Were God to deny his own goodness by doing something contrary thereto or wherein his goodness were not expressed, we should arrive at the impossible conclusion that he denied himself. But this would not follow if he were not to communicate his goodness to anything : since it would suffer nothing by not being communicated.

Reply to the Thirteenth Objection. Although the Word of God. proceeds from the Father naturally, it does not follow that creatures proceed from God naturally. The Father by his words *speaks* his creatures according as they are in him : and in him they are as producible not necessarily but voluntarily.

Reply to the Fourteenth Objection. The last end is not the communication of the divine goodness, but that goodness itself for love of which God wills to communicate it. He works for his goodness' sake not as desiring to have what he has not, but as wishing to communicate what he has : for he acts not from desire, but from love, of the end.

Reply to the Fifteenth Objection. As in God there is naught but good, so is there naught but what is necessary. But it does not follow that whatsoever proceeds from him does so of necessity.

Reply to the Sixteenth Objection. As stated above God's will inclines naturally to his goodness : so that he cannot will but what is becoming to him, namely the good. Yet he is not determined to this or that good : wherefore it does not follow that the goods which exist proceed from him necessarily.

Reply to the Seventeenth Objection. Though the same nature is in the Father, Son and Holy Ghost it has not the same mode of existence in each one of the three, and when I say ' mode of existence ' I mean in respect of the relations. In the Father nature is considered as not received from another : in the Son, as received from another. Consequently we must not infer that whatsoever belongs to the Father by virtue of his nature, belongs also to the Son or the Holy Ghost.

Reply to the Eighteenth Objection. The effect follows from the action according to the mode of the principle of the action : wherefore since the divine will which has no necessary connection with creatures is considered, in our way of thinking, to be the principle of the divine action in regard to creatures, it does not follow that the creature proceeds from God by natural necessity, although the action itself is God's essence or nature.

Reply to the Nineteenth Objection. The creature is like God as regards general conditions, but not as to the mode of participation : thus being is in God otherwise than in creatures, and so too is goodness. Hence although from the first good all goods derive, and all beings from the first being, yet all do not derive supreme goodness from the sovereign good, nor from the necessary being do all things proceed of necessity.

Reply to the Twentieth Objection. God's will is his essence : wherefore his working by his will does not prevent his working by his essence. God's will is not an intention in addition to his essence, but is his very essence.

ARTICLE XVI

CAN A MULTITUDE OF THINGS PROCEED FROM ONE FIRST THING ?

Sum. Th. I, Q. xlvii, A. 1 : *C.G.* II, xxxix–xlv : III, xcvii

THE sixteenth point of inquiry is whether many things can proceed from one : and seemingly the answer should be in the negative.

1. As God is essentially good and consequently the sovereign good, so is he essentially and supremely one. Now inasmuch as he is good nothing can proceed from him but what is good. Therefore inasmuch as he is one, only one thing can proceed from him.

2. As good is convertible with being, so also is one.

Now the creature is like God in that it has being, as stated above. Therefore as it is like God in goodness, so must it be like him in unity, and thus from the one God one creature should proceed.

3. As good and evil taken in general are mutually opposed by way of privation, although they are contraries considered as differentiating habits; so one and many are opposed to each other by way of privation (*Metaph.* x, 3). Now by no means do we say that wickedness proceeds from God, but from a defect in second causes. Neither therefore should we say that God is the cause of multitude.

4. Cause and effect should be proportionate to each other, forasmuch as single things cause single things and universal things cause universal, according to the Philosopher (*Phys.* ii, 3). Now God is the most universal of all causes. Therefore his proper effect is the most universal of all, namely being. Now it is not because things have being that there is not multitude, since diversity and distinction are the cause of multitude, and all things agree in point of being. Therefore multitude is not from God, but from second causes whence each thing derives its particular condition of being, whereby it is differentiated from others.

5. Every effect has its proper cause. But one cannot be proper to many. Therefore one cannot be the cause of many.

6. You will say perhaps that this is true of natural but not of voluntary causes.—On the contrary the craftsman is the cause of his work by his will. But that work comes from the craftsman in accordance with the proper form thereof existing in the mind of the craftsman. Therefore even in voluntary effects each one requires its proper cause.

7. There ought to be conformity between cause and effect. God is altogether one and simple. Therefore there should be neither multitude nor composition in the creature which is his effect.

8. One effect cannot proceed immediately from a diversity of agents. Now as the cause is appropriate to the effect, so is the effect to its cause. Therefore from one same cause there cannot proceed many immediate effects: and thus the same conclusion follows.

9. In God it is the same power that begets, spirates and creates. Now the power to beget terminates in one only, and likewise the power to spirate: because in the Trinity there can be but one Son and one Holy Ghost. Therefore the creative power also terminates in one only.

10. But you will say that the universe of creatures is somewhat one with regard to order.—On the contrary the effect should be like its cause. But the unity of God is not a unity of order, since in God there is no before and after nor higher and lower. Consequently unity of order does not suffice to make it possible that many things be made by one God.

11. One simple thing has but one action. Now one action has but one effect. Therefore one simple thing can produce but one effect.

12. The creature proceeds from God not only as the effect from its effective cause, but also as the exemplate from its exemplar. Now one exemplar has but one proper exemplate. Therefore only one creature can proceed from God.

13. God is cause of things by his intellect. Now an agent by intellect acts by the form in his intellect. Wherefore since there is but one form in the divine intellect, it would seem that only one creature can proceed from it.

14. But you will say that although the form in the divine intellect is one in substance since it is the divine essence, we may nevertheless consider therein a certain plurality by reason of various respects to various creatures, so that there is a logical plurality.—On the contrary these several respects are either in the divine intellect or solely in our mind. In the first case it will follow that there is plurality and not supreme simplicity in the divine intellect. In the second case, it will follow that God does not produce a variety of creatures except by means of our reason, and consequently that he produces a variety of creatures through various respects to creatures, which respects exist only in our reason. This is what we are endeavouring to show, namely that multitude does not proceed from God immediately.

15. God brings things into being through his intellect

apprehending them. Now in him there is but one apprehension : since his act of intelligence is his essence which is one. Therefore he produces but one creature.

16. That which has no being save in the mind is not a creature of God, for such things would seem to be vanity, as chimeras and the like. Now multitude is only in the reason, because it signifies an abstraction that does not exist in reality. Therefore God is not the cause of multitude.

17. According to Plato (*Tim.*) the best produces the best. Now the best can only be one. Since then God is best of all things, only one thing can be produced by him.

18. Every agent that acts for an end produces an effect as near to the end as possible. Now God in producing the creature ordains it to an end. Therefore he makes it as near to the end as possible. But this can be done only in one way. Therefore he produces only one creature.

19. It is unjust to deal unequally to various recipients, unless these be already unequal either in merit or in some other diversity of condition. Now no diversity precedes God's work, otherwise he would not be the first cause of all. Therefore when he first created things he did not bestow unequal gifts on his creatures. But diversity and multitude of creatures are in respect of their receiving more or less of the divine gifts (*Cœl. Hier.* iv). Therefore when God first created things he did not produce a multitude.

20. God communicates his goodness to creatures according to their capacity. Now the nature of higher creatures was capable of such perfection and dignity as to be the causes of lower creatures : because the more perfect things can act on those which are less perfect and communicate their perfection to them. Therefore seemingly God produced the lower creatures by means of the higher, and thus he did not produce immediately more than one creature, whatever it be, higher than the others.

21. The more immaterial a form the more active it is, as being more remote from potentiality : since a thing acts forasmuch as it is in act and not as in potentiality. Now in an angel's mind there are forms of things and these forms are more immaterial than the forms that are in natural things.

Now seeing that natural forms are causes of like forms, it would seem that a fortiori the forms in an angel's mind produce like forms of natural things. But diversity and consequently multitude of things result from the form. Therefore seemingly multitude did not proceed from God except by means of the higher creatures.

22. Whatsoever God makes is one thing. Therefore only one thing proceeds from him : and thus he is not the cause of multitude.

23. God understands but one thing, because he understands nothing outside himself (*Metaph.* xii, 9). Now he is cause of things by his intellect. Therefore he causes but one thing.

24. Anselm says (*Monolog.* viii) that in God the creature is the creative essence. Now the creative essence is but one. Consequently in God the creature is one only. But the creature is produced by God according to the same way as it pre-existed in God. Therefore only one creature proceeds from God and consequently multitude is not from him.

On the contrary it is written (Wis. xi, 21) : *Lord, thou hast disposed all things in number, weight and measure.* But there is no number without multitude. Therefore multitude is from God.

Again, God's power surpasses that of any other thing. Now one point can be the beginning of many lines. Thus then can God, though he is one, be the beginning of many creatures.

Again, that which is proper to unity as such is most appropriate to that which is supremely one. Now it is proper to unity to be the principle of multitude. Therefore it is most appropriate to God who is supremely one to be the cause of multitude.

Again, Boëthius says (*Arith.*) that God brought things into being according to a numerical exemplar. Now the exemplate is like the exemplar. Therefore he produced things in multitude and number.

Again it is written (Ps. ciii, 24) : *Thou hast done all things in wisdom.* Now seeing that it belongs to a wise man to set things in order, it follows that there must be order and consequently multitude in all the things done by wisdom. Therefore the multitude of things is from God.

I answer that the impossibility of many things proceeding from one immediate and proper principle would seem to arise from the cause being determined to its effect, so that it would seem due and necessary that from such and such a cause such and such an effect should proceed. Now there are four causes two of which, the material and the effective cause to wit, precede the effect as to intrinsic being; while the end precedes it if not in being yet in intention; and the form precedes it in neither way considered as form, since the effect has its being by the form and consequently its being is simultaneous with that of the effect. But in so far as the form is the end it precedes the effect in the intention of the agent. And although the form is the end of the operation, being the end that terminates the operation of the agent, nevertheless every end is not a form. For there is in the intention an end that is not the end of the operation, as in the case of a house. The form of the house is the end terminating the operation of the builder: but his intention does not terminate there but in a further end, namely a dwelling-place, so that the end of the operation is the form of a house, that of the intention, a dwelling-place. Accordingly the necessity of such and such effects coming into being cannot arise from the form as such, since thus it is simultaneous with the effect, but it must arise either from the power of the effective cause, or from the matter, or from the end whether of the intention or of the operation. Now it cannot be said that the effect of God's action is necessitated by matter: because seeing that he is the author of all being, nothing in any way whatsoever having being is presupposed to his action, so that one be bound to say that owing to the disposition of matter his action must produce this or that effect. Likewise neither can it arise from the effective power: because seeing that his active power is infinite, it is not determined to one effect save to that which were equal to him, and this cannot be competent to any effect. Wherefore if it be necessary that he produce an effect beneath himself, his power considered in itself is not determined to any particular distant degree, so that it be necessary for such and such an effect to be produced by his active power. Likewise neither can it arise from the end of the intention. For this end is the divine goodness, which gains nothing from the production of the effects.

Again it cannot be wholly represented by those effects nor be wholly communicated to them, so that one be able to say that it were necessary for an effect of God to be such and such in order wholly to participate of God's goodness, since it is possible for an effect to participate thereof in many ways, so that no effect is rendered necessary by the end. Necessity arises from the end when the intention of the end cannot be fulfilled, either not at all or not conveniently, without this or that thing. It remains therefore that necessity in God's works cannot arise except from the form which is the end of operation. For seeing that the form is not infinite it has determined principles without which it cannot exist, and a determined mode of existence; thus we might say, for instance, supposing that God intends to make a man, that it is necessary and due that he give him a rational soul and an organic body, without which there is no such thing as a man. It is the same with the universe. That God wished to make the universe such as it is, was not made necessary or due, either by the end or by the power of the effective cause, or by the potentiality of matter, as we have proved. But given that he wished to make the universe such as it is, it was necesssary that he should produce such and such creatures whence such and such a form of universe would arise. And seeing that the perfection of the universe requires both diversity and multitude in things, inasmuch as it cannot be found in one thing on account of the latter's remoteness from the perfection of the first good, it was necessary on the supposition of that intended form that God should produce many and diverse creatures; some simple, some compound, some corruptible, some incorruptible.

Through failing to note this some philosophers wandered from the truth. Because they did not understand that God is the author of the universe, some of them maintained that matter was self-existent and that matter itself necessitated diversity among the things evolved therefrom. Some of them would make things to differ according to the rarity or density of matter, like the early physicists who could not see further than the material cause.—Others traced this diversity to the action of some effective cause, whereby different effects were produced according to a difference of matter. Thus Anaxagoras held that a divine intelligence produced a diversity of things by freeing them from the commixture of matter. Thus also Empedocles explained by attraction and repulsion the various differences and affinities arising from diversity of matter. That these were in error is shown for two reasons. First, because they did not hold that all being flows from the first and supreme being, as we proved above (A. 5). Secondly, because according to them it would follow that the order and distinction of the parts of the universe arose from chance, since they were necessitated by the requirements of matter.—Others, like Avicenna and his school (*Metaph.* ix, 4), ascribed the plurality and diversity of things to a necessity arising from the effective cause. He said that the first being by understanding himself produced one effect only, namely the first intelligence which of necessity fell short of the simplicity of the first being, since potentiality began to be united to act, and that which receives being from another is not its own being, but a potentiality as it were in respect thereof. And so from this first intelligence, in as far as it understands the first being, another and lower intelligence proceeds, and inasmuch as it understands its own potentiality it produced the heavenly body which it moves, and inasmuch as it understands its act it produces the soul of the first heaven. Thus through a number of intermediate causes there arose in consequence diversity among things. This opinion also cannot stand. First, because it would have the divine power limited to one effect which is the first intelligence. Secondly, because it makes other substances besides God to be the creators of other creatures, and we have shown this to be impossible (A. 4). Moreover this opinion like those already mentioned would imply that the beauty arising from the order of the universe is the result of chance, since it ascribes the diversity of things not to the intention of an end, but to the determination of active causes in respect of their effects.

Others, like Plato and his followers, erred regarding the necessity imposed by the final cause. For he said that the universe as to its actual conformation was the necessary outcome of the divine goodness as understood and loved by God, so that the sovereign good produced the very good. This indeed may be true if we look only at what is and not at what might be. This universe consisting of the things that actually exist is very good, and it is due to the sovereign goodness of God that it is very good. Nevertheless God's goodness is not so tied to this universe that it could not have produced a better or one that is less good.

Others again erred through failing to note the necessity resulting from the formal cause, but only that which is due to the divine goodness. Thus the Manicheans considering that God is supremely good, thought that only those creatures proceed from God that are the best of creatures, those, namely, which are spiritual and incorruptible: and they ascribed corporeal and corruptible beings to another principle. The error of Origen although contrary to this comes from the same source (*Peri Archon* i, 7, 8). He considered God as supremely good and just, and for this reason he believed that at first he created only the best, i.e. rational creatures all equal to one another: and that these by their free-will acted in various ways well or ill, and he maintained that from this resulted the various degrees of things in the universe. He held that those rational creatures which turned to God were promoted to the ranks of the angels, and to the various orders according to the degree of their merits: while on the other hand the remaining rational creatures who by their free-will sinned, were in his opinion cast into the ranks of the lower world and bound to bodies: some which sinned less grievously were bound to the sun, moon and stars, some to human bodies, some transformed into demons. Both of these errors apparently disregard the order of the universe and confine their observation to its individual parts. For the very order of the universe is sufficient proof that from one principle, without any previous difference of merits, originated various degrees among creatures for the perfection of the universe, which by its multiplicity and variety of creatures reproduces that which in the divine goodness pre-existed without composition or distinction. Even so the perfection of a house or of the human body requires diversity of parts, since neither would be complete if all its parts were of the same condition, for instance, if every part of the human body were an eye, since the functions of the other parts would be wanting : or if every part of the house were the roof, the house would be imperfect and fail of its purpose which is to shelter from rain and disaster. Accordingly we must conclude that the multitude and diversity of creatures proceeded from one principle, not on account of a necessity imposed by matter, not on account of a limitation in power, not on account of goodness or a necessity imposed by goodness, but from the order of wisdom, in order that the perfection of the universe might be realised in the diversity of creatures.

Reply to the First Objection. Inasmuch as God is one, that which he produced is one, not only because each thing is one in itself, but because all things taken together are in a sense one perfect thing, and this kind of unity requires diversity of parts, as we have already shown.

Reply to the Second Objection. The creature is like God in unity, inasmuch as each creature is one in itself, and all together are one by unity of order, as stated above.

Reply to the Third Objection. Wickedness consists entirely in privation of being, whereas multitude results from being. Even the difference between one being and another is a being. Wherefore since God is not the cause of a thing tending to non-being, but is the author of all being, he is not the principle of evil, but he is the cause of multitude. It must be observed, however, that unity is twofold. There is a unity that is convertible with being : it adds nothing to being save that it excludes division, and it excludes multitude—in so far as multitude results from division—not extrinsic multitude that is composed of unities as parts, but intrinsic multitude that is opposed to unity :

since when we say that a thing is one we do not deny the existence of others extrinsic thereto with which it constitutes a multitude, but we deny its division into many. The other kind of unity is the principle of number, and to the idea of being it adds that of measure : it is this kind of unity that multitude excludes, since number results from the division of continuity. Yet multitude does not entirely exclude unity, since when a whole is divided the parts still remain undivided : but it does exclude unity of the whole : whereas evil considered in itself excludes the good, since in no way does it constitute a good nor is it constituted thereby.

Reply to the Fourth Objection. The relation of being to the things comprised under the head of being is not the same as that of animal or any other genus to its species. The species adds to the genus : as man adds to animal a difference that is not included in the essence of the genus : thus animal denotes merely the sensitive nature which does not contain rationality; whereas the things comprised under being add nothing extraneous to the notion of being. Wherefore it does not follow that the cause of an animal as such, is the cause of the rational nature as such. But it follows that the cause of being as such must be the cause of all the various kinds of being, and consequently of the entire multitude of beings.

Reply to the Fifth Objection. Appropriateness of cause to effect regards the likeness of the effect to its cause. Now the likeness of the creature to God consists in its being a faithful reproduction of what previously existed in God's intellect and will : even as the products of the craftsman's art are like him in so far as they express his artistic ideas and witness to his intention of producing them. For just as the natural agent acts by its form, so does the craftsman act by his intellect and will. Accordingly God is the proper cause of each creature, inasmuch as he understands each creature and wills it to be. The statement that the same thing cannot be proper to many is true of appropriateness of equality and does not apply to the case in point.

The Reply to the Sixth Objection is clear from what has been said.

Reply to the Seventh Objection. Although there is a certain likeness between the creature and God, it is not one of equality. Hence it does not follow that because unity in God is altogether free of multitude and composition therefore the same unity is to be found in the creature.

Reply to the Eighth Objection. Although an effect cannot surpass its cause, a cause can surpass its effect : and consequently several effects can proceed from one cause although one effect cannot proceed immediately from several causes.

Reply to the Ninth Objection. Although in God the generative and the creative power is really the same, they do not connote the same respect : the generative power connotes relationship to that which proceeds by nature, and which therefore can be but one : whereas the creative power implies relationship to something that proceeds by the will, and which consequently need not be one.

Reply to the Tenth Objection. As we have already indicated, although the creature imitates the unity of God, it does not follow that its unity is of the same kind as God's.

Reply to the Eleventh Objection. Although God's action is one and simple, for it is his essence : we must not infer that it has only one effect, but that it has many : because from God's action effects proceed according to the order of his wisdom and the decree of his will.

Reply to the Twelfth Objection. When the exemplate is a perfect copy of the exemplar, there can be but one copy of one exemplar, except accidentally through the copies differing in matter. Creatures, however, are not perfect representations of their exemplar : wherefore they can imitate it in various ways so that there can be many exemplates. There is but one perfect mode of imitation, for which reason there can be but one Son who is the perfect image of the Father.

Reply to the Thirteenth Objection. Although the form in the divine intellect is but one really, it is many logically by reason of its manifold respect to creatures, inasmuch as creatures are perceived to represent that form in many ways.

Reply to the Fourteenth Objection. These **various**

respects to creatures are not only in our intellect but also in God's. And yet there are not in the divine intellect different ideas by which God understands; for he understands by one only which is his essence, but they are many as understood by him. Even as we understand that the creature can imitate God in many ways, so also does God understand this: and consequently he understands the various respects of creatures to him.

Reply to the Fifteenth Objection. Even as God understands all things by one, so does he understand them all by one act of apprehension: because the act of the intelligence must needs be one or many according to the unity or plurality of the principle of understanding.

Reply to the Sixteenth Objection. Although multitude apart from many things is only in the mind, multitude in many things is an objective reality: even so animal in general is only in the mind, but the animal nature is in individuals. Consequently both multitude and animal nature must be traced to God as their cause.

Reply to the Seventeenth Objection. The universe as created by God is the best possible in respect of the things that actually exist; but not in respect of the things that God is able to create.

Reply to the Eighteenth Objection. This argument would hold if that which is done in order to obtain an end can gain the end wholly and perfectly by way of equality: and this is not the case in the question at issue.

Reply to the Nineteenth Objection. This argument which is used by Origen (*Peri Archon* i, 7, 8) is not very convincing. There is no injustice in dealing unequally with equal persons except when one is giving them their due: and this cannot be said of the first creation of things. That which is given out of pure liberality may be given more or less liberally as the giver wills and as his wisdom dictates.

Reply to the Twentieth Objection. Although other creatures are beneath the angels, their production requires infinite power in their maker, inasmuch as they are brought into being by creation, since they are not made from pre-existent matter. Consequently we must hold that all creatures as not being made from pre-existent matter are created by God immediately.

Reply to the Twenty-first Objection. Since being is the term and proper effect of creation, it is impossible that the things created by God receive their forms from the angels, because all being derives from a form.

Reply to the Twenty-second Objection. Whatsoever God makes is indeed one in itself, yet this unity, as stated above, does not exclude all manner of multitude, since that multitude whereof unity is a part remains.

Reply to the Twenty-third Objection. When the Philosopher says that God understands nothing outside himself he does not mean that God does not understand things that are outside him, but that even those things that are outside God are seen by him not outside but in him, because he knows all things in his essence.

Reply to the Twenty-fourth Objection. The creature is said to be in God in two ways. First as in its governing cause and preserver of its being: and in this sense the creature is understood as already existing apart from the Creator, so that we may say that the creature derives its being from the Creator. For the creature is not understood to be preserved in being except as already having being in its proper nature, in respect of which being the creature is distinguished from God. Wherefore in this sense the creature as existing in God is not the creative essence. Secondly the creature is said to be in God inasmuch as it exists virtually in its effective cause or as the thing known in the knower. In this sense the creature, as existing in God, is the very essence of God according to Jo. i, 3 : *That which was made, in him was life*. Nevertheless although the creature as existing in God thus, is the divine essence, there is not, in this sense, only one creature in God but many : because the divine essence is an adequate medium for knowing different creatures, and a sufficient power to produce then.

ARTICLE XVII

HAS THE WORLD ALWAYS EXISTED ?
Sum. Th. I, Q. xlix, A. 1: *C.G.* II, xxxiv, xxxvii

THE seventeenth point of inquiry is whether the world has always existed : and it would seem that it has.

1. A thing never fails in that which is proper to it. Now according to Dionysius (*De Cœl. Hier.* iv) it is proper to the divine goodness to communicate itself to the things that exist ; and this was done by the creation. Since then the divine goodness always was it would seem that it has always brought creatures into being, and that consequently the world has always existed.

2. God does not refuse a creature that which it is capable of having according to its nature. Now there are creatures the nature of which is capable of having been always, for instance, the heavens. Therefore seemingly it was granted to the heavens to have been always. But given that the heavens existed we must allow that other creatures existed as the Philosopher proves (*De Cœlo* ii, 3). Therefore it it would appear that the world has always existed. The minor premiss is proved as follows. That which is incorruptible is capable of having always been, since were it capable of being only for a certain fixed time, it would not exist for ever, and therefore would not be incorruptible. Now the heavens are incorruptible : and consequently are capable of being always.

3. It will be replied that the heavens are not absolutely incorruptible, since they would fall away into nothingness if God did not preserve them in being.—On the contrary we must not conclude that a statement is possibly or contingently true from the fact that it would be false if the consequence were false : thus it is necessarily true that man is an animal, and yet it would be false if the consequence were false, namely that man is a substance. Consequently we must not conclude that the heavens are corruptible from the fact that they would cease to exist on the supposition that God withdrew his sustaining power from creatures.

4. As Avicenna proves (*Metaph.* ix, 4) every effect in comparison with its cause is necessary, since if given the cause the effect does not follow of necessity, even when the cause is present it will be possible for the effect to follow or not. Now that which is possible does not become actual except through something actual: so that besides the aforesaid cause we shall need another cause to make the effect emerge from the potentiality whereby it was possible for it to be or not to be on the presupposition of its cause. Whence it follows that given a sufficient cause the effect follows of necessity. Now God is the sufficient cause of the world. Therefore as God always was, so also was the world.

5. Whatsoever preceded time has always been: for eviternity did not precede time but began with time. Now the world was before time, since it was created in the first instant of time, which clearly was before time: for it is written (Gen. i, 1): *In the beginning God created heaven and earth*, where a gloss notes, *that is in the beginning of time*. Therefore the world existed from eternity.

6. That which remains unchanged always produces the same effect, unless it be hindered. Now God is always the same according to Psalm ci, 28: *Thou art always the selfsame*. Since then God cannot be hindered in his action on account of the infinity of his power, it would seem that he always produces the same effect: so that as he produced the world at some time, it would seem that he always produced it from eternity.

7. As man necessarily wills his own happiness so God necessarily wills his own goodness and whatsoever pertains to it. Now it belongs to God's goodness to bring creatures into being. Therefore God wills this of necessity, and seemingly willed to do so from eternity, even as from eternity he willed his own goodness.

8. It may be said that it belongs to God's goodness to bring creatures into being, but not to do so from eternity.— On the contrary it is more bountiful to give quickly than tardily: and the bounty of God's goodness is infinite. Therefore seemingly he gave being to creatures from eternity.

9. Augustine says (*Confess.* vii, 4): *In thee to be able is to*

will, and to will is to do. Now God from eternity willed to create the world : otherwise he would have changed, if the will to create came to him anew. Since then there is no inability in God, it would seem that he created the world from eternity.

10. If the world was not always, before it existed it was either possible for it to exist or it was impossible. If it was not possible, it was impossible and consequently it was necessary for it not to be : and thus it would never have been brought into being. And if it was possible for it to be, there was some potentiality in respect thereof, and consequently a subject or matter, since potentiality demands a subject. But if there was matter there was also form, since matter cannot be entirely devoid of form. Therefore there was a body composed of matter and form, and consequently the entire universe.

11. Whatsoever becomes actual after being potential, is brought from potentiality to actuality. Hence if before the world actually existed it was possible for it to exist, we must infer that the world was brought from potentiality to actuality, and consequently that matter preceded and was eternal ; so that we come to the same conclusion as before.

12. An agent that begins to act anew is moved from potentiality to actuality ; and this cannot be said of God who is utterly immovable. Therefore it would seem that he does not begin anew to act, but that he created the world from eternity.

13. If a voluntary agent begins to do what he already willed but has not done yet, we must suppose that something has occurred to induce him to do it now, which did not induce him before, but stirs him to action as it were. But it cannot be said that before the world existed there was something besides God to offer him a fresh inducement to act. Since then he purposed from eternity to create the world (otherwise something new would have occurred to his will) it would seem that he made the world from eternity.

14. Further, nothing besides God's goodness moves the divine will to act. Now the divine goodness is always the

same. Therefore God's will also is always bent on the production of creatures, and thus he produced them from eternity.

15. That which is always in its beginning and always in its end, never begins and never ceases, because a thing is after it has begun and before it has ceased. Now time is always in its beginning and end, because time is nothing but an instant which is the end of the past and the beginning of the future. Hence time never begins nor ends but is always: and consequently movement also and things that are subject to movement, in fact, the whole world : since there is no time without movement, nor movement without movables, nor movable things apart from the world.

16. It will be said perhaps that the first instant of time is not the end of the past nor the last beginning of the future. —On the contrary the *now* of time is always considered as flowing, wherein it differs from the *now* of eternity : and that which flows passes from one thing to another. Consequently every *now* passes from a previous to a following *now*, and there cannot be a first or last *now*.

17. Movement follows that which can be moved, and time follows movement. Now the first movable being circular has neither beginning nor end, for it is not possible to indicate the actual beginning or end of a circle. Therefore neither time nor movement has a beginning, and the same conclusion follows as above.

18. It will be said that although a circular body has no beginning of its magnitude, it has a beginning of its duration. —On the contrary duration of movement follows the measure of magnitude, because, according to the Philosopher (*Phys.* iv, 11), magnitude, motion and time are mutually proportionate. Hence if there be no beginning of the magnitude of a circular body neither will there be a beginning of the magnitude of movement or of time, and consequently there will be no beginning of their duration, since their duration, especially that of time, is their magnitude.

19. God is the cause of things by his knowledge : and knowledge connotes relation to the thing knowable. Since then relatives are by nature simultaneous, and God's know-

ledge is eternal, it would seem that things were produced by him from eternity.

20. God precedes the world either in the order of nature only, or by duration. If only in the order of nature, as a cause precedes its synchronous effect, it would seem that creatures must have existed, like God, from eternity. And if he precede the world in duration, there must have been a duration prior to that of the world, so as to constitute a *before* and *after* in duration ; and this implies time. Therefore the world was preceded by time and consequently by movement and movable things : and we come to the same conclusion as before.

21. Augustine (*De Trin.* v, 16) says : *I dare not assert that God was not Lord from eternity.* Now so long as he was Lord he had creatures for his subjects. Therefore we must not assert that creatures are not from eternity.

22. God was able to create the world before he created it, else he were impotent. Likewise he knew that he could, else he were ignorant. And apparently he willed, else he were envious. Therefore it would seem that he did not wait to begin creating creatures.

23. Whatsoever is finite can be communicated to a creature. Now eternity is something finite : else nothing could extend beyond it, and yet it is written (Exod. xv, 18) : *The Lord shall reign for eternity and beyond.*[1] Therefore one would infer that a creature is capable of being eternal, and that it was becoming to the divine goodness to produce creatures from eternity.

24. Whatsoever has a beginning has a measure of its duration. Now time cannot have a measure of its duration : for it cannot be measured by eternity, since then it would have been always : nor by eviternity, since then it would last for ever : nor by time, since nothing is its own measure. Therefore time had no beginning, and consequently neither had movable things, nor the world.

25. If time had a beginning, this was either in time or in an instant. It did not begin in an instant, for in an instant there is not yet time : nor did it begin in time, for in that

[1] Douay and A.V. *For ever and ever.*

case no time would precede the term of time, since before a thing begins to exist it is nothing. Consequently time had no beginning and the same conclusion follows as before.

26. God from eternity was the cause of things : otherwise we should have to say that he was at first their potential and afterwards their actual cause ; so that there would be something already in existence to reduce him from potentiality to act : and this is impossible. Now nothing is a cause unless it has an effect. Therefore the world was created by God from eternity.

27. Truth and being are convertible : and many truths are eternal, such as that man is not an ass, and that the world was to be, and many similar truths. Therefore it would seem that many beings are from eternity, and not God alone.

28. But it may be said that all these are true by the first truth which is God.—On the contrary, the truth of this proposition, ' The world will exist,' differs from the truth of this proposition, ' Man is not an ass,' because granted, though it is impossible, that the one is false, the other remains true. But the first truth cannot alter. Therefore these propositions are not true by the first truth.

29. According to the Philosopher (*Categor* 5.) a statement is true or false according as the thing is so or not. If, then, many propositions are true from eternity, it would seem that the things signified by them have existed from eternity.

30. With God ' to speak ' and ' to make ' are the same according to Psalm xxxii, 9, *He spake and they were made.* Now God spoke from eternity, otherwise the Son who is the Father's Word would not be co-eternal with the Father. Therefore God's work is eternal and the world was made from eternity.

On the contrary it is said (Prov. viii, 24 *seqq.*) in the words of divine Wisdom : *The depths were not as yet and I was already conceived, neither had the fountains of waters as yet sprung out. The mountains with their huge bulk had not as yet been established : before the hills was I brought forth. He had not yet made the earth, nor the rivers, nor the poles of the world.* Therefore the poles of the world, the rivers and the earth were not always.

Again according to Priscian, the younger in point of time are keener in point of intelligence. But keenness of intelligence is not infinite: therefore the time during which it increases is not infinite and consequently neither is the world.

Again it is written (Job xxiv, 19): *With inundation the ground by little and little is washed away.* Now the earth is not infinite: so that if time were infinite the earth would by now have been wholly washed away: and this is clearly false.

Again it is evident that God naturally preceded the world as a cause precedes its effect. But in God duration and nature are the same, therefore God preceded the world by duration, and thus the world was not always.

I answer that we must not hesitate to hold that, as the Catholic faith teaches, the world has not always existed. This cannot be disproved by any physical demonstration.

In order to make this clear we must observe that as we have shown in a previous question in God's works we cannot assign a necessity on the part of the material cause, nor on the part of the active power of the agent, nor on the part of the ultimate end, but only on the part of the form which is the end of the work, since if the form be presupposed it is requisite that things be such as to be fit for such and such a form. Hence we must speak of the production of this or that particular creature otherwise than of the production of the whole universe by God. When we speak of the production of a particular creature, it is possible to gather the reason why it is such and such, from some other creature, or at least from the order of the universe to which every creature is ordained, as a part to the form of the whole. But when we speak of the production of the whole universe, we cannot point to any other creature as being the reason why the universe is such and such. Wherefore since neither on the part of the divine power which is infinite, nor of the divine goodness which stands not in need of creatures, can a reason be assigned for the particular disposition of the universe:

this reason must be found in the mere will of the Creator: so that if it be asked why the heavens are of such and such a size, no other reason can be given except that their maker willed it so. For this reason too, as Rabbi Moses says, Holy Writ exhorts us to consider the heavenly bodies, since we gather from their disposition how all things are subject to the will and providence of a Creator. For no reason can be given for the distance of this star from that one, or for any other dispositions that we observe in the heavens, save the ordinance of divine wisdom: wherefore it is written (Isa. xl, 26): *Lift up your eyes on high and see who hath created these things.* Nor does it matter if someone say that the distance in question results from the nature of the heavens or heavenly bodies, even as a certain quantity is appointed to every natural thing, because just as the divine power is not confined to this rather than to that quantity, so is it not confined to a nature that requires one particular quantity rather than to a nature that requires another quantity. Consequently it makes no difference whether it be a question of quantity or of nature: although we grant that the nature of the heavens is not indifferent to any quantity in particular, and that there is no inherent possibility of the heavens having any other quantity than that which they actually have. But this cannot be said of time or the duration of time. For time like place is extraneous to things: wherefore although there is no possibility in the heavens with respect to another quantity or inherent accident, yet is there a possibility with regard to place and position, since the heavens have a local movement; and with regard to time, since time ever succeeds time, even as there is succession in movement and ubiety: wherefore it cannot be said that neither time nor ubiety result from the heavens' nature, as was the case with quantity. It is clear then that the appointment of a fixed quantity of duration for the universe depends on the mere will of God, even as the appointment of a fixed quantity of dimension. Consequently we cannot come to a necessary conclusion about the duration of the universe, so as to prove demonstratively that the world has always existed.

Some, however, through failing to observe that the universe was made by God, were unable to avoid erring in this question about the beginning of the world. Thus the earliest physicists recognised no effective cause and maintained that uncreated matter was the cause of all things, and thus they were compelled to hold that matter had always existed. For seeing that nothing brings itself from non-existence into being, that which begins to exist must be caused by something else. These asserted—either that the world was always in continual existence, because they recognised none but natural agents which being confined to one mode of action, of necessity always produced the same effects ;—or that the world had an interrupted existence ; thus Democritus held the world, or rather worlds, to be in a continual state of formation and destruction on account of the chance movements of atoms.

Since, however, it seemed unreasonable that all the congruities and utilities to be found in nature should be due to chance, whereas they obtain either always or in the majority of cases : and seeing that nevertheless this would follow if there were no other cause but matter, and especially that there are some effects which cannot be sufficiently explained by the causality of matter, others like Anaxagoras posited an intellect as active cause, or like Empedocles, attraction and repulsion. Yet they did not hold these to be the active causes of the universe, but likened them to other particular agents whose activity consists in the transformation of matter from one thing into another. Consequently they were compelled to assert that matter is eternal, through not having a cause of its existence : but that the world had a beginning, because every effect of a cause which acts by movement follows its cause in duration, since such effect does not exist before the end of the movement, which end is preceded by the initial movement, co-existent with which is the agent that initiates the movement.

Aristotle (*Phys.* viii, 1), observing that if it be said that the efficient cause of the world acted by movement, it would follow that one would have to proceed to infinity, since every movement must be preceded by another movement, maintained that the world has always existed. He argued not from the position that the world was made by God, but from the position that an agent which begins to act must be moved: thus considering the particular and not the universal cause. Wherefore in order to prove the eternity of the world he based his arguments on movement and the immobility of the prime mover: and hence if we consider them carefully, his arguments seem to be those of one who is arguing against a position, so that at the commencement of *Phys.* viii, having introduced the question of the eternity of movement, he begins by citing the opinions of Anaxagoras and Empedocles, his object being to argue against them. Those who came after Aristotle, however, considering that the whole universe was produced by God through his will and not by movement, endeavoured to prove the eternity of the world from the fact that the will does not wait to do what it intends, except on account of some new occurrence or change, even though we be compelled to imagine it in the succession of time, in that one wills to do this or that now and not sooner. Yet these fell into the same error as those mentioned before. For they considered the first agent as being like an agent which exercises its activity in time and yet acts through its will. Such an agent is not the cause of time but presupposes it: whereas God is cause even of time, since time is included in the universality of the things made by God: and therefore seeing that we are considering the production of all being by God, the fact that he made it then and not sooner does not enter the question. For this considers time as though it preceded the making instead of being conditional on the making. But if we consider the making of the universality of creatures among which time itself is included, we must consider why such and such a measure was affixed to time, and not why the making was at such and such a time. The fixing of the measure to time depends on the mere will of God, who willed that the world should not have always been, but should have a beginning, even as he willed the heavens to be neither greater nor smaller than they are.

Reply to the First Objection. It is proper to (divine)

goodness to bring things into being through the will of which it is the object. Consequently it does not follow that because the divine goodness always existed therefore things brought into being always existed, but that they were produced according to the disposition of the divine will.

Reply to the Second Objection. The heavenly body being incorruptible is capable of always being : but no capability whether of being or of operating regards the past, but only the present or the future : since no man exercises a power over his past actions, for he cannot cause to have been done that which he has not done : but he has the power to do it now or in the future. Consequently the capability in the heavens of being always regards not the past but the future.

Reply to the Third Objection. The fact that the heavens would return into nothingness if God ceased to uphold them does not make them corruptible simply. Seeing, however, that the preservation of the creature by God depends on God's unchangeableness, not on natural necessity (in which case it would be absolutely necessary), and is necessary solely on the supposition that God wills and has unchangeably decreed that preservation, it may be granted that the heavens are corruptible in a restricted sense, in so far as their incorruptibility is dependent on God.

Reply to the Fourth Objection. Every effect carries a necessary relationship to its effective cause whether natural or voluntary. But we have already proved (A. 15) that God is the cause of the world not by a necessity of his nature, but by his will : wherefore it was necessary for the divine effect to follow not whenever the divine nature existed, but when the divine will decreed that it should follow, and in the very manner that he willed.

Reply to the Fifth Objection. A thing may precede time in two ways. First, before the whole of time, and before anything belonging to time. In this way the world did not precede time, because the instant wherein the world began, though not time, is something belonging to time, not indeed a part but the starting-point of time. In another way a thing is said to precede time because it is before the completion of time : and time is not complete before the instant that is preceded by another instant : in this sense the world preceded time. It does not follow from this that the world is eternal, since the instant of time that precedes time is not eternal.

Reply to the Sixth Objection. Since every agent produces its like, an effect must follow from an effectively operating cause, so as to bear a likeness to its cause. Now as that which proceeds from a cause that acts by its nature bears a likeness thereto in that it has a form like the form of its cause, so that which proceeds from a voluntary agent bears a likeness thereto in that it has a form like its cause, forasmuch as the effect is the reproduction of something in accordance with the will, as instanced in the work produced by the craftsman. But the will appoints not only the form of the effect but also the place, time and all other conditions thereof : so that the effect of the will follows when the will decides and not as soon as the will is. For the likeness of the effect to the will is not in the point of being but in the point of disposal by the will. Consequently, though the will remain ever the same, it does not follow that its effect should flow from it from eternity.

Reply to the Seventh Objection. God necessarily wills his own goodness and whatsoever is necessarily connected with his goodness. Such is not the production of creatures, and consequently the objection fails.

Reply to the Eighth Objection. Since God made creatures in order to manifest himself, it was more fitting and more to the purpose that they should be made in suchwise as to manifest him in a more becoming manner and more clearly. Now he is more clearly manifested by creatures if they be not from eternity, because this brings into greater evidence the fact that he brought them into being and that he does not need them, and that they are entirely dependent on his will.

Reply to the Ninth Objection. God's will to create the world was eternal ; not that the world should exist from eternity, but that it should be made when he actually did make it.

Reply to the Tenth Objection. Before the world was it was possible for the world to be made, not by a passive potentiality, but by the active power of the agent.—Or we may reply that it was possible not by reason of some power, but because the terms of the proposition, ' The world exists ' are not in contradiction to each other. According to the Philosopher (*Metaph.* v, 12) a thing may be said to be possible in this way without reference to a potentiality.

This suffices for the reply to the Eleventh Objection.

Reply to the Twelfth Objection. This argument stands in the case of an agent that begins a new action, whereas God's action is eternal, since it is his substance. He is said, however, to begin to act in reference to a new effect that results from his eternal action according to the disposition of his will which is considered as the principle of his action in relation to the effect. For the effect follows from the action according to the condition of the form that is the principle of that action : even so a thing is heated by the action of the fire according to the degree of heat in the fire.

Reply to the Thirteenth Objection. This argument considers the agent that produces its effect in time without being the cause of time : this does not apply to God as stated above (A. 15).

Reply to the Fourteenth Objection. If movement be taken strictly God's will is not moved : but it is said to be moved, metaphorically speaking, by its object : and thus God's goodness alone moves his will, according to the saying of Augustine (*Gen. ad lit.* viii, 22) that God moves himself independently of place and time. Nor does it follow that creatures were produced whenever God's goodness existed, because creatures proceed from God not as though they were due or necessary to his goodness, since it does not need them, nor does he gain anything by them, but by his mere will.

Reply to the Fifteenth Objection. Since the first succession of time was caused by movement (*Phys.* iv, 12) it is true that every instant is a beginning and an end of time, even as it is true that every moved thing is in a beginning and in an end of movement: so that if we suppose that movement neither always existed nor will always exist, there will be no need to say that every instant is a beginning and an end of time ; for there will be an instant which will be only a beginning, and an instant which will be only an end. Hence this objection argues in a circle and consequently does not prove : but it serves the purpose of Aristotle who employs it to attack a position as we have said above. In fact, many arguments serve to rebut an opinion on account of the statements advanced by its holders, and yet in themselves are not absolute demonstrations.

Reply to the Sixteenth Objection. An instant is indeed always considered as flowing, yet not always as flowing from one thing to another, but sometimes as only flowing from something, for example, the last instant of time, sometimes as flowing only towards something, as the first instant.

Reply to the Seventeenth Objection. This argument does not prove that movement has always existed, but that circular movement can be always, because from mathematical principles we cannot with certainty draw conclusions about movement: hence Aristotle (*Phys.* viii, 8) does not infer the eternity of a movement from its being circular, but from the fact that a movement is eternal he shows that it must be circular, because no other movement can be eternal.

This suffices for the reply to the Eighteenth Objection.

Reply to the Nineteenth Objection. Things knowable are related to our knowledge as God's knowledge is to creatures: because God's knowledge is the cause of creatures and things knowable are the cause of our knowledge. Wherefore even as things are knowable even without our knowing them (*De Categor.* 7), so is it possible for God to have knowledge without the knowable thing having existence.

Reply to the Twentieth Objection. God does indeed precede the world by duration, not of time but of eternity, since God's existence is not measured by time. Nor was there real time before the world, but only imaginary ; thus now we can imagine an infinite space of time running with eternity and preceding the beginning of time.

Reply to the Twenty-first Objection. If the relation of lordship be regarded as consequent to the action whereby God actually governs creatures, then God was not Lord from eternity. But if it be regarded as consequent to the power of governing, then it belongs to God from eternity. Nor does it follow that creatures must have existed from eternity except potentially.

Reply to the Twenty-second Objection. This is Augustine's argument (*Contra Maxim.* ii, 7, 8, 23) to prove that the Son is co-eternal and co-equal with the Father. But this argument is not applicable to the world, because as the Son's nature is the same as the Father's it requires to be co-eternal and co-equal with the Father's, otherwise were this denied him it would savour of envy. The nature of the creature, however, does not require this: and consequently the comparison fails.

Reply to the Twenty-third Objection. The Greek text reads: *The Lord shall reign for age upon age and beyond:* and Origen, as quoted by a gloss, says that by *age* we are to understand the space of one generation the limits of which are known to us: by *age upon age* we are to understand an immense space of time which has an end, yet unknown to us: and that God's reign will extend even beyond this. Hence 'eternity' here means the duration of time. Anselm, however (*Proslog.* xix, xx), takes eternity to mean eviternity, which has no end: and yet God is said to reign beyond it, because in the first place eviternal things can be thought of as non-existent; secondly, because they would not be if God ceased to uphold them, so that of themselves they do not exist: thirdly, because they have not their whole existence at once, but are subject to successive change.

Reply to the Twenty-fourth Objection. That which has a beginning must have a measure of its duration in so far as it begins through movement. But time does not begin thus by creation, wherefore the argument does not prove. However, it may be said that every measure is measured by itself within its own genus : thus a line is measured by a line, and time by time.

Reply to the Twenty-fifth Objection. Time is not like permanent things which have their whole substance at once : so that there is no need for the whole of time to exist as soon as it begins. Consequently it is not untrue that time begins in an instant.

Reply to the Twenty-sixth Objection. God's action is eternal, but its effect is not, as we have stated above : hence though God was not always cause, inasmuch as his effect was not always, it does not follow that he was not cause potentially, since his action was always, unless we refer the potentiality to the effect.

Reply to the Twenty-seventh Objection. According to the Philosopher (*Metaph.* vi, 4) truth is in the mind, not in things, for it is the equation of thought and thing. Wherefore whatsoever has been from eternity has been true by the truth of the divine mind, which truth is eternal.

Reply to the Twenty-eighth Objection. Whatsoever things are said to be true from eternity do not vary in their truth, but are true by the one same truth of the divine mind, with reference nevertheless to various things as future in their own being : so that we are able to indicate a certain distinction in that truth resulting from their various relations.

Reply to the Twenty-ninth Objection. The saying of the Philosopher refers to our mental or oral statements, since the truth of our thought or words is caused by things already evident : whereas the truth of the divine mind is the cause of things.

Reply to the Thirtieth Objection. On the part of God there is no difference between 'to make' and 'to speak,' for God's action is not an accident but his substance : nevertheless 'to make' connotes the effect actually existing in its own nature, whereas 'to speak' does not.

The arguments on the contrary side, although they prove what is true, are not demonstrative except the first which is based on authority. The argument taken from the growth of intelligence in the course of time, does not prove that time must have had a beginning : since possibly the study of the sciences may have been frequently interrupted, and subsequently taken up anew after a long interval, as the Philosopher observes. Again the soil is not so much eaten away by erosion on one part of the earth's surface without a corresponding increase taking place elsewhere through the combination of the elements. And the duration of God, although it be identified with the divine nature in reality, differs therefrom logically : so that it does not follow that God preceded the world in duration from the fact that he preceded it naturally.

ARTICLE XVIII

WERE THE ANGELS CREATED BEFORE THE VISIBLE WORLD ?
Sum. Th. I, Q. lxi

THE eighteenth point of inquiry is whether the angels were created before the visible world : and it would seem that they were.

1. Damascene (*De Fide Orthod.* ii, 3) quotes Gregory Nazianzen as saying that *at first God devised the angelic and heavenly powers, and the devising was the making thereof.* Therefore he created the angels before making the visible world.

2. Should it be said that 'first' here denotes order of nature not of duration ; on the contrary, Damascene (*l.c.*) cites two opinions on this point : one of which states that the angels were created first, while the other holds the contrary. Now no one ever denied that the angels were in the order of nature created before visible creatures. Therefore we must take it to refer to the order of duration.

3. Basil says (*Hexæm.* hom. i) : *Prior to this world there existed a nature that is intelligible to our understanding :* and subsequently he states that this is the angelic nature. Therefore it would seem that the angels were created before this world.

4. The Scriptures enumerate those things that were

created together with the visible world without any mention of the angels. Therefore it would seem that the angels were not created together with the visible world but before.

5. That which is directed to the perfection of another as its end is subsequent thereto. Now the visible world is directed to the perfection of the intellectual creature since, according to Ambrose (*In Hexæm.* i, 5), God who by nature is invisible produced a visible work in order to make himself known thereby. But he could only be made known to a rational creature. Therefore the rational creature was made before the visible world.

6. Whatsoever precedes time precedes the visible world, since time began together with the visible world. Now angels were created before time, since they were created before the day, as Augustine says (*Gen. ad lit.* i, 9). Therefore the angels were created before the visible world.

7. Jerome says (*Super Ep. ad Tit.* i, 2) : *Six thousand years of our time have not yet elapsed, before which for how many ages, for how long think you the angels served God and to his command owed their existence?* Now the visible world began with our time. Therefore the angels were in existence before the visible world.

8. A wise man produces his effects in due order. Now the angels precede visible creatures in point of excellence. Therefore they should have been brought into being first by God who is the supremely wise Master-Craftsman.

9. God inasmuch as he is good makes others share in his goodness. Now angels were capable of being dignified by preceding the visible creature in point of duration. Therefore seemingly this was vouchsafed them by God's sovereign goodness.

10. Man is described as being a lesser world by reason of his likeness to the greater world. Now man's more noble part, his heart to wit, is formed before the other parts, according to the Philosopher (*De Gen. Animal.* ii, 4). Therefore seemingly the angels, who are the more noble part of the greater world, were created before visible creatures.

11. According to Augustine (*Gen. ad lit.* ii, 7, 8), Scripture in the work of the second and following days divided the

formation of things into three stages : for first it states that God said : *Let there be a firmament made :* then : *And it was so done,* and, thirdly : *God made the firmament.* The first of these refers to the existence of things in the Word ; the second to the existence in the angelic mind, of creatures to be made ; the third to the creature's existence in its own nature. Now when creatures were yet to be made they did not exist. Therefore angels existed and had knowledge of the visible things of nature before the latter existed.

12. It might be said, however, that it is a question of the making of creatures as to their formation and not as to their first creation.—On the contrary, in the opinion of Augustine (*Gen. ad lit.* i, xv), the creation of visible nature did not precede its formation in point of time. Hence if angels existed before the formation of visible creatures, they also existed before its creation.

13. God's speaking was the cause of creatures being made. Now seemingly this cannot refer to the birth of the Word, since this was from eternity and not repeated in course of time : and yet Scripture tells of God speaking from day to day. Nor can it refer to audible speech, both because there was as yet no man to hear the voice of God speaking, and because before the formation of light it would have been necessary for some other body to be formed, since an audible voice is not produced except by means of a body. It would seem then that it refers to the spiritual speech whereby God spake to the angels : and consequently that the angels' knowledge is presupposed as a cause for the production of visible creatures.

14. As observed above, Holy Writ employs three expressions in relating the creation ; whereof the first refers to the existence of things in the Word, the second to their existence in the angelic knowledge, the third to their existence in their own nature. Now the first of these precedes the second in point both of duration and of causality. Therefore likewise the second, namely the angelic knowledge, precedes the third, namely the existence of the visible creature, both in duration and causality.

15. Order is required in the issue of things from their source no less than in their advancement to their end. Now according to Dionysius (*Eccl. Hier.* v) it is God's ruling that the lowest things should be brought to their end by the intermediate. Therefore in like manner corporeal creatures being the lowest proceed from God by the angelic creatures who hold the middle position : wherefore the angels precede corporeal creatures as a cause precedes its effect.

16. It is unbecoming that things utterly disparate should be associated together. Now angels and visible creatures are altogether disparate. Therefore they were not associated together in the creation by being formed at the same time. And it would be a perversion of order if they were created after visible creatres. Therefore they were created before them.

17. It is written (*Ecclus.* i, 4) : *Wisdom hath been created before all things:* and this cannot refer to the Son of God who is the Wisdom of the Father : since he was not created but begotten. Therefore the angelic wisdom which is a creature was formed before all things.

18. Hilary says (*De Trin.* xii) : *No wonder that we believe that our Lord Jesus Christ was before all ages seeing that even the angels were created by God before the world.* Now the Son of God preceded all ages not only in order of dignity but also in duration. Therefore the angels also preceded the visible world.

19. The angelic nature stands between the divine and the corporeal natures : and eviternity, which measures the angels' existence, stands between eternity and time. Now by his eternity God preceded the angels and the visible creature. Therefore by their eviternity the angels preceded the visible world.

20. Augustine (*De Civ. Dei* xi, 9) says that the angels were always in existence. But it cannot be said that corporeal creatures were always in existence. Therefore the angels preceded the corporeal creature.

21. The movements of corporeal creatures are directed by the ministrations of spiritual creatures, according to Augustine (*De Trin.* iii, 1) and Gregory (*Dial.* iv). Now

the mover precedes that which he moves. Therefore angels preceded visible creatures.

22. Dionysius likens God's action on things to the action of fire on the things which it burns. Now fire acts on the nearer bodies before those that are distant. Therefore God's goodness produced angelic creatures which are nearest to him before corporeal creatures which are distant from him: and thus the angels existed before the world.

On the contrary, it is written at the commencement of Genesis: *In the beginning God created heavens and earth,* where Augustine explains the heavens to mean the angelic nature and the earth the corporeal nature. Therefore the angels were created together with corporeal things.

Again, the gloss of Strabo on the same text states that the heavens refer to the empyrean which was inhabited by the holy angels as soon as it was created. Therefore the angels were created at the same time as the empyrean which is a visible creature.

Again, man is described as the lesser world on account of his likeness to the greater world. Now man's soul is made at the same time as his body. Therefore in the greater world the angelic and the corporeal creature were made at the same time.

I answer that all the Catholic Doctors are agreed that the angels have not always existed inasmuch as they were made from nothing. Some, however, held that the angels were not made at the same time as the visible world but before: a conclusion to which they were led by various reasons. Some held that it was not God's original intention to form corporeal creatures, and that his production of the latter was occasioned by the merits or demerits of spiritual creatures. Thus Origen maintained that in the first instance God made all the immaterial and rational creatures. These, he said, were all equal, for the divine justice required them to be so: since without injustice there could apparently be no reason for inequality in endowments, except diversity of merit and demerit. Consequently he maintained that the diversity which we observe among creatures was preceded by a diversity of merit and demerit, so that those spiritual creatures which were more faithful to God were promoted to the higher orders among the angels, and those who sinned more grievously were chained to the baser and viler bodies: so that this very diversity of merits required that various degrees of bodies should be produced by God.

Augustine refutes this opinion (*De Civ. Dei* xi, 23). For it is clear that God's goodness is the sole reason for his producing creatures both spiritual and corporeal, inasmuch as his creatures which out of his goodness he has fashioned reproduce his uncreated goodness according to their mode. Wherefore Scripture says of each of God's works and afterwards of all of them together: *God saw all the things that he had made, and they were very good;* as though to say that God had formed creatures in order that they might have goodness. On the other hand in the aforesaid opinion corporeal creatures were formed not because it was good for them to be, but that the wickedness of the spiritual creature might be punished. Moreover it would follow that the order we perceive to exist in the universe is the result of chance, forasmuch as various rational creatures happened to sin variously: for had all sinned equally, there would be no difference of nature in bodies, according to this opinion.

Hence others rejecting this opinion held that spiritual substances were created before corporeal substances because they perceived that the nature of the former surpasses the entire range of corporeal nature: and they maintained that the created spiritual nature, even as it ranks between God and the corporeal creature in the order of nature, so is it placed between them in point of duration. Seeing that this opinion was held by such great doctors as Basil, Gregory Nazianzen and others we must not condemn it as being erroneous: but if we consider carefully yet another opinion held by Augustine and other doctors and now more generally accepted, we shall find that the latter is the more reasonable of the two. For we must consider the angels not only absolutely, but also as a part of the universe: and there is all the more reason for doing so inasmuch as the good of the universe is of greater weight than the good of any individual creature, even as the good of the whole is of greater import than that of a part. Now it became the angels, considered as part of the universe, to be created together with corporeal creatures. Because of one whole there should seemingly be one making. And if the angels were created apart, they would seem utterly alienated from the order of corporeal creatures, and to constitute as it were another universe by themselves. Hence we must conclude that the angels were created together with corporeal creatures, yet without prejudice to the other opinion.

This suffices for the replies to the first three Objections which follow the lines of the second opinion.

Reply to the Fourth Objection. According to Basil (*Hexæm.* homil. i) the lawgiver Moses at the commencement of Genesis began by relating the origin of visible creatures, omitting spiritual creatures who had been created before: the reason for this omission being that he was addressing himself to an unlettered people incapable of grasping spiritual things. Augustine on the other hand held that by the heavens Moses denoted the spiritual creature and by the earth the corporeal, when he wrote: *In the beginning God created heaven and earth.* And the reason why he expressed the creation of the angels under the metaphor of the heavens and not clearly may be the same as that given above, namely because the people were uncultured. Also in order to avoid idolatry to which they were inclined, and of which they would be afforded an occasion if they were told of other spiritual substances besides one God, and ranking above the heavens; and all the more seeing that these very substances were called gods by the gentiles. According to Strabo and others before him, the heavens in the text quoted signify the empyrean which is the abode of the holy angels, by the figure of metonymy, the container being put for the content.

Reply to the Fifth Objection. According to Augustine (*Gen. ad lit.* v, 5) the angels' knowledge of God is not derived from visible creatures: wherefore the visible creature was made that it might manifest God not to the angels, but to the rational creature which is man: so that this proves to be the end of creatures. Now the end though it is first in intention is the last in execution, wherefore man was made last.

Reply to the Sixth Objection. According to Augustine (*Super Gen.* i, 5) the creation of heaven and earth did not precede in duration the formation or production of light, wherefore he does not mean to say that the spiritual nature was created before the first day by a priority of duration, but by a kind of natural order: because the spiritual substance and formless matter considered in their respective essences are not subject to the changes of time. Consequently we cannot infer that the spiritual creature was formed before the corporeal, since even before the formation of light mention is made of the creation of the corporeal creature denoted by the earth. According to others the creation of heaven and earth belongs to the first day, because together with them time was created: although the division of time into day and night began with light: hence time is stated to be one of the four things first created, namely the angelic nature, the empyrean heaven, formless matter and time.

Reply to the Seventh Objection. Jerome is expressing himself in accordance with the opinion of the early doctors.

Reply to the Eighth Objection. This argument would avail were each creature brought into being as existing absolutely by itself: for then it would be fitting for each one to be created separately according to the degree of its goodness. Seeing, however, that all creatures are produced as parts of one universe, it was fitting that all should be produced together so as to form one universe.

Reply to the Ninth Objection. Although it would conduce to a certain dignity of the spiritual creature were it created before the visible creature, it would not conduce to the dignity and unity of the universe.

Reply to the Tenth Objection. Although the heart is formed before the other members, there is but one continual generation of the animal's body, the heart is not formed by a separate generation, and the other members afterwards by a succession of generations at various intervals. This does not apply to the creation of the angels and corporeal creatures, as though they were produced by one formative act, the spiritual creature first and the whole universe by a continuous production: because successive production applies to things produced from matter, in which one part is nearer than another to the final completion. Consequently there was no place for succession in the first creation of things, although it may obtain in the formation of things from created matter. Wherefore the doctors who held that the angels were created before the world, maintained that the creation of the former was entirely distinct from the creation of bodies, and that there was a long interval between. Moreover there is need for the heart in an animal to be formed first, because its activity conduces to the formation of the other members: whereas no spiritual creature co-operates in the creation of corporeal creatures since God alone can create. Hence the Commentator (*Metaph.* xi, com. 44) finds fault with Plato for asserting that God after creating the angels committed to them the creation of corporeal creatures.

Reply to the Eleventh Objection. Augustine is referring to the making of corporeal creatures as regards not their first creation but their formation.

Reply to the Twelfth Objection. If it be maintained that all things were created together in their form and matter, the spiritual creature is said to have known the corporeal creature that was to be made, not that this formation was future in point of time, but because it was known as future forasmuch as it was perceived in its cause wherein it existed potentially: even so one who considers a box in the principles from which it is made may be said to know it as something to be made.

Reply to the Thirteenth Objection. God's speaking refers to the eternal generation of the divine Word in whom from eternity was the type of all things to be made. Nor does the frequent repetition in each work of the phrase 'God said' imply that God spoke in time: for although the Word is one in himself he contains the proper type of every single creature. Accordingly God's word prefaces each work as the proper type of the work to be produced, lest the work being complete, it be necessary to ask why that particular work was done, whereas it had already been stated before the production of the work, that ' God spoke ' : even so when we wish to indicate the cause of a thing we begin with knowledge of the cause.

Reply to the Fourteenth Objection. The existence of things in the Word is the cause of their existence in themselves : whereas the existence of things in the angelic mind is not the cause of their existence in themselves : wherefore the comparison fails.

Reply to the Fifteenth Objection. A thing is directed to its end by means of its operation : whereas it is not brought into being by its operation, but only by the operation of its effective cause. Hence it is more fitting that the higher creatures should co-operate with God in bringing things to their end than in their production.

Reply to the Sixteenth Objection. Although corporeal and spiritual creatures are disparate in regard to their own proper natures, they are connected in regard to the order of the universe. Hence the necessity for them to be created together.

Reply to the Seventeenth Objection.[1] According to Augustine (*Conf.* xii, 15) these words of Ecclesiasticus refer to created wisdom abiding in the angelic nature, and he holds that it was created first by priority not of duration but of dignity. According to Hilary (*De Synod.*) they refer to the uncreated wisdom, namely the Son of God : and it is said to be both created and begotten, as may be gathered from Proverbs viii, and various other passages of Scripture, in order to exclude any imperfection from the birth of God's Son. Thus creation implies imperfection on the part of the creature in so far as it is made from nothing, but it implies perfection on the part of the Creator, who produces creatures without himself being changed. On the other hand birth implies perfection in the son in so far as he receives the nature of the begetter, while it implies imperfection in the begetter after the manner of generation here below, inasmuch as begetting is accompanied by change or

[1] Cf. *Sum. Theol.* I, Q. xli, A. 3, *ad* 4.

division of substance in the begetter. Hence the Son of God is said to be both created and begotten, in order that creation may exclude change in the begetter, and birth exclude imperfection in the begotten, the two combining to give us one perfect idea.

Reply to the Eighteenth Objection. Hilary's statement is in accordance with the opinion of the early doctors.

Reply to the Nineteenth Objection. God is the cause of the angelic nature, but the latter is not the cause of the corporeal nature: and thus there is no comparison.

Reply to the Twentieth Objection. The angels are said to have been always in existence, not that they were from eternity but from all time, because whenever time was the angels were. In this sense corporeal creatures were always.

Reply to the Twenty-first Objection. The mover does not of necessity precede in point of time the thing moved, but in dignity, as for instance, the soul precedes the body.

Reply to the Twenty-second Objection. In the action of fire on bodies a twofold order is to be observed, of position and of time. There is order of position in its every action, because all its actions are affected by position, and its activity bears more on the bodies nearest to it: wherefore by spreading it becomes less effective so that at last it is entirely spent. On the other hand order of time does not affect all the actions of fire, but only those that are accompanied by movement. Hence as fire illumines and heats bodies, in heating there is order of position and time; but in illumination which is not movement but the term of a movement there is only order of position. Since then God's action in creating is without movement the comparison is true, not as regards order of time but as regards order of position. Because in spiritual action the various degrees of nature correspond to diversity of position in corporeal action. Accordingly the comparison of Dionysius is verified in this that as fire is more effective on the bodies nearest to it, so God bestows his goodness more plentifully on those that are nearest to him in the degree of worthiness.

ARTICLE XIX

WAS IT POSSIBLE FOR THE ANGELS TO EXIST BEFORE THE VISIBLE WORLD ?

Sum. Th. I, Q. lxi, A. 3

THE nineteenth point of inquiry is whether it were possible for the angels to exist before the visible world : and seemingly it was impossible.

1. Two distinct things that cannot be in the same place require a difference of place. Now it is universally agreed that two angels cannot be in the same place. Hence it is inconceivable that there be two distinct angels unless there be two distinct places. Now there was no place before the visible creature, for place according to the Philosopher (*Phys.* iv, 4) is a space occupied by a body. Therefore the angels could not exist before the visible world.

2. The production of the corporeal creature nowise deprived the angels of their natural power. Hence if it was possible for the angels to exist outside a place before the visible world was made, it would be possible even now that the visible world has been created : and this apparently is not true, because if they were not in a place they would be nowhere and thus they would seem not to exist at all.

3. Boëthius says that every created spirit needs a body. Now an angel is a created spirit. Therefore he needs a body and consequently could not exist before the corporeal creature.

4. To this it may be replied that an angel needs a body not for his existence but for his ministrations.—On the contrary, the angelic ministrations are exercised where we are, namely in this world. Now the angels have a corporeal place besides our abode, namely the empyrean heaven. Therefore it is not only in order to minister to us that they need a body in a corporeal place.

5. It is impossible to imagine 'before' and 'after' without time. Now if the angels had existed before the world, the beginning of the angels' existence would have preceded the beginning of the visible world. Consequently

time would have begun before the visible world, and that is impossible, since time follows movement, and movement is consequent to the thing moved. Therefore it was impossible for the angels to exist before the world.

On the contrary whatsoever does not involve a contradiction God can do in his creatures. Now no contradiction is involved if the angels exist while the visible creature exists not. Therefore it was not impossible for God to create the angels before the world.

I answer that, as Boëthius says (*De Trin.*) in speaking of God, we must not be led astray by our imagination, nor indeed should we in speaking of any corporeal things whatsoever: because seeing that the imagination is founded upon our senses, according to the Philosopher (*De Anima* iii, 3), it cannot rise above quantity which is the subject of sensible qualities. Through failing to note this, and to transcend their imagination, some have been unable to understand that anything can exist without being situated somewhere. For this reason some of the philosophers of old said that what is not in a place is not at all (*Phys.* iv, 3) : and through the same error some of the moderns have maintained that angels cannot exist without a corporeal creature, through thinking angels to be like things which they imagine to occupy different places. This is in contradiction with the opinion of those of old who held the angels to have existed before the world. It is also prejudicial to the dignity of the angelic nature which being naturally superior to the corporeal creature is nowise dependent thereon. Therefore absolutely speaking it was possible for the angels to exist before the world.

Reply to the First Objection. Two angels cannot be in the same place, not because they are distinct from each other, but because this would confuse their operations: hence the argument does not prove.

Reply to the Second Objection. Even now nothing prevents angels from not being in a place if they so will: although they are always in a place on account of the order by virtue of which the spiritual creature presides over the corporeal, as Augustine states (*De Trin.* iii).

Reply to the Third Objection. As Boëthius himself explains, angels need bodies only for their ministrations and not for the perfection of their nature.

Reply to the Fourth Objection. The angels are in the empyrean heaven as being a place befitting contemplation, not as though contemplation were impossible elsewhere.

Reply to the Fifth Objection. This 'before' and 'after' do not prove that there was real time before the world but only imaginary time, as we have stated above when discussing the eternity or creation of the world.

SECOND BOOK
(QUESTIONS IV–VI)

APPROBATIO ORDINIS.

NIHIL OBSTAT:
GABRIEL COYLE, O.P., S.T.L.
THOMAS GILBY, O.P., S.T.L., PH.D.

IMPRIMATUR:
BERNARDUS DELANY, O.P.,
Prior Provincialis Angliae.

In festo Sti. Bernardi.
20 *Aug.* 1933.

NIHIL OBSTAT:
GEORGIUS D. SMITH, S.TH.D., PH.D.,
Censor deputatus.

IMPRIMATUR:
✠ JOSEPH BUTT,
Vicarius generalis.

WESTMONASTERII,
die 5 *Octobris,* 1933.

CONTENTS

QUESTION IV. OF THE CREATION OF FORMLESS MATTER

ARTICLE   PAGE

I. DID THE CREATION OF FORMLESS MATTER PRECEDE IN DURATION THE CREATION OF THINGS? - - - 1

II. WAS MATTER FORMED ALL AT ONCE OR BY DEGREES? - 23

QUESTION V. OF THE PRESERVATION OF THINGS BY GOD

I. ARE THINGS PRESERVED IN THEIR BEING BY GOD? - 75

II. CAN GOD ENABLE A CREATURE TO KEEP ITSELF IN EXISTENCE BY ITSELF AND WITHOUT GOD'S ASSISTANCE? - 86

III. CAN GOD ANNIHILATE A CREATURE? - - - - 87

IV. IS THERE A CREATURE THAT OUGHT TO BE OR ACTUALLY IS ANNIHILATED? - - - - - - - 97

V. WILL THE HEAVENLY MOVEMENT CEASE AT ANY TIME? - 104

VI. CAN ANY MAN KNOW WHEN THE MOVEMENT OF THE HEAVENS WILL CEASE? - - - - - - 119

VII. WILL THE ELEMENTS REMAIN WHEN THE HEAVENS CEASE TO BE IN MOTION? - - - - - - - 125

VIII. WILL ACTION AND PASSION REMAIN IN THE ELEMENTS AFTER THE HEAVENS HAVE CEASED TO BE IN MOTION? 134

IX. WILL PLANTS, ANIMALS AND MINERALS REMAIN AFTER THE END OF THE WORLD? - - - - - 138

X. WILL HUMAN BODIES REMAIN AFTER THE HEAVENLY MOVEMENT HAS CEASED? - - - - - 145

QUESTION VI. ON MIRACLES

I. CAN GOD DO ANYTHING IN CREATURES THAT IS BEYOND NATURE, AGAINST NATURE, OR CONTRARY TO THE COURSE OF NATURE? - - - - - - 150

II. CAN EVERYTHING THAT GOD DOES WITHOUT NATURAL CAUSES OR CONTRARY TO THE COURSE OF NATURE BE CALLED A MIRACLE? - - - - - - 162

III. CAN SPIRITUAL CREATURES WORK MIRACLES BY THEIR NATURAL POWER? - - - - - - 167

IV. CAN GOOD ANGELS AND MEN WORK MIRACLES BY SOME GIFT OF GRACE? - - - - - - - 178

CONTENTS

ARTICLE	PAGE
V. DO THE DEMONS ALSO CO-OPERATE IN THE WORKING OF MIRACLES?	183
VI. HAVE ANGELS AND DEMONS BODIES NATURALLY UNITED TO THEM?	188
VII. CAN ANGELS OR DEMONS ASSUME BODIES?	201
VIII. CAN AN ANGEL OR DEMON BY MEANS OF AN ASSUMED BODY EXERCISE THE FUNCTIONS OF A LIVING BODY?	208
IX. SHOULD THE WORKING OF A MIRACLE BE ATTRIBUTED TO FAITH?	213
X. ARE DEMONS FORCED TO WORK MIRACLES BY SENSIBLE AND CORPOREAL OBJECTS, DEEDS OR WORDS?	221

ON THE POWER OF GOD

QUESTION IV
OF THE CREATION OF FORMLESS MATTER

THERE are two points of inquiry : (1) Whether the creation of formless matter preceded in duration that of things ? (2) Whether matter was informed all at once or by little and little ?

ARTICLE I
DID THE CREATION OF FORMLESS MATTER PRECEDE IN DURATION THE CREATION OF THINGS ?
Sum. Th. I, Q. lxvi, A. 1 ; QQ. lxvii, lxix

THE first point of inquiry is whether the creation of formless matter preceded in duration the creation of things : and it would seem that it did not.

1. Augustine says (*Gen. ad lit.* xv) that formless preceded informed matter as the voice precedes the song. Now the voice precedes the song not in duration but only in nature. Therefore formless matter precedes informed things not in duration but only in nature.

2. It might be said that Augustine is speaking of matter with regard to the formation that results from the elemental forms which were in matter from the very beginning.—On the contrary, as water and earth are elements, so also are fire and air. Now Scripture in referring to the formless state of matter mentions earth and water. Consequently if matter from the beginning had the forms of the elements, Scripture would also have mentioned fire and air.

3. The substantial form together with matter are the cause of the accidental qualities according to the Philosopher (*Phys.* i). Now the active and passive qualities are the accidental properties of the elements. Hence, if substantial forms were in matter from the beginning, it follows that the active and passive qualities were there also, so that there was no formlessness there apparently.

4. But it will be said that there was formlessness or confusion as regards the position of the elements.—On the contrary according to the Philosopher (*De Cælo et Mundo* iv, text. 25) every element has a place corresponding to its form : for the elements occupy their respective places by virtue of their respective forms. Hence if from the beginning matter had substantial forms, it follows that each element was in its proper place, so that there was no confusion of elements in respect of which matter could be called formless.

5. If matter be called formless for no other reason but that the elements had not yet their proper and natural place, it would seem to follow that matter is said to be informed by the fact that the elements were allotted their natural positions. But this is not verified in the work of distinction, where certain waters are placed above the heavens, whereas water's natural place is beneath the air and immediately above the earth (*De Cælo et Mundo* iv). Therefore the formless state of matter was not owing to the aforesaid confusion of place.

6. It will be said perhaps that the waters are stated to be above the heavens in so far as they are raised above them by evaporation.—On the contrary as philosophers prove, the vaporised waters cannot be raised above the entire atmosphere, in fact they do not rise more than half way : and consequently much less can they rise above fire and yet further above the heavens.

7. The formless state of matter is expressed in the words (Gen. i, 2), *The earth was void and empty.* Now matter is said to be void in respect of the power of production, and to be empty in respect of adornment, according to the explanation of holy men, so that the text refers to the things that move on the face of the earth. Consequently the formless condition

of matter does not refer to place, nor did it precede in duration the formation of matter.

8. He who can give all at once is less liberal if he give by degrees, wherefore it is written (Prov. iii, 28) : *Say not to thy friend : Go and come again, and to-morrow I will give to thee.* Now God was able to give perfect being to things at once. Hence since he is supremely liberal he did not make matter formless before giving it a form.

9. Movement from centre to centre results from the elements occupying their natural position. Now the formless state of matter gives evidence that there was movement from centre to centre, because the vaporised waters as we are told arose above the earth. Therefore the elements had already their natural positions.

10. Rarity and density are the causes of things being heavy and light (*Phys.* iv). Now rarity and density were already in the elements, for we are told that the waters were more rarefied than now. Therefore things were heavy or light, and the elements had their respective positions which belong to them according as they are heavy or light.

11. In this formless condition of things it is clear that the earth had its position, and we are given to understand that it was covered with the waters when we read (Gen. i, 9) : *Let the waters that are under the heaven be gathered together into one place, and let the dry land appear.* Therefore the other elements likewise had their respective positions so that there was no formlessness in matter.

12. From a perfect agent issues a perfect effect, since every agent produces its like. Now God is the most perfect agent. Therefore from the very first he produced perfect matter, which consequently was formed since the form is the perfection of matter.

13. If formless matter preceded the formation of things in duration, matter existing in that condition either was entirely devoid of form, or it had some kind of form. If it was altogether without form, it was only potential and not actual, and consequently it was not yet created, since existence is the term of creation. If, on the other hand, it had some kind of form, this was either an elemental form, or the form of a

mixed body. If it was an elemental form, it had either one form or several. If several, there was already diversity on account of the divers elemental forms. If one only, it follows that one particular elemental form naturally precedes the others in matter, and thus one element would be the origin of the others. This was the theory of the early physicists who held that there is only one element, and this is refuted by the Philosopher (*De Gener. et Corrup.* ii). And if it had the form of a mixed body, it follows that the form of a compound naturally precedes the elemental forms in matter : and this is clearly false, because a compound is made by something that sets the elements in motion so as to produce the form of the compound. Therefore it is impossible that matter was at first formless and afterwards formed.

14. It will be said perhaps that matter had the elemental forms but not in the same way as now, since the waters were more rarefied, and in the form of vapour, mixed with the air.—On the contrary, each elemental form requires a particular measure of rarity or density that is essential to it. Now the rarity which enables a thing to rise into the air surpasses the condition of water which is naturally heavier than air. Consequently if the waters were so rarefied that in the shape of vapour they rose into the air, they no longer retained the nature of water : and thus the elemental forms were not in matter, whereas we have stated the contrary to be the case.

15. The various kinds of things were formed from formless matter during the works of the six days. Now among the works of the six days the firmament was formed on the second day. Hence, if formless matter was subject to the elemental forms it would follow that the heavens were made from the four elements, and this is refuted by the Philosopher (*De Cœlo et Mundo* i).

16. The natural body is compared to its shape as matter to its form. Now a natural body cannot be without a shape. Therefore matter cannot be without a form.

17. If matter was without a form when it was first created, the gathering of the waters which took place on the third day would never have been. But this would seem impossible :

because if the waters covered the earth on all sides, there was no place into which they could be gathered together. Hence seemingly formless matter did not precede the formation of things. That the waters covered the earth on all sides is apparent from the fact that the elements were separate (*De Cælo et Mundo* iii, text. 56).

18. It will be said perhaps that there were hollow places under the surface of the earth into which the waters subsided, so that the earth provided a place for the waters to congregate.—On the contrary such hollows or caverns in the earth are caused by rocks upholding the surface and preventing it from subsiding: and this could not apply to the case in point since rocks are compounded of the elements, and it would follow that mixed bodies existed before the formation of the elements. Therefore such cavernous places were impossible.

19. If there were such hollow places in the earth they could not be empty: and so they would be full of air or water: and this would seem to be impossible since it is contrary to the nature of either to be underneath the earth.

20. The water that covered the earth on all sides was either in its natural place or not. If it was, it could not be removed thence except by violence, since otherwise than by force a body is not moved from where it rests naturally. But this is not in keeping with the original institution of things whereby nature was established, since nature is incompatible with violence. On the other hand if this position of the water was violent, the water could by its nature return to the disposition which it lacked, since a thing returns naturally from a place in which it is situated by force. Consequently the gathering together of the waters into one place should not be ascribed to the work of formation.

21. Things were created in accordance with their natural order. Now distinction is naturally prior to confusion, thus a simple thing is naturally prior to a compound. Hence it was not fitting to the institution of things that they should be at first in a state of confusion and afterwards be made distinct.

22. A process from actuality to potentiality is more suitable to the corruption of things than to their institution: because things are made by becoming actual from being potential. Now to proceed from compound things to the elements, is to proceed from the actual to the potential, since the elements are as matter in relation to the form of the compound. Therefore it was not suitable to the institution of things that they should first of all be in a state of confusion and composition, and afterwards be made distinct.

23. This would seem to savour of the errors of the ancient philosophers: namely of Empedocles who held that the parts of the world were divided from one another by repulsion whereas previously they had been united by attraction: and of Anaxagoras who held that at first all things formed one mass, and that afterwards the mind began to make distinctions by analysing this confused and composite mass. These opinions have been sufficiently refuted by later philosophers. Therefore we must not hold that by a priority of duration matter was in a formless and confused state before its information.

1. On the contrary Gregory (*Moral.* xxxii) commenting on Ecclus. xviii, 1: *He that liveth for ever created all things together*, says that all things were created together in their substantial matter but not in their specific form: and this would not be unless the substantial matter existed before receiving specific forms. Therefore formless matter preceded the formation of things in point of duration.

2. Again, that which is not cannot exercise an operation. Now formless matter exercises an operation, since it is appetent of a form (*Phys.* iii). Therefore matter can be without a form, and thus it is not unreasonable to suppose that formless matter preceded the formation of things in point of duration.

3. Again, God can do more than nature. Now nature makes a potential thing to be actual. Therefore God can make that which is a being simply to be potential: and thus he could make matter without a form.

4. Again, we must not deny the existence of what Scripture declares to have been: for as Augustine says (*De Trin.* v)

no Christian contradicts the statements of Holy Writ. Now the divine Scriptures assert that at one time the earth was void and empty. Therefore we must not deny this. And in whatever sense the words be explained they imply that matter was formless. Therefore at some time the substance of matter was in existence before its formation, otherwise it would never have been formless.

5. Again, we have shown (A. 18) that spiritual and corporeal creatures were made at the same time. Now the formless state in the spiritual creature preceded its formation in point of duration. Therefore the same is to be said of the corporeal creature. The minor premise is proved as follows. The formation of the spiritual creature denotes its conversion to the Word whereby it was enlightened. And as soon as light was made light was divided from darkness, which in the spiritual creature denotes sin. But there could be no sin in the angels in the first instant of their creation, because in that case the demons would never have been good angels. Therefore the spiritual creature was not formed in the first instant of its creation.

6. Again, the material of which a thing is made precedes even in time that which is made from it. Now God created the earth from invisible matter (Gen. i, 2[1]) which according to Augustine (*Super Gen.* i, 15) was formless matter. Therefore formless matter preceded the formation of the earth. The major premise is proved thus. According to the Philosopher (*Phys.* i) things are said to be made in two ways. First thus : if I say : ' This is made so and so *per se* ' which belongs to a subject, for example, ' a man is made white ' ; or, ' This is made so and so accidentally ' namely from a privation or contrary, for example ' A not-white or a black thing is made white.' Secondly, as when I say ' This is made from so and so ' : this does not refer to the subject except by reason of a privation. For we do not say that a white man is made from a man, but that a white thing is made from a not-white or a black thing, or from a black or not-white man. Accordingly that from which a thing is made is either a privation or contrary, or it is matter subject to

[1] Septuagint version.

privation or contrary. And in either case that from which a thing is made must precede in point of time, since contraries cannot be in the same subject together, nor can matter be subject at the same time to privation and form. Therefore that from which a thing is made precedes in time that which is made from it.

7. Further, the action of nature as far as possible imitates the action of God even as the action of a second cause imitates that of the first cause. Now the process of nature's action is from the imperfect to the perfect. Therefore God also at first in order of time produced something imperfect and afterwards perfected it, and thus formless matter preceded its formation.

8. Again, Augustine says that when Scripture mentions earth and water in the words of Genesis (i, 2), *The earth was void and empty, and the spirit of God moved over the waters*, the sense is not that they were already earth and water, but that they could be. Hence primary matter at one time had not as yet the nature of earth and water, but was able to have it : and consequently matter without a form preceded its formation. I answer that as Augustine says (*Conf.* xii) this question admits of a twofold discussion, one regards the true answer to the question itself, the other regards the sense of the text in which Moses inspired by God tells the story of the world's beginning.

As to the first discussion two things are to be avoided : one is the making of false statements especially such as are contrary to revealed truth, the other is the assertion that what we think to be true is an article of faith, for as Augustine says (*Confess.* x), *when a man thinks his false opinions to be the teaching of godliness, and dares obstinately to dogmatise about matters of which he is ignorant, he becomes a stumbling block to others.* The reason why he says that such an one is a stumbling block is because the faith is made ridiculous to the unbeliever when a simple-minded believer asserts as an article of faith that which is demonstrably false, as again Augustine says in his commentary (*Gen. ad lit.* i). As regards the other discussion two things also are to be avoided. One is to give to the words of Scripture an interpretation manifestly false : since falsehood cannot underlie the divine Scriptures which we have received from the Holy Ghost, as neither can there be error in the faith that is taught by the Scriptures. The other is not to force such an interpretation on Scripture as to exclude any other interpretations that are actually or possibly true : since it is part of the dignity of Holy Writ that under the one literal sense many others are contained. It is thus that the sacred text not only adapts itself to man's various intelligence, so that each one marvels to find his thoughts expressed in the words of Holy Writ ; but also is all the more easily defended against unbelievers in that when one finds his own interpretation of Scripture to be false he can fall back upon some other. Hence it is not inconceivable that Moses and the other authors of the Holy Books were given to know the various truths that men would discover in the text, and that they expressed them under one literary style, so that each truth is the sense intended by the author. And then even if commentators adapt certain truths to the sacred text that were not understood by the author, without doubt the Holy Ghost understood them, since he is the principal author of Holy Scripture. Consequently every truth that can be adapted to the sacred text without prejudice to the literal sense, is the sense of Holy Scripture.

Having laid down these principles we must observe that commentators have given to the opening chapter of Genesis various explanations, none of which is contrary to revealed truth : and as far as concerns the question in point they may be divided into two groups in respect of their twofold interpretation of the formless state of matter indicated at the beginning of Genesis by the words, *The earth was void and empty.* Some understood these words to mean that matter was formless in the sense that it actually had no form but that all forms were in it potentially. Now matter of this kind cannot exist in nature unless it receive formation from some form : since whatever exists in nature exists actually, and actual existence comes to a thing from its form which is its act, so that nature does not contain a thing without a form. Moreover, since nothing can be included in a genus that is not contained specifically in some division of the genus, matter cannot be a being unless it be determined to some specific mode of being, and this cannot be without a form. Consequently if formless matter be understood in this sense it could not possibly precede its formation in point of duration, but only by priority of nature, inasmuch as that from which something is made naturally precedes that which is made from it, even as night was created first. This was the view taken by Augustine. Others took the view that the formless state of matter does not denote absence of all form in matter, but the absence of natural finish and comeliness : in which sense it is quite possible that matter was in a formless state before it was formed. This would seem in keeping with the wise ordering of its Maker who in producing things out of nothing did not at once bring them from nothingness to the ultimate perfection of their nature, but at first gave them a kind of imperfect being, and afterwards perfected them : thus showing not only that they received their being from God so as to refute those who assert that matter is uncreated ; but also that they derive their perfection from him, so as to refute those who ascribe the formation of this lower world to other causes. Such was the view of Basil the Great, Gregory and others who followed them. Since, however, neither opinion is in conflict with revealed truth, and since both are compatible with the context, while admitting that neither may be held, we must now deal with the arguments advanced on both sides.

Reply to the First Objection. Augustine is speaking of formless matter as devoid of all form, in which case we must needs say that its formless state preceded its formation by priority of nature alone. In the next Article we shall state his view on the order of the formation.

Reply to the Second Objection. There are several opinions on this point. Philo is said to have understood that the Book of Genesis in mentioning the number and order of the elements speaks of earth and water in the strict sense. The waters are indicated as being above the earth, since it is written (i, 9) : *Let the waters be gathered together into their own place, and let the dry land appear.* Above these two he places

CREATION OF FORMLESS MATTER

the air as being mentioned in the words : *The Spirit of the Lord moved over the waters*, where he takes ' spirit ' to denote the air : and takes the ' heaven ' to mean fire, because it is located above all the others. Seeing however that Aristotle proved (*De Cælo* i) that the heavens cannot be made of fire, as indicated by their circular movement, Rabbi Moses agrees with Aristotle, and while adopting Philo's view as to the three first elements, contended that fire is denoted by the darkness, because in its own sphere fire does not give light : and he holds that the situation of fire is indicated in the words : *Upon the face of the deep*. He holds also that by the heavens we are to understand the Fifth Essence.

As Basil, however (*Hom.* ii, *in Hexæm.*), observes that Scripture is not wont to signify the air by the *Spirit of the Lord*, and that by mentioning the extremes it implies the intermediate elements : and with reason inasmuch as it is evident to the senses that water and earth are bodies, whereas air and fire are not so intelligible to unlettered minds such as those for whose instructions the Scriptures were given.

According to Augustine (*Dial.* lxv, qu. 21) the earth and water mentioned before the formation of light, do not denote the completely formed elements, but formless matter void of all species. Moreover the formless state of matter is signified by these two elements rather than the others, because they are more akin to a formless state as having more matter and less form, and again because they are better known to us and indicate to us more clearly the matter of the other elements. Also formless matter is signified by two rather than by one element only, lest if one only were mentioned we might be led to think that this one alone was formless matter.

Reply to the Third Objection. In the opinion of Basil and other holy men the formless state of things in the beginning did not imply that the elements lacked their natural qualities : since each had its respective forms both substantial and accidental.

Reply to the Fourth Objection. The situation of the elements may be considered in two ways. First as regards their respective natures : and in this way fire naturally contains air, air water, and water earth. Secondly, as regards the necessity of generation which belongs to the middle place : and thus it is necessary that the surface of the earth be partly covered by water, so as to favour the generation and preservation of mixed bodies, especially of perfect animals which require air for breathing. We must reply, then, that this primordial formless state did not affect the situation natural to the elements considered in themselves (for all the elements had it) but the situation that was competent to them in respect of the generation of mixed bodies. This situation was not perfect as yet, seeing that mixed bodies had not yet been produced.

Reply to the Fifth Objection. With regard to the waters that are above the heavens there have been various opinions. Origen is credited with the view that they denote spiritual natures. But this cannot be reconciled with the text, since it is not competent to the nature of a spiritual being to occupy a situation, as though the firmament intervened between them and the lower corporeal waters, according to the text (i, 6). Hence others hold that the firmament signifies the neighbouring airy sky above which the waters are raised by evaporation and become rain-clouds : and then the airy heaven stands between the higher vaporised waters that float in the space of the mid-air, and the aqueous body which is seen to be situated on the earth. Rabbi Moses agrees with this explanation, which nevertheless would seem to be incompatible with the context : since the text goes on to say (verses 16, 17) that God made two great lights and the stars, and that he set them in the firmament of the heaven. Consequently others maintain that the firmament signifies the starry heaven, and that the waters situated above the heavens are of the same nature as the elemental waters, but that they are set there by divine providence in order to temper the power of the fire of which they held the entire heaven to consist, according to Basil. In support of this view some according to Augustine (*Gen. ad lit.* ii, 4, 5) advanced two arguments. One was that since water by means of evaporation can rise into mid-air where the rains are produced, if it be yet more rarefied and divided into yet smaller particles (for it is indefinitely divisible like all continuous bodies) it will be able by reason of its rarefaction to rise above the starry heaven, and remain there in a position becoming to its nature. The other argument is that in the star Saturn, whose heat must be extreme on account of the rapidity of its movement by reason of the length of its orbit, the effects of cold are observed, and they pretend that this is occasioned by the neighbourhood of the water which has a cooling effect on this star.

But this explanation we consider to be defective in that it ascribes to the Scriptures statements that are proved evidently to be false.—First, as regards position, for it would seem to upset the natural situation of bodies. Because since a body should occupy a higher position according as it is more formal, it would seem inconsistent with the nature of things that water, which is the most material of all bodies with the exception of earth, should be set even above the starry heaven. Moreover it would seem out of keeping that things of the same species should be allotted different natural places, which would be the case if the element of water were partly immediately above the earth and partly above the heavens. Nor is it enough to reply that God by his omnipotence upholds those waters against their nature, above the heavens, since we are discussing the nature that God gave to things, and not the miracles that he may have been pleased to work in them ; as Augustine says (*ibid*. ii, 1). —Secondly, the argument about rarefaction and divisibility of the waters is altogether futile. For though mathematical bodies are indefinitely divisible, natural bodies have a fixed term to their divisibility, since every form demands a certain quantity even as other accidents in accordance with its nature. Hence neither can rarefaction of water continue indefinitely, but it reaches a fixed term which is the rarity of fire. Moreover, water might continue to be rarefied until it was no longer water, but air or fire, if the bounds of water's rarity were exceeded. Nor would it be possible for water naturally to rise above the positions of air and fire, unless it lost the nature of water so as to surpass their rarity. Nor again would it be possible for an elemental body which is corruptible to become more formal than the heavens which are incorruptible, and thus be set above them naturally.—Thirdly, the second argument is utterly trivial. Heavenly bodies as philosophers show are not susceptible to impressions from foreign bodies. And it was impossible for Saturn to be cooled by those waters, without the stars of the eighth sphere being affected by them in the same way: whereas many of these stars are observed to have a heating influence.

Wherefore one would prefer to offer an explanation which would leave the text of Scripture unassailable, by suggesting that those waters are not of the same nature as our elemental water, but are of the nature of the Fifth Essence, being transparent like the waters here below, even as the empyrean shines like our fire. Some call them crystalline, not that they are frozen into the form of crystals, since according to Basil (*Hom.* iii *in Hexæm.*) only a silly child or an imbecile could imagine such things about the heavens: but on account of their solidity, even as it is written about all the heavens (Job xxxvii, 18) that they are *strong as though they were made of molten brass*. This heaven according to astronomers is the ninth sphere. Hence Augustine does not adopt any of these explanations but dismisses them as doubtful; thus he says (*ibid.* 5): *Howsoever these waters may be there and of what kind they may be, one thing is certain, they are there. Surely the written Word has greater authority than the combined genius of men.*

The *Sixth Objection* we grant.

Reply to the Seventh Objection. If according to the exposition of Basil (*Hom.* iv *in Hexæm.*) and his followers we take the earth to signify the element of earth, we may consider it first as the principle from which certain things originate, plants for instance, of which it is the mother so to speak (*De Veget.*) so that in their respect it was void before it produced them, since we say that a thing is void or vain if it fail to attain its proper effect or end. Secondly, we may consider it as the abode and place of animals, in respect of which it is described as empty.—Or, according to the text of the Septuagint which reads '*invisible* and *incomposite,*' part of the earth was invisible through being covered with water, as also because light was not yet produced so as to render it visible ; while it was incomposite because there were as yet no plants and animals to adorn it, nor was it as yet a fit place for their generation and conservation. If, however, the earth signifies primary matter, as Augustine maintains (*Dial.* lxv, qu. 21), then it is said to be void in comparison with the composite body in which it subsists, because a void is opposite to firmness and solidity ; while it is described as being empty in comparison with the forms which were lacking to its potentiality. Hence Plato (*Tim.*) compares the receptivity of matter to place, inasmuch as place received that which is located therein : and ' empty ' and ' full ' are terms which are properly applied to a place. Again matter considered in its formless condition is described as invisible, inasmuch as it lacks form which is the principle of all knowledge ; and incomposite since it only subsists in a composite state.

Reply to the Eighth Objection. It pertains to the liberality of a giver not only that he give quickly, but also that he give ordinately and each gift at a suitable time. Hence when the text continues, *When thou canst give at present*, we must understand the possibility not only of giving absolutely, but also of giving most suitably. Wherefore, in order to observe a suitable order God gave his creatures at first an imperfect state, so that by degrees they might proceed from nothingness to perfection.

Reply to the Ninth Objection. As we have already stated the situation connatural to the elements was in the elements : hence the objection does not avail against this opinion.

The same answer applies *to the Tenth and Eleventh Objections.*

Reply to the Twelfth Objection. A perfect agent produces a perfect effect : but this effect need not be simply perfect from the very beginning as regards its nature, and it will suffice if it be perfect in keeping with that stage of its existence : even so a child may be described as perfect immediately after its birth.

Reply to the Thirteenth Objection. According to the view

that we are defending for the nonce matter is not said to be formless as though it were devoid of all form ; or as though it had but one form—either with a potentiality to all forms, as the ancient physicists maintained who asserted that there was only one primary element ;—or virtually containing many other forms, as happens in mixed bodies. The various elemental forms were in various parts of matter, which nevertheless was said to be formless, because it had not as yet received the forms of mixed bodies, to which forms the forms of the elements were in potentiality : and because the elements were not as yet suitably placed for the production of such bodies, as we have already stated.

Reply to the Fourteenth Objection. Nothing, not even the authority of the book of Genesis or any argument of reason, binds us to say that at the beginning the elemental forms were not in matter in the same way as they are now : although possibly vapours arose from the waters, as happens now, and then perhaps in greater volume seeing that the earth was wholly covered by the waters.

Reply to the Fifteenth Objection. There are several opinions about the firmament which was created on the second day.

Some hold that this firmament is not distinct from the heaven which is stated to have been made on the first day : and they contend that Scripture at first announces the works collectively, and afterwards explains how they were done in the course of the six days. This is the view expressed by Basil in his *Hexæmeron*.

Others maintain that the firmament created on the second day is distinct from the heaven stated to have been made on the first, and this view admits of a threefold explanation.—Some asserted that the heaven created on the first day signifies the spiritual creature whether formed or still unformed, and that the firmament fashioned on the second day is the corporeal heaven that we see. This is the opinion of Augustine (*Gen. ad lit.* i, 9 : *Confess.* xii).—Others contend that the heaven created on the first day is the empyrean, and that the firmament created on the second day is the starry heaven visible to us. This is the view of

Strabo (*Gloss. Ord. in* Gen. i).—Others maintain that the heaven made on the first day is the starry heaven, and that the firmament made on the second day signifies the region of the air in the neighbourhood of the earth, and separating waters from waters, as stated above. Augustine alludes to this opinion (*Gen. ad lit.* ii, 1) which is that of Rabbi Moses. If this last explanation be adopted it is easy to solve the difficulty : because the firmament made on the second day has not the nature of the fifth essence, so that, as regards the firmament, there is no reason why in its production there should not have been a process from formlessness to formation, whether in respect of rarefaction through the rising vapours being diminished by the gathering together of the waters, or in respect of its position through the air taking the place of the receding waters. On the other hand in the case of the first three opinions which hold the firmament to denote the starry heaven, there is no need to ascribe to the heaven a process from formlessness to formation, as though it acquired a new form, since Scripture does not bind us to ascribe such a process to the lower elements. But we must understand that the firmament was endowed with a power in respect of the generation of mixed bodies and that its formation consisted in this : even as we have already said about the formation of the lower elements in relation to the generation of mixed bodies (*ad* 4, *ad* 13) : since as the lower elements are the matter from which mixed bodies are formed, so the firmament is the active cause of mixed bodies. Hence we may take the division of the lower from the higher waters to be like that of two extremes which are distinguished from each other by a mean that has some affinity with both. Thus the lower waters are subject to change inasmuch as through the movement of the firmament they become the matter of mixture, whereas the higher waters are not. According to the opinion of Augustine (*Super Gen.* ii, 11) if we suppose formless matter to have preceded its formation in point of time, there is no great difficulty, since we must ascribe some kind of matter to a heavenly body, seeing that the latter also has movement. Hence there is nothing to prevent such matter preceding its formation by priority of nature, although no kind of formation accrued to it from time. Nor are we therefore bound to say that the heavenly body and the lower elements have one nature in common, although they have a common name, earth or water for instance, in the opinion of Augustine : because this unity is not one of substance but of proportion in so far as any matter is considered from the viewpoint of its potentiality to its form.

Reply to the Sixteenth Objection. This is clear from what has already been said, since the formless condition of matter does not imply that it is devoid of all form but is to be taken as already explained.

Reply to the Seventeenth Objection. The opinion of Augustine (*Dial.* lv, qu. 21) who held that the earth and water previously mentioned signify not the elements but primary matter is not incompatible with the gathering together of the waters. Thus he says himself (*Gen. ad lit.* ii, 7, 8) that as the words *Let a firmament be made* indicate the formation of the heavenly bodies on the second day, so the words *Let the waters be gathered together* signify the formation of the lower elements on the third day. Hence as the words *Let the waters be gathered together* mean that the water received its form, so the words *Let the dry land appear* denote the same with regard to the earth. The reason for these words being used in the formation of these elements instead of words significant of making—e.g. ' Let water ' or ' earth be made '—as when the heaven was mentioned, e.g.—*Let a firmament be made*, was in order to indicate the imperfection of their forms and their affinity to formless matter. The expression *gathered together* is used in connection with water to denote its mobility ; and the word *appear* in connection with the earth to signify its stability. Hence Augustine says (*Gen. ad lit.* ii, 11) : *Of the waters it is said ' Let them be gathered together ' and of the earth ' Let it appear,'* because *water glides and flows away, whereas the earth abides.*

If, however, we adopt the view of Basil and other holy men who said that in both cases the same earth is signified, and likewise the same water but differently disposed before and after, several replies are suggested. Some said that part of the earth was not under water, and that the waters which covered the inhabitable parts were by God's command gathered together thither. This is disproved from the text itself by Augustine (*Super Genes.* i, 12) who says : *If part of the earth was bare whither the waters could be gathered together, then the dry land appeared already and this is contrary to the context.* Hence others said that the waters were rarefied and nebulous and afterwards condensed and gathered into a smaller place. But this involves no less a difficulty, both because they were not real waters if they had the form of vapour, and because they would have occupied a place in the air, and the difficulty remains to find a place for the air. Consequently others say that there were hollow places in the earth which by God's operation could receive the multitude of waters. But against this would seem to be the fact that it is accidental if one part of the earth be further than another from the centre : whereas in this formation of things they received their natural shape, as Augustine says (*Super. Genes*, vi, 6). Wherefore it would seem better to hold with Basil (*Hom.* iv, *in Hexæm.*) that the waters were distributed over various parts of the earth and afterwards *gathered together*, an explanation which would seem to be warranted by the text making use of this expression : for even if the waters covered the whole earth, they would not need to be everywhere as deep as they are now in some parts.

Reply to the Eighteenth Objection. Seeing that mineral bodies do not show any evident superiority of excellence over the elements as living bodies do, they are not described as having been formed apart from the elements, and we understand them to have been produced at the same time as the elements. Hence nothing prevents the existence of hollow places before the waters were gathered together, so that the earth could afterwards provide room for the waters to be gathered together in the depressions of its surface. However, the words used by Augustine in his allusion to this view (*Gen. ad lit.* i, 12) seem to mean that these hollow places did not already exist beneath the surface, but that they were formed on the surface of the earth when the waters were gathered together. These in fact are his words : '*By subsiding in all directions the earth was able to provide these hollow places into which the waters flowing and rushing together were received, and the dry land appeared in those parts that the waters had abandoned.*' The same view is expressed by Basil (*Hom.* iv, *in Hexæm.*) : *When the waters were commanded to gather together, a place for their gathering was at once formed, so that by God's command sufficient place was provided to receive the confluence of the many waters.* It may be that sufficient place was made by the depressions in the earth's surface, even as certain parts are accidentally higher as hills and mountains.

Reply to the Nineteenth Objection. If the hollow places did not already exist in accordance with what we have said in the last reply, this objection is to no purpose. If, however, they were already in existence we reply that altogether it is unnatural for water or air to be situated beneath the earth if this be left to itself, it is not so if the earth be hindered somewhat in its movement. Thus in caverns beneath the earth we find that the earth is supported by pillars which arise through the air from the floor, since nature abhors a vacuum. But if it be contended that the shallow waters spread over the whole surface of the earth were subsequently gathered together into greater depths, as stated above, these objections will fall to the ground.

Reply to the Twentieth Objection. If we consider the situation natural to the elements and befitting their nature absolutely, then it is natural for water to cover the whole earth on all sides just as it is natural for the air to cover the waters. But if we consider the elements in relation to the generation of mixed bodies, in which the heavenly bodies also take an active part, then their natural situation is that which was given to them afterwards. Hence as soon as the dry land appeared in some part of the earth we are told at once that the plants were produced. That the heavenly bodies should exercise an active influence on the elements is not contrary to nature, as the Commentator says (*De Cœl. et Mund.* iii) : thus the ebb and flow of the sea, although it is not the natural movement of water as a heavy body, since it is not towards the centre, nevertheless is natural to water as moved by a heavenly body instrumentally. Much more truly may this be said of the divine action on the elements whose whole nature subsists thereby. As regards the point at issue both these actions would seem to concur in the gathering together of the waters, the divine action principally, and that of the heavenly body in a subordinate degree. Hence immediately after the formation of the firmament the text refers to the gathering of the waters together. Moreover the very nature of water furnishes us with a likely explanation. In the elements the container is more formal than the content, according to the Philosopher (*Phys.* viii); hence water fails to be a perfect container of the earth in so far as it is not so perfectly formal, as fire and air, being more akin to the density of the earth than to the rarity of fire.

Reply to the Twenty-first Objection. The state of confusion ascribed to the world in its beginning, did not consist in a mingling of the elements, but was by way of contrast with the present state of things, the various parts of the world being distinct from one another and favourable to the generation and preservation of living beings.

This suffices for the *Replies to the Twenty-second and Twenty-third Objections.*

We must now deal with the arguments on the other side which support Augustine's view.

1. Gregory's words express the view that we have already upheld. They do not mean, however, that when things were first created the matter of all things was made devoid of all specific forms, but without certain forms, namely those of living things, and without the order requisite for their generation, as we have explained above (*ad* 4, *ad* 13).

2. Appetence of form is not an act of matter but a certain relationship in matter in respect of a form, in so far as matter has the form potentially, as the Commentator states (*Phys.* i, 81).

3. Were God to make a mere potential being he would do less than nature which makes actual beings. The perfection of all actions depends on the term to which it tends rather than that from which it originates. Moreover the very

argument involves a contradiction, namely that anything be made that is pure potentiality: since what has been made must needs be so long as it is (*Phys.* vi): and what is purely potential, is not simply.

4. If, as Augustine holds, the words of Scripture, *The earth was void and empty* signify matter utterly devoid of form we are not to suppose that it was ever actually so, but that its nature was such if we consider it apart from inherent forms.

5. The formation of a spiritual creature may be understood in two ways: first by the infusion of grace, secondly by the consummation glory. The first, according to Augustine's opinion, was bestowed on the spiritual creature from the first moment of its creation: and in that case the darkness from which the light was divided does not signify the sin of the wicked angels, but the formless state of the nature, which was not formed as yet but remained to be formed by subsequent works (*Gen. ad lit.* i). —Or, as he says elsewhere (*ibid.* iv) the day signifies God's knowledge, and the night the creature's knowledge which is indeed darkness in comparison with God's (*ibid.*). Or, if the darkness signifies the sinful angels, then this distinction refers to their sin not as actually committed but as foreseen by God: wherefore he says in his work addressed to Orosius (*Dial.* lxv *QQ.* qu. 24): *Foreseeing that some of the angels would fall through pride, by the ordinance of his unfailing prescience he divided the good from the bad, calling the bad darkness and the good light.*

The second formation does not belong to the creation of things at the beginning, but rather to their continuation and government by divine providence. For this last, according to Augustine, is true of all those things in which the operation of nature is required, namely that they come at length to this formation: because by the movement of their free-will some turned to God and remained standing, others turned from him and fell.

6. The world is said to have been made of invisible matter, not that formless matter preceded the world in point of time, but by priority of nature. Likewise privation was not at

any time in matter before the advent of a form, but matter taken as formless is taken as having a privation.

7. It is owing to the imperfection of nature that operates by movement that it proceeds from the imperfect to the perfect: because movement is the act of that which is imperfect. God, however, by reason of the perfection of his power was able at once to give being to perfect things: hence the comparison fails.

8. The words of Augustine do not mean that matter was in such potentiality to the elemental forms that it had none of them: but that considered in its essence it includes no form actually, but is in potentiality to them all.

ARTICLE II

WAS MATTER FORMED ALL AT ONCE OR BY DEGREES?
Sum. Th. I, Q. lxvii-lxxii

THE second point of inquiry is whether matter was formed all at once or by degrees: and seemingly it was formed by degrees.

1. It is written (Judith ix, 4) *Thou hast done the things of old and hast devised one thing after another.* Now, with God to devise is to act according to Damascene (*De Fide Orthod.* ii, 3) hence the text quoted continues: *And what thou hast designed hath been done.* Therefore things were made in a certain order and not all at once.

2. Several parts of time cannot be together at once, because the whole of time is successive. Now according to Genesis i, things were formed at various times. Therefore seemingly things were formed by degrees and not all at once.

3. It will be said, perhaps, that according to Augustine (*De Civ. Dei* ii, 7, 9) those six days are not the days or divisions of time to which we are accustomed, but a six-fold manifestation of things to the angelic mind corresponding to the six classes of things[1]—On the contrary day is caused by the presence of light, whereupon it is written (Gen. 1, 5)

[1] *Sum. Theol.*, P. I, Q. lviii, art. 6.

that God *called the light day*. And light properly speaking is not found in spiritual creatures but only in a metaphorical sense. Therefore neither can the angels' knowledge be called day properly speaking. Consequently it would seem not to be a literal exposition of the text to take day as signifying the angelic knowledge. The minor premise is proved thus: Nothing that is a direct object of the senses properly is applicable to the spiritual world: for such things as are common to sense and spirit are not sensible except indirectly, for instance substance, power, virtue and the like. Now light is the direct object of the sense of sight. Hence it cannot be applied properly speaking to spiritual things.

4. An angel has two ways of knowing things, in the Word and in their own nature: consequently ' day ' must refer to the one or the other. It cannot signify his knowledge of things in the Word since this is only one in relation to all those things: because an angel, whatsoever things he knows, knows them simultaneously and by one knowledge, seeing that he knows them in the Word. Thus there would be but one day. On the other hand if it refer to his knowledge of things in their respective natures, it would follow that there were many more than six days, inasmuch as there are many genera and species of creatures. Hence it would seem that the six days cannot refer to the angelic knowledge.

5. It is written (Exod. xx, 9, 10): *Six days shalt thou labour . . ., but on the seventh day is the Sabbath of the Lord thy God: thou shalt do no work on it:* and afterwards the reason is given (verse 11): *For in six days the Lord made heaven and earth and the sea and all things that are in them, and rested on the seventh day.* Now in permitting work on six days and forbidding it on the seventh the Law speaks of days in the literal and material sense. Therefore the days ascribed to God's works are to be taken in the material sense.

6. If day signifies the angels' knowledge it follows that to make a thing in a day is nothing else but to produce it in the knowledge of the angels. But it does not follow that if a thing is produced in the angels' knowledge it therefore exists in its own nature, but only that it is known by the angels. Consequently we should not be informed about the creation

of things in their respective natures, which is contrary to Scripture.

7. The knowledge of any single angel differs from that of any other. If then day signifies an angel's knowledge, there should be as many days as there are angels, and not only six as Scripture tells us.

8. Augustine (*Gen. ad lit.* ii, 7, 8) says that by the words, *God said: Let . . . be made* we are to understand that the thing to be made pre-existed in the Word : that by the words, *It was so* we understand that knowledge of the thing was produced in the intellectual creature : and by the words, *God made* we understand that the thing was made in itself. If then *day* signifies the angels' knowledge, then having said of this or that work, *And it was so* in reference to the angelic knowledge, it was superfluous to add, *The evening and morning were the first*—or the *second day*.

9. But it will be said that these words are added to indicate the spiritual creature's twofold manner of knowing things. One is his knowledge of things in the Word and this is called morning, or morning knowledge : the other is his knowledge of things in their respective nature, and this is called evening, or evening knowledge.—On the contrary, though an angel can at the same time consider several things in the Word, he cannot at the same time consider several things in his own nature, since he understands different things in their respective natures by means of different species. If then each of the six days has both morning and evening, there must needs have been some kind of succession in the six days, and consequently the formation of things did not take place all at once.

10 Several actions cannot proceed from one power at the same time, any more than one straight line can terminate at one end in more than one point : since power terminates in action. Now the consideration of things in the Word and in their respective natures is not one but several actions. Therefore morning and evening knowledge are not simultaneous, and thus again it follows that there was succession in those six days.

11. As stated above (A. 1) Augustine explains the division

of light from darkness as that of the formed creature from the informed matter which had yet to be formed: so that after one creature had been formed on the part of its matter there still remained another creature to be formed, and consequently matter was not formed all at once.

12. According to Augustine the angels' morning knowledge signifies their knowledge of the Word in whom they knew the creatures yet to be made. But this would not be the case if the creatures whose formation is assigned to the following days were formed at the same time as the angels. Therefore all things were not created at the same time.

13. In spiritual matters a day is spoken of by way of comparison with the material day. Now in the material day morning precedes evening. Therefore in these days evening should not have been mentioned before the morning: *Evening and morning were the first day.*

14. Between evening and morning is night, and between morning and evening is midday. Hence as Scripture mentions evening and morning, it should have mentioned midday also.

15. Every material day has both evening and morning. But this is not the case with these seven days: for the first has no morning, and the seventh has no evening. Therefore it is unreasonable to compare these days with ours.

16. It might be said that the first day has no morning because morning signified that knowledge of the creature yet to be made which the angel received from the Word: and, before being made, the spiritual creature could not receive from the Word any knowledge of its own future making.—On the contrary from this it follows that the angel at one time existed whereas other creatures were not yet made, but were still to be made. Therefore all things were not made at the same time.

17. The spiritual creature does not acquire knowledge of things beneath it from those things themselves: and thus he does not need their presence in order to know them. Consequently before those things were made he could know them as things to be made in their respective nature and not only in the Word: so that knowledge of a thing to be made

would seem to belong to the evening as well as the morning knowledge: and thus according to the foregoing exposition, the second day should have had neither morning nor evening.

18. Those things which are first simply are first in an angel's knowledge: since the fact that things which are last are first known to us is due to our acquiring knowledge through our senses. Now the types of things in the Word are simply prior to the things in themselves. Therefore the angels' knowledge of things in the Word precedes his knowledge of things in their respective natures and consequently the morning should have been mentioned before the evening and this is contrary to the text of Scripture.

19. Things that differ specifically cannot combine to form one. Now knowledge of things in the Word and in their respective natures differ specifically, since the medium of knowledge is entirely different in either case: and, consequently, according to the foregoing exposition, morning and evening could not make one day.

20. The Apostle (1 Cor. xiii, 8, 10) says that *knowledge will be destroyed* in heaven: and this only refers to the knowledge of things in their respective natures, which is the evening knowledge. Now in heaven we shall be as the angels (Mat. xxii, 30). Therefore evening knowledge is not in the angels.

21. Knowledge of things in the Word surpasses knowledge of them in their respective natures more than the sun's brightness surpasses candle-light. But sunlight renders useless the light of a candle: and therefore much more does the morning knowledge of the angels render their evening knowledge useless.

22. Augustine (*Gen. ad lit.* vii, 24, 25) queries whether Adam's soul were made apart from his body at the same time as the angels or at the same time as his body. But there would be no purpose in discussing this question if all things were made at the same time, because then the human body was made at the same time as the angels. It would seem then that in Augustine's opinion all things were not made at the same time.

23. The portion of earth from which man's body was made

had the form of slime according to Genesis ii, 7 : and it had not yet the form of a human body. Therefore forms were not all at the same time produced in matter.

24. An angel's knowledge of a thing in its own nature can be no other but his knowledge through the species bestowed on him by nature : for it cannot be said that he acquires species from the things perceived, since he lacks sensorial organs. Now these species bestowed on the angels are independent of corporeal things : and thus even before things existed angels could know them in their respective natures. Consequently from the fact that angels knew a thing in its own nature we cannot argue that it was brought into being : wherefore the explanation given above would seem unreasonable.

25. The morning knowledge whereby the angels knew things in the Word must needs have been through some species, since all knowledge is such. Now it could not be through a species issuing from the Word, because such a species would be a creature, so that the knowledge produced by it would be evening rather than morning knowledge, since evening knowledge is that which is produced by means of a creature. Nor may it be said that the aforesaid knowledge was acquired by means of a species that is the Word himself, since in that case the angel would see the Word; which he did not do before he was beatified, because the beatific vision consists in seeing the Word. But the angels were not beatified in the first instant of their creation, as neither did the demons sin in that first instant. Therefore if morning signifies the knowledge which angels have in the Word, we must infer that all things were not created at the same time.

26. It will be said, perhaps, that in that instant the angels saw the Word as the type of things to be created, but not as the end of the Blessed.—On the contrary there is only a relative difference between the Word considered as end and considered as type. Now the knowledge of God's relation to creatures is not beatific, seeing that this relation in reality is in the creature rather than in God : and it is only the vision of the divine essence that is beatific. Consequently,

as regards the bliss of those who see the Word, it matters not whether they see him as the end of beatitude or as a type.

27. Prophets also are said to have seen the future in the *mirror of eternity*, inasmuch as they saw the divine mirror as reflecting future events : and then there would be no difference between the angel's morning knowledge and the knowledge of a prophet.

28. It is written (Gen. ii, 5) that God *made every plant of the field before it sprung up in the earth, and every herb of the ground before it grew*. Now the herbs were brought forth on the third day. Hence some things were made before the third day, and all were not made at the same time.

29. It is written (Ps. ciii, 24) that God *made all things in wisdom*. Now a wise man does things in an orderly way (*Metaph.* i, 2). Therefore, seemingly, God did not make all things together, but in order of time and by degrees.

30. It might be said that though order of time was not observed in the creation, the order of nature was.—On the contrary in the order of nature the sun, moon and stars precede the plants, for it is clear that they are causes of plants : and yet we are told that the heavenly lights were made after the plants. Therefore the order of nature was not observed.

31. The heavenly firmament naturally precedes earth and water, and yet Scripture mentions these before the firmament which we are told was made on the second day.

32. The subject naturally precedes its accident. Now light is an accident and its first subject is the firmament. Therefore the creation of light would not precede that of the firmament.

33. Animals that walk are more perfect than those which swim or fly, principally by reason of their likeness to man : and yet the creation of fishes and birds is related before that of terrestrial animals. Therefore the right order of nature was not observed.

34. Fishes and birds seemingly do not in their respective natures differ from each other more than from terrestrial animals : and yet we are told that fishes and birds were

created on the same day. Therefore the days do not correspond to various kinds of things, but rather to various successive times : and then all things were not created at the same time.

1. On the contrary it is written (Gen. ii, 4, 5) : *These are the generations of the heaven and the earth when they were created in the day that the Lord made the heaven and the earth, and every plant of the field.* Now we are told that the plants of the field were created on the third day : while heaven and earth were made on the first day, or even before all days. Hence the things made on the third day were created on the same day as those which were made on the first day or before all days : and thus in like manner all things were made at the same time.

2. Again it is written (Job xl, 10) : *Behold Behemoth whom I made with thee.* Now according to Gregory (*Moral.* xxxii, 9) Behemoth signifies the devil, who was made on the first day or before all days : while man, to whom the Lord's words are addressed, was made on the sixth day. Hence things made on the sixth day were created together with those that were made on the first day : and so we arrive at the same conclusion as before.

3. Again, parts of the universe depend on one another, especially the lower on the higher parts. Therefore it was impossible for some parts to be made before others, especially the lower before the higher.

4. Again there is a greater difference between corporeal and spiritual creatures than between one corporeal creature and another. Now, as we have already shown, the spiritual and corporeal creatures were made at the same time. Therefore, a fortiori, all spiritual creatures were made at the same time.

5. Again by reason of the immensity of his power God works in an instant : and thus the work of each day was accomplished suddenly and instantaneously. Therefore there is no sense in saying that he waited until the next day to do his next work, and remained idle for a whole day.

6. Further if the days mentioned in the story of the creation were ordinary days, it is difficult to understand how

the night could be wholly distinct from the day, and light from darkness. For if the light which we are told was made on the first day enveloped the whole earth, nowhere was there darkness, which is the earth's shadow cast on the side opposite to the light that causes day. And if that light by its movement revolved around the earth so as to cause day and night, then there was always day on one side, and night on the other, and consequently night was not wholly divided from the day, and this is contrary to Scripture.

7. Again the division between day and night is caused by the sun and other heavenly luminaries, wherefore it is written in the story of the fourth day (verse 14) : *Let there be lights made in the firmament of the heaven* and the text continues *and let them be for signs and for seasons and for days and years.* Seeing then that the effect does not precede its cause, it cannot be that the first three days were of the same kind as the days which are regulated by the sun : and consequently the mention of those days is no proof that things were made one after the other.

8. Moreover if then there was some other light which by its movement caused day and night, there must have been some vehicle with a circular movement to carry this other light and cause a succession of day and night. Now this vehicle would be the firmament which we are told was made on the second day. Therefore at least the first day could not be the same kind of day as those we have now, nor likewise as the other days of the text.

9. Again if that light was made that it might produce day and night, it would also do so now : for it is unreasonable to say that it was made solely to serve this purpose for the three days that preceded the creation of the sun, and that afterwards it ceased to exist. But there is no other light now besides the sun that causes day and night. Therefore neither during those three days was there any other corporeal light to cause the distinction between day and night.

10. Someone might say that this light was afterwards resolved into the solar body.—On the contrary whenever a thing is made out of pre-existent matter, it is composed of a matter susceptive of a succession of forms. But such is

not the matter of which the sun or any other heavenly body is composed, because in them there is no contrariety (*De cœl. et mund.* i). Therefore it is impossible that the sun was afterwards formed out of that light.

I answer that in the supposition that formless matter did not precede its formation in point of time but only in point of origin (and it could not be otherwise if formless matter signify matter entirely devoid of form) it follows of necessity that the formation of things was simultaneous, since it is not possible for any part of matter to be even for an instant entirely formless. Besides, as regards that particular part, matter would precede its formation in point of time. Wherefore if we adopt the opinion of Augustine as discussed in the preceding article, there is no reason to propose the question at the head of this article, and we must state at once that all things were formed at the same time, except in so far as it remains for us to explain in what sense we are to take the six days mentioned by Scripture. For if we are to take them to be like the days we have now, this would be in contradiction with the aforesaid opinion, since then we should have to hold that the formation of things took place during a series of days.

Augustine explains these days in two ways. First in his opinion (*Gen. ad lit.* i, 17) the distinction of light from darkness signifies the distinction of formed from formless matter which awaited its form, the difference being one not of time but of the order of nature. He holds that the order between formlessness and formation according as all things are ordered by God is implied by day and night, for day and night are an ordering of light and darkness. He says that evening denotes the termination of the work done: and morning the future beginning of the work, future not in the order of time but in the order of nature: for the first work contains already a kind of indication of the future work to be done. According to this view we must take the days as being distinct from one another inasmuch as there were various formations and consequently a lack of various forms.

Since however it would follow from this that the seventh day also was distinct from the first six, if these also were distinct from one another (whence it would seem to follow either that God did not make the seventh day, or that he made something after the seven days wherein he completed his work) he (Augustine) maintained in consequence that all these seven days were but one, namely the angelic knowledge, and that the number refers to the distinction between the things they knew rather than to a distinction of days : in other words that the six days signify the angel's knowledge in reference to the six classes of things created by God, while one day signifies the angel's knowledge in reference to the Maker's rest, in that he rested in himself from the things he had made : so that evening signifies knowledge of a thing in its own nature, and morning, knowledge in the Word.

According to other holy men these days denote order of time and succession in the production of things. In their opinion there was order not only of nature but also of time and duration in the works of the six days : for they contend that as matter was in a formless condition before its formation, so also one formation preceded another in the order of time. Because (as stated in the preceding article) by the formless condition of matter they did not understand the lack and exclusion of all form (since heaven, water and earth by which they understood the heavenly bodies, were already in existence, besides spiritual substances, and the four elements under their respective forms) but the mere absence and exclusion of the due distinction and perfect comeliness of each thing, in that it was lacking in that finish and beauty now to be seen in the corporeal creature. Thus we can gather from the text of Genesis, that the corporeal nature was lacking in a threefold beauty, for which reason it is described as being formless.[1]—The heavens and the entire diaphanous body lacked the comeliness and beauty of light : and this is denoted by the ' darkness.' The element of water lacked due order and distinction from the element of earth : and this lack of form is designated by the word ' deep,' which signifies a certain inordinate immensity of the waters according to Augustine (*Cont. Faust.* xxii, 11).—The earth lacked a twofold beauty : one which it acquired by

[1] Cf. *Sum. Th.*, I, Q. lxvi, A. 1.

the withdrawal of the waters, and this is signified by the words : *And the earth was void and empty*—or *invisible*, because it could not be seen by reason of the waters covering it on all sides : the other which it acquires through being adorned with plants, and this is indicated when it is said that it was *empty* or *incomposite*, i.e. unadorned. Thus then before the work of distinction Scripture mentions a manifold distinction as already existing in the elements of the world from the beginning of its creation. First it mentions the distinction between heaven and earth in so far as the heaven signifies the entire transparent body which includes fire and air on account of their transparency which they have in common with the heaven. Secondly it mentions the distinction of the elements as regards their substantial forms, by naming water and earth which are more perceptible to sense, and thus implying the others which are less apparent. Thirdly it mentions positional distinction : for the earth was beneath the waters which concealed it, while the air which is the subject of darkness is indicated as being above the waters in the words, *Darkness was over the face of the deep*. Accordingly the formation of the first body, namely the heaven, took place on the first day by the production of light whose illuminating property was communicated to the sun and heavenly bodies which already existed in respect of their substantial forms, and thus their formlessness of darkness was removed. From this formation resulted the distinction of movement and time, namely of night and day, since time is consequent to the movement of the higher heaven. Hence the text mentions the distinction of light and darkness : since the cause of light was in the substance of the sun, and the cause of darkness was in the opaqueness of the earth : so that while there was light in one hemisphere, there was darkness in the other, and again in the one hemisphere light at one time and darkness at another. This is expressed in the words, *He called the light day, and the darkness night.*—On the second day took place the formation and distinction of the middle body, namely water, by the formation of the firmament in that it was given parts and order. Thus under the name of water are comprised all transparent bodies : so that the firmament or starry heaven produced on the second day, not in substance, but as to a certain accidental perfection, divided the waters that are above the firmament (from those that are beneath it). By the firmament is meant the whole transparent heaven without the stars, known also as the 'aqueous' or crystalline heaven. Philosophers say that it is the ninth sphere and the first moving body, which causes the whole heaven to revolve as a daily movement, and producing by that movement a continuity of generation. In like manner the starry heaven by its zodiacal movement causes diversity in generation and corruption, by approaching to or receding from us and by the varying power of the stars. The waters beneath the firmament are the other corruptible transparent bodies. Consequently these lower transparent bodies signified under the name of waters received from the firmament a certain order and were divided into fitting parts.—On the third day was formed the lowest body, namely the earth, in so far as it was freed of its watery covering, and the lowest division was made of the sea from the dry land. It was thus not unfitting that the text having expressed the formless condition of the earth in the words, *The earth was invisible* or *empty*, should signify its formation in the words *And let the dry land appear*, and the waters being *gathered together into one place apart from the dry land, and God called the dry land Earth, and the gathering together of the waters he called Seas :* and whereas the earth was hitherto *void* and *empty* he adorned it with plants and herbs.—On the fourth day took place the adornment of the first part of the corporeal creature, which had been divided on the first day, the adornment to wit of the heavens by the creation of the luminaries. These as to their substance were created from the beginning, but whereas then their substance was formless now on the fourth day it is formed, not indeed with a substantial form, but by receiving a certain fixed power, inasmuch as these luminaries were endowed with certain powers for certain effects, as evinced by the different effects produced by solar, lunar or stellar rays. Dionysius (*Div. Nom.* iv) refers to this distinction of powers when he says that the light of the sun was formed on the fourth day, whereas hitherto it had been formless. If Scripture makes no mention of these luminaries from the outset but only on the fourth day, it was according to Chrysostom in order to keep the people from idolatry, by showing that the luminaries were not gods, seeing that they did not exist from the beginning.—On the fifth day, the second part of corporeal nature which had been divided on the second day was adorned by the creation of birds and fishes. Wherefore on this fifth day Scripture mentions the waters and the heavenly firmament, so as to show that the fifth day corresponds to the second, where mention was made of the waters and firmament. On this day then by God's word the birds and fishes in their respective natures were brought into actual being from the already created elemental matter in order to adorn the air and the water which are a fitting medium for their animal movements.— On the sixth day the third part of corporeal nature and the lowest body, namely the earth, was adorned by the creation of terrestrial animals to which it is connatural to move on the earth. Hence just as in the work of creation the text indicates a threefold division of corporeal creatures, the first signified under the name of heaven, the middle signified under the name of water, and the lowest signified under the name of earth; while the first part, i.e. the heaven was distinguished on the first day and adorned on the fourth, the middle part, i.e. the waters, distinguished on the second day and adorned on the fourth, as we have stated; so was it fitting that the lowest part, i.e. the earth which was distinguished on the third day, should be adorned on this the sixth day by the terrestrial animals being brought into actual existence and divided into various species.

From all this it is clear that Augustine differs from other holy men in his explanation of the works of the six days.— First, by the earth and water first created he understands primal matter utterly devoid of form, and by the creation of the firmament, the gathering together of the waters and by the uncovering of the dry land he understands the introduction of substantial forms into corporeal matter. Whereas the other saints take the earth and water first created to signify the elements of the world existing each under its own form, and the subsequent works to indicate some kind of division of the already existing bodies through their receiving certain powers and accidental properties, as stated above.—Secondly they differ in respect of the production of plants and animals : since the other saints say that these were actually produced in their respective natures during the work of the six days, whereas Augustine holds that they were produced only potentially.—Thirdly in holding (*Gen. ad lit.* iv, 34) that all the works of the six days took place at the same time Augustine apparently does not differ from the others as to the manner in which things were produced.— First, because both views agree in saying that in the first production of things matter was the subject of the substantial forms of the elements, so that primal matter did not precede the substantial forms of the elements of the world by a priority of duration.—Secondly because both opinions are agreed that in the first production of things by the work of creation plants and animals were not brought into actual but only potential existence, inasmuch as they could be educed from the elements by the power of God's word.

There is however a fourth point in which they differ. According to the other saints after the first production of the creature when the elements of the world and the heavenly bodies as to their substantial forms were produced, there was a time when there was no light : also when the firmament was not yet formed, or the transparent body adorned and made distinct : also when the earth was still covered with the waters, and as yet the luminaries were not formed. This is the fourth point wherein they differ from the view of Augustine who (l.c.) held that all these things were formed together in the same instant of time.

That the works of the six days according to the other saints were produced not simultaneously but by degrees, was not owing to lack of power in the Creator who could have produced all things at once, but was directed to the manifestation of God's wisdom in the production of things, in that when he made things out of nothing he did not at once bring them from nothingness to their ultimate natural perfection, but conferred on them at first an imperfect being, and afterwards perfected them, so that the world was brought gradually from nothingness to its ultimate perfection. Thus different days corresponded to the various degrees of perfection, and it was shown that things derived their being from God, against those who contended that matter was uncreated, and that moreover he is the author of their perfection, against those who ascribed the formation of the lower world to other causes.

The first explanation of these things namely that held by Augustine is the more subtle, and is a better defence of Scripture against the ridicule of unbelievers: but the second which is maintained by the other saints is easier to grasp, and more in keeping with the surface meaning of the text. Seeing however that neither is in contradiction with the truth of faith, and that the context admits of either interpretation, in order that neither may be unduly favoured we now proceed to deal with the arguments on either side.

Reply to the First Objection. In the divine works order of nature and origin and not of duration was observed. Formless spiritual and corporeal natures were formed first by priority of nature and origin. And though both natures were formed at the same time; inasmuch as the spiritual nature naturally transcends the corporeal, its formation preceded that of the corporeal nature in the order of nature. Again since an incorruptible corporeal nature transcends a corruptible nature, it behoved the former to be formed first in the order of nature. Wherefore on the first day the formation of the spiritual nature is signified by the creation of light, whereby the mind of the spiritual creature was illumined through its conversion to the Word. On the second day the formation of the corporeal nature heavenly and incorruptible, is signified by the creation of the firmament, which we understand to include the production of all the heavenly bodies and their distinction in respect of their various forms. —On the third day the formation of the corporeal nature of the four elements is signified by the gathering together of the waters and the appearance of the dry land.—On the fourth day the adornment of the heaven is signified by the creation of the luminaries, and this in the order of nature should precede the adornment of the waters and the earth which took place on the following days. Thus God's works were wrought in order indeed, not of duration but of nature.

Reply to the Second Objection. Things were not formed by degrees nor at various times : all these days which the text assigns to God's works are but one day described as present to each of the six classes of things and numbered accordingly : even so God's Word *by whom all things were made* is one, namely the Son of God, and yet we read repeatedly *God said* . . . And just as those works persevere in his subsequent works which are propagated from them by the agency of nature, so do those six days continue throughout the succeeding time. This may be made clear as follows. The angelic nature is intellectual and is properly described as light, and thus the enlightening of the angel should be called day. Now the angelic nature when things were first created was given the knowledge of these things, so that in a manner of speaking the light of the angel's intellect was made present to the things created, in so far as they were made known to the light of his mind. Hence this knowledge of things, implying that the light of the angelic intellect is made present to the things known, is called day : and various days are distinguished and ordered according to the various classes and order of the things known. Thus the first day is the knowledge of God's first work in forming the spiritual creature and converting it to the Word.—The second day is the knowledge of the second work whereby the higher corporeal creature was formed by the creation of the firmament.—The third day is the knowledge of the third work of the formation of the corporeal creature in respect of the lower part, namely the earth, water and neighbouring air.—The fourth day is the knowledge of the fourth work or the adornment of the higher part of the corporeal creature, that is of the firmament by the creation of luminaries.—The fifth day is the knowledge of the fifth divine work whereby the air and water were adorned by the creation of birds and fishes.—The sixth day is the knowledge of God's sixth work, namely of the adornment of the earth by the creation of terrestrial animals.—The seventh day is the angelic knowledge as referred to the Maker's rest in that he rested in himself from the production of new works.

Now since God is all light, and *there is no darkness in him*, God's knowledge in itself is pure light : whereas the creature through being made from nothing contains within itself the darkness of potentiality and imperfection, and consequently the knowledge of which a creature is the object must needs be mingled with darkness. Now a creature may be known in two ways : either in the Word, as the outcome of the divine scheme, and thus the knowledge of it is called ' morning knowledge,' because as the morning is the end of darkness and the beginning of light, so the creature, whereas before it was not in existence, receives a beginning of light from the light of the Word. Secondly a creature is known as existing in its own nature : and this is called ' evening knowledge,' because as the evening is the end of light and verges into night, so the creature as subsistent in itself terminates the operation of the light of the divine Word, in that it is made thereby, and of itself would fall into the darkness of its deficiencies were it not upheld by the Word. And so this knowledge being divided into morning and evening is called day : for just as in comparison with the Word's knowledge it is darksome, so in comparison with that ignorance which is darksome, it is light. In this way we may observe a certain circular movement of day and night, inasmuch as the angel knowing himself in his own nature referred this knowledge to the praise of the Word as his end, and in the Word as principle received the knowledge of the next work. And as this morning is the end of the preceding day so is it the beginning of the next day : for day is a part of time and the effect of light. And the distinction of those first days is not a distinction of different times, but refers to the spiritual light according as divers and distinct classes of things were made known to the angelic mind.

Reply to the Third Objection. The statement that light properly speaking is not in spiritual things, is untrue. For Augustine (*Gen. ad lit.* iv, 24) says that in spiritual things light is better and more certain ; also that *light* is said of

Christ otherwise than *stone*; for he is *light* properly speaking, and *stone* metaphorically. The reason is that *all that is made manifest is light* (Eph. iv, 13) : and manifestation belongs more properly to spiritual than to corporeal things. Hence Dionysius (*Div. Nom.* iv) numbers light among the intelligible names of God, and intelligible names belong properly to the spiritual world. In proof of the opposite statement it is said that the name light was first employed to signify the cause of manifestation to sight : and in this way light is a quality directly perceptible to sense, and is not properly applied to spiritual things. It is however extended by common use so as to signify anything that causes a manifestation in any kind of knowledge ; so that it bears this signification in ordinary language and in this way light belongs more properly to spiritual things.

Reply to the Fourth Objection. As we have stated above, these days are differentiated not in respect of succession in knowledge, but according to the natural order of the things known. Hence Augustine (*De Civ. Dei* xiv, 7, 9) holds that these seven days are one day represented by things in seven ways. Consequently the order of the days should be referred to the natural order of the works, which are assigned to days, each day corresponding to certain things which by the angelic intellect are known simultaneously in the Word.

Reply to the Fifth Objection. The six days wherein God is said to have created the heaven, the earth, the sea and all that are in them, do not signify a succession of time, but the angelic knowledge as referred to six classes of things created by God, while the seventh day is the angel's knowledge as referred to the rest of the Maker. For in Augustine's opinion (*Gen. ad lit.* iv, 15) God is said to have rested on the seventh day inasmuch as he revealed to the angelic mind the rest whereby he rested in himself from the things created, whereby he is happy in himself and needs not creatures, being all-sufficient to himself : and this knowledge Augustine calls day.—God is said to have rested from work on the seventh day, because afterwards he did nothing new that in some way did not already exist either materially or causally or in respect of some specific or generic likeness in the works of the six days.—And whereas after the completion of all his works God rested in himself on the seventh day, Scripture and the Law commanded the seventh day to be kept holy. For then especially is a thing holy when it rests in God; thus things dedicated to God (e.g. the tabernacle, the vessels, the ministers) are called holy things. Now the seventh day was dedicated to the worship of God and for this reason it is said to be kept holy. Accordingly as God after producing six classes of creatures and making them known to the angelic mind, rested not indeed in the things he had created as though they were his end, but in himself and from the things he had created: inasmuch as he himself is his own beatitude (since he is not made happy by making things, but through being all-sufficient to himself and needing not the things he made),—even so are we to learn to rest not in God's works nor in ours, but from work and in God in whom our happiness consists. In fact for this very reason was man commanded[1] to labour in his own works for six days, and to rest on the seventh, applying himself to the worship of God and resting in the meditation of divine things, wherein his sanctification chiefly consists.

Again the newness of the world proves in a striking manner the existence of God and that he needs not creatures: wherefore man was commanded in the Law to rest and hold festival on the seventh day which saw the completion of the world, in order that the novelty of the world produced all at once and the six different classes of things might keep man in continual remembrance of God, and lead him to give thanks to him for the great and fruitful boon of the creation, so as to rest his thoughts in him as his end, in this life by grace, in the future life by glory.

Reply to the Sixth Objection. Every new work of God as referred to the angelic knowledge is called a day: and as there were but six classes of things created in the beginning by God and made known to the angelic intellect, as stated above, so are there but six days: to which the seventh is added, namely the same angelic knowledge as referred to God's rest in himself. For God produced nothing in nature,

[1] Exod. xx, 9, 10; Deut. v. 13, 14.

without first, in the order of nature, making it known to the angel's mind.

The *Reply to the Seventh Objection* is clear from what has been said : because these days are not differentiated in relation to a difference in the angelic knowledge, but by the different primordial works as referred to that knowledge : so that those first days are distinct in reference to different works and not in reference to different knowledges. Hence these six days are distinct according as the light of the angelic mind is shed on the six classes of things made known to it.

Reply to the Eighth Objection. According to Augustine these three denote the threefold being of things. First, their being in the Word : for things have being in the divine art which is his Word, before they have being in themselves : and this is signified by the words, *God said : Let . . . be made,* i.e. *He begot the Word in whom things were before they were made.*—Secondly, things have being in the angelic mind, because God created nothing in nature, without having previously revealed its nature to the angelic mind : and this is signified in the words, *it was so done,* namely by the outpouring of the Word into the angel's intellect.—Thirdly, things have being in their own nature : and this is signified when it is said, *He made.* For even as the art to which the creature is fashioned is in the Word before it is produced in the creature so in the order of nature was knowledge of that same art in the angelic mind before the creature was produced. Thus the angel has a threefold knowledge of things, namely as they are in the Word, as they are in his mind, and as they are in their respective natures. The first is called ' morning ' knowledge, while the other two are included in ' evening ' knowledge : and in order to indicate this twofold mode of a spiritual creature's knowledge of things, it is said : *Evening and morning were one day.* Accordingly by these six days wherein we read that God made all things, Augustine understands (*De Civ. Dei* xi, 9) not these ordinary days that are measured by the course of the sun, since we are told that the sun was created on the fourth day, but one day, that is the angelic knowledge made present to the six classes of things. Thus even as the presence of a corporeal luminary by its shining on this lower world makes a temporal day, so the presence of the spiritual light of the angelic mind by its shining on creatures makes a spiritual day : so that in his opinion these six days are differentiated according as the light of the angel's intellect shines on the six classes of things made known to it : and the first day is his knowledge of God's first work, the second day, his knowledge of the second work, and so on.   Consequently these six days differ not in the order of time or of the succession of things, but in the natural order of the things known, in so far as one thing was known before another in the order of nature.   And just as in a natural or material day the morning is the beginning and the evening the end and term, even so the angel's knowledge of each work in its original being, namely as having its being in the Word, is called ' morning knowledge ' : while the knowledge thereof in respect of its ultimate being, and as existing in its own nature, is called ' evening knowledge.'   For the origin of everything's being lies in the cause whence it issues : while its term lies in its recipient which terminates the action of its cause.   Wherefore the first knowledge of a thing is the consideration thereof in the cause whence it comes : while the ultimate knowledge of a thing is the consideration of that thing in itself.   Since then the being of things issues from the eternal Word as from their original principle, and this issue terminates in the being that things have in their respective natures, it follows that knowledge of things in the Word which has for its object their first and original being, should be called ' morning knowledge,' by way of comparison with the morning which is the beginning of day : whereas knowledge of a thing in its own nature, which has for its object its ultimate and terminated being, should be called ' evening knowledge ' since the evening ends day.   Hence as the six classes of things in relation to the angelic knowledge differentiate the days, even so the unity of the thing known which is knowable by various modes of cognition constitutes the unity of the day, which itself is divided into evening and morning.

Reply to the Ninth Objection.   An angel is unable directly and principally to understand in their own natures several without first, in the order of nature, making it known to the angel's mind.

The *Reply to the Seventh Objection* is clear from what has been said : because these days are not differentiated in relation to a difference in the angelic knowledge, but by the different primordial works as referred to that knowledge : so that those first days are distinct in reference to different works and not in reference to different knowledges. Hence these six days are distinct according as the light of the angelic mind is shed on the six classes of things made known to it.

Reply to the Eighth Objection. According to Augustine these three denote the threefold being of things. First, their being in the Word : for things have being in the divine art which is his Word, before they have being in themselves : and this is signified by the words, *God said : Let . . . be made*, i.e. *He begot the Word in whom things were before they were made.*—Secondly, things have being in the angelic mind, because God created nothing in nature, without having previously revealed its nature to the angelic mind : and this is signified in the words, *it was so done*, namely by the outpouring of the Word into the angel's intellect.—Thirdly, things have being in their own nature : and this is signified when it is said, *He made*. For even as the art to which the creature is fashioned is in the Word before it is produced in the creature so in the order of nature was knowledge of that same art in the angelic mind before the creature was produced. Thus the angel has a threefold knowledge of things, namely as they are in the Word, as they are in his mind, and as they are in their respective natures. The first is called ' morning ' knowledge, while the other two are included in ' evening ' knowledge : and in order to indicate this twofold mode of a spiritual creature's knowledge of things, it is said : *Evening and morning were one day*. Accordingly by these six days wherein we read that God made all things, Augustine understands (*De Civ. Dei* xi, 9) not these ordinary days that are measured by the course of the sun, since we are told that the sun was created on the fourth day, but one day, that is the angelic knowledge made present to the six classes of things. Thus even as the presence of a corporeal luminary by its shining on this lower world makes a temporal day, so the presence of the spiritual light of the angelic mind by its shining on creatures makes a spiritual day: so that in his opinion these six days are differentiated according as the light of the angel's intellect shines on the six classes of things made known to it: and the first day is his knowledge of God's first work, the second day, his knowledge of the second work, and so on. Consequently these six days differ not in the order of time or of the succession of things, but in the natural order of the things known, in so far as one thing was known before another in the order of nature. And just as in a natural or material day the morning is the beginning and the evening the end and term, even so the angel's knowledge of each work in its original being, namely as having its being in the Word, is called ' morning knowledge ': while the knowledge thereof in respect of its ultimate being, and as existing in its own nature, is called ' evening knowledge.' For the origin of everything's being lies in the cause whence it issues: while its term lies in its recipient which terminates the action of its cause. Wherefore the first knowledge of a thing is the consideration thereof in the cause whence it comes: while the ultimate knowledge of a thing is the consideration of that thing in itself. Since then the being of things issues from the eternal Word as from their original principle, and this issue terminates in the being that things have in their respective natures, it follows that knowledge of things in the Word which has for its object their first and original being, should be called ' morning knowledge,' by way of comparison with the morning which is the beginning of day: whereas knowledge of a thing in its own nature, which has for its object its ultimate and terminated being, should be called ' evening knowledge ' since the evening ends day. Hence as the six classes of things in relation to the angelic knowledge differentiate the days, even so the unity of the thing known which is knowable by various modes of cognition constitutes the unity of the day, which itself is divided into evening and morning.

Reply to the Ninth Objection. An angel is unable directly and principally to understand in their own natures several things, but he is well able to understand several things indirectly as related to one intelligible object. And whereas all things that were produced in their respective natures, were in the order of nature first impressed in the shape of images on the angelic mind, the angel by knowing himself, at the same time, so to say, knows those six classes of things in their natural mutual co-ordination, since by knowing himself, he knows whatsoever has being in himself.

Reply to the Tenth Objection. One power can exercise two operations at the same time, if one of these is referred and ordered to the other; thus it is evident that the will at the same time wills the end and the means, and the intellect at the same time understands the premises and the conclusions through the premises, provided that it knows the conclusions. Now the angels' 'evening knowledge' is ordered to their 'morning knowledge,' according to Augustine (*Dial.* lxv *QQ.* qu. 26 : *Super Genes.* ii, 3, 8), just as natural knowledge and love are ordered to heavenly knowledge and love. Wherefore nothing hinders an angel from having at the same time 'morning' and 'evening' knowledge, just as natural and heavenly knowledge are together. For one power cannot exercise at the same time two operations that proceed from two species of the same kind, if the one be not ordered to the other (and such are all created non-subsistent intelligible species), so that an angel cannot at the same time produce several intellectual acts by means of several concreated species. But if those two operations proceed from forms generically different and disparate one of which is ordered to the other (and such are a subsistent uncreated form, and a non-subsistent created form), then they can be produced simultaneously. Wherefore since the angel's knowledge of things in their respective natures, which is called 'evening' knowledge is exercised by means of a created non-subsistent intelligible species, while his knowledge of things in the Word, which is called 'morning' knowledge is exercised through the subsistent essence of the Word ; and since these two are generically distinct and disparate, yet one is ordered to the other, it follows that both knowledges can be exercised at the same time. The reason is that a concreated species inhering in the intellect is not incompatible with the union of the intellect to the essence of the Word, which actuates the intellect not in respect of being but only in respect of understanding, inasmuch as it is disparate and of a higher order, and this same inherent species and whatsoever of perfection there is in the created intellect are by way of a material disposition to that union and blessed vision whereby things are seen in the Word. Hence just as disposition to a form and the form itself can coexist in that which is actually complete, so the inhering intelligible species coexists with the intellect's union to the essence of the Word, in the intellect's perfect operation. Wherefore a twofold operation issues simultaneously from the intellect of the blessed angel; one by reason of its union to the essence of the Word and whereby it sees things in the Word, and this is called 'morning' knowledge; the other by reason of the species inhering to it, whereby it sees things in their own nature, and this is called 'evening' knowledge. Neither of these actions is weakened or lessened by attention to the other, on the contrary it is strengthened, seeing that the one leads to the other, even as the imagination of what one has seen is more vivid when the thing is actually present to the eye. For the action whereby the blessed see the Word and things in the Word is the reason of their every action. And when of two actions one is the reason of the other or is ordered to the other, both of them can be exercised at once by the same power. In that case the one power terminates in different actions in respect of different species mutually ordered the one to the other, not in the same respect but in different respects. For species that differ in genus and order, or that are disparate, can be united together in respect of a perfect act, for instance colour, smell and taste in fruit. Now the divine essence, whereby the angel's intellect sees things in the Word is uncreated and self subsistent: the essence of an angel whereby he sees always himself and things as having being in himself is created and self-subsistent by reason of the being he had received and by which his intellect subsists; and the infused or concreated intelligible species, whereby he sees things in their own nature is non-subsistent:

wherefore these three are different in order and genus, and disparate, so that the first is as it were the reason of the others, and the second the reason of the third : consequently the angelic intellect will be able to have a threefold operation in respect of those three forms. Even so the soul of Christ at the same time understands things by the species of the Word, as by infused, and by acquired species.

Reply to the Eleventh Objection. Just as in the opinion of Augustine (*Ad Oros.* qu. xxi) the informity of matter preceded its formation by priority not of time but of order (as sound and voice precede the song), so the formation of the spiritual nature signified in the creation of light, since this is more noble than the corporeal nature, preceded the formation of the latter in the order of nature and origin but not of time. Now the formation of the spiritual nature consists in its being enlightened so as to adhere to the Word, not indeed by perfect glory, with which it was not created, but by perfect grace with which it was created. Accordingly by this light the distinction was made from darkness, to wit from the formless condition of the corporeal creature as yet unformed, yet in the order of nature to be formed afterwards. Because the formation of the spiritual creature may be taken in two ways. First, as denoting the infusion of grace, second, as denoting the conservation of glory. The former according to Augustine was vouchsafed the spiritual creature from the very first instant of its creation, in which case the darkness from which the light was divided does not denote the sin of the wicked angels, but the formless condition of nature which was not yet formed, but in the order of nature was to be formed in the subsequent works (*Gen. ad lit.* i, 5, 6, 7).—Or again (*Super Gen.* iv, 22, 23) *day* signifies God's knowledge, *night* the creature's, which latter is darkness in comparison with God's (*ibid.*).—Or again if darkness be taken to signify the wicked angels, then this distinction refers to their sin not as present but as future to God's foreknowledge. Hence (*Ad Oros.* qu. xxiv) he says : *God foreseeing that some of his angels would fall through pride, by the unchangeable order of his foreknowledge, divided the good from the wicked, and called the wicked darkness, the good, light.*

The second formation of the spiritual nature does not belong to the beginning of things, but rather to their course in which they are governed by divine providence. Hence the distinction of light from darkness, if by darkness we understand the sins of the demons, must be taken in reference to God's foreknowledge. Wherefore Augustine says (*De Civ. Dei* xi, 19) that he alone could divide light from darkness who before the angels fell could foresee that they would fall. But if by darkness we understand the formless condition of matter yet to be formed, the order is signified not of time but of nature between the formations of both natures.

Reply to the Twelfth Objection. If we suppose that all things were created at the same time as to both matter and form, then the angel is said to have been cognisant of the future creation of the corporeal creature, not as though the corporeal creature were future in point of time, but because it was known as future inasmuch as it was seen in its cause in which it existed already as something that could issue therefrom. Thus he who knows a chest in the materials of which it is made, may be said to know the chest as a future thing. For the knowledge of a thing in the Word is called 'morning' knowledge, whether the thing is already made or has to be made, and refers indifferently to present or future things, since it is conformed to the divine knowledge whereby God knows all things simply before they are made as well as after they have been made. Nevertheless all knowledge of a thing in the Word refers to that thing as yet to be made, whether it be already made or not, in so far as 'yet to be made' indicates not time but the issue of the creature from its Creator. Even so the artificer has in his art the knowledge of the work he produces, but that knowledge refers to the work as something he intends to make even when it has already been made. Wherefore for this reason, although the corporeal creature was made at the same time as the spiritual nature, the angel is nevertheless said to have known the corporeal creature in the Word as something yet to be made, for the reason already given.

Reply to the Thirteenth Objection. Even as morning precedes evening, so the 'morning' precedes the 'evening' knowledge in the order of nature, not in respect of one and the same work but in respect of different works. Nevertheless 'evening' knowledge of a prior work is understood to precede 'morning' knowledge of a later work. For the work of the first day was the creation of light, whereby we understand the formation of the angelic nature by the enlightenment of grace; while the knowledge whereby the spiritual creature knows himself is consequent to its being in his own nature. Hence in the order of nature the spiritual creature knew himself in his own nature by 'evening' knowledge whereby he knew himself as already created, before he knew himself in the Word in whom he knew God's work as something yet to be done. Accordingly in this knowledge whereby the good angels knew themselves they did not rest, as making themselves the object of their fruition and their own end, because then they would become night as the wicked angels who sinned, but they referred their knowledge to the praise of God. Thus by his knowledge of himself the good angel was converted to the contemplation of the Word, and this was the beginning of the following day, because in the Word he received knowledge of the following work, namely the firmament. Now just as in continuous time the same 'now' belongs to two periods of time, inasmuch as it is the end of the past and the beginning of the future, even so the 'morning' knowledge of the second day terminates the first day and begins the second day, and so on to the seventh day. Consequently on the first day *evening* alone is mentioned, since the angel first had 'evening' knowledge of himself, and that evening knowledge went forward to 'morning' knowledge, in so far as from contemplation of himself he advanced to the contemplation of the Word, and to the *morning*, of the next day by receiving in the Word the 'morning' knowledge of the next work. Thus then 'morning' knowledge of one and the same work after the first work naturally precedes the 'evening' knowledge of the same work: but 'evening' knowledge of a previous work naturally precedes 'morning' knowledge of a later work: wherefore as the first day had only an evening, so the seventh day through signifying contemplation of God which being faultless never wanes has only a morning.

Reply to the Fourteenth Objection. Augustine gives the name of ' morning ' knowledge to that which is in full light, so that it includes ' mid-day ' knowledge : in fact he calls it sometimes ' day ' sometimes ' morning ' knowledge.—Or else it may be said that all knowledge of the angelic intellect has a mixture of darkness on the part of the knower, so that no knowledge of an angelic intellect can be called ' mid-day ' knowledge, but only that knowledge whereby God knows all things in himself.—Again, since God is all light and *no darkness is in him,* the knowledge, of God, being all light, may in itself and absolutely be called ' mid-day ' knowledge : whereas a creature being made from nothing has the darkness of potentiality and imperfection, and consequently the knowledge of a creature is mixed with darkness. This mixture is signified by *morning* and *evening,* for as much as a creature can be known in two ways.—First in the Word, according as the creature issues from the divine art, and thus the knowledge thereof is called ' morning ' knowledge ; because as morning is the end of darkness and the beginning of light, so the creature after darkness, namely after non-existence, receives a beginning of light from the Word.— Secondly the creature is knowable in its own nature by means of a created species, and such knowledge is called ' evening ' knowledge, since just as evening is the end of light and verges into night, even so the creature as subsistent in itself is the end of the operation of the Word who is light, in that it is made by him, and so far as it is concerned tends to the darkness of non-existence unless it were upheld by the Word. And yet this knowledge is called *day,* because as in comparison with the knowledge of the Word it is darksome, so in comparison with ignorance which is altogether darksome, it is called light ; even so the life of the just man is said to be darksome as compared with the life of glory, and yet is called light in comparison with the life of the wicked.— Again seeing that morning and evening are parts of a day, and that ' day ' in the angels is knowledge illumined by the light of grace, it follows that ' morning ' and ' evening ' knowledge extend only to the gratuitously bestowed knowledge of the good angels, so that the enlightened angel's knowledge of God's works is called *day*, and the days are distinguished in reference to the various kinds of divine works as known, and are arranged according to their order. Now each of those works is known by the enlightened angel in two ways. First in the Word or by the species of the Word, and this is called ' morning ' knowledge. Secondly, in its own nature, or by a created species. In this knowledge the good angels do not rest as making it their end, because they would become night like the wicked angels : but they refer that knowledge to the praise of the Word and the light of God in whom they know all things as in their source. Wherefore this knowledge of the creature being referred to God is not called ' night ' : which it would be were they to rest therein, since they would become night through making a creature the object of their fruition. Accordingly ' morning ' and ' evening ' knowledge are divisions of the day, i.e. the knowledge which the good enlightened angels have of the works of creation. Now the good angels' knowledge of a creature, whether through a created or an uncreated medium, has always an element of obscurity ; and so it is not called ' mid-day ' knowledge as the knowledge of God in himself is ; nor is it called ' night,' as that knowledge of a creature which is not referred to the divine light, but it is called ' morning ' and ' evening ' knowledge, for this reason that evening as such terminates in the morning. Hence not all knowledge of a thing in its nature can be called ' evening ' knowledge, but only that which is referred to the glory of the Creator. Thus the knowledge which the demons have of things cannot, strictly speaking, be called either ' morning ' or ' evening ' knowledge : because ' morning ' and ' evening ' in reference to the angelic knowledge are not to be likened to it on all points but only in the point of beginning and end.

Reply to the Fifteenth Objection. Although created in grace, the angel was not beatified from the very beginning of his creation, nor did he see God's Word in his essence : wherefore neither had he ' morning ' knowledge of himself, which signifies knowledge of a thing through the species of the Word. But at first he had 'evening' knowledge of himself inasmuch as he knew himself in himself naturally, for this reason that in everyone natural knowledge precedes supernatural knowledge, as being the latter's foundation, and an angel's knowledge naturally follows his being in his own nature: so that when he was first created he had not 'morning' but 'evening' knowledge of himself. This knowledge he referred to the praise of the Word and by so doing he merited 'morning' knowledge. It is significant then that the first day is stated to have had only an evening and not a morning, which evening passed into morning: because the spiritual creature which, we are told, was made on the first day, knew itself as soon as it was made. This was 'evening' knowledge, and by referring it to the praise of the Word, it merited the 'morning' knowledge of the next work. For not every knowledge of a thing in its nature can be called 'evening' knowledge but only that which is referred to the praise of the Creator: since evening recedes and ends with the morning. Hence the knowledge which the demons acquire by themselves about things is neither 'morning' nor 'evening' knowledge: but this can only be said of the knowledge gratuitously bestowed on the good angels. Accordingly the knowledge of things in their respective natures, if it be referred to the praise of the Word, is always 'evening' knowledge: nor does the fact that it is so referred make it 'morning' knowledge, but it makes it terminate therein, and by so doing the angel merits to receive 'morning' knowledge. And just as the first day which signifies the formation and knowledge of the spiritual creature in its own nature, has only an evening, so too the seventh day has only a morning in that it signifies the contemplation of God which being faultless never wanes, and which corresponds to the angels' knowledge in reference to God's rest in himself, while to rest in God is the enlightenment and sanctification of everything. For in that God ceased to fashion new creatures he is said to have completed his work and to have rested in himself from his works. And just as God rests in himself alone, and is happy in the enjoyment of himself, even so we are made happy by enjoying him alone, and thus he makes us to rest in him both from his works and from our own. Accordingly the first day which corresponds to the knowledge which the spiritual creature enlightened by the light of grace had concerning itself, has only an evening : whereas the seventh day which corresponds to the angelic knowledge in reference to God's rest and fruition in himself has only a morning, because in God there is no darkness. For God is stated to have rested on the seventh day inasmuch as he revealed to the angels his own rest whereby he rested in himself from the things he had made. It is the knowledge of this rest that Augustine (*Dial.* lxv, qu. 26) calls *day*. And since the creature's rest whereby it stands firm in God, has no end, in like manner God's rest whereby he rests in himself from the things he has made, in that he needs them not, has no end, for he will never need them : hence it is that the seventh day which corresponds to that rest has not an evening but a morning; whereas the other days which correspond to the angelic knowledge in reference to things, have both morning and evening, as already stated.

Reply to the Sixteenth Objection. As we have already explained, it is possible to know a thing already made as something yet to be made, if it be considered in the causes whence it issues : and thus the angels received knowledge in the Word of things to be made, for the Word is the supreme art of things. Because all knowledge of a thing in the Word, otherwise ' morning ' knowledge, is said to have for its object the thing as ' yet to be made,' whether or not it be already made ; since ' yet to be made ' indicates not time but the issue of the creature from the Creator, as stated above (*ad* 14). Wherefore though the corporeal creature was made at the same time as the spiritual nature, the angel is said by ' morning ' knowledge to know in the Word the thing as something yet to be made. Why the first day had no morning but only evening has been explained in the previous Reply.

Reply to the Seventeenth Objection. The spiritual creature does not derive his knowledge from things : he understands them naturally by means of innate or concreated species.

Now the species in an angel's mind do not equally refer to the present and the future. Present things have actually a likeness to the forms in the angelic mind, so that by those forms the present can be known : whereas future things are not yet actually like those forms, so that by those forms the future cannot be known, since knowledge is effected by an actual assimilation of the known to the knower. Wherefore, as an angel does not know the future as such, he needs the presence of things in order that by the forms impressed on him he may know things in their respective natures : because before these latter are made, they are not assimilated to those forms. Moreover 'evening' and 'morning' knowledge are differentiated on the part not of the thing known but of the medium of knowledge. 'Morning' knowledge results from an uncreated medium that transcends the nature both of the knower and of the thing known : and for this reason knowledge of things through the species of the Word is called 'morning' whether the things be already made or remain yet to be made : whereas 'evening' knowledge is effected by means of a created medium that is proportionate both to the knower and to the thing known, whether the latter be already made or remain yet to be made.

Reply to the Eighteenth Objection. Although the angel has being in the Word before he has being in his own nature, nevertheless seeing that knowledge presupposes the existence of the knower, he could not know himself before he existed. Now his knowledge of himself in his own nature is natural to him, whereas his knowledge of the Word is supernatural. Hence it behoved him to know himself first in his own nature, before knowing himself in the Word : because in everyone natural knowledge precedes supernatural as its foundation. Other things, however, by his 'morning' knowledge he knew in the Word by a priority of the natural order before knowing them in their respective natures by his 'evening' knowledge : so that in respect of the subsequent works morning preceded evening, as already stated.

Reply to the Nineteenth Objection. As one complete science includes various particular sciences, whereby various conclusions are known, so also the one angelic knowledge which is a kind of whole comprises 'morning' and 'evening' knowledge as its parts, even as morning and evening are parts of the day, albeit disparate. Because things that are mutually disparate if ordered to each other can constitute one whole: thus matter and form which are disparate, constitute one composite; and again flesh, bones and sinews are parts of one composite body. Now the divine essence whereby things are known in the Word by 'morning' knowledge is the prototype of all the concreated forms in the angelic mind, seeing that these derive from it as from their exemplar, and through them things are known in their own nature by 'evening' knowledge: even as the angel's essence is the type whereby he understands the being which he knows; yet it is not a perfect type, for which reason he needs other superadded forms. Consequently when an angel sees God in his essence, as also himself and other things by means of concreated species, in a way of speaking he understands one thing: thus because light is the reason for seeing colour, therefore when the eye sees both light and colour it sees in a manner of speaking one visible thing. And although these operations are distinct in reality, seeing that the operation whereby he sees God is everlasting and is measured by participated eternity, and the operation whereby he understands himself is everlasting and is measured by eviternity, while the operations whereby he understands other things by innate species is not everlasting but one succeeds the other, nevertheless since one is ordered to the other, and one is the formal reason as it were of the other, they are so to speak one thing: because where one thing is on account of another there is but one (*Top.* iii, 2), so that when several operations are mutually ordered the one to the other, they can be simultaneous and constitute one whole.

Reply to the Twentieth Objection. Whereas the intellect is the abode of intelligible species, it follows that the science of setting in order the intelligible species, in other words the intellect's skill and ability in using those species must remain after death, even as the intellect itself which is the abode of those species. On the other hand the manner in which it actually uses them in the present state of life, namely by turning to phantasms which dwell in the sensible powers, will not remain after death : because seeing that the sensible powers will be destroyed, the soul will be unable either by the species acquired in this life, or by the species acquired by it in its state of separation, to understand by turning to phantasms; but it will be able to do so in a manner befitting the mode of being that it will have in likeness to the angels. Hence knowledge will be destroyed not as to the habit, nor as to the substance of the cognitive act that takes its species from the species of the object, but as to the manner of knowing, which will not be by conversion to the phantasms; and this is the meaning intended by the Apostle.

Reply to the Twenty-first Objection. The light caused in the air by the sun and that produced by a candle are of the same kind, and seeing that two forms of the same kind cannot coexist in a perfect state in the same subject, it follows that sun and candle together produce one light in the air. Now the divine essence whereby things are known in the Word differs in kind from the species whereby an angel knows a thing in its nature : wherefore the comparison fails. For when perfection is come the opposite imperfection is made void : thus on the advent of the vision of God, faith which is of things unseen is made void. But the imperfection of 'evening' knowledge is not opposed to the perfection of 'morning' knowledge, since knowledge of a thing in itself is not opposed to knowledge of it in its cause : nor again does it involve a contradiction that a thing be known through two mediums one of which is more perfect than the other : even so we may hold the same conclusion by a demonstration and a probable medium. In like manner the same thing may be known by an angel in the uncreated Word and through an innate species; since the one is not opposed, in fact rather is it a material disposition, to the other. Now perfection by its advent removes the opposite imperfection. But the imperfection of nature is not opposed to the perfection of heavenly bliss, in fact it underlies it, just as the imperfection of potentiality underlies the perfection of form : and the form removes not potentiality but the privation to which it is opposed. In like manner the imperfection of natural knowledge is not opposed to the perfection of the beatific knowledge but underlies it as a material disposition. Hence the angel can know things by a created medium in their own nature ; and this is ' evening ' and natural knowledge ; and at the same time by the essence of the Word, which is beatific and ' morning ' knowledge." And these two knowledges do not hinder each other, since the one is ordered to the other, and is by way of a material disposition to the other.

Reply to the Twenty-second Objection. Augustine (*Super Gen.* v, 12, 14) holds that at the very beginning of creation certain things specifically distinct were produced in their respective natures, such as the four elements produced from nothing, as well as the heavenly bodies and spiritual substances : for this kind of production requires no matter either out of which or in which a thing is made. Also that other things are stated to have been created in their seed-forms, for example animals, plants and men, and that these were all subsequently produced in their respective natures in that work by which God after the six days attends to nature previously established, of which work it is said (Jo. v, 17) : *My Father worketh until now.* Moreover he holds that in the production and distinction of things we should see an order not of time but of nature : inasmuch as all the works of the six days were wrought in the one instant of time either actually, or potentially in their seed-forms, in that afterwards they could be made from pre-existent matter either by the Word, or by the active forces with which the creature was endowed in its creation. Wherefore in regard to the first man's soul which, he suggests without asserting it, was created actually at the same time as the angels, he does not hold that it was created before the sixth day, although he holds that on the sixth day it was actually made, and the first man's body as to its seed-forms : for God endowed the earth with a passive potentiality so that by the active power of the Creator man's body could be formed therefrom. Accordingly the soul was actually made at the same time as the body was made in its passive potentiality to God's active power.—Or again, seeing that in truth according to Aristotle (*De anima* ii), the soul is not a complete species in itself but is united to the body as the latter's form, and is naturally a part of human nature, we must infer that the first man's soul was not brought into actual existence before the formation of the body, but was created and infused into the body at the same time as the body was formed, even as Augustine holds (*Super Gen.* x, 17) with regard to other souls. For God produced the first things in their perfect natural state, according as the species of each one required. Now the rational soul being a part of human nature has not its natural perfection except as united to the body. Hence it naturally has its being in the body, and existence outside the body is non-natural to it: so that it was unfitting for the soul to be created without the body.

If then we adopt the opinion of Augustine on the works of the six days, it may be said that as in those six days the body of the first man was not actually formed and produced, but only potentially in its seed-forms : even so his soul was not produced then actually and in itself, but in its generic likeness; and thus preceded the body during those six days not actually and in itself, but in respect of a certain generic likeness, inasmuch as it has an intellectual nature in common with the angels. Afterwards however, in the work whereby God attends to the creature already produced, the soul was actually created at the same time as the body was formed.

The *Reply to the Twenty-third Objection* is clear from what has been said. The human body was not brought into actual existence in those six days, as neither were the bodies of other animals, but only in the shape of seed-forms, since God in creating the elements planted in them certain forces or seeds, so that either by the power of God, or by the influence of the stars or by seminal propagation animals might be produced. Accordingly those things that were actually produced in those six days were created not by degrees but at the same time, while the others were brought into existence as seed-forms in their like.

Reply to the Twenty-fourth Objection. As we have already said in the Reply to the Sixteenth Objection, knowledge of things by innate species that are proportionate to things is called 'evening' knowledge and is of things as subsisting in their respective nature, whether already made or yet to be made. And although those species are related equally to the present or future, the things themselves that are present or future are not equally related to the species: because present things are actually assimilated to the species and thus can be actually known thereby; whereas future things are not actually assimilated to them, wherefore it does not follow that they can be known by them. And 'evening' knowledge which is of things in their respective natures is not so called because the angels take from things the species whereby they understand them, but because by the species received at their creation they understand things as subsisting in their respective nature.

Reply to the Twenty-fifth Objection. In Augustine's opinion (*Super Gen.* ii, 8) the angels from the very beginning saw the things to be made by the Word. The things which, we are told, were made in the works of the six days were all made at the same time: wherefore those six days were all from the very outset of the creation, and consequently the good angels must have known the Word and creatures in the Word from the very beginning. Creatures have a threefold being as already stated. First in the divine art which is the Word: this is signified when it is said: *God said: Let . . . be made,* i.e. *He begot the Word in whom such and such a work was before it could be made.* Secondly, they have being in the angelic intelligence, and this is signified in the words, *It was so done,* to wit by the outpouring of the Word. Thirdly they have being in themselves and in their respective natures. In like manner the angel has a threefold knowledge of things, —of things as existing in the Word, as existing in his own mind, and as existing in their respective natures. Again the angel has a twofold knowledge of the Word: a natural knowledge whereby he knows the Word by his likeness shining forth in his (the angel's) nature, wherein consists his natural beatitude, and which he can obtain by his natural powers; and a supernatural and beatific knowledge whereby he knows the Word in his (the Word's) essence, and in this his supernatural beatitude consists, which surpasses his natural powers.

By either of these the good angel knows things or creatures in the Word : by his natural knowledge, however, he knows things in the Word imperfectly : whereas by his beatific knowledge he knows things in the Word with greater fullness and perfection.

The first knowledge of things in the Word was received by the angel at the instant of his creation, wherefore it is stated in *De Eccl. Dogmat.* that *the angels who persevered in the happy state wherein they were created, possess the good they have, not by nature but by grace.* Again Augustine[1] (*De Fide ad Pet.* iii) says : *The angelic spirits received from above the gift of eternity and beatitude when they were created in their spiritual nature.* Yet they were not thereby beatified simply, seeing that they were capable of greater perfection, but in a restricted sense, i.e. in relation to the time being. Thus the Philosopher (1 *Ethic.* x) says that some are happy in this life, not simply, but *as men.* The second or beatific knowledge was bestowed on the angels not from the beginning of their creation, since they were not created in a state of perfect beatitude, but from the moment they were beatified by perfect conversion to the good. Accordingly all these six classes of things were created at the same time together with the angels, and in the same instant the angel by natural knowledge knew in the Word whatsoever afterwards he knew in the Word more fully by supernatural knowledge, which the angels received immediately on their referring their natural self-knowledge to the praise of the Word : and this same natural knowledge being measured by eviternity, is always coexistent with their supernatural knowledge of the Word, and with their knowledge through innate species, of creatures in their respective natures. Hence these three cognitions are co-existent, nor does one properly speaking follow the other : although the knowledge of things in the Word, be they already made or yet to be made, is called ' morning ' knowledge : while the knowledge of things through a created

[1] *Fulgentius.*

medium in their own nature, be they present or future, is called ' evening ' knowledge.

Reply to the Twenty-sixth Objection. It is not possible that an angel see the Word or divine essence as the type of things to be made, without seeing it as the end of the Blessed and the object of beatitude : since the divine essence in itself is the object of beatitude and the end of the Blessed. For it is not possible to see the divine essence as the type of things to be made without seeing it in itself ; wherefore the whole argument is granted.

Reply to the Twenty-seventh Objection. Some with the object of distinguishing between prophetic and beatific knowledge, contended that the prophets see the divine essence itself which they call the *mirror of eternity*, not however in the way in which it is the object of the Blessed and the end of beatitude, but as the type of things to be done, inasmuch as it contains the types of future events,[1] as stated in the argument. But this is impossible, since God in his very essence is the object of beatitude and the end of the Blessed, according to the saying of Augustine (*Conf.* v, 4) : *Happy whoso knoweth thee, though he know not these,* i.e. creatures. Now it is not possible to see the types of creatures in the very essence of God without seeing it also, both because the divine essence is the type of all things that are made (the ideal type of the thing to be made adding nothing to the divine essence save only a relationship to the creature) ; and because knowledge of a thing in itself (and such is the knowledge of God as the object of heavenly bliss) precedes the knowledge of that thing as related to something else (and such is the knowledge of God as containing the types of things). Wherefore it is impossible for prophets to see God as containing the types of creatures yet not as the object of heavenly bliss. And since they do not see the divine essence as the object of heavenly bliss (both because vision does away with prophecy (1 Cor. xiii, 9, 10)— and because the beatific vision denotes knowledge of God not as distant but as near, since he is seen face to face), it follows that prophets do not see the essence of God as the

[1] Cf. *Sum. Th.* II–II, Q. clxxiii. A. 1.

type of future events, nor do they see things in the Word as the angels did by 'morning' knowledge. For the prophetic vision is not the vision of the very essence of God, nor do they see in the divine essence itself the things that they do see, as the angels did: but they see them in certain images according as they are enlightened by the divine light as Dionysius says (*Cœl. Hier.* iv). These images illumined by the divine light have more of the nature of a mirror than the divine essence, inasmuch as in a mirror are formed images from other things, and this cannot be said of God. Yet the prophet's mind thus enlightened may be called a mirror in so far as a likeness of the truth of the divine foreknowledge is reflected therein, and for this reason it is called the *mirror of eternity* as reflecting by means of those images the foreknowledge of God who in his eternity sees all things as present before him. Hence the prophet's knowledge bears a greater resemblance to the angel's 'evening' than to his 'morning' knowledge: since the 'morning' knowledge is effected through an uncreated medium, and the prophet's through a created medium, that is by species impressed on him or illumined by the divine light, as stated above.

Reply to the Twenty-eighth Objection. In Augustine's opinion the words, *Let the earth bring forth the green herb* do not signify that plants were actually produced then in their own nature, but that the earth then received certain forces of production to be brought into action in the work of propagation: so that we may understand that the earth did then bring forth the green herb and the fruit-tree yielding fruit in the sense that then it was made capable of bringing them forth. This is confirmed by the authority of Scripture (*Gen.* ii, 4, 5) where we read: *These are the generations of the heaven and the earth when they were created in the day that the Lord God made the heaven and the earth, and every plant of the field before it sprung up in the earth, and every herb of the ground before it grew.* Whence two conclusions are to be inferred. First, that all the works of the six days were created on the day when God made heaven and earth and every plant of the field, so that the plants, which are stated to have been made on the third day were produced at the same time as heaven and earth were created by God. Secondly, that the plants were brought forth then, not into actual existence, but only in certain seed-forms, inasmuch as the earth was enabled to produce them. This is signified when it is stated that God brought forth every plant of the field before it actually sprung up in the earth by the work of administration, and every herb of the ground before it grew. Accordingly before they actually grew above the earth they were produced causally in the earth.

It is also confirmed by the following argument. In those first days God produced the creature in its cause, in its origin, or in actual existence, by a work from which he rested subsequently, and yet afterwards in the administration of things which he had made, he continues to work even until now in the work of propagation. Now the production of plants from the earth into actual existence belongs to the work of propagation, since the powers of the heavenly body as father, and of the earth as mother suffice for their production. Hence the plants were not actually produced on the third day but only in their causes: and after the six days they were brought into actual existence in their respective species and natures by the work of government. Consequently before the plants were produced causally, nothing was produced, but they were produced together with the heaven and the earth. In like manner the fishes, birds and animals were produced in those six days causally and not actually.

Reply to the Twenty-ninth Objection. It belongs to the wisdom of an artificer whose works, like God's, are all perfect, to make neither the whole separate from its chief part, nor the parts separate from the whole : since neither the whole separate from the chief part, nor the parts separate from the whole have perfect being. Since then the angels in their various species, together with the heavenly bodies and the four elements are the chief parts constituting the one universe, inasmuch as they are mutually ordered to one another and of service the one to the other ; it follows that it belongs to God's wisdom to produce the whole universe, together with all its parts at the same time and not by degrees.

The reason whereof is that of one whole together with all its parts there should be but one production, and that to produce the one before the other is a mark of weakness in the agent. Now God has infinite power without any weakness, and the universe is his principal effect. Wherefore he created by one single productive act the whole universe together with all its principal parts. And although in the production of the universe no order of time was observed, the order of nature and origin was observed. For according to Augustine the work of creation preceded the work of distinction in the order of nature but not of time ; likewise the work of distinction preceded the work of adornment in the order of nature. The work of creation consisted in the making of heaven and earth : and by the heaven we are to understand the production of the spiritual nature in a formless condition : and by the earth, the formless matter of corporeal beings. These two, as Augustine says (*Conf.* xii, 8), being outside time, considered in their essence are not subject to the alternations of time : wherefore the creation of both is described as taking place before all days. Not that this formless condition preceded formation by a priority of time, but only in the order of nature and origin, as sound precedes song. Again in his opinion, one formation does not precede another in point of duration, but only in the order of nature. According to this order we must needs give the first place to the formation of the highest spiritual nature, signified in the making of light on the first day, inasmuch as the spiritual nature surpasses the corporeal in dignity and eminence, wherefore it behoved it to be formed first : and it is formed by being enlightened, so as to adhere to the Word of God. Now just as in the natural order spiritual and divine light surpasses the corporeal nature in dignity and eminence, so also do the higher bodies surpass the lower. Hence on the second day mention is made of the formation of the higher bodies, when it is said, *Let a firmament be made*, whereby it is signified that a heavenly form was bestowed on formless matter which existed already not in point of time but in the order of origin only. The third place is given to the impression of the elemental forms on formless matter, existing already by a priority not of time but of origin and nature. Hence by the words, *Let the waters be gathered together and let the dry land appear,* we are to understand that corporeal matter received the substantial form of water so that it was enabled to carry out that movement, as also the substantial form of earth so that it became visible as dry land : because water *glides and flows away, whereas the earth abides* (*Gen. ad lit.* ii, 11). Moreover under the name of water, according to Augustine, we are to understand that the other higher elements also were formed.

In the following three days corporeal nature is stated to have been adorned. It behoved the parts of the world to be first in the order of nature formed and distinguished and afterwards each part to be adorned by being filled with their respective occupants. On the first day, as stated, the spiritual nature was formed and distinguished ; on the second the heavenly bodies were formed and distinguished, and on the fourth adorned ; on the third day the lower bodies, namely, air, water and earth were formed and distinguished : of which the air and water as being of greater dignity were adorned on the fifth day ; and the earth, being the lowest body, was adorned on the sixth day. Thus the perfection of the divine works corresponds to the perfection of the number six which is the sum and product of its aliquot parts, one, two and three : in that one day was deputed to the formation and distinction of the spiritual creature : two days to the formation and distinction of the corporeal nature, and three to its adornment (thus $1+2+3=6$: $6\times1=6$: $2\times3=6$ and $3\times2=6$). Since then six is the first perfect number, it fittingly denotes the perfection of things and of the divine works. Accordingly there is nothing to show that the order of the divine works was one of time and not of nature.

Reply to the Thirtieth Objection. The luminaries were produced in actual and not virtual existence like the plants : thus the firmament has no power productive of luminaries, as the earth has enabling it to bring forth plants. Hence Scripture does not say : *Let the firmament produce lights,* as it says : *Let the earth bring forth the green herb,* i.e. let it have the power to produce them. Wherefore the luminaries actually existed before the plants did, although the latter were produced virtually and in their causes before the luminaries were brought into actual existence. Moreover it has been stated that the order of production preceded in the order of nature the work of adornment; and the luminaries belong to the adornment of the heavens, while the plants, especially as regards their virtual existence, do not belong to the adornment of the earth, but rather to its perfection. For seemingly only such things belong to the perfection of the heavens and the earth as are intrinsic to the heavens and earth; while adornment is one of those things that are distinct from them: even so a man is perfected by his proper parts and forms, but is adorned by his clothes or something of the kind. Now things become mutually distinct especially by local movement whereby they are separated the one from the other. Hence the work of adornment comprises in a special way the production of those things that are endowed with movement whether in the heavens or on the earth. According to Ptolemy the luminaries are not fixed in the heavens but have a movement independent of that of the spheres, while in the opinion of Aristotle, the stars are fixed to the spheres; and really do not move except with the movement of the spheres: nevertheless the movements of the luminaries and stars is perceptible to the senses whereas that of the spheres is not. Moses coming down to the level of an unlettered people, described things as they appear, by saying that the luminaries are an adornment of the heavens.—Plants are not part of the earth's adornment, only the animals are: because a thing belongs to the adornment of the place wherein it has real or apparent movement, and not where it remains motionless; and the plants cling to the earth by their roots, so that they are not part of its adornment but form part of its perfection. As to the stars although they have no movement of themselves, they have an accidental and apparent movement; while the plants have no movement at all. Consequently in the order of nature it behoved the plants which belong to the intrinsic perfection of part of the universe to be produced before the luminaries which belong to the adornment of the heavens.

Reply to the Thirty-first Objection. According to Augustine (*Super Gen. contra Manich.* i, 5, 7) the earth and water mentioned at the beginning before the creation of the firmament do not signify the elements of earth and water, but primal matter devoid of all forms and species. Moses, seeing that he was addressing an unlettered people could not mention primal matter, except under the guise of things known to them and most akin to a formless condition through having more matter and less form. For this reason he expresses it by combining a twofold comparison, and instead of calling it earth only or water only, he calls it earth and water, lest if he mentioned only one of these, it might be thought that primal matter was really that and nothing else. Yet it bears a certain likeness to earth, inasmuch as it supports and underlies forms as the earth supports plants and other things. Again earth of all the elements has the least specification, being more solid and allied to matter, and less formal than the others. It bears also this likeness to water, that it has a natural aptitude for receiving various forms: because humidity which is becoming to water renders things impressionable and easy to fix. Accordingly the earth is said to be '*void and empty*' or '*invisible and incomposite,*' because matter is known by its form: so that considered in itself, it is said to be '*invisible,*' i.e. unknowable, and *void* inasmuch as the form is the end for which matter craves (because a thing is said to be *void* when it fails to obtain its end): or it is called *void* in comparison with the composite wherein it subsists, because a void is opposed to firmness and solidity. It is said to be *incomposite*, because it cannot subsist outside a composite, and lacks the beauty of actual existence. It is said to be *empty* because its potentiality is filled by the form: hence Plato (*Tim.*) identified matter with place, inasmuch as the receptivity of matter is somewhat like to the receptivity of place, in that while the same matter remains, divers forms succeed one another, just as divers bodies succeed one another in one place. Hence terms that are predicated of place are by comparison predicated of matter, so that matter is said to be empty because it lacks the form which fills the capacity and potentiality of matter. Thus, then, formless primal matter in the order of nature and origin preceded the formation of the firmament, and the latter in the order of nature preceded the earth and water mentioned on the third day, as stated above.

Reply to the Thirty-second Objection. Augustine (*De Civ. Dei* xi, 33) holds that it was not fitting for Moses to omit the production of the spiritual creature : and so he contends that in the words, *In the beginning God created heaven and earth*, *heaven* signifies the spiritual creature as yet unformed, and *earth*, formless corporeal matter. And seeing that the spiritual nature is more worthy than the corporeal, it behoved it to receive its formation first. Accordingly the formation of the spiritual nature is signified in the creation of light which denotes spiritual light ; because the formation of a spiritual nature consists in its being enlightened so as to adhere to the Word of God, not indeed by perfect glory in which it was not created, but by that which is conferred with the light of grace in which it was created : and this spiritual light preceded the firmament in the order of nature.

But in the opinion of other holy men the light created on the first day was corporeal, and was produced in the heaven created on the first day together with the substance of the sun as regards the common nature of light, while on the fourth day it received definite powers for the production of definite effects.

Reply to the Thirty-third Objection. The order of the production of these animals, since they belong to the adornment of the parts of the universe, depends on the order of the parts they adorn rather than on their own excellence. Now air and water which are adorned by fishes and birds as being more worthy in the order of nature precede the earth which is adorned by the animals that walk on its surface : wherefore it behoved the production of flying creatures and of fishes or swimming creatures to precede that of the creatures that walk.—It might also be said that in the process of generation perfection follows imperfection, and is ordered in such wise that the more imperfect things are produced first in the order of nature: because this process requires that the more perfect a thing is and the greater its likeness to the active cause, the later its production in point of time, although in the order of nature and dignity it takes precedence. For this reason since man is the most perfect of all animals, it behoved him to be made after all the others and not immediately after the heavenly bodies, which are not reckoned in relation to the lower bodies in the order of generation, since they have no matter in common with them, but one that is altogether disparate.

Reply to the Thirty-fourth Objection. Birds and fishes as regards the matter from which they are produced have more in common with each other than with terrestrial animals. Fishes and birds are said to be produced from the waters: the former from the more solid parts, the latter from the more subtle portion that was resolved into vapour so as to be a mean between air and water: hence the birds arose into the air, while the fishes sank into the deep. Now animals are assigned to various days or to one day according as their bodies are produced from different matters or from the same matter. Since then fishes and birds are said to be produced from the waters inasmuch as, considering their respective temperaments in comparison with the temperament peculiar to the common genus, they have more water in their composition than other animals have, whereas other animals are said to have been produced from the earth, hence it is that one day is assigned to the production of fishes and birds, and another day to the production of the terrestrial animals. Moreover the production of animals is related solely with respect to their being intended for the adornment of parts of the world: wherefore the days on which the animals were produced are distinguished solely with respect to their likeness or difference in the point of adorning some part of the world. As to fire and air seeing that the common people do not regard them as parts of the world, Moses does not mention them expressly but comprises them with the intermediate element namely water, especially as regards the lower parts of the air. Consequently one day is assigned to the birds and fishes which adorn the water and the air as to its lower part which is akin to water: while one other day is assigned to all the terrestrial animals.

If, however, preference be given to the opinion of Gregory and others, the arguments against this view must now be dealt with. These authors hold that between the days in question there was a succession of time, and that things were produced by degrees, so that when heaven and earth were created, there was as yet no light, nor was the firmament formed, nor were the waters removed from the face of the earth, nor the heavenly lights produced.

1. On the day when God created heaven and earth, namely the heavenly bodies and the four elements with their substantial forms, he also created every plant of the field, not actually or before it sprang up from the earth, but potentially so that afterwards on the third day it was produced into actual existence.

2. According to Gregory (*Moral.* xxxii, 9) when God created the angel, he created man also, not actually or in himself, but potentially or in his likeness, in so far as he is like the angels in regard to his intellect. Afterwards on the sixth day man was produced actually in himself.

3. The disposition of a thing that is already complete is not the same as its disposition while yet in the making: wherefore although the nature of a perfect and complete world requires that all the essential parts of the universe exist together, it could be otherwise when the world was as yet in its beginning : thus in a complete man there cannot be a heart without his other parts, yet in the formation of the embryo the heart is fashioned before any other part. It may also be replied that in this beginning of things the heavenly bodies and all the elements with their substantial forms were produced together with the angels, all of which are the principal parts of the universe ; and that on the following days, something was done in the nature already created, and pertaining to the perfection and adornment of the parts already produced.

4. Although the Greek doctors maintained that the

spiritual creature was created before the corporeal, the Latin doctors held that the angels were created at the same time as the corporeal nature, so as to ensure the simultaneous production of the universe in respect of its principle parts. For seeing that corporeal creatures are one in created matter, and that the matter of corporeal creatures was created at the same time as the angels, it may be said that all things were in a sense created at the same time either actually or potentially. Now angels have not matter in common with the corporeal creature : wherefore when the angels were created, corporeal nature would nowise have been created, and consequently neither the universe : and so it is reasonable that they should be created together with the corporeal nature. Accordingly all corporeal things were created at the same time, not actually but in respect of matter in some way formless ; and afterwards by degrees they were brought into actual existence by the distinction and adornment of the already existing creature.

5. Even as a creature has not being of itself so neither has it perfection otherwise than from God : so in order to indicate that the creature has being from God and not of itself, it was his will that it should come into existence after non-existence : and in order to indicate that the creature has not perfection of itself, it was God's will that it should be at first imperfect, and afterwards by degrees be perfected by the work of distinction and adornment. It may also be replied that it behoved the creation of things to show forth not only the might of God's power but also the order of his wisdom, so that things having precedence in nature have priority of production : wherefore it was not due to inability on the part of God as though he needed time for his works, that all things were not produced, distinguished and adorned at the same time, the reason of all this being that the order of wisdom might be observed in the production of things. Hence it was fitting that different days should be assigned to the different states of the world. After the work of creation the following work in every case added a new state of perfection to the world : wherefore in order to indicate this perfection and newness of state, it was God's

will that one day should correspond to each distinction and adornment, and not because he was weak or tired.

6. The light which, we are told, was made on the first day was the light of the sun, according to Gregory and Dionysius, which, together with the substance of the luminaries, which is the subject of that light, was produced on the first day as regards the common nature of light. On the fourth day, the luminaries were endowed with a definite power for the production of definite effects : thus we observe that the rays of the sun have a different effect from those of the moon, and so forth. For this reason Dionysius (*Div. Nom.* iv) says that this light was the light of the sun, but as yet formless as regards that which was the sun's substance, and was endowed with an illuminating power in a general way : and that afterwards it was formed on the fourth day, not indeed with a substantial form, since it has that on the first day, but as regards certain accidental additions by receiving definite powers for the production of definite effects. Accordingly when this light was produced, the light was divided from the darkness in a triple respect. First in respect of its cause, since the cause of light was the sun's substance, while the cause of darkness was the opaqueness of the earth. Secondly in respect of place, since there was light in one hemisphere and darkness in the other. Thirdly, in respect of time, since in the one hemisphere there was light at one time, and darkness at another. This is indicated in the words of Genesis i, 5, *He called the light day and the darkness night*. Hence that light neither covered the earth on all sides, since in one hemisphere there was light, and darkness in the other : nor was there always light on one side and darkness on the other, but in the same hemisphere there was day at one time and darkness at another.

7. The heaven has a twofold movement. One is the diurnal movement which is common to the whole heaven and causes day and night. This movement would seem to have been produced on the first day, when the formless substance of the sun and other luminaries was produced. The other is its own peculiar movement, which differs in the various heavenly bodies, whose movements bring about the

differences of days, months and years. On the first day was produced the common division of time into day and night by the diurnal movement which is common to the whole heaven, and may be said to have begun on the first day. Wherefore on the first day mention is made only of the distinction of day and night produced by the diurnal movement common to all the heavens. On the fourth day was made the distinction as regards the difference of days and seasons, in that one day is warmer than another, one season warmer than another, and one year warmer than another: all of which result from the special and proper movements of the stars, which movements may be understood to have commenced on the fourth day. Hence it is that on the fourth day mention is made (*ibid.* 14) of the difference between days, seasons and years: *And let them be for seasons and for days and for years*: and this difference results from their respective movements. Accordingly those first three days that preceded the formation of the luminaries were of the same kind as the days that are now regulated by the sun as regards the common division of time into day and night resulting from the diurnal movement common to the whole heaven, but not as regards the special differences of days resulting from those proper movements.

8. Some say that the light stated to be created on the first day was a luminous cloud, which subsequently when the sun was made, was resolved into the surrounding matter. But this is not likely, seeing that in the beginning of Genesis Scripture relates the establishment of nature in that condition wherein it was to remain, so that it should not be said that anything was made which after a little while ceased to exist. Hence others say that this luminous cloud still exists but united to the sun in such a manner that it cannot be distinguished from it. But in this case this cloud would be superfluous, whereas nothing in God's works is void of purpose or superfluous. Wherefore yet others say that the body of the sun was formed from this cloud. But this again is inadmissible, if we suppose the solar body not to be composed of the four elements but actually incorruptible: since in that case its matter is not susceptive of different

forms. Consequently we have to say with Dionysius (*Div. Nom.* iv) that this light was the light of the sun, of a formless sun however, in respect of what was already the substance of the sun : and that it had an illuminating power in a general way, and that on the fourth day it received a special definite power for the production of its peculiar and particular effects. And thus day and night resulted from the circular movement whereby this light approached and receded. Nor is it unlikely that the substances of the spheres which by their common diurnal movement caused this light to revolve, existed from the very beginning, and that subsequently they received certain powers in the works of distinction and adornment.

9. The production of light signifies that the property of luminosity and transparency which is reducible to the genus of light was then bestowed on all luminous and diaphanous bodies. And since the sun is the principle and source of light, by illuminating both higher and lower bodies, therefore Dionysius by the light in question understands the formless light of the sun, which by the common diurnal movement divided the day from the night, even as it does now.

10. And thus the tenth argument is solved, since that light was not a cloud in its very substance that afterwards ceased to be. It might however be called a cloud as resembling one in respect of a property, in that as a luminous cloud receives from the sun a light that is less bright than its source, even so in those first three days the substance of the sun had an imperfect and as it were formless light which was afterwards perfected on the fourth day : wherefore the substance of the sun was then luminous, since from the moment in which it was created it had its substantial form : yet the sun is stated to have been formed from it on the fourth day, not in substance, but by the addition of a new power, just as a man from being ignorant of music becomes musical not in substance but in capacity.

QUESTION V

OF THE PRESERVATION OF THINGS BY GOD

THERE are ten points of inquiry : (1) Whether things are preserved in their being by God, or do they of themselves continue to exist independently of all divine action. (2) Whether God can enable a creature to continue in existence of itself alone. (3) Whether God can annihilate a creature. (4) Whether any creature is or will be annihilated. (5) Whether the heavenly movement will cease at any time. (6) Whether it is possible for a man to know when the heavenly movement will cease. (7) Whether the elements will remain when the heavenly movement ceases. (8) Whether action and passion will remain in the elements when the heavenly movement ceases. (9) Whether plants, dumb animals and minerals will remain after the end of the world. (10) Whether human bodies will remain when the heavens cease to be in motion.

ARTICLE I

ARE THINGS PRESERVED IN THEIR BEING BY GOD ?
III *Contra Gent.* lxv, lxvii, xliv. *Sum. Th.* I, Q. civ. A. 1

THE question at issue is about the preservation of things in their being by God : and the first point of inquiry is whether they continue to exist independently of all divine action : and seemingly they do.

1. It is written (Deut. xxxii, 4) : *God's works are perfect.* Accordingly it is argued thus. A perfect thing is that which lacks nothing, according to the Philosopher (*Phys.* iii). Now a thing lacks something in its very being if it cannot exist without the assistance of an external agent. Such a

thing therefore is not perfect, and consequently the works of God are not such.

2. It may be said that God's works are not simply perfect but only in regard to their nature.—On the contrary a thing is perfect as to its nature if it has all that its nature is capable of having. Now whatsoever has all that its nature is capable of having, is able to continue in existence, even if God cease to preserve it from without. If then some creatures are perfect in their nature they can continue to exist without God keeping them in existence. The minor premise is proved thus. The preservation of things is a work of God: hence is is said (Jo. v. 17): *My Father worketh even till now, and I work* (cf. Augustine, *Gen. ad lit.* x): and when an agent works, the effect receives something. Wherefore as long as God preserves things the things preserved receive something from God, and thus whatsoever needs to be preserved has not all that it is capable of having.

3. A thing is not perfect unless it fulfils its purpose. Now the principles of a thing are intended for the purpose of preserving the being thereof. If then the created principles of things are unable to keep things in existence, it follows that they are imperfect, and are not God's works: which is absurd.

4. God is the efficient cause of things. Now the effect remains when the action of the efficient cause ceases: thus the builder ceases to act yet the house remains; the flame that caused the fire may cease to burn yet the fire caused by it continues. Therefore even if God's actions cease altogether, creatures can continue to exist.

5. But someone will say that lower agents are the causes of things becoming but not of their existence: so that the existence of an effect remains when the causes of its becoming have been removed: whereas God is the cause of things not only in their becoming but also in their being. Wherefore things cannot continue to exist if the divine action ceases.— On the contrary every thing generated has being by its form. If then the lower generating causes do not cause existence, they will not be causes of forms: and consequently forms that are in matter are not produced by forms in matter,

which is contrary to the opinion of the Philosopher (*Metaph.* vii, 8) who asserts that a form which is in this or that flesh and bones is produced by a form that is in this or that flesh and bones: and it will follow that forms in matter are produced by forms outside matter, which was Plato's view, or by the giver of forms, as Avicenna contended (*Metaph.* ix, 4, 5).

6. Things whose being is as yet in the state of becoming cannot continue after the agent has ceased to act, as instanced in movement, fire and the like, whereas those in actual existence can continue even after the agent has been removed. Hence Augustine (*Gen. ad lit.* viii, 12) says: *By the presence of light the air is not made (permanently) lightsome, but is being made lightsome, for if it had been made (permanently) lightsome, it would not continue to be made lightsome, and if the light were removed it would remain lightsome.* Now there are many creatures whose being is not in a state of becoming but of actual existence, such as the angels and all bodies. Therefore creatures can remain in existence after God has ceased to act.

7. Lower generating causes, as proved above, cause the existence of the things they generate; not, however, as principle and first, but as second causes. Now the first cause of existence which is God, does not give the things he produces the beginning of existence except through the second causes mentioned above. Wherefore neither does he give them continuance of existence, since one and the same thing derives both being and continuance of being from the same cause. Wherefore things generated are kept in existence by their essential principles, when second active causes have ceased: and consequently even when the first cause, namely God, withdraws his activity.

8. If a thing cease to exist this is either by reason of its matter or because it is produced from nothing. But matter is not a cause of corruption except through being subject to contrariety; and there is not in all creatures matter subject to contrariety. Hence those things in which there is no matter subject to contrariety, such as the heavenly bodies and angels, cannot cease to exist by reason of matter.

Nor can they cease to exist through being produced from nothing since from nothing nothing comes, and nothing has no action, and consequently does not cause a thing to be corrupted. Therefore if all divine action were to cease, such things would not cease to exist.

9. The form begins to be in matter in the last instant of a thing's becoming when it is no longer in the state of becoming but of actual existence. Now in Avicenna's opinion (*Metaph.* ix, 4, 5) the forms of generated things are inserted in matter by an active intelligence which is the giver of forms. Wherefore that intelligence is the cause of being and not only of becoming so that by its action things can be kept in existence apart from God's action.

10. The substantial form also is a cause of existence: so that if the cause of a thing's existence also keeps it in existence, it follows that the form of a thing suffices to keep it in existence.

11. A thing is kept in existence by its matter inasmuch as this upholds the form. Now according to the Philosopher (*Phys.* i, 82 : *De Cælo et Mundo*, i, 20) matter is ungenerated and incorruptible, so that it is not produced by a cause, and, therefore remains even when all action of an efficient cause ceases. Wherefore it will be possible for things to remain in existence after the action of the first efficient cause, namely God, has ceased.

12. It is written (Ecclus. xxxiii, 15) : *Look upon all the works of the most High. Two and two, and one against another.* Now some of God's works need his action to keep them in existence. Therefore as against these there must be some of God's works which do not need to be kept in existence by him.

13. The natural appetite cannot be null and void. Now everything has a natural appetence for the preservation of its existence. Wherefore a thing is able of itself to remain in existence, else its natural appetite would be frustrated.

14. Augustine says (*Enchir.* x) that God makes each thing good, and all things together very good ; for which reason it is written (Gen. i, 31) : *God saw all the things that he had made and they were very good.* Accordingly the

universe of creatures is very good and the best of all since *best produces best* according to Plato (*Tim.*). Now it is better not to need another thing for one's preservation in existence, than to need another for that purpose. Therefore the universe of creatures needs no other to keep it in existence.

15. Heavenly bliss is something created in the nature of the blessed. Now heavenly bliss is a state rendered perfect by the accumulation of all goods according to Boethius (*De Consol.* iii, 2): and this must needs include continuance in existence, which is one of the greatest goods. Therefore there is a creature that can of itself remain in existence.

16. Augustine says (*De Civ. Dei* vii, 30) that God so governs things by his providence that he allows them to exercise their own movements. Now the proper movement of nature since it proceeds from nothing is to return to nothing. Therefore God allows the nature that comes from nothing to return to nothing: and consequently he does not keep things in existence.

17. A recipient that is contrary to what it has received does not preserve it but destroys it. Thus we observe that when a natural agency produces in a subject an effect by violence, this effect remains for a time in the subject opposed to it, after the natural agent has ceased to act: thus after the fire has ceased to act, heat remains in the water heated, but only for a time. Now God's effects are received not in a contrary but in nothing, since he is the author of the whole substance of a thing. Much more then will the divine effects remain, be it only for a time, after God's action has ceased.

18. Form is the principle of knowledge, operation and existence. Now a form without assistance from without can be a principle of operation and knowledge. Therefore it can also be a principle of existence, so that after all divine action has ceased, things can be kept in existence by their forms.

On the contrary it is written (Heb. i, 8): *Upholding all things by the word of his power:* and the gloss remarks: *Even as all things were created by him, so by him are they preserved unchangeable.*

Again, Augustine says (*Gen. ad lit.* iv, 12) : *The might of the Creator and the power of the Almighty is the cause of existence in every creature ; and if the ruling power of God were withdrawn from his creatures, their form would at once cease and all nature would collapse ;* and further on : *The world would not stand for one instant, if God withdrew his support.* Again, Gregory says (*Moral.* xvi, 37) that all things would fall into nothingness were they not upheld by the hand of the Almighty.

Again, in the book *De Causis* (prop. ix) it is said : *Every intelligence derives its immobility* i.e. stability and essence, *from that goodness which is the first cause.* A fortiori therefore other creatures are not stabilised in existence save by God.

I answer that without any doubt whatever it must be admitted that things are preserved in existence by God, and that they would instantly be reduced to nothing were God to abandon them. The proof of this may be expressed as follows. An effect must needs depend on its cause. This is part of the very nature of cause and effect ; and is evidenced in formal and material causes, seeing that on the removal of any of its material or formal principles, a thing at once ceases to exist, because such principles enter into its essence. The statement applies to efficient causes even as to formal and material causes : since the efficient cause produces a thing by inducing the form or disposing the matter. Hence a thing depends equally on its efficient cause, its matter and its form since through the one it depends on the other. As to final causes the same is to be said of them as of efficient causes : because the end is a cause only for as much as it moves the efficient cause to act, since it comes first not in existence but in the intention. Consequently there is no action where there is no final cause (*Metaph* iii, 2). Accordingly the existence of a thing made depends on its efficient cause inasmuch as it depends on the form of the thing made. Now there can be an efficient cause on which the form of the thing made does not depend directly and considered as a form, but only indirectly : thus the form of a generated fire does not depend on the generating fire directly and by reason of its species, seeing that it occupies the same degree in the order of things, and the form of fire is in the same way in both the generated and in the generating fire, and is distinguished therefrom only by a material distinction, through being seated in another matter. Hence since the generated fire has its form from some cause, this same form must depend on some higher principle, that is the cause of that form directly and in respect of its very species. Now seeing that properly speaking the existence of a form in matter implies no movement or change except accidentally, and since no bodies act unless moved, as the Philosopher shows, it follows of necessity that the principle on which the form depends directly must be something incorporeal, for the effect depends on its active cause through the action of a principle. And if a corporeal principle be in some way the cause of a form, this is due to its acting by virtue of an incorporeal principle and as its instrument. In fact this is necessary in order that the form begin to exist, inasmuch as it does not begin to exist otherwise than in matter : because matter cannot be subject of a form unless it have a particular disposition, since the proper act should be in its proper matter. When, therefore, matter is in a disposition unsuitable to a particular form, it cannot directly receive that form from an incorporeal principle on which the form directly depends, so that there is need for something to transmute the matter : and this will be a corporeal agent whose action consists in moving something. This corporeal agent acts by virtue of the incorporeal principal, and its action terminates in this or that form, inasmuch as this or that form is in the corporeal agent either actually (as in universal agents) or virtually (as in equivocal agents). Accordingly these lower corporeal agents are not the cause of the forms in things made, except to the extent of their causality in transmuting matter, since they do not act except by transmuting, as stated above (Q. iii, AA. 7, 8) : and this is by transmuting matter and educing the form from the potentiality of matter. Hence the form of the thing generated depends naturally on the generator in so far as it is educed from the potentiality of matter, but not as to its absolute existence. And, therefore, when the act of the generator ceases, the eduction of the form from potentiality into actual being, that is the *becoming* of the thing generated, ceases, whereas the form itself whereby the thing generated has its existence, does not cease. Hence it is that the existence of the thing generated, but not its becoming, remains after the action of the generator has ceased. On the other hand, forms that do not exist in matter, such as intellectual substances, or that exist in matter nowise disposed to the form, such as the heavenly bodies wherein there are no contrary dispositions, must proceed from a principle that is an incorporeal agent that acts not by movement, nor do they depend on something for their *becoming* without depending on it also for their *being*. Wherefore just as when the action of their efficient cause which acts by movement ceases, at that very instant the becoming of the thing generated ceases, even so when the action of an incorporeal agent ceases, the very existence of things created by it ceases. Now this incorporeal agent by whom all things, both corporeal and incorporeal are created, is God, as we have proved above (Q. iii, AA. 5, 6, 8), from whom things derive not only their form but also their matter. And as to the question at issue it makes no difference whether they were all made by him immediately, or in a certain order as certain philosophers have maintained. We conclude then that with the cessation of the divine operation, at the same instant all things would fall into nothingness, as we have proved by the authorities quoted in the arguments '*On the contrary.*'

Reply to the First Objection. God's creatures are perfect in their nature and order: and their perfection requires among other things that they be kept in existence by God.

Reply to the Second Objection. God does not create things by one action and preserve them by another. The existence of permanent things is not divisible except accidentally in so far as it is subject to some kind of movement: and in itself is in an instant. Hence God's action which is the direct cause of a thing's existence is not distinct as the principle of its being and as the principle of its continuance in being.

Reply to the Third Objection. As long as the essential

principles of a thing remain, so long does that thing continue to exist: but those very principles would cease to be, were the divine action to cease.

Reply to the Fourth Objection. These lower agents cause a thing as to its *becoming*, but not as to its existence properly speaking: whereas God is the direct cause of existence: wherefore the comparison fails. Hence Augustine says (*Gen. ad lit.* iv, 12): *When a man is building a house and goes away, the building remains after he has ceased to work and gone: whereas the world would not stand for a single instant if God withdrew his support.*

Reply to the Fifth Objection. Inasmuch as corporeal agents do not act except by transmuting, and as nothing is transmuted except by reason of matter, the causality of corporeal agents cannot extend beyond things that in some way are in matter. The Platonists together with Aricenna through denying the eduction of forms from matter were obliged to hold that natural agents merely dispose matter, and that the form is induced by a principle that is separate from matter. On the other hand if with Aristotle we hold substantial forms to be educed from the potentiality of matter, natural agents will dispose not only matter but also the substantial form, only, however, in regard to its eduction from the potentiality of matter into actual existence, as stated above (Q. iii, AA. 9, 11): so that they will be principles of existence as considered in its inchoation but not as considered absolutely.

Reply to the Sixth Objection. Some of the forms that begin to exist in matter through the action of a corporeal agent are when produced perfect both in their specific nature and in their being in matter, like the form of their generator: the reason being that the matter does not retain contrary principles: and such forms remain after the action of their generator, until the time of their corruption. Other forms however when produced are perfect in their specific nature, but have not perfect being in matter: thus heat in hot water has the perfect species of heat, but not perfect being which depends on the hold that the form has on the matter, inasmuch as the matter retains the form that is contrary to the quality of heat. Forms of this description can remain for a short time after the action of the agent, but are prevented from remaining for long by the contrary principle that is in the matter. Again other forms when produced in matter are imperfect both in species and in being: as for instance light which is produced in the air by a luminous body: for light in the air is not a perfect natural form as light in the luminous body, but rather after the manner of an *intention*. Hence just as a man's likeness does not remain in a mirror save as long as the mirror is in front of him, even so neither does light remain in the air when the luminous body is no longer present. For these *intentional* beings depend on the natural forms of bodies directly and not only accidentally, so that they no longer remain in existence after the action of the agent has ceased. Wherefore suchlike things are said to be in a state of becoming on account of the imperfection of their being, whereas perfect creatures are not said to be in a state of becoming although they have an imperfect being, and God who made them never ceases to uphold them.

Reply to the Seventh Objection. The action of a corporeal agent does not extend beyond movement, so that it is the instrument of the first agent in the eduction of forms from potentiality to actuality which education is by movement: but not in their preservation, except in so far as through some kind of movement matter is made to retain the disposition which renders it appropriate to the form: it is thus in fact that the lower bodies are kept in existence through the movement of the heavenly bodies.

Reply to the Eighth Objection. If the divine action were to cease, the creature also would cease to exist, not through the presence of a contrary in its matter, since that would cease to exist at the same time as the matter, but because the creature is made from nothing: and yet not in the sense that nothingness conduces actually to the corruption of the creatures, but that it does not act for its preservation.

Reply to the Ninth Objection. Even the giver of forms, **if** we suppose with Avicenna that it is something apart from God, must cease to exist if God who is its cause cease to act.

Reply to the Tenth Objection. The form also would cease to exist if the aforesaid action were to cease, so that it could no longer be a principle of existence.

Reply to the Eleventh Objection. Matter is said to be ungenerated because it is not produced by generation : but this does not exclude its being produced by God, seeing that every imperfect thing must needs originate from a perfect one.

Reply to the Twelfth Objection. In God's works the presence of one contradictory does not argue the presence of its opposite (for then it would follow that since some of his works are created, there must be some that are not created) although this is true if we apply it to other kinds of opposition. But the things to which the objection refers are in contradictory opposition to each other ; wherefore the argument does not prove.

Reply to the Thirteenth Objection. It is true that everything has a natural desire to be kept in existence, not however by its own action but by its cause.

Reply to the Fourteenth Objection. The universe of creatures is the best, not simply, but in the genus of created things : so that nothing prevents something from being better.

Reply to the Fifteenth Objection. The goods, the accumulation of which makes the state of beatitude perfect, have their source in the creature's union with its cause : since the beatitude of the rational creature consists in enjoying God.

Reply to the Sixteenth Objection. Properly speaking tendency to nothingness is not a movement of nature, which always has a tendency to the good ; but it is a defect of nature that it tends to nothingness, so that the argument is based on a false supposition.

Reply to the Seventeenth Objection. A violent agent that produces a violent impression is the cause of that impression as to its *becoming* and not simply as to its being, as explained above (*ad* 6). Wherefore as soon as the agent ceases to act the impression may last for a time but not for long on account of its imperfection.

Reply to the Eighteenth Objection. Just as a form cannot be a principle of existence, unless we presuppose some previous principle, even so neither can it be a principle of operation since God works in everything as we have shown above (Q. iii, A. 6) : nor again of knowledge, since all knowledge derives from the uncreated light.

ARTICLE II

CAN GOD ENABLE A CREATURE TO KEEP ITSELF IN EXISTENCE BY ITSELF AND WITHOUT GOD'S ASSISTANCE ?

THE second point of inquiry is whether God can make a creature able of itself to keep itself in existence independently of God ; and seemingly he can do so.

1. To create is more than to keep oneself in existence. Now a creature could have received the power to create according to the Master (*Sent.* v, 4). Therefore it could have received the power to keep itself in existence.

2. The power of God over things surpasses the power of our intellect. Now our intellect can understand a creature apart from God. Much more therefore can God make a creature able of itself to keep itself in existence.

3. There is a creature made to God's image (Gen. i, 26). Now according to Hilary (*De Synod.*[1]) an image is the undivided and united likeness of one thing adequately representing another: so that an image can be adequate to the thing of which it is the image. Seeing then that God needs no other to keep him in existence, it would seem that he could communicate this to a creature.

4. The more perfect the agent the more perfect an effect can it produce. Now natural agents can produce effects which are able to remain in existence without their causes. Therefore *a fortiori* God can do this.

On the contrary God can do nothing that is prejudicial to his own authority : and it would be prejudicial to his dominion if anything could exist without his upholding it. Therefore God cannot do this.

I answer that God's omnipotence does not imply that he can make two contradictories true at the same time. Now the statement that God can produce a thing

[1] Super i. can. Synod. Ancyr.

which does not need to be upheld by him involves a contradiction. For we have already proved that every effect depends on its cause in so far as it is its cause. Accordingly the statement that a thing needs not God to uphold its existence implies that it is not created by God: while the statement that such a thing is produced by God implies that it is created by him. Wherefore just as it would involve a contradiction to say that God produced a thing that was not created by him, even so it would involve a contradiction were one to say that God made a thing that did not need to be kept in existence by him. Wherefore God is equally unable to do either.

Reply to the First Objection. Since to create is to be the cause of something, and only that which has no cause needs not to be kept in existence by another, it is clear that not to need to be kept in existence by another is more than to create : even as to have no cause is more than to be a cause. Moreover it is not altogether true that the power of creating is communicable to a creature, seeing that it is the act of the first agent as we have shown above (Q. iii, A. 4).

Reply to the Second Objection. Although the intellect is able to understand a creature without understanding God, it cannot understand a creature not being kept in existence by God, since this involves a contradiction, as if one were to say that a creature is not created by God, as stated above (Q. iii, A. 5).

Reply to the Third Objection. Equality is essential to an image, not absolutely speaking but of a perfect image : such an image of God is not a creature but the Son of God ; wherefore the argument proves nothing.

The *Reply to the Fourth Objection* may be gathered from what has been already said in the preceding answer.

ARTICLE III

CAN GOD ANNIHILATE A CREATURE ?
Sum. Th. I, Q. civ, A. 3

THE third point of inquiry is whether God can annihilate a creature : and seemingly he cannot.

1. Augustine says (*QQ.* lxxxiii, qu. 2) that God does not cause things to tend to non-existence. But this would be the case were he to annihilate a creature. Therefore God cannot annihilate a creature.

2. Corruptible creatures whose existence is more unstable than that of others, do not cease to exist save through the action of some active cause: thus fire is extinguished by some counteracting agency. Much less therefore can other creatures cease to exist otherwise than through some agency. If then God were to annihilate a creature, this would not be except through some kind of action. But this cannot be done through an action: since every action, proceeding as it does from an actual being, must terminate in an actual being, because every maker produces its like. Now an action whereby an actual being is produced in no way annihilates. Therefore God cannot annihilate a thing.

3. Whatsoever happens accidentally must be traced to something that is intended directly. Now no active cause produces imperfection and corruption save accidentally, since nothing acts without intending a good, according to Dionysius (*Div. Nom.* iv): thus the purpose of fire in destroying water is not to deprive the water of its form, but to introduce its own form into the matter. Wherefore imperfection cannot be caused by an agent, without some perfection being caused at the same time. Now where a perfection is produced there is not annihilation. Therefore God cannot annihilate a thing.

4. Nothing acts except for an end: since the end moves the effective cause. Now the end of God's action is his own goodness: and this is indeed obtained by his producing things, so that they are made in likeness to their producer, but not by his annihilating them, since thereby they would be utterly deprived of that likeness. Therefore God cannot annihilate a thing.

5. So long as the cause remains its effect must needs remain also: because if this were not necessary, it would be possible, given a cause, for its effect to be or not to be; and then it would need something else to determine its being: and thus the cause would not suffice for the existence of its

effect. But God is the sufficient cause of things. Therefore as long as God exists things must needs remain in existence. Now God cannot prevent his own remaining in existence. Therefore he cannot reduce creatures to non-existence.

6. It will be said that God would not be the actual cause if things were to be annihilated.—On the contrary, God's action is his being, wherefore Augustine says (*De Doctr. Christ.* i, 32) that God's existence is the reason of our existence. Now his existence was never new to him. Therefore he never ceases to act, and will always be an actual cause.

7. God cannot act against common sense, e.g. he cannot make the whole larger than its part. Now all wise men are agreed that the rational soul is immortal. Therefore God cannot cause it to be annihilated.

8. The Commentator says (*Metaph.* xi, com. 41) that if a thing in itself can either be or not be, nothing else can make it be of necessity. Wherefore whatsoever creatures have being of necessity do not admit of the intrinsic possibility of being or of not being. Now such are all incorruptible things, e.g. incorporeal substances and heavenly bodies. Therefore in none of these is there the possibility of not being: so that if they be left to themselves through God withdrawing his action from them, they will not cease to exist: and thus seemingly God cannot annihilate them.

9. The thing received does not remove the potentiality of the recipient; but it may perfect it. If then there exist a thing which potentially does not exist, it cannot receive anything that will remove this potentiality: and consequently a thing that in itself contains the possibility of not existing, cannot receive from anything else the necessity of existing.

10. Whatever causes a generic difference belongs to the essence of things, for the genus is part of a thing's definition. Now certain things differ generically in the point of being corruptible or incorruptible (*Metaph.* x, 10). Therefore everlastingness or incorruptibility is part of such things' essence. Now God cannot deprive a thing of what is essential to it, thus he cannot make a man not to be an animal and yet remain a man. Therefore he cannot cause incorruptible

things not to last for ever, and thus he cannot reduce them to nothing.

11. A corruptible thing can never be changed so as to become naturally incorruptible (for the incorruptibility of bodies rising from the dead is a gift not of nature but of glory) and the reason for this is that corruptible and incorruptible differ generically, as stated above. Now if a thing which has an intrinsic possibility not to exist, could be made by something else to exist of necessity, a corruptible thing might be changed into an incorruptible one. Therefore a thing which has an intrinsic possibility not to exist cannot possibly acquire necessity of existing from another : and so we come to the same conclusion as above.

12. If creatures have no necessity of existing except in so far as they depend on God, and if they depend on God in so far as he is their cause, their necessity of existing must correspond to the mode of causality whereby God is their cause. Now God is the cause of things not of necessity but by his will, as we have proved above (Q. iii, A. 15). Therefore necessity in things will be such as it is in things that are produced by the will. Now things effected by the will are not necessary simply and absolutely : their necessity is only conditional, inasmuch as the will is not determined by necessity to one particular effect. It follows then that in things nothing is absolutely necessary, but only conditionally: even as it is necessary that Socrates move if he runs ; or walk if he wishes to walk and is not prevented from so doing. Whence it would seem to follow that no creature is simply incorruptible, and that all are corruptible : which cannot be admitted.

13. Just as God is the sovereign good so is he the most perfect being. Now inasmuch as he is the sovereign good, it is unbecoming to him to be the cause of the evil of sin. Therefore inasmuch as he is the most perfect being it is unbecoming to him to cause things to be annihilated.

14. Augustine says (*Enchir.* xi) that God is so good that he would never allow evil to be done, were he not so powerful that he can produce a good from any evil whatsoever. But no good would result if creatures were to be annihilated.

Therefore God cannot allow creatures to return to nothingness.

15. The distance from nothing to being is no less than from being to nothing. Now it belongs to an infinite power to produce a being from nothing on account of the infinite distance. Therefore only an infinite power can reduce a being to nothing. But no creature has infinite power. Hence if we take away the action of the Creator, a creature cannot be reduced to nothing : and yet only on the supposition that God's action be removed was it said that he can annihilate things. Therefore nowise can God reduce creatures to nothing.

On the contrary Origen says (*Peri Archon*) : *That which was given can be taken away and lost.* Now creatures were given existence by God. Therefore it can be taken from them : so that God can reduce them to nothing.

Again, that which depends on God's simple will, can also cease if it be God's will. Now the creature's whole being depends on God's simple will, since he is the cause of things by his will and not by natural necessity. Therefore if it be his will creatures can be annihilated.

Again, God is not more indebted to creatures after they begin to exist than he was before they began to exist. Now, before they came into existence, he could, without prejudice to his goodness, abstain from bringing them into being, since his goodness nowise depends on creatures. Therefore without prejudice to his goodness God can withdraw his action from creatures, with the result as proved above (A. 2) that they would cease to exist. Therefore God can annihilate creatures.

Again, as we have proved (A. 1) God, by the same action, produces and upholds things. Now God was able not to produce creatures. Therefore he can likewise abstain from upholding them : and thus he can annihilate them. *I answer that* things made by God may be said to be possible to him in two ways. First with regard to the power of the agent alone : thus before the world was made, it was possible for the world to exist, not by a possibility inherent to the creature, which did not exist, but only by the power of God, who was able to bring the world into being. Secondly in respect of a possibility inherent to the thing made : thus it is possible for a composite body to be corrupted. Accordingly if we consider the possibility of non-existence in reference to things made, there have been two opinions on this point. Avicenna (*Metaph.* viii, 6) held that all things except God have in themselves a possibility of being and of non-being. Because seeing that being is something besides the essence of a created thing, the very nature of a creature considered in itself has a possibility of being, while it only has necessity of being from another whose nature is its being, and which therefore by its nature exists of necessity ; and this is God. On the other hand the Commentator (*Metaph.* xi, text. 41 : and *De Subst. Orb.*) holds a contrary opinion, to wit that certain things were created in whose nature there is no possibility of non-being inasmuch as a thing that has in its nature a possibility of non-being, cannot acquire everlastingness from without, so as to become by its very nature everlasting. The latter opinion would seem more reasonable. Because possibility of being and non-being does not belong to a thing save by reason of its matter which is pure potentiality. And matter since it cannot exist without a form cannot have a potentiality in respect of non-being, save as, while existing under some form it retains the possibility of receiving another form. Accordingly it may happen in two ways, that a thing's nature does not include the possibility of non-being. First, because that thing is a pure form subsistent in its own being, such as incorporeal substances which are entirely immaterial. For if a form through being in matter is the principle of existence in material things, and a material thing cannot cease to exist save by losing its form, it follows that when a form subsists by itself it can nowise cease to exist, even as neither can existence be separated from itself. Secondly, because the matter has no potentiality in respect of another form, and the whole of its potentiality is determined by one form : such are the heavenly bodies in which there is no contrariety of forms. Accordingly a possibility of non-being is in the nature of those things alone whose matter is subject to contrariety of forms : whereas it belongs to other things by their nature to exist of necessity, all possibility of non-existence being removed from their nature. And yet this does not imply that their necessity of existence is not from God: since one necessity may cause another (*Metaph.* v). For the created nature to which everlastingness belongs is produced by God. Moreover in those things which contain a possibility of non-being the matter remains, while the forms change: thus, when things are generated, they are educed from potentiality into actuality by generation even as, when they are corrupted, they are reduced from actuality so as to return to a state of potentiality. It follows then that in all created natures there is no such potentiality whereby a thing is made to have the possibility of tending to non-existence.

If on the other hand we consider the power of God the Maker of things, we must observe that a thing is said to be impossible to God in two ways. First, because it is impossible in itself, in that by its very nature it is outside the scope of any power whatsoever: such are things that involve a contradiction. Secondly, because the opposite of that thing is necessary: and this occurs in two ways with respect to an agent. First on the part of a natural active power that is confined to one effect: thus the power of a hot thing is confined to heating: in this way God the Father begot the Son necessarily and cannot but beget him. Secondly, on the part of the ultimate end to which everything tends of necessity: thus man necessarily desires happiness and cannot possibly desire to be unhappy: and likewise God necessarily wills his goodness, and cannot possibly will things that are incompatible with it: for example we say that God cannot lie or wish to lie. Now the simple non-existence of creatures is not in itself impossible as involving a contradiction (else they had existed from eternity: and the reason of this is that they are not their own being): thus in the statement, *The creature does not exist at all*, the predicate is not in conflict with the definition of the subject, whereas it is in the sentence, *Man is not a rational animal*: for sentences of the latter kind imply a contradiction and are impossible in themselves. Likewise God did not produce creatures by natural necessity, as though his power were determined to the existence of creatures, as we have proved above (A. 3). Likewise God's goodness does not depend on creatures, as though it could not be without them : seeing that it gains nothing by them. It remains then that it is not impossible for God to reduce things to nothing : since he is not under the necessity of giving them being, except on the presupposition of his decree and foreknowledge, in that he decreed and foresaw that he would keep things in existence for ever.

Reply to the First Objection. If God were to reduce creatures to nothing, he would not be the cause of their tendency to non-existence : because it would result not from his causing non-existence in them, but from his ceasing to give them existence.

Reply to the Second Objection. Corruptible things cease to exist, in so far as their matter receives another form, with which its previous form was incompatible : wherefore their corruption requires the action of a certain agent, whereby the new form is educed from its potential state into actual existence. Whereas if God were to annihilate a thing, there would be no need for any action, and it would suffice if God were to withdraw the action whereby he gives things existence : thus the absence of the sun's action in enlightening the air causes the absence of light in the air.

Reply to the Third Objection. This argument would avail, if God could by some action annihilate things : but this is not so, rather would it be by ceasing from action.

Reply to the Fourth Objection. Where there is no action we need not require an end. But seeing that even cessation from action cannot be in God save by his will, and that the will's object is the end, it might be possible to ascribe an end even in the annihilation of things : so that as in the production of things, the end was the manifestation of God's abundant goodness, so in the annihilation of things the end could be the sufficiency of his goodness, seeing that it is so self-sufficing as to need nothing from without.

Reply to the Fifth Objection. The effect both follows its cause and derives its mode from the cause ; wherefore effects consequent upon an act of the will, proceed from the will at the time appointed by the will ; and not necessarily as soon as the will has decreed their existence. And thus since creatures proceed from God by his will, they come into being when it is God's will that they should be, not of necessity or simultaneously with God's will, otherwise they would have existed from eternity.

Reply to the Sixth Objection. The action whereby God made things may be considered from a twofold point of view : it may be considered in its substance and in its relation to its effect. The substance of that action since it is the divine essence is eternal and cannot but be ; whereas the relation to its effect depends on the divine will : because every action of a maker produces its effect according to the exigency of the principle of that action : thus fire imparts heat according to the measure of its own heat. Hence seeing that God's will is the principle of the things made by him, his action bears a relation to his effects according as his will determines. Hence though God's action cannot cease in its substance, its relation to his effects might cease, if he so willed.

Reply to the Seventh Objection. A principle of common sense is one whose opposite involves a contradiction, for instance, ' A whole is greater than its part,' because it is contrary to the definition of a whole that it be not greater than its part. Now it is not contrary to common sense that a rational soul cease to exist, as we have already made clear : but it is in common sense that the nature of the rational soul be incorruptible. Wherefore if God were to reduce a human soul to nothing this would not be through the soul's having some inherent possibility of non-existence, as stated above.

Reply to the Eighth Objection. A thing whose nature contains the possibility of non-existence does not acquire from an external source the necessity of being so that this necessity be contained in its nature, since this would involve a contradiction, to wit the possibility of a nature's non-existence together with the necessity of its existence ; but there is nothing to prevent its acquiring incorruptibility by grace or glory. Thus by virtue of the union of the soul with its principle Adam's body was in a way incorruptible through the grace attached to the state of innocence, and the bodies of the risen dead will be incorruptible by the grace belonging to the state of glory. On the other hand a nature which does not include the possibility of non-existence is not prevented from acquiring from another source the necessity of existence, since whatsoever perfection it has, it has received it from another : wherefore if its cause withdraw its action, it would cease to exist, not on account of its inherent potentiality to non-existence, but on account of God's power to cease giving existence.

Reply to the Ninth Objection. It has been sufficiently shown that things which are incorruptible by nature are not to be supposed, as the objection supposes, to have at first a potentiality to non-existence which potentiality is removed by something received from God : whereas in things which are incorruptible by grace, there underlies in their nature a possibility of non-existence, which however is entirely voided by grace through the power of God.

Reply to the Tenth Objection. If by ceasing to uphold them God were to reduce incorruptible creatures to nothing, he would not by so doing deprive their nature of its everlastingness, so that it would remain without being everlasting : but their whole nature would cease to exist through their cause ceasing to exercise its influence over them.

Reply to the Eleventh Objection. That which is by nature corruptible cannot be changed so as to become naturally incorruptible, and vice versa : although that which is corruptible by nature can be made to last for ever by the superaddition of glory. Yet it does not follow that certain corruptible things become naturally incorruptible, since were their cause to withdraw they would cease to exist.

Reply to the Twelfth Objection. Although incorruptible creatures depend on God's will, which can either give or not give them existence, nevertheless by that same will they are gifted with the absolute necessity of existence, in so far as they are created in a nature wherein there is no potentiality to non-existence : because every creature is such as God willed it to be, as Hilary says (*De Synod*).

Reply to the Thirteenth Objection. Although God is able to reduce creatures to nothing, he cannot as long as they continue to exist, cease to be the cause of their existence. Now he is their cause both efficient and final. Accordingly just as he cannot cause an existing creature not to owe its existence to him, even so he cannot cause that creature not to be ordered to his goodness. Wherefore since the evil of sin removes the order of which he is the end, inasmuch as sin is aversion from the highest good ; it follows that God cannot be the cause of the evil of sin, although he can be the cause of annihilation, by ceasing altogether to uphold a creature.

Reply to the Fourteenth Objection. Augustine is speaking of the evil of sin : and even if he were referring to penal evil, the annihilation of things would be no evil, because every evil since it is a privation is based upon good, as Augustine says (*Enchir.* xi). Hence just as there was no evil before things were created, so neither would there be any evil were God to annihilate all things.

Reply to the Fifteenth Objection. No creature has the power either of making something from nothing or of reducing a thing to nothing. The fact that if God ceased to uphold creatures they would return to nothing is not due to a creature's action but to its defect, as stated above.

ARTICLE IV

IS THERE A CREATURE THAT OUGHT TO BE OR ACTUALLY IS ANNIHILATED ?

THE third point of inquiry is whether any creature is to be annihilated, or is actually annihilated : and seemingly the answer should be in the affirmative.

1. Just as a finite power cannot move in an infinite time, even so by no finite power can a thing exist for an infinite time. Now all corporeal power is finite (*Phys.* viii).

Therefore no body has the power to exist for an infinite time. But there are bodies that cannot be corrupted, because nothing is contrary to them, like the heavenly bodies. Therefore at some time they must of necessity be annihilated.

2. That which is directed to the attainment of an end is no longer needed where the end has been reached: thus a ship is necessary that we may cross the sea, but we no longer need it after crossing the ocean. Now corporeal creatures were made for the sake of the spiritual creature, in order to help it to reach its end. When therefore the spiritual creatures arrive at their ultimate end they no longer need corporeal creatures: and since there is nothing superfluous in God's works it would seem that at the last end of all things every corporeal creature will cease to exist.

3. Nothing accidental is infinite. Now existence is accidental to the creature according to Avicenna (*Metaph.* viii, 4); wherefore Hilary (*De Trin.* vii) distinguishes God from his creatures by stating that *there is no accident in God*. Therefore no creature will last for ever, and all creatures will at some time be reduced to nothing.

4. The end should correspond to the beginning. Now creatures had their beginning after nothing had existed but God. Therefore creatures will return to an end wherein there will be absolutely nothing in existence.

5. That which has no power to exist always, cannot endure for ever. And that which has not always been has no power to exist always. Therefore that which was not always cannot endure for ever. But creatures were not always. Therefore they cannot last for ever, and thus they will at length be annihilated.

6. Justice requires, if a man is ungrateful for a benefit bestowed or acquired, that he should be deprived of it. Now by committing mortal sin man proved himself ungrateful. Therefore justice demands that he be deprived of all the benefits he has received from God, among which is his very existence: also God's judgement on sinners will be just according to the Apostle (Rom. ii, 2). Therefore they will be annihilated.

7. The words of Jeremias are to the point (x, 24): *Correct*

me O Lord, and yet with judgement and not in thy fury, lest thou bring me to nothing.

8. It will be said perhaps that God's punishments are even less severe than what is deserved, on account of his mercy which in his judgements is always mingled with justice : so that God does not exclude sinners entirely from a share in his benefits.—On the contrary, mercy is not shown to man by granting him what it were better for him not to have : and it were better for the damned not to be at all than to be thus, as evidenced by the words about Judas (Matt. xxvi, 24) : *It were better for him had that man not been born.* Therefore it is no part of God's mercy that the damned be kept in existence.

9. Things that have no matter in their composition are altogether, i.e. utterly destroyed when they disappear (*Metaph.* iii) : for instance accidents. Now accidents frequently disappear. Therefore some things are reduced to nothing.

10. The Philosopher (*Phys.* vi) argues that if a continuous quantity is composed of indivisible parts, it must be resolved into indivisible parts. Whence we may infer that everything is resolved into the elements from which it is produced. Now all creatures are produced from nothing. Therefore all at some time will be resolved into nothing.

11. It is written (2 Pet. ii, 10) : *The heavens shall pass away with great violence.* But they cannot pass away by corruption so as to be changed into some other body, since they have no contrary. Therefore they will pass away into nothing.

12. Again to the point are the words of Psalm ci, 26, 27 : *The heavens are the works of thy hands : they shall perish,* and of Luke xxi, 63 : *Heaven and earth shall pass away.* On the contrary it is written (Eccles. i, 4) : *The earth standeth for ever :* and again (*ibid.* iii, 14) : *I have learned that all the works which God hath made continue for ever.* Therefore creatures will not be annihilated.

I answer that the created universe will never be annihilated. And notwithstanding that corporeal creatures have not always existed they will last nevertheless for ever as to their substance : although it has been maintained by some that at the final consummation all corruptible creatures will be reduced to nothing, an opinion that has been ascribed to Origen, who however apparently does not assert it as his own but rather as a view held by others.

In support of this solution to the question we may argue from a twofold source. First from the divine will, on which the existence of creatures depends. Although considered in itself God's will about creatures is indifferent to opposite things, since it is not more bound to one alternative than to another, yet it is necessitated in a way of speaking through the granting of a supposition. For even as in creatures that which is indifferent to opposite things is necessitated through a supposition being made (thus it is possible for Socrates to sit or not to sit, but while he sits, it is necessary that he sit), so too the divine will which, considered in itself, can will either a certain thing or its opposite—for instance, to save or not to save Peter—cannot will not to save Peter so long as he wills to save him. And whereas God's will is unchangeable, if it be supposed that he wills a certain thing at some time, on that supposition it is necessary that he will it always, although it is not necessary if he will a thing to last for a time, that he also will it to last for ever. Now he who wills a thing for its own sake, wills it to last for ever, for the very reason that he wills it for itself : because if he wills a thing to exist for a time, and afterwards not to exist, he wills that thing to exist for the perfection of something else, and when this latter is perfected, he no longer wills the thing that he only willed that this other thing might be made perfect. Now God wills the created universe for its own sake, although he wills its existence for his own sake : for these two are not incompatible with each other. Because God wills creatures to exist for his goodness' sake, namely that they may imitate and reflect it ; which they do inasmuch as from it they derive their being, and subsist in their respective natures. Consequently it amounts to the same whether we say that God made all things for himself according to the text of Proverbs xvi, 4, *The Lord hath made all things for himself,* or that he made creatures that they might exist, according to Wisdom, i, 14, *He created all things that they might be.* Wherefore from the very fact that God made creatures it is to be inferred that he willed them to last for ever, and seeing that his will is unchangeable the opposite will never happen.

Secondly, from the very nature of things. God fashioned each nature in such a way as not to deprive it of its property. Hence on the words of Romans xi, 24, *Contrary to nature thou wert grafted,* a gloss says that *God who is the author of nature does not act contrary to nature,* although at times in support of the faith he performs in creatures works that surpass nature. Now it is a natural property of those immaterial things which have no contrary that they last for ever, since in them there is no potentiality to non-existence, as we have shown above. Thus even as he does not deprive fire of its natural inclination to rise, so neither does he deprive the aforesaid things of their everlastingness by reducing them to nothing.

Reply to the First Objection. According to the Commentator (*Metaph.* xi, comm. 41) although all potentiality residing in a body is finite it does not follow that every body has a finite potentiality to exist : seeing that bodies that are actually corruptible have no potentiality, finite or infinite, to exist but only to be moved. This solution however apparently does not solve the difficulty. Potentiality to exist may be taken not only in the sense of a passive potentiality that is on the side of matter, but also in the sense of an active power which is on the part of the form which cannot be lacking to incorruptible things : because power of existence is proportionate to the degree in which a form is in a thing : wherefore the Philosopher (*De Cælo et Mundo,* i) holds that certain things have the virtue and power to last for ever. Accordingly we reply otherwise as follows. From the fact that a thing lasts for an infinite time we cannot infer that it has an infinite potentiality to exist, unless it be itself measured by time either directly, as movement, or indirectly, as the existence of things that are subject to movement, and are for a certain period of time, beyond which they cannot last. Now the existence of a heavenly body is not affected by time or movement, since it is utterly unchangeable. Wherefore from the fact that the heaven lasts for an infinite time, it does not acquire infinity of existence, seeing that it is altogether outside the continuance of time : for which reason theologians say that it is measured by eviternity. Therefore the heaven does not require an infinite power in order to last for ever.

Reply to the Second Objection. Just as one part of an army is related both to another part and to the commander-in-chief, so too the corporeal creature is directed both to assist in the perfecting of the spiritual, and to reflect the divine goodness. The latter it will do for ever, though it cease to do the former.

Reply to the Third Objection. If we speak of substantial existence, then existence is not described as an accident as though it were in the genus of accident (for it is the act of an essence) but by a kind of similitude, inasmuch as like an accident it is not part of the essence. And yet even if it were in the genus of accident nothing prevents it from lasting for ever, seeing that proper accidents are of necessity in their respective substances, so that nothing hinders them from being in them for ever. On the other hand accidents that adhere to their subjects accidentally are nowise everlasting by nature : but the substantial existence of a thing cannot be an accident of this kind, because it is the act of its essence.

Reply to the Fourth Objection. Before things existed, there was no nature having everlastingness as a property, as there was when things had been created. Moreover it would conduce to a certain perfection of the spiritual creature that things did not always exist, since this is a distinct proof that God is the cause of things : whereas no good would result if all things were annihilated. Hence the comparison fails between the beginning and the end.

Reply to the Fifth Objection. Those things that will last for ever have the power to last for ever ; but they did not always have this power, wherefore they did not always exist.

Reply to the Sixth Objection. Although in justice God

could deprive of existence and annihilate a creature that sins against him, yet it is a more becoming justice that he keep it in existence to punish it : and this for two reasons. First, because in the former case justice would have no admixture of mercy, since nothing would remain to which he might show mercy : and yet it is written (Ps. xxiv, 10) that *all the ways of the Lord are mercy and truth*. Secondly, because in the second case justice is more in proportion with sin, and this in two respects. In the first place, when a sin is committed the will rebels against God, whereas nature does not, but observes the order assigned to it by God : so that the punishment should be such as to afflict the will by hurting the nature which the will had abused : whereas if the creature were utterly annihilated, nature would be hurt indeed, but the will would not be afflicted. In the second place, seeing that sin contains two things, aversion from the incommutable good, and conversion to transient good, aversion results from conversion, since no sinner intends to turn away from God, but seeks the enjoyment of a temporal good which is incompatible with the enjoyment of evil. Wherefore as the pain of loss corresponds to the aversion of sin, while the pain of sense corresponding to the conversion is inflicted for the actual sin, it is fitting that the pain of loss should not be without the pain of sense : whereas if the creature were annihilated there would be eternal pain of loss, but the pain of sense would cease.

Reply to the Seventh Objection. The judgement mentioned by the prophet signifies the infliction of a congruous punishment in proportion to sin, as explained above : and the fury from which he prays to be delivered is that which excludes the moderation of mercy.

Reply to the Eighth Objection. A thing is said to be better either because it includes a greater good, and thus it is better for the damned to exist than not to exist : or because it excludes an evil, since even absence of evil is reckoned a good by the Philosopher (*Ethic.* v., 8). The words of our Lord quoted are to be taken in the latter sense.

Reply to the Ninth Objection. Although forms and accidents have no matter in their composition, they have matter in which they exist and from the potentiality of which they are educed : wherefore when they cease to be, they are not utterly annihilated, but remain in the potentiality of matter as before.

Reply to the Tenth Objection. Even as creatures are made from nothing, so are they reducible to nothing, if so it pleased God.

Reply to the Eleventh and Twelfth Objections. The sense of the passages quoted is not that the substance of the world will perish, but that its outward appearance will vanish according to the Apostle (1 Cor. vii, 31).

ARTICLE V

WILL THE HEAVENLY MOVEMENT CEASE AT ANY TIME ?

Sum. Th. Suppl., Q. xci, A. 2

THE fifth point of inquiry is whether the movement of the heavens will cease at any time : and seemingly it will not.

1. It is written (Gen. viii, 22) : *All the days of the earth, seed time and harvest, cold and heat, summer and winter, night and day, shall not cease.* Now all these result from the movement of the heavens. Therefore as long as the earth remains the movement of the heavens will continue. But *the earth will stand for ever* (Eccles. i, 4). Therefore the movement of the heavens will also last for ever.

2. It might be said that the passage quoted refers to the earth as serving man in his present state of life, wherein by sowing and reaping he gathers a harvest for the support of his animal life ; but not as serving him in the state of glory, when it will last for ever for the greater enjoyment of the good.—On the contrary it is written (Jer. xxxi, 35, 36) : *Thus saith the Lord who giveth the sun for the light of the day, the order of the moon and of the stars for the light of the night, who stirreth up the sea and the waves thereof roar, the Lord of hosts is his name. If these ordinances shall fail before me* . . . *then also the seed of Israel shall fail so as not to be a nation*

before me for ever. Now this does not refer to Israel in the flesh, seeing that by reason of their dispersion they can no longer be called a nation. Wherefore it must refer to the spiritual Israel, who will be in the truest sense a nation before the Lord, when they shall see God in his essence. Therefore in the state of beatitude the laws aforesaid which are consequent upon the movement of the heavens, will not cease, and consequently neither will the movement of the heavens.

3. According to the Philosopher (*Phys.* ii) anything that is rendered necessary by something that is already necessary, is itself absolutely necessary; thus an animal's death is necessary being necessitated by matter. Now the operations of incorruptible things, among which we must reckon the heavenly movement, are for the sake of the substances of those things whose operations they are, so that apparently they are rendered necessary by something that is already necessary; while the contrary obtains in corruptible things, whose substance is for the sake of their operations, so that their necessity depends on something subsequent to them, as the Commentator remarks (*ibid.*) therefore the heavenly movement is necessary absolutely and so it will never cease.

4. The end of the heavenly movement is that the heavens by their movement may be likened to God, inasmuch as they pass from potentiality to actuality by coming into new positions, which they actually acquire successively: inasmuch as a thing is so far like God, who is pure act, as it is itself actual. Now this end would cease if movement were to cease: so that, since movement does not cease unless the end which is its purpose is obtained, the movement of the heavens will never cease.

5. It might be said that the heavenly movement is not for this end, but for the completion of the number of the elect, and that when this is complete the heavens will cease to be moved.—On the contrary nothing is for the sake of that which is of less account, because the end is of more account than the means, for it is the cause of goodness in the means. Now the heavens, inasmuch as they are incorruptible, are of more account than things subject to generation and corruption. Wherefore it is not to be said that the movement

of the heavens is for the sake of some generation in this lower world, whereby nevertheless the number of the elect might be made complete.

6. Yet it might be said that the movement of the heavens is not for the generation of the elect as its principal end, but as its secondary end.—On the contrary that which is put in motion in order to secure the end of the movement continues in motion even when a secondary end has been obtained. If then generation whereby the number of the elect is made complete is a secondary end of the celestial movement, this movement does not cease when that number is reached.

7. All that is in potentiality is imperfect until it is made actual. Now in the consummation of the world, God will not leave anything imperfect. Since then the heaven's potentiality to ubiety is not actualised otherwise than by movement, it would seem that the heavenly movement will not cease even at the consummation of the world.

8. If the causes of a certain effect be incorruptible and invariable the effect will be everlasting. Now all the causes of the celestial movement are incorruptible and invariable, whether we refer to the moving cause or to the thing itself that is moved. Therefore the movement of heaven will last for ever.

9. That which is receptive of everlastingness will never be deprived of its everlastingness by God, as instanced in angels, the rational soul and the substance of heaven. Now the heavenly movement is susceptive of everlastingness, since circular movement alone can last for ever according to the Philosopher (*Phys.* viii). Therefore the movement of heaven will last for ever, like other things that have a natural aptitude to be everlasting.

10. If heaven cease to be moved this cessation will either be in an instant or in time. If in an instant, it will follow that a thing is at rest and in motion at the same time : because seeing that it was in motion during the whole of the preceding time, we must agree that it was in motion at any given instant of that time. Now in this given instant in which it was stated that heaven was at rest, it was natural

to the heaven to be in motion, since rest and motion apply to the same subject : and this instant belongs to the preceding time inasmuch as it is its term. Therefore heaven would be moved in that instant. Yet it was agreed that it was at rest therein. Therefore in the same instant it would be at rest and in motion, which is impossible. On the other hand if this cessation be in time, it follows that there will be time after the celestial movement. But there is no time without movement of heaven : wherefore the heavenly movement will continue after it has ceased, and this again is impossible.

11. If the heavenly movement is ever to cease, it follows that time which is its measure will cease also (*Phys.* iv). But time cannot cease : therefore the celestial movement cannot cease. Proof of the minor premise :—Anything that is always in its beginning and its end, never began and will never cease, because everything is subsequent to its beginning and previous to its end. Now the only thing we can seize on in time is an instant, and this is the beginning of the future and the end of the past : so that time is ever in its beginning and end. Therefore time will never cease.

12. The celestial movement is natural to heaven, as their respective movements are to heavy and light bodies (*De Cœlo* i). There is this difference, however, that elemental bodies exercise their natural movement only when they are outside their proper place, whereas the heaven is moved even while it is in its proper place. Whence we may infer that the relation of an elemental body to its natural movement when it is outside its proper place is like the relation of the heaven to its natural movement when it is in its proper place. Now an elemental body when outside its proper place does not rest unless it be forced. Therefore the heavenly body cannot rest unless it be forced. But this is inadmissible. For since nothing violent can endure for ever, it would follow that this heavenly rest does not last for ever, and that at length the heavens would begin again to be moved, which is ridiculous. Therefore we must not say that the heavenly movement will cease at some time.

13. Things that succeed one another should have some kind of order and mutual proportion. But there is no

proportion between the finite and the infinite. Therefore it is unreasonable to assert that heaven is moved for a finite time, and afterwards is at rest for an infinite period : and yet this must be said if the heavenly movement began and will end and will never begin again.

14. The more excellent likeness to God is that which is in respect of a more excellent act : thus man's likeness to God by reason of his rational soul is more excellent than that of a dumb animal, which is by reason of its sensitive soul. Now the second act is more excellent than the first ; thus consideration is better than knowledge. Therefore the heaven's likeness to God in respect of its second act which is to cause things in this lower world is more excellent than its likeness in respect of brightness which is its first act. If then in the consummation of the world the chief parts of the world will be bettered, it would seem that the heaven will not cease to be moved when it is filled with a greater brightness.

15. Magnitude, movement and time are in sequence to one another in respect of division and finitude or infinitude (*Phys.* vi, text. 18, 37, 38, 39). Now there is neither beginning nor end in a circular magnitude. Therefore neither is there any end in a circular movement : so that the heavenly movement being circular it would seem that it will never have an end.

16. It might be replied to the last objection that although a circular movement may have no end considered in its nature, it will have an end by the will of God.—On the contrary Augustine says (*Gen. ad lit.* ii) : *In discussing the origin of the world, we do not ask what God can do, but what the nature of things allows of being done.* Now the consummation of the world corresponds to its origin, as the end corresponds to the beginning. Therefore in discussing the end of the world we must not have recourse to the divine will, but to the nature of things.

17. The sun by its presence causes light and day in this lower world, and by its absence it produces darkness and night. Now the sun cannot be present in both hemispheres except by movement. Therefore if the heavenly movement

cease, the sun by its presence will make it to be always day in one part of the world, and in the other part by being always absent it will cause a continual night : so that the latter part will not be bettered but will be worse off in the consummation of the world.

18. That which is indifferent to two things will either cling to both or to neither. Now the sun so far as its nature is concerned is indifferent to any particular position in the heavens. Therefore it will either occupy everyone or none. But it cannot occupy none, since every sensible body is somewhere. Therefore it must occupy them all : and this is impossible except by successive movement. Therefore it will always be in movement.

19. At the end of the world none of the things that will remain will lose their perfection, inasmuch as they will not be worse off in that state but will be bettered. Now movement is a perfection of the heavens : because movement is the perfection of the thing moved as such (*Phys.* ii. text. 16) and because by movement the heavens acquire perfect goodness (*De Cæl.* ii, text. 66). Therefore at the end of the world the heavens will not cease to be moved.

20. No body ever attains to the degree of a spiritual nature. Now it belongs to a spiritual nature to have perfect goodness without movement (*De Cæl. et Mund.* ii, text. 62 *seqq.*). Wherefore the heaven will never attain to perfect goodness if its movement ceases : and this is contrary to the nature of the world's consummation.

21. Nothing is removed except by its contrary. Now there is nothing contrary to the heavenly movement (*De Cæl. et Mund.* i, text 10, 15). Therefore the heavenly movement will never cease.

On the contrary it is written (Apoc. x, 5, 6) : *The angel whom I saw standing upon the sea and upon the earth lifted up his hand to heaven, and he swore by him that he liveth for ever and ever. . . . that time shall be no longer.* Now time will endure as long as the heavens are moved. Therefore at some time the heavens will cease to be moved.

Again it is written (Job xiv. 12) : *Man when he is fallen asleep shall not rise again till the heavens be broken ; he shall not awake nor rise up out of his sleep.* Now we must not understand that the heavens will be broken in their substance, because this will always remain, as proved above. Therefore when the dead shall rise again, the heavens will be broken in the sense that their movement will cease.

Again, commenting on Rom. viii, 22, *Every creature groaneth and travaileth even until now,* a gloss of Ambrose[1] says : *All the elements labour to fulfil their various duties ; thus the sun and moon, not without toil, run their appointed courses. This they do for our benefit : so that when we are removed hence, they will rest.* Therefore at the resurrection of the saints the movements of the heavenly bodies will cease.

Again, Isidore (*De Ord. Creatur.*) writes : *After the judgement the sun will receive the reward of his labour, thenceforward neither sun nor moon shall set :* which is impossible as long as the heavens are in motion. Therefore the heavens will then cease to be moved.

I answer that following the teaching of holy men we hold that at some time the celestial movement will cease, although this be a matter of faith rather than of demonstration by reason. In order to make clear wherein this question offers difficulty, it must be observed that the heavenly movement is not natural to the heavenly body in the same way as the elemental body's movement is natural to the elemental body. The latter movement has in the thing movable its principle not only material and receptive but also formal and active : because the form of the elemental body follows that movement, even as other natural properties result from essential principles : wherefore in these things the generator is said to be the mover inasmuch as it gives the form that results from the movement. But this does not apply to a heavenly body. Because as nature ever tends to one definite effect through not being indifferent to many, it is impossible that any nature tend to movement as such, since in every movement there is a certain absence of uniformity, inasmuch as the thing moved passes from one mode of being to another, and uniformity in the thing moved is contrary to the definition of movement. In consequence nature never

[1] Pseudo-Ambrose, among S. Ambrose's Works.

inclines to movement for the sake of movement, but for the sake of some definite result to be obtained by movement : thus a heavy body is inclined by nature to rest in the centre, wherefore it tends to a downward motion, for the reason that by such a movement it will reach that place. On the other hand the heaven by its movement does not reach a ' whereabouts ' to which it is inclined by nature, because every ' whereabouts ' is the beginning and end of a movement : so that its natural movement cannot result, so to say, from a tendency of a natural inherent power, in the same way as the natural movement of fire has an upward tendency. Now circular movement is said to be natural to the heaven, in so far as it has a natural aptitude for that kind of movement, so that it contains in itself the passive principle of that movement, while the active principle of this movement is some separate substance, such as God, or an intelligence, or a soul according to some ; as to which of these it may be it matters not to the question at issue. Accordingly no argument for the permanence of this movement can be taken from the nature of a heavenly body wherein there is only aptitude for movement : and we seek one from a separate active principle. And seeing that every agent acts for an end, we must consider what is the end of the heaven's movement : because if this end be such as to require that this movement should cease at some time, then the heavens will at length cease to be moved ; while if rest is inconsistent with that end, then its movement will last for ever : for it cannot be said that it will cease through a change in its moving cause, since God's will like his nature is unchangeable, and through it whatever intermediate causes produce the heavenly movement may have become unchangeable likewise.

Now in making this observation three things must be avoided. In the first place we must not say that the heaven is moved for the sake of being moved : as we have said that it exists for the sake of existing, wherein it is like God. The reason is that movement by its very nature cannot be regarded in the light of an end, since it is a tendency to something else : so that it answers to the definition of means rather than of an end. This is confirmed by the fact that movement is the act of that which is imperfect (*De Anima* iii, 7; *Phys.* iii): while the end is the ultimate perfection.—Secondly, we must not say that the heavenly movement is for the sake of something less excellent than the heavens: because since the end specifies the means it ought to be more worthy than the means. Now the action of a more noble agent may happen to terminate in a less noble effect, but not as the end intended by that action: thus the safety of a peasant is an end secured by the king's government, yet the king's government does not seek that peasant's safety as its end, for it seeks something better, namely the common good. Consequently it cannot be admitted that the generation of beings in this lower world is the end of the heavenly movement, although it is its effect and term: since both heaven itelf is more excellent than this lower world, and its movement than the movements and changes that take place here below.—Thirdly, we must not suppose the end of the heaven's movement to be something indefinite, since to take the indefinite as a final cause is to destroy the end and the very nature of good (*Metaph.* ii). Because it is impossible to reach the indefinite; and nothing is moved to that which it cannot obtain (*De Cœlo et Mundo*, i). Wherefore it cannot be said that the end of the celestial movement is to attain to that for which it has no potentiality: although Avicenna would seem to say so. But this it cannot possibly obtain: since while it is actually in one position it is in its previous position potentially.

Wherefore we must assign as the end of the heavenly movement something that the heaven can obtain by its movement, that is distinct from its movement and more excellent.

This admits of a twofold solution. The first is that we assign as the end of the heavenly movement something in the heavens themselves and coexistent with movement. With this in view some philosophers held that the end of the heavenly movement is its likeness to God in causing, which takes place during the movement. In this view it is not becoming for this movement to cease, since were it to cease the end resulting from the movement would cease also. The second solution is that we assign as the end of the heavenly movement something outside heaven that is obtained by that movement, and which can remain when that movement ceases : and this is the view that we adopt. We hold then that the movement of the heavens is for the completion of the number of the elect. For the rational soul is more excellent than any body whatsoever, even than the heavens : wherefore there is nothing unreasonable in supposing that the end of the heavenly movement is the multiplication of rational souls ; not indeed indefinitely, since this could not result from the movement of the heavens ; and it could in that case be moved to something that it could not obtain. Therefore it is a definite number of souls that is the end of the heavenly movement : and when this is reached the movement will cease.

Now though either of these views can be upheld, the second, which is of faith, seems the more probable, and this for three reasons. First because it differs not whether we say that a certain thing's end is its likeness to God in some particular respect, or the thing itself with this likeness : just as we have said above that the end of things may be said to be either their being made like to God's goodness, or their nature as likened to God. Wherefore to say that the end of things is to be like God in causing is the same as to say that their end is to cause. Now to cause cannot be an end since it is an operation which implies an effect and tends to something else. Moreover in operations of this kind the effect is better than the operation (*Ethic.* i, 1), so that suchlike operations cannot be the end of the operator, for they do not perfect the maker but the thing made : and thus the thing made is more correctly the end (*Metaph.* ix : *Ethic.* i, 1). Now the things that are produced by the heavenly movement cannot be the end of that movement since they are less excellent than the heavens, as stated above. Wherefore it is unreasonable to hold that the end of the heavenly movement is likeness to God in causing.—Secondly, since the heavenly movement is produced by an external active principle, while the heavens themselves have merely the natural aptitude for that movement, as stated above, it follows that the heavens are moved and act as an instrument : for such is the disposition of an instrument, as may be seen in the productions of art : thus the axe has nothing more than the aptitude for its particular movement, while the principle of this movement is in the craftsman. Hence as philosophers say, that which moves through being itself moved, moves as an instrument. Now in the instrumental action there cannot be an end in the instrument save accidentally in so far as the instrument is considered as a thing made and not as an instrument. Consequently it is not probable that the end of the heavenly movement is a perfection of the heavens : rather is it something outside the heavens.—Thirdly, if likeness to God in causing is the end of the heavenly movement, this likeness will be found chiefly in the production of that which is produced by God immediately, to wit the rational soul : to the production of which the heavenly movement conduces by disposing the matter. So that it is more probable that the end of the heavenly movement is the number of the elect than a likeness to God in causing generation and corruption as the philosophers say. For this reason we grant that the heavens will cease to be in motion when the number of the elect is complete.

Reply to the First Objection. The text refers to the duration of the earth as subject to change : for it is thus that it receives the seed and gives the harvest. So long as the earth is in that state the heavens will not cease to be in motion.

Reply to the Second Objection. The text quoted refers not to the carnal but to the spiritual Israel : not indeed as in God's presence by seeing him face to face in his heavenly home, but as a wayfarer in the presence of God by faith. Hence the words of the text resemble those of our Lord to his disciples (Matt. xxviii, 20) : *Behold I am with you . . . until the consummation of the world.*

Reply to the Third Objection. The preposition *propter* (for the sake of) indicates a cause : sometimes it indicates a final cause which comes into being afterwards, and sometimes it indicates a material or efficient cause, which precedes. Now when it is stated that in incorruptible things acts are for the sake of the agents, ' for the sake of ' indicates not the final but the efficient cause on account of which, and not of the end, there is necessity in those actions. Accordingly the celestial movement, if we refer it to that which is in motion, is not necessitated thereby as by its efficient cause, as we have proved, but it is necessitated by its mover: which being a voluntary mover necessitates the movement according as it is determined by the order of divine wisdom, and not so that it last for ever.

Reply to the Fourth Objection. The end of the heaven's movement cannot consist in its becoming like God by actually reaching to various successive positions which previously it occupied potentially: both because this is indefinite, as we have shown, and because while on the one hand it becomes like God by reaching positions actually which it occupied before potentially, on the other hand it becomes less like God by the fact that positions previously actual become potential.

Reply to the Fifth Objection. Although things subject to generation and corruption are inferior to the heavens, the rational soul is superior to the heavenly body: and yet the former is produced by God into being in matter dispersed by the heavenly movement.

Reply to the Sixth Objection. According to the teaching of faith the completion of the number of the elect is not the secondary but the principal end of the heaven's movement. It is not, however, its ultimate end because the ultimate end of everything is the divine goodness, inasmuch as creatures in some way attain thereto either by likeness or by rendering the service they owe God.

Reply to the Seventh Objection. It is not true that a thing is to be described as imperfect by reason of any potentiality therein that has not been given actuality: this is true only when actuality makes the thing complete. A man is not imperfect because being potentially in India he is not actually there: but he will be imperfect if he lack knowledge or virtue which are his natural perfections.

Now heaven is not perfected by its position as these lower bodies which are preserved by occupying their proper positions. Wherefore although its potentiality to be in this or that position be never given actuality, it does not follow that it is imperfect. In fact if we consider heaven in itself it does not acquire greater perfection by being in one position than by being in another : it is indifferent to all positions, since it is moved naturally to any one. Now this indifference conduces to rest rather than to perpetual movement, unless we take into account the will of Him who moves it and intends its end. Thus certain philosophers explained the earth's rest in the centre by assigning as its cause the equidistance of the centre to each part of the heaven's circumference.

Reply to the Eighth Objection. Though all the causes of the celestial movement are everlasting, nevertheless the mover on whom its necessity depends, moves by his will : nor is it necessary that he move it for ever, but only according to the exigency of the end.

Reply to the Ninth Objection. The heaven's capacity of perpetual movement is not to be confused with its capacity of existing for ever. Its existence depends on its natural principles, from which it acquires the necessity of existing, in that they exclude the possibility of non-existence, as we have shown above : whereas its nature does not include perpetual movement but only an aptitude thereto, and the necessity of that movement being perpetual depends on its mover. Hence also according to the Commentator (*Metaph.* ii : *De Subst. Orb.*) the heaven has everlasting movement which it receives from an intrinsic principle. Wherefore even those who hold that this movement will never cease, say that the cause of its duration and everlastingness is God's will. And yet the unchangeableness of God's will does not, as they contend, necessarily prove the everlastingness of the celestial movement : because his will is not shown to be changeable if he wish different things to succeed one another according to the exigency of the end which he wills unchangeably. We must, therefore, seek the reason for an everlasting movement in the end rather than in the unchangeableness of the mover.

Reply to the Tenth Objection. The heavenly movement will end in an instant : and in that instant there will be neither movement nor rest, but the end of movement and the beginning of rest. The subsequent rest will not be in time, because rest is measured by time not directly, but indirectly (*Phys.* iv) : so that the rest of a body not subject to any kind of movement is in no way measured by time. Yet, not to draw the line too fine, one might say that after movement there will be not rest but a certain immobility in the heavens.

Reply to the Eleventh Objection. Even as the celestial movement will cease, so also will time be no more, as appears from the text quoted from the Apocalypse. The last instant of all time will indeed be the end of the past, but not the beginning of the future : because that an instant be at once both the end of the past and the beginning of the future obtains in a continuous circular movement in which every point is both beginning and end in respect of different parts. Hence if the celestial movement cease, just as there will be an ultimate indivisible point of movement, so will there be of time.

Reply to the Twelfth Objection. We have already said that it is not on account of an active inclination of its formal principle to such a movement that the heaven's movement is natural, as in the case of the elements : so that it does not follow, if the heavens cease to be in motion, that their rest is therefore violent.

Reply to the Thirteenth Objection. If the celestial movement were not for the sake of something else, we should expect to find some kind of proportion between that movement, and the subsequent rest, in the supposition that the movement is not everlasting. But whereas it is ordinated to another end, this proportion must be referred to the end and not to the subsequent rest. Accordingly we are to understand that God in bringing all creatures into being out of nothing, himself instituted the first perfection of the universe, consisting in the principal parts thereof, and the various species of things : and that in order to give it its final perfection, consisting in the completion of the ranks of the blessed, he ordained the various movements and operations of creatures, some of which are natural, for instance, the movement of the heavens and the activities of the elements, whereby matter is prepared to receive rational souls, while others are voluntary such as the ministrations of the angels who are *sent to minister for them who shall receive the inheritance of salvation.* Wherefore when this consummation has been attained to remain for ever without change, those things that were ordained thereto will cease for ever.

Reply to the Fourteenth Objection. This argument takes into consideration the second act that is an operation abiding in the operator and is the end of the operator and therefore excels the form of the operator. But the second act which is an action tending to something made is not the end of the agent, nor does it excel the agent's form, unless the thing made excel that which makes it, as things produced by act excel the instruments as being the ends of the latter.

Reply to the Fifteenth Objection. It is true that there is no actual beginning or end in a circular magnitude, yet it is possible to indicate a beginning or end therein in respect of an inception or termination of some kind of movement.

Reply to the Sixteenth Objection. At the beginning of the world nature was being established; wherefore in discussing its beginning we must not omit what is proper to nature. On the other hand at the end of the world the operation of nature will attain the end appointed by God: wherefore in discussing it we must have recourse to God's will which determined that end.

Reply to the Seventeenth Objection. When the heavens cease to be in motion, although the sun will always remain to the one side of the earth, there will not be utter darkness and gloom on the other side, because God will give brightness to the elements. Hence it is written (Apoc. xxi, 23): *The city hath no need of the sun nor of the moon . . . for the glory of God hath enlightened it.* And no inconsistency will follow if the part which was inhabited by the Saints receive a greater light.

Reply to the Eighteenth Objection. Though the heaven

is indifferent to any position that is possible to it, its movement is not for the purpose of obtaining a position but for something else : wherefore in whatever position it remains, it matters not so long as its movement has achieved its purpose.

Reply to the Nineteenth Objection. Although movement is the act of that which is moved it is the act of that which is imperfect. Hence if a thing is deprived of movement we must not infer that it is deprived of a perfection simply, especially if it acquires nothing by its movement. When the Philosopher says that by movement heaven acquires perfect goodness, he is expressing himself according to the first of the above-mentioned opinions about the end of the celestial movement, which end is consistent with the movement being everlasting.

Reply to the Twentieth Objection. The perfection of a spiritual nature is that it can be the cause of other things without being moved itself, a perfection to which the heavens can never attain. Nevertheless the heavens will not for this reason be worse off than before, inasmuch as their end does not consist in causing other things, as stated above.

Reply to the Twenty-first Objection. The heavens will cease to be in motion not on account of anything contrary to their movement, but solely on account of the will of their mover.

ARTICLE VI

CAN ANY MAN KNOW WHEN THE MOVEMENT OF THE HEAVENS WILL CEASE?

Sum. Th. Suppl., Q. lxxxviii, A. 3

THE sixth point of inquiry is whether man can know when the movement of the heavens will cease : and it would seem that this is impossible.

1. According to Augustine (*De Civ. Dei*) the sixth age is from the coming of Christ to the end of the world.

Now it is known how long the previous ages lasted. Therefore it is possible to know how long this age is to last, by comparing it with the others, and thus we can tell when the movement of the heavens will cease.

2. The end of everything corresponds to its beginning. Now the beginning of the world has been known by revelation ever since Moses wrote : *In the beginning God created heaven and earth.* Therefore it is possible to know about the end of the world by revelation delivered to us in the Scriptures.

3. It is said that the reason for our uncertainty about the end of the world is that man may ever be solicitous for the state of his soul. But the uncertainty about his death is enough to ensure that solicitude on his part. Therefore there was no need for uncertainty about the end of the world, except perhaps for the sake of those in whose lifetime the end of the world will come.

4. It is related of some that they received a revelation of their approaching death, the Blessed Martin for instance. And Augustine says (*Ep. ad Oros.*) that each one will appear at the judgement as he was in death : so that there is the same reason for concealing the day of one's death as for hiding the day of judgement. Consequently the day of judgement which concerns all should have been revealed in the Scriptures whereby all are taught.

5. A sign is intended for the purpose of making something known. Now certain signs of the Lord's coming at the end of the world are given in the Gospels (Matt. xxiv, Luke xxi) and by the Apostle (1 Tim. iv, 2 Tim. iii, 2 Thess. ii). Therefore seemingly it is possible to know the time of the Lord's coming and of the end of the world.

6. No man is reproved or punished here below for what does not lie in his power. Now in Scripture some are reproved and punished for ignorance of the times. Thus our Lord spoke to the Pharisees (Matt. xvi, 3) : *You know how to discern the face of the sky : and can you not know the signs of the times ?* and (Luke xix, 44) he says : *They shall not leave in thee a stone upon a stone, because thou hast not known the time of thy visitation.* Again (Jerem. viii, 7) : *The kite in the air hath known her time : the turtle, the swallow and the stork*

have observed the time of their coming, but my people have not known the judgement of the Lord. Therefore the day of judgement or the time of the end of the world can be known.

7. At his second coming Christ will appear more manifestly than at his first : since then *every eye shall see him, and they also who pierced him* (Apoc. i, 7). Now his first coming was foretold in Scripture even as to the exact time of its happening (Dan. ix). Therefore one would think that his second coming also should have been foretold as to its precise date.

8. Man is said to be a little world because he bears a likeness to the greater world. Now the end of a human life can be definitely foreseen. Therefore the end of the world can be foreknown.

9. Great and small, long and short are relative terms whereby one thing is compared to another. Now the time from Christ's coming until the end of the world is described as being short, according to 1 Corinthians, vii, 29, *Time is short*, and again (*ibid.* x, 11), *Upon whom the ends of the world are come*, and (1 Jo. ii, 18), *It is the last hour*. Therefore this is said in comparison with the preceding time : and consequently at least it can be known that the time between Christ's coming and the end of the world is much shorter than from the beginning of the world to the coming of Christ.

10. Augustine says (*De Civ. Dei*, xx, 16) that fire which will consume the surface of the earth at the end of the world will be caused by a conflagration of all the fires of the world. Now by observing the movement of the heavens it is possible to know how long it will take the heavenly bodies, which are the natural generators of heat in this lower world, to be in the most favourable position to bring about this result, so that this universal conflagration be effected by the concurrent action of the heavenly bodies and the fires of the lower world. Therefore it is possible to know when the end of the world will be.

On the contrary it is said (Matt. xxiv, 36) : *Of that day and hour no one knoweth, no not the angels of heaven.*

Again, if this were to be revealed to anyone, especially should it have been revealed to the Apostles, who were appointed to teach the whole world. Yet when they asked about the final coming of the Lord they received the following answer (Act. i, 7) : *It is not for you to know the times or moments which the Father hath put in his own power.* Much less then was it revealed to others.

Again, We are not forbidden to believe the revelation which we have received in the Scriptures. Now the Apostle (2 Thess. ii, 2) forbids us to believe any sort of announcement *as if the day of the Lord were at hand.* Therefore we must beware of the impostors who endeavour to foretell the time of the day of the Lord : hence he goes on to say : *Let no man deceive you by any means.*

Again, Augustine says (*Ad Hesych.* ep. cxcix) : *Can we, I ask you, define the time of his coming, in such a way that at least we can say that he will come within, for instance, the next hundred years, or within any number of years greater or less ?* But we are entirely ignorant about this. Therefore we cannot know whether the end of the world will be within any given number of years, whether ten thousand or twenty thousand, or two or three.

I answer that the exact time of the end of the world is utterly unknown, except to God and to Christ as man. The reason of this is that there are two ways in which we can know the future, by natural knowledge and by revelation. By natural knowledge we foresee certain future events in their causes which we see present, and from which we look forward to their effects—either with the certainty of science if the causes be such as to produce their effects of necessity, or by conjecture, if the causes be such as to produce their effects in the majority of cases, as an astronomer foresees a future eclipse, and a physician future death. In this way it is impossible to foreknow the exact time of the end of the world, because the cause of the heaven's movement and its cessation is no other but the will of God, as we have shown ; and we cannot by our natural powers know that cause. Other results of the heaven's movement or of any other sensible cause can be foreknown by natural knowledge, such as the destruction of some particular part of the earth, which was hitherto inhabitable and afterwards becomes uninhabitable. By revelation however, though it be possible for it to be known if such were God's will, it is not becoming that it should be revealed except to Christ as man : and this for three reasons. First, because the world will not come to an end until the number of the elect is complete, which completion is as it were the fulfilment of the whole of divine predestination ; wherefore it is not fitting that the end of the world should be revealed except to him who has received the revelation of the whole of divine predestination, that is to Christ as man, through whom the whole predestination of the human race is in a manner fulfilled. Wherefore it is said (Jo. v, 20) : *The Father loveth the Son and showeth him all things which himself doth.*—Secondly, because through our not knowing how long the present state of the world will last, whether for a short or for a long time, we look upon the things of this world as though they were soon to pass away : wherefore it is said (1 Cor. vii, 31) *They that use this world* (let them be) *as if they used it not, for the fashion of this world passeth away.*—Thirdly that men may ever be prompt to look forward to God's judgement, through being in utter ignorance of its exact time, wherefore it is written (Mt. xxiv, 42) : *Watch . . . because you know not what hour your Lord will come.* Hence, as Augustine says (*Ad Hesych.* ep. cxcix) *he who says that he knows not when the Lord will come whether after a short or after a long time is in agreement with the words of the Gospel. And of two who say that they know, his is the more dangerous statement who says that Christ will come soon or that the end of the world is at hand,* since this might occasion men to disbelieve in the end of the world if it fails to happen when it was foretold.

Reply to the First Objection. As Augustine says (*QQ.* lxxxiii, qu. 57) the last age of the world corresponds to the last stage in a man's life, which does not last for a fixed number of years as the other stages do, but lasts sometimes as long as all the others together, and even longer. Wherefore the last age of the world cannot be assigned a fixed number of years or generations.

Reply to the Second Objection. The revelation of the world's beginning was useful in showing that God is the cause of all things. But harm rather than good would result from knowledge of the end of the world : so that the comparison fails.

Reply to the Third Objection. Man is naturally solicitous not only for himself but also for the good estate of the community whereof he is a part, for instance, of the household, or city or even of the whole world. Consequently in order that man might be on his guard there was need for both things to be hidden from him, the end of his own life and the end of the world.

Reply to the Fourth Objection. The revelation of the end of one's own life is a particular revelation, while the revelation of the end of the whole world is connected with the revelation of the whole of divine predestination : so that the comparison fails.

Reply to the Fifth Objection. These signs were given in order to declare the future end of the world at some time, but not the exact date of its end. Thus among those signs there are some that have been seen almost from the beginning of the world, for instance, that *nation shall rise against nation* and that there will be *earthquakes in places*, although these things will happen more frequently towards the end of the world ; but in what measure, we cannot know.

Reply to the Sixth Objection. This reproof of our Lord refers to those who knew not the time of his first coming, but not to those who are in ignorance of the time of his second coming.

Reply to the Seventh Objection. Christ's first coming opened to us the way to merit by faith and the other virtues : hence on our part it was necessary for us to have knowledge of his first coming, so that by believing in him who was come we might obtain merit through his grace. But in his second coming rewards will be given according to merit, so that on our part it will be a question not of action or of knowledge but of receiving : wherefore there is no need for us to know the exact time of that coming. However, this day is said to be manifest, not as though it were clearly foreknown, but because it will be manifest when it comes.

Reply to the Eighth Objection. The life of man's body depends on certain things already existing and of the material order, whence it is possible to have some foreknowledge of his coming end. It is not thus with the whole world : wherefore in this particular there is no comparison, although there are certain points in which man the lesser world is like the greater world.

Reply to the Ninth Objection. These words of Scripture that would seem to indicate shortness of time or nearness of the end, are not so much to be referred to the amount of time as to a certain disposition of the present state of the world. For no other state will succeed that of the Law of the Gospel which has brought things to perfection, and succeeded the Old Law as the Old Law succeeded the Law of Nature.

Reply to the Tenth Objection. This conflagration of the world-fires is not supposed to be the outcome of some natural cause, so that it be possible by observing the movement of the heavens to foresee when it will happen : but it will take place at the bidding of God's will.

ARTICLE VII

WILL THE ELEMENTS REMAIN WHEN THE HEAVENS CEASE TO BE IN MOTION ?

Sum. Th. Suppl., Q. lxxiv, A. 5, Q. xci, A. 4

THE seventh point of inquiry is whether the elements will remain when the heavens cease to be in motion, and seemingly they will not.

1. It is written (2 Pet. iii, 10, 12) that at the end of the world *the elements shall melt with heat.* Now when a thing is melted it remains no more. Therefore the elements will not remain.

2. But, it will be said, they will remain in substance, though not as to their active and passive qualities.—On the contrary, if the cause remains the effect remains. Now essential principles cause the proper accidents. Since then the active and passive qualities are the proper accidents of the elements, it would seem, as long as the essential

principles remain, without which the substance cannot exist, that the active qualities must also remain.

3. An inseparable accident is never actually separated from its subject. Now heat is an accident inseparable from fire. Therefore fire cannot remain without retaining heat : and the same applies to the other elements.

4. But, it will be said, this will be done by the power of God, so that the elements will remain without their active and passive qualities, though is impossible naturally.—On the contrary, as nature was established at the beginning of the world, so will it be consummated at the end of the world. Now, in speaking of the beginning of the world, according to Augustine (*Gen. ad lit*, ii) we must consider not what God can do but what nature requires. Therefore this is also to be considered in discussing the end of the world.

5. Active and passive qualities are in all the elements. And a gloss of Bede on the text of Peter quoted above says that the fire which will be kindled at the end of the world will *entirely engulf two of the elements, and will restore the others to a better fashion*. Therefore the destruction of the elements cannot refer to their active and passive qualities, since in that case it would not be said that only two elements would be consumed.

6. But, it will be said, the active qualities, to wit heat and cold, are most prominent in two elements, fire and water, and for this reason these two are stated to be absorbed.—On the contrary at the end of the world the elements will be bettered, according to Augustine (*Gen. ad lit*. xii, 16). Now the agent is more noble than the patient. Therefore those elements should remain in which active qualities are prominent, rather than those which betray passive qualities.

7. Augustine (*Super Gen*. iii, 10) says that water and earth are passive, while fire and air are active. Therefore if certain elements are to be absorbed on account of their active power, it would seem that these should be fire and air rather than earth and water.

8. Heavy and light are natural qualities of the elements

just as hot and cold, wet and dry. If then the latter qualities do not remain in the elements, neither do the former. Now it is by reason of the nature of heaviness and lightness that the elements have their natural places: so that if the elemental qualities do not remain after the end of the world, they will have no special place, so that the earth be below and fire up above.

9. The elements were made for the use of man on his road to beatitude. Now the means cease when the end has been obtained. Therefore the elements will cease to exist when, at the end of the world, man will have obtained his final reward in heaven.

10. Matter is for the sake of the form that it acquires by generation. Now the elements are as matter in relation to all mixed bodies. Since then there will be no further generation of mixed bodies after the end of the world, it would seem that the elements will not remain.

11. On Luke xxi, 33, *Heaven and earth shall pass away*, the (interlinear) gloss adds, *having cast aside their previous form*. Since then the form gives being, it would seem that the elements will no longer exist after the end of the world.

12. According to the Philosopher (*Metaph*. x) corruptible and incorruptible are not included in the same genus, and similarly therefore neither are mutable and immutable. If then a thing be transformed from mutability to immutability, it would seem that it no longer remains in its natural genus. Now the elements will be changed from mutability to immutability because the (interlinear) gloss on Matthew v, 18, *Till heaven and earth pass*, says: *Till they pass from mutability to immutability*. Therefore the elements will not retain their present nature.

13. The present disposition of the elements is natural: hence if this disposition be removed so as to give place to another, this will be unnatural to them. Now that which is unnatural and violent cannot last for ever, according to the Philosopher (*De Cælo et Mundo*, ii: iii). Consequently this latter disposition cannot remain for ever in the elements, and they would return to the former, which would seem inadmissible. Therefore the elements in their

substance will cease to exist, and not only their disposition, their substance remaining.

14. That alone can be incorruptible and ingenerable whose entire matter underlies the form for which it has a potentiality: as instanced in the heavenly bodies. Now this cannot apply to the elements: because the matter that underlies the form of one element has a potentiality for the form of another. Therefore the elements cannot be incorruptible, and consequently cannot last for ever.

15. That which has no power to exist for ever cannot be everlasting. Now the elements have no power to exist for ever, because they are corruptible. Therefore they cannot last for ever when the heavens cease to be in motion.

16. But, it will be said, the elements are incorruptible as a whole, though they be corruptible in their parts.—On the contrary it is on account of the movement of the heavens that one part of an element is destroyed and another generated: for it is thus that the element is preserved as a whole. Hence when the heavenly movement ceases there will be no longer an assignable cause for the preservation of the whole element.

17. The Philosopher says (*Phys.* viii) that the movement of the heavens is the source of life to all things in nature; and Rabbi Moses says that the heavenly movement is to the universe what the beating of the heart is to the animal, in that the life of the whole animal depends thereon. Now when the heart ceases to beat, all the parts of the animal cease to live. Therefore when the heavens cease to move, all the parts of the universe will perish: and thus the elements will not remain.

18. Everything has its being from its form. Now the heavenly movement is the cause of forms in this lower world: and this is proved from the statement of philosophers who assert that nothing here below acts for the production of a species except by virtue of the heaven's movement. Therefore when this ceases, the elements will cease to exist, since their forms will be destroyed.

19. At the presence of the sun the higher elements always overcome the lower, as happens in summer on account of the

strength of the heat : whereas at the absence of the sun the opposite happens. Now when the heavens cease to be in motion, the sun will always be on one side of the earth, and absent from the other. Therefore on the one side the cold elements will be entirely destroyed, and the hot on the other side : so that the elements will not remain when the heavenly movement ceases.

On the contrary a gloss of Ambrose[1] on Romans viii, 20, *The creature was made subject to vanity*, says: *All the elements labour to fulfil their offices . . . wherefore they will rest when we are taken up to heaven.* Now only that which exists can be said to rest. Therefore the elements will remain at the end of the world.

Again, the elements were made for the manifestation of the divine goodness : and then most of all will there be need to manifest the divine goodness when all things will receive their final consummation. Therefore the elements will remain at the end of the world.

I answer that all are agreed in holding that the elements in some way will remain, and in some fashion pass away : but opinions differ as to the manner of remaining and passing away.

Some have maintained that all the elements will remain as regards their matter, but that some will receive a higher form, namely water and fire, which will receive the form of the heavens. Thus it will be possible to give the name of heaven to three of the elements, namely to air (which by reason of its nature is sometimes called the heaven in Scripture) and to water and fire which will assume the form of the heavens. Hereby would be verified the words of Apocalypse xxi, 1, *I saw a new heaven and a new earth*, because *heaven* would include the three elements, fire, air and water. However this view is impossible : because the elements are not in potentiality to receive the form of the heaven, inasmuch as the latter has no contrary, and all the matter that has a potentiality for the heavens' form underlies that form. Moreover it would follow that the heavens could be generated and corrupted : which the Philosopher proves to be

---

[1] Pseudo-Ambrose quoted by Lombard.

false (*De Cœlo et Mundo*, i). Again the argument in support of this view is frivolous : because as Basil says (*Hom. in Hexæm.*) *Scripture in mentioning the extremes includes those that come between.* Thus when we read (Gen. i, 1) that *In the beginning God created heaven and earth,* the creation of heaven and earth includes the intermediate elements. Moreover sometimes all the lower things are comprised in the word *earth.* Thus in Psalm cxlvii, 7, the words *Praise the Lord from the earth* are succeeded by these, *Fire, hail,* etc. Hence there is no reason why we should not say that by the renewal of heaven and earth Scripture intended also the renewal of the intermediate elements, or that *earth* includes all the elements.

Wherefore others hold that all the elements will remain as to their substance, not only in respect of their matter but also as regards their substantial forms. For just as, in the opinion of Avicenna, the elemental forms remain in a mixed body, while their active and passive qualities remain not in full force but reduced to a mean ; so will it be possible in the last state of the world for these elements to remain without these qualities. This would seem in agreement with what Augustine says (*De Civit. Dei* xvi) : *In this world-conflagration the qualities of the corruptible elements that were suitable to our bodies will be entirely destroyed by fire, and the elemental substance will have those qualities which by a wondrous change will be suitable to immortal bodies.* But this does not seem a reasonable view. First because, since the active and passive qualities are proper accidents of the elements, they must needs be caused by the essential principles of the latter, so that as long as the essential principles remain, it is impossible for these qualities to cease, save by violence, in which case they would not cease for long. Wherefore neither does the opinion of Avicenna seem probable, when he asserts that the elements retain their forms actually in a mixed body—although they do retain them but only virtually as the Philosopher says : since it would follow that the various elemental forms remain in the various parts of matter. Now this would not happen unless they were also distinct as to position : so that the mixture would not be real but only apparent. Moreover in a mixed body the qualities of one element counteract the qualities of another : and this cannot apply to the final consummation of the world, when all violence will cease.—Secondly because, since the active and passive qualities belong to the integrity of the elements' nature, it would follow that the elements will remain in a state of imperfection. Hence Augustine in the passage quoted refers not to the active and passive qualities, but to the dispositions of things subject to generation, corruption and alteration.

Seemingly then the question is best solved by saying that the elements will remain in their substance with their natural qualities, but that generation, corruption and alteration resulting from their action on one another will cease, because it is by means of these that the elements are ordinated to the completion of the number of the elect, even as the heaven by means of its movement. The substance, however, of the elements will remain even as the substance of heaven. The reason is that since the universe will remain for ever, as we have proved already, it follows that whatsoever belongs to the perfection of the universe must remain as to its substance. Now this applies to the elements inasmuch as they are essential parts of the universe, as the Philosopher proves (*De Cœlo et Mundo*, ii). For if the universe is a circular body it must have a centre, and this is the earth : and given the earth which is heavy absolutely as occupying the centre, there must be its contrary namely fire which is light absolutely : because if one contrary exists in nature, the other must exist also. Now given the extremes, we must posit the middle : wherefore we must posit air and water, which are heavy in comparison with fire, and light in comparison with earth : one of which is nearer to the earth than the other. Hence from the very conformation of the universe it is evident that the elements are essential parts thereof.—This is also made clear if we consider the order of causes to their effects. Thus even as heaven is the universal active cause of things that are generated, so the elements are their universal matter. Hence the perfection of the universe requires that the elements remain in their substance. Moreover by their very nature they have an aptitude to remain thus. The reason is that corruption occurs in mixed bodies otherwise than in the elements. Mixed bodies contain within themselves the active principle of corruption, through being composed of contraries: whereas the elements have an outside contrary but are not composed of contraries, wherefore they do not contain an active principle of corruption, but only a passive principle, inasmuch as their matter has an aptitude to receive another form than that which they actually have. It is due to this principle that generation and corruption in the elements are natural movements or changes, and not to any active principle as the Commentator says (*Phys.* ii). Accordingly even as it is possible for the movement of a heavenly body to cease without suffering violence, while the body itself remains, because the active principle of its movement is external to it, as stated above; so too is it possible that the elements cease to be corrupted and remain in their substance, when the external cause of their corruption ceases, which cause must be reduced to the heavenly movement which is the first principle of generation and corruption.

Reply to the First Objection. This melting of the elements does not mean that their substance will be destroyed but that they will be refined by the fire which will go before the face of the Judge. After being thus refined the elements will remain in their substance and natural qualities, as we have stated.

The Second and Third Objections are granted.

Reply to the Fourth Objection. At the beginning of the world the nature of bodies was established in accordance with its being ordained to generation and corruption, whereby the number of the elect is made complete. But at the end of the world the substance of the elements will remain as being ordained to the perfection of the universe. Consequently there will be no need in that final state for the elements to retain all that they needed at the beginning of the world.

Reply to the Fifth Objection. Bede's gloss does not mean that two elements will be thus destroyed in their substance, but that they will be changed in their state. This is especially evident in the case of two elements, namely air and water to which according to some the gloss refers: although others take it to refer to fire and water in which the active qualities are most prominent.

Reply to the Sixth Objection. Action depends on the agent rather than on the patient for the simple reason that the agent ranks above the patient. Hence when the elements will no longer be subject to change and mutual reaction, it is more fitting to describe this as a withdrawal of active forces rather than of passive qualities.

Reply to the Seventh Objection. If we consider action and passion in the elements with respect to the essential principles it is true, as Augustine says, that water and earth are passive, while fire and air are active, because fire and air have more of form which is the principle of action, and earth and water have more of matter which is the principle of passivity. But if we consider them with respect to active and passive qualities which are the immediate principles of action, then fire and water are more active, while earth and air are more passive.

The Eighth Objection is granted.

Reply to the Ninth Objection. The elements considered in their mutability were made for man on his way to heaven; but in the point of their substance, they were made both for the perfection of the universe, and for the substance of man which is composed of them.

Reply to the Tenth Objection. At the end of the world not all mixed bodies will cease to exist since human bodies will remain. It is therefore fitting, if some of the elements remain in the body of man who is the lesser world, that they should all remain in the greater world.

Reply to the Eleventh Objection. The form to be cast aside by the elements is their mutability, and not that form which is their principle of existence.

Reply to the Twelfth Objection. The elements will lose their changeable disposition, because they will cease to be changed; but they will not lose their changeable nature.

Reply to the Thirteenth Objection. The elements'

disposition to generation, corruption and change is natural to them as long as the heavens continue to be in motion, but it will not be so after this movement has ceased.

Reply to the Fourteenth Objection. This argument proves that in the elements there is a material, but not an active, principle of corruption : hence they undergo no change, when the heavenly movement ceases which is the cause of their being changed.

Reply to the Fifteenth Objection. Just as an element has no power to last for ever, inasmuch as it can be destroyed by an extrinsic agent, even so it has none but a material principle of corruption, as stated above.

Reply to the Sixteenth Objection. As long as the heavens continue to be in motion the elements as a whole are incorruptible, while here and there they are generated or destroyed. When, however, the heavens cease to be in motion there will be another cause of their incorruptibility, namely that whereas they cannot be destroyed save by an extrinsic cause, when the heavenly movement ceases, that extrinsic cause will cease also.

Reply to the Seventeenth Objection. The heaven's movement gives life to all nature in its state of mutability which will cease at the end of the world.

Reply to the Nineteenth Objection. Although the eduction of forms from matter depends on the celestial movement, their preservation depends on higher causes as already explained.

Reply to the Twentieth Objection. The sun causes heat by movement according to the Philosopher (*De Cœlo et Mundo,* ii), wherefore when movement ceases there will no longer be a cause of corruption in the elements, which results from excess of heat.

ARTICLE VIII

WILL ACTION AND PASSION REMAIN IN THE ELEMENTS AFTER THE HEAVENS HAVE CEASED TO BE IN MOTION ?

THE eighth point of inquiry is whether action and passion will remain in the elements after the heavens have ceased to be in motion : and seemingly they will.

1. Natural forces are confined to one effect: thus the power of fire, being a natural force, is adapted for heating, and not for not heating. Now, as we have said before (A. 7), at the end of the world fire and other elements will retain their powers. Therefore it will be impossible for fire and the other elements not to be active.

2. As the Philosopher says (*De Gener. Anim.* i) mutual action and passion require the agent and patient to be alike in matter and unlike in form. Now when the heavens cease to be moved, this will be the case, since their substance will remain, and their essential principles will be unchanged. Therefore after the cessation of the heavenly movement there will be action and passion in the elements.

3. The cause of action and passion in the elements is that in the elemental matter there is ever an appetence for another form, although by the one form it is perfected. Now matter will retain this appetence even after the heavens have ceased to be moved; inasmuch as the whole potentiality of matter will not be fulfilled by one form. Therefore action and passion will remain in the elements at the end of the world.

4. That which belongs to the perfection of an element will not be taken from it. Now it belongs to the perfection of everything to produce its like, because diffusion of being derives from the sovereign good to all beings. Therefore seemingly after the end of the world the elements will produce their like: and thus action and passion will be in them.

5. Just as it is proper to fire to be hot, so is it proper to fire to heat: because as heat results from the essential principles of fire, so heating results from heat. If then at the end of the world fire and its heat remain, it would seem that it will continue to heat.

6. All bodies in contact with one another, in some way alter one another (*De Gener. Anim.* i). Now in that state of the world the elements will be in contact with one another. Therefore they will alter one another: and thus there will be action and passion.

7. At the end of the world *the light of the moon shall be as the light of the sun, and the light of the sun shall be sevenfold*

(Isa. xxx, 26). But the sun and moon by their light illumine the lower bodies now : wherefore *a fortiori* will they then illumine them : so that there will remain some kind of action and passion in this lower world, since light will be reflected from the nearest bodies to the furthest.

8. The saints with their eyes will see the things of this world. Now things cannot be seen unless there be action and passion, because the organ of sight is passive to the visible object. Therefore there will be action and passion even after the cessation of the heavenly movement.

On the contrary if the cause be removed the effect is removed also. Now the heavenly movement is the cause of action and passion in these corporeal things according to the Philosopher's teaching (*Metaph.* i : *De Cœlo* ii). Therefore after the cessation of the heaven's movement, there will be no more action and passion in this lower world.

Again, there can be no action and passion in bodies without movement. But if the first movement which is that of heaven (*Phys.* viii) cease, all subsequent movements will cease also. Therefore with the cessation of the celestial movement, action and passion will cease in this lower world.

I answer that according to the book *De Causis* when the first cause withdraws its action from the effect, the second cause must needs withdraw its action therefrom, inasmuch as the second cause acts only by reason of the action of the first cause by virtue of which it acts. And since every agent acts for as much as it is actual, the order of active causes will be according to the order of their actuality. Now the lower bodies are less actual than the heavenly bodies, because their potentiality is not made wholly complete by act, inasmuch as their matter underlying one form retains a potentiality to another form. This does not obtain in the heavenly bodies, since their matter has no potentiality to another form, so that their potentiality is wholly terminated by the form that they have. Again, the separate substances have yet more perfect actuality than even the heavenly bodies, because they are not composed of matter and form, but are subsistent forms, falling short however of

God's actuality who is his own being, which does not apply to other separate substances. Thus it is to be observed that as the elements also surpass one another in their degrees of actuality, water being more specific than earth, air more than water, and fire more than air, even so is it in the heavenly bodies and in separate substances. Accordingly the elements act by virtue of the heavenly bodies, and the heavenly bodies by virtue of separate substances: so that when the separate substances cease to act, the action of the heavenly body must cease also, and when this ceases the action of the elemental body must also cease.

It must be observed however that a body has a twofold action: one according to a property of a body, inasmuch as it acts by movement (for it is proper to a body that it be moved so as to move and act), the other by attaining to the order of separate substances and receiving a share in their mode of operation: thus lower natures are wont to share in a property of a higher nature, for instance certain animals share in a certain likeness to prudence which is proper to man. This latter action of a body does not aim at the transformation of matter, but at communicating a certain likeness to its form to the 'medium,' which may be compared to the spiritual 'intention' which things impress on the senses or intelligence: thus the air receives the light of the sun, and the 'medium' receives a reflection of coloured images. Now both these actions are caused here below by the heavenly bodies. Thus fire by its heat transforms matter by virtue of a heavenly body; and visible bodies reflect their images in the medium by the power of light, the source whereof is in a heavenly body. Hence if both these actions on the part of a heavenly body were to cease, no action would remain in this lower world. But if the heavens were to cease to be in motion, the first action would cease, but not the second: and consequently when the heavenly movement ceases, in this lower world the action whereby the 'medium' is illumined and affected by sensible things will continue, but not the action whereby matter is transformed and which results in generation and corruption.

Reply to the First Objection. The power of fire is indeed

confined to heating, but on the presupposition of those prior causes that are required for fire to act.

Reply to the Second Objection. Likeness in matter and contrariety of form are not sufficient for action and passion in this lower world, unless the heavenly movement be presupposed by virtue of which all the lower active powers act.

Reply to the Third Objection. Matter is not sufficient for action without an active principle. Wherefore the appetence of matter is not a sufficient proof of action in the elements, without the heavenly movement which is the first principle of action.

Reply to the Fourth Objection. Things of lower degree never attain to the perfection of their superiors. Now it is the exclusive perfection of the Supreme Agent that he is so perfect that he can act without the aid of any other agent: and consequently this can never be the case with inferior agents.

Reply to the Fifth Objection. Provided that fire acts then it is true that its proper action is to heat; yet its action is dependent on something else, as already stated. The same solution applies to the *Sixth Objection:* inasmuch as for the elements to act, contact is not enough unless we presuppose the movement of the heavens.

We grant the two remaining arguments, since they do not apply to actions whereby matter is transformed, but to actions whereby species are multiplied by a kind of spiritual *intention.*

ARTICLE IX

WILL PLANTS, ANIMALS AND MINERALS REMAIN AFTER THE END OF THE WORLD?

Sum. Th. Suppl., Q. xci, A. 5

THE ninth point of inquiry is whether plants, animals and minerals will remain after the last judgement: and seemingly they will.

1. It is written (Eccles. iii, 14): *I have learnt that all the*

works which God hath made continue for ever. Now minerals, plants and dumb animals are the works of God. Therefore they will remain for ever.

2. It might be said that these words refer to those of God's works which in some way are ordained to incorruption : for instance the elements, though corruptible in part are incorruptible as a whole.—On the contrary, as the elements are incorruptible as a whole, while corruptible in part, so the things mentioned are incorruptible in the species, although the individuals are corruptible. Therefore it would seem that those things also remain for ever.

3. The intention of nature cannot be frustrated, because nature's intention consists in its being guided to its end by God. Now by generation and corruption nature intends to assure the perpetuity of the species. Therefore, unless these things be preserved in their species, nature's intention will be abortive : and this is impossible, as stated.

4. The beauty of the universe will belong to the glory of the blessed, for which reason holy men say that for the greater glory of the blessed the elements of the world will be raised to a better state. Now plants, minerals and dumb animals belong to the beauty of the universe. Therefore they will not be utterly destroyed in the state of perfect bliss.

5. It is written (Rom. i, 20) : *The invisible things* of God . . . *are clearly seen, being understood by the things that are made :* and among these things may be reckoned plants and animals. Now in that state of perfect bliss it will be necessary for man to see the invisible things of God. Therefore it is unfitting that those works of God be destroyed.

6. It is written (Apoc. xxii, 2) : *On both sides of the river was the tree . . . bearing twelve fruits.* Since then the text refers to the consummate bliss of the saints in heaven, it would seem that in that state the plants will remain.

7. From the divine being all beings derive the desire to exist for ever, in so far as they are likened to the first being which is everlasting. Now that which things derive through their likeness to the divine being will not be taken from them in the final consummation. Therefore plants and animals will remain for ever, at least in their species.

8. In that final state of universal consummation things will not be deprived of that which pertains to their perfection. Now the work of adornment was a kind of consummation of the work of creation. Wherefore since animals belong to the work of adornment, it would seem that they will not cease to exist in that final state of the world.

9. Animals and plants no less than the elements are of use to man in his state as wayfarer. Now the elements will remain[1]. Therefore animals and plants will also, and consequently they will not cease to exist.

10. The more a thing shares in a property of the first everlasting being namely God, the more seemingly is it also everlasting. Now plants and animals have a greater share than the elements in the divine properties: inasmuch as the elements have only existence, whereas plants have life, and animals in addition to this have knowledge. Therefore animals and plants should last for ever rather than the elements.

11. As Dionysius says (*Div. Nom.* vii) it is an effect of divine wisdom that the lower nature at its highest point is in conjunction with the lowest point of the higher nature. Now this will not be true if animals and plants cease to exist, because in no point do the elements attain to human perfection, whereas certain animals do in a measure: and plants come near to animals, and minerals which are immediately above the elements approach to the plants. Therefore at the end of the world, seeing that nothing should be destroyed belonging to the order of divine wisdom, it would seem that animals and plants should not cease to exist.

12. If when the world was created animals and plants had not been produced, the world would not have been perfect. But the world will be more perfect in the end than at the beginning. Therefore seemingly all animals and plants will remain.

13. Certain minerals and dumb animals are appointed for the punishment of the damned: for instance (Ps. x, 7): *Fire, brimstone and storms of wind shall be the portion of their*

---

[1] The Latin text is evidently incomplete: see the Reply.

cup, and (Isa. lxvi, 24) : *Their worm shall not die, and their fire shall not be quenched.* Now the punishment of the damned will be everlasting. Therefore seemingly animals and minerals will remain for ever.

14. The elements contain the germs of mixed bodies, animals and plants according to Augustine (*De Trin.* iii, 8, 9). Now these germs would be to no purpose if these things were not produced from them. Since then at the end of the world the elements will remain and consequently the germs they contain, and seeing that none of God's works are frustrated, it would seem that animals and plants will remain when the world is renewed.

15. The final cleansing of the world will be by the action of fire. But some minerals are of such strong composition that they are not consumed by fire, gold for instance. Therefore one would think that these at least will remain after that fire.

16. The universal is everlasting : yet it does not exist save in individuals. Therefore it would seem that the individuals of every universal will last for ever : and consequently dumb animals, plants and minerals will always exist.

On the contrary Origen says (*Peri Archon*) : *We must not think that animals whether tame or wild, or trees or rocks will reach that final state.*

Again, animals and plants are ordained for man's animal life : hence it is written (Gen. ix, 3[1]) : *Even as the green herbs have I delivered all things for your meat.* But man's animal life will come to an end. Therefore animals and plants will also cease to exist.

I answer that in that renewal of the world no mixed body will remain except the human body. In support of this view we shall proceed in the order prescribed by the Philosopher (*Phys.* ii) namely by considering first the final cause, then the material and formal principles and lastly the moving causes. The end of minerals, plants and animals is twofold. One is the completion of the universe, to which end all the parts of the universe are ordained : yet the aforesaid things are not ordained to this end as though by their very nature

[1] Cf. *ibid.* i, 29.

and essentially they were required for the universe's perfection, since they contain nothing that is not to be found in the principal parts of the world (namely the heavenly bodies and the elements) as their active and material principles. Consequently the things in question are particular effects of those universal causes which are essential parts of the universe, so that they belong to the perfection of the universe only in the point of their production by their causes, and this is by movement. Hence they belong to the perfection of the universe not absolutely speaking but only as long as the latter is in motion. Wherefore as soon as movement in the universe ceases these things must cease to exist.—The other end is man, because as the Philosopher says (*Polit.* i, 5) things that are imperfect in nature are ordained to those that are perfect, as their end, with the result that as he says (*ibid.*) since an animal's life is imperfect as compared with a man's which is perfect simply, and a plant's life as compared with an animal's: it follows that plants are for animals being prepared by nature to be the latter's food; and animals are for man, to whom they are necessary as food and for other purposes. Now this necessity lasts as long as man's animal life endures. But this life will cease in that final renewal of the universe, because the body will rise not natural but spiritual (1 Cor. xv, 44): hence animals and plants will also cease to exist then.

Again this is consistent with the matter and form of these things: for since they are composed of contrary elements, they contain within themselves an active principle of corruption. Wherefore if they were prevented from corrupting by an external principle only, this would be in a manner violent and inconsistent with perpetuity, since that which is violent cannot last for ever according to the Philosopher (*De Cœlo et Mundo*, i). Nor have they an internal principle to preserve them from corruption, because their forms are in themselves corruptible through not being self-subsistent but depending on matter for their being. Consequently they cannot remain for ever identically the same; nor specifically the same when generation and corruption cease.

The same conclusion follows from the consideration of

the moving cause. In plants and animals to be is to live, and in corporeal things this cannot be without movement. Hence animals die when the heart ceases to beat, and plants when they lack nourishment. Now these things have no moving principle that is not dependent on the first movable: since the very souls of animals and plants are wholly subject to the influence of the heavenly bodies. Therefore when the heavenly movement ceases it will be impossible for them to retain movement or life. It is evident then that at the renewal of the world the aforesaid things will be unable to remain.

Reply to the First Objection. All God's works *continue for ever* either in themselves or in their causes : in this way animals and plants will remain because the heavenly bodies and the elements will remain.

Reply to the Second Objection. Perpetuity of species and not of the individual is secured by generation which will cease when the heavens cease to be in motion.

Reply to the Third Objection. Nature's intention is to perpetuate the species as long as the heavenly movement continues whereby that perpetuity is assured.

Reply to the Fourth Objection. The things in question conduce to the beauty of the universe as regards the changeable state of the world, and man's animal life, and not otherwise, as stated above.

Reply to the Fifth Objection. In heaven the saints will not need to *see the invisible things of God* in creatures as they do in the present life to which the Apostle refers : but they will see the invisible things of God in themselves.

Reply to the Sixth Objection. The tree of life in the words quoted signifies Christ or Wisdom of whom it is written (Prov. iii, 18) : *She is a tree of life to them that lay hold upon her.*

Reply to the Seventh Objection. The desire to exist for ever is in creatures by reason of their likeness to God, in each one however, according to its mode.

Reply to the Eighth Objection. As stated above, the work of creation whereby the earth was adorned with animals and plants was accomplished in reference to the first consummation of the world, wherein the world was given a state of changeableness directed to the completion of the number of the elect, but not simply in reference to the final consummation of the world.

Reply to the Ninth Objection. The elements are said to be rewarded[1] not in themselves, because in themselves they had no merit; but because men will be rewarded in them, inasmuch as their brightness will conduce to the glory of the elect. As to plants and animals they will be of no use to man like the elements which will be as it were the place of their glory: hence the comparison fails.

Reply to the Tenth Objection. Although plants and animals are better than the elements in respect of life and knowledge: nevertheless in respect of simplicity which conduces to incorruptibility, the elements are more like God.

Reply to the Eleventh Objection. In man himself there is a conjunction of natures, inasmuch as in him the nature of a mixed body is united to the nature of plants and animals.

Reply to the Twelfth Objection. The perfection of the world at the creation was not the same as the perfection of the world at its consummation, as already stated: wherefore that which belonged to its first perfection need not belong to its second perfection.

Reply to the Thirteenth Objection. The worm that is mentioned as part of the punishment of the wicked is not to be taken literally but metaphorically, and according to Augustine (*De Civit. Dei*, xx) signifies the remorse of their conscience. Other like expressions, if there be any, should be interpreted in the same way.

Reply to the Fourteenth Objection. The germs contained in the elements do not suffice to produce an effect without the aid of the heavenly movement: wherefore when the heavens cease to be in motion it does not follow that there will still be animals and plants; nor does it follow that these germs are useless, since they belong to the perfection of the elements.

Reply to the Fifteenth Objection. Although there are certain things that are not consumed by fire for the nonce, yet as Galen says there is nothing that fire will not consume in time,

---

[1] Cf. *Sum. Th.* Suppl., Q. xci, A. 4, *On the contrary*, . . .

if it remain long enough in the fire : and yet the fire of that world-conflagration will be much more fierce than the fire to which we are used. Besides, the action of the fire will not be the sole cause of the destruction of mixed bodies, since there will also be the cessation of the heavenly movement.

Reply to the Sixteenth Objection. There are three ways of looking at the universal ; and in each way it is true that the universal is after a manner everlasting. We may consider the universal in one way as apart from any kind of being : and thus it is true that the universal lasts for ever, rather by abstraction of the cause determining it to a definite duration than by assigning the cause of its perpetuity : for it does not belong to the nature of a universal to exist at one time more than at another. In this way also primal matter is said to be one. Secondly, we may consider the universal in respect of the being it has in individuals : and thus again it is true that it exists always, since whenever the individual exists its universal exists. In the same way it is said to be everywhere, because it is wherever its individual exists, even though there are many places where its individual is not : so that neither is the universal there. Thirdly, the universal may be considered in respect of the being it has in the mind : and thus again it is true that the universal is everlasting, especially in the mind of God.

ARTICLE X

WILL HUMAN BODIES REMAIN AFTER THE HEAVENLY MOVEMENT HAS CEASED ?
Sum. Th. I, Q. lxxvii, A. 8

THE tenth point of inquiry is whether human bodies will remain after the cessation of the heavenly movement : and seemingly they will not.

1. It is written (1 Cor. xv, 50) : *Flesh and blood cannot possess the Kingdom of God.* Now the human body is composed of flesh and blood. Therefore at the end of the world human bodies will not remain.

2. All mixtures of the elements are caused by the movement of the heavens, because alteration is required in a mixture. Now the human body is a mixture of the elements. Therefore when the heavens cease to be in motion it cannot remain.

3. Necessity arising from matter is absolute (*Phys.* ii). Now in a body composed of contrary elements there is necessity for corruption arising from the very matter. Therefore it is necessary for such bodies to be corrupted: and it is impossible for them to remain after the state of generation and corruption. Since then human bodies answer to this description, it follows that at the end of the world they cannot possibly remain.

4. Man in common with dumb animals has a sensible body. Now the sensible bodies of dumb animals will not remain at the end of the world. Neither therefore will human bodies remain.

5. The end of man is a perfect assimilation to God. Now seeing that God has no body, the soul without the body is more like God than when united to the body. Therefore in the state of final beatitude the soul will be without the body.

6. Man's perfect beatitude requires the perfect operation of his intelligence. Now the intellectual soul's operation is more perfect when the soul is separated from the body than when it is united to it : because *a united force is stronger than a divided one* (*De Causis*). Now a separate form is self-united, while forms united to matter are as it were scattered in many directions. Therefore in the state of perfect bliss the soul will not be united to the body.

7. The elements that form a mixed body have a natural inclination to be in their proper places. Now a natural inclination cannot be in vain : for which reason that which is against nature cannot be everlasting. Consequently the elements in a mixed body must of necessity tend to their proper places at some time or other, so that the mixed body will be corrupted. Therefore after the state of corruption human bodies will not remain, since they are a mixture of the elements.

8. Every natural movement of any body whatsoever

depends on the movement of the heavens. Now the movement of the heart without which there can be no life in a man's body, is a natural movement. Therefore it cannot continue when the heavens cease to be in motion, and thus man's body will not continue to live.

9. The members of a man's body for the most part are directed to purposes befitting his animal life, as instanced in the veins, stomach and the like which are for the purpose of nourishment. Now animal life will not remain in man in the state of bliss. Therefore neither will the members of his body remain (otherwise they would be useless) and consequently not the body itself.

On the contrary it is written (1 Cor, xv. 53) : *This corruptible must put on incorruption.* Now *this corruptible* signifies the body. Therefore the body will remain, clothed in incorruption.

Again it is written (Phil. iii, 22) : *Who will reform the body of our lowness made like to the body of his glory.* But Christ never did and never will put aside the body which once for all he reassumed in his resurrection ; according to Romans vi, 9 : *Christ having risen again from the dead dieth no more.* Therefore the saints also will live for ever with the bodies in which they rose again : and thus human bodies will remain after the end of the world.

I answer that as Augustine states (*De Civ. Dei* xxii, 26) Porphyry held that the human soul in order to be perfectly happy must avoid all bodies, so that in his opinion the soul cannot be united to the body in the state of perfect bliss. Origen (*Peri Archon*) refers to this opinion when he says that some maintained that the saints would eventually lay aside the bodies resumed at the resurrection, so that being made like God they might live in perfect happiness. This opinion, besides being contrary to faith (as may be gathered both from the authorities quoted and from many others), is also contrary to reason. For there can be no perfect happiness where nature itself is not perfect. And since the union of soul and body is natural, besides being substantial and not accidental, the soul's nature cannot be perfect unless it be united to the body : wherefore the soul separated from the body cannot have the ultimate perfection of beatitude. For this reason Augustine (*De Gen. ad lit.* xii, 35) says that the souls of the blessed do not as perfectly enjoy the sight of God before the resurrection as after : wherefore the human body will need to be united to the soul in the final state of beatitude. The above-mentioned opinion is a sequel to the position of those who hold that the soul is united to the body accidentally, as a sailor to his ship or a man to his clothes. For this reason Plato, as Gregory of Nyssa relates (*De Anima* x), said that man is a soul clothed with a body. But this cannot stand : for man would not be a *per se* being but an accidental being : nor would he be in the genus of substance but in that of accident, as being something clothed or shod.

Moreover it is evident that the arguments given above which refer to mixed bodies, cannot apply to man : because man is ordained to the perfection of the universe as an essential part thereof, since there is in him something that is not even virtually contained either in the elements or in the heavenly bodies, namely the rational soul. Again man's body is ordained to him, not only in his animal life but for the perfection of his nature. And although his body is composed of contrary elements it will contain an incorruptible principle, that will be able to preserve it without violence, inasmuch as it is intrinsic to him. And it will suffice as a principle of movement when the heavenly movement ceases, since it does not depend on the latter.

Reply to the First Objection. Flesh and blood signify the corruption of these things, wherefore the text continues : *Neither shall corruption possess incorruption.*

Reply to the Second Objection. Movement causes mixture in the making : but its preservation comes from the substantial form, and besides, from principles yet higher than the heavens. This has been explained in previous articles.

Reply to the Third Objection. By its perfect union with God the soul will have complete sway over the body : so that although matter, if left to itself, is corruptible, it will acquire incorruption by the power of the soul.

Reply to the Fourth Objection. In man the sensitive

faculty derives from an incorruptible principle, namely the rational soul : whereas in dumb animals it derives from a corruptible principle. Wherefore man's sensitive body can last for ever while that of the dumb animal cannot.

Reply to the Fifth Objection. The soul is more like God when united to the body than when separated from it, because its nature is then more perfect. For a thing is like God forasmuch as it is perfect, although God's perfection is not of the same kind as a creature's.

Reply to the Sixth Objection. The human soul is not capable of being multiplied in the same way as material forms which can be divided if their subject be divided : but remains in itself in its simplicity and unity. Hence its operation will not be hindered by its union with the body when the body will be wholly subject to it. Now indeed it is hindered by its union with the body, because its power over the body is not perfect.

Reply to the Seventh Objection. The elements' natural inclination towards their proper places will be retained in the body through the power of the soul, lest the elements be destroyed : because the elements will have a more perfect place in the human body than in their own places.

Reply to the Eighth Objection. The movement of the heart will result in man from the nature of the rational soul which is independent of the celestial movement : wherefore it will not cease when that of the heavens ceases.

Reply to the Ninth Objection. All the body's members will remain, not indeed for the purposes of the animal life, but from the perfection of human nature.

QUESTION VI

ON MIRACLES

THERE are ten points of inquiry. (1) Can God do anything in creatures, that is beyond natural causes, or against nature, or contrary to the course of nature? (2) Whether anything that God does against nature or against the course of nature can be called a miracle? (3) Can spiritual creatures work miracles by their own natural power? (4) Can good angels and men work miracles by a gift of grace? (5) Do the demons co-operate in the working of miracles? (6) Have angels or demons bodies naturally united to them? (7) Can angels or demons assume bodies? (8) Can an angel or demon by means of an assumed body exercise the operations of a living body? (9) Should the working of a miracle be ascribed to faith? (10) Are demons compelled by sensible and corporeal objects, deeds or words to work the miracles which appear to be done by the arts of magic?

ARTICLE I

CAN GOD DO ANYTHING IN CREATURES THAT IS BEYOND NATURE, AGAINST NATURE, OR CONTRARY TO THE COURSE OF NATURE?[1]

(Con. Gen. iii, 98, 99, 100).

THE first point of inquiry is whether God can do anything in creatures that is beyond or against nature, or contrary to the course of nature: and seemingly he cannot.

1. The (ordinary) gloss on Romans xi, 24, *Contrary to nature thou wert grafted*, says: *God the author of all natures does nothing against nature.*

[1] See above Q. i, A. 3

2. Another gloss on the same passage observes: *God can no more act against the law of nature than he can act against himself.* Now he can nowise act against himself because *he cannot deny himself* (2 Tim. ii, 13). Therefore he cannot act against the order of nature.

3. Just as the order of human justice derives from divine justice, so does the order of nature derive from divine wisdom since it is this that *ordereth all things sweetly* (Wis. viii, 1). Now God cannot act against the order of human justice: further, he would be the cause of sin which alone is contrary to the order of justice. Since then God's wisdom is no less than his justice, it would seem that neither can he act against the order of nature.

4. Whenever God works in creatures through the innate laws of nature, he does not act against the course of nature. Now God cannot fittingly work in a creature independently of the innate laws of nature. Therefore he cannot fittingly work against the course of nature. The minor proposition is proved as follows. Augustine says (*De Trin.* iii, 11, 12) that visible apparitions were shown to the patriarchs by means of the angelic ministrations, inasmuch as God governs bodies through spirits. In like manner he governs the lower bodies through the higher (*ibid.* 4): and it may also be said that he directs all effects through their causes. Since then the laws of nature are implanted in natural causes, it would seem that God cannot fittingly work in natural effects, except by means of the natural laws: and thus he will do nothing contrary to the course of nature.

5. God cannot make yes and no to be true at the same time: because since this is incompatible with the very nature of being as such, it is also incompatible with a creature: and the first of things created was being (*De Causis*, p. 54). Now the aforesaid principle, being the first principle of all, to which all others are reduced (*Metaph.* iv), must be implied in every necessary proposition, and its opposite in every impossible proposition. Since then things that are contrary to the course of nature are impossible in nature, for instance that a blind man be made to see, or a dead man to live, they imply the opposite of the aforesaid

proposition. Therefore God cannot do what is contrary to the course of nature.

6. A gloss on Ephesians iii says that God does not change his will so as to act against the causes which he had established by his will. Now God established natural causes by his will. Therefore he neither does nor can do anything contrary to them, inasmuch as he cannot change: for to do anything contrary to that which one has deliberately decided would seem to point to a change in one's will.

7. The good of the universe is a good of order, and to this the course of nature belongs. But God cannot act against the good of the universe, since it is due to his sovereign goodness that all things are good in relation to the order of the universe. Therefore God cannot do anything contrary to the order of nature.

8. God cannot be the cause of evil. Now according to Augustine (*De Nat. Boni* iv) evil is the privation of measure, form and order. Therefore God cannot do anything contrary to the course of nature which belongs to the order of the universe.

9. It is written (Gen. ii, 2) that *on the seventh day God rested from all the work which he had done*, and this because as the (ordinary) gloss observes, he ceased to produce new works. Now in the works of the six days he did nothing contrary to the course of nature: wherefore Augustine (*Gen. ad. lit* ii) says that in discussing the works of the six days we do not ask what God might have done miraculously, but what was compatible with nature which he established then. Therefore neither did God afterwards do anything contrary to the course of nature.

10. According to the Philosopher (*Metaph.* vii) nature causes order in all things. Now God cannot do anything that is not in order, since according to Romans xiii, 1: *Those that are of God are well ordered*[1] Therefore he cannot do anything contrary to nature.

11. Nature no less than human reason is from God. But

---

[1] This text is invariably quoted by S. Thomas as though the Latin read: *Quae sunt a Deo, ordinata sunt*, whereas the correct reading is *Quae autem (potestates) sunt, a Deo ordinatae sunt.*

God cannot act against the principles of reason, for instance that the genus be not predicated of its species, or that the side of a square be not proportionate to the diameter. Neither therefore can he act against the principles of nature.

12. The entire course of nature derives from divine wisdom even as the products of art proceed from art, according to Augustine in his commentary on Jo. i, 3, 4 : *That which was made, was life in him.* Now a craftsman does nothing against the principles of his art except by mistake : and this cannot happen to God. Therefore God does nothing contrary to the course of nature.

13. The Philosopher says (*Phys.* ii, text 78) that the manner in which a thing is done follows its natural aptitude to be done in that way. Now what has a natural aptitude to be done as it is done, is not done against nature. Therefore nothing is done contrary to nature.

14. Anselm says (*Cur Deus Homo* xx) that God cannot do what is in the least way unbecoming. Now it is unbecoming for the course of nature to be changed, while it is becoming for it to be observed. Therefore it is impossible that God act against the course of nature.

15. Knowledge is to falsehood, as power to the impossible. Now God cannot know what is naturally false. Therefore he cannot do what is contrary to the course of nature, since this is naturally impossible.

16. That which is impossible of itself is more impossible than that which is accidentally impossible, since that which is of itself so and so is more than other things so and so. Now it is accidentally impossible for that which has been not to have been : and yet God cannot do this according to Jerome[1] and the Philosopher (*Ethic.* vi, 2). Therefore neither can God do things that are contrary to the course of nature and impossible in themselves, for instance that a blind man see.

17. According to the Philosopher (*Ethic.* iii, 1) an action is compulsory when its principle is external, and the person compelled contributes nothing to it. Now nature cannot contribute to things that are done against the course of

---

[1] *Ad Eustoch, De cust. Virg.*

nature : and thus if they are done by God they will be compulsory and will not last. But this cannot be admitted, since the blind retain their sight after having it restored by God.

18. Every genus is divided into potentiality and act (*Phys.* iii) : and passive potentiality comes under potentiality, while active potentiality comes under act : wherefore nature has no passive potentiality without a corresponding active potentiality, since they come under the same genus, as again the Commentator states (*Metaph.* ix, text. 11, 17). Now there is no natural active potentiality directed to things contrary to the course of nature : and consequently neither is there a natural passive potentiality. But when a creature has no passive potentiality in respect of a thing, this is said to be impossible, although by virtue of his omnipotence God can do all things. Therefore things that are contrary to the course of nature are impossible through something lacking to creatures, although not by reason of a defect in God's powers.

19. Whatsoever God has done once it would not be unbecoming if he did it always. Yet it would be unbecoming were he to produce all natural effects independently of their natural causes, because in that case natural things would be deprived of their operations. Therefore it is unbecoming for him to produce at times an effect in this lower world without the agency of natural causes : and if he acts by their means he does nothing against the course of nature. Therefore God does nothing contrary to the course of nature.

20. A natural cause is ordained to its effect essentially, and vice versa. Now God cannot deprive a thing of that which is essential to it, so long as the thing remains : for instance, that a man be not an animal. Therefore he cannot produce an effect without the natural cause that is essentially ordained to that effect : for instance he cannot give sight without the natural causes whence sight is produced.

21. It is unfitting for a greater good to be neglected for a lesser good. Now the good of the universe is greater than any particular good of any thing whatsoever : wherefore Augustine says (*Enchir.* x) that God made every single

thing good, and all things together very good, for the order of the universe. Therefore it is unfitting that God for the spiritual good of an individual man or of a nation, change the course of nature which belongs to the order of the universe, wherein its good consists. Therefore God never does anything contrary to the course of nature.

On the contrary, nature cannot restore a habit to one who is deprived of it: yet this can be done by God: thus it is written (Mt. xi, 5): *The blind see, the deaf hear*, etc. Therefore God does something contrary to the order of nature. Again, the power of a higher being is not dependent on or limited by the power of a lower being. Now God is above nature. Therefore his power is not limited by that of nature: so that nothing prevents him from acting against the order of nature.

I answer that, without any doubt God can work in creatures independently of created causes, just as he works in all created causes, as shown elsewhere: and by working independently of created causes he can produce the same effects and in the same order as he produces them by their means: or even other effects and in a different order: so that he is able to do something contrary to the common and customary course of nature. We shall realise how true this is if we consider the views that have been held in opposition to this truth. These are three in number.

The first is that of some early philosophers who contended that these corporeal things do not derive their existence from any higher cause; thus some of them, as Anaxagoras, said that an intelligence was the cause of some kind of movement in them, for instance, a movement of segregation. According to this opinion natural forms which are the principles of natural actions cannot be influenced, nor their actions hindered, by any supernatural cause: so that nothing can happen contrary to the course of nature, which is unchangeably regulated by these corporeal causes. Now this opinion is false: because the supreme being must needs be the cause of being in all things (*Metaph.* ii, text. 4), just as that which is supremely hot is the cause of heat in all other things. We have treated this point more fully elsewhere (*Sum. Theol.*,

P. I, Q. xliv, A. 1) when we proved that nothing can exist unless it be made by God.

A second opinion in opposition to this truth was held by other philosophers who asserted that God is the cause of all by his intellect. They maintained however that God has a universal knowledge of things inasmuch as he knows himself, and that he himself is the source of all being, but that he has no proper knowledge of each individual being. But, said they, from common and universal knowledge individual effects do not follow except by means of particular knowledge. Thus, if I know that all fornication is to be avoided, I shall not avoid this particular action unless I know that it is fornication. Accordingly they said that particular effects do not proceed from God except in a certain order by means of other causes, of which the higher are more universal, and the lower more particular: and according to this view God is unable to do anything contrary to the order of nature. But this opinion is false: for since God knows himself perfectly, he must needs know all that is in him in any way whatsoever. Now in him is the likeness of every one of his effects, inasmuch as there can be nothing that does not imitate him: and thus it follows that he has proper knowledge of all things, as we have proved elsewhere (*Sum. Theol.*, P. I, Q. xiv).

The third opinion opposed to the aforesaid truth is that of some philosophers who said that God produces things by natural necessity: so that his works are confined to the course of things appointed by nature, and thus he is unable to act against it. But this again is evidently false: since above all those things that act of natural necessity there must be something that determines nature to one mode of action, as elsewhere (*Sum. Th.*, P. I, Q. xix, A. 4) we have proved. It is impossible then that God the first agent act of natural necessity: and this again has been proved in several ways in another question (*ibid.* A. 3 and above Q. iii, A. 15).

These three points being established, namely that God is the author of being in all things of nature; that he has proper knowledge and providence in respect of each individual; and that he does not act of natural necessity, it follows that he can act independently of the course of nature in the production of particular effects—either as regards being by producing in natural things a new form which nature is unable to produce, for instance, the form of glory ; or by producing a form in a particular matter, as sight in a blind man : or as regards operation, by restraining the action of nature from doing what it would naturally do, for instance, by hindering fire from burning (Dan. iii, 49, 50), or water from flowing, as happened in the Jordan (Jos. iii, 13).

Reply to the First Objection. Both God and nature act against individual nature : for instance, it is against the nature of this or that particular fire that it be extinguished : wherefore the Philosopher says (*De Cælo et Mundo*, ii) that corruption, decrepitude, and in general all defects are contrary to nature : whereas nothing in nature acts against universal nature. For particular nature denotes the relation of a particular cause to a particular effect, while universal nature denotes the relation of the first agent in nature, which is the heavens, to all agents in the lower world. And seeing that none of the lower bodies acts save by virtue of the heavenly body, it is impossible for any natural body to act against universal nature : while the very fact that anything acts against a particular nature, is in accord with universal nature. Now just as the heaven is the universal cause in respect of lower bodies, so God is the universal cause in respect of all beings, and in comparison with him even the heaven is a particular cause. For nothing prevents one and the same cause from being universal in relation to things below it, and particular in relation to those above it : thus if we take the predicables, animal is universal in relation to man, and particular in relation to substance. Accordingly just as by the power of the heavens something can happen that is contrary to this or that particular nature, and yet not contrary to nature simply, since it is in accord with universal nature : even so by the power of God something can occur that is contrary to universal nature which is dependent on the power of the heavens ; without being contrary to nature simply, since it will be in accord with the supremely universal nature, dependent on God in relation to all creatures. It is in this sense that Augustine in the gloss quoted says that God does nothing contrary to nature : wherefore he goes on to say, because *the nature of each thing is what God does in it.*

The *Reply to the Second Objection* is evident from what has just been said : because in that gloss Augustine refers to the supreme law of nature which is God's ordinance with regard to all creatures.

Reply to the Third Objection. As we have already explained although God can do something contrary to the relation between one creature and another, he cannot do anything contrary to a creature's relation to himself. Now the justice of a man consists chiefly in his being duly referred to God : so that God cannot do anything contrary to the order of justice. On the other hand the course of nature is dependent on the relation of one creature to another, wherefore God can act against the course of nature.

Reply to the Fourth Objection. Just as God can produce effects in nature without employing natural causes, so also can he without the ministry of the angels : but the reason for his doing so is not the same in both cases. He acts independently of natural causes in order that being unable to ascribe the effect to visible causes we may be compelled to attribute it to some higher cause, and that thus a visible miracle may be a manifestation of the divine power. But the activities of the angels are not visible ; wherefore their ministrations do not hinder us from ascribing something to the divine power. For this reason Augustine does not say that God is unable to work without the ministry of the angels, but that he does not do so.

Reply to the Fifth Objection. Just as God cannot make *yes* and *no* to be true at the same time, so neither can he do what is impossible in nature in so far as it includes the former impossibility. Thus for a dead man to return to life clearly involves a contradiction if we suppose that his return to life is the natural effect of an intrinsic principle, since a dead man is essentially one who lacks the principle of life. Wherefore God does not do this but he makes a dead man to regain life from an extrinsic principle : and this involves no contradiction. The same applies to other things that are impossible to nature, and which God is able to do.

Reply to the Sixth Objection. God does not change his will when he does anything contrary to natural causes : because from eternity he foresaw and decreed that he would do what he does in time. Wherefore he so ordered the course of nature, that by his eternal decree he preordained whatsoever he would at some time do independently of that course.

Reply to the Seventh Objection. When God does anything outside the course of nature he does not put aside the entire order of the universe wherein its good consists, but the order of some particular cause to its effect.

Reply to the Eighth Objection. Penal evil is contrary to the order between one part of the universe and another part : and in like manner every evil that is a defect of nature. But sinful evil is contrary to the order between the whole universe and its last end, inasmuch as the will in which sinful evil resides, is deprived by sin of its order in relation to the last end of the universe. Wherefore God cannot be the cause of this evil : since he cannot act against the latter order, although he can act against the former.

Reply to the Ninth Objection. God does not work miracles except in creatures that already exist, and in some way existed already in the works of the six days. Hence miraculous works, in a manner of speaking, existed already materially in the works of the six days, although it was not befitting that anything should be done miraculously contrary to the course of nature, when nature itself was being established.

Reply to the Tenth Objection. Nature is the cause of order in all natural things, but not in all things absolutely speaking.

Reply to the Eleventh Objection. The logician and the mathematician consider things in their abstract principles, so that in logic and mathematics nothing is impossible except what is contrary to the abstract notion of a thing. These things involve a contradiction and consequently are of themselves impossible. Such impossibilities God cannot do. On the other hand the physicist studies individual matter, wherefore he reckons as an impossibility, even that which is impossible to an individual. But nothing prevents God from being able to do what is impossible to lower agents.

Reply to the Twelfth Objection. The divine art is not fully extended in producing creatures : so that God can by his art do something otherwise than the course of nature requires. Hence although he can do something contrary to the course of nature it does not follow that he can act against his art : since even a human craftsman can by his art produce another work in a different way to that in which he produced a previous work.

Reply to the Thirteenth Objection. The Philosopher refers to things that are done in nature : for such things are so done as they have a natural aptitude to be done.

Reply to the Fourteenth Objection. It is fitting that the course of nature be observed forasmuch as it is ordained by divine providence : wherefore if it be in the order of divine providence that something be done otherwise, there is no reason why it should not be.

Reply to the Fifteenth Objection. A thing cannot be said to be false simply or false relatively in the same way as a thing is impossible simply or impossible relatively : if a thing is false at all, it is false simply. Hence God cannot know falsehood, even as he cannot do what is simply impossible. And yet just as he can do what is relatively impossible, so is he able to do what is relatively unknown.

Reply to the Sixteenth Objection. All accidental things are to be reduced to something *per se*; wherefore nothing prevents that which is accidentally impossible from being more impossible when reduced to that which is impossible in itself : thus snow by its whiteness dazzles the eyes more than the whiteness of the wall does, because the whiteness of the snow is greater than that of the wall. In like manner that Socrates did not run is an impossibility because it is reduced to a *per se* impossibility, namely that the past has not been ; which involves a contradiction. Consequently nothing prevents this from being more impossible than that which is impossible relatively, although accidentally it is not impossible.

Reply to the Seventeenth Objection. In every natural thing there is natural order and relationship to all higher causes: and therefore things that happen to lower bodies through the influence of the heavenly bodies, are not compulsory, although they may seem contrary to the natural movements of these lower bodies, as evidenced in the ebb and flow of the sea consequent upon the movement of the moon. And much less compulsory is what God does in this lower world.

Reply to the Eighteenth Objection. A higher active force can produce a higher effect with the same material: thus nature can produce gold out of earth and a mixture of other elements, which art cannot do. Hence it is that the same thing has a potentiality for various effects, according to its relation to various agents. Wherefore nothing prevents created nature from being in potentiality to certain effects that can be produced by the power of God, and which cannot be produced by a lower power: this potentiality of nature is called obediential forasmuch as every creature obeys its Creator.

Reply to the Nineteenth Objection. Every created thing is ordered to its own operation by God: and thus it is not unfitting if by divine providence a certain effect is produced without the co-operation of nature.

Reply to the Twentieth Objection. Although God produces an effect without the action of its natural cause, he does not destroy the relation between cause and effect. Thus the fiery furnace retained its relation to burning, although it burned not the three children in the furnace.

Reply to the Twenty-first Objection. When God does anything contrary to the course of nature, the whole order of the universe is not subverted, but the course resulting from the relation between one particular thing and another. Hence it is not unfitting if at times something is done contrary to the course of nature for man's spiritual welfare which consists in his being ordered to the last end of the universe.

ARTICLE II

CAN EVERYTHING THAT GOD DOES WITHOUT NATURAL CAUSES OR CONTRARY TO THE COURSE OF NATURE BE CALLED A MIRACLE?

Sum. Th. I, Q. cv, A. 7

THE second point of inquiry is whether everything can be called a miracle that God does without natural causes or against the order of nature: and seemingly the answer should be in the negative.

1. We may gather from Augustine (*Super Joan. Tract.* viii: *De Trin.* iii, 5)[1] that a miracle is *something difficult which seldom occurs, exceeding the faculty of nature and so far surpassing our hopes as to compel our astonishment.* Now God sometimes acts against the course of nature even in very little things, for instance when he made wine from water (Jo. ii), and yet he did this without natural causes. Therefore not everything that God does independently of natural causes should be called a miracle.

2. That which often happens should not be described as occurring seldom. Yet at the time of the apostles God often wrought works without natural causes; thus it is related (Acts v. 15) that *they brought forth the sick into the streets,* etc. Hence such things were not of rare occurrence, and consequently were not miracles.

3. What nature can do is not above the faculty of nature. Now sometimes without natural causes God does things that could be done by nature: as when our Lord healed Peter's mother-in-law of the fever with which she was stricken. This then was not beyond the faculty of nature and was not miraculous.

4. A dead man cannot live again through the action of a natural cause. Now the saints look forward to the resurrection of the dead when God will raise all the dead to life at the end of the world: wherefore we say in the creed: *I look for the resurrection of the dead.* Therefore not everything that God does beyond the faculty of natural causes,

---

[1] *De Utilitate credendi* xvi.

surpasses human hope; wherefore such a thing is not a miracle.

5. The creation of heaven and earth, or the creation of a rational soul is a work of God surpassing other active causes: for God alone can create, as we have proved above (Q. iii, AA. 1, 4: *Sum. Th.*, P. I., Q. xlv, A 5). Yet these cannot be called miracles, since they are not done for the manifestation of grace, for which purpose alone miracles are wrought according to Augustine, but for the establishment of nature. Therefore not everything that God does beyond the faculty of nature is a miracle.

6. The conversion of a sinner is a work of God beyond the faculty of nature: and yet it is not a miracle, but rather the end of a miracle, since miracles are wrought in order that men be converted to God. Therefore not everything that God does beyond the faculty of nature is a miracle.

7. It is more astonishing if a thing be done by one who is less powerful than if it be done by one who is more powerful. Now God is more powerful than nature: yet nature's works are not called miracles, for instance, the healing of a sick man, or the like. Much less then should it be called a miracle when it is wrought by God.

8. Monsters are contrary to nature, and yet they are not described as miraculous. Therefore not everything that is contrary to nature is miraculous.

9. Miracles are wrought in confirmation of the faith. Now the Incarnation of the Word was not intended as an argument in confirmation, but to be an object, of faith. Therefore it was not a miracle: and yet it was the work of God alone without the action of any other cause. Therefore not everything that God does beyond the faculty of nature is a miracle.

On the contrary, Augustine[1] says that things follow a threefold course: they may be either natural or voluntary or marvellous. Now those things which God does beyond the faculty of natural causes belong neither to the course of nature, nor to the course of voluntary things, since neither nature nor created will has any effective part in them.

[1] Anselm, *De Pecc. Orig.* xi.

Therefore they belong to the order of wonders : and thus they are miracles.

Again, Richard of St. Victor says that a miracle is a work of the Creator manifestive of divine power. Now this applies to those of God's works which surpass natural causes. Therefore they are miracles.

I answer that the word miracle is derived from *mirari* (to be astonished). Now two things concur in making us astonished, as we may gather from the Philosopher (*Metaph.* i, 2). One is that the thing which astonishes us has a hidden cause : the second is that in that which astonishes us we perceive something that would seem to be in contradiction with the cause of our wonder : thus someone might be astonished if he saw iron rising towards a magnet, through not knowing the magnet's power, since apparently the iron ought by its natural movement to tend downwards. This happens in two ways : for a thing may be wonderful in itself, or it may be wonderful to us. A thing is wonderful to us, when the cause of that which astonishes us is hidden, not simply, but to this or that individual, and when the thing at which we marvel has in reality no disposition inconsistent with the marvellous effect, but only in the opinion of the person who marvels. The result is that what is wonderful or astonishing to one person, is not wonderful or astonishing to another : thus one who knows of the magnet's power through having been taught or had experience of it, is not astonished at the aforesaid effect : whereas an ignorant person is astonished.—A thing is wonderful or marvellous in itself when its cause is simply hidden, and when the thing has a contrary disposition to the visible effect. Such things may be called not only actually or potentially wonderful, but also miracles, as having in themselves a cause for admiration. Now the most hidden cause and the furthest removal from our senses is God who works most secretly in all things : wherefore those effects are properly called miracles, which are produced by God's power alone on things which have a natural tendency to the opposite effect or to a contrary mode of operation : whereas effects produced by nature, the cause of which is unknown to us or to some of us, as also those effects, produced by God, that are of a nature to be produced by none but God, cannot be called miraculous but only marvellous or wonderful. For this reason a miracle in its definition is described as being above the order of nature in the words *exceeding the faculty of nature*, to which on the part of the thing done corresponds the word *difficult*. Again it is described as transcending our knowledge, in the words *so far surpassing our hopes as to compel admiration*, to which on the part of the thing done correspond the words *which seldom occurs :* since when we are accustomed to an occurrence it becomes more familiar to our knowledge.

Reply to the First Objection. The *difficulty* mentioned in the definition of a miracle refers to the greatness of the thing not in itself, but in comparison with the faculty of nature : wherefore every effect is reckoned to be difficult that God works in any little thing, if that effect surpasses the faculty of nature.

Reply to the Second Objection. A miracle is described as seldom occurring because it is contrary to the usual course of nature, even were it to be repeated day after day. Thus the transubstantiation of bread into Christ's body occurs every day, yet it ceases not to be miraculous : because the things that happen generally in the whole order of the universe are to be described as usual occurrences rather than what happens in one individual thing alone.

Reply to the Third Objection. It is customary to divide the miraculous works of God into those which are done above, those which are done against, and those which are done without nature.—A miracle is *above* nature when God produces an effect which nature is wholly incapable of producing. This happens in two ways. First, when God induces into matter a form which nature is utterly unable to induce, for instance, the form of glory which God will induce into the bodies of the elect ; and again the Incarnation of the Word. Secondly when nature, although able to induce a particular form into some matter, is unable to induce it into this particular matter : thus nature is able to produce life, but not to produce it in this corpse. A miracle is *contrary* to nature, when nature retains a disposition contrary to the effect produced by God : for instance when he prevented the three children in the furnace from being hurt, while the fire retained the power to burn ; and when the waters of the Jordan stood (Jos. iii, 16) while retaining the force of gravity ; and again when a virgin gave birth to a son.—A miracle is done by God *without* nature, when he produces an effect that nature can produce, but in a manner of which nature is incapable. This may be either through lack of the instruments which nature is wont to employ, as when Christ changed water into wine (Jo. ii) : for nature can do this in a certain way, the water absorbed by the vine for the purpose of nourishment being converted in due time into the juice of the grape by the process of assimilation : or, because the effect is produced by God more copiously than when produced by nature, for instance, the frogs that were brought forth in Egypt (Exod. viii, 6) : or because it is produced in less time than nature can produce it, as when a person is instantly cured through the prayer of a saint, for nature could have done this, yet not at once but by degrees, not now but at another time : for instance, the miracle already quoted wrought on Peter's mother-in-law. Evidently then all such works, if we take into account both the substance and the manner of the thing done, surpass the faculty of nature.

Reply to the Fourth Objection. The coming resurrection of the dead is beyond the hope of nature, but not beyond the hope of grace. This twofold hope is mentioned (Rom. iv, 18) : *Who against hope believed in hope.*

Reply to the Fifth Objection. Heaven, earth and rational souls in the natural order cannot be created by any cause other than God : wherefore the creation of these is not a miracle.

The same answer applies *to the Sixth Objection* as regards the conversion of a sinner.

Reply to the Seventh Objection. Nature's works are also God's works, but the miracles wrought by God are not wrought by nature : and thus the argument does not conclude. Moreover, the action of nature is manifest to us, whereas God is a hidden cause : for which reason God's works are more wonderful to us than the works of nature.

Reply to the Eighth Objection. Monsters are a result that is contrary to a particular nature, but not to universal nature.

Reply to the Ninth Objection. In the words of the saints the Incarnation is the miracle of miracles, because it is greater than all other miracles, and because all other miracles are ordered to it. For this reason not only does it lead us to believe in other articles of faith, but other miracles lead us to believe in it : since nothing prevents one miracle from leading to faith in another, as, for instance, the raising of Lazarus leads us to believe in a future resurrection.

ARTICLE III

CAN SPIRITUAL CREATURES WORK MIRACLES BY THEIR NATURAL POWER ?

Sum. Th. I, Q. cx, AA. 1 seqq. : *Con. Gen.* iii, 103

THE third point of inquiry is whether spiritual creatures can work miracles by their natural power : and seemingly they can.

1. That which can be done by a lower power, can *a fortiori* be done by a higher power. Now the power of a spiritual creature surpasses that of a corporeal creature : wherefore it is written (Job xli, 24) : *There is no power upon earth that can be compared with him.* Therefore a spiritual creature can produce the same effects as nature. But when a natural effect is produced, not by a natural but by a hidden cause, it is a miracle. Therefore the spiritual creature can work miracles.

2. The more actual a thing is the more is it active, inasmuch as activity is in proportion to actuality. Now the forms that are in rational creatures are more actual than the forms which are in corporeal creatures, because they are more immaterial : and consequently they are more active. But the forms that are in a corporeal nature produce their like

in nature. Much more therefore are the forms in the mind of a spiritual creature capable of doing this : so that a rational creature can produce natural effects without natural causes : and this is a miracle.

3. An angel's intelligence is more akin to the divine intelligence than a man's is. Now in the human intelligence there are active forms residing in the practical intellect, such as the forms of art. Much more then are these active forms in an angel's intelligence : inasmuch as it is evident that the ideas in the divine intellect are supremely active.

4. It might be said that the active forms in the angelic mind are employed in the production of effects by means of a corporeal agent in the same way as forms in the human mind.—On the contrary any power that cannot come into action except by means of a corporeal instrument, is uselessly bestowed on one who has no bodily organs : thus the power of locomotion would be useless to an animal unless it had the means to move. But an angel has not a body naturally united to him. Therefore his power needs no corporeal agent in order to do its work.

5. Any power whose field of action exceeds that of its organ can perform some actions without that organ : thus since the eye's field of action is not equal to the whole power of the soul, the latter performs many actions without the eye. Now a body cannot be in proportion to the whole power of an angel. Therefore an angel can produce certain effects without employing corporeal agents : and thus seemingly he can work miracles by his natural power.

6. An angel's power surpasses all corporeal power more than the body of the heavens surpasses the elements. Now certain effects are produced in this lower world by the power of a heavenly body independently of the action of the active and passive qualities that are the forces proper to the elements. Much more then can certain effects be produced in nature by the power of an angel, without the aid of the powers of natural bodies.

7. According to Augustine (*De Trin.* iii, 4) *all bodies are governed by God through the rational spirit of life;* and Gregory says the same (*Dial.* iv. 6) : so that seemingly the

movements of the heavens and of all nature are controlled by the angels even as the movements of the human body are controlled by the soul. Now the soul produces forms in the body independently of the natural active forces of the body: thus a mere fancy makes a man grow hot or cold, or become feverish or even leprous according to physicians. *A fortiori* then it is possible that by the mere concept of the angel who moves the heavens certain effects be produced in this lower world without the action of natural causes: and thus an angel can work a miracle.

8. It will be said perhaps that this is due to the fact that the soul is the form of the body, whereas an angel is not the form of a corporeal creature.—On the contrary—whatsoever effects result from the soul's operation, are produced by the soul as moving, and not as informing the body: since by its operation it is not the body's form but its mover. Now the aforesaid effects of the soul on the body are consequent upon impressions of the soul in imagining something. Therefore they are produced by the soul as mover but not as form.

9. The reason why God can work wonders is because his power is infinite. Now in *De Causis* (Prop. xvi) it is stated that the power of an intelligence is infinite especially over the lower world. This can be proved from the fact that an intelligence causes the heavenly movement, as proved above, which has a natural aptitude to be everlasting: and only an infinite power can cause an everlasting movement (*Phys.* viii). Therefore it would seem that angels can work miracles even by their natural power.

10. It is also stated in *De Causis* (Prop. xvii) that a united force is stronger than one that is divided: and the Commentator says that the power of an intelligence the more it is concentrated and united, the greater and stronger it is, and the more capable of working wonders. Now the Commentator is speaking there of an intelligence's natural power, since he knew not of the power of grace. Therefore by his natural power an angel can work miracles.

11. But to this it might be replied that an angel can work wonders not by his own power, but by employing the forces implanted in nature by God, in order to produce the desired

result.—On the contrary, these natural germs which contain the active forces of nature cannot be employed so as to produce a certain effect otherwise than by local movement. Now seemingly it amounts to the same that bodies obey or do not obey a spiritual substance whether as to local movement or as to other kinds of movement: since all natural movement has its distinctive and definite mover. Hence if angels have at their command the use of these germs in the production of an effect in nature by means of local movement, they will also be able by the movements of alteration or of generation to induce a form into matter by their mere command: and this is to work wonders.

12. The power to induce a form into matter, and the power to prevent its induction are in the same genus: thus the form of fire is induced into matter by the power of a body, and it is also the power of a body that prevents the induction of that form. Now a natural agent is prevented by the power of a spiritual creature from inducing a form into matter. Thus it is related that by virtue of some particular writing a man was not burnt after being cast into a furnace: and clearly this was not the work of God who protects his saints from torture on account of their merits and not for the sake of any writing: so that this must have been a work of the devil's power. It would seem therefore, with equal reason, that a spiritual creature can at will induce a form into matter without any corporeal agency. And yet one would reckon it a miracle that a man be not burnt when cast into the fire, as in the case of the three children.

13. A form that is in the imagination or in the senses is superior to a form in corporeal matter forasmuch as it is more immaterial. Now a spiritual creature can produce a form in the imagination or senses, so that a thing appears otherwise than it is. Thus Augustine says (*De Civit. Dei* xviii, 18): *Verily the demons do not create substantial beings, they only change the outward appearance of things created by the true God:* and afterwards he adds that they do this by acting on the imagination. Much more therefore can an angel produce a form in corporeal matter: and thus the same conclusion follows as before.

14. To this it might be replied that the demon's action on the imagination does not consist in the production of new forms but in the composition and division of forms already existing.—On the contrary the soul is a more noble being than a corporeal nature. If then a demon can by his power produce what is the proper operation of the sensitive soul, namely composition and division of images, one would think that *a fortiori* he is able by his power to produce the operations of a corporeal nature: and thus the same conclusion follows as before.

15. As power is to power so is operation to operation. Now an angel's power does not depend on the power of a corporeal creature. Neither then does his operation depend on that of a corporeal creature: and therefore he can work miracles independently of natural causes.

16. Just as to make a thing out of nothing argues infinite power by reason of the infinite distance between being and nothing; even so is it possible to a finite power to reduce a thing from potentiality to act. Now the angels' power surpasses all other finite powers. Therefore by his power an angel can bring into actuality all the forms that are in the potentiality of matter, without the action of any natural cause: and thus the same conclusion follows as before.

17. An agent that is hindered acts not but is passive. Now the angel that acts on corporeal things is in no way passive to them. Therefore he is not prevented in his action from working miracles by acting independently of natural causes.

On the contrary God works miracles inasmuch as nature is subject to him. But it is not subject to the angels: since *he hath not subjected unto angels the world (to come)* (Heb. ii, 5). Therefore angels cannot work miracles by their natural power.

Again, Augustine (*De Trin.* ii, 10) after carefully discussing this question, concludes: *It is good for me to be mindful of my limitations, and I would have my brethren remember theirs, lest human weakness should go further than is safe. How angels do these things, or rather how God does them through his angels, my sight is not keen enough to see, my reason too diffident to unravel, my mind too slow to grasp; nor can I answer with assurance all the queries that could be made on this matter, as though I were an angel myself, or a prophet, or an apostle.* Wherefore employing the same moderation, without dogmatizing and without prejudice to a better opinion, we shall discuss the question so far as reason and authority will avail to elucidate it.

It must be observed then that in regard to the point at issue philosophers have disagreed. Avicenna held that the spiritual substance which moves the heavens produces effects in the lower bodies not only by means of the celestial movement but even independently of any bodily action: for he contended that corporeal matter is much more obedient to the concept and command of the aforesaid spiritual substance than to any counter agents in nature or to any corporeal agent. It was owing to this cause, he maintained, that sometimes unwonted disturbances take place in the air, and extraordinary cures of diseased persons; which we call miracles. He gives as an instance the movement of the body by the soul inasmuch as when the latter is affected by a mere imagination, the body without any corporeal agency, is affected by heat or cold, by fever or even by leprosy. This view is quite in keeping with the principles laid down by him. For he holds that natural agents do no more than dispose matter: and that substantial forms are bestowed by a spiritual substance which he calls the giver of forms: the result being that matter in the natural course obeys the spiritual substance as regards the reception of the form therefrom. No wonder then if a spiritual substance produce certain forms in matter outside the ordinary course of corporeal agents and by the sole command of its will. For if matter obeys a separate substance in receiving a substantial form, it is only reasonable that it obey also in receiving the dispositions to a form: for this clearly requires less power. In the opinion of Aristotle, however, and of those who follow him, the above view cannot stand. Aristotle in fact advances two arguments to prove that forms are not stamped on matter by a separate substance, but are brought into act from the potentiality of matter by the action of a form existing in matter. The first of these arguments is given in *Metaph.* vii, 8, and is based on the principle which he there proves, that what is made is properly speaking the composite, and not form or matter : since it is the composite which properly speaking has being. Now every agent produces its like : wherefore that which gives existence to natural things by generation, must needs be something composite and not a form without matter, in other words it cannot be a separate substance. The other argument, to be found in *Phys.* viii, is that whereas the same thing has a natural aptitude to produce always the same effect, and since that which is generated or corrupted or altered, increased or diminished is not always in the same condition, it follows that whatsoever generates or moves with the aforesaid kinds of movement is not always in the same condition, but passes from one state to another. But this cannot be a separate substance, because all such substances are unchangeable, and anything that is changed is a body (*Phys.* vi). Consequently the immediate cause of the reduction of a form into act by generation or alteration, is a body passing from one mode of being to another through accession and recession by local motion. Hence it is that a separate substance is by its command the immediate cause of local movement in a body, by means of which it causes other movements whereby the thing moved acquires a new form. Now this is reasonable. For local movement is the first and most perfect movement, in that it does not change a thing inwardly but only in point of its place which is external to it : wherefore a corporeal nature receives its first movement, which is local, from a spiritual nature. Accordingly the corporeal nature obeys the bidding of the spiritual in the point of its natural relation to local movement, but not as regards the reception of a form. This of course is to be understood in reference to the created spiritual nature whose power and essence are confined to a definite genus, and not to the uncreated spiritual substance whose power is infinite, and not confined to a particular genus and the laws governing that genus. In this point faith is in agreement with this opinion : thus Augustine (*De Trin.* iii, 8, 9) says that corporeal matter does not obey the mere will of the angels. However, the teaching of faith differs somewhat from the position of the philosophers. The philosophers mentioned held that separate substances by their bidding move the heavenly bodies with local movement: and that in this lower world local movement is not caused immediately by a separate substance, but by other causes, natural, voluntary or violent. Thus the commentator Alexander ascribes to the activity of the heavenly bodies all the effects which we ascribe to angels or demons in this lower world. But this seems insufficient: because these effects do not follow a definite course, like those which are produced by the natural action of the higher or lower bodies. Besides there are certain effects that altogether surpass the powers of a heavenly body, for instance, the sudden changing of rods into snakes, and many similar ones. But faith asserts that not only heavenly bodies cause local movement by their bidding, but that other bodies also do so, at God's behest or with his permission. Accordingly by their command they cause local movement in those bodies that have a natural active power to produce a particular effect which however Augustine (*Super Gen.* ix, 17) calls the seeds of nature. It follows that their operations will not be miraculous but should rather be described as an art. For miraculous effects are produced by a supernatural cause without recourse to the action of nature: whereas it belongs to art to employ the action of natural principles, in producing an effect which either nature cannot produce, or at least not so efficiently. Hence the Philosopher says (*Phys.* ii) that *art both copies nature, and makes things which nature cannot make, and sometimes assists nature*: thus the physician helps nature to heal by employing those things which have a natural healing power in the process of alteration and digestion. Now in the production of like effects the good or bad angel's art is more efficacious and leads to better results than the art of man: and this for two reasons. First, because seeing that corporeal effects in this lower world depend chiefly on the heavenly bodies, then is an art most effective when the heavenly body's power acts in co-operation with it. Thus in farming and medicine it is useful to notice the movements and position of the sun, moon and stars, whose powers are much better known to the angels by their natural knowledge than to men. Hence they are better fitted to choose the hour at which the power of a heavenly body is more likely to co-operate in producing the desired result. This apparently is the reason why necromancers observe the position of the stars when they invoke the demons.—The second reason is that angels are better acquainted than men with the active and passive powers of the lower bodies, and are therefore able to employ them effectively with greater ease and expedition seeing that bodies move locally at their command. Hence again physicians produce more wonderful results in healing, because they are better acquainted with the powers of natural things.—We may add as a third reason that an instrument acts not only by its own power but also by the power of its mover. Thus a heavenly body produces a certain effect by virtue of the spiritual substance which moves it, for instance, it causes life in animals engendered from corrupt matter; and natural heat as the instrument of the vegetal soul conduces to the formation of flesh. Therefore it is not unreasonable to suppose that natural bodies themselves, forasmuch as they are moved by a spiritual substance, produce a greater effect. We may gather this from the words of Gen. vi, 4 where we read: *Giants were upon the earth in those days. For after the sons of God went into the daughters of men, and they brought forth children, these are the mighty men, men of renown:* and the (ordinary) gloss commenting on this text observes that it is not incredible that men of this kind were born of women who consorted with demons. It is therefore evident that angels whether good or wicked are unable to work miracles by their natural power: but they can produce certain wonderful effects in which their action is after the manner of an art.

Reply to the First Objection. It is true that the natural power of an angel or demon is greater than the natural power of a body; but it does not extend so far as to induce form into matter immediately, but only by means of a body.

Hence it does this more excellently than a body since the first mover excels the second in action.

Reply to the Second Objection. The forms of natural things in the angelic mind are more actual than forms existing in matter : wherefore they are the immediate principle of a more perfect operation namely of understanding. But they are not the immediate principle of that operation which is the transmutation of matter ; but they operate through the medium of the will, and the will through the (motive) power, which power is the immediate cause of local movement, by means of which they are the cause of other movements, and a kind of cause of the induction of form into matter.

Reply to the Third Objection. The forms in the human mind do not produce artifacts save through the will, the motive power, the natural organs and the craftsman's tools.

Reply to the Fourth Objection. A power that can employ an organ which serves it in all its operations must have that organ united to it ; thus the eye is united to the faculty of sight. But no body could serve an angel so far as to equal his power : hence an angel has not a body actually united to him. For this reason those philosophers who held that separate substances produce no effects here below except by means of the heavens, said that a spiritual substance is united to the heavens as its instrument, and this they called the heavens' soul : and that besides this there is another spiritual substance, not united to the heavens, by which the heavens' soul is moved as a man is moved by the object of his desire, and this spiritual substance they called intelligence.

Reply to the Fifth Objection. Although an angel causes the movement of the heavens, he can by his act of intelligence bring his action to bear on things here below, independently of the heavens' movement, and of any body whatsoever, by moving other bodies : and yet he is unable to induce a form into matter without employing a corporeal agent.

Reply to the Sixth Objection. The heaven being a corporeal agent can be the immediate cause of alteration and information : but it is not so with the angels.

Reply to the Seventh Objection. In the natural order the

soul by its bidding moves the body locally: because its appetitive power commands the movement, and the body obeys its bidding, and this is effected by the motive powers affixed to the organs and derived by the body from the soul which informs the body. Other alterations such as heat, cold and the like derive from the soul by means of local movement. It is also evident that imagination gives rise to a passion whereby in some way the movements of the heart and spirits are affected: and that when the latter are drawn towards the heart or diffused throughout the members the body is likewise affected: and this may lead to disease especially if the matter be so disposed.

This suffices for the *Reply to the Eighth Objection.*

Reply to the Ninth Objection. An angel's power is said to be infinite over the lower world, inasmuch as his power is not enclosed in matter, and consequently is not confined by an inferior recipient. But it is not infinite in respect of things above it, as already stated: because the angel receives a finite nature from God, so that his substance is confined to a particular genus, and consequently his power is confined to a particular mode of action: and this cannot be said of God.

Reply to the Tenth Objection. Although an angel does wonderful things as the result of art, they are not miracles, as we have stated above.

Reply to the Eleventh Objection. Although the local movements of the lower bodies as well as other movements are brought about by certain fixed natural causes: the corporeal creature in the natural order obeys the spiritual as regards local movement, but not as regards other movements, for the reason already given: and especially if the power of the spiritual creature is not confined to a particular body, as the soul's power is to the body united to it.

Reply to the Twelfth Objection. Just as a created spiritual substance cannot by its command give form to matter, even so it cannot by its command prevent a form from being given to matter by a natural agent: and if it does this sometimes, it is by putting a natural obstacle in the way, even though this may not be perceptible to human senses: especially since it can move the flame of a fire locally, so as not to approach the combustible.

Reply to the Thirteenth Objection. A separate spiritual substance can by its natural power influence the imagination; not indeed by introducing forms into the organ of imagination at his bidding, but by raising a kind of commotion of the spirits and humours. For it is evident that if these be disturbed, phantoms appear, as instanced in those who are insane or asleep. Besides it is said that certain natural things are effective in producing this distrubance in the imagination, and that magicians make use of them in order to produce illusory visions.

This suffices for the *Reply to the Fourteenth Objection.*

Reply to the Fifteenth Objection. Even as an angel surpasses a heavenly body in respect of power, so also does he in respect of operation, as stated above: yet not to the extent of inducing form into matter immediately and by his mere bidding.

Reply to the Sixteenth Objection. A finite power can educe something from potentiality to act; but not any finite power, nor in any way: because every finite power has a fixed mode of action.

Reply to the Seventeenth Objection. Even though an agent be not hindered it cannot do what is beyond its power; thus fire cannot make a thing cold although there is nothing to prevent it. Hence from the fact that an angel cannot induce a form into matter by his bidding we may infer, not that he is prevented from doing this by some extrinsic agent, but that his natural power does not extend to this.

ARTICLE IV

CAN GOOD ANGELS AND MEN WORK MIRACLES BY SOME GIFT OF GRACE ?

Sum. Th, I, Q. cx, A. 4

THE fourth point of inquiry is whether good angels and men can work miracles by some gift of grace: and it would seem that they can.

1. The angelic orders were established for no other purpose than their operations. Now an order of angels was appointed for the working of miracles: thus Gregory says in a homily (*In Evang.* xxxiv) that signs and miracles are usually wrought by the Virtues. Therefore angels can work miracles by a gift of grace.

2. It is written (Acts vi. 8): *Stephen full of grace and fortitude did great signs and wonders among the people.* Now grace would not be mentioned first unless the subsequent acts were a consequence thereof. Therefore even men can work miracles by the power of grace.

3. A gift of grace is not given except for the sake of what the recipient may do thereby. Now some received the gratuitous gift to work miracles: thus it is said (1 Cor. xii, 9, 10): *To another is given the grace of healing in one Spirit; to another the working of miracles.* Therefore by a gift of grace the saints can work miracles.

4. To this it may be replied that saints are said to work a miracle not by doing it themselves but by impetrating God for the miracle to be done.—On the contrary prayer becomes impetration through those things that make it acceptable to God, namely faith, charity and other virtues pertaining to sanctifying grace. Therefore saints need no gratuitous gift in order to work miracles.

5. Gregory (*Dial.* ii, 30) says that *those who are devoutly united to God, if the necessity should arise, not unfrequently perform signs in both these ways, working wonders sometimes by their prayers, sometimes by their power.* Now when any one does a thing by his power, he does it by his own act and not merely by impetration. Therefore angels and holy men work miracles by their own action.

6. According to Anselm (*De Pecc. Orig.* xi) there is a threefold course in things, the natural, the voluntary and the wonderful. Now in the natural course of things angels act as standing between God and natural bodies: thus Augustine (*De Trin.* iii, 4) says: *All bodies are governed by God through the rational spirit of life;* and Gregory says (*Dial.* iv. 5): *In this visible world all dispositions are executed through invisible creatures.* The same applies to the voluntary

course of things: for the angels stand between us and God and are the bearers of the light that they receive from him. Therefore also in the course of wonderful things the angels are intermediaries, inasmuch as miracles are worked through their agency.

7. To this it will be replied that angels are intermediaries as acting not by their own power but by the power of God.—On the contrary, whoever acts by the power of another, is in some way the cause of the effect produced by that power. If then the angels act by the divine power in working miracles, they also are in some way the cause thereof.

8. The Old Law was given by God miraculously, wherefore it is related (Exod. xix, 16) that *thunders began to be heard and lightning to flash, and a very thick cloud to cover the mount.* Now the Law was given by the angels (Gal. iii, 19). Therefore miracles are wrought by the angels.

9. Augustine says (*De Doctr. Christ.* i) : *Whosoever possesses a thing and gives it not although he would suffer no loss by giving it, does not possess it as it ought to be possessed.* Now God has the power to work miracles, and he would lose nothing by imparting it to others. Therefore if he has not bestowed it on others, it would seem that he has not that power as it ought to be possessed. Hence one would infer that God has given to angels and men the power to work miracles.

On the contrary it is written (Ps. lxxi, 18) : *Who alone worketh great wonders.*

Again, according to Bernard (*De Disp. et Præcept.*) none save the maker of a law can change that law or dispense therefrom : thus in human affairs the emperor alone can change the law, since it was he who made it. Now God alone framed the law of nature's course. Therefore he alone can work miracles by acting independently of the natural course.

I answer that angels inasmuch as they are ministers of the divine power can by a gift of grace do things that surpass their natural power of action : in fact it may be said that angels take an active part in working miracles in three ways.—First, by impetration ; and this way may be common to both men and angels.—Secondly, inasmuch as by their natural power they dispose matter for the working of a miracle : thus it is said that they will collect the dust of the dead who by God's power will return to life. This way, however, is peculiar to the angels : since human spirits, through being united to bodies, cannot act on external objects save by means of the body to which in a sense they are chained.—Thirdly, by co-operation. This way, however, Augustine leaves without coming to a decision. Thus (*De Civ. Dei*, xxii, 9) he says : *Whether God himself does all these things by himself in his unsearchable way, or by his ministers, or by the souls of the martyrs, or by men as yet in the body, or by the angels to whom he issues his invisible commands (the martyr's part consisting in prayer and impetration but not operation) or by some other way incomprehensible to mortals, in any case these miracles are witnesses of that which proclaims that flesh will rise again to eternity.* Gregory, however (*Dial.* ii, 31), appears to give a decisive answer to the question. He says that holy men even in this life work miracles not merely by prayer and impetration but also authoritatively, and therefore by co-operation : and he proves this both by reason and by examples. His reason is that if men were given the power to become the sons of God, it is not strange that by that power they can work miracles. The examples he offers are that of Peter, who without any previous prayer, pronounced sentence of death on the lying Ananias and Sapphira by mere denunciation (Acts v, 4, 9) : and of the Blessed Benedict who *looked on the bonds of a poor countryman and thus loosened them more speedily than it were possible to human hands.* Wherefore he concludes that the saints work miracles sometimes by prayer, sometimes by power. We must now discuss how this may be possible.

It is evident that God alone works miracles by his sole command. Now we find that the divine commands reach the lower rational spirits, namely the souls of men, by means of the higher spirits, namely the angels, as in the promulgation of the Old Law. In the same way the divine command can, through the angelic and human spirits, reach corporeal creatures through whom in a manner of speaking the divine decrees are intimated to nature. Accordingly human and angelic spirits act somewhat as instruments of the divine power for the accomplishment of a miracle. This does not mean that they are possessed of a permanent habitual power, since then they would be able to work miracles whenever they chose to do so. In fact Gregory declares this to be impossible (l.c.) and proves his assertion by quoting the example of Paul, who prayed that the sting might depart from him (2 Cor. xii, 9) yet his prayer was not granted; and of Benedict, who against his will was detained by the storm that was granted through his sister's prayer. The saints' power to co-operate with God in the working of miracles may be taken to be something after the manner of imperfect forms[1] called 'intentions,' which are not permanent and are only evoked at the presence of the principal agent, even as light in the air, and movement in an instrument. Accordingly the gratuitous gift that is the grace of miracles or of healing can denote a power of this kind: so that this grace which is given that a man may work supernaturally, is like the grace of prophecy which is given that a man may know supernaturally, and by virtue of which the prophet cannot prophesy when he lists, but only when the spirit of prophecy moves him, as Gregory proves (*Hom. in Ezech.* i). Nor is it strange if in this way God uses the spiritual creature as an instrument in order to produce wondrous effects in corporeal nature, seeing that he also uses corporeal creatures instrumentally in the sanctification of spiritual creatures, for instance in the sacraments.

This suffices for the Replies to the Objections, since it is true that God alone works miracles by his authority: and it is also true that he communicates to creatures the power to work miracles, according to the creatures' capacity and the order of divine wisdom: to the effect that a creature may work a miracle ministerially by grace.

[1] Cf. *Sum Th.* II–II, Q. clxxi, A.2.

ARTICLE V

DO THE DEMONS ALSO CO-OPERATE IN THE WORKING OF MIRACLES?

THE fifth point of inquiry is whether the demons also co-operate in the working of miracles: and it would seem that they do.

1. It is said (Mt. xxiv, 24): *There shall arise false Christs and false prophets, and shall show great signs and wonders.* Now such things they will not do save by the power of the demons. Therefore demons co-operate in the working of miracles.

2. The sudden healing of a sick man is a miracle: thus Christ worked a miracle when he healed Peter's mother-in-law (Lk. iv). But the demons also can do this: since a sick man may be quickly cured by using medicine: and the demons, being by nature rapid in their movements, and well acquainted with the healing properties of medicines, can apply these so efficaciously, that the sick man is cured at once. Therefore they can work miracles.

3. It is a miracle to make the dumb speak. But it is a yet greater miracle to make a dog speak or sing: and Simon Magus is stated to have done this by a demon's power. Therefore a demon can work miracles.

4. Valerius Maximus relates (*Fact. et Dict. Mem.* i, 8) that the statue of Fortune situated at Rome on the Latin Way, spoke not once but twice thus: *It is well that you have looked on me oh matrons; rightly have you hallowed me.* Now it is a greater miracle for stones than for the dumb to speak: and yet the latter is miraculous. Therefore seemingly demons can work miracles.

5. History tells us as related by Augustine (*De Civ. Dei* x, 26) that a certain Vestal Virgin in proof of undefiled chastity carried water from the Tiber in a leaky jug, and yet the water was not spilt. Now this could not happen unless the water by some non-natural power were prevented from falling: which was certainly a miracle when the Jordan was divided and the waters stood still. Therefore demons can work miracles.

6. It is much more difficult to change a man into a dumb animal than water into wine. Now the change of water into wine (Jo. ii) was miraculous. Therefore *a fortiori* is it a miracle to change a man into a dumb animal. Yet men are changed into dumb animals by the demon's power; thus Varro relates, as Augustine states (*De Civ. Dei* xviii, 16 *seqq.*), that when the companions of Diomedes were returning from Troy they were changed into birds, which for a long time afterwards flew around the temple of Diomedes: also that the famous sorceress Circe changed the companions of Ulysses into beasts, and that some Arcadians after crossing a swamp were changed into wolves. Therefore demons can work miracles.

7. Job's trials were evidently brought about through the agency of the devil, since the Lord gave the latter power over all that Job had (Job i, 12). Now these trials were not effected without a miracle, as evinced by the fire coming down from heaven, and the wind that destroyed his house, resulting in the death of his children. Therefore demons can work miracles.

8. It was a miracle that Moses changed his rod into a serpent (Exod. vii, 10). Therefore it would seem that demons can work miracles.

9. The working of miracles is further removed from man's than from the angels' power. Now miracles are sometimes wrought by wicked men: thus the wicked are made to say (Mt. vii, 22): *Have not we prophesied in thy name . . . and done many miracles?* Therefore real miracles can be wrought by demons also.

10. On the contrary, at the time of Antichrist the devil will be able to do works of very great power: for *he must be loosed a little time* (Apoc. xx, 3), which refers to the time of Antichrist. But he will not then work real miracles, since it is clearly stated (2 Thess. ii, 9) that the time of Antichrist will be *in all power and signs and lying wonders.* Therefore the demons cannot work miracles.

I answer that just as the good angels by grace can do something surpassing the power of nature, so the wicked angels being restrained by divine power are unable to do as much as they might by their natural powers. The reason of this is that as Augustine says (*De Trin.* iii, 9) some things the angels would be able to do if they were permitted to do them, which however they cannot do because they are not permitted to do them. (Hence the angels are said to be ' bound ' in that they are prevented from doing things to which their natural powers could extend ; and to be ' loosed ' when by the divine decree they are permitted to do what their nature enables them to do.) While as he says (*ibid.*) some things they cannot do even if permitted to do them, because the kind of nature bestowed on them by God does not permit of their doing such things. Accordingly God does not give them the power to do things that surpass the faculty of their nature, because seeing that a miraculous work is a divine witness to God's power and truth, if the demons whose whole will is diverted to evil, were to receive the power to work miracles, God would vouch for their falsehood, which is repugnant to his godness. Hence at times they perform by God's permission only such works as seem miraculous to men, and which are within the limits of their natural power. Even so, as explained above (A. 4) by their natural power they can produce as art produces things, those effects only that result from the natural forces contained in bodies, which obey them in respect of local movement ; and thus they can employ them in producing an effect in a very short time. Now by means of these powers it is possible for bodies to undergo real transformation : inasmuch as in the natural course one thing is generated from another. Besides this they can by working some kind of change in a body, for instance by disturbing the organ of the imagination,[1] in respect of the various spirits and humours, make things that do not really exist to appear to the imagination : an effect that may be produced by means of certain external bodies, by the application of which things appear different to what they really are, as in cases of delirium or insanity.

Accordingly demons can work wonders in us in two ways : first by means of real bodily transformation : secondly by disturbing the imagination so as to delude the senses. But

[1] Cf. *Sum. Th.* I, Q. cxi, AA. 3, 4.

neither of these works is miraculous but is like the work of a craftsman, as explained above (A. 4) : wherefore it must be said simply that demons cannot work real miracles.

Reply to the First Objection. Signs and wonders denote things that can be done by natural power, yet to men are marvellous ; or again that are done by deceiving the senses ; as explained above.

Reply to the Second Objection. Nothing prevents a man from being cured more quickly by the devil's art than by nature left to itself : since we find that the same is true of human art. It does not seem however that the demons can cure a man all at once (although certain other effects they can produce almost suddenly) because the medicines that are applied to a man's body effect his cure instrumentally, nature being the principal agent. Wherefore the medicines applied should be such as can be made to act by nature : and if too many were applied they would be not conducive but prejudicial to health. Hence it is that diseases which are by nature incurable, are also incurable by demons. It is different with effects that depend on an external agent as their principal cause. It must be observed, however, that if demons were to effect a sudden cure it would not be a miracle, since to be successful they would have to employ natural forces.

Reply to the Third Objection. Speaking dogs and like works of Simon the magician were quite possibly done by trickery and not in very truth. If, however, they were genuine, it matters not : since the demon did not give a dog the power of speech miraculously as when it is given to the dumb ; but by some kind of local movement he made sounds to be heard like words composed of letters and syllables. It is thus that we may understand Balaam's ass to have spoken, although in this case it was by the action of a good angel.

The same answer applies *to the Fourth Objection* about the statue : for this was done by a devil producing sounds like human speech by means of a movement in the air.

Reply to the Fifth Objection. It is not unlikely that in commendation of chastity the true God through his good angels worked this miracle of the jug holding the water, because whatever good was in the heathens was from God. If, however, it was the work of the demons, this is not inconsistent with what has been said. Local rest and movement are from principles of the same genus, since the same nature that makes a thing move locally makes it rest locally. Wherefore just as demons can move bodies locally so can they prevent them being moved. Nor is it a miracle, as it is when it is done by God, because it results from the demon's natural power in respect of this particular effect.

Reply to the Sixth Objection. These transformations of which Varro speaks were not real but apparent: they were effected by the demon working on a man's imagination by introducing therein a bodily image, as Augustine says (*De Civ. Dei* xviii, 18).

Reply to the Seventh Objection. By God's permission the devils can by a movement of the air cause disaster, even as this may be the natural result of the wind's movements. It was in this way that Job's trials were brought about by the work of the demons.

Reply to the Eighth Objection. The (ordinary) gloss mentions two opinions about the works of Pharaoh's magicians. According to one view the rods were not really changed into serpents, but only in appearance by a kind of conjuring trick. But Augustine, quoted in the same gloss says that the change was real. And he proves this with a certain amount of likelihood from the fact that Scripture uses the same word in speaking of the rods of the magicians and the rod of Moses, which of course was changed into a real serpent. Yet the demons' work in changing the rods into serpents was no miracle, since they did it by means of seed collected together, with which they were able to corrupt the rods and change them into serpents. But what Moses did was a miracle, since this was done by the power of God without the co-operation of any power of nature.

Reply to the Ninth Objection. Men of evil life are sometimes the heralds of truth, wherefore God works miracles to vouch for the truth of their message: but this cannot be said of the demons.

Reply to the Tenth argument advanced in a contrary sense. It is stated that the devil's power will be let loose at the time of Antichrist, inasmuch as he will be permitted to do many things that he is not allowed to do now : hence he will do many things with the result that those will be seduced who deserved to be seduced for not assenting to the truth. And he will do some things by trickery, wherein there will be neither a true nor a miraculous result. He will also by a real transformation of bodies do some things wherein although the results be real they will not be miraculous, since they will be effected through natural causes. These are called lies on account of the intention with which he will do them, namely to induce men, by his wonderful works, to believe in his lies.

ARTICLE VI

HAVE ANGELS AND DEMONS BODIES NATURALLY UNITED TO THEM ?
Sum. Th. I, Q. li, A. 1

THE sixth point of inquiry is whether angels and demons have bodies naturally united to them : and it would seem that they have.

1. Every animal is composed of a body naturally united to a soul. Now angels and demons are animals ; for Gregory says in a homily for the Epiphany (*Hom.* x *in Ev.*) that *as the Jews were rational beings it was fitting that the message should be brought to them by a rational animal, an angel to wit :* and of the demons Augustine says (*Gen. ad lit.* iii, 10) : *The demons are animals of the atmosphere because their nature is akin to that of aerial bodies.* Therefore angels and demons have bodies naturally united to them.

2. Origen says (*Peri Archon* i, 6) that of all spiritual creatures God alone has no body. Since then angels and demons are spiritual creatures, it would seem that they have bodies naturally united to them.

3. The imagination, and the irascible and concupiscible

faculties are powers employing organs. Now these powers are in demons and likewise in angels: thus Dionysius says (*Div. Nom.* iv) that *the wickedness of the devil is anger in the irascible, lust in the concupiscible and licence in the imagination.* Therefore they have bodies naturally united to them.

4. Angels are either composed of matter and form or they are not. If they are, they must have bodies: because seeing that matter considered in itself is one (since it is not differentiated save by a form) it follows that in all divers things composed of matter there must be divers forms received into divers parts of matter: for the same matter cannot receive divers forms. Now diversity of parts in matter is inconceivable without division of matter; likewise division without dimension, since without these substance is indivisible (*Phys.* i). Consequently all things composed of matter must be dimensioned and therefore bodies.—On the other hand if angels are not composed of matter and form, they are either self-subsistent forms or forms united to bodies. If they are self-subsistent forms, it follows that they do not derive their being from another: because since the form as such is the principle of being, that which is a pure form has not its being from a cause, but is only a cause of being in other things. And if they are forms united to bodies, these bodies must be united to them naturally: because union of form with matter is natural. It remains then that we must needs admit one of these three, namely that angels are bodies, or are uncreated substances, or have bodies naturally united to them. But the first two are impossible. Therefore we must admit the third.

5. A form as such is that whereby something is informed. Wherefore a pure form informs without being in any way informed: and this belongs to God alone, who is the supreme beauty whence all things are beautiful, as Augustine says *De Civ. Dei* viii (*QQ.* lxxxiii, qu. 23). Therefore angels are not pure forms, and consequently are forms united to bodies.

6. Just as the soul is unable to produce an effect in external bodies, except by means of corporeal instruments, so neither can an angel without corporeal powers, which he uses as instruments. Now the soul for the purpose of its

activities has a body naturally united to it. Therefore angels have also.

7. The first movement in bodies is that whereby a body is moved by an incorporeal substance. Now the first movement is of that which moves itself (*Phys.* viii) because that which is (so and so) of itself precedes that which is (so and so) through another. Therefore that which is moved immediately by an incorporeal substance is moved as being moved of itself. But this is impossible unless the incorporeal substance that causes movement be united to the body naturally. Since then angels and demons move bodies immediately (A. 2) it would seem that they have bodies naturally united to them.

8. It is better to live and give life than to live only, just as light is more perfectly in that which shines and enlightens than in that which shines only. Now the human soul lives and quickens the body naturally united to it. Therefore the angel lives not less perfectly than the soul.

9. The movement of a body that has various movements is the movement of a thing that moves itself: because that which has only one movement seemingly does not move itself (*Phys.* viii). Now the celestial body is moved with various movements. Thus the planets according to astronomers are said at times to move forwards, at other times backwards and sometimes to be stationary. Therefore the movement of the higher bodies is of things which move themselves, so that they are composed of corporeal and of spiritual substance. But this spiritual substance is not a human soul, nor is it God. Therefore it is an angel: and consequently an angel has a body naturally united to him.

10. Nothing acts beyond its species. Now the heavenly bodies cause life in the world below, as instanced in animals engendered of putrid matter by the power of the celestial bodies. Since then a living substance excels one that is not living, as Augustine says (*De Vera Relig.* 29, 55) it would seem that the heavenly bodies have life and thus have spiritual substances naturally united to them: so that we come to the same conclusion as before.

11. The first movable thing is the heavenly body. Now

the Philosopher proves (*Phys.* viii) that all moved things are reduced to the first movable that is moved of itself. Therefore the heaven is moved of itself : and thus it is composed of a body that is moved and an immovable mover which is a spiritual substance and so the same conclusion follows as before.

12. According to Dionysius (*Div. Nom.* vii) divine wisdom has so ordained that the highest point of the lower nature is in contact with the lowest point of the higher nature. Now the highest point in corporeal nature is the heavenly body, since it transcends all other bodies. Therefore it is in contact with the spiritual nature and is united to it ; and thus the same conclusion follows as before.

13. The body of the heavens is more excellent than the human body, even as the everlasting surpasses the corruptible. Now the human body is naturally united to a spiritual substance. Therefore *a fortiori* the heavenly body is, seeing that the more noble body has the more noble form : and thus we come to the same conclusion as before.

14. Certain animals are formed from the earth, for instance men and beasts ; some from water, as fish and birds, according to Genesis i. Therefore there must be some formed from air, some from fire and some from celestial matter. Now the latter cannot be other than angels and demons, for seeing that these are the more noble bodies they must have the more noble souls. Therefore angels and demons are animals and have bodies naturally united to them

15. Plato also seems to favour this view : thus in the Timœus he says that there are animals solid as the earth, others akin to liquid, others subtle as the air, others akin to the gods : and these must be the angels. Consequently the angel is an animal, and the same conclusion follows as before.

16. Nothing is moved except a body (*Phys.* vi). Now an angel is moved. Therefore he is either a body or naturally united to a body.

17. The Word of God is above the angels : and he is united to a body. Therefore it is not beneath the dignity of an angel to be united to a body naturally.

18. Porphyry says (*Prædic.*, *De Differentia*) that the word 'mortal' in the definition of a man distinguishes us from the gods, whereby only the angels can be meant. Therefore the angels are animals, and thus have bodies naturally united to them.

On the contrary, Damascene (*De Fid. Orth.* ii, 3) says that an angel is an intellectual substance, ever movable, free and incorporeal.

Again, it is stated in *De Causis* (Prop. 7) that an intelligence is a simple substance: and the Commentator says (*ibid.*) that it is neither a magnitude nor spread over a magnitude. Now an angel is an intelligence, as is clearly indicated by Dionysius (*Div. Nom.* vii) who calls the angels divine minds and intelligences. Therefore an angel is neither a body nor united to a body.

Again, angels and souls differ in the point of incapability and capability of union to a body: so that if an angel were united to a body, he would nowise differ from a soul; which cannot be admitted.

Again, there is a spiritual substance that is dependent on a body as regards its beginning and its end, for instance the vegetal and sensible soul: there is also a spiritual substance dependent on a body as regards its beginning and not as regards its end, to wit, the human soul. Therefore there will be a spiritual substance that needs not a body, either as to its beginning or as to its end: and this can be no other but an angel or a demon. That there be one which needs a body as to its end and not as to its beginning, is impossible.

Again, there is a form, e.g. of a stone, that is neither a soul nor a spirit: and there is a form that is a soul but not a spirit, e.g. of a dumb animal: and there is a form that is both soul and spirit, e.g. the form of a man. Therefore there will be a form that is a spirit but not a soul: and such is an angel. Hence an angel is not united to a body naturally, since this enters into the definition of a soul.

I answer that, the ancients were divided in opinion concerning incorporeal substances.

Some of the philosophers of old contended that there was

no such thing as an incorporeal substance and that all substances are bodies : and Augustine (*Confess.*) confesses that at one time he fell into this error. This opinion, however, was refuted by the philosophers. Aristotle rejected it (*Phys.* viii) for this reason that there must be some infinite moving power, since otherwise it would not produce a perpetual movement. Again he proves that every power of a magnitude must be finite whence it follows that there must be a power that is wholly incorporeal, in order to produce a continual movement. Again he proves the same conclusion in another way (*Metaph.* xii). Act precedes potentiality both by nature and in time, absolutely speaking : although in this or that individual that passes from potentiality to act, potentiality precedes act in point of time. But seeing that it must be brought into actuality by something that is already actual, it follows that absolutely speaking act precedes potentiality even in time. Wherefore since every body is in potentiality, as its mutability shows, there must needs be an everlasting unchangeable substance that precedes all bodies. A third argument in support of the same conclusion may be taken from the principles of the Platonists. Finite and individual being must needs be preceded by a being that is infinite : thus if we find fire having a finite and so to speak participated nature in iron, we must expect to find the nature of fire in something that is fire essentially. Hence seeing that being and all other perfections and forms are found to have a finite nature in that they are received into matter, we infer that there must pre-exist an incorporeal substance wherein there is the perfection of being not in a finite manner but with a certain universal fullness. The reason why they were led into the error of maintaining that all substance is corporeal was that their intelligence being unable to rise above their imagination whose object is wholly corporeal they were unable to reach the knowledge of incorporeal substances which the intelligence alone can grasp.

Others admitted the existence of incorporeal substances : but they supposed them to be united to bodies, and they denied that any incorporeal substance could be found that is not the form of a body. Hence they contended that God himself is the world-soul: thus Augustine (*De Civ. Dei* iv, 31) states that Varro held God to be a soul that governs the world by movement and reason. Hence he said that the whole world is God on account of its soul and not by reason of its body, just as a man is said to be wise in respect of his soul, not of his body. For this reason heathens worshipped the whole world and its parts. This opinion also was refuted by the philosophers for several reasons. First because a power united to and informing a body has a restricted action through being united to a particular kind of body: wherefore since there must needs be a universal agent exercising its influence on all bodies, inasmuch as the first mover cannot be a body, as we have proved, it follows that there must be some incorporeal being that is not united to a body. Hence Anaxagoras posited a subsistent intellect, that it might be able to command (*Phys.* viii), because to command belongs to one who is above those who are commanded, and is neither subject nor bound to them in any way.—Secondly, because if every incorporeal substance be united to a body as the form thereof, it would follow that the first thing to be in motion moves itself like an animal, as being composed of a corporeal and a spiritual substance. Now that which moves itself does so by its will inasmuch as it is appetent of something: for the appetite is a moved mover, while the appetible object is a non-moved mover. Consequently above the incorporeal substance united to a body there must be something higher to move it as the appetible object moves the appetite: and this must be an intelligible good: since this is appetible as being good simply, whereas the appetible object of sense is sought, as being this particular good and at this particular moment.

Now an intelligible good must be incorporeal, since were it not devoid of matter it could not be an object of intelligence: wherefore it must needs be intelligent, seeing that a substance is intelligent through being free of matter. Therefore above the substance that is united to a body, there must be another higher substance that is incorporeal or intellectual and not united to a body. This is the proof given by Aristotle (*Metaph.* xi) ; for it cannot be said that a thing which sets itself in motion seeks nothing outside itself: since it would never be in motion, inasmuch as the purpose of motion is to obtain something that is extrinsic in some way or other.—Thirdly, because that which sets itself in motion may be moved or not moved (*Phys.* viii), wherefore if something that is moved by itself be continually in motion, the continuance of its motion must needs be due to something outside that is wholly immovable. Now we observe that the heaven whose soul they held to be God is in continual motion : wherefore above the substance that animates the world—if there be such a substance—there must be a yet higher substance, that is not united to a body, and is self-subsistent. Those who contended that every substance is united to a body were apparently led astray through thinking that matter is the cause of susbistence and individuality in all beings, as it is in corporeal beings : wherefore they thought that incorporeal substances cannot subsist outside a body : as suggested by way of objection in the Commentary on *De Causis.*

Accordingly Plato and Aristotle rejected these opinions and held that certain substances are incorporeal, some united to bodies, some not united to any body. Plato according to Macrobius (*Super Somn. Scip.* i) posited two separate substances, namely God the father of the whole universe and occupying the highest place : and beneath him the mind of God which he called the paternal intelligence containing the types or ideas of all things. He also held that many incorporeal substances are united to bodies: some united to heavenly bodies, and these the Platonists called gods ; some united to air-like bodies, whom they called demons. Hence Augustine (*De Civ. Dei* viii, 16) quotes the following definition of the demons as given by Apuleius : *Demons are animals with a rational mind, a passive and immortal soul.* Moreover, the heathens who adopted the ideas of Plato held that divine worship was to be given to all these incorporeal substances on account of their immortality. Further, they believed that incorporeal substances are united to the grosser terrestial bodies, those namely that are akin to earth and water, to wit the souls of men and of other animals. Aristotle agrees with Plato on two points, and differs from him in two. He agrees with him in that he believes in a supreme substance neither corporeal nor united to a body, and in holding the heavenly bodies to be animate: but he differs from him by maintaining the existence of several incorporeal substances not united to a body, corresponding to the various heavenly movements: and again in denying the existence of air-like animals, and he did so with reason. First, because a mixed body is superior to an elemental body, especially as regards the form: since the elements are the matter of mixed bodies. Wherefore incorporeal substances which are the highest of all forms ought to be united to mixed bodies and not to the elements. Now there can be no mixed body in which there is not a preponderance of earth and water in point of the quantity of matter, since even the higher elements are more active through being more formal: and if these latter were to preponderate, the proportion due to a mixture would not be observed, seeing that the higher elements would altogether subdue the lower. Consequently it is not possible that incorporeal substances be united as forms to aerial bodies, but to mixed bodies in which the earthy and watery matter preponderates.—Secondly, because a homogeneous and uniform body must needs have the same form in the whole and in its parts. Now the body of the air is all of one nature: so that if any spiritual substances be united to any parts of the air, they must also be united to the whole: and thus the whole air will be animated, which seemingly is an absurd thing to say, although some of the ancients were of this opinion (*De Anima* i), holding that the air is full of gods. —Thirdly, because if a spiritual substance has no other powers besides intellect and will, it were useless for it to be united to a body, since these operations are performed independently of the body: inasmuch as every form of a body executes some of its actions in dependence on the body. If however a spiritual substance has other powers (as apparently the Platonists held to be the case with the demons, for they said that these had a passive soul, and passions are only in the sensitive part of the soul, as is proved in *Phys.* viii), it needs to be united to an organic body, so as to be able to perform the actions of such powers by means of determinate organs. But an aerial body cannot satisfy this condition, since it is shapeless. It follows then that spiritual substances cannot be naturally united to aerial bodies. As to whether incorporeal substances be united as forms of heavenly bodies Augustine leaves the question unsolved (*Gen. ad lit.* ii), while Jerome would seem to assert it as a fact in his commentary on Ecclesiastes i, 6, *The Spirit goeth forward surveying all places round about,* as also Origen (*Peri Archon,* i, 7). Several modern writers consider this to be disproved by the fact that since according to Scripture the number of the blessed is composed exclusively of men and angels, these spiritual substances would not be reckoned either among human souls or among the angels who are incorporeal. However Augustine (*Enchir.* lviii) considers this also doubtful: *It is by no means certain whether the sun, moon and stars belong to the same company,* namely of the angels: *although some are of opinion that they are bodies of light without sense or intelligence. Yet without any doubt whatever the teaching of both Plato and Aristotle differs from the doctrine of faith inasmuch as we hold that there are many substances not united to bodies, many more indeed than any of these admit.* And this would seem the more probable view, for three reasons. First, because as the bodies above are of higher rank than those below, even so incorporeal substances rank higher than bodies: and the bodies above excel those below, inasmuch as the earth compared to the heavens is as a point in comparison with a sphere, as proved by astronomers. Hence incorporeal substances according to Dionysius (*Cœl. Hier.* xiv.) surpass the entire multitude of material species; and this is indicated (Dan. vii, 10): *Thousands of thousands ministered to him and ten thousand times a hundred thousand stood before him.* Moreover it is in keeping with the outpouring of the divine goodness that it should bring into existence in greater profusion those things that are the noblest in nature. And seeing that the higher things do not depend on the lower, nor are their powers confined to the things here below, we must not limit their activities to the phenomena of the lower world.—Secondly, because in the order of natural things, we find many degrees intervening between natures that are distant from each other: thus between animals and plants, there are imperfect animals which are like plants in being fixtures, and are like animals in having sensation. Since then the supreme substance which is God is farthest removed from corporeal nature, it seems reasonable that there should be many intervening degrees of nature, and not only those substances which are principles of movement.—Thirdly, because since God exercises not only a universal providence over corporeal beings, but also a particular providence over individuals, in which as stated above (A. 1) at times he works independently of the order of universal causes: we must posit the existence not only of incorporeal substances who serve God in administering the universal causes of nature, namely the movements of heavenly bodies, but also of others who administer to God's particular works in individuals, especially as regards man whose mind is not subject to the heavenly movements. Accordingly following the truth of faith we assert that angels and demons have not bodies naturally united to them, but are wholly incorporeal as Dionysius says.

Reply to the First Objection. In several passages of his works Augustine makes use of the Platonic view about angels and demons having bodies, without actually agreeing with it. Hence (*De Civ. Dei* xxi, 10) treating of the punishment of the demons he follows up both the opinion of those who said that demons have aerial bodies, and the view of those who say that they are wholly incorporeal. Gregory describes an angel as being an animal, in the broad sense of the term, namely as indicating any animate being.

Reply to the Second Objection. On many points Origen adopts the views of the Platonists: thus he seems to have been of the opinion that all created incorporeal substances are united to bodies: and yet he does not state this positively, but suggests it as by no means certain, and at the same time mentions the other view.

Reply to the Third Objection. Without doubt Dionysius

maintained that angels and demons are incorporeal. He employs the terms anger and concupiscence metaphorically for an inordinate will, and imagination as signifying the erring choice of their intelligence, inasmuch as *every wrongdoer is ignorant* according to the Philosopher (*Ethic.* iii, 1) and *they err who work evil* (Prov. xiv).

Reply to the Fourth Objection. Even if angels be composed of matter and form, this argument does not prove that they are bodies; unless we suppose that angels and bodies have the same matter. It might be said indeed that the matter of bodies is distinct not by dimensional division but by relation to forms of different kinds, since potentiality is proportionate to act. But we would rather believe that angels are not composed of matter and form, but are pure self-subsistent forms. Nor does it follow from this that they were not created, because a form is a principle of existence, as that whereby a particular thing is, although the existence both of form and of matter in the composite proceeds from the one agent. Hence if there be a created substance that is a pure form it can have an efficient but not a formal principle.

Reply to the Fifth Objection. According to the Philosopher (*Phys.* ii) there is an order of precedence even in formal causes: so that nothing prevents a form resulting from the participation of another form: and thus God who is pure being, is in a fashion the species of all subsistent forms that participate of being but are not their own being.

Reply to the Sixth Objection. In the natural order an angel's power is higher and therefore more universal than the power of a human soul: wherefore it could not have a corporeal organ that would adequately correspond to the action which it exercises on external bodies: and consequently it was not fitting for it to be bound to certain corporeal organs, as the soul is by union with the body.

Reply to the Seventh Objection. The first thing moved is that which moves itself by reason of the immovable mover: hence if the immovable mover moves either a body naturally united to it, or one that is not so united, the relation of priority remains the same.

Reply to the Eighth Objection. The soul united to the body quickens the body not only effectively but also formally: and absolutely speaking to quicken the body thus is less than to be self-quickening only. Because the soul is able to quicken the body inasmuch as it has the lowest degree of being which can be common to the soul and body when united together: whereas the being of an angel is higher in degree, and therefore cannot be thus communicated to a body: wherefore it lives only and does not quicken formally.

Reply to the Ninth Objection. That the planets seem to have a backward and forward movement and sometimes to be stationary is not due to a variable movement of one and the same movable, but to the various movements of different movables, whether we put it down to eccentrics and epicycles according to Ptolemy, or to a difference of movements in the poles, as others maintain. And yet even if the heavenly bodies vary in their movements this does not prove that their movement is caused by a voluntary mover that is united rather than separated from them.

Reply to the Tenth Objection. Even if the heavenly bodies be inanimate, they are moved by a living separate substance by whose power they act, even as an instrument by the power of the principal agent, and thus they cause life in things below them.

Reply to the Eleventh Objection. The Philosopher brings his arguments to two alternative conclusions, namely that all things moved must be reduced either directly to an immovable mover, or to a self-mover, part of which is an immovable mover: although he seems to prefer the latter alternative. If, however, anyone give preference to the former, nothing unreasonable is implicated in (the Philosopher's) arguments.

Reply to the Twelfth Objection. That which is highest in bodies reaches the lowest degree of the spiritual nature by participating of its properties, for instance by being incorruptible, but not by being united to it.

Reply to the Thirteenth Objection. The human body is inferior to the heavenly body as regards matter: yet it has a more noble form, if heavenly bodies are inanimate:—more noble, that is, in itself, but not as informing the body: because the form of heaven perfects its matter in a more excellent way, by making it incorruptible, than the rational soul perfects the body. The reason is because the spiritual substance that moves heaven is of too high a dignity to be united to a body.

Reply to the Fourteenth Objection. Bodies cannot be aerial for reasons already given. And this suffices for the *Reply to the Fifteenth Objection* which proceeds on the lines of Plato's opinion.

Reply to the Sixteenth Objection. An angel's movements are not by commensuration of the angel with space, like the movements of a body: and the term is used equivocally when we speak of the movements of angels and of bodies.

Reply to the Seventeenth Objection. The Word of God is not united to a body as informing it: for in that case the Word and the flesh would become one nature: and this is heretical.

Reply to the Eighteenth Objection. Porphyry follows the opinion of Plato when he gives the name of gods to the demons whom he held to be animals as well as the heavenly bodies.

ARTICLE VII

CAN ANGELS OR DEMONS ASSUME BODIES?

THE seventh point of inquiry is whether angels or demons can assume bodies: and it would seem that they cannot.

1. A body cannot be united to an incorporeal substance except either in being or in movement. Now angels cannot have bodies united to them in being, because they would then be naturally united to them, which is contrary to what has been said (A. 6). Hence it follows that they cannot be united to bodies except as moving them. But this does not amount to assumption: since then angels and demons would assume every body that they move, which is clearly false: for an angel moved the tongue of Balaam's ass, and yet we do not say that he assumed it. Therefore we cannot say that angels or demons assume bodies.

2. If angels or demons assume bodies, this is not because they need to, but either for our instruction (as regards the good angels) or for our deception (as regards the wicked angels). But in either case an imaginary vision would be enough. Therefore seemingly they do not assume bodies.

3. God appeared to the Patriarchs in the Old Testament, even as angels are stated to have done, as Augustine proves (*De Trin.* iii, 11, 12). Now we must not say that God assumed a body, except in the mystery of the Incarnation. Therefore neither do angels assume bodies when they appear.

4. Just as it naturally becomes the soul to be united to a body, so is it naturally becoming to an angel not to be united to a body. Now the soul cannot leave the body at will. Therefore neither can an angel assume a body.

5. No finite substance can perform several operations at the same time. Now an angel is a finite substance. Therefore he cannot at the same time administer to us and assume a body.

6. There should be proportion between assumed and assumer. But there is no proportion between an angel and a body, since they belong to wholly different genera and are therefore incompatible with each other. Therefore an angel cannot assume a body.

7. If an angel assume a body, this will either be a heavenly body or one with the nature of the four elements. But it cannot be a heavenly body, since the body of the heavens cannot be divided, or forced out of its place. Nor can it be an igneous body, for then he would consume the other bodies with which he came into contract : nor an aerial body, since air is shapeless : nor an aqueous body, for water does not retain shape : nor an earthly body, since they disappear suddenly, like the angel who appeared to Tobias. Therefore they do not assume any kind of body.

8. Every assumption terminates in some kind of union. But none of the three kinds of unity mentioned by the Philosopher (*Phys.* i) can result from an angel and a body : thus they cannot be one by continuity, nor by indivisibility, nor logically. Therefore an angel cannot assume a body.

9. If angels assume bodies, the bodies assumed by them

either really are or are not as they appear to be. If they really are, since sometimes they appear as men, the body assumed by them will be a real human body: which is impossible, unless we say that an angel assumed a man, which would seem to be improbable. And if they are not, this again is seemingly unfitting, since pretense is unbecoming to the angels of truth. Therefore in no way does an angel assume a body.

10. As stated above (AA. 3, 4, 5) angels and demons cannot produce effects in the bodies of the lower world except by means of natural forces. Now the forces of nature are not implanted in bodies for the purpose of forming the human body otherwise than by the special process of generation, and from a special seed: and it is plain that angels do not assume a body in this way. And the same argument applies to the other bodily shapes in which angels appear at times. Therefore this cannot result from their assuming bodies.

11. In order to put a body in motion the mover must influence the body moved. But it cannot do this without some kind of contact: and seeing that an angel cannot be in contact with a body, it would seem that he cannot move a body, nor consequently assume one.

12. Someone will reply to this that angels by their command move bodies with local movement.—On the contrary *Mover and moved must be together* (*Phys.* viii). But from the fact that an angel commands something by his will it does not follow that he is together with the body that is said to be moved by him. Therefore he cannot command it by his mere will.

13. As stated above (AA. 3, 4, 5) a body's movement does not obey the mere will of an angel as regards its information. Now shape is a kind of form. Therefore by his mere command an angel cannot shape a body so that it have the appearance of a man, or of something of the kind wherein he may appear.

14. The (interlinear) gloss on Ps. x, 5), *the Lord is in his holy temple*, says that although the demons exercise an external power over idols they cannot reside in them, nor

consequently in other bodies. But if they assume bodies they must be in the bodies assumed. Therefore we must not say that they assume bodies.

15. If they assume bodies, they are united either to the whole body or to part of it. If they are united to a part only, they will be unable to move the whole body, unless they move one part by means of another: and this would seem to be impossible, unless the assumed body has organs appointed for movement, and this is peculiar to animate bodies. And if he be united immediately to the whole body, the angel must needs be in each part of the body assumed, and of course, wholly in each part, since he is indivisible. Hence he will be in several places at the same time, which belongs to God alone. Therefore an angel cannot assume a body.

On the contrary it is related (Gen. xviii, 2) that the angels who appeared to Abraham came to him in assumed bodies: and the same is said of the angel who appeared to Tobias.

I answer that, some of those who believe the statements of Scripture about angelic apparitions, say that an angel never assumes a body: thus Rabbi Moses who holds this view, says that all the apparitions of angels related in the Scriptures, are prophetic, i.e. imaginary visions, the seer being either awake or asleep. But this does not safeguard the truth of Scripture: because the very expressions used by Scripture indicate what things are genuine facts and what are prophetic visions. Thus when we are to understand an apparition to be a mere vision, it employs words denoting a vision; for example (Ezech. viii, 3): *The spirit lifted me up between the earth and the heaven and brought me in the vision of God in Jerusalem.* Wherefore it is clear that when a thing is simply stated as a fact, we are to take it as such: and this applies to many apparitions in the Old Testament. We must admit then without any qualification that the angels do sometimes assume a body, by fashioning a sensible body, and offering it to external or corporeal vision: even as at other times by producing forms in the imagination they cause themselves to appear in imaginary visions. This is fitting for three reasons. First and chiefly, because all the apparitions of the Old Testament were ordered to that apparition whereby the Son of God appeared visibly on the earth, as Augustine says (*De Trin.* iii, 11, 12). Wherefore since the Son of God took to himself a real body, and not an imaginary one as the Manicheans pretended, it was fitting that the angels also should appear to men by assuming real bodies.—A second reason may be gathered from the words of Dionysius in his letter to Titus. Thus he says there that among other reasons why in the divine Scriptures divine things are made known to us under sensible signs, there is this—that the whole man may be perfected by participating as far as possible in divine things, by grasping the intelligible truth not only by his intellect, but also by perceiving it in sensible nature by means of sensible forms which are images as it were of divine things. Hence in like manner seeing that angels appear to man in order to perfect him, it is fitting that they not only enlighten his intelligence by intellectual vision, but also that they profit his imagination and exterior senses by imaginary visions, namely of the bodies they assume. Wherefore this threefold vision is mentioned by Augustine (*Gen. ad lit.* xi, 7, 24).—A third reason may be that although the angels are by nature above us, it is possible for us by grace to attain to equality and fellowship with them—*They will be as the angels in heaven* (Mt. xxii, 30). Hence in order to give proof of their companionability and kinship in our regard, they conform to us, in so far as it becomes them, by assuming a body : and thus by assuming what is ours, they enable our minds to rise to what is peculiar to them : even so the Son of God by descending to us, raised us to things divine.—As to the demons, when they transform themselves into angels of light, they endeavour to deceive us by doing what the good angels do for our profit.

Reply to the First Objection. An angel does not assume every body that he moves. To assume is to take to oneself (*ad se sumere*). Accordingly an angel assumes a body, not that he may unite it to his nature as a man takes food : nor to unite it to his person, as the Son of God took human nature ; but in order to represent himself, in the same way as intelligible things can be represented by sensible objects.

Thus an angel is said to assume a body when he fashions himself a body in such a way that it is adapted to represent him, as Dionysius explains by saying that the bodily shapes signify the angelic properties (*Cœl. Hier.* v).

Reply to the Second Objection. As already stated not only imaginary but also corporeal vision is useful for our instruction.

Reply to the Third Objection. As Augustine says (*De Trin.* iii, 11, 12) all the apparitions of God related in the Old Testament were effected by the ministry of the angels, who fashion certain forms imaginary or corporeal, whereby they lead the seer's mind to God; even as it is possible to lead man to God by sensible signs. Accordingly in these apparitions the angels assumed the bodies that appeared: yet God is said to have appeared in them, because he was the end whereto the angels intended to raise man's mind by means of these representations. Hence in these apparitions Scripture sometimes states that God appeared and sometimes an angel.

Reply to the Fourth Objection. Nothing has a power that surpasses its being, since everything's power rises from its essence or presupposes it. And since the soul is united by its being to the body as the form thereof, it is not in its power to release itself from union with the body: and in like manner it is not in the angel's power to unite himself in his being to a body as its form: but he can assume a body in the manner indicated above, to which body he is united as its mover, and as a figure to its shape.

Reply to the Fifth Objection. These two operations, the assumption of a body and ministering to us are ordered the one to the other: so that there is nothing to prevent both being done at the same time.

Reply to the Sixth Objection. Between an angel and a body there cannot be proportion of commensuration, since their respective magnitudes are not in the same genus and are altogether disparate. But nothing prevents an angel from having a certain relationship to a body such as that of a mover to the thing moved, or of a figure to its shape; and this may be called proportion.

Reply to the Seventh Objection. An angel can assume a body from any element, as well as from several elements mixed together. It is, however, more fitting that he assume a body from the air, which condenses easily so as to take and retain shape and reflect various colours from other bodies, as may be seen in the clouds : so that as far as the present question is concerned there is no difference between pure air and steam or smoke which tend to the nature of air.

Reply to the Eighth Objection. The division referred to is that of simple unity : the union of an angel with a body does not produce unity of this kind but a relative unity, such as that of the mover and thing moved, or figure and shape, as stated above.

Reply to the Ninth Objection. The appearances of the body assumed by an angel are real as regards what is perceptible to the senses, as this is the *per se* sensible, for example colour and shape, but not as regards the specific nature which is accidentally sensible. Nor does this implicate any pretence on the part of the angel, since he does not present himself to human eyes under the guise of a man in order to be taken for a man, but that angelic virtues may be indicated by means of human characteristics : thus neither are metaphors false whereby certain things are signified by their likeness to others.

Reply to the Tenth Objection. Although the natural forces of bodies do not suffice to produce the real species of a human body except by the way of generation, they suffice to produce a resemblance to a human body as regards colour, shape and like external accidents. This would seem to apply particularly to certain of these accidents which can be produced by the local movement of certain bodies, whereby vapours are condensed or rarefied, and clouds given various shapes.

Reply to the Eleventh Objection. An angel in moving a body induces the movement therein, and touches it not by corporeal but by spiritual or virtual contact.

Reply to the Twelfth Objection. A (body's) power must needs execute the angel's behest, so that he must be in virtual contact with the body that he moves.

Reply to the Thirteenth Objection. Shape is a form that can be produced in matter by cutting, condensing, vaporising or fashioning, or some like kind of movement: wherefore the same does not apply to this kind of forms as to others.

Reply to the Fourteenth Objection. We may understand something as being in a body in two ways. First as contained within the dimensions of the body: and in this way nothing prevents a demon from being in a body. Secondly as present in the essence of a thing by giving it being and operating therein: this belongs to God alone, although he is not an essential part of anything. Moreover the sense of the gloss is that the demons were not in idols as idolaters imagined them to be, namely so that the idol and the indwelling spirit were one being.

Reply to the Fifteenth Objection. An angel in the same way as the soul is wholly in each part of the assumed body: for though he is not, as the soul is, the form of that body he is its mover: and *mover and moved must be together.* Yet it does not follow that he is in several places at the same time, because the whole assumed body in relation to the angel is as one place.

ARTICLE VIII

CAN AN ANGEL OR DEMON BY MEANS OF AN ASSUMED BODY EXERCISE THE FUNCTIONS OF A LIVING BODY?

THE eighth point of inquiry is whether an angel or demon by means of an assumed body can exercise the functions of a living body: and seemingly he cannot.

1. Whoever is competent to have the power to exercise a certain function, is competent to have anything that is required for the exercise of that function, else the power would be useless to him. Now the functions of living bodies cannot be exercised without bodily organs. Since then an angel has no bodily organs naturally united to him, it would seem that he cannot exercise these functions.

2. The soul excels nature. But an angel cannot make nature act except by means of natural forces. Much less

therefore can he produce the functions of the soul in an inanimate body.

3. Of all the operations of the soul that are exercised through organs, those of the senses are more akin to intellectual operation which is proper to an angel. But an angel cannot feel or imagine through an assumed body. Much less then can he exercise the other functions of the soul.

4. Without a voice there can be no speech: and voice is sound emitted from an animal's mouth. Since then the angel who uses an assumed body is not an animal, seemingly he cannot use it to speak; much less for other actions, seeing that speech being a sign of intelligence is apparently most akin to him.

5. In one and the same individual the ultimate operation of the vegetal soul is generation: for an animal feeds and grows before generating. Now it cannot be said that an angel, or a body assumed by him, feeds or grows. Therefore an assumed body cannot generate.

6. Someone will reply that an angel or demon can generate through an assumed body, not by means of seed from that body, but by conveying seed from a man to a woman: even as he produces certain real natural effects by employing appropriate seeds.—On the contrary, animal seed is effective chiefly by natural heat: and if a demon were to transport seed from a distance, it would seem impossible to prevent the natural heat from evaporating. Therefore a man cannot be generated in this way.

7. If this were possible, from such seed a man would be generated in proportion to the power of human seed. Hence those who are stated to have been begotten by demons would not be of higher stature and greater strength than others who are generated in the usual way from human seed. Whereas it is stated (Gen. vi, 4): *After the Sons of God went into the daughters of men, and they brought forth children (giants were born)*[1] *these are the mighty men of old, men of renown.*

8. Food is taken by eating: so that if angels do not feed in their assumed bodies, seemingly neither do they eat.

9. To show the reality of his risen human body, Christ

---

[1] The words in brackets are not in the Vulgate.

after his resurrection willed to eat. Now this would have been no proof of his resurrection if angels or demons in their assumed bodies were able to eat: and it certainly was a proof. Therefore angels or demons cannot eat through their assumed bodies.

1. On the contrary it is said of the angels who appeared to Abraham (Gen. xviii, 9): *When they had eaten, they said to him: Where is Sara thy wife?* Therefore angels both eat and speak in their assumed bodies.

2. Commenting on Gen. vi, 2, *The sons of God* etc. Jerome says: *The hebrew word* אלהים *has either a singular or a plural signification: for it means both God and gods. Hence Aquila dared to say that the sons of gods are gods, thereby meaning saints or angels.* Therefore apparently the angels generate.

3. Just as nothing is without purpose in human art, so neither is there in the art of the angels. Now there would be no purpose in their assuming bodies disposed as organic bodies, unless they used the organs. Therefore seemingly in their assumed bodies they exercise functions corresponding to the various organs: for instance, they see with the eyes, hear with the ears and so forth.

I answer that an action takes its species from two sources, the agent, and its term: thus heating differs from cooling in that the former proceeds from heat and terminates in heat, while the latter proceeds from cold and terminates in cold. Properly speaking action like movement takes its species from its term; whereas it takes its naturality from its source. For movement and action are said to be natural when they proceed from an intrinsic source. We must note then that some of the functions of the soul not only proceed from the soul as their source, but also terminate in the soul and the animate body. Such like actions cannot be ascribed to angels in their assumed bodies; for they are neither of the same species (as when performed by us) nor are they natural to the angel: for instance, sensation, growth, nourishment and the like. For sensation follows a movement from things to the soul; likewise nourishment and growth consist in generating something that is added to the living body. On the other hand some actions of the soul have the soul as their source, but terminate in an external effect : and if this effect can be produced by mere bodily division or local movement, it may be said that the angel in his assumed body performs such an action, as regards a specific likeness in the effect : but the action will not be truly natural, but like a natural action : thus speech is produced by movement of the organs and air, and eating, by division of food and its transmission throughout the body. Hence speech when ascribed to angels in assumed bodies is not really natural speech but an imitation thereof by producing a like effect : and the same applies to eating. Wherefore it is written (Tob. xii, 18, 19) : *When I was with you . . . I seemed indeed to eat and to drink with you ; but I use an invisible meat and drink.* If, however, the effect requires to be the result of a transformation, it cannot be produced by an angel : except perhaps by means of a natural action, as in the case of generation.

Reply to the First Objection. An angel does not perform these actions naturally, wherefore he needs not to have the corresponding organs naturally united to him.

Reply to the Second Objection. As stated above, an angel does not perform real operations of the soul but imitations of them.

Reply to the Third Objection. We have said (in the body of the Article) why sensation cannot be ascribed to angels in assumed bodies.

Reply to the Fourth Objection. As stated above, an angel's speech in an assumed body is not real but an imitation of speech.

Reply to the Fifth Objection. Generation is never ascribed to good angels : concerning the demons, however, there are two opinions. Some say that even the demons are unable to generate in their assumed bodies, and this for the reasons given in the objections. Others, however, are of opinion that they can, not indeed by seed from the body assumed, or by virtue of their own nature, but by employing the seed of a man for the purpose of generation, one and the same demon being succubus to a man and transferring the seed thus received by acting as incubus to a woman. This may be reasonably held, since demons cause also other natural things by using appropriate seeds, as Augustine says (*De Trin.* iii, 8, 9).

Reply to the Sixth Objection. A demon is able to remedy the evaporation of the semen, both by rapidity of movement, or by employing such means as will retain the natural heat in the semen.

Reply to the Seventh Objection. Without doubt a generation that is effected in the way mentioned is the result of the force in the human seed. Wherefore a man begotten in this way is the child not of the demon but of the man whose seed was employed. And yet it is possible that stronger and bigger men be begotten in this way; because the demons who seek to be admired for their feats, can observe the position of the stars, and the respective temperaments of the man and woman so as to produce such an effect: and especially if the seed through being used by them as instrument receive thereby an increase of power.

Reply to the Eighth Objection Eating is ascribed to angels in assumed bodies, not for the purpose of growth, but as the mere act of eating: likewise it is ascribed to Christ after whose resurrection no addition could be made to his body. There is this difference however, that in Christ's case eating was real, since he had a vegetal soul, and so there could be an increase in the truth of his nature. But in neither case was the food changed into flesh and blood, but was resolved into prejacent matter.

This suffices for the *Reply to the Ninth Objection.*

Solution of the first argument in the contrary sense. We have explained in the body of the Article in what sense eating and speaking are to be ascribed to an angel.

Solution of the second argument. The sons of God denote the sons of Seth, who were sons of God by grace, and of the angels by imitation. The sons of men are the sons of Cain, who abandoned God and lived according to the flesh.

Solution of the third argument. The angels assume the organs of sense, not to use them, but as signs: hence although they do not sense by them, they do not assume them to no purpose.

ARTICLE IX

SHOULD THE WORKING OF A MIRACLE BE ATTRIBUTED TO FAITH?

Sum. Th. II–II, Q. clxxviii, AA. 1, 2.

THE ninth point of inquiry is whether the working of a miracle should be ascribed to faith : and seemingly it should not.

1. The gratuitous graces differ from the virtues, in that the virtues are common to all holy persons, whereas the gratuitous graces are divided among various persons, according to 1 Corinthians xii, 4 : *There are diversities of graces.* Now the working of miracles belongs to a gratuitous grace, wherefore it is said (*ibid.* 10.) : *To another the working of miracles.* Therefore the working of miracles is not to be set down to faith.

2. It will be replied that it is ascribed to faith as the meritorious cause, and to the gratuitous grace as the executive cause.—On the contrary a gloss[1] says : *Sometimes prophecy, the working of miracles, the casting out of devils is not due to the merit of the worker but to the invocation of Christ's name.* Therefore seemingly it is not to be ascribed to faith.

3. Charity is the source and root of merit, and without it formless faith cannot merit. Hence if the working of miracles be put down to faith by reason of merit, it should be ascribed still more to charity.

4. Since holy men work miracles by praying, the working of miracles should be ascribed chiefly to that virtue which causes prayers to be heard : and this is charity. Thus it is said (Mt. xviii, 19) : *If two of you shall consent upon earth concerning anything whatsoever they shall ask it shall be done to them by my Father who is in heaven :* and (Ps. xxxvi, 4) : *Delight in the Lord and he will give thee the requests of thy heart.* For it is charity that makes man delight in the Lord through love of God, and consent with his fellow men through

[1] The Ordinary Gloss on Mt. vii, 22, *Lord have we not prophesied, etc.*

love of his neighbour. Therefore the working of miracles should be set down to charity.

5. It is said (Jo. ix, 31): *We know that God doth not hear sinners*. Now charity alone removes sins, for as it is written (Prov. x, 12) *charity covereth all sins*. Therefore the working of miracles should be attributed to charity and not to faith.

6. Holy men work miracles not only by impetration but also authoritatively, as Gregory says (*Dial*. ii, 30): and this is due to man's union with God, so that the divine power comes to his aid. Now charity causes this union, for *he who is joined to the Lord*, i.e. by charity, *is one spirit* (1 Cor. vi, 17). Therefore the working of miracles is to be ascribed to charity.

7. Envy is especially opposed to charity, since charity rejoices in the good things for which envy grieves. Now according to a gloss on Gal. iii, 1, *envy by bewitching men produces an evil effect in them*. Therefore the working of miracles is to be put down to charity.

8. The intellect is not a principle of action except through the medium of the will. Now faith is in the intellect, and charity is in the will. Therefore neither does faith work save through charity: *Faith that worketh by charity* (Gal. v. 6). Therefore just as virtuous deeds are ascribed to charity rather than to faith, so also is the working of miracles.

9. All other miracles are directed to the Incarnation of Christ which is the miracle of miracles. Now the Incarnation is ascribed to charity (Jo. iii, 16): *God so loved the world, as to give his only begotten Son*. Therefore other miracles are to be ascribed not to faith but to charity.

10. It was a miracle that Sara old and barren bore a son to an old man: and this is ascribed to hope (Rom. iv, 18): *Who against hope believed in hope*. Therefore the working of miracles is to be ascribed to hope and not to faith.

11. A miracle is something difficult and unusual as Augustine says (*Tract*. viii *in Joan: De Trin*. iii, 5). Now difficult things are the object of hope. Therefore the working of miracles should be attributed to hope.

12. A miracle is a sign of the divine power. Now just as charity corresponds to goodness which is appropriated to the Holy Ghost, and as faith corresponds to truth which is appro-

priated to the Son : even so hope corresponds to power which is appropriated to the Father. Therefore the working of miracles should be ascribed to hope.

13. Augustine says (*QQ.* lxxxiii, qu, 79) that wicked men sometimes work miracles by *outward signs of righteousness.* Therefore the working of miracles is to be set down to righteousness, and not to faith.

14. It is stated (Acts vi, 8) that *Stephen full of grace and fortitude did great wonders and signs among the people.* Therefore seemingly it should be ascribed to fortitude.

15. Our Lord said to his disciples (Mt. xvii, 20) when they were unable to cast out devils : *This kind is not cast out but by prayer and fasting.* Now the casting out of devils is reckoned among miracles : and fasting is an act of the virtue of abstinence. Therefore the working of miracles belongs to abstinence.

16. Bernard says that to be constantly with women without falling is more than to raise the dead. Now that belongs to chastity. Therefore it belongs to chastity to work miracles, and not to faith.

17. That which is derogatory to faith should not be ascribed to faith. Now miracles are derogatory to faith since unbelievers ascribe them to the magic acts. Therefore miracles should not be set down to faith.

18. The faith of Peter and Andrew is commended by Gregory (*Hom.* v. *in Evang.*) for that they believed without seeing miracles. Therefore miracles are derogatory to faith and the same conclusion follows as before.

19. Given the cause the effect follows. If then faith be the cause of miracles being wrought, all who believe would work miracles : and this is clearly false. Therefore it does not belong to faith to work miracles.

On the contrary it is said (Mk. xvi, 17) : *These signs shall follow them that believe. In my name they shall cast out devils,* etc.

Again our Lord said (Mt. xvii, 19) : *If you have faith as a grain of mustard-seed you shall say to this mountain : Remove from hence hither, and it shall remove : and nothing shall be impossible to you.*

Again, if A which is the opposite of B causes C which is the opposite of D, then B is the cause of D. Now unbelief is a cause which hinders the working of miracles: thus it is said (Mk. vi, 5, 6) of Christ: *He could not do any miracles there* (i.e. in his own city) *only that he cured a few that were sick, laying his hands upon them, and he wondered because of their unbelief,* and (Mt. xvii, 18) it is related that when the disciples asked our Lord: *Why could not we cast him out? Because of your unbelief,* said he. Therefore faith is the cause of the working of miracles. I answer that holy men work miracles in two ways, according to Gregory (*Dial.* ii, 30) namely by impetration and authoritatively. Now in both ways faith renders a man fit to work miracles. For faith makes a man deserve that a miracle be wrought in answer to his prayer: and this is clear for the following reason. It is to be observed that whereas in natural things all particular causes derive the effectiveness of their action from the universal cause, a particular and proper effect is ascribed to a particular cause. We have an example of this in the active forces of the lower bodies in relation to the power of the heavenly body; and in the lower spheres which while following the movement of the first sphere, have each one their proper movements: and it is the same with the virtues whereby we merit. For they all derive their efficacy in meriting from charity, which unites us to God from whom we merit, and perfects our will whereby we merit, and yet each virtue merits a certain particular reward proportionately corresponding to it: thus humility merits exaltation, and poverty merits the kingdom. Hence sometimes when a man has lost charity, although he merits nothing condignly by acts of other virtues, yet through the divine liberality he may be repaid for these acts by certain congruous benefits, at any rate in this life. Wherefore it is said that a man may sometimes congruously merit an increase of worldly goods by deeds generically good which he has done while deprived of charity. In this way then faith merits the working of miracles, although the root of the merit is charity.

Three reasons may be given for this. First, because miracles are arguments of faith, inasmuch as when something is done above the faculty of nature, it provides a proof of that which surpasses the natural faculty of reason : hence it is said (Mk. xvi, 20) : *They going forth preached everywhere : the Lord working withal, and confirming the word with signs that followed.*

The second reason is because faith is based chiefly on the divine power, which it conceives as being the motive or medium of assent to things which appear to be above reason : wherefore the divine power in miraculous works comes especially to the assistance of faith.

The third reason is because miracles are wrought independently of natural causes : and faith takes its arguments not from reasons pertaining to nature and the senses but from things pertaining to God.

Hence just as poverty in worldly goods merits spiritual riches, and humility merits heavenly exaltation, even so faith through despising as it were things done naturally, merits after a fashion the working of miracles which are wrought above the faculty of nature.

In like manner faith makes a man suitable to work a miracle authoritatively. Three reasons will make this clear. First, because as already stated (A. 4) holy men are said to work miracles authoritatively, not as though they were the chief authors of miracles, but because as divine instruments they announce, as it were, to natural things the divine command which nature obeys when miracles are wrought. Now it is by faith that God's words dwell in us, because faith is a kind of participation in God's truth : wherefore faith disposes a man to the working of miracles.

Secondly, because holy men who work miracles authoritatively, act by the power of God working in nature. For God's action is compared to the whole of nature, as the soul's action to the body : and the body is transmuted by the soul above the order of natural principles, especially by a persistent imagination whereby the body is heated whether through desire or through anger, or is even constitutionally changed so as to become feverish or leprous. Accordingly a man will be disposed to the working of miracles by that which gives persistence and stability to his apprehension. And a firm faith does this : and therefore firmness of faith conduces in no small measure to the working of miracles. This is made evident (Mt. xxi, 21) where it is said : *If you shall have faith and stagger not, not only this of the fig-tree shall you do, but also if you shall say to this mountain, Take up and cast thyself into the sea, it shall be done :* and (Jas. i, 6), *Let him ask in faith nothing wavering.*

Thirdly, because miracles wrought authoritatively are done by way of command, and therefore a man is especially fitted to work miracles authoritatively by that which fits him to command : and this is a certain aloofness and withdrawal from those whom he has to command. Thus Anaxagoras says that the intellect is not mixed with the body, so that it may govern it. Now faith withdraws the mind from the domain of nature and sense, and sets it on the foundation of things intelligible. Consequently faith renders a man fit to work miracles authoritatively. For this reason those virtues are most conducive to the working of miracles, which withdraw a man's mind from those things which are most material: such as continence and abstinence which withdraw man from the preference of those things which engage his mind in sensible things. But other virtues which direct man in the administration of temporal things, do not so dispose him to the working of miracles.

Reply to the First Objection. The working of miracles is ascribed to the gratuitous grace as its proximate principle, and to faith as a disposition to the gratuitous grace.

Reply to the Second Objection. Though sometimes a sinner works a miracle, this is not due to his merit—that is, not to his condign merit—but to a certain congruity, inasmuch as he holds constantly to the faith in witness whereof God works the miracle.

Reply to the Third Objection. Charity through being a greater virtue than faith makes faith meritorious : yet faith more congruously merits in a special way the working of miracles. For faith is a perfection of the intellect, whose act consists in the thing understood being, after a fashion, in the intellect : whereas charity is a perfection of the will, whose act consists in its tending to the thing in itself. Wherefore by charity man abides in God and becomes one with him: whereas by faith divine things abide in us: for which reason it is said (Heb. xi, 1) that faith *is the substance of things to be hoped for.*—Moreover miracles are wrought in confirmation of faith, and not of charity.

Reply to the Fourth Objection. As stated, charity merits the granting of prayers, as the universal source of merit: but faith merits in a special way the working of miracles, as we have said above (*Reply Obj.* 3).

Reply to the Fifth Objection. According to a gloss on this passage[1] these are the words of the blind man, who had not yet fully received the sight of wisdom: wherefore they contain an untruth. God does at times hear sinners; but this is owing to his liberality and not to their merits: so that their prayer is impetratory but not meritorious; even as sometimes the prayer of a just man is meritorious but not impetratory: for impetration regards the object of the petition and is wholly gratuitous, whereas merit regards the merited reward and is a matter of justice.

Reply to the Sixth Objection. As we have already said (*Reply Obj.* 3) charity unites man to God as drawing man to God: but faith draws divine things to us.

Reply to the Seventh Objection. Envy could not have an evil effect by bewitching men, unless a fixed imagination conduced to that effect.

Reply to the Eighth Objection. This argument proves that faith merits through charity, and this has been granted (*Reply Obj.* 3). Moreover the objection holds in those actions which a man does by his own power, and wherein the intellect directs the will that commands the executive power. But in those actions where the divine power is executive, faith alone which is based on the divine power suffices for action.

Reply to the Ninth Objection. This argument considers the miracle as wrought by God whose every action in creatures is motived by love. Thus God's love did not permit him to be barren as Dionysius says (*Div. Nom.* iv). But we are

---

[1] Augustine (*Tract.* xliv in *Joan*).

considering the miracle as done by man : wherefore the objection is not to the point.

Reply to the Tenth Objection. The working of miracles is not properly ascribed to hope : because the object of hope is a thing to be obtained, wherefore it is only about eternal things. But faith is of things both eternal and temporal : and thus it can extend to things that have to be done. For this reason in the words quoted the chief place is given to hope rather than to faith : *He believed in hope.*

Reply to the Eleventh Objection. The object of hope is something difficult to obtain, not difficult to do.

Reply to the Twelfth Objection. God's power corresponds to hope, inasmuch as he is above all in majesty ; and the possession of this is the object of hope. But the power itself as effective of miracles is the base on which faith is founded chiefly.

Reply to the Thirteenth Objection. Outward signs of righteousness come from that faith whereby the whole Church is justified, according to Rom. iii, 22, *The justice of God through faith in Christ Jesus.*

Reply to the Fourteenth Objection. The martyrs showed fortitude in suffering and constancy in confessing on account the firmness of their faith.

Reply to the Fifteenth Objection. Abstinence also conduces to the working of miracles, but not in the same degree as faith.

Reply to the Sixteenth Objection. Though it be difficult to be constantly with women and not to fall, it is not a miracle properly speaking, since it depends on a created power, namely the free-will.

Reply to the Seventeenth Objection. The abuse of miracles by those who spoke ill of them does not detract from their efficacy in confirming the faith of those who were well disposed.

Reply to the Eighteenth Objection. The faith of Peter and Andrew is commended on account of their readiness to believe : and this was all the more enhanced as they needed fewer reasons for believing ; and miracles by their very nature are to be reckoned among these reasons.

Reply to the Nineteenth Objection. Faith is not a sufficient cause of working miracles, but a disposition thereto. And miracles are wrought according to the ordering of divine providence, which gives men suitable remedies for various causes and in many ways.

ARTICLE X

ARE DEMONS FORCED TO WORK MIRACLES BY SENSIBLE AND CORPOREAL OBJECTS, DEEDS OR WORDS?

THE tenth point of inquiry is whether demons by sensible and corporeal objects, deeds, or words, be forced to work the miracles that seem to be wrought by magic: and seemingly they can.

1. Augustine (*De Civ. Dei* x, 9) quotes Porphyry as saying that a certain man in Chaldea was seized with envy and by adjuring the spiritual powers, bound them with his imprecations not to grant the prayers of any other. And (*ibid.* 21) he says: *Unless the demons first gave the information, it was not possible to know what any one of them desired or disliked, by what name he was to be invoked or compelled.* Therefore demons are compelled to produce magical effects.

2. Whosoever does a thing against his will is in some way compelled. Now demons sometimes do a thing against their will when they are adjured by magicians. Thus it is always the devil's will to lead men into sin: and yet a man may be incited to base love by magic, and by the same art may be freed from the violence of the incitement. Therefore demons are compelled by magicians.

3. It is related of Solomon that he performed certain exercises and thereby compelled the demons to quit bodies that were obsessed by them. Therefore demons can be compelled by adjuration.

4. If demons come when evoked by a magician this is because they are either enticed or compelled. But they are not always evoked by being enticed: since sometimes they are adjured through things they hate, for instance through

the virginity of the imprecator, whereas they themselves are ever inciting men to concubinage. Therefore seemingly they are sometimes compelled.

5. It is the devil's constant aim to turn man away from God. Nevertheless they obey the summons when they are adjured through things that imply that they revere God, for instance by invoking God's majesty. Therefore they do this not willingly but under compulsion.

6. If so be that they are enticed by sensible objects it is not as animals are enticed by food, but as spirits are drawn by such signs as give pleasure, for instance different kinds of stones, herbs, trees, animals, chants, rites, as Augustine says (*De Civ. Dei* xxi, 6). Yet apparently they are not drawn by signs; for only those are drawn by signs who make use of signs, and these are only those who are possessed of senses: inasmuch as a sign is that which besides the impression it makes on the senses brings something else to our knowledge. Therefore demons are in no way enticed but are only compelled.

7. A certain man said to Jesus (Mt. xvii, 14): *Lord have pity on my son, for he is a lunatic and suffereth much:* and (Mk. ix, 16) it is said: *I have brought my son to thee, having a dumb spirit.* Now the (ordinary) gloss observes on the words quoted from Matthew: *Him Mark calls deaf and dumb whom Matthew describes as a lunatic, not that the moon obeys the demons, but that the demon by observing the moon's course has an evil influence on man.* It would seem, then, that by observing the heavenly bodies and other material things the demons may be compelled to do this or that.

8. Seeing that demons sinned by pride it is hardly likely that they are enticed by things that are derogatory to their superior nature. Yet they are adjured by invocations of their power and by the most incredible falsehoods, all of which is derogatory to their knowledge. Hence Augustine (*De Civ. Dei* x, 11) quotes Porphyry as saying: *Why should a weak man threaten, or seek by falsehood to extract the truth? for he will threaten to make the heavens fall and do other like things impossible to man, that the gods like silly children overawed by false and absurd threats may obey his behest.* There-

fore the demons are evoked not by being enticed but by being compelled.

9. The demon's endeavour is to bring men to idolatry: and they compass this chiefly by their presence in images. Now if they came of their own accord, they would always come to such things. But they come only at certain times, and when invoked by certain chants and rites, and then only to certain consecrated or rather execrated images. Demons therefore are invoked not by being enticed but by compulsion.

10. Sometimes demons are invoked by magic art in order that they may turn men to base love. But demons endeavour to do this of their own accord : wherefore there would be no use in enticing them to do this if they did so whenever they were invoked. Now they do not so always. Therefore when they do they are invoked, not as being enticed but as being compelled.

On the contrary, it is written (Job xli, 24) : *There is no power upon earth that can be compared with him*, namely the devil. Now a greater power is not compelled by a lesser. Therefore nothing on earth can compel the demons.

Again, to be invoked and to be compelled apply to different subjects : we invoke those who are above, and we compel those who are beneath, according to Porphyry. Now demons come when called : therefore they are not compelled.

Should anyone say that they are compelled by the power of God : I reply, on the contrary, that to compel the demons by (calling upon) the power of God is the effect of the gift of grace whereby the order of heavenly powers is fulfilled. Now this gift is not in unbelievers and wicked men like sorcerers. Therefore neither can the demons be compelled by invoking the divine power. Again, it is no sin to do what is done chiefly by the divine power, for instance to work miracles. If then magicians were to compel the demons by the power of God, they would not sin in employing the magic arts ; which is plainly false. Therefore the demons cannot in any way be compelled by magic.

I answer that there have been many opinions about the things done by the magic arts. Some, like Alexander, have said that the effects produced by magic are the result of powers and energies engendered in the lower world by the forces in these lower bodies combined with an observation of the heavenly movements. Hence Augustine (*De Civ. Dei* x, 1) states that Porphyry believed that it is possible for men to employ herbs, stones, animals, certain sounds and voices, figures and various forms of trickery as well as by observing the movement of the stars in the revolution of the heavens, to conjure up forces conducive to the various effects of the stars. This opinion seems to be inadequate : since, although the natural forces of higher and lower bodies may suffice to produce some of the results ascribed to witchcraft, such as certain transmutations of bodies, nevertheless there are certain results of magic that are altogether beyond the scope of material forces. For it is plain that speech can only come from an intelligence : and magicians cause spoken answers to be heard ; wherefore this must proceed from an intelligence, especially seeing that these answers sometimes convey information about hidden matters. Nor can it be said that this is done by influencing the imagination alone by some kind of trickery : because in that case these voices would not be heard by all the bystanders, nor could they be heard by those who are awake and have the use of their senses. It follows then that these answers proceed either from the mind of the magician or from some outside intellectual agency.

The former is impossible for two reasons. First, because a man's mind cannot by its own power come to the knowledge of hidden matters except through matters known to him : so that by its will it is unable to effect the revelation of hidden matters, which is produced by the magic arts, since the principles of reason are insufficient to lead to the knowledge of those hidden matters. Secondly, because if the magician's mind produced these results by its own power, it would not need to resort to invocations or other like external means.

It is clear, therefore, that these results of magic are produced by some external spirits : not however by righteous and good spirits ; and this is clear for two reasons. First, because good spirits would not associate themselves with wicked men, such as are the majority of magicians; secondly, because they would not co-operate with man in wrong-doing, which is often the result of magic. It remains then for us to conclude that they are produced by evil spirits whom we call demons.

These demons may be said to be compelled in two ways: first by a higher power that forces them to act of necessity: secondly, by way of enticement, even as a man is said to be compelled to do something when he is drawn by his desire. In neither way, however, properly speaking, can demons be compelled by material things: unless we suppose them to have aerial bodies naturally united to them and consequently sensible affections like other animated beings: thus Apuleius believed that demons are animals with aerial bodies and passive souls.[1] For in that case they could be compelled in either way by a corporeal power; either of the heavenly bodies (by whose action they might be led to certain passions) or of these lower bodies which might be to them an object of pleasure: thus Apuleius says that *they delight in the smoke of sacrifices and such like things.* This opinion, however, has been shown to be false in the previous Articles.

We conclude then that the demons which give success to the magic art may be both compelled and enticed. They are compelled by a higher being: sometimes by God himself, sometimes through the divine power by holy angels and men. Thus the demons are said to be curbed by the angelic order of Powers. Holy men, even as they participate in the gift of the Virtues inasmuch as they work miracles, so do they share in the gift of the Powers inasmuch as they cast out devils. Sometimes too they are compelled by superior demons; and this compulsion alone can be effected by means of magic. They may also be compelled, being as it were enticed, by the magic arts, not indeed by means of corporeal things for their own sake, but for the sake of something else. First because they are aware that the result for which they are invoked can be more easily produced by such corporeal things: and they want their power to be an object of

---

[1] See above A. 6.

admiration : and for this reason they are more ready to obey the summons when they are invoked under certain constellations. Secondly, in so far as these corporeal things are signs of certain spiritual things that please them. Hence Augustine (*De Civ. Dei* xxi, 6) says that demons are enticed by these things not as animals are by food, but as spirits by signs. For seeing that men in token of their subjection to God offer sacrifice and prostrate themselves, the demons delight in having such tokens of reverence offered to them. Moreover different demons are enticed by different signs as corresponding better to their various vices. Thirdly, they are enticed by those corporeal things which lead men into sin : for this reason they are enticed by lies or anything that deceives men or leads them into sin.

Reply to the First Objection. Demons are said to be compelled by magic art in the ways given above.

Reply to the Second Objection. The demon is quite content if by preventing an evil and promoting a good he makes it easier for him to draw men into familiar converse with him, and to become an object of admiration to them : thus they even transform themselves into angels of light (2 Cor. xi, 14).

Reply to the Third Objection. If Solomon performed these exorcisms when he was in a state of grace, they could derive the power to compel the demons from the power of God. But if it was after he had turned to the worship of idols, so that we have to understand that he performed them by magic arts, these exorcisms had no power to compel the demons, except in the manner explained above.

Reply to the Fourth Objection. The demons come when invoked by virgins, in order to lead men to think that they are divine, as though they loved purity.

Reply to the Fifth Objection. Again, by coming when adjured by the invocation of the divine majesty, they wish men to think that they are not utterly banished by the justice of God. For they do not desire to be as gods, as altogether equal to God, but rejoice in receiving from men divine worship under him.

Reply to the Sixth Objection. Demons are not said to be enticed by signs as though they used signs, but seeing that men are wont to employ signs, they take pleasure in the signs employed by men on account of what they signify.

Reply to the Seventh Objection. As the ordinary gloss observes (*ibid.*) demons afflict men more at certain phases of the moon, in order to bring God's creatures into evil repute, by the fact that men believe them to serve the demons and thus deceive men.

Reply to the Eighth Objection. Although such lies would seem derogatory to the demons' power : yet it pleases them that men believe in these lies : because the devil is a liar and the father of lies.

Reply to the Ninth Objection. The demons become present to images when invoked at certain hours and by certain signs, for reasons already given.

Reply to the Tenth Objection. Although the demons ever desire to draw men into sin : they endeavour to do so all the more when they have a greater incentive, and when there is a likelihood of a greater number being drawn into sin.

THIRD BOOK
(QUESTIONS VII–X)

NIHIL OBSTAT:
F. VINCENTIUS McNABB, O.P., S.T.M.
F. GABRIEL COYLE, O.P., S.T.L.

IMPRIMATUR:
F. BERNARDUS DELANY, O.P.,
Prior Provincialis Angliae.

In festo SS. Rosarii, B.V.M.
die 1 Octobris, 1933.

NIHIL OBSTAT:
GEORGIUS D. SMITH, PH.D., S.TH.D.,
Censor deputatus.

IMPRIMATUR:
✠ JOSEPH BUTT,
Vicarius generalis.

WESTMONASTERII,
die 19 Octobris, 1933.

CONTENTS

QUESTION VII. THE SIMPLICITY OF THE DIVINE ESSENCE

ARTICLE	PAGE
I. IS GOD SIMPLE?	1
II. IS GOD'S ESSENCE OR SUBSTANCE THE SAME AS HIS EXISTENCE?	7
III. IS GOD CONTAINED IN A GENUS?	14
IV. DO 'GOOD,' 'WISE,' 'JUST' AND THE LIKE PREDICATE AN ACCIDENT IN GOD?	18
V. DO THESE TERMS SIGNIFY THE DIVINE ESSENCE?	24
VI. ARE THESE TERMS SYNONYMOUS?	33
VII. ARE THESE TERMS ASCRIBED UNIVOCALLY OR EQUIVOCALLY TO GOD AND THE CREATURE?	39
VIII. IS THERE ANY RELATION BETWEEN GOD AND THE CREATURE?	46
IX. ARE THESE RELATIONS BETWEEN A CREATURE AND GOD REALLY IN CREATURES THEMSELVES?	50
X. IS GOD REALLY RELATED TO THE CREATURE SO THAT THIS RELATION BE SOMETHING IN GOD?	55
XI. ARE THESE TEMPORAL RELATIONS IN GOD AS LOGICAL RELATIONS?	62

QUESTION VIII. OF THOSE THINGS THAT ARE PREDICATED OF GOD RELATIVELY FROM ETERNITY

I. ARE THE RELATIONS PREDICATED OF GOD FROM ETERNITY REAL OR ONLY LOGICAL RELATIONS?	66
II. IS RELATION IN GOD THE SAME AS HIS SUBSTANCE?	74
III. DO THE RELATIONS CONSTITUTE AND DISTINGUISH THE PERSONS OR HYPOSTASES?	81
IV. IF MENTAL ABSTRACTION BE MADE OF THE RELATIONS, DO THE DIVINE HYPOSTASES REMAIN?	90

QUESTION IX. OF THE DIVINE PERSONS

I. OF THE PERSONS AS COMPARED TO THE ESSENCE, SUBSISTENCE AND HYPOSTASIS	96
II. WHAT IS MEANT BY A PERSON?	101

CONTENTS

ARTICLE	PAGE
III. CAN THERE BE A PERSON IN GOD?	107
IV. IN GOD DOES THE TERM 'PERSON' SIGNIFY SOMETHING RELATIVE OR SOMETHING ABSOLUTE?	110
V. ARE THERE SEVERAL PERSONS IN GOD?	119
VI. IN SPEAKING OF GOD CAN THE WORD 'PERSON' BE RIGHTLY PREDICATED IN THE PLURAL?	131
VII. ARE NUMERAL TERMS PREDICATED OF THE DIVINE PERSONS?	134
VIII. IS THERE ANY DIVERSITY IN GOD?	146
IX. ARE THERE ONLY THREE PERSONS IN GOD: OR ARE THERE MORE OR FEWER THAN THREE?	149

QUESTION X. THE PROCESSION OF THE DIVINE PERSONS

I. IS THERE PROCESSION IN GOD?	167
II. IS THERE BUT ONE PROCESSION IN GOD, OR ARE THERE MORE?	176
III. OF THE ORDER BETWEEN PROCESSION AND RELATION IN GOD	191
IV. DOES THE HOLY GHOST PROCEED FROM THE SON?	194
V. WOULD THE HOLY GHOST STILL BE DISTINGUISHED FROM THE SON IF HE DID NOT PROCEED FROM HIM?	213

ON THE POWER OF GOD

QUESTION VII

THE SIMPLICITY OF THE DIVINE ESSENCE

THERE are eleven points of inquiry : (1) Whether God is simple. (2) Whether God's substance or essence are the same as his being. (3) Is God in any genus ? (4) Whether ' good,' ' just,' ' wise ' and the like predicate an accident in God. (5) Whether the aforesaid terms signify the divine substance. (6) Whether these terms are synonymous. (7) Whether these terms are said of God and creatures univocally or equivocally. (8) Is there any relation between God and the creature ? (9) Whether the relations between God and creatures are really in creatures. (10) Whether God is really related to the creature, so that the relation be something in God. (11) Whether temporal relations are in God only logically.

ARTICLE I

IS GOD SIMPLE ?

Sum. Th. I, Q. iii

THE first point of inquiry is whether God is simple : and seemingly he is not.

1. From one simple thing only one thing can naturally proceed : for the same always produces the same according to the Philosopher (*De Gener.* ii). But many things come from God. Therefore he is not simple.

2. If a simple thing is reached the whole of it is reached. Now God is reached by the blessed : for as Augustine says (*De videndo Deum*[1]), *to reach God with the mind is great*

[1] *Ad Paulinam,* Ep. cxlvii.

happiness. If, then, God is simple he is wholly reached by the blessed. Now that which is wholly reached is comprehended. Therefore God is comprehended by the blessed: which is impossible. Therefore God is not simple.

3. The same thing cannot be several kinds of cause. Now God is several kinds of cause (*Metaph.* xi). Therefore there must be various things in him: and consequently he is composite.

4. Whatsoever contains one thing in addition to another is composite. Now in God there is one thing besides another, namely property and essence. Therefore there is composition in God.

5. It will be replied that the property is the same thing as the essence. On the contrary, affirmation and negation are not true of the same. Now the divine essence is common to the three Persons, whereas the properties are incommunicable. Therefore property and essence are not the same.

6. A thing is composite if different predicaments are predicated of it. Now substance and relation are predicated of God, according to Boethius (*De Trin.*). Therefore God is composite.

7. In everything there is substance, power and operation, according to Dionysius (*Cæl. Hier.* xi): wherefore seemingly operation follows power and substance. Now there are several divine operations. Therefore there is plurality and composition in the divine substance.

8. Wherever there is plurality of forms there must be composition. Now in God there is plurality of forms, for as the Commentator says (*Metaph.* xi, com. 18), all forms exist actually in the first mover, even as they are potentially in primal matter. Therefore composition is in God.

9. Whatsoever is added to a thing that has complete being is accidental to it. Now certain things are said of God since the beginning of time, such as that he is the Creator and the Lord. Therefore these things are in him accidentally. But an accident with its subject forms a kind of composition. Therefore composition is in God.

10. Where there are several things there is composition.

Now in God there are three persons, and there are three things according to Augustine (*De Doct. Christ.* i, 5). Therefore composition is in God.

On the contrary, Hilary says (*De Trin.* viii) : *God is not composed of several things as man is, as though what he has were distinct from him who has it.* Again Boethius says (*De Trin.*) : *He is truly one since there is no number in him.* Now where there is composition there is number. Therefore God is incomposite and utterly simple.

I answer that we must hold that God is altogether simple : and for the nonce this may be proved by three arguments. The first is as follows. We have proved (Q. iii, A. 5) in a former discussion, that all beings proceed from a first being which we call God. Now although in one and the same thing that is at one time in act, at another time in potentiality, potentiality precedes act in time but follows it in nature : yet absolutely speaking act precedes potentiality not only in nature, but also in time, since everything that is in potentiality is made actual by some being that is in act. Accordingly the being that made all things actual, and itself proceeds from no other being, must be the first actual being without any admixture of potentiality. For were it in any way in potentiality, there would be need of another previous being to make it actual. Now in every composite of whatsoever kind of composition there must needs be a mixture of act and potentiality : because of the things whereof it is composed, either one is in potentiality to the other, as matter to form, subject to accident, genus to difference, or all the parts together are in potentiality to the whole, since parts are reducible to matter, and the whole is reducible to form (*Phys.* ii) so that no composite is first act. But the first being which is God must needs be pure act, as we have proved (Q. i, A. 1). Therefore it is impossible that God be composite : and thus it follows that he is utterly simple. The second reason is because seeing that composition requires difference in the component parts, these different parts require an agent to unite them together : since different things as such are not united. Now every composite has being through the union of its component parts. Therefore every composite depends on a pre-existing agent : and consequently the first being which is God, from whom all things proceed, cannot be composite. The third reason is because the first being, which is God, must needs be most perfect and consequently supremely good : since the principles of things are not imperfect, as Pythagoras and Leucippus contended. Now the supremely good is that in which there is nothing lacking in goodness, even as the supremely white is that in which there is no admixture of blackness. But this is impossible in any composite thing because the good that results from the composition of its parts, and whereby the whole is good, is not in any single part. Wherefore the parts are not good with the goodness proper to the whole. Consequently that which is supremely good must be supremely simple and void of all composition. This argument is given by the Philosopher (*Metaph.* xi) and by Hilary (*De Trin.* vii), where he says that *God who is light is not composed of things that are dim, nor is he who is strength composed of things that are weak.*

Reply to the First Objection. Aristotle does not mean that a multitude cannot proceed from one. For since an agent produces its like, and since an effect falls short of reproducing its cause, it follows that where we find unity in the cause we shall find multiplicity in the effects : thus in the sun's power all the forms of generable bodies are, in a fashion, one, and yet they are diversified in its effects. Hence it is that by its one power a thing is able to produce various effects : thus fire by its heat liquefies and solidifies, softens and hardens, flames and blackens : and man by the power of his reason acquires various sciences and produces various works of art. Wherefore *a fortiori* God by his one simple power is able to create many things. The Philosopher means then that a thing so long as it remains the same does not produce different effects at different times, if it act by natural necessity : except perhaps accidentally, through diversity of matter, or the intervention of another agent : but this is not to the point.

Reply to the Second Objection. God is attained by the mind of the blessed, whole but not wholly, because the mode of God's knowableness infinitely surpasses the mode of a created intellect : and thus the created intellect cannot understand God as perfectly as he is understandable, and consequently he cannot comprehend him.

Reply to the Third Objection. By reason of one and the same thing God is considered by us as having different kinds of causality : because in that he is the first act, he is an active cause, he is the exemplar of all forms, and he is supreme goodness and consequently the final cause of all things.

Reply to the Fourth Objection. Property and essence in God differ not in reality but only logically : for paternity itself is the divine essence, as we shall show further on (Q. viii, A. 1).

Reply to the Fifth Objection. As the Philosopher says (*Phys.* iii, 3), nothing prevents contradictory statements being verified about one same thing from different points of view : thus the same identical point from different aspects is the beginning and end (of a line) : and considered as the beginning it is not the end and vice versa. Wherefore since essence and property are the same in reality but differ logically, nothing prevents the one being common and the other incommunicable.

Reply to the Sixth Objection. In God the absolute and the relative do not differ really, but only logically as stated above : wherefore we cannot infer that there is composition in him.

Reply to the Seventh Objection. God's operation may be considered from the point of view either of the operator or of the work done. If we consider it on the part of the operator, then in God there is but one operation and this is in his essence : for he produces his effects not by an action that is between him and the thing done, but by his intelligence and will which are his very being. If, however, we consider God's operation on the part of the work done, then there are various operations, and various effects of the divine operation : but this does not argue composition in him.

Reply to the Eighth Objection. The form of the effect has a different mode of being in the natural agent and the agent by art. The form of the effect is in the natural agent inasmuch as the agent produces an effect of like nature, since every agent produces its like. Now this happens in two ways. When the effect bears a perfect likeness to the agent, as proportionate to the agent's power, then the form of the effect is in the agent in the same degree: thus it is in univocal agents, for instance fire generates fire. When, however, the effect is not perfectly likened to the agent, as being improportionate to the agent's power, then the form of the effect is not in the same degree in the agent but in a higher degree: this is the case in equivocal agents, for instance the sun generates fire. On the other hand in agents by art, the form of the effect pre-exists in the same degree but not in the same mode of being: because in the effect the form has material being, whereas in the mind of the craftsman it has intelligible being. Now whereas a thing may be in the intellect as the thing which we understand, and as the species whereby we understand, art-forms are in the intellect as that whereby we understand: because it is through conceiving the form of his art-work that the craftsman produces that work in matter. Accordingly the forms of things are in God in both ways. Because while his action in reference to things is from his intellect, it is not without the action of nature. But whereas here below the craftsman's art acts by virtue of an extraneous nature which it employs as an instrument, as a brickmaker uses fire to bake his bricks: on the other hand God's art employs no extraneous nature in its action, but produces its effect by virtue of his own nature. Hence the forms of things are in the divine nature as in the power that produces them, but not according to the same degree, since no effect is equal to that power. Consequently all forms that are manifold in his effects are in his power as one thing, so that their multiplicity argues no composition in him. Likewise in his intellect there are many things understood through one thing which is his essence. Now it is no proof of composition in one who understands that he understand many things by one: wherefore neither from this point of view does it follow that there is composition in God.

Reply to the Ninth Objection. Relations that are ascribed to God in time, are in him not really but only logically: because real relation is where one thing really depends on another either simply or in a certain respect. Hence knowledge bears a real relation to what is knowable, whereas the relation of the thing knowable to knowledge is only logical according to the Philosopher (*Metaph.* v, text. 20). Since then God depends on no other being, but on the contrary all things depend on him, other things bear a real relation to God, while his relation to them is only logical, for the reason that our intelligence is unable to understand that A is related to B without conceiving a corresponding relation of B to A.

Reply to the Tenth Objection. Plurality of Persons does not argue composition in God. The Persons may be considered in two ways. First, in reference to the Essence with which they are identical: so that there is no composition here. Secondly, in reference to one another, and thus they are regarded as mutually distinct not as united together: wherefore from this point of view again there is no composition: since every composition implies union.

ARTICLE II

IS GOD'S ESSENCE OR SUBSTANCE THE SAME AS HIS EXISTENCE?

Sum. Th. I, Q. iii, AA. 3, 4

THE second point of inquiry is whether God's essence or substance is the same as his existence: and seemingly it is not.

1. Damascene says (*De Fid. Orth.* i, 1, 3): *That God is, is evident to us; but what he is in substance and nature is utterly incomprehensible and unknown.* Now the same thing cannot be both known and unknown. Therefore God's existence is not the same as his substance or essence.

2. But it will be replied that God's existence is unknown to us even as his substance, as regards what it is.

On the contrary, these two questions are different: *Is he?*

and *What is he?* and we know the answer to the former, but not the answer to the latter, as evinced from the authority quoted. Therefore that which in God corresponds to the question *Is he?* is not the same as that which corresponds to the question *What is he?* and existence corresponds to the former question and substance or nature corresponds to the latter.

3. Again it will be replied that God's existence is known not in itself but through its likeness in creatures.

On the contrary, in the creature there is existence and substance or nature, and since it has both from God it is likened to God in both, because an agent produces its like. If then God's existence is known through the likeness of created existence, it follows that his substance is known through the likeness of created substance: and thus we would know not only that God is but also what he is.

4. A thing is said to differ from another by reason of its substance: nor can one thing differ from another by reason of that which is common to all things: wherefore the Philosopher says (*Metaph.* ii, 3) that *being* should not be placed in a definition, since it would not differentiate the thing defined from another. Consequently the substance of a thing that is distinct from other things cannot be its being, since being is common to all things. Now God is something distinct from all other things. Therefore his being is not his substance.

5. Things are not distinct if they have not a distinct being. Now the being of A is not distinct from B's being considered as being but considered as in this or that nature. Hence a being that is in a nature that is not distinct from its being will not be distinct from any other being: and thus it will follow, if God's substance is his being, that he is the common being of all things.

6. Being to which no addition can be made is being common to all things. Now if God is his own being no additions can be made to his being: and then his being will be common to all. Consequently he can be predicated of everything, and will enter into the composition of everything: which is heretical and contrary to the statement of

the Philosopher who says (*De Causis,*[1] prop. xx) that the first cause rules all things without being mingled with them.

7. Nothing that implies concretion should be said of a thing that is utterly simple. Now such is existence: for it would seem that existence is to essence as whiteness is to the white thing. Therefore we should not say that God's substance is his existence.

8. Boethius says (*De Hebdom.*[2]): *Whatsoever has being participates of that which is being, and thus has being; and participates of something else, and thus it is this or that thing.* Now God has being. Therefore, besides his being, there is something else in him whereby he is a particular thing.

9. That which is most imperfect should not be ascribed to God who is most perfect. Now existence is most imperfect like primal matter: for just as primal matter may be determined by any form, so being, inasmuch as it is most imperfect, may be determinated by all the proper predicaments. Therefore as primal matter is not in God, so neither should existence be an attribute of the divine substance.

10. That which signifies something as an effect should not be ascribed to the first substance which has no beginning. Now such is existence, for every being has existence through its essential principles. Therefore it is unfitting to say that God's substance is its own existence.

11. A proposition is self-evident wherein a thing is predicated of itself. But if God's substance is its own existence, the subject and predicate will be identical in the proposition, *God exists.* Wherefore it will be a self-evident proposition; yet this is not true seemingly, since it can be demonstrated. Therefore God's existence is not his substance.

On the contrary, Hilary says (*De Trin.* vii): *In God existence is not an accident but subsisting truth.* Now that which is subsisting is the substance of a thing. Therefore God's existence is his substance.

Again, Rabbi Moses says that *God is a being but not in an essence, is living but not with life, is powerful but not with*

---

[1] The *Liber de Causis* ascribed to Gilbert de la Porrée (1076–1154) is an abridged translation of the *Institutio Theologica* of Proclus, a neoplatonic philosopher of the fifth century.

[2] Alias, *An omne quod est sit bonum.*

power, wise but not with wisdom. Therefore in God essence is not distinct from existence.

Again, a thing is properly denominated from what it is: since the name of a thing denotes its essence and quiddity (*Metaph.* iv). Now of all God's names *He who is* (Exod. iv) is the most appropriate to him. Hence as this name is given to him in respect of his existence, it would seem that God's very existence is his essence.

I answer that in God there is no distinction between existence and essence. In order to make this clear we must observe that when several causes producing various effects produce one effect in common in addition to their various effects, they must needs produce this common effect by virtue of some higher cause to which this effect properly belongs. The reason for this is that since a proper effect is produced by a particular cause in respect of its proper nature or form, different causes having different natures and forms must needs have their respective different proper effects: so that if they have one effect in common, this is not the proper effect of any one of them, but of some higher cause by whose virtue they act: thus pepper, ginger and the like which differ in characteristics have the common effect of producing heat; yet each one has its peculiar effect differing from the effects of the others. Hence we must trace their common effect to a higher cause, namely fire to whom that effect properly belongs. Likewise in the heavenly movements each planet has its peculiar movement, and besides this they have all a common movement which must be the proper movement of some higher sphere that causes them all to revolve with the daily movement. Now all created causes have one common effect which is *being*, although each one has its peculiar effect whereby they are differentiated: thus heat makes a thing *to be* hot, and a builder gives *being* to a house. Accordingly they have this in common that they cause *being*, but they differ in that fire causes fire, and a builder causes a house. There must therefore be some cause higher than all other by virtue of which they all cause being and whose proper cause is *being*: and this cause is God. Now the proper effect of any cause proceeds therefrom in likeness to its nature. Therefore *being* must be the essence or nature of God. For this reason it is stated in *De Causis* (prop. ix) that none but a divine intelligence gives being, and that *being* is the first of all effects, and that nothing was created before it.

Reply to the First Objection. 'Being' and 'is' may be taken in two ways (*Metaph.* x, 13, 14). Sometimes they signify the essence of a thing and the act of being, and sometimes they denote the truth of a proposition even in things that have no being: thus we say that *blindness is* because it is true that a man is blind. Accordingly when Damascene says that God's existence is evident to us, the existence of God is taken in the second sense and not the first. For in the first sense God's existence is the same as his essence, and as his essence is unknown so also is his existence. In the second sense we know that God is, because we conceive this proposition in our mind from his effects.

This suffices for the *Replies to the Second and Third Objections*.

Reply to the Fourth Objection. God's being which is his essence is not universal being, but being distinct from all other being: so that by his very being God is distinct from every other being.

Reply to the Fifth Objection. As stated in *De Causis* (prop. iv) God's being is individualised and distinct from every other being by the very fact that it is self-subsistent being, and is not something additional to a nature that is distinct from its being. Now every other being that is not subsistent must be individualised by the nature and essence that subsists in that being: and of such beings it is true that the being of A is distinct from the being of B by the fact that it is the being of another nature: even so if there were one heat existing of itself without matter or subject, by that very fact it would be distinct from every other heat, just as heats existing in a subject are not differentiated otherwise than by their subjects.

Reply to the Sixth Objection. Being to which no addition is made is universal being, though the possibility of addition thereto is not incompatible with the notion of universal being: whereas the divine being is being to which no addition can be made and this enters into the very notion of the divine being: wherefore the divine being is not universal being. Thus by adding the difference *rational* to animal in general we do not add anything to the notion of animal in general: and yet it is not incompatible with the idea of animal in general that an addition to it be possible: for this enters into the notion of irrational animal which is a species of animal.

Reply to the Seventh Objection. The mode of signification of the names we give things is consequent upon our mode of understanding: for names signify the concepts of our intellect (*Peri Herm.* i). Now our intellect understands being according to the mode in which it finds it in things here below from which it gathers its knowledge, and wherein being is not subsistent but inherent. Now our reason tells us that there is a self-subsistent being: wherefore although the term *being* has a signification by way of concretion, yet our intellect in ascribing *being* to God soars above the mode of its signification, and ascribes to God the thing signified, but not the mode of signification.

Reply to the Eighth Objection. The saying of Boethius refers to things that have being by participation and not by their essence: since that which has being by its essence, if we stress the terms, should be described as *being itself* rather than as *that which has being.*

Reply to the Ninth Objection. Being, as we understand it here, signifies the highest perfection of all: and the proof is that act is always more perfect than potentiality. Now no signate form is understood to be in act unless it be supposed to have *being.* Thus we may take human nature or fiery nature as existing potentially in matter, or as existing in the power of an agent, or even as in the mind: but when it has being it becomes actually existent. Wherefore it is clear that *being* as we understand it here is the actuality of all acts, and therefore the perfection of all perfections. Nor may we think that being, in this sense, can have anything added to it that is more formal and determines it as act determines potentiality: because *being* in this latter sense is essentially distinct from that to which it is added and whereby it is determined. But nothing that is outside the range of being can be added to *being*: for nothing is outside its range except *non-being*, which can be neither form nor matter. Hence *being* is not determined by something else as potentiality by act but rather as act by potentiality: since in defining a form we include its proper matter instead of the difference: thus we define a soul as the act of an organic physical body. Accordingly this *being* is distinct from that *being* inasmuch as it is the *being* of this or that nature. For this reason Dionysius says (*Div. Nom.* v) that though things having life excel those that merely have being, yet being excels life, since living things have not only life but also being.

Reply to the Tenth Objection. The order of agents follows the order of ends, in that the last end corresponds to the first agent and in due proportion other ends to other agents in their order. Take, for example, the ruler of a state, the commander of the army and a private soldier: the ruler is clearly the first in the order of agents; at whose orders the commander goes forth to the war; and under him is the private soldier who engages in hand-to-hand combat at the orders of his commander. Now the end of the private soldier is to overthrow his opponent, and this is directed yet further to the victory of the army, which is the end of the commander-in-chief; and this again is directed to the welfare of the state or kingdom, which is the end of the ruler or king. Accordingly *being* which is the proper effect and end of the operation of the first agent must occupy the position of last end. Now although the end is first in the intention, it is last in execution, and is the effect of other causes. Therefore created *being*, which is the proper effect corresponding to the first agent, is caused from other principles, and yet the first cause of *being* is the first principle of all.

Reply to the Eleventh Objection. A proposition may be self-evident in itself and yet not self-evident to this or that individual; when, to wit, the predicate belongs to the definition of the subject, which definition is unknown to him: thus if he knew not what is a whole, he would not know this proposition, *A whole is greater than its part.* The reason is that such propositions become known when their terms are known (*Poster. Anal.* i). Now this proposition, *God is*, is in itself self-evident, since the same idea is expressed in both subject and predicate : but with regard to us it is not self-evident, because we know not what God is : so that for us it needs to be proved, though not for those who see God in his essence.

ARTICLE III

IS GOD CONTAINED IN A GENUS ?
Sum. Th. I, Q. iii, A. 5

THE third point of inquiry is whether God is contained in a genus : and seemingly he is.

1. Damascene says (*De Fide Orth.* iii, 4) : *Substance in God denotes the common species of the three Persons like in species : hypostasis signifies an individual, for instance the Father, Son and Holy Ghost, Peter or Paul.* Thus God is compared to the Father, Son and Holy Ghost as a species to individuals. Now wherever there is a species with individuals, there is a genus : since the species is composed of genus and difference. Therefore seemingly God is contained in a genus.

2. Things which are in no way different are identical. But God is not identical with other things : therefore in some way he is different from them. Now that which is different from something else differs therefrom by some difference. Therefore there is a difference in God, whereby he differs from other things. But it is not an accidental difference, since nothing in God is accidental, as Boethius says (*De Trin.*). And every substantial difference makes a division of a genus. Therefore God is contained in a genus.

3. Things may be the same either in genus, or in species, or in individual (*Topic.* i, 6). Therefore things may also differ in these ways, since if one of two opposites admits of multiplicity, the other does so too. Therefore God is distinct from a creature either in individual only, or in number and species, in which case he will be in the same genus as

the creature, and consequently will be contained in a genus : or he will differ from the creature in genus, and then he will be in another genus from the creature : because diversity results from numbers, so that difference of genus implies a number of genera. Therefore in any case God must be contained in a genus.

4. Anything to which the generic difference of substance applies belongs to the genus (of substance). Now the generic difference of substance is self-subsistence, which is most applicable to God. Therefore God is in the genus of substance.

5. Anything that can be defined must be in a genus. Now God can be defined, for he is said to be pure act. Therefore God is contained in a genus.

6. Whatsoever is predicated of another essentially and of other things besides, is compared to that thing either as its species or as its genus. Now all things predicated of God are predicated of him essentially, since all the predicaments when applied to God refer to his essence, as Boethius says (*De Trin.*). And it is clear that they are applicable not only to God but to other things besides. Therefore they are compared to God either as the species to the individual, or as the genus to its species, and in either case God must be contained in a genus.

7. A thing is measured by a measure of its own genus (*Metaph.* x). Now according to the Commentator (*ibid.*) God is the measure of all substances. Therefore God is in the same genus as other substances.

On the contrary whatsoever is contained in a genus contains something in addition to the genus, and therefore is composite. But God is utterly simple. Therefore he is not contained in a genus.

Moreover, whatsover is contained in a genus can be defined, or else comprised under something that is defined. But this cannot apply to God since he is infinite. Therefore he is not in a genus.

I answer that God is not contained in a genus, and for the nonce this may be proved by three arguments. The first argument is that nothing is assigned to a genus by reason of its *being* but by reason of its quiddity; and this is clear from the fact that the *being* of a thing is proper to that thing and distinct from the *being* of anything else: whereas the essence may be common. Hence the Philosopher (*Metaph.* ii, 3) says that *being* is not a genus. Now God is *Being* itself: wherefore he cannot be in a genus.

The second reason is that although matter is not a genus nor form a difference, nevertheless the notion of the genus is taken from the matter, and the notion of the difference from the form: for instance, in man the sensible nature whence he derives his animality is material in relation to his reason whence derives the difference of rationality. For an animal is that which has a sensitive nature, and a rational being is one that has reason. Hence in everything that is contained in a genus there must be composition of matter and form, or of act and potentiality: and this cannot be in God who is pure act as we have shown (A. 1). Therefore he cannot be in a genus. The third reason is that as God is simply perfect he contains the perfections of all genera: for this is what is meant by being simply perfect (*Metaph.* v). Now that which is contained in a genus is confined within the limits of that genus. Wherefore God cannot be in a genus: for in that case his essence would not be infinite nor absolutely perfect, but his essence and perfection would be confined within the limits of a definite genus.

Hence it is also evident that God is neither a species nor an individual, nor is there difference in him. Nor can he be defined, since every definition is taken from the genus and species. Wherefore neither can we demonstrate anything about him save from his effects, since the middle proposition of an *a priori* demonstration is a definition.

Reply to the First Objection. Damascene uses the word species metaphorically and not in the strict sense. God's name (i.e. God) is like a species in that it is predicated essentially of several distinct individuals: but it cannot be called a species strictly speaking, since a species is not identically the same in each individual but only logically: whereas the same identical divine essence is common to the three

Persons: wherefore Father, Son and Holy Ghost are one God, but Peter, Paul and Mark are not one man.

Reply to the Second Objection. A distinction is to be noted between difference and diversity according to the Philosopher (*Metaph.* x). Diversity is absolute and is applied to things which are not the same: whereas difference is relative, since that which is different differs in a certain respect. Accordingly if we take the term *different* strictly, it is not true that *things which are in no way different are the same:* but if we take the term *different* in a broad sense it is true: and in this sense we grant that God differs from other things. It does not follow, however, that he differs by reason of a difference, but that he differs from other things by reason of his essence: for this must needs be the case in first principles and simple things. Thus man differs from a donkey by the difference of rationality: but rationality is not distinguished from a donkey by a still further difference (since thus there would be no end to the process), for it differs therefrom by itself.

Reply to the Third Objection. God is said to be diverse in genus from the creature, not as though he were contained in another genus, but because he is altogether outside a genus.

Reply to the Fourth Objection. According to Avicenna (*Metaph.* iii, 8) substance is not rightly defined as a self-subsistent being: for *being* cannot be the genus of a thing according to the Philosopher (*Metaph.* ii, 3), because nothing can be added to being that has not a share of being, and a difference should not be a part of the genus. If, however, substance can be defined notwithstanding that it is the most universal of genera, its definition will be *a thing whose quiddity is competent to have being not in a subject.*[1] Hence the definition of substance cannot be applied to God, whose quiddity is not distinct from his being. Wherefore God is not contained in the genus of substance but is above all substance.

Reply to the Fifth Objection. God cannot be defined: because whatsoever is defined is comprehended by the intellect of him that defines it; and God is incomprehensible to

---

[1] Cf. *Sum. Th.* I, Q. iii, A. 5, *ad* 1 : III, Q. lxxvii, A. 1, *ad* 2.

the intellect. Hence it is not a definition of God when we say that he is pure act.

Reply to the Sixth Objection. It is essential to a genus that it be predicated univocally. Now nothing can be predicated univocally of God and the creature, as we shall prove further on (A. 7). Hence although things predicated of God are predicated of him substantially they are not predicated of him generically.

Reply to the Eighth Objection. Although God does not belong to the genus of substance as contained in a genus, as a species or an individual is contained in a genus : yet we may say that he is in the genus of substance by reduction as its principle, even as a point is in the genus of continuous quantity, and unity in the genus of number. In this way he is the measure of all substances, as unity is the measure of all numbers.

ARTICLE IV

DO ' GOOD,' ' WISE,' ' JUST ' AND THE LIKE PREDICATE AN ACCIDENT IN GOD ?

Sum. Th. I, Q. iii, A. 6 : xiii, 6

THE fourth point of inquiry is whether *good, wise, just* and the like predicate an accident in God : and it would appear that they do.

1. A predicate that signifies not the substance but something consequent upon the nature of a thing is an accidental predicate. Now Damascene (*De Fide Orthod.*) says that *good, just* and *holy* when said of God, are consequent to his nature and do not signify his essence. Therefore they predicate an accident in God.

2. But it was replied that Damascene is referring to the mode of signification of these terms.

On the contrary, a mode of signification that results from the generic nature must have a real foundation : since when the predicate of a proposition is a genus it denotes the substance of the subject, for it is an essential predication. Now the mode of signification of the terms in question is consequent upon the nature in respect of the genus : for they are in the genus of quality, which by its very nature bears a relation to the subject : for a quality is whereby we are disposed in this or that way (*quales*). Therefore this mode of signification must be based on a reality ; in other words the things signified by these words are consequent upon the nature of the thing of which they are predicated and therefore accidents.

3. But it will be said that these terms are not predicated of God in reference to their genus, which is quality ; because the expressions we apply to God are not to be taken in their strict sense.

On the contrary, the species is falsely predicated of that which is not included in the genus : thus if a thing is not an animal it is untrue to say that it is a man. If then the genus of the aforesaid, which is quality, is not predicated of God, these terms will be not only improperly but also falsely predicated of God : and consequently it will be untrue to say that God is just or holy : and this cannot be admitted. Therefore we must conclude that these terms are predicated of God accidentally.

4. According to the Philosopher (*Phys.* i, 2) that which really has being, namely substance, is never an accident : wherefore in like manner a *per se* accident is always an accident. Now justice, wisdom and the like are *per se* accidents. Therefore in God also they are accidents.

5. Whatsoever we find in created things is copied from God who is the exemplary form of all things. Now wisdom, justice and so on are accidents in creatures. Therefore they are accidents in God.

6. Wherever there is quantity and quality there is accident. Now in God, seemingly, there is quantity and quality : because in him there is likeness and equality : thus we say that the Son is like and equal to the Father : and likeness is oneness in quality, and equality is oneness in quantity. Therefore there are accidents in God.

7. A thing is measured by the first of its genus. Now God is the measure not only of substances but also of all accidents, since he is the creator of both substance and accident. Therefore in God there is not only substance but also accidents.

8. If A can be understood apart from B, B is accidental to A. Thus Porphyry (*Praedic.* cap. *de accidente*) proves that things which are separable are accidents, since we can conceive a white crow, and a white Ethiopian. Now it is possible to conceive God apart from goodness, according to Boethius (*De Hebd.*).[1] Therefore goodness denotes an accident in God, and for the same reason the others.

9. Two things should be considered in the meaning of a name, namely that from which it is taken and the thing to which it is given : and in both respects this term ' wisdom ' would appear to denote an accident. For it is taken from the fact that it makes a man wise, which seemingly is the act of wisdom ; while the thing to which it is given is a quality. Therefore in every respect this and similar terms signify an accident in the subject of which they are predicated : and therefore it is an accident in God.

On the contrary, Boethius says (*De Trin.*) that God, inasmuch as he is a simple form, cannot be a subject. Now every accident is in a subject. Therefore there can be no accident in God.

Moreover every accident is dependent on something else. But no such thing can be in God, since that which is dependent must have a cause : and God is the first cause and has no cause whatsoever. Therefore no accidents can be in God.

Again, Rabbi Moses says that in God suchlike terms do not signify tendencies in addition to his substance. Now every accident denotes a tendency in addition to the substance of its subject. Therefore these terms do not denote accidents in God.

Again, an accident is something that can be present or absent without the destruction of its subject. But this is impossible in God, since he is unchangeable, as proved by the Philosopher (*Phys.* viii, 5). Therefore accidents cannot be in God.

I answer that without any doubt whatever we must hold that there are no accidents in God. For our present purpose it will suffice to prove this by three arguments.

The first argument is that no nature, essence or form can

---

[1] Alias, *An omne quod est sit bonum.*

receive the addition of something extraneous : although that which has a nature, form or essence can receive something extraneous thereto, thus humanity contains nothing but what belongs intrinsically to humanity. This is clear from the fact that if anything be added to or subtracted from definitions which indicate the essence of a thing, the species is changed, as is the case with numbers, as the Philosopher observes (*Metaph.* viii). Man, however, who has humanity, can have something else which is not contained in the notion of humanity, such as whiteness and the like which are not humanity but in the man. Now in every creature there is a distinction between the one who has a thing and the thing which he has. In composite creatures there is a twofold difference ; since the supposit or individual has the nature of its species —thus a man has humanity—and also has being : for a man is neither humanity nor is he his own being. Wherefore a man can have an accident, but his humanity or his being cannot. In simple substances there is only one difference, that namely between essence and existence. Thus in the angels every supposit is his own nature, since the quiddity of a simple being is the simple being itself according to Avicenna (*Metaph.* v), but it is not its own being, so that the quiddity subsists in its own being. In these substances therefore there can be an intelligible but not a material accident. On the other hand in God there is no distinction between haver and the thing had, or between participator and the thing participated : indeed he is both his own nature and his own being, wherefore nothing in him can be adventitious or accidental. This argument is apparently indicated by Boethius (*De Hebd.*)[1] when he says : *That which has being can have something in addition to its being : but that which is being, has nothing besides itself.*

The second reason is that since an accident is extraneous to the essence of its subject, and things that are diverse are not united together save by some cause, it follows, if any accident accrue to God, that this is due to some cause. It cannot, however, be due to some extrinsic cause, since it would follow that this extrinsic cause acts on God, and is previous to him,

[1] *Ibid.*

even as the mover precedes that which is moved and the maker that which is made : for an accident is produced in a subject by an extrinsic cause acting on the subject in which the accident is produced. Again it cannot be due to an intrinsic cause as happens with *per se* accidents whose cause is in their subject. For a subject cannot both cause and receive an accident on the same count, since no power moves itself into action : wherefore it must receive the accident on one count, and cause it on another, and thus it will be composite : thus certain things receive an accident on account of their matter, and cause it on account of the nature of their form. Now we have shown (A. 1) that God is not composite. Therefore no accident can possibly be in him.

The third argument is that accident is compared to subject as act to potentiality, since it is a kind of form thereof. Wherefore since God is pure act without any admixture of potentiality, he cannot be the subject of an accident.

Accordingly from the foregoing we conclude that in God there is not composition of matter and form or of any essential parts, nor of genus and difference, nor of subject and accidents : and that the aforesaid terms do not predicate an accident in God.

Reply to the First Objection. Damascene is speaking of these names not as to what they predicate of God, but as to the reason why we predicate them of him. For we take these terms on account of their signification from certain accidental forms that we observe in creatures. In fact from this it is his intention to show that the expressions employed by us in speaking of God do not signify his essence.

Reply to the Second Objection. Although quality is the genus of human goodness, wisdom and justice, it is not their genus if we take them as predicated of God, because quality as such is a being forasmuch as it qualifies the subject in which it is. But wisdom and justice are denominated not from this but rather from a certain perfection or act : wherefore such things are predicated of God by reason of their difference and not of their genus. Hence Augustine says (*De Trin.* v, 1): *As far as we can, let us conceive goodness that is not a quality, and greatness that is not a quantity-* Wherefore we cannot conclude that such things are consequent to God's nature.

Reply to the Third Objection. If good and just were predicated of God univocally, it would indeed follow that their predication is false if we do not predicate their genus of him: but as we shall show further on (A. 7) nothing is predicated univocally of God and the creature.

Reply to the Fourth Objection. The wisdom that is an accident is not in God: his is another wisdom not univocally so called: hence the argument does not prove.

Reply to the Fifth Objection. The exemplate is not always a perfect reproduction of the exemplar; so that sometimes the exemplate reproduces defectively and imperfectly that which is in the exemplar: especially is this the case in exemplates that are taken from God who is an exemplar surpassing all proportion of the creature.

Reply to the Sixth Objection. Likeness and equality are ascribed to God not as though there were quality and quantity in him, but because we ascribe to him certain things which imply quality and quantity in us: for instance, when we say that God is great, wise, and so forth.

Reply to the Seventh Objection. Accidents are not beings save in relation to substance as the first being: wherefore we infer that accidents are measured by some first thing that is not an accident, but a substance.

Reply to the Eighth Objection. If we understand a thing in its essence then it is true that anything which does not enter into that consideration is accidental: since given that we understand it in its essence, we must needs understand whatsoever pertains to its essence; thus if we understand what a man is, we must needs understand what is an animal. Here, however, we do not see God in his essence, but consider him in his effects. Wherefore nothing prevents us from considering him in his effect that is *being*, without considering him in his effect that is *goodness;* and this is what Boethius intends to say. Yet it must be observed that although we may understand God somewhat without understanding his goodness; we cannot understand God and understand that he is not good—thus we cannot understand man and understand that he is not an animal—for this would be to deny God's essence which is goodness. On the other hand the saints in heaven who see God in his essence, by seeing God see his goodness.

Reply to the Ninth Objection. The term *wisdom* in its application to God is true as regards that from which it is taken. It is not taken, however, from the fact that it makes a man wise, but from its being a habit perfecting the intellect. For knowledge as such is referred to the thing known, whereas as an accident it is referred to the knower: and the possession of wisdom is accidental to man but not to God.

ARTICLE V

DO THESE TERMS SIGNIFY THE DIVINE ESSENCE?
Sum. Th. I, Q. xiii, A. 12

THE fifth point of inquiry is whether these terms signify the divine essence: and seemingly they do not.

1. Damascene says (*De Fide Orthod.* i, 4): *We must not think that the terms we employ in speaking of God denote what he is in his substance: rather do they indicate what he is not, or some kind of relationship, or something to be excluded from him, or else such things as are consequent to his nature or action.* Now the *being* that is predicated of a thing substantially denotes what that thing's substance is. Therefore these terms are not predicated of God substantially as indicating his essence.

2. No term that signifies the essence of a thing can truly be denied of that thing. For Dionysius says (*Cœl. Hier.* ii) that *negations about God are true, but affirmations are vague.* Therefore these terms do not signify God's essence.

3. According to Dionysius (*Div. Nom.* iii) these expressions signify the outpouring of divine goodness into things. But God does not pour out his substance on things. Therefore such expressions do not signify the divine essence.

4. Origen says that God is called wise because he fills us with wisdom. Now this denotes not the divine essence but

a divine effect. Therefore these terms do not signify the divine essence.

5. The first cause is denominated only from its first effect (*De Causis*, prop. xvi) which is the intelligence. Now when a cause is denominated from its effect, the predication connotes not the essence but the cause. Therefore expressions that are ascribed to God do not predicate his essence but his causality.

6. Words signify the concepts of the intellect, as the Philosopher says (*Peri Herm.* i). Now we are unable to understand the divine essence; since as Damascene says (*De Fide Orth.* i, 4) we know not what he is but that he is. Therefore we cannot give him a name nor employ words to express his essence.

7. According to Dionysius (*Div. Nom.* iv) all things participate of the divine goodness. But all do not participate of the divine essence which is only in the three Persons. Therefore God's goodness does not denote his essence.

8. We cannot know God except from his likeness in creatures: thus the Apostle says (Rom. i, 20) that *the invisible things of God from the creation of the world are clearly seen being understood by the things that are made*. Now we name him according as we know him. Therefore we do not name him except from his likeness in creatures. But when we name a thing from its likeness to another, such a name is predicated of it not essentially but metaphorically: inasmuch as it is said secondly of God and first of the thing whence the simile is taken: whereas that which signifies the essence of a thing is said of that thing first.

9. According to the Philosopher (*Metaph.* viii) that which signifies the essence, denotes that and nothing else. Wherefore if this word *good* signifies the divine essence, there will be nothing in the divine essence that is not signified thereby: even so there is nothing in the essence of man that is not signified by this word *man*. But this word *good* does not signify *wisdom*: so that wisdom will not be the divine essence, and for the same reason neither will the other terms. Therefore all these words cannot possibly signify the divine essence.

10. As quantity is the cause of equality, and quality the cause of likeness, so is essence the cause of identity. If then all these expressions signify God's essence, they would no longer indicate equality or likeness but rather identity between God and us : so that a creature might be identified with God from the fact that it imitates his wisdom, goodness and so forth : and this is absurd.

11. Nothing can be contrary to nature in God who is the source of all nature : nor does he anything contrary to nature according to the (ordinary) gloss on Romans xi, 24 : *Contrary to nature thou wert grafted.* Now it is contrary to nature that an accident be substance. Since then wisdom, justice and the like are *per se* accidents, they cannot be substance in God.

12. When we say that God is good, *good* is a complex term. But there would be no complexity if God's goodness were his very substance. Therefore seemingly *good* does not denote God's substance ; and the same reason applies to all similar expressions.

13. Augustine says that God eludes every conception of our intelligence, so that it cannot grasp him. But this would not be so if these terms signified the divine essence, since God would correspond to a conception of our intellect. Therefore they do not signify the divine essence.

14. Dionysius says (*Myst. Theol.* i) that man is best united to God by realising that in knowing God he knows nothing about him. But this would not be so if these ideas and expressions of man's reflected God's very essence. Therefore the same conclusion follows as before.

On the contrary, Augustine says (*De Trin.* vii, 7) : *In God to be is to be mighty, or wise ; such is his simplicity that whatsoever you may say of him is his essence.*

Again, Boethius says (*De Trin.*) that under whatsoever predicament, except relation, we predicate things of God they all refer to his essence : thus although *just* apparently indicates a quality, it signifies his essence : the same applies to *great* and so forth.

Again all things that are ascribed to another by way of participation presuppose one to whom they are ascribed *per se* and essentially. Now these expressions are applied to creatures by way of participation. Since then they are reduced to God as their first cause, it follows that they are said of God essentially, and thus it follows that they signify his essence.

I answer that some have maintained, and Rabbi Moses most emphatically, that these terms when predicated of God do not signify the divine essence. He says in effect that these expressions are to be taken in reference to God in two ways. First, as indicating a likeness of effect: and that God is said to be *wise*, not that wisdom is something in him, but because in his effects he acts like a wise man, namely by directing each one to its due end; again that he is said to be a *living* God inasmuch as he acts like a living being, in that he acts of himself. Secondly, by way of negation: so that when we say God lives we do not mean that life is something in him, but that God has not that mode of existence which is in things inanimate. Likewise when we say that God is an intelligent being, we do not mean that intelligence is really in him, but that he has not that mode of existence whereby dumb animals exist: and so on. In either case, however, this explanation is apparently insufficient and objectionable. The first, for two reasons. First, because according to this explanation there would be no difference in saying *God is wise*, or *God is angry* or *God is a fire:* since he is said to be angry because he acts like an angry man by punishing; for angry men are wont to act thus. Also he is said to be a fire, because he acts like fire when he cleanses, and fire does this in its own way. Now this is contrary to the view taken by the saints and prophets in speaking of God: since certain things they affirm of him and deny others: for they assert that he is living, wise and the like, and deny that he is a body or subject to passions. But in the opinion we are discussing anything may be said or denied of God with equal reason. The second reason is that since, as our faith teaches and as he also grants, creatures have not always existed, it follows that we could not say that God was wise or good before the existence of creatures. For it is evident that before creatures existed he did nothing as regards his effects, neither as good nor as wise. Now this is altogether contrary to sound faith : unless perhaps he meant to say that before the existence of creatures God would be called wise, not that he worked as being wise, but because he could do so : and then it would follow that wisdom denotes something in God and consequently is his essence, since whatsoever is in God is his essence. The second explanation appears likewise to be unsatisfactory : because there is not a specific term that does not exclude from God some mode of being that is unbecoming to him. For every specific term includes the difference whereby the opposite species is excluded : thus the term *lion* includes the difference *quadruped* which differentiates a lion from a bird. Accordingly if predicates about God were employed merely for the purpose of exclusion, just as we say that God is *living* because, according to him (Rabbi Moses), God has not being in the same way as inanimate creatures : even so might we say that God is a lion because he has not the mode of being of a bird. Moreover the idea of negation is always based on an affirmation : as evinced by the fact that every negative proposition is proved by an affirmative : wherefore unless the human mind knew something positively about God, it would be unable to deny anything about him. And it would know nothing if nothing that it affirmed about God were positively verified about him. Hence following Dionysius (*Div. Nom.* xiii) we must hold that these terms signify the divine essence, albeit defectively and imperfectly : the proof of which is as follows.

Since every agent acts inasmuch as it is actual and consequently produces its like, the form of the thing produced must in some manner be in the agent : in different ways, however. When the effect is proportionate to the power of the agent, this form must be of the same kind in the maker and the thing made : for then maker and thing made are of the same species, and this is the case in all univocal causes : thus man begets a man, and fire generates fire. When, however, the effect is improportionate to the power of the cause, the form is not of the same kind in both maker and thing made, but is in the agent in a more eminent way. Because according as the form is in the agent, the latter has the power to produce the effect: so that if the whole power of the agent is not reflected in the thing made, it follows that the form is in the maker in a more eminent way than in the thing made. This is the case in all equivocal agents, for instance when the sun generates fire. Now it is plain that no effect equals the power of the first agent which is God, else only one effect would proceed from his one power. But seeing that from his one power many and various effects proceed, it is evident that every effect of his falls short of the power of its cause. Consequently no form of a divine effect is in the effect in the same degree as in God: and yet they must needs be in him in a more eminent way. Wherefore all forms which in the various effects are distinct and different from one another are united in him as in one common power: even so all the forms produced by the power of the sun in this lower world are in the sun in respect of its one power, to which all things generated by the sun's action are assimilated as regards their forms. In like manner the perfections of creatures are assimilated to God in respect of his one simple essence. Since then our intellect takes its knowledge from creatures, it is informed with the likenesses of perfections observed in creatures, namely of wisdom, power, goodness and so forth. Wherefore just as creatures by their perfections are somewhat, albeit deficiently, like God, even so our intellect is informed with the species of these perfections. Now whenever an intellect is by its intelligible form assimilated to a thing, that which it conceives and affirms in accordance with that intelligible species is true of that thing to which it is assimilated by its species: inasmuch as knowledge is assimilation of the mind to the thing known. Hence it follows that whatsoever the intellect informed with the species of these perfections conceives or asserts about God, truly exists in God who corresponds to each one of these species inasmuch as they are all like him. Now if such an intelligible species of our intellect were equal to God in its likeness to him, our intellect would comprehend him, and the intellect's conception would be a perfect definition of God, just as a walking animal biped is a perfect definition of a man. However, this species does not perfectly reflect the divine essence, as stated above, and therefore although these terms which our intellect attributes to God from such conceptions signify the divine essence, they do not signify it perfectly as it exists in itself, but as it is conceived by us.

Accordingly we conclude that each of these terms signifies the divine essence, not comprehensively but imperfectly. Wherefore this name *He Who Is* is most becoming to God, since it does not ascribe any particular form to God, but signifies *being* without any limitation. This is the meaning of Damascene (*De Fide Orthod.* i, 12) when he says that the name *He Who Is* denotes *a boundless sea of substance*. This solution of the question is confirmed by the words of Dionysius (*Div. Nom.* i) : *Since all things are comprised in the Godhead simply and without limit, it is fitting that he should be praised and named on account of them all*. *Simply*—because the perfections which are in creatures by reason of various forms are ascribed to God in reference to his simple essence : *without limit*, because no perfection found in creatures is equal to the divine essence, so as to enable the mind under the head of that perfection to define God as he is in himself. A further confirmation may be found in *Metaph.* v, where it is stated that the simply perfect is that which contains the perfections of all genera : which words the Commentator expounds as referring to God.

Reply to the First Objection. Damascene means to say that these expressions do not signify what God is by defining and including his essence as it were : wherefore he goes on to say that this name *He Who Is* which denotes God's essence indefinitely is most becomingly ascribed to God.

Reply to the Second Objection. Although Dionysius says that there is truth in denying these expressions of God he does not say that there is untruth in affirming them, but that their signification is vague : because as regards the thing signified they are truly ascribed to God, since in a way it is in him, as we have shown. But as regards their mode of signification they can be denied of God, since each of these terms denotes a definite form, and in this way they are not ascribed to God as we have already stated. Wherefore absolutely speaking they can be denied of God, because they are not becoming to him in the way signified: since this mode is according to the way in which they are in our intellect, as already stated, whereas they are becoming to God in a more eminent way. For this reason the affirmation of them is described as vague as being not altogether fitting on account of the difference of mode. Hence, according to the teaching of Dionysius (*Myst. Theol.* i; *Cœl. Hier.* ii; *Div. Nom.* ii, iii), these terms are applied to God in three ways. First, affirmatively: for instance, *God is wise:* since we must needs say this of God because in him there is a likeness to the wisdom that derives from him.—Nevertheless seeing that wisdom in God is not such as that which we understand and name, it can be truly denied, so that we may say: *God is not wise.*—Again, since wisdom is not denied of God as though he were lacking in wisdom, but because in him it transcends the wisdom we indicate and name, we ought to say that *God is super-wise.* Accordingly Dionysius explains perfectly by these three ways of ascribing wisdom to God, how these expressions are to be applied to God.

Reply to the Third Objection. These expressions are said to denote the divine outpourings, because they are first employed to signify these outpourings as existing in creatures, while from the likeness thereof to God the human mind is led to ascribe the same expressions to God in a higher degree.

Reply to the Fourth Objection. The saying of Origen does not mean that when we say *God is wise*, the sense is that God is the cause of wisdom; but that as we have explained from the wisdom which he causes our intellect is led to ascribe supereminent wisdom to God.

Reply to the Fifth Objection. When we say that God is intelligence, we name him after his effect. But a name that signifies the essence of his effect cannot be applied to him definitively in the same way as it signifies that essence. Wherefore this name, although it is applicable to him in a way, is not applicable as his name: since that which a name signifies is the definition. On the other hand it is applicable to the effect as its name.

Reply to the Sixth Objection. This argument proves that we cannot give God a name that defines or includes or equals his essence : since we do not know to that extent what God is.

Reply to the Seventh Objection. Just as all things participate in God's goodness not in identity but in likeness thereto : so also do they participate in a likeness of God's being. But there is a difference : for goodness implies the relationship of cause, since good is self-diffusive : whereas being connotes mere existence and quiescence.

Reply to the Eighth Objection. An effect includes something whereby it is like its cause, and something whereby it differs therefrom : and this by reason of its matter or something of the kind. Take for example a brick hardened by fire : the clay is heated by the fire and thus becomes like the fire : then it is condensed and hardened, and this is due to the nature of the material. Accordingly if we ascribe to the fire that wherein the brick is likened to it, it will be ascribed to it properly in a more eminent degree and with priority : because fire is hotter than the brick : and it is hot in a more eminent way, since the brick is hot by being made hot, while the fire is hot by nature. On the other hand if we ascribe to the fire that wherein the brick differs from the fire, it will be untrue, and any term that signifies this condition of dissimilarity cannot be said of fire unless metaphorically. Thus it is false to say that fire, the most subtle of bodies, is dense. It can, however, be described as hard on account of the violence of its action, and the difficulty to quench it. Accordingly in creatures there are certain perfections whereby they are likened to God, and which as regards the thing signified do not denote any imperfection, such as being, life, understanding and so forth : and these are ascribed to God properly, in fact they are ascribed to him first and in a more eminent way than to creatures. And there are in creatures certain perfections wherein they differ from God, and which the creature owes to its being made from nothing, such as potentiality, privation, movement and the like. These are falsely ascribed to God : and whatsoever terms imply suchlike conditions cannot be ascribed to God otherwise than metaphorically, for instance lion, stone and so on, inasmuch as matter is included in their definition. They are, however, ascribed to him metaphorically by reason of a likeness in their effects.

Reply to the Ninth Objection. This argument considers that which signifies substance definitively and comprehensively: but none of these expressions denote the divine essence thus, as stated above.

Reply to the Tenth Objection. Although these perfections in God are his very substance, they are not the very substance of the creature, wherefore in their respect the creature is not said to be the same as God but like him.

Reply to the Eleventh Objection. It would be contrary to nature if wisdom in God were of the same kind as that which is an accident: but this is not the case as we have already stated. Nor is the authority quoted to the point: for God makes nothing against nature in himself, because he makes nothing in himself.

Reply to the Twelfth Objection. When we say *God is good*, this term *good* is complex not as reflecting any composition in God, but on account of the composition in our intellect.

Reply to the Thirteenth Objection. God eludes the conception of our intellect because he transcends all that our mind conceives of him; but not so that our intellect is in no intelligible way likened to him.

Reply to the Fourteenth Objection. It is because human intelligence is not equal to the divine essence that this same divine essence surpasses our intelligence and is unknown to us: wherefore man reaches the highest point of his knowledge about God when he knows that he knows him not, inasmuch as he knows that that which is God transcends whatsoever he conceives of him.

ARTICLE VI

ARE THESE TERMS SYNONYMOUS?
Sum. Th. I, Q. xiii, A. 4: *C.G.* I, 35

THE sixth point of inquiry is whether these terms are synonymous: and apparently they are.

1. Synonyms are terms that have exactly the same meaning. Now all these terms when applied to God signify the same thing: for they denote the divine essence, which is altogether simple and one, as we have proved. Therefore these terms are all synonymous.

2. Damascene says (*De Fide Orth.* i. 11) that in God all things are one except ingenerability, generation and procession. Now terms that signify the same are synonymous. Therefore all the terms applied to God, except those that signify personal properties are synonyms.

3. Things that are identical with one and the same thing are identical with one another. Now in God wisdom is identical with his substance, and so also are his will and his power. Wherefore in God wisdom, power and will are absolutely the same thing: and thus these terms are synonymous.

4. It will be replied that these terms signify one thing indeed, but from different points of view, and therefore are not synonyms.—On the contrary a point of view that has no objective reality is untrue and futile: so that if there are many such points of view, while the thing itself is only one, it would seem that these points of view are futile and false.

5. But someone will reply that these points of view are not futile, since something in God corresponds to them.—On the contrary creatures are likened to God inasmuch as they were made by him in likeness to his idea. Now plurality of ideas or points of view does not connote a plurality of relations in God to the creature: since by his essence he is the idea of all things. Neither then does anything in the divine essence correspond to the points of view from which we describe God from his likeness to his creatures.

6. That which is supremely one cannot be the root and foundation of multitude. Now the divine essence is supremely one. Therefore it cannot be the root and foundation of the different points of view of these expressions.

7. Difference of relations that are really in God, causes a distinction of Persons. If then something in God corresponds to the mutual relations of the attributes there would

be a number of persons corresponding to the number of attributes: and thus there would be more than three persons in God which is heretical. Wherefore seemingly these expressions are altogether synonymous.

On the contrary it is futile to put words together that are synonymous, for instance, ' clothes and garments.' If then these words are synonymous it will be futile to say *God is good, God is wise:* but this is not so.

Again, to deny one synonym about anything is to deny the others. Yet some have denied God's power without denying his knowledge or goodness. Therefore these words are not synonymous.

Again, this is proved from the Commentator who says (*Metaph.* xi) that these expressions when applied to God are not synonymous.

I answer that all those who have considered the question are agreed in saying that these terms are not synonymous. This view offers no difficulty to those who held that these expressions signify not God's essence, but certain notions added to his essence, or modes of the divine action in its effects, or the denial of what they signify in creatures. But given that they signify the divine essence, as we have proved (A. 5), the question would seem to present considerable difficulty: since then we have all these terms with one simple signification, namely the divine essence. But it must be observed that the signification of a term does not refer to the thing immediately but through the medium of the mind: because words are the tokens of the soul's impressions, and the conceptions of the mind are images of things, according to the Philosopher (*Peri Herm.* i).

Now terms may be hindered from being synonymous either by reason of the things signified, or on the part of the notion conveyed by the term and to signify which the term is employed. Wherefore the terms which are applied to God cannot be hindered from being synonymous by reason of their signifying different things, according to what has been said above, but only by the various aspects consequent to the conception of the mind. Hence the Commentator (*Metaph.* xi) says that multiplicity in God is only according to differences in the intellect and not in being, and we express the same when we say that he is one in reality and many things logically. Now these various aspects which are in our mind cannot be such that nothing corresponds to them on the part of the thing: since the things which these aspects regard are ascribed to God by the mind. Wherefore if there were nothing in God, either in himself or in his effect, corresponding to these points of view, the intellect would be in error in attributing them to him, and all propositions expressive of such attributions would be false ; which is inadmissible. Now there are certain aspects to which nothing corresponds in the thing understood : but the things thus conceived the mind does not attribute to things as they are in themselves, but only as they are understood : for example, the aspect of genus or species and other intellectual 'intentions'; since in the things themselves that are outside the mind there is nothing that is a likeness of the notion of genus or species. And yet the intellect is not in error: for the things reflected by these notions, namely genus and species, are not attributed by the intellect to things as existing outside the mind but only as existing therein. Because just as the intellect understands things existing outside the mind, so does it, by reflecting on itself, understand that it understands them : wherefore just as the intellect has a conception or notion to which the thing as existing outside the mind corresponds, so has it a conception or notion to which the thing corresponds as understood : for instance, to the notion or conception of a man there corresponds the thing outside the mind, while nothing but the thing as understood corresponds to the notion or conception of the genus or species. But it is impossible that such be the meaning of these expressions that are applied to God : for in that case the intellect would not attribute them to him as he is in himself but as he is understood : and this is plainly false ; for when we say *God is good*, the sense would be that we think him to be so, but that he is not so in reality.

Accordingly some hold that the meanings of these terms connote various corresponding divine effects : for they maintain that when we say *God is good*, we indicate God's essence together with a connoted effect, the sense being *God is and causes goodness*, so that the difference in these attributions arises from the difference in his effects. But this does not seem right : because seeing that an effect proceeds in likeness to its cause, we must needs understand a cause to be such before its effects are such. Wherefore God is not called wise because he is the cause of wisdom : but because he is wise, therefore does he cause wisdom. Hence Augustine says (*De Doct. Christ.* ii, 32) that *because God is good, therefore we exist, and inasmuch as we exist we are good.* Moreover according to this view it would follow that these expressions are attributed to the creature before the Creator : just as health is attributed first to a healthy man and afterwards to that which gives health, since the latter is called healthy through being a cause of health.—Again if when we say *God is good* we mean nothing more than *God is and is the cause of goodness*, it would follow that we could equally predicate of him the names of all the divine effects, for instance, that *God is heaven* since he is the cause of heaven. —Again this is clearly false if it refer to actual causality : because then we could not say that God was good, wise or the like from eternity, for he did not cause things actually from eternity. If on the other hand it refer to virtual causality, so that God be called good because he is and has the power to infuse goodness ; then we shall have to say that the term *good* signifies that power. Now that power is a supereminent likeness of its effect even as the power of any equivocal agent. Thus it would follow that the intellect in conceiving goodness is like that which is in God and is God : so that something that is in God and that is God corresponds to the notion or conception of goodness.

We must say then that all these many and diverse notions correspond to something in God of which they are likenesses. For it is plain that one form can have but one specific likeness proportionate to it : while there can be many imperfect likenesses, each one of which falls short of a perfect representation of the form. Since then, as we have proved above, the ideas we conceive of the perfections we observe in creatures are imperfect and improportionate likenesses of the divine essence, nothing prevents the same one essence from corresponding to all these ideas, as being imperfectly represented thereby. So that all these conceptions are in the mind as their subject, but in God as the foundation of their truth. For the idea that the intellect has of a thing is not true unless that thing corresponds to the idea by its likeness to it. Accordingly the cause of difference or multiplicity in these expressions is on the part of the intellect, which is unable to compass the vision of that divine essence in itself, but sees it through many faulty likenesses thereof which are reflected by creatures as by a mirror. Whereof if it saw that very essence, it would not need to use many terms, nor would it need many conceptions.

For this reason God's Word, which is his perfect concept, is but one: wherefore it is written (Zach. xiv, 9): *In that day there shall be one Lord, and his name will be one*—when God's very essence will be seen, and knowledge of God will not be gathered from creatures.

Reply to the First Objection. These terms signify one thing indeed, but under different aspects, as stated above: hence they are not synonyms

Reply to the Second Objection. Damascene means that in God all things are one in reality except the personal properties which constitute a real distinction of Persons: but he does not deny a logical difference in the terms that are attributed to God.

The Reply to the Third Objection is clear from what has just been said: because as wisdom and goodness are in reality the same as the divine essence, so are they identical with each other: and yet they differ logically, as stated.

Reply to the Fourth Objection. It has already been explained that though God is absolutely one, yet these many concepts or notions are not false, because to all of them one and the same thing corresponds albeit imperfectly represented by them: but they would be false if nothing corresponded to them.

Reply to the Fifth Objection. Since in God there is absolute unity, and multiplicity in creatures, just as God understands many creatures by one intelligible species which is his essence, while there is a manifold relationship of God to creatures : even so in our intellect which mounts up to God from the multiplicity of creatures, there must be many species having relations to one God.

Reply to the Sixth Objection. These different aspects are founded on the divine essence not as their subject but as on the source of truth, or as on that which is represented by all of them : and this is not in conflict with God's simplicity.

Reply to the Seventh Objection. Paternity and Sonship are mutually opposed : so that they require a real distinction of supposits : whereas goodness and wisdom are not opposite to each other.

ARTICLE VII

ARE THESE TERMS ASCRIBED UNIVOCALLY OR EQUIVOCALLY TO GOD AND THE CREATURE ?

Sum. Th. I, Q. xiii, A. 5 : *C.G.* I, xxxii *seqq.*

THE seventh point of inquiry is whether these terms are attributed to God and creatures univocally or equivocally.

1. Measure and the thing measured must be in the same genus. Now God's goodness is the measure of all created goodness, and the same applies to his wisdom. Therefore they are said of creatures univocally.

2. Things are like which have a common form. Now the creature can be likened to God, according to Genesis i, 26, *Let us make man to our own image and likeness.* Therefore there is a community of form between God and the creature. Now something can be predicated univocally of things that have a common form. Therefore something can be predicated univocally of God and the creature.

3. More or less makes no difference in the species. Now whereas God is called good and the creature also is called good, the difference seems to be that God is better than the creature. Therefore goodness in God and the creature is of the same species and consequently is predicated univocally of both.

4. There is no comparison possible between things of different genera, as the Philosopher proves (*Phys.* vii), thus we cannot compare the speed of alteration with the speed of local movement. But we compare God to the creature: thus we say that God is supremely good, and that the creature is good. Therefore God and the creature are in the same genus and consequently something can be predicated of them univocally.

5. Nothing can be known except through a homogeneous species: thus whiteness in a wall would not be known by its image in the eye unless the two were homogeneous. Now God by his goodness knows all beings, and so forth. Therefore God's goodness and the creature's are homogeneous: and consequently good is predicated univocally of God and the creature.

6. The house that the builder has in his mind and the material house are homogeneous. Now all creatures came from God as a work proceeds from the craftsman. Therefore goodness that is in God is homogeneous with the goodness that is in the creature: wherefore we come to the same conclusion as before.

7. Every equivocal agent is reduced to something univocal. Therefore the first agent which is God must be univocal. Now something is predicated univocally of a univocal agent and its proper effect. Therefore something is predicated univocally of God and the creature.

1. *On the contrary* the Philosopher says (*Metaph.* x, 7) that nothing except in name is common to the eternal and the temporal. Now God is eternal and creatures temporal. Therefore nothing but a name can be common to God and creatures: and consequently these terms are predicated equivocally of God and the creature.

2. Since the genus is the first part of a definition, a difference of genus causes equivocation: so that if a term be employed to signify something in different genera it will be equivocal. Now wisdom as attributed to a creature is in the genus of quality: wherefore seeing that it is not a quality in God, as we have shown, it would seem that this word *wisdom* is predicated equivocally of God and his creatures.

3. Nothing can be predicated except equivocally of things that are in no way alike. Now there is no likeness between creatures and God: for it is written (Isa. xl, 18): *To whom then have you likened God?* Therefore seemingly nothing can be predicated univocally of God and creatures.

4. But it will be replied that although God cannot be said to be like a creature, a creature can be said to be like God.

On the contrary, it is written (Ps. lxxxii, 2): *O God, who shall be like to thee?* as if to say: *None.*

5. A thing cannot be like a substance in respect of an accident. Now wisdom in a creature is an accident, and in God is the substance. Therefore man cannot be like God by his wisdom.

6. Since in a creature being is distinct from form or nature, nothing can be like being itself by its form or nature. Now these terms when predicated of a creature signify a form or nature: while God is his own very being. Therefore a creature cannot be like God by these things that are predicated of a creature: and thus the same conclusion follows as before.

7. God differs more from a creature than number from whiteness. But it is absurd to liken a number to whiteness or vice versa. Therefore still more absurd is it to liken a creature to God: and again the same conclusion follows.

8. Things that are like have some one thing in common: and things that have one thing in common have a common predicate. But nothing whatever can be predicated in common with God. Therefore there can be no likeness between God and the creature.

I answer that it is impossible for anything to be predicated univocally of God and a creature: this is made plain as follows. Every effect of an univocal agent is adequate to the agent's power: and no creature, being finite, can be adequate to the power of the first agent which is infinite. Wherefore it is impossible for a creature to receive a likeness to God univocally. Again it is clear that although the form in the agent and the form in the effect have a common ratio, the fact that they have different modes of existence precludes their univocal predication: thus though the material house is of the same type as the house in the mind of the builder, since the one is the type of the other; nevertheless *house* cannot be univocally predicated of both, because the form of the material house has its being in matter, whereas in the builder's mind it has immaterial being. Hence granted the impossibility that goodness in God and in the creature be of the same kind, nevertheless *good* would not be predicated of God univocally: since that which in God is immaterial and simple, is in the creature material and manifold. Moreover being is not predicated univocally of substance and accident, because substance is a being as subsisting in itself, while accident is that whose being is to be in something else. Wherefore it is evident that a different relation to being precludes an univocal predication of being. Now God's relation to being is different from that of any creature's: for he is his own being, which cannot be said of any creature. Hence in no way can it be predicated univocally of God and a creature, and consequently neither can any of the other predicables among which is included even the first, *being*: for if there be diversity in the first, there must be diversity in the others: wherefore nothing is predicated univocally of substance and accident.

Others, however, took a different view, and held that nothing is predicated of God and a creature by analogy but by pure equivocation. This is the opinion of Rabbi Moses, as appears from his writings. This opinion, however, is false, because in all purely equivocal terms which the Philosopher calls equivocal *by chance*, a term is predicated of a thing without any respect to something else: whereas all things predicated of God and creatures are predicated of God with a certain respect to creatures or vice versa, and this is clearly admitted in all the aforesaid explanations of the divine names. Wherefore they cannot be pure equivocations. Again, since all our knowledge of God is taken from creatures, if the agreement were purely nominal, we should know nothing about God except empty expressions to which nothing corresponds in reality. Moreover, it would follow that all the proofs advanced about God by philosophers are sophisms : for instance, if one were to argue that whatsoever is in potentiality is reduced to actuality by something actual and that therefore God is actual being, since all things are brought into being by him, there will be a fallacy of equivocation ; and similarly in all other arguments. And again the effect must in some way be like its cause, wherefore nothing is predicated equivocally of cause and effect ; for instance, *healthy* of medicine and an animal.

We must accordingly take a different view and hold that nothing is predicated univocally of God and the creature : but that those things which are attributed to them in common are predicated not equivocally but analogically. Now this kind of predication is twofold. The first is when one thing is predicated of two with respect to a third : thus being is predicated of quantity and quality with respect to substance. The other is when a thing is predicated of two by reason of a relationship between these two : thus being is predicated of substance and quantity. In the first kind of predication the two things must be preceded by something to which each of them bears some relation : thus substance has a respect to quantity and quality : whereas in the second kind of predication this is not necessary, but one of the two must precede the other. Wherefore since nothing precedes God, but he precedes the creature, the second kind of analogical predication is applicable to him but not the first.

Reply to the First Objection. This argument avails in the case of a measure to which the thing measured can be equal or commensurate : but God is not a measure of this kind since he infinitely surpasses all that is measured by him.

Reply to the Second Objection. The likeness of the creature to God falls short of univocal likeness in two respects. First it does not arise from the participation of one form, as two hot things are like by participation of one heat : because what is affirmed of God and creatures is predicated of him essentially, but of creatures, by participation : so that a creature's likeness to God is as that of a hot thing to heat, not of a hot thing to one that is hotter. Secondly, because this very form of which the creature participates falls short of the nature of the thing which is God, just as the heat of fire falls short of the nature of the sun's power whereby it produces heat.

Reply to the Third Objection. *More* and *less* may be considered from three points of view, and predicated accordingly. First when it is only a question of the quantity of the thing participated : thus snow is said to be whiter than the wall, because whiteness is more perfect in the snow than in the wall, and yet it is of the same nature : and consequently such a difference of *more* or *less* does not cause a difference of species. Secondly when the one is predicated participatively and the other essentially : thus we might say that goodness is better than a good thing. Thirdly when the one same term is ascribed to one thing in a more eminent degree than to another, for instance, heat to the sun than to fire. These last two modes of *more* and *less* are incompatible with unity of species and univocal predication : and it is thus that a thing is predicated *more* and *less* of God and creatures, as already explained.

Reply to the Fourth Objection. When we say that God is better or that he is the sovereign good we compare him to creatures not as though he participated of the same generic nature as creatures, like the species of a genus ; but as the principle of a genus.

Reply to the Fifth Objection. Inasmuch as an intelligible species has a higher mode of existence, the knowledge arising therefrom is the more perfect : for instance, the knowledge arising from the image of a stone in the mind is more perfect than that which results from the species in the senses. Hence God is able to know things most perfectly in his essence, inasmuch as in his essence is the supereminent but not homogeneous likeness of things.

Reply to the Sixth Objection. There is a twofold likeness between God and creatures. One is the likeness of the creature to the divine mind, and thus the form understood by God and the thing itself are homogeneous, although they have not the same mode of being, since the form understood is only in the mind, while the form of the creature is in the thing. There is another likeness inasmuch as the divine essence itself is the supereminent but not homogeneous likeness of all things. It is by reason of this latter likeness that good and the like are predicated in common of God and creatures: but not by reason of the former, because when we say *God is good* we do not mean to define him from the fact that he understands the creature's goodness, since it has already been observed that not even the house in the mind of the builder is called a house in the same sense as the house in being.

Reply to the Seventh Objection. The equivocal agent must precede the univocal: because the latter's causality does not extend to the whole species (else it were its own cause) but only to an individual member of the species. But the equivocal agent's causality extends to the entire species: and consequently the first agent must be an equivocal agent.

1. *Reply to the First Argument* on the contrary side. The Philosopher refers to things that are common physically, not logically. Now things that have a different mode of existence have nothing in common in respect of that being which is considered by the physicist, but they may have some common 'intention' that the logician may consider. Moreover, even from the physicist's point of view the elemental and the heavenly body are not in the same genus: but in the view of the logician they are. However, the Philosopher does not mean to exclude analogical but only univocal community: since he wishes to prove that the corruptible and the incorruptible have not a common genus.

2. Difference of genus excludes univocation but not analogy. In proof of this, *healthy* is applied to urine in the genus of *sign*, but to medicine in the genus of *cause*.

3. In no sense is God said to be like the creature, but contrariwise: for as Dionysius says (*Div. Nom.* x), *likeness is not reciprocated between cause and effect, but only in co-ordinates:* thus a man is not said to be like his statue, but vice versa, the reason being that the form wherein the likeness consists is in the man before it is in the statue. Hence we do not say that God is like his creatures but vice versa.

4. According to Dionysius (*ibid.*) when it is said that no creature is like God this is to be understood as referring to effects which are imperfect and beyond all comparison fall short of their cause : nor does this refer to the quantity of the thing participated but to the other two modes, as explained above (Reply to Third Objection).

5. A thing cannot be like substance in respect of an accident, so that the likeness regard a form of the same kind : but there may be the likeness that is between cause and effect : since the first substance must needs be the cause of all accidents.

6. *The Sixth Argument* is answered in like manner.

7. Whiteness is not in the genus of number, nor is it the principle of a genus : wherefore they do not admit of comparison. Whereas God is the principle of every genus, and consequently all things are somewhat likened to him.

8. This argument refers to things that have a common genus or matter : which does not apply to God and the creature.

ARTICLE VIII

IS THERE ANY RELATION BETWEEN GOD AND THE CREATURE ?

Sum. Th. I, Q. xiii, A. 7 : Q. xxviii, A. 4 : Q. xxxii, A. 2

THE eighth point of inquiry is whether there be any relation between God and the creature : and it would seem that there is none.

1. According to the Philosopher (*De Praedic.* v) relatives are simultaneous. But creatures cannot be simultaneous with God : since in every way he precedes creatures. Therefore there cannot be any relation between God and a creature.

2. Things that are related can be compared in some way. But there is no comparison between God and a creature : since things that differ in genus are not comparable with one another, for instance, a number and a line. Therefore there is no relation between God and a creature.

3. Relative and co-relative belong to the same genus.

But God is not in the same genus as the creature. Therefore we cannot predicate a relation between them.

4. A creature cannot be in opposition to the Creator: because one opposite is not the cause of the other. Now relatives are in opposition to each other. Therefore there cannot be a relation between a creature and God.

5. Anything of which something new can be predicated, may be said in a sense to become. Consequently if something be said of God in relation to the creature, it follows that in a sense God becomes: which is impossible, seeing that he is unchangeable.

6. Whatsoever is predicated of a thing is predicated either essentially or accidentally. Now expressions that denote relation to creatures are not predicated of God essentially, since essential predicates are predicated necessarily and always: nor are they predicated accidentally. Therefore such relations can nowise be predicated of God.

On the contrary Augustine says (*De Trin.* v, 13) that the Creator is related to the creature as the master to his servant.

I answer that relation differs from quantity and quality in that quantity and quality are accidents residing in the subject, whereas relation, as Boethius says (*De Trin.*), signifies something not as adhering to a subject but as passing from it to something else : wherefore de la Porrée said that relations are not adherent but assistant,[1] which is true in a sense as we shall show further on. Now when a thing is attributed to someone as proceeding from him to another this does not argue composition between them, as neither does action imply composition with the agent. And for this reason the Philosopher proves (*Phys.* v) that there can be no movement in relation : since without any change in the thing that is related to another, the relation can cease for the sole reason that this other is changed. Thus it is clear with regard to action that there is no movement in respect of action except metaphorically and improperly speaking, just as we say that one who passes from inaction into action is changed : and this would not be the case if

---

[1] *Sum. Th.* I, Q. xxviii, A. 2.

relation or action signified something abiding in the subject. Hence it is evident that it is not incompatible with a thing's simplicity to have many relations towards other things: indeed the more simple a thing is the greater the number of its concomitant relations: since its power is so much the less limited and consequently its causality so much the more extended. Wherefore it is stated in *De Causis* (prop. xvii) that a united force is less confined than a distributed force. Now we must needs admit a relation between a principle and the things which proceed from it; and not only a relation of origin inasmuch as a result springs from its source, but also a relation of distinction, seeing that an effect must needs be distinct from its cause, for nothing is its own cause. Accordingly from God's supreme simplicity there results an infinite number of respects or relations between creatures and him, inasmuch as he produced creatures distinct from himself and yet somewhat likened to him.

Reply to the First Objection. Those relatives are naturally simultaneous which have the same reason for their mutual relationship, for instance, father and son, master and servant, double and half. But when there is not the same reason on either side for referring one thing to another, then relatives are not naturally simultaneous, but one naturally precedes the other: as the Philosopher states with regard to sense and the sensible object, knowledge and the thing knowable (*De Praed.* v). Wherefore it clearly does not follow that God and the creature are naturally simultaneous, since there is not the same reason on either side for one being referred to the other. It is not necessary, however, even in relatives that are naturally simultaneous that the subjects be naturally simultaneous, but only the relations.

Reply to the Second Objection. Not all the things that are related can be compared to each other, but only those that are related in respect of one quantity or quality, so that one may be described as greater, better, whiter and so on than the other. But different relations can be compared to each other even if they belong to different genera: since things that differ generically differ from one another.

And yet although God is not in the same genus as the creature as a thing contained in a genus, he is nevertheless in every genus as the principle of the genus : and for this reason there can be relation between the creature and God as between effect and principle.

Reply to the Third Objection. The subjects of things mutually related need not be in the same genus, but only the things themselves that are thus related : thus quantity is said to be distinct from quiddity. And yet as we have already said it is not the same with God and creatures as with things differing generically and nowise co-ordinated to one another.

Reply to the Fourth Objection. Relative opposition differs in two ways from other kinds of opposition. First in the latter one thing is said to be opposite to another inasmuch as it excludes it,—as negation excludes affirmation,—and in this respect is opposed to it : and opposition of privation and habit, and of contrariety includes opposition of contradiction (*Metaph.* iv). But it is not thus with things that are opposed relatively. For son is not opposed to father by excluding him, but on account of the nature of his relationship to him. Hence follows the second difference : because in other kinds of opposition one of the opposites is always imperfect by reason of the negation attaching to privation and one of the contraries. But this is not necessarily so in relative opposition, indeed it is possible to consider both relatives as perfect, as is especially evident in equiparent relatives and in relatives of origin, for instance, things that are equal to or like one another, father and son. Wherefore relation is more attributable to God than other kinds of opposition. By reason of the first difference relative opposition may be observed between the creature and God, but not any other kind : seeing that it is owing to God that creatures are affirmed rather than excluded ; and yet creatures have a certain relationship to God. By reason of the second difference, in the divine Persons (in whom there can be no imperfection) there can be relative opposition and no other, as we shall show further on (Q. viii).

Reply to the Fifth Objection. To become is to be changed properly speaking : wherefore just as a thing is not changed in respect of a relation except accidentally, to wit through a change in the thing to which the relation is consequent, so neither is a thing said to become in respect of a relation, except accidentally. Thus a body through a change in its quantity becomes equal (to another), yet the change is not essentially connected with equality but is related thereto accidentally. And yet a thing does not need to be changed in order that a relation begin to be predicated of it: but it suffices that a change occur in one of the extremes: since the cause of relationship between two is something inherent in both. Consequently from whichever extreme a change is wrought in that which caused the relationship, the relationship between them ceases. Accordingly from the fact that a change is wrought in the creature, a relation begins to be attributed to God. Hence he cannot be said to become except metaphorically; inasmuch as he is like a thing that becomes, through something new that is said about him: thus we say (Ps. lxxxix, 1): *Lord, thou art become our refuge.*

Reply to the Sixth Objection. When these relations begin to be ascribed to God on account of some change wrought in creatures, it is evident that the cause of their being attributed to him is on the part of the creature, and that they are predicated of God accidentally. But as Augustine says this does not imply an accident in God, but refers to something outside him and compared to him accidentally: for God's existence does not depend on creatures as neither does the builder's existence depend on the house: wherefore just as it is accidental to the builder that the house exists, so is it accidental to God that the creature exists. For we say that anything without which a thing can exist is accidental to it.

ARTICLE IX

ARE THESE RELATIONS BETWEEN A CREATURE AND GOD REALLY IN CREATURES THEMSELVES?

THE ninth point of inquiry is whether these relations between creatures and God are in creatures themselves: and it would seem that they are not.

1. There are certain relations which posit nothing real on either side; as Avicenna says (*Metaph.* iv, 10) of the relation between entity and non-entity. Now no relatives are further apart than God and the creature. Therefore this relation posits nothing real on our side.

2. We must not assert anything that leads to an indefinite process. Now if relation to God is something real in a creature, we shall have to go on indefinitely: since that relation will be a creature, if it be something real, and therefore will likewise bear a relation to God, and so on indefinitely. Therefore we must not assert that relation to God is something real in a creature.

3. Nothing has a relation except to one definite thing (*Metaph.* iv): thus *double* is not related to anything but *half;* and *father* is not related except to *son*, and so on. Therefore there must be correspondence between the things that are related and those to which they are related. Now God is simply one being. Therefore there can be no real relation in creatures to him.

4. The creature is related to God inasmuch as it proceeds from him. Now the creature proceeds from God as to its very substance. Therefore it is related to God by its substance and not by an additional relation.

5. A relation is a kind of mean between the related extremes. But there can be no real mean between God and the creature which is created by him immediately. Therefore relation to God is nothing real in the creature.

6. The Philosopher (*Metaph.* iv) says that if the reality of things depended on our opinion and perception, whatsoever we perceive would be real. Now it is clear that all creatures are dependent on the perception or knowledge of their Creator. Therefore all creatures are referred to God by their substance and not by an inherent relation.

7. It would seem that the more things are distant from one another the less are they related. Now there is a greater distance between the creature and God than between one creature and another. But seemingly the relation between one creature and another is nothing real: for since it is not a substance, it must he an accident and consequently

must be in a subject, and therefore cannot be removed therefrom without the subject being changed: and yet we have asserted the contrary to be the case with relations. Therefore the creature's relation to God is nothing real.

8. Just as a created being is infinitely distant from non-being, so also is it infinitely distant from God. But there is no relation between created being and absolute non-being, according to Avicenna (*Metaph.* iv, 10). Neither therefore is there a relation between created being and uncreated being.

On the contrary Augustine says (*De Trin.* v, 16): *It is evident that whatever begins to be predicated of God whereas it was not predicated of him before is said of him relatively*: relatively, that is, not to an accident in God (as if something had accrued to him), but, without doubt, to an accident in the thing in relation to which God begins to be predicated. Now an accident is something real in its subject. Therefore relation to God is something in the creature.

Again, whatsoever is related to a thing through being changed is really related thereto. Now the creature is related to God through being changed. Therefore it is really related to God.

I answer that relation to God is something real in the creature. To make this clear we must observe that as the Commentator says (*Metaph.* xi, text. 19), seeing that of all the predicaments relation has the least stability, some have thought that it should be reckoned among the predicables because the predicaments (*prima intellecta*) have an objective reality and are the first things to be understood by the intellect: whereas the predicables (*secunda intellecta*) are certain 'intentions' consequent to our mode of understanding: inasmuch as by a second act the intellect reflects on itself, and knows both the fact that it understands and the manner of its understanding. According then to this view it would follow that relation has no objective reality, but exists only in the mind, even as the notion of genus or species and of 'second substances'. But this is impossible: because nothing is assigned to a predicament unless it has objective reality: since logical being is divided against the being that is divided by the ten predicaments (*Metaph.* v).

Now if relation had no objective reality, it would not be placed among the predicaments. Moreover the perfection and goodness that are in things outside the mind are ascribed not only to something absolute and inherent to things but also to the order between one thing and another: thus the good of an army consists in the mutual ordering of its parts, to which good the Philosopher (*Metaph.* x) compares the good of the universe. Consequently there must be order in things themselves, and this order is a kind of relation. Wherefore there must be relations in things themselves, whereby one is ordered to another. Now one thing is ordered to another either as to quantity or as to active or passive power: for on these two counts alone can we find in a thing something whereby we compare it with another. For a thing is measured not only by its intrinsic quantity but also in reference to an extrinsic quantity. And again by its active power one thing acts on another, and by its passive power is acted on by another: while by its substance and quality a thing is ordered to itself alone and not to another, except accidentally: namely inasmuch as a quality, substantial form or matter is a kind of active or passive power, and forasmuch as one may ascribe to them a certain kind of quantity: thus one thing produces the same in substance; and one thing produces its like in quality; and number or multitude causes dissimilarity and diversity in the same things; and dissimilarity in that one thing is considered as being more or less so and so than another,— thus one thing is said to be whiter than another. Hence the Philosopher (*Metaph.* v) in giving the species of relations, says that some are based on quantity and some on action and passion. Accordingly things that are ordered to something must be really related to it, and this relation must be some real thing in them. Now all creatures are ordered to God both as to their beginning and as to their end: since the order of the parts of the universe to one another results from the order of the whole universe to God: even as the mutual order of the parts of an army is on account of the order of the whole army to its commander (*Metaph.* xii). Therefore creatures are really related to God, and this relation is something real in the creature.

Reply to the First Objection. That between one creature and another there is a relation which posits nothing in either extreme is not due to the distance between them, but to the fact that certain relations are based not on any order in things, but on an order which is only in our intellect: but this does not apply to the order of creatures to God.

Reply to the Second Objection. The relations themselves are not related to something else by any further relation but by themselves because their very essence is relative. It is not the same with things whose essence is absolute, so that this does not lead to an indefinite process.

Reply to the Third Objection. The Philosopher concludes (*ibid.*) that if all things are related to the supreme good, the supreme good must be infinite by nature: and accordingly an infinite number of things can be related to that which is infinite by nature. Such is God, since the perfection of his essence is not confined to any genus, as we have stated above. For this reason an infinite number of creatures can be related to God.

Reply to the Fourth Objection. The creature is related to God by its essence as cause of that relation, and by that same relation, formally: thus a thing is said to be like in quality, causally; and by its likeness, formally: and for this reason the creature is said to be like God.

Reply to the Fifth Objection. When it is said that the creature proceeds from God immediately, we exclude an intermediate creative cause, but not the intermediate real relationship which arises naturally from the creature's production, even as equality results immediately from quantity: thus a real relation follows naturally the production of created substance.

Reply to the Sixth Objection. Creatures depend on God's knowledge as an effect depends on its cause, and not as though their very existence consisted in that knowledge, so that for a creature to exist would mean nothing else but that it is known by God. This was the view of those who contended that whatsoever is perceived is real, and that the reality of things depends on our thoughts and perception, so that to exist would be nothing but to be an object of perception or thought.

Reply to the Seventh Objection. The very relation that is nothing but the order between one creature and another may be considered as an accident, or as a relation. Considered as an accident it is something adhering to a subject; but not considered as a relation or order, for then it is mere towardness, something passing as it were from one thing to another and assisting that which is related. Accordingly a relation is something inherent, but not because it is a relation: thus action as action is considered as issuing from the agent; but, as an accident, is considered as inherent to the active subject. Wherefore nothing prevents such an accident from ceasing to exist without any change in its subject, because it is not essentially complete through its existence in its subject but through transition into something else: and if this be removed the essence of this accident is removed as regards the action, but remains as regards its cause: even so, if the matter be removed, the heating is removed, although the cause of heating remain.

Reply to the Eighth Objection. There is no order between created being and non-being, but there is between created and uncreated being, hence the comparison fails.

ARTICLE X

IS GOD REALLY RELATED TO THE CREATURE SO THAT THIS RELATION BE SOMETHING IN GOD?

THE tenth point of inquiry is whether God be really related to the creature so that this relation be something in God: and seemingly the answer should be in the affirmative.

1. There is a real relation in the mover to that which it moves: wherefore the Philosopher (*Metaph.* v) reckons the relation between mover and moved to be a species of the predicament relation. Now God is compared to the creature as mover to that which is moved. Therefore he is really related to the creature.

2. It will be replied that he moves creatures without any change in himself; wherefore he is not really related to the thing moved. On the contrary, the presence of one of two relative opposites in a thing is not a reason for attributing the other to the same thing: thus a thing is not double because it is a half, nor is God Father because he is Son. Accordingly if mover and moved are mutually related, it does not follow that where there is the relation of *mover* there must be the relation of *moved*. Hence that God is not moved does not hinder him from having the relation of mover to moved.

3. As the father gives being to the son so does the Creator give being to the creature. But the father is really related to the son. Therefore the Creator is also really related to the creature.

4. Terms that are predicated of God properly and not metaphorically indicate the thing signified as being in God; and among terms of this kind Dionysius (*Div. Nom.* i) reckons *Lord.* Wherefore the thing signified by this word *Lord* is really in God. But it is a relation to the creature. Therefore, etc.

5. Knowledge relates to the thing knowable (*Metaph.* v). Now God is compared to creatures as known to the thing known. Therefore in God there is a relation to creatures.

6. The thing moved always bears a relation to its mover. Now the will is compared to the thing willed as the thing moved to its mover: because the appetible object is a mover that is not moved (*Metaph.* xii). Since then it is God's will that things exist, for *he hath done all things whatsoever he would* (Ps. cxiii, 11), it would seem that he is really related to the creature.

7. If God is not related to creatures, the only reason would seem to be that he is not dependent on them and is far above them. But the heavenly bodies likewise are independent of elemental bodies and surpass them almost out of all proportion. Wherefore it would follow that there is no real relation in the higher bodies to the lower world.

8. All names are taken from forms: and forms are something inherent to the things whereto they belong. Since

then God is named from his relation to creatures, it would seem that these relations are something in God.

9. Proportion—for instance that of double to half—is a real relation. Now seemingly there is a proportion in God to the creature: since there must be proportion between mover and the thing moved. Therefore it would seem that God is really related to creatures.

10. Whereas *understanding* is an image of the thing (understood), and *words* are signs of things, according to the Philosopher (*Peri Herm.* i), these two are ordered differently in disciple and teacher. The teacher begins with the things whence he has gathered the knowledge in his intellect, and expresses that knowledge in words, while the disciple begins with the words through which he arrives at the ideas in the intellect of the teacher, and thence at the knowledge of things. Now whatsoever is said about these relations must first of all come to the knowledge of a teacher. Consequently with him these relative terms correspond to the ideas in his intellect and these ideas correspond to an objective reality: wherefore seemingly these relations are real.

11. These relative terms which are predicated of God in time signify relations that are either predicamental (*secundum esse*) or transcendental (*secundum dici*). If their relativity is transcendental they posit nothing real in either extreme. But according to what has been said this is false, since they really exist in the creature as related to God. Therefore they signify predicamental relation, and consequently they posit something real in both extremes.

12. It is in the nature of relatives that given one the other follows, and if one be removed the other is also removed. If then there is a real relation in the creature, there must be in God a real relation to the creature.

On the contrary Augustine says (*De Trin.* v, 16): *It is clear that whatsoever is said of God relatively is an accident in the thing to which God begins to be referred.* Hence it would seem that these relations are attributed to God not by reason of something in him but on account of something outside him: so that they posit nothing real in him.

Again, as the knowable thing is the measure of knowledge,

so is God the measure of all things, as the Commentator says (*Metaph.* x). Now the knowable thing is not referred to knowledge by a real relation existing in it, but rather by the relation of knowledge to it, as the Philosopher says (*Metaph.* v). Therefore seemingly neither is God related to the creature by a real relation in him.

Again, Dionysius says (*Div. Nom.* ix): *Likeness is not reciprocal between cause and effect, for an effect is said to be like its cause and not vice versa.* Now the same would seem to apply to other relations as to that of likeness. Therefore seemingly neither is there reciprocity in the relations between God and the creature, and we cannot argue that because the creature is really related to God, therefore is God really related to the creature.

I answer that the relations whereby we refer God to creatures are not really in God. To make this clear we must observe that since a real relation consists in the order of one thing to another, as already stated, a real relation is mutual in those things alone wherein on either side there is the same reason for mutual order: and this applies to all relations consequent to quantity. For since the notion of quantity is independent of all objects of sense, it is the same in all corporeal natures. And for the same reason that a quantitative thing A is really related to the quantitative thing B, B is really related to A. Now between one quantity, considered absolutely, and another there is the order deriving from measure and thing measured, under the name of whole and part and other such things that result from quantity.

On the other hand in relations arising from action and passion or active and passive power there is not always order of movement on both sides. Because that which has the nature of being patient, moved or caused must always have an order to the agent or mover, seeing that the effect is always perfected by its cause and dependent thereon: so that it is ordered to it as the cause of its perfection. Now agents, whether movers or causes, sometimes have an order to their respective patients, whether moved or caused, inasmuch, to wit, as the good or perfection of the mover or agent is to be found in the effect, patient or thing moved.

This is especially evident in univocal agents which by their action produce their like in species, and consequently perpetuate their species as far as this is possible. This is also evident in all other things which move, act or cause through themselves being moved; because by their very movement they are ordered to produce effects; and again in all those things where any good accrues to the cause from its effect. And there are some things to which others are ordered but not vice versa, because they are wholly foreign to that genus of actions or power from which that order arises: thus knowledge has a relation to the thing known, because the knower by an intelligible act has an order to the thing known which is outside the soul. Whereas the thing itself that is outside the soul is not touched by that act, inasmuch as the act of the intellect does not pass into exterior matter by changing it; so that the thing which is outside the soul is wholly outside the genus of intelligible things.

For this reason the relation which arises from the act of the mind cannot be in that thing. The same applies to sense and the sensible object: for although the sensible object by its own action affects the organ of sense, and consequently bears a relation to it, just as other natural agents have a relation to the things on which they act, nevertheless it is not the alteration of the organ that perfects the act of perception, but the act of the sensitive power; to which act the sensible object outside the soul is altogether foreign. In like manner a man who stands to the right of a pillar bears a corresponding relation to the pillar by reason of his motive power whereby he is competent to be to the right or to the left, before or behind, above or below. Wherefore such-like relations in man or animal are real, but not in the thing which lacks that power. In like manner again money is external to the action whereby prices are fixed, which action is a convention between certain persons: and man is outside the genus of those actions whereby the artist produces his image. Hence there is not a real relation either in a man to his image, or in money to the price, but vice versa. Now God does not work by an intermediary action to be regarded as issuing from God and terminating in the creature: but his action is his substance and is wholly outside the genus of created being whereby the creature is related to him. Nor again does any good accrue to the creator from the production of the creature: wherefore his action is supremely liberal as Avicenna says (*Metaph.* viii, 7). It is also evident that he is not moved to act, and that without any change in himself he makes all changeable things. It follows then that there is no real relation in him to creatures, although creatures are really related to him, as effects to their cause.

In this matter Rabbi Moses erred in many ways, for he wished to prove that there is no relation between God and the creature, because seeing that God is not a body he has no relation to time or place. Thus he considered only the relation which results from quantity and not that which arises from action and passion.

Reply to the First Objection. The natural mover or agent moves and acts by an intermediary movement or action that is between the mover and the thing moved, between the agent and the patient: wherefore in this intermediary, at least agent and patient, mover and thing moved must come together. Wherefore the agent as such is not outside the genus of the patient as such: and consequently each has a real relation to the other, especially seeing that this intermediary action is a perfection proper to the agent so that the term of that action is a perfection of the agent. This does not apply to God, as stated above: and thus the comparison fails.

Reply to the Second Objection. The fact that the mover is moved is not the cause of its relation of mover being a real relation, but a sign thereof. For the fact that it moves through being moved shows that from one point of view it belongs to the same genus as the thing moved; and again from the fact that by its movement it is moved to a certain end it follows that this end is its good.

Reply to the Third Objection. The father, being an univocal agent gives the nature of his own genus to his son: but God does not thus give being to the creature: hence the comparison fails.

Reply to the Fourth Objection. The denomination *lord* comprises three things in its signification: namely, first, power to compel subjects; secondly, arising from that power, relation to those subjects; thirdly, a relation in those subjects to their lord, since one relative implies the other. Accordingly the term *lord* retains its meaning in God as regards the first and third, but not the second. Hence Ambrose (*De Fide* i, 1) says that this name *lord* is a name of power, and Boethius says that dominion is the power of compelling slaves.

Reply to the Fifth Objection. God's knowledge has not the same relation to things as ours has: since it is related to them as their cause and measure, inasmuch as things are true so far as by his knowledge God ordained them. On the other hand things are the cause and measure of our knowledge. Wherefore just as our knowledge bears a real relation to things and not vice versa, so are things really related to God's knowledge and not vice versa. Or we may reply that God understands other things by understanding himself, wherefore his knowledge is related directly not to things but to the divine essence.

Reply to the Sixth Objection. The appetible object that moves the appetite is the end, and the means do not move the appetite save on account of the end. Now the end of the divine will is nothing else than the divine goodness. Hence it does not follow that other things bear the same relation to the divine will as the mover does to that which it moves.

Reply to the Seventh Objection. The heavenly bodies are related to the lower bodies by real relations arising from quantity, inasmuch as on either side there is quantity of the same kind; and again by real relations arising from action and passion, because the action whereby being themselves moved they move other things is intermediary and is not their very substance, since by being a cause of lower things they obtain a certain good.

Reply to the Eighth Objection. That from which a thing is denominated need not always be its natural form, and it suffices for it to be expressed, grammatically speaking, by way of a form : thus a man is denominated from an action, his apparel and the like which are not really forms.

Reply to the Ninth Objection. If by proportion is meant a definite excess, then there is no proportion in God to the creature. But if proportion stands for relation alone, then there is relation between the Creator and the creature : in the latter really, but not in the former.

Reply to the Tenth Objection. Although the teacher begins with things, the ideas of things are received by the teacher's mind otherwise than in nature, because that which is received into another follows the mode of the recipient : and it is plain that ideas are in the teacher's mind immaterially, but materially in nature.

Reply to the Eleventh Objection. This distinction between predicamental and transcendental relatives does not prove the relations in question to be real. Certain predicamental relative terms do not signify a real relation, for instance, right and left as ascribed to a pillar : and some transcendental relative terms signify real relations, for instance, knowledge and sensation. Because relatives are said to be predicamental when terms are employed to signify the relations themselves, while they are said to be transcendental when the terms are employed to signify qualities or something of the kind primarily, from which relations arise. Nor as regards the question at issue does it matter whether they be real or logical relations.[1]

Reply to the Twelfth Objection. Although given one relative the other follows, this does not imply that both are posited in the same way : and it suffices that one be real and the other logical.

ARTICLE XI

ARE THESE TEMPORAL RELATIONS IN GOD AS LOGICAL RELATIONS ?

THE eleventh point of inquiry is whether these temporal relations are in God as logical relations : and it would seem that they are not.

[1] Cf. *Sum. Th.* I, Q. xiii, A. 7, ad 1.

THE DIVINE ESSENCE

1. An idea to which nothing real corresponds is idle and vain, according to Boethius (*Super Proem. Porphyr. in Praedicab.*). Now these relations are not really in God, as proved above. Therefore it is vain and idle for the reason to attribute them to him.

2. That which has only a logical existence is not ascribed to things except according as they are in the mind, for instance genus, species and order. Now these temporal relations are not ascribed to God according as he is only in our mind, since if they were, then, to say that God is Lord because we understand him to reign over creatures would have no objective reality, which is clearly false. Therefore these relations are not in God as logical relations.

3. This name *Lord* signifies a relation since it is a predicamental relative. But Lordship is not merely a logical relation in God. Therefore neither are these relations in God only logical.

4. If there were no created intelligence God would still be Lord and Creator. But there would be no logical relations if there were no created intelligence. Therefore *God* and *Lord* and the like do not denote merely logical relations.

5. That which has existence in our mind only has not existed from eternity. Now some of God's relations to the creature have been from eternity, such as the relations implied in the terms *knowledge* and *predestination*. Therefore such are not merely logical relations in God.

On the contrary, names signify ideas or concepts (*Peri Herm.* i). Now it is plain that these names are relative terms. Therefore these relations must be logical.

I answer that just as a real relation consists in order between thing and thing, so a logical relation is the order of thought to thought; and this may occur in two ways. First, when the order is discovered by the mind and attributed to that which is expressed in a relative term. Such are the relations attributed by the mind to the things understood as such, for instance, the relations of genus and species: for the mind discovers these relations by observing the order between that which is in the mind and that which is outside the mind, or again the order between one idea and another.

Secondly, when these relations arise from the mode of understanding, namely when the mind understands one thing in its relation to another, although that relation is not discovered by the intellect but follows by a kind of necessity its mode of understanding. Such relations are attributed by the intellect not to that which is in the intellect but to that which has objective reality. This happens forasmuch as certain things not mutually related are understood in relation to one another, although the mind does not understand them to be related, for in that case it would be in error. Now in order that two things be related they must each have existence, be distinct from each other (for nothing bears a relation to itself), and be referable to the other. Now the mind sometimes conceives two things as having existence, whereas one or neither of them is a being: as when it considers two futures, or one present and one future, and considers one in relation to the other by placing one before the other: wherefore such relations are purely logical since they arise from the mode of understanding. And sometimes the mind considers one thing as though it were two, and considers them in the light of a certain relationship: as when a thing is said to be identical with itself, and such a relation is purely logical. Sometimes the mind considers two things as referable to each other, whereas there is no relation between them, in fact one of them is itself essentially a relation: as when a relation is said to be accidental to its subject, wherefore such a logical relation has merely a logical relationship to anything else. Again the mind sometimes considers something in relation to another inasmuch as it is the term of the relationship of another thing to it, and yet itself is not related to the other: as when it considers something knowable as terminating the relationship of knowledge to it ; and thus it imputes to the thing knowable a certain relation to knowledge, and such a relation is purely logical. In like manner our mind attributes to God certain relative terms, inasmuch as it considers God as the term of the creature's relation to him: wherefore such relations are purely logical.

Reply to the First Objection. In these relations there is

something objective corresponding to them, namely the relation of the creature to God. For just as a thing is said to be knowable relatively, not in reference to knowledge but because knowledge refers to it (*Metaph.* v), even so God is spoken of relatively because creatures are related to him.

Reply to the Second Objection. This argument considers those relations that are discovered by reason and attributed to things that are in the mind. The relations in question, however, are not of this kind but arise from the mode of understanding.

Reply to the Third Objection. Just as a man is identical with himself really and not only logically (although such a relation is merely logical) inasmuch as the cause of the relation is real, namely substantial identity, which the mind considers in the light of a relation : even so the power to compel subjects is in God really, and our mind considers it in relation to the subjects on account of the subjects' relation to God : and thus he is called *Lord* really, although in him the relation is merely logical. For the same reason it is evident that he would be Lord even if there were no created mind in existence.

Hence the *Reply to the Fourth Objection* is clear.

Reply to the Fifth Objection. As stated above God's knowledge is related essentially not to the creature but to the essence of the Creator whereby God knows all things.

QUESTION VIII

OF THOSE THINGS THAT ARE PREDICATED OF GOD RELATIVELY FROM ETERNITY

THERE are four points of inquiry : (1) Whether relations predicated of God from eternity and signified by the names *Father* and *Son* are real or logical relations. (2) In God is relation his substance ? (3) Do the relations constitute and distinguish the persons and hypostases ? (4) If the relations be mentally abstracted do the hypostases remain in God ?

ARTICLE I

ARE THE RELATIONS PREDICATED OF GOD FROM ETERNITY REAL OR ONLY LOGICAL RELATIONS ?

C.G. IV, xiv : *Sum. Th.* I, Q. xxviii, A. 1

WE have now to inquire into the relations attributed to God from eternity : and the first point of inquiry is whether the relations attributed to God from eternity and signified by the names *Father* and *Son* be real or only logical relations. It would seem that they are not real.

1. According to Damascene (*De Fid. Orth.* i, 11) *in the subsistent Trinity there is something common and identical, and if there be any distinction or diversity this is in our knowledge and understanding.* Now the Persons are distinct by their relations. Therefore in God the relations are merely logical.

2. Boethius says (*De Trin.* iv) : *Relation in the Trinity of the Father to the Son and of both to the Holy Ghost is like the relation of the same to the same.* Now the relation of identity is purely logical. Therefore such are the relations of paternity and filiation.

3. In God there is no real relation to the creature, because

he produced creatures without any change in himself, as Augustine says (*De Trin.* v, 16). Now much more true is it that the Father produced the Son, and the Son proceeded from the Father without any change taking place. Therefore in God there is no real relation in the Father to the Son or vice versa.

4. Things that are not perfect, such as privation, matter and movement, are not attributed to God. Now of all things relation has the most unstable being, so much so that some have reckoned it among the predicables; according to the Commentator (*Metaph.* xi). Therefore there can be no relation in God.

5. In creatures there is always composition of the 'relation and its subject': for one thing cannot inhere to another without composition. Now there can be no composition in God. Therefore there cannot be real relation in him.

6. Things that are absolutely simple differ from one another by themselves. Now the divine Persons are absolutely simple. Therefore they differ by themselves and not by any relations: and consequently there is no need of putting relations in God, since the only reason for doing so is to distinguish the Persons.

7. Just as the relations are properties of the divine Persons so are the absolute attributes properties of the essence. Now the absolute attributes have only a logical being in God. Therefore the relations in God are merely logical.

8. A perfect thing lacks nothing (*Phys.* iii). Now the divine substance is most perfect, and consequently lacks nothing that pertains to its perfection. Therefore there is no need to place relations in God.

9. Seeing that God is the first beginning and last end of things, anything that is reducible to something previous cannot be in God, but only those things to which others are reduced: thus the movable is reducible to the immovable, and the accidental to the essential; wherefore God is not moved, and nothing in him is accidental. Now everything that denotes 'to-another' being is reducible to absolute or 'to-itself' being. Therefore in God nothing is relative to another but all is absolute.

10. By his very nature God exists of necessity. Now everything that by its very nature exists of necessity is absolute : for the relative cannot exist without its correlative. But that which by its very nature exists of necessity, does not cease to exist when something else is removed. Therefore no real relations are in God.

11. As stated in the preceding question (A. 9) every real relation arises from some kind of quantity or from action or passion. But there is no quantity in God : for in the words of Augustine (*De Trin.* v, 1)[1] God is *great without quantity*. Nor is there number in him, as Boethius says (*De Trin.*), whence relations could arise, although there is number resulting from relations. Hence if there be real relations in God they must be attributed to him in respect of some action of his. Not, however, in respect of the action whereby he brings creatures into being, since in the preceding question (A. 10) it was proved that there is no real relation in God to creatures. Nor again in respect of the personal action ascribed to God, such as generation : for seeing that in God to beget belongs to a distinct hypostasis, and distinction arises only from relation, it will be necessary for the relation to precede such an action, so that it cannot result from it. Accordingly we must conclude that, if any real relation in God arises from his action, it must be consequent upon his eternal or essential action of intelligence or volition. But even this is impossible, since such an action results in the relation between the one who understands and the thing understood, and such a relation in God cannot be real : else in God he who understands and that which he understands would be really distinct, which is clearly false, since each is predicated of each Person : for not only does the Father understand, but also the Son and the Holy Ghost : and likewise each of them is understood. Wherefore seemingly no real relation is in God.

12. Man's natural reason can attain to the knowledge of the divine mind : for it has been demonstrated by philosophers that God is intelligence. If then real relations which in God are said to distinguish the Persons arise from the

---

[1] *Contra Ep. Manich. quam vocant, Fund.* xv.

action of the intellect, it would seem possible for human reason to discover the Trinity of Persons, and this would no longer be an article of faith. *For faith is the substance of things to be hoped for, the evidence of things that appear not* (Heb. xi, 1).

13. Relative opposition is divided against other kinds of opposition: and the latter cannot be ascribed to God. Neither therefore can relative opposition.

On the contrary Boethius says (*De Trin.*) that *relation alone multiplies the Trinity.* Now this multiplication is not merely logical but is real, for as Augustine says (*De Trin.* i, 3), *Father, Son and Holy Ghost are three things.* Therefore the relations in God are not merely logical but real.

Again, that which is real is constituted by something real. Now the relations in God are properties which constitute the Persons; and person signifies something real. Therefore the divine relations also must be real.

Again, generation is more perfect in God than in creatures. Now in creatures generation produces a real relationship, namely that of father and son. Therefore *a fortiori* relations in God are real.

I answer that those who follow the teaching of the catholic faith must hold that the relations in God are real. The catholic faith teaches that there are in God three Persons of one Essence. Now number results from some kind of distinction · wherefore in God there must be some distinction not only in respect of creatures who differ from him in nature, but also in respect of someone subsisting in the divine nature. But this distinction cannot regard anything absolute, since whatsoever is predicated of God absolutely denotes the divine essence, so that it would follow that the divine Persons differ essentially, which is the heresy of Arius. It follows then that the divine Persons are distinct only by their relations. Now this distinction cannot be merely logical, because things that are only logically distinct can be predicated of one another: thus we say that the beginning is the end, because one point in reality is both beginning and end (of a line) although there is a logical distinction. Hence it would follow that the Father is the Son and the Son the Father: because seeing that names are given in order to distinguish things, it would follow that the divine Persons differ only in name, which is the heresy of Sabellius. It remains thus to be said that the relations in God are something real: how this may be we must endeavour to discover by following the statements of holy men, although reason is unable to do so fully.

We must observe then that since a real relation cannot be conceived unless it arise from quantity or from action or passion, it follows that we must posit relation in God according to one of these modes. Now in God there cannot be quantity either continuous or discrete, nor anything bearing a likeness to quantity, except number arising from and presupposing relation; and unity, which regards the essence, the consequent relation of which is not real but merely logical, as, for instance, the relation implied in the word *same*, as we have stated in the preceding question (A. 11). It follows then that we ascribe to God the relation that arises from action: not indeed the action that passes into something passive, since nothing is passive in God in whom there is no matter, and there is no relation in God to what is outside him, as we have proved (Q. vii, A. 10). Consequently real relation in God must follow the action that remains in the agent, and in God these are intelligence and volition, since sensation through being effected by means of a corporeal organ cannot be attributed to God who is wholly incorporeal. For this reason Dionysius (*Div. Nom.* xi) says that in God Fatherhood is perfect, i.e. not corporeally or materially but intelligibly. Now the one who understands may have a relation to four things in understanding: namely to the thing understood, to the intelligible species whereby his intelligence is made actual, to his act of understanding, and to his intellectual concept. This concept differs from the three others. It differs from the thing understood, for the latter is sometimes outside the intellect, whereas the intellectual concept is only in the intellect. Moreover the intellectual concept is ordered to the thing understood as its end, inasmuch as the intellect forms its concept thereof that it may know the thing understood.

It differs from the intelligible species, because the latter which makes the intellect actual is considered as the principle of the intellect's act, since every agent acts forasmuch as it is actual : and it is made actual by a form, which is necessary as a principle of action. And it differs from the act of the intellect, because it is considered as the term of the action, and as something effected thereby. For the intellect by its action forms a definition of the thing, or even an affirmative or negative proposition. This intellectual concept in us is called properly a word, because it is this that is signified by the word of mouth. For the external utterance does not signify the intellect itself, nor the intelligible species, nor the act of the intellect, but the concept of the intellect by means of which it relates to the thing. Accordingly this concept or word by which our intellect understands a thing distinct from itself originates from another and represents another. It originates from the intellect through an act of the intellect : and it is the likeness of the thing understood. Now when the intellect understands itself this same word or concept is its progeny and likeness, that is of the intellect understanding itself. And this happens because the effect is like its cause in respect of its form, and the form of the intellect is the thing understood. Wherefore the word that originates from the intellect is the likeness of the thing understood, whether this be the intellect itself or something else. And this word of our intellect is extrinsic to the essence of the intellect (for it is not the essence but a kind of passion thereof), yet it is not extrinsic to the intellect's act of intelligence, since this act cannot be complete without it. If then there be an intellect whose act of intelligence is its very essence, it follows that this word is not extrinsic to the essence of that intellect even as it is not extrinsic to its act of intelligence. Such is the divine intellect : since in God to be and to understand are the same. Wherefore his word is not outside his essence, but co-essential with it. Accordingly in God we find the origin of one from another, namely a word proceeding, and one from whom the word proceeds without prejudice to the unity of the essence. For whenever one thing originates from another there must be a real relation —either only on the part of that which originates, when it receives not the same nature as its principle, as in the creature's origination from God—or on the part of both, when to wit that which originates attains to the nature of its principle, as when a man is begotten, and a real relation results between father and son. Now in God the Word is co-essential with its principle, as we have proved. It follows then that in God there is a real relation both on the part of the Word and on the part of the Speaker.

Reply to the First Objection. In the divine Persons there is essential unity, but there is a logical distinction by reason of the relation which does not differ from the Essence really but only logically, as we shall state further on.

Reply to the Second Objection. Relation in the divine Persons bears a certain likeness to the relation of identity if we consider the unity of Essence: whereas if we consider the origin of one (Person) from another in the same nature we must conclude that these relations are real.

Reply to the Third Objection. Just as God undergoes no change in producing his creature, so is he not changed in the production of his Word. Yet the creature does not attain to the divine essence and nature, wherefore the divine essence is not communicated to the creature. For this reason the relation of God to the creature does not result from anything in God but only with respect to something done on the part of the creature. On the other hand the Word is produced as co-essential with God himself; wherefore God is related to his Word in respect of something in God and not only with respect to something on the part of the Word. For then is there a real relation on one side and not on the other, when the cause of the relation is on one side and not on the other: for instance, the relation between the knowable object and knowledge results from the act of the knower and not from anything that he may know.

Reply to the Fourth Objection. Relation has a most unstable existence, if this belongs to it alone: but it is not so in God, for in him relation has no other existence than that of the substance, as we shall show further on in the next Article. Hence the argument fails.

Reply to the Fifth Objection. This argument considers the real relation whose being is distinct from the substance in which it is. But this is not so in the case in point, as we shall show further on.

Reply to the Sixth Objection. Since the divine Persons differ by their relations only, they do not differ otherwise than by themselves, for the relations are the very Persons who subsist, as we shall prove (A. 4).

Reply to the Seventh Objection. The essential attributes which are properties of the essence are in God really and not logically. For God's goodness is something real, and so is his wisdom and so forth, although they are not distinct from his essence otherwise than logically: and the same applies to the relations, as we shall prove further on.

Reply to the Eighth Objection. God's substance would be imperfect were there anything in it distinct therefrom. But in God relation is his substance, as we shall prove further on: wherefore the objection fails.

Reply to the Ninth Objection. The movable and the accidental are reducible to something previous as the imperfect to the perfect. For an accident is imperfect: and movement is the act of what is imperfect. But relation sometimes follows from the perfection of a thing, as in the case of the intellect, since it follows the operation which is its perfection. Hence the divine perfection does not hinder us from ascribing relations to God, as it forbids us to ascribe movement and accident to him.

Reply to the Tenth Objection. That which necessarily exists of itself is not related to anything extraneous, but nothing prevents it from being related to something within it. Wherefore as it is not said to be necessary through another, it is said to be necessary of itself.

Reply to the Eleventh Objection. Real relation in God follows the action of his intellect, not as though this real relation were that of the one who understands to what he understands, but to his word: for the word and not the thing understood proceeds from him who understands.

Reply to the Twelfth Objection. Although natural reason is able to succeed in proving that God is intelligence, it is not able to discover adequately his mode of understanding. Just as we are able to know that God is but not what he is: even so we are able to know that God understands, but not how he understands. Now to understand by conceiving a word belongs to the mode of understanding: wherefore reason cannot prove this adequately, but it can form a kind of conjecture by comparison with what takes place in us.

Reply to the Thirteenth Objection. In other kinds of opposition one of the extremes is always by way of being imperfect or non-existent, or with an admixture of non-entity: since negation excludes being and privation is a negation, and of two contraries one always includes a privation. Hence other kinds of opposition cannot be in God, whereas relative opposition can because on neither side does it imply imperfection.

ARTICLE II

IS RELATION IN GOD THE SAME AS HIS SUBSTANCE?

Sum. Th. I, Q. xxviii, A. 2 : *C.G.* IV, xiv

THE second point of inquiry is whether in God relation is his substance: and seemingly it is not.

1. That *no substance is a relation* is a self-evident proposition like *no substance is a quantity.* Neither then is God's substance a relation.

2. It will be replied that God's substance is a real and not merely a logical relation. On the contrary an idea to which nothing real corresponds is idle and vain. But nothing is vain in God. Therefore it is not possible that relation in God differ logically from his substance.

3. The divine Persons are distinct by their relations: for *relation alone multiplies the Trinity,* according to Boethius (*De Trin.*). If then the divine Persons are not distinct in substance, seeing that the relations add nothing real to the substance but only a logical consideration, it will follow

that the distinction between the divine Persons is only logical; which is the heresy of Sabellius.

4. The divine Persons are not distinct by anything absolute: because it would follow that they are distinct in essence, since what is said of God absolutely signifies his essence; for instance, goodness, wisdom and so forth. If then the relations are the same thing as the divine essence it will follow either that the divine Persons are not distinct by the relations, or that they are distinct in essence.

5. If relation is the same thing as God's very substance, it will follow that just as God and his greatness belong to the predicament of substance, since God is his own greatness, so likewise Paternity will belong to the predicament of substance: so that whatsoever is said of God will be said in reference to his substance, which is contrary to the statement of Augustine (*De Trin.* v, 4, 5) that not all the things said of God refer to his substance: for relations are ascribed to God such as that of Father and Son.

6. Whatsoever is said of the predicate may be said of the subject. But if relation is God's very essence, it will be true to say: *The divine essence is Paternity*, and with equal reason: *Filiation is the divine essence*: and thus it would follow that *Filiation is Paternity*.

7. Things that are the same admit of the same predicates: thus the Philosopher says (*Top.* i): *The slightest difference that we may assign will show that the things are not the same.* Now we predicate of the divine essence that it is wise, that it created the world and so on: while such things, apparently, are not predicated of Paternity and Filiation. Therefore in God relation is not the divine essence.

8. That which distinguishes the divine Persons is not the same thing as that which neither distinguishes them nor is itself distinguished. Now in God relation distinguishes while essence neither distinguishes nor is distinguished. Therefore they are not the same thing.

9. One and the same thing cannot by its essence be the cause of contraries except accidentally. Now distinction which in God results from relation is contrary to unity, the

principle of which is the essence. Therefore relation and essence are not the same thing.

10. If two things are the same with each other, where one is there is the other. If then the divine essence is the same thing with Paternity, wheresoever is the divine essence there will be Paternity. But it is in the Son. Therefore Paternity is also: which is clearly false.

11. In God relation and essence differ at least in our conception of them. Now where the concept or definition differs, there is a different being; since a definition states the quiddity of a thing's being. Hence in God the being of the relation will differ from the being of the substance. Consequently relation and substance differ in being, and therefore really.

12. According to the Philosopher (*Praedic.*) the being of relation is to be 'to-another.' Therefore the being of relation and not the being of substance consists in respect to another. Therefore relation and substance are not the same in being; and we come to the same conclusion as before.

13. Augustine says (*De Trin.* v, 4, 5) that something is said of God not substantively but relatively. Now that which signifies the divine substance is predicated substantively. Therefore in God relation does not signify the essence: and the same conclusion follows.

14. Augustine says (*De Trin.* vii, 6) that God is not God in the same way as he is Father. Now he is God by the divine essence, but Father by Paternity. Therefore the essence is not Paternity: wherefore in God the relations are not the divine substance.

On the contrary, whatsoever is in God is God, as Augustine says (*De Trin.* v, 5). Now relation is in God, as Paternity in the Father. Therefore relation is God himself and the divine substance.

Again every supposit containing things that are different is composite. Now in the person of the Father there is Paternity and the essence: wherefore if Paternity and the divine essence are two things it will follow that the person of the Father is composite; and this is clearly false. It follows therefore that in God relation is the very substance.

I answer that given that there are relations in God we are bound to say that they are the divine essence : else we would have to say that there is composition in God and that the divine relations are accidents, since whatsoever adheres to a thing besides its substance is an accident. It would also follow that something that is not the divine substance is eternal ; and all these things are heretical.

Accordingly to make the matter clear we must observe that some of the nine kinds of accident are defined with regard to the nature of an accident, for the nature of an accident is to inhere ; wherefore I describe those as defined with regard to the nature of an accident which are defined as inhering to a subject, such as quantity and quality. On the other hand relation is not defined with regard to its nature as an accident, for it is described not as being in a subject but as having a respect to something extraneous. For this reason the Philosopher (*Metaph.* v) says that knowledge as a relation is not in the knower but in the thing known. Hence through taking note of the manner of signification in relative terms some said that they are not adherents but as it were assistants to substance, because they denote a kind of medium between the related substance and that to which it is related. From this it was necessary to infer that in creatures relations are not accidents, since the being of an accident is to be in (a subject). Hence certain theologians of the school of Gilbert de la Porrée extended this opinion to the divine relations, and contended that the relations are not in the divine Persons but are assistants to them as it were. And seeing that the divine essence is in the Persons it followed that the relations are not the divine essence : and since every accident adheres (to a subject) it followed that they are not accidents : and in this sense they took the saying of Augustine quoted above, namely that relations are not predicated of God either substantively or accidentally. But from this opinion it follows that relation is not an objective reality but only a subjective idea : since every real thing is either a substance or an accident. For this reason some of the ancients reckoned relation among the predicables, as the Commentator remarks (*Metaph.* xi, com. 19) : wherefore the followers of de la Porrée are compelled to hold that the divine relations are merely logical. Thus it would follow that the distinction between the Persons is not real : which is heretical.

Accordingly we must reply that a thing may be adherent and yet not be defined as adherent : even as action is not defined as being in but from the agent, and yet it is clear that it is in the agent. In like manner although relation is not defined as adhering yet it needs must be adherent : that is to say when it is a real relation, for if it be a logical relation it is not adherent. And just as in creatures it must be an accident, so in God it must be the substance, since whatsoever is in God is his substance. Therefore real relations must be the divine substance, yet they have not the mode of substance, but receive another mode of predication differing from those things that are predicated of God substantively.

Reply to the First Objection. No substance that is in a genus can be a relation, because it is confined to one genus and is therefore excluded from another. The divine essence, however, is not in the genus of substance, but is above every genus, and comprises the perfection of all genera. Wherefore nothing prevents its including that which pertains to relation.

Reply to the Second Objection. Substance and relation differ logically and in that thing which is God something corresponds to both : yet not a different thing to each but one and the same. Moreover it is most appropriate that one thing should correspond to two points of view, when its nature comprises that thing perfectly : and thus it is in the case in point.

Reply to the Third Objection. Although relation does not add a thing to the essence, but only a point of view, yet it is itself a thing, even as goodness is a thing in God, and yet it does not differ from the essence otherwise than logically ; and the same applies to wisdom. Wherefore just as things which pertain to goodness or wisdom, such as intelligence and so on, are really in God, even so that which is proper to a real relation, namely opposition and distinction, is really in God.

Reply to the Fourth Objection. The essential attributes not only signify that which is the divine essence, but they also signify it in a certain way, since they signify something as existing in God : and for this reason a difference in respect of anything absolute would reflect on the divine essence. On the other hand the divine relations, though they signify that which is the divine essence, they do not signify it by way of essence, since they do not convey the idea of existence in something, but of reference towards something else. Hence the distinction arising from the divine relations does not point to a distinction in the essence but only to respect to another by way of origin, as explained above.

Reply to the Fifth Objection. Although the relation is the divine substance, it does not convey the idea of substance, as already explained : wherefore it is not predicated substantively, because to be predicated thus belongs to the mode of signification.

Reply to the Sixth Objection. This argument applies to the *per se* predicables. Now a thing is predicated *per se* of something when the predication regards the proper nature of that thing ; whereas if the predication arises not from the proper nature but from identity, it is not even *per se* predication. Hence when it is said, *The divine essence is Paternity*, Paternity is predicated of the divine essence on account not of a logical but of a real identity : and the same applies if essence be predicated of Paternity, as already stated ; because essence and relation differ logically. Wherefore this argument falls into the fallacy of accident : because although there is no accident in God, there is a certain likeness to an accident, inasmuch as things which are predicated of one another in respect of an accident while differing logically have but one subject.

Reply to the Seventh Objection. According to the Philosopher (*Phys.* iii, 3) it is not things which are in any way the same that receive the same predicates but only those that have the same definition. Now the divine essence and Paternity, although the same in reality, have not the same definition : wherefore it does not follow that whatsoever is predicated of the one is predicated of the other. It must be observed, however, that certain things follow the definitions of essence and relation : wherefore one of these removes the other ; thus neither does essence distinguish nor is relation common. On the other hand certain things imply a certain difference from the definition of essence or relation, not in their principle signification but in their mode of signifying : and these are predicated of essence or relation, although not properly : such are adjectives and verbal substantives, e.g. good, wise, to understand, to will : because suchlike terms as to the thing signified, signify the essence ; yet they signify it as though it were a supposit and not in the abstract. For this reason good, wise, creating and the like are most appropriately predicated of the Persons and of the concrete essential names such as God, Father ; yet they may be predicated, albeit improperly, of the essence in the abstract and not taken as a supposit. Still less properly are they predicated of the relations : because they are applicable to the supposit in respect of the essence and not of the relation : thus God is good or creative through having his essence—not through having a relation.

Reply to the Eighth Objection. That which causes a distinction and that which neither distinguishes nor is distinguished can be the same in reality but not logically.

Reply to the Ninth Objection. The unity of the essence is not opposed to the distinction of the relations : wherefore it does not follow that relation and essence are causes of contraries.

Reply to the Tenth Objection. If two things be the same both really and logically, wherever the one is there must the other be. But this does not necessarily apply when they are the same really but not logically : thus the same instant is the beginning of the future and the end of the past : yet not the beginning of the future but that which is the beginning of the future is said to be in the past. In like manner we do not say that Paternity is in the Son, but that which is Paternity, the essence.

Reply to the Eleventh Objection. In God there is no being save that of the essence, even as there is no (act of) understanding but the intellect : and therefore as in God there is but one act of understanding, so is there but one being Wherefore it can nowise be granted that in God the being of the relations is distinct from the being of the essence. Now the definition of a thing does not signify its being but its being this or that, namely what that thing is. Wherefore two definitions of one thing do not prove that it has a twofold being, but that it can be said in two ways of that thing that it is : thus we may say of a point what it is as a beginning, and what it is as an end, on account of the different definitions of beginning and end.

Reply to the Twelfth Objection. Since in creatures relation is an accident its being is to be in something, and not to have a respect to some other thing : but considered as a relation its being is to have respect to something else.

Reply to the Thirteenth Objection. Relatives are said not to be predicated of God substantially, because they are not predicated as something existing in a substance, but as having a respect to something else, yet not as though that which they signify were not the substance.

Reply to the Fourteenth Objection. God is said not to be God in the same way as Father on account of the different ways of signifying godhead and paternity, as explained above.

ARTICLE III

DO THE RELATIONS CONSTITUTE AND DISTINGUISH THE PERSONS OR HYPOSTASES ?

Sum. Th. I, Q. xxx, A. 1 : Q. xl. A. 2

THE third point of inquiry is whether the relations constitute and distinguish the Persons or Hypostases : and seemingly they do not.

1. Augustine says (*De Trin.* vii, 1) : *Every relative expression signifies something besides the relation expressed : thus a master is a man, a slave is a man.* Now the Persons in God are expressed relatively. Therefore they are something

besides the relative term : and consequently they are not constituted by the relations : for if you remove that which constitutes a thing it is no longer a thing.

2. It will be replied that in God that which is besides Paternity is the Father.

On the contrary it is evident that Father is also a relative term. If then through Paternity being relative the Person must contain something besides Paternity, for the same reason beside being Father the Person must contain something that is not relative.

3. Augustine says (*ibid.*) that in no sense can the Father be referred to himself, but whatsoever is said of him is in relation to the Son. Thus the same conclusion follows as before.

4. One may reply that what the Father is besides the relation is the essence.

On the contrary whatsoever is in a relative besides the relation is referred to the other thing by that relation, as may be seen from the examples which he gives : thus man is related to servant by the relationship of dominion. Now the essence in God is not related, since it neither begets nor is begotten. Therefore this cannot be said of the essence but of the subject of the relation, which subject begets or is begotten.

5. A thing is considered in itself before we refer it to another. Now nothing is constituted by that which comes after it in our consideration of it. Therefore the hypostasis of the Father is not constituted by its relation to something else.

6. In God hypostases are more perfect than in us. But in us properties neither constitute nor distinguish hypostases, but are signs of distinction in hypostases already constituted. Therefore neither in God do the relations which are properties constitute or distinguish the hypostases.

7. Logically the generating hypostasis precedes generation, since the generator is understood to be the principle of generation : and logically generation precedes Paternity, since relations follow actions or passions (*Metaph.* v). Therefore logically the hypostasis of the Father precedes Paternity, and consequently is not constituted by it, as neither is the hypostasis of the Son by Filiation.

8. No form is constituted or distinctive outside its own genus; thus whiteness constitutes and distinguishes a white from a black thing in point of quality: likewise length constitutes and differentiates a thing in point of quantity. Therefore neither is relation constitutive or distinctive outside the genus of relation. But a hypostasis belongs to the genus of substance. Therefore relation neither constitutes nor distinguishes the hypostasis.

9. In God relation is the divine essence: wherefore if it constitutes and distinguishes the hypostasis, this is either *quâ* the divine substance or *quâ* relation. Not, however, *quâ* divine essence, because since this is common to the three Persons it cannot be the principle of their distinction: nor again *quâ* relation, because relation does not signify anything self-subsistent 'which is the meaning of the word hypostasis,' but merely reference to another. Therefore relation nowise distinguishes or constitutes the hypostasis.

10. In God nothing constitutes or distinguishes itself. Now the relations are themselves the hypostases: for just as Godhead and God do not differ, so neither do Paternity and Father. Therefore the relations neither constitute nor distinguish the hypostases.

11. One should not ask how two things are distinct unless they have something in common which is distinguished by something added in each of them: thus animal is common to man and horse, and is distinguished as rational and irrational by the addition of differences: wherefore we may ask how man and horse differ. Whereas things which have nothing in common so as to be distinguished in the foregoing manner are distinct by themselves and not by any distinguishing principle. Now two divine hypostases have nothing common but the essence, and this is not in any way distinguished by relations. Therefore it should be said not that the hypostases are distinguished by the relations, but that they are distinct by themselves.

12. Nothing causes what it presupposes. But relation presupposes distinction, since thereby one thing is referred to another, and otherness implies distinction. Therefore relation cannot be a principle of distinction.

13. Richard of S. Victor (*De Trin.* iv, 15) says that in the angels the hypostases are distinguished by quality alone, and in God by origin alone. Now origin differs logically from relation, as generation from Paternity. Therefore the hypostases are distinguished not by relation but by origin.

14. According to Damascene (*De Fide Orth.* iii, 6, 7) the divine hypostases are distinguished by their properties. Now it is the property of the Father that he begot the Son, according to Augustine,[1] and of the Son that he is born of the Father. Therefore the Father and the Son are distinguished by generation and birth. But these denote origin, therefore the Father and the Son are distinguished by origin and not by relation.

15. There are some relations in God which neither constitute nor distinguish the hypostases, such as equality and likeness. Therefore neither do the other relations, such as Paternity and Filiation, constitute and distinguish the hypostases.

On the contrary Boethius says (*De Trin.*) *that in God relation alone multiplies the Trinity.* Now multitude in the Trinity arises from constituted and distinct hypostases. Therefore relation alone constitutes the Persons and hypostases.

Moreover things are distinguished only by what is not predicated of them in common. Now the relations alone are predicated of the divine Persons severally and not in common according to Augustine (*De Trin.* v, 8). Therefore the Persons and hypostases in God are distinguished by the relations alone.

I answer that there are two opinions on this question. The first is that in God relations neither constitute nor distinguish the hypostases but show that they are constituted and distinct. In order to elucidate the point it must be observed that this word *hypostasis* denotes an individual substance, one to wit that cannot be predicated of several. Hence genera and species in the predicament of *substance*, such as man or animal, cannot be called hypostases, since they are predicated of several: whereas Socrates and Plato

---

[1] Fulgentius, *De Fide ad Petrum*, ii.

are called hypostases because they are predicated of one only. Accordingly if, as Jews and pagans assert, there is no Trinity in God, there is no need to ask what constitutes or distinguishes the hypostasis since this is nothing but the divine essence : because by his very essence God is something undivided in itself, and distinct from all things that are not God. Seeing, however, that the Catholic Faith teaches that there is one essence in three Persons, it is inconceivable that the divine essence distinguish and constitute the hypostasis in God : because we understand the Godhead as constituting God, and as common to the three Persons and therefore as predicated of several subjects and not as an incommunicable hypostasis. In like manner nothing that is said of God absolutely can be understood as distinguishing and constituting the hypostases in the Persons, since what is predicated of God absolutely conveys the notion of something essential. Wherefore that which constitutes and distinguishes the hypostasis in the divine Persons must be that which before anything else is not predicated of several but exclusively of one. Now there are two things that fulfil this condition, relation and origin, and generation and Paternity (or birth and Filiation), which although they are really but one thing in God, differ nevertheless logically and in their mode of signification. Logically the first of these is origin, for relation seemingly follows origin. Wherefore this opinion holds that the divine hypostases are constituted and distinguished by their origin, and this is indicated when we say *A is from B*, and *from B is A :* and that the relations of Paternity and Filiation logically follow the constitution and distinction of the Persons, and indicate the constitution and distinction of the hypostases. Thus the fact that one is called Father shows that another originates from him : and the fact that one is called Son shows that he originates from another. Nor does it follow from this opinion that the divine hypostases, if not distinguished by their relations, are distinguished by something absolute, since the origins themselves imply relation : seeing that as father denotes relationship to a son, so does begetter to one begotten.

Nevertheless this opinion seemingly is void of foundation. For a thing may be understood to distinguish and constitute the hypostasis in two ways. It may be taken for the principle whereby the hypostasis is formally constituted and distinguished; as man is constituted by humanity, and Socrates by ' socrateity ' : or it may be taken for the way as it were to distinction and constitution : thus we might say that Socrates is a man by his generation which is the way to the form whereby he is constituted formally. It is clear then that a thing's origin cannot be understood as constituting and distinguishing except in reference to that which constitutes and distinguishes formally : since if humanity were not produced by generation, never would a man be constituted by generation. Consequently it cannot be said that the hypostasis of the Son is constituted by its nativity, except in so far as we take its nativity as terminating in something whereby the hypostasis is formally constituted. Now the relation in which nativity terminates is filiation. Therefore the hypostasis of the Son must be formally constituted and distinguished by Filiation and not by its origin : nor by the relation implied in the origin, since the relation implied in the origin like the origin itself denotes something not as yet subsistent in the nature but as tending thereto. And since all hypostases of the same nature have the same constitutive and distinguishing principle, it follows that in like manner on the part of the Father we must understand that the hypostasis of the Father is constituted and distinguished by Paternity, and not by active generation nor by the relation implied thereby.

This is the second opinion, namely that the relations constitute and distinguish the Persons and hypostases : and it may be explained as follows. As already proved, Paternity is the same as the divine essence : and likewise the Father is the same as God : wherefore Paternity by constituting the Father constitutes God. And just as Paternity, although it is the divine essence, is not common as the essence is : even so although the Father is the very same thing as God, he is not common as God is, but proper. Accordingly God the Father as God is something common as having the divine nature, and as Father is something proper and distinct from the other Persons. Hence he is a hypostasis, which signifies that which subsists in a nature and is distinct from others : so that Paternity by constituting the Father constitutes the hypostasis.

Reply to the First Objection. The divine Persons are something besides a relation : this is the essence which is not spoken of relatively. This is what Augustine means to say as may be seen by studying his words carefully.

Hence we grant the *Second and Third Objections.*

Reply to the Fourth Objection. Although relation is not attributed to the essence as though it were a form, it is attributed to it as identical with it. For even if we do not say that the essence begets or is related, we do say that it is a generation and relation. However, relative terms are predicated of the essential names in the concrete even by way of information : thus we say that God begets God, and that God is related to God, inasmuch as relation and essence are understood as having a common supposit, as we have shown : although the essential names themselves are not distinct. Wherefore apart from the relative terms the essential names are understood in the concrete, since through the relations they have a relative signification.

Reply to the Fifth Objection. In each divine hypostasis we speak of something that is absolute : this belongs to the essence, and in our way of thinking precedes the divine relations. Yet that which we conceive as absolute, since it is common, does not regard the distinction of the hypostases : so that it does not follow that we must conceive the hypostasis as distinct before we understand its relation.

Reply to the Sixth Objection. In lower things hypostases are distinct in essence, so that the properties which result from the essence cannot be the principle of distinction, but are signs thereof. But the divine hypostases are nowise distinct in essence : wherefore the properties must be the principle of this distinction.

Reply to the Seventh Objection. Two things are requisite to constitute a hypostasis. First it must be self-subsistent and undivided in itself : secondly it must be distinct from other hypostases of the same nature. If, however, there be no other hypostases of the same nature it will still be a hypostasis, even as Adam when there were not as yet other hypostases in human nature. Hence the generating hypostasis must always be presupposed to generation, in so far as it is self-subsistent and undivided in itself, but not as distinct from other hypostases of the same nature, if other hypostases of the same nature originate solely by this kind of generation : thus Adam was not distinct from other hypostases of the same nature before the formation of the woman from his rib, and the birth of his children. But in God the hypostases are not multiplied except by the procession of the other Persons from one. Wherefore we understand the Person of the Father as subsistent before we understand him as begetting, and not as distinct from the other hypostases of the same nature which do not proceed unless we presuppose this generation. And although the divine relations constitute the hypostases and thus make them subsistent, they do this inasmuch as they are the divine essence : because a relation as such neither has nor can give subsistence, for this belongs to a substance alone. On the other hand the relations as such distinguish, for it is as such that they are mutually opposed. It follows then that the relation of Paternity, inasmuch as it constitutes the hypostasis of the Father (which it does as identical with the divine substance) is presupposed to generation, but inasmuch as it distinguishes, generation is presupposed to Paternity. As regards the Son there is no further difficulty : because birth logically precedes the hypostasis of the one born, for we conceive it as the way to it : since generation is the way to substance.

Reply to the Eighth Objection. As we have already stated in God relation is something besides relation ; for it is God's very substance in reality : wherefore it can constitute something subsistent and not merely relative.

Reply to the Ninth Objection. As already stated relation as such distinguishes the hypostasis : while as identical with the divine essence it constitutes the hypostasis, and does both inasmuch as it is both relation and divine essence.

Reply to the Tenth Objection. In God the abstract and the concrete do not differ in reality, since in God there is neither accident nor matter : they differ only in their manner of signification, inasmuch as we understand the Godhead as constituting God and God as having Godhead : the same applies to Paternity and the Father, for though they are really the same thing, they differ in their mode of signification.

Reply to the Eleventh Objection. Although in God nothing is really common save the one essence, there is a logical community in the divine Persons in the fact that each is a supposit of the essence. This community is indicated in all concrete essential names, that signify the supposit in general : for instance, *God is one who has the Godhead.* Accordingly it is logically common to the three Persons to be a supposit of the divine nature, although the three Persons are not one supposit, but three : even as Socrates and Plato are two men although it is logically common to them to be a man. Now a difference is sought not only in things that have something real in common, but even in those that have something in common logically.

Reply to the Twelfth Objection. Relation presupposes the distinction of the other genera such as substance and quantity ; and sometimes also of action and passion : whereas it does not presuppose but causes the distinction arising from towardness : thus the relation of *double* presupposes the relation of great and small, whereas it does not presuppose but causes the relation of 2 to 1. In God, however, there is no other than relative distinction.

Reply to the Thirteenth Objection. Richard says that the Persons are distinct by their origin, inasmuch as they are distinguished by relations of origin.

Reply to the Fourteenth Objection. Augustine[1] uses the words *begot the Son* and *is the Father* as having the same meaning : wherefore he sometimes speaks of *origin* instead of *relation.*

Reply to the Fifteenth Objection. The relations of equality and likeness cannot cause a distinction of Persons in God, rather do they presuppose it. Likeness is sameness of quality

[1] Fulgentius.

in things that differ, and equality is sameness of quantity in things that are distinct. Thus it is clear that distinction of supposits is presupposed to both likeness and equality.

ARTICLE IV

IF MENTAL ABSTRACTION BE MADE OF THE RELATIONS, DO THE DIVINE HYPOSTASES REMAIN?

Sum. Th. I, Q. xl, A. 3

THE fourth point of inquiry is whether if we make mental abstraction of the relations the divine hypostases remain: and it would seem that they do remain.

1. In the created world everything is made to a likeness of what is in God. Now if we make abstraction of the relations and properties of the human hypostasis there still remains the hypostasis. Therefore the same applies to God.

2. It is not owing to the same reason that the Father is someone and that he is the Father: for the Son also is someone and yet he is not the Father. Hence if we remove Paternity from the Father he is still someone. Now he is someone inasmuch as he is a hypostasis. Therefore if we remove Paternity by mental abstraction, the hypostasis of the Father still remains.

3. Seeing that we understand a thing through its definition, we can understand anything even if abstraction be made of what is not included in its definition. Now relation is not included in the definition of a hypostasis. Therefore we can make abstraction of the relation and still understand the hypostasis.

4. Jews and heathens understand that there is a hypostasis in God, for they conceive him to be a self-subsistent being: yet they do not understand Paternity, Filiation and like relations in him. Therefore if we make abstraction of such relations the hypostases still remain in God.

5. That to which anything is added remains when the addition is removed: thus *man* adds *rational* to *animal* (since man is a rational animal): wherefore if we remove *rational, animal* remains. Now *person* adds a property to

hypostasis: for *person* signifies a *hypostasis distinguished by a property of dignity.*[1] Therefore if by abstraction we remove property from the Person, the hypostasis remains.

6. Augustine says (*De Trin.* vii, 2) that the Word is begotten Wisdom. Now *wisdom* presupposes the hypostasis and *begotten* presupposes the property. Therefore if we remove from the Word that he is begotten, his hypostasis still remains: and the same applies to the other Persons.

7. If we make abstraction of Paternity and Filiation there still remain in God the One (proceeding) from another and One from whom another (proceeds). But these denote the hypostases. Therefore abstraction being made of the relations the hypostases remain in God.

8. Though the constituent difference be removed the genus remains. Now the personal properties by constituting the Persons are in God as constituent differences. Therefore if these properties be removed, the genus *person* or hypostasis remains.

9. Augustine says (*De Trin.* v, 6) that if we remove the fact that (this Person) is the Father, it still remains that he is *unbegotten.* Now *unbegotten* is a property that can have no other subject but a hypostasis. Therefore if we make abstraction of Paternity, the hypostasis of the Father still remains.

10. As the relations are properties of the hypostases, so are the attributes properties of the essence. Now if we make abstraction of an essential attribute we still conceive the divine substance: thus Boethius says (*De Hebd.*) that if by abstraction we remove goodness from God, it still remains that he is God. Therefore in like manner if we remove the relations, the hypostases still remain in God.

11. According to Boethius (*Super Proœm. Porphyr. in Praed.*) it is proper to the intellect to separate things that are naturally united. Now property and hypostasis are really united in God. Therefore the intellect can separate them.

12. It is possible to conceive a thing after removing what it contains: thus we can conceive a subject after an accident

---

[1] *Sum. Th.* I, Q. xxix, A. 3, ad 2.

has been removed from it. Now the divine relations are said to be in the hypostases. Therefore after the relations have been removed by abstraction the hypostases remain.

On the contrary, in God no distinction is possible except by the relations. Now the hypostasis denotes something distinct. Therefore the hypostases do not remain if the relations be removed. For seeing that in God there are only two modes of predication, namely substantive and relative, if the relations be removed nothing remains to be predicated except substantively: and such are things that regard the essence, so that the hypostases will no longer be distinct.

I answer that as stated above (A. 3) some have contended that in God the hypostases are not constituted or distinguished by the relations but only by their origin. And they held relation to be consequent to the origin of the Person as terminating and completing it, so as to indicate a certain dignity. Wherefore since person is thought to denote dignity, they said that the hypostasis with the added relation is conceived to constitute the Person; and thus they held the relations to constitute the Person and not the hypostasis. In this sense it is customary with some to call these relations Personalities: and consequently just as with us if we remove from a man that which pertains to dignity and makes him a person, his hypostasis remains, even so in God if we mentally abstract these personal relations from the Persons they say that the hypostases but not the Persons will remain. Seeing, however, that as we have proved above (A. 3) these relations both constitute and distinguish the hypostases, we must hold the contrary opinion that abstraction being made of these relations neither the Persons nor the hypostases remain: because if the constituents of a thing be removed the thing itself cannot remain.

Reply to the First Objection. Neither relations nor properties constitute the human hypostasis, whereas we have proved that they constitute the divine hypostasis: wherefore the comparison fails.

Reply to the Second Objection. From the same cause the Father is someone and is the Father: the same that is, really and not only logically, yet with a logical distinction, either as that of generic and specific, or of common and proper. Thus it is plain that from the same form man is an animal and is a man (since one thing has not several actually distinct substantial forms) : yet from his soul inasmuch as it is a sensible soul, he is only an animal, and from his soul as both sensible and rational, he is a man. Hence a horse is an animal but is not a man ; because its sensible soul is not the same sensible soul as that of a man, and for that reason it is not the same individual animal as a man. The same applies to the question in point. The Father is someone and is the Father on account of the relation : but he is someone on account of the relation considered in general : while that he is a particular someone is due to this particular relation which is Paternity. For this reason again the Son, in whom is a relation, but not the relation of Paternity, is someone, but he is not that particular someone that is the Father.

Reply to the Third Objection. The definition of a thing may include something in two ways : explicitly, i.e. actually, or implicitly, i.e. potentially. The definition of an animal does not include the rational soul explicitly and actually, for then every animal would have a rational soul : but it includes it implicitly and potentially, because an animal is a sensible animate substance. Now just as *soul* includes *rational soul* potentially, so does *animated being* contain *rational being* potentially : so that where the definition of *animal* is actually applied to *man*, *rational* must be included in the definition of animal explicitly, for as much as animal is the same as man. It is thus in the case in point : for hypostasis considered in general is a distinct substance, wherefore since there can be no distinction in God except by reason of relation, when I say 'divine hypostasis' it must of necessity be conceived as distinct by reason of a relation. Hence although relation is not included in the definition of the hypostasis that is a man, it is included in the definition of a divine hypostasis.

Reply to the Fourth Objection. Jews and heathens do not conceive the essence as distinct except from things of another nature, and such distinction arises from the divine essence itself. We, however, conceive the hypostasis as distinct from that which is of the same nature, and from which it cannot be distinguished otherwise than by relation alone. Hence the objection proves nothing.

Reply to the Fifth Objection. The manner of definition differs in accidents and substances. Substances are not defined by something outside their essence : wherefore the first thing included in the definition of a substance is the genus, which is predicated essentially of the thing defined. Whereas an accident is defined by something outside its essence, namely by its subject, on which it depends for its being. Hence in its definition the subject takes the place of the genus : for instance, ' Simous means flat-nosed.' Accordingly just as, if we remove the difference from the definition of a substance the genus remains, even so if we remove the accident (which takes the place of the difference) from the definition of an accident the subject remains. There is, however, a difference. When the difference is removed the genus remains, but not identically the same : thus if we remove *rational*, the same identical animal which is *rational animal* does not remain ; whereas when from the definition of an accident we remove that which takes the place of the difference the same identical subject remains, thus the same nose remains when we remove the curved or ' pug ' shape. This is because an accident does not complete the essence of its subject as the difference completes the essence of the genus. When therefore we say, ' a person is a hypostasis distinguished by a property pertaining to dignity,' hypostasis is included in the definition of person not as subject but as genus. Wherefore if we remove the property pertaining to dignity the hypostasis does not remain the same identically or specifically but only generically, and as applied to non-rational substances.

Reply to the Sixth Objection. When we say, *The Word is Begotten Wisdom*, ' Wisdom ' stands for the hypostasis, although it does not signify it. Hence it does not include the property in its signification, and so it is necessary to add it : thus I might say that *God is the Begotten Son.*

Reply to the Seventh Objection. He that proceeds from

another and he from whom another proceeds do not differ from Filiation and Paternity save as common from proper : since *Son* denotes him who is from another by generation, and *Father* signifies him from whom another is by generation : unless we contend that *he who is from another* and *he from whom another is* denote the origin, while *Father* and *Son* denote the consequent relations. But we have already made it plain that the hypostases are constituted not by their origins but by their relations.

Reply to the Eighth Objection. After abstraction of the constituent difference, the genus remains in common but not in any species or individual.

Reply to the Ninth Objection. Augustine does not mean to say that God the Father remains unbegotten if we abstract his Paternity, except perhaps in so far as *unbegotten* would then denote a condition of nature and not a property of the Person. His intention was to show that if we abstract the Paternity, *unbegotten* may still remain in general : since it is not necessary that whatsoever is unbegotten be the Father.

Reply to the Tenth Objection. The notion of goodness does not constitute the notion of the essence, in fact good is conceived as informing being. On the other hand the property constitutes the hypostasis : wherefore the comparison fails.

Reply to the Eleventh Objection. Although the mind is able to separate certain things that are united, it cannot do so in every case : for it cannot separate things one of which enters into the definition of the other ; thus it cannot separate animal from man. Now property enters into the definition of the hypostasis : wherefore the objection does not prove.

Reply to the Twelfth Objection. If one removes that which is in another as subject or place, that in which it was remains : but it is not so if we remove that which is part of a thing's essence : thus man no longer remains if we remove *rational :* and in like manner if we remove the property, the hypostasis does not remain.

QUESTION IX

OF THE DIVINE PERSONS

THERE are nine points of inquiry. (1) Of the Person as compared with the essence, subsistence and hypostasis. (2) What is a person? (3) Can there be a Person in God? (4) In God does this word *Person* mean something relative or something absolute? (5) Are there a number of Persons in God? (6) Is it right to predicate Person plurally in God? (7) How are numeral terms predicated of God, positively or in a removing sense? (8) Is there diversity in God? (9) Are there only three Persons in God, or more or less than three?

ARTICLE I

OF THE PERSONS AS COMPARED TO THE ESSENCE, SUBSISTENCE AND HYPOSTASIS

Sum. Th. I, Q. xxix, A. 2

WE are inquiring about the divine Persons, and the first point of inquiry is about the Persons in comparison with the essence, subsistence and hypostasis: and it would seem that they are absolutely the same.

1. Augustine (*De Trin.* vii, 3) says that the Greeks mean the same when they acknowledge three hypostases in God, as the Latins when they acknowledge three Persons. Wherefore hypostasis and Person signify the same.

2. But it will be replied that the person differs from the hypostasis in that the latter signifies an individual of any nature in the genus of substance, whereas a person denotes an individual of none but a rational nature.

On the contrary, Boethius says (*De Duab. Nat.*) that the Greeks employ the term hypostasis to denote only an individual of rational nature. If, then, person signifies an individual of rational nature, hypostasis and person are absolutely the same.

3. Names are taken from our idea of the things they signify. Now individuality conveys the same idea in things of a rational nature as in other substances. Therefore an individual of rational nature should not have a special name rather than other individuals in the genus of substance, as though there were a difference between hypostasis and person.

4. Subsistence is taken from subsisting. Now nothing subsists besides individuals in the genus of substance, in which are accidents and ' second substances ', namely genus and species (*Praedic.*). Therefore only individuals in the genus of substance are subsistences. But an individual in the genus of substance is a hypostasis or person. Therefore subsistence is the same as hypostasis and person.

5. It will be replied that genera and species in the genus of substance subsist, since to subsist belongs to them according to Boethius (*loc. cit.*).

On the contrary, to subsist is to exist by oneself. Hence what exists only in another does not subsist. Now genera and species are only in something else : for they are only in ' first substances,' and if these latter be removed, nothing of the former can possibly remain (*Praedic.* Substantia). Hence to subsist does not belong to genera and species, but only to individuals in the genus of substance : so that we must still conclude that subsistence is the same as hypostasis.

6. Boethius (*Comment. Praedic.*) says that οὐσία, i.e. essence, signifies that which is composed of matter and form. Now this must be an individual, since matter is the principle of individuation. Therefore the essence signifies the individual, and thus person, hypostasis, essence and subsistence are the same.

7. The essence is signified by the definition, since a definition tells us what a thing is. Now the definition of a natural thing that is composed of matter and form, includes not only the form but also the matter, according to the Philosopher (*Metaph.* vi). Therefore the essence is something composed of matter and form.

8. It will be replied that the essence denotes the common nature, while the other three, namely subsistence, hypostasis and person, signify an individual in the genus of substance. On the contrary, universal and particular are to be found in every genus. Now in other genera there are not different names for the particular and the universal ; thus quality and quantity are denominated in the same way whether in general or in particular. Neither therefore in the genus of substance should there be different names to denote a universal and a particular substance : wherefore one would think that these terms have the same signification.

On the contrary, Boethius says (*Comment. Praed.*) that οὐσία, i.e. essence, signifies that which is composed of matter and form ; that ὀυσίωσις, i.e. subsistence, signifies the form, and hypostasis the matter. Therefore they differ.

Moreover the same conclusion would seem to follow from the fact that the same author (*De Duab. Nat.*) explains the difference between these terms.

I answer that the Philosopher (*Metaph.* v) says that substance may be taken in two ways. In one sense it is the ultimate subject which is not predicated of another : and this is the individual in the genus of substance : while in another sense it is the form or nature of a subject. The reason for this distinction is that several subjects may have a common nature ; thus several men have in common the nature of man. Hence the need of distinguishing that which is one from that which is multiple : for the common nature is signified by the definition which indicates what a thing is : so that this common nature is called the essence or quiddity. Wherefore whatsoever a thing contains pertaining to the common nature is included in the signification of the essence, whereas this cannot be said of all that is contained in the individual substance. For if whatsoever is in the individual substance were to belong to the common nature, there would be no possible distinction between individual substances of the same nature. Now that which is in the individual substance besides the common nature is individual matter (which is the principle of individuation) and consequently individual accidents which determine this same matter. Accordingly the essence is compared to the individual substance as a formal part thereof, for instance, human nature in Socrates. Hence in things composed of matter and form, the essence is not quite the same as the subject, and consequently it is not predicated of the subject: for we do not say that Socrates is his human nature. On the other hand in simple substances there is no difference between essence and subject, seeing that in them there is no individual matter to individualise the common nature, but their very essence is a subsistence. This is clear from what the Philosopher says (*Metaph.* vii), and from Avicenna, who says (*Metaph.*) that a simple thing is its own quiddity. Now two things are proper to the substance which is a subject. The first is that it needs no external support but is supported by itself: wherefore it is said to subsist, as existing not in another but in itself. The second is that it is the foundation to accidents by sustaining them, and for this reason it is said to substand. Accordingly substance which is a subject, inasmuch as it subsists, is called οὐσίωσις or subsistence, but inasmuch as it substands it is called hypostasis by the Greeks, and 'first substance' by the Latins. It is clear then that *hypostasis* and *substance* differ logically but are one in reality. *Essence*, however, in material substances is not the same as they really, nor yet is it altogether diverse since it is by way of a formal part: but in immaterial substances it is altogether the same in reality while differing logically. *Person* adds a definite nature to the *hypostasis*, since it is nothing more than a hypostasis of rational nature.

Reply to the First Objection. Inasmuch as person adds nothing but the rational nature to the hypostasis, it follows that hypostasis and person are absolutely the same in rational nature; thus seeing that man adds rational to animal, it follows that a rational animal is a man. Hence Augustine's statement is true when he says (*De Trin.* vii, 4) that Greeks mean the same when they acknowledge three hypostases in God, as the Latins when they acknowledge three Persons.

Reply to the Second Objection. The word *hypostasis* in

Greek in its proper signification denotes an individual substance of any nature, but through use it has come to mean only an individual of rational nature.

Reply to the Third Objection. Just as it is proper to an individual substance to exist by itself, so is it proper to it to act by itself. For nothing acts but an actual being : for which reason as heat exists not by itself so neither does it act by itself, but the hot thing heats by its heat. Now to act by themselves is becoming in a higher degree to substances of a rational nature than to others : since rational substances alone have dominion over their actions, so that it is in them to act or not to act, while other substances are acted on rather than act themselves. Hence it was fitting that the individual substance of rational nature should have a special name.

Reply to the Fourth Objection. Although nothing subsists but the individual substance which is called a hypostasis, it is not said to subsist for the same reason as it is said to substand : it is said to subsist as not existing in another, and to substand inasmuch as other things are in it. Hence if there were a substance that exists by itself without being the subject of an accident, it could be called a subsistence but not a substance.

Reply to the Fifth Objection. Boethius expresses himself according to the opinion of Plato, who held genera and species to be separate subsistent forms devoid of accidents ; and in this view they could be called subsistences but not hypostases. Or we may reply that genera and species are said to subsist, not because they themselves subsist, but because in their natures individuals subsist, apart from all accidents.

Reply to the Sixth Objection. In material substances essence denotes something composed of matter and form ; not indeed of individual but of common matter : thus the definition of man which signifies his essence, includes flesh and bones but not this flesh and these bones. On the other hand individual matter is included in the meaning of hypostasis and subsistence in material things.

This suffices for the *Reply to the Seventh Objection.*

Reply to the Eighth Objection. Accidents are not individualised save by their subjects. Substance alone is individualised by itself and its proper principles; hence it is fitting that only in the genus of substance should the particular have a special name.

The arguments advanced in a contrary sense may be granted. But it must be noted that Boethius in his commentary on the *Categories* takes these terms in a different sense from that in which they are usually employed and as he uses them in his work *De Duabus Naturis*. Thus he applies the term *hypostasis* to matter as the first substanding principle, whereby the 'first substance' is enabled to underlie accidents: since a simple form cannot be a subject, as he also says (*De Trin.*). Again he applies the term οὐσίωσις to the form as the principle of being: because by it is a thing actual: while he employs οὐσία or essence as indicating the composite. Whence he shows that in material substances both form and matter are essential principles.

ARTICLE II

WHAT IS MEANT BY A PERSON?

Sum. Th. I, Q. xxix, AA. 1, 3

THE second point of inquiry is the meaning of the word person. Boethius (*De Duab. Nat.*) defines it as *an individual substance of rational nature:* and it would seem that this definition is incorrect.

1. According to the Philosopher (*Metaph.* vii) no singular thing can be defined. Now a person is an individual in the genus of substance as already stated. Therefore it cannot be defined.

2. To this it will be replied that although that which is a person is singular, the idea of a person is something common, and this suffices to make it possible to define it.

On the contrary, that which is common to all individual substances of rational nature, is the 'intention' of singularity, which is not in the genus of substance. Therefore in the definition of person we should not give substance the place of the genus.

3. But it will be replied that this word *person* does not denote a mere intention, but an intention together with its subject.

On the contrary, the Philosopher (*Metaph.* vii) proves that a compound of subject and accident cannot be defined: because such a definition would be nugatory. For seeing that the definition of an accident includes the subject, e.g. nose in the definition of Simous, it will be necessary in defining a compound of subject and accident to express the subject twice; once for itself and once for the accident. If, then, person signifies the intention together with the subject it will be futile to define it.

4. The subject of this common intention is an individual. If then person denotes the intention together with its subject, it will still follow that in defining person the individual will be defined, which cannot be done.

5. An intention is not included in the definition of a thing, nor accident in the definition of a substance. Now person denominates a thing and a substance. Therefore it is unfitting to include individual in the definition of person, since it denotes both an intention and an accident.

6. A thing in whose definition substance is expressed as the genus must be itself a species of substance. Now person is not a species of substance, for then it would be condivided with other species of substance. Therefore it is unfitting in defining person to express substance as the genus.

7. Substance is divided into first and second. Now second substance cannot have a place in the definition of person: since a contradiction of terms would be involved in saying *individual substance,* inasmuch as 'second substance' is a universal substance. Likewise it cannot denote a 'first substance,' for a 'first substance' is an individual substance, so that it would be futile to add *individual* to *substance* in defining *person*. Therefore it is unfitting to include *substance* in the definition of *person*.

8. The term *subsistence* is seemingly more akin than *substance* to *person:* thus we say that there are three subsistences in God, as likewise three Persons: whereas we do not say there are three substances, but one. Therefore it

were better to define person as a subsistence than as a substance.

9. If you multiply the thing defined you multiply the genus included in the definition : thus many men are many animals. Now there are three persons and not three substances in God. Therefore substance should not be expressed as the genus in the definition of person.

10. Rational is a difference of animal. Now person is to be found in things that are not animals, viz. in the angels and in God. Therefore *rational* should not be expressed as the difference in defining person.

11. Nature is only in movable things, since it is the principle of movement (*Phys.* ii, 1). Now essence is in things both movable and immovable. Therefore it were better in defining person to include essence rather than nature, seeing that person is found to be both in movable and immovable things, since there are persons in men, angels and God.

12. The definition should be convertible with the thing defined. Now not every individual substance of rational nature is a person. For the divine essence *quâ* essence is not a person, else in God there would be one Person even as there is one essence. Therefore the aforesaid definition of person is unsuitable.

13. Human nature in Christ is an individual substance of rational nature : for it is neither an accident nor a universal substance, nor is it of irrational nature : and yet in Christ it is not a person, since it would follow that the divine Person in assuming human nature assumed a human person. Thus there would be two persons in Christ, the divine Person assuming and the human person assumed, which is the heresy of Nestorius. Therefore not every individual substance of rational nature is a person.

14. The soul separated by death from the body is not said to be a person ; yet it is an individual substance of rational nature. Therefore this is not a suitable definition of person.

I answer that as explained above it is reasonable that the individual in the genus of substance should have a special name : because a substance is individualized by its proper principles, and not by something extraneous as an accident is by its subject. Again it is reasonable that among individual substances the individual of rational nature should have a special name, because as stated above it belongs to it properly and truly to act by itself. Wherefore just as the word *hypostasis* according to the Greeks, or 'first substance' according to the Latins is the special name of an individual in the genus of substance, even so the word *person* is the special name of an individual of rational nature: so that *person* is a special name under both these heads. Hence to indicate that it is in a special manner an individual in the genus of substance, it is stated that it is *an individual substance;* and to indicate that it is in a special manner (an individual) of rational nature it is added *of rational nature.* Accordingly by describing it as a substance we exclude accidents from the notion of person, for no accident can be a person, and by adding *individual* we exclude genera and species in the genus of substance, since they cannot be called persons: and by adding *of rational nature* we exclude inanimate bodies, plants and dumb animals which are not persons.

Reply to the First Objection. Three points are to be noted in an individual substance: first, the generic and specific nature existing in the individual: second, such a nature's mode of existence, inasmuch as the generic and specific nature in the individual substance exists as proper to that individual and not as common to many: third, the principle whence arises this mode of existence. Now just as a nature considered in itself is common, so also is that nature's mode of existence: for we do not find human nature existing in things except as individualized in this or that man: since there is not a man that is not a particular man, except in the opinion of Plato who posited separate universals. But the principle of that mode of existence, namely the principle of individuation, is not common, but differs in each individual: for this particular thing is individualized by this matter, and that one by that matter. Accordingly just as the term denoting the nature is common and definable, e.g. *man* or *animal,* so too is the term denoting the nature together with such a mode of existence, e.g. *hypostasis* or *person.* On the other hand the term that includes in its signification a determinate principle of individuality, is neither common nor definable, e.g. Socrates or Plato.

Reply to the Second Objection. Not only is the intention of singularity common to all individual substances, but also the generic nature together with that particular mode of existence. In this way the term *hypostasis* denotes a nature of the genus *substance* as individualized; while the term *person* denotes only a rational nature with that particular mode of existence. For this reason neither hypostasis nor person is a term of intention, like *singular* and *individual*, but denotes a thing only, and not a thing together with an intention.

This suffices for the *Replies to the Third and Fourth Objections.*

Reply to the Fifth Objection. Whereas the essential differences of things are often unknown and unnamed, we are sometimes under the necessity of employing accidental differences to denote substantial distinctions, as the Philosopher teaches (*Metaph.* viii). Thus it is that *individual* is included in the definition of person, in order to indicate an individual mode of existence.

Reply to the Sixth Objection. The division of substance into 'first' and 'second' is not a division into genus and species, since 'second' substance covers nothing that is not covered by 'first' substance: but it is a division of a genus according to different modes of existence. Thus 'second' substance denotes the generic nature in itself absolutely, while 'first' substance signifies that nature as individually subsistent: wherefore the division is analogous rather than specific. Accordingly person is contained in the genus *substance*, although not as a species, but as defining a specific mode of existence.

Reply to the Seventh Objection. Some hold that *substance* is included in the definition of *person*, inasmuch as it signifies a hypostasis; but since the definition of hypostasis includes *individual* as opposed to community of universality and to part (for no universal or part of a thing, e.g. a hand or a foot, can be called a hypostasis) they say that *individual* is added in the definition of *person*, inasmuch as *individual* excludes the community of assumability: for they hold that human nature in Christ is a hypostasis but not a person. Wherefore, say they, to exclude assumability, *individual* is added in the definition of person. This, however, would seem contrary to the intention of Boethius who (*De Duab. Nat.*) by the term *individual* excludes universals from the definition of *person*. Hence it is better to say that in the definition of *person substance* does not stand for *hypostasis* but for that which is common to 'first' substance, i.e. hypostasis and 'second' substance, and is divided into both: so that this common (substance) by the addition of *individual* is narrowed down to the hypostasis, and thus to say : *An individual substance of rational nature*, is the same as to say : *A hypostasis of rational nature.*

Reply to the Eighth Objection. In view of what we have just said, this argument does not prove. *Substance* does not stand for *hypostasis*, but for that which is common to all substance in whatever sense it be taken. If, however, *substance* were to stand for *hypostasis* the objection would remain inconclusive : because the substance that is a hypostasis, is more akin to person than is subsistence, since person conveys the idea of subject like a 'first' substance, and not merely the idea of subsistence, as subsistence does. But seeing that the term *substance* is employed even by the Latins to denote the *essence*, therefore in order to avoid error we do not speak of three substances, as we do of three subsistences. The Greeks, however, who have the word hypostasis as distinct from οὐσία do not hesitate to acknowledge three hypostases in God.

Reply to the Ninth Objection. Just as we speak of three Persons in God so may we speak of three individual substances : but of only one substance that is the essence.

Reply to the Tenth Objection. *Rational* is the difference of animal, inasmuch as *reason* whence it is taken denotes discursive knowledge, such as is in angels but not in man nor in God. But Boethius takes *rational* in a broad sense for *intellectual*, and this is common to man, angels and God.

Reply to the Eleventh Objection. In the definition of *person* nature is not to be taken according as it is the principle of movement, in which sense it is defined by the Philosopher (*Phys.* ii, 1) but as defined by Boethius (*De Duab. Nat.*) according as it is the *specific difference giving each thing its form.* And since the difference completes the definition and confines the thing defined to its species, it follows that the term *nature* is more suitable in the definition of person which is special to certain substances, than the term *essence* which is most common.

Reply to the Twelfth Objection. In the definition of person *individual* signifies that which is not predicated of several; and in this sense the divine essence is not an individual substance by predication, inasmuch as it is predicated of several persons, although it is individual in itself. However, Richard of S. Victor (*De Trin.* iv, 18, 23) amends the definition of Boethius as applied to the divine Persons; and says that a person is *the incommunicable existence of the divine nature,* so as to indicate by the term *incommunicable* that the divine essence is not a Person.

Reply to the Thirteenth Objection. Seeing that an individual substance is something complete existing by itself, human nature in Christ, inasmuch as it was assumed into the divine Person, cannot be called an individual substance such as is a hypostasis, any more than a hand, a foot or anything that does not subsist by itself apart from anything else: and for this reason it does not follow that it is a person.

Reply to the Fourteenth Objection. The separated soul is a part of rational nature and not a whole rational human nature: wherefore it is not a person.

ARTICLE III

CAN THERE BE A PERSON IN GOD?
Sum. Th. I, Q. xxix, A. 3

THE third point of inquiry is whether there can be a person in God: and seemingly the reply should be in the negative.

1. According to Boethius (*De Duab. Nat.*) the word *person* is taken from *personating:* for masked men were called

persons, because they personated something in comedies and tragedies. But it is unbecoming for God to be masked except perhaps metaphorically speaking. Therefore the term person should not be applied to God except perhaps metaphorically.

2. As Damascene says (*De Fide Orth.* i, 1, 2, 4), it is impossible for us to know what any of the things are which we ascribe to God, as regards the sense in which they apply to him. Yet what a person is we know by the above-given definition (A. 2). Therefore *person* is not applicable to God, at least in the sense of the aforesaid definition.

3. God is not in a genus : because since he is infinite he cannot be confined within the limits of any genus. Now *person* signifies something in the genus of substance. Therefore *person* is not to be applied to God.

4. There is no composition in God. But *person* signifies something composite : for an individual of human nature, which is a person, is extremely composite : besides, the parts of the definition of *person* show that *person* is a composite thing. Therefore there is no person in God.

5. There is no matter in God. But matter is the principle of individuation. Since then a person is an individual substance, the term cannot be applied to God.

6. Every person is a subsistence. But God cannot be called a subsistence, for he is not subject to anything. Therefore he is not a person.

7. Person is comprised under hypostasis. Now there cannot be a hypostasis in God, since there are no accidents in him, and *hypostasis* denotes the subject of an accident as stated above (A. 1). Therefore there is no person in God.

The contrary is plain from the authority of Athanasius in the Creed, *Quicumque vult*, etc., and of Augustine (*De Trin.* vii, 6), and from the general usage of the Church who being taught of the Holy Ghost cannot err.

I answer that, as stated above, *person* denotes a certain nature with a certain mode of existence. Now the nature which *person* includes in its definition is of all natures the most exalted, to wit that nature which is intellectual in regard to its genus. Likewise the mode of existence signified by the word *person* is most exalted, namely that a thing exists by itself. Since then whatsoever is most excellent in creatures should be attributed to God, it is becoming that the word *person* should be attributed to God, even as other terms which are said of God properly.

Reply to the First Objection. Two things must be considered in a name: that which it is intended to signify, and that from which it is taken for the purpose of signification. For a name is often given to signify a certain thing, but is taken from an accident or an action or an effect of that thing, and yet these are not the chief signification of the name which denotes rather the very substance or nature of the thing. Thus the word *lapis* (stone) is taken from *laesio pedis* (hurting the foot), yet it does not signify this, but rather a body wherein such an accident is frequently found: so that *laesio pedis* belongs to the etymology of the word *lapis* rather than to its meaning. Accordingly when it is not the intended signification of a term that is appropriate to God, but some property by way of likeness, then such a term is applied to God metaphorically. Thus God is called a lion, not that the lion's nature is to be attributed to God, but on account of the lion's strength. When, however, that which the term signifies is appropriate to God, it is applied to God in its proper sense, for instance, good, wise and the like, although sometimes the source from which such terms are taken is not applicable to God. Thus although to personate as a masked man, whence comes the term *person*, is not to be attributed to God, yet that which the word signifies, namely *that which subsists in an intellectual nature* is appropriate to God: and for this reason the term *person* is ascribed to God in its proper sense.

Reply to the Second Objection. Both the word *person* and the definition of person given above are applicable to God: not, however, so as to be a definition of God, since there is more in God than is signified by the term. Hence the definition of the term does not define what God is.

Reply to the Third Objection. Although God is not in the genus of substance as a species, he belongs to the genus of substance as the principle of the genus.

Reply to the Fourth Objection. It is accidental to *person* as such that it is composite, because the complement or perfection required for personality is not to be found at once in one simple thing, but requires a combination of several, as is to be observed in men. But in God together with supreme simplicity there is supreme perfection : wherefore in him there is *person* without composition. As to the parts which combine to make the definition of *person* they do not argue composition in *person* except in material substances : and *individual*, being a negation, does not imply composition through being added to substance. Hence the only composition that remains is that of individual substance, i.e. hypostasis with the nature : which two in immaterial substances are absolutely one and the same thing.

Reply to the Fifth Objection. In material things whose forms are not self-subsistent but adherent to matter the principle of individuation must needs come from matter : whereas immaterial forms, being self-subsistent, are individualized by themselves, because from the very fact that a thing is self-subsistent, it cannot be predicated of several. Consequently there is no reason why there should not be an individual substance and a person in immaterial things.

Reply to the Sixth Objection. Although there is no composition in God by reason whereof we might be able to understand subjection of one thing to another in him, nevertheless by an act of the mind we consider his being apart from his substance as subject to his being, and from this point of view call it subsistence.

Reply to the Seventh Objection. Though there are no accidents in God, there are personal properties of which the hypostases are the subjects.

ARTICLE IV

IN GOD DOES THE TERM 'PERSON' SIGNIFY SOMETHING RELATIVE OR SOMETHING ABSOLUTE ?
Sum. Th. I, Q. xxix, A. 4

THE fourth point of inquiry is whether this term *person* signifies something relative or something absolute in God : and seemingly it signifies something absolute.

1. Augustine says (*De Trin.* vii, 4) that *when John states that there are three who bear witness in heaven, the Father, the Word and the Holy Ghost, if it be asked, Three what? the answer is, Three persons.* Now the query *What?* refers to the essence. Therefore in God *person* signifies the essence.

2. Augustine (*ibid.* 6) says that in God to be and to be a person are the same. Now in God *to be* denotes the essence and not a relation. Therefore *person* does so also.

3. Augustine (*loc. cit.*) says: *Person is predicated* (of the Father) *absolutely not with respect to the Son or the Holy Ghost: just as he is called God, great, good or just absolutely.* Now all these denote the essence and not a relation. Therefore *person* does so also.

4. Augustine (*ibid.* 4) says that although *the term essence is common to them*, namely the Father, Son and Holy Ghost, so that each one is called the essence, yet the term *person* is common to them. But relation in God is not common but distinctive. Therefore *person* does not signify relation in God.

5. It will be replied that in God *person* is common logically and not really. On the contrary, there are no universals in God: hence Augustine (*ibid.* 6) rejects the opinion of those who said that the *essence* in God is like a genus or species, and *person* like a species or individual. Now that which is common logically and not really is common after the manner of a universal. Hence in God *person* is common not merely logically but really, so that it cannot denote a relation.

6. A term does not denote things of different genera except equivocally: thus *acute* is applied equivocally to the sense of taste and to a mathematical figure. Now it is evident that *person* does not signify a relation in angels and man, but something absolute. Therefore if it signifies a relation in God, it will be employed equivocally.

7. That which is accidental to the thing signified by a term is beside the term's signification; thus *white* which is accidental to man is beside the signification of *man.* Now the thing signified by the word *person* is an individual substance of rational nature, since according to the Philosopher

(*Metaph.* iv) the description of what a word means is its definition: and it is accidental to such a substance that it be related to something else. Therefore relation is beside the signification of the word *person*.

8. It is inconceivable that any term be predicated of a thing to which the meaning of that term is seen to be inappropriate: thus if we understand that a certain thing is not a rational animal it is inconceivable that such a thing be a man. Now Jews and pagans acknowledge God to be a person; yet they do not acknowledge relations in him, whereas we ascribe them to him according to faith. Therefore *person* does not signify these relations in God.

9. But to this it will be replied that Jews and pagans err in their views about God: and thus we cannot argue from their opinion.—On the contrary neither an erroneous opinion not truth itself can change the meaning of a word: so that if the word *person* does not signify relation in the opinion of those who err about God, neither will it do so with those who think aright about him.

10. According to the Philosopher (*Peri Herm.* i) words are signs of ideas. Now the idea conceived of the word *person* is the idea of a ' first ' substance. Therefore this word *person* signifies a ' first ' substance, than which nothing is more absolute, since it is self-existent. Therefore the word *person* does not signify a relation, but something absolute.

11. But to this it may be replied that the word *person* signifies a relation after the manner of a substance.—On the contrary, this is a self-evident proposition: *No relation is a substance*, just as this: *No quantity is a substance*, according to the Philosopher (*Poster.* i). If then the word *person* signifies the substance as we have already proved, it cannot possibly signify a relation.

12. Opposite terms cannot be true of the same thing. Now self-existence and existence by another are opposite terms. If then *person* signifies substance which is a self-existent being, it cannot signify a relation.

13. A term that signifies a relation, is referred to something that it co-signifies, for instance, master and servant. Now it is clear that *person* has no reference to something

else. Therefore it does not signify a relation, but something absolute.

14. *Person* is as it were *one by itself (per se una)*. Now unity in God regards the essence. Therefore *person* signifies essence and not relation.

15. To this it will be replied that this word signifies one distinct thing, and since distinction in God arises from relation, *person* must signify relation.

On the contrary, the Son and Holy Ghost are said to be distinguished by the mode of their origin ; because the Son proceeds by way of the intellect as Word, and the Holy Ghost by way of the will, as Love. Therefore distinction in God is not through the relations alone : and consequently it does not follow that *person* signifies relation.

16. If relation causes distinction in God, while person is something distinct without causing distinction, relation cannot be signified by the word *person*.

17. The relations in God are called properties : whereas the person is something underlying the properties. Therefore it does not signify relation.

18. There are four relations in God, paternity, filiation, procession, common spiration : for innascibility which is the fifth notion is not a relation. But the word person signifies none of these : because if it signified paternity, it would not be said of the Son ; if it signified filiation, it would not be said of the Father ; if it signified the procession of the Holy Ghost, it would be said neither of the Father nor of the Son ; and if it signified the common spiration, it would not be said of the Holy Ghost. Therefore the word *person* does not signify relation.

On the contrary Boethius says (*De Trin.*) that *every term that refers to the persons signifies relation*. Now no term refers to the persons more than *person* itself. Therefore the word *person* signifies relation.

Again, in God under Person are included the Father, the Son and the Holy Ghost. But these names signify relation. Therefore *person* does also.

Again, nothing absolute is divided in God. But *person* is divided. Therefore it is not absolute but relative.

I answer that the term *person* in common with the absolute names of God is predicated of each Person, and does not in itself refer to anything else, and in common with the names signifying relation it is divided and predicated of several: wherefore it would seem that *person* admits of both significations absolute and relative. How the name *person* can admit of both significations has been explained in various ways.

Some say that *person* signifies both, but equivocally. They assert that in itself it expresses the essence absolutely both in the singular and in the plural, like the name *God*, or *good* or *great:* but that owing to the insufficiency of names employed in speaking of God, the holy fathers in the Council of Nicea accommodated the term *person* so that it could be employed sometimes in a relative sense, especially in the plural, as when we say that Father, Son and Holy Ghost are three Persons, or with the addition of a disjunctive term, as when we say: *One is the Person of the Father, another of the Son*, or: *The Son is distinct from the Father in Person.* And that when it is predicated in the singular absolutely, it may equally signify the essence or the relation, as when we say: *The Father is a Person*, or: *The Son is a Person.* Apparently this is the opinion of the Master (I., D. xxv): but this does not seem to be a satisfactory explanation. For it was not without reason taken from the very signification of the word, that the holy fathers inspired by God chose this term to express a profession of the true faith: and all the more seeing that they would have provided an occasion for error in affirming three Persons, if the word *person* signified the essence absolutely.

Wherefore others said that it expresses at the same time essence and relation but not equally; the one directly and the other indirectly. Some of them maintained that it expresses the essence directly and the relation indirectly: while others took the contrary view. Yet neither opinion solves the difficulty: for if it signifies the essence directly it should not be predicated in the plural, and if it signifies the relation directly, it should not be predicated absolutely or of each Person. Hence others said that it signifies both directly : and some of them said that it expresses equally both essence and relation, and neither more than the other.

But this is unintelligible : since that which does not signify one thing signifies nothing : wherefore according to the Philosopher (*Metaph.* iv) every term signifies one thing in one sense. Hence others said that it signifies relation as affecting the essence : but it is difficult to see how this is possible inasmuch as relations do not determine the essence in God. And so others said that the relation does not express the absolute, i.e. the substance which is essence, but the substance which is hypostasis, since this is determined by a relation. This is indeed true, but does not make us any wiser, seeing that the meaning of hypostasis or subsistence is less clear than that of person.

Accordingly to elucidate the matter it must be noted that, according to the Philosopher (*Metaph.* iv), the proper definition of a term is its signification. Now when a term is predicated of a thing which is directly included in the signification of that term as the determinate in the indeterminate, that thing is said to be classed under that term : but if it is not directly included in the term's signification it is said to be coupled with it. Thus *animal* signifies a sensible animate substance, and *white* signifies a colour that dilates the sight : while *man* is included directly in the idea of *animal* as the determinate in the indeterminate ; for *man* is a sensible animate substance, having a rational soul : and is included under *white*, not directly, however, since white is outside his essence. Hence man is classed under the term *animal*, but is coupled with the term *white*. And since that which comes under a common denomination is related to the common name as the determinate to the indeterminate, that which was included becomes the thing signified by the addition of a determining word to the common term : thus a rational animal is a man. But we must observe that a thing is signified in two ways, formally and materially. Formally a term signifies that which it was chiefly intended to signify and this is the definition of the term : thus *man* signifies something composed of a body and a rational soul. Materially a term signifies that which is requisite for that definition: thus *man* signifies something that has a heart, brain and such parts as are required in order that the body be animated with a rational soul.

Accordingly we reply that the term person signifies nothing else but an individual substance of rational nature. And since under an individual substance of rational nature is contained the substance, individual, i.e. incommunicable and distinct from others, whether of God, of man or of angels, it follows that a divine Person must signify something subsistent and distinct in the divine nature, just as a human person signifies something subsistent and distinct in human nature: and this is the formal signification of a person whether divine or human. Since, however, that which is distinct and subsistent in human nature is nothing else than something individualized and differentiated from others by individual matter, it follows that this is the material signification when we speak of a human person. But the only thing that is distinct and incommunicable in the divine nature is relation, since all that is absolute is common and undivided. Now in God relation is really the same as the essence. And as in God essence is identical with the one who has the essence (e.g. the Godhead is identical with God), so also is relation the same as the one who is related. Consequently relation is the same as that which is distinct and subsists in the divine nature. It is evident then that *person* commonly speaking signifies an individual substance of rational nature; while a divine *Person* in its formal signification denotes a distinct being subsistent in the divine nature. And seeing that this can be nothing else but a relation or a relative being, it follows that in its material signification it denotes a relation or a relative being. Hence it may be said that it signifies a relation by way of substance not *quâ* essence but *quâ* hypostasis, even as it signifies a relation not *quâ* relation but *quâ* relative: e.g. as signifying *Father* not as signifying *Paternity*. For in this way the signified relation is included indirectly in the signification of the divine Person, which is nothing but something distinct by a relation and subsistent in the divine essence.

Reply to the First Objection. *What?* queries not only the essence but also sometimes the supposit, for instance: *What swims in the sea? Fish.* And so the answer to *what?* is the person.

Reply to the Second Objection. It is on account of the mode of signification of this word *person*, that Augustine says: *In God to be and to be a Person are the same.* For it does not signify by way of relation as *Father* and *Son* do.

Reply to the Third Objection. It is due to the formal signification of *person* that it is predicated absolutely without reference to another.

Reply to the Fourth Objection. In God *essence* is common in reality, but person only logically, like the word relation.

Reply to the Fifth Objection. In God there are no differences of being since there is but one being in him. Now this is incompatible with the idea of universal, wherefore there is no universal in him, although there is in him one thing logically and not really.

Reply to the Sixth Objection. The fact that *person* designates one thing in God and another in man must be referred to a difference in suppositality rather than in the signification of the word *person:* and equivocation arises from a difference in signification but not in suppositality.

Reply to the Seventh Objection. Although relation is accidental to the common signification of *person*, it is not accidental to the divine Person, as we have proved above.

Reply to the Eighth Objection. This argument considers the formal and not the material signification of the term : and the same answer applies *to the Ninth Objection.*

Reply to the Tenth Objection. A 'first' substance is said to be absolute as being independent of another. In God, however, the relative term does not exclude the absolute that depends on another, but the absolute that is not related to another.

Reply to the Eleventh Objection. This proposition, *No relation is a substance* is self-evident if it refer to relation and substance that are in a genus. God, however, is not confined within the limits of a genus, but contains in himself the perfections of all genera. Wherefore relation and substance are not really distinct in him.

Reply to the Twelfth Objection. Self-existent is opposed to non-self-existent and not to that which is related to another.

Reply to the Thirteenth Objection. The word *person* does not itself refer to a relation, but by its mode of signification.

Reply to the Fourteenth Objection. In God *one* is common to essence and relation : thus we say that the essence is one, and that the Father is one.

Reply to the Fifteenth Objection. It may be that this different mode of procession whereby the Son is said to proceed by way of intellect, and the Holy Ghost by way of will, does not suffice for a personal distinction between the Holy Ghost and the Son, since in God will and intellect are not really distinct. If, however, it be granted that this suffices to make a distinction between them, it is clear that each is distinct from the Father by a relation, in that one of them proceeds from the Father by generation, the other by spiration, and these relations constitute their Persons.

Reply to the Sixteenth Objection. Just as relation signifies as causing distinction in God, so is that which is related signified as being distinct. Now in God relation and the thing related are not distinct, as neither are essence and that which is : hence in God that which distinguishes and that which is distinct are one and the same.

Reply to the Seventeenth Objection. In God property is not an accident, but is really the same as the thing whose property it is : although it differs therefrom logically. Accordingly *person* does not signify relation as a property, but as the essence underlying the property.

Reply to the Eighteenth Objection. Although there cannot be a universal without singulars, it can be understood apart from them and consequently signified. Hence it follows that if there are no singulars there is no universal : but it does not follow that unless some one singular be misunderstood or signified amiss, the universal is not understood or signified. Thus the word *man* does not signify any one individual man but only man in general : and in like manner the word *person*, although it does not signify paternity or filiation or common spiration or procession, it nevertheless signifies relation in general in the way already explained, even as the word *relation* does in its own particular way.

ARTICLE V

ARE THERE SEVERAL PERSONS IN GOD?
Sum. Th. I, Q. xxx, A. 1

THE fifth point of inquiry is whether there are several persons in God: and seemingly there are not.

1. Boethius says (*De Trin.*): *That is truly one in which there is no number.* But God is most truly one. Therefore number is not in him.

2. It will be replied that in God there is not number simply but a number of Persons.

On the contrary, from a qualified statement we may always infer a simple statement provided the qualification has not the effect of diminishing: thus from the proposition, *There is a white man,* it follows that *there is a man,* but from the proposition, *There is a dead man,* it does not follow that *there is a man.* Now when we say a *number of persons* the qualification does not diminish since *person* is something most complete. Therefore if in God there is a number of persons, it follows that there is number simply.

3. Unity is opposed to number according to the Philosopher (*Metaph.* x, text 20). But opposite things are not in the same subject. Since then in God there is supreme unity there cannot be number or plurality in him.

4. Wherever there is number there is plurality of units: and where there are several units there is manifold being, because the being of one unit is distinct from the being of another unit. If then there be number in God there must be manifold being and manifold essence; which is clearly false.

5. Just as unity is undivided so is there division in number. But there cannot be division in God since there is no composition in him. Therefore there cannot be number in God.

6. Every number has parts, for it is composed of units. But there are no parts in God, since there is no composition in him. Therefore number is not in God.

7. We should not attribute to God anything wherein the creature differs from him. Now the creature differs from God in that it is produced in a certain number, according to Wisdom xi, 21 : *Thou hast ordered all things in measure and number and weight.* Therefore we should not ascribe number to God.

8. Number is a species of quantity. But there is no quantity in God, inasmuch as if any quantitative expression were predicated of God he would be substantially changed, as says Boethius (*De Trin.*). Therefore either there is no number in God, or it belongs to his substance ; which is contrary to the faith.

9. Wheresoever is number there are those things to which number is liable, such as addition, subtraction, multiplication and division, and the like which result from number. But these cannot be in God. Therefore number cannot be in God.

10. Every number is finite. Therefore the infinite cannot be numbered. Since then God is infinite there cannot be number in him.

11. To this it might be replied that God though infinite to us is finite to himself.

On the contrary, that which belongs to God in himself is truer than that which belongs to him as compared to us. If then God is finite to himself and infinite to us he is more truly finite than infinite : and this is clearly false.

12. According to the Philosopher (*Metaph.* x) number is multitude measured by unity. But God is a measure, himself unmeasured. Therefore no number is in God.

13. In a nature that differs not from its supposit, it is impossible to have several supposits of that nature : since for this reason is it possible to have several men in the one human nature, that the individual man is not his own humanity : wherefore the multiplication of individuals in the one human nature is consequent to the diversity of individual principles, which are not part of the common

nature. Whereas in immaterial substances wherein the very nature of the species is the subsisting supposit, there cannot be several individuals of one species. Now in God there is the most complete identity of nature and supposit, because the divine being itself which is the divine nature, is subsistent. Therefore there cannot be in God several supposits or persons.

14. *Person* is the name of a thing : hence where there is not a number of things there is not a number of persons. Now there is not a number of things in God : for Damascene says (*De Fide Orth.* i, xi) that in God the Father, Son and Holy Ghost are really one thing, though logically and in our way of thinking they are distinct. Therefore in God there is not a number of persons.

15. There cannot be a number of things in one without composition. Now God is one : wherefore if in God there are several persons which is the same as several things, it follows that there is composition in him, and this is incompatible with his simplicity.

16. The absolute is more perfect than the relative. Now the absolute properties, namely the essential attributes such as wisdom, justice and so on, do not constitute so many persons in God. Neither therefore do the relative properties such as paternity and filiation.

17. That which differentiates things from one another stands in relation to them as their constituent difference. If then the divine Persons are distinguished by their relations, these latter must be the constituent differences of the Persons ; and consequently there will be composition in the divine Persons, inasmuch as the difference constitutes the species by being added to the genus.

18. Things that are distinguished by specifically different forms must themselves differ specifically : thus man and horse differ specifically as being rational and irrational. Now paternity and filiation are specifically different relations. If then the divine Persons are distinguished by the relations only, they must differ specifically, and consequently will not be of one nature ; which is against the faith.

19. It is inconceivable that several supposits have one

being. Now in God there is but one being. Therefore there cannot be several supposits or persons in him.

20. Since creation is the proper act of God alone, it must proceed from each supposit of the divine nature. Now it is impossible that this action, inasmuch as it is one, proceed from several supposits, because one action is from but one agent. Therefore there cannot be several supposits or persons in the divine nature.

21. Here below, difference in properties does not make a difference in supposits: thus one supposit of human nature is not distinct from another through the one being white and the other black; but through the diversity of individual matter which is the substance of each individual. If then in God there is no distinction save that which arises from relative properties, there cannot be in him a number of supposits or persons.

22. The highest creatures are more like God than the lowest. Now in the lowest creatures there are several supposits in one nature, whereas in the highest creatures, which are the heavenly bodies, there are not. Therefore in God there are not several persons in one nature.

23. The Philosopher (*De Cœlo et Mun.* i) says that when the whole perfection of a species is in one supposit there are not several supposits of that nature, and that for this reason there is but one world because it consists of its whole matter. Now the whole perfection of the divine nature is in one supposit. Therefore in the one nature there are not several supposits or persons.

24. To this it may be replied that the fullness of joy requires the companionship of several in the divine nature, because there is no pleasure in possessing a thing unless we share it with a companion, according to Boethius. Moreover perfect love is to love another as oneself.—On the contrary, to depend on another for the fullness of one's joy and love is an indication of insufficient goodness in oneself. Hence the Philosopher says (*Ethic.* ix, 4) that the wicked through finding no pleasure in their own company seek the companionship of others: whereas the good seek to commune with themselves through finding pleasure in so doing. Now

the divine nature cannot lack a sufficiency of goodness. Wherefore since one supposit of the divine nature has in himself all fullness of joy and love, there is no need to put several supposits or persons in God.

On the contrary it is written (1 Jo. v 7): *There are three who give testimony in heaven, the Father, the Word and the Holy Ghost.*

Again Athanasius says in the Creed: *All the three Persons are co-eternal and co-equal with one another.* Therefore in God there is a number of Persons.

I answer that the plurality of Persons in God is an article of faith, and natural reason is unable to discuss and adequately understand it though we hope to understand it in heaven when we shall see God in his essence, and faith will be succeeded by vision. The holy fathers, however, being pressed by those who gainsaid the faith, were compelled to discuss this and other matters of belief, yet humbly and reverently withal, and avoiding any pretence to comprehension. Nor is such a discussion without its use since it enables the mind to perceive some glimpse of the truth sufficient to steer clear of error. Wherefore Hilary (*De Trin.* ii) says: *Believing this*, namely the plurality of Persons in God, *set forth, run, persevere, and though I may know that you will not reach, I shall acclaim your progress. He who religiously pursues the infinite, although he will never catch up with it, will progress so long as he continues.*

In order then to throw some light on this question and especially in accordance with the elucidations of Augustine, we must observe that we must attribute to God every perfection that is in creatures, as regards the essence of the perfection absolutely but not as regards the way in which it is in this or that one. Thus goodness or wisdom is not in God as an accident as it is in us, although in him is supreme goodness and perfect wisdom. Now in creatures nothing is more excellent or more perfect than to understand: a sign of which is that of all creatures intellectual substances are the highest and are said to be made to God's image in respect of their intelligence. It follows then that understanding is in God as well as whatsoever is essential thereto, although it belongs to God in one way and to creatures in another. Now for the act of understanding it is essential that there be one who understands and something understood. And that which is understood in itself is not the thing that is known by the intellect, since this thing is at one time only potentially understood and is outside the person who understands, as when a man understands a material thing, for instance a stone, an animal or something of the kind: whereas the thing understood must be in the person who understands and must be one with him. Now the intelligible species is the likeness of the thing understood, which likeness informs the intellect for the purpose of understanding. For the intellect cannot understand except in so far as it is actuated by this likeness, just as nothing else can act as being in potentiality but only as actuated by a form. Accordingly this likeness is as the principle in the act of understanding, just as heat is the principle of calefaction, and not as the term of understanding. Consequently that which is the first and direct object in the act of understanding is something that the intellect conceives within itself about the thing understood, whether it be a definition or proposition according to the two operations of the intellect mentioned in *De Anima*, iii. Now this concept of the intellect is called the interior word and is signified by means of speech: for the spoken word does not signify merely the thing understood, or the intelligible form thereof or the act of understanding, but the concept of the intellect through which it signifies the thing: as when I say, *Man*, or, *Man is an animal*. And in this respect it matters not whether the intellect understands itself, or something else: since just as when it understands another thing from itself it forms a concept of that thing which is expressed orally, so also when it understands itself it forms a concept of itself which also can be expressed by word of mouth. Since then in God there is the act of understanding, and since in understanding himself he understands all other things, it follows that there must be in him an intellectual concept which is absolutely essential to the act of understanding. And if we were able to comprehend the divine act of understanding so as to grasp what it is and how it takes place, just as we grasp our own act of understanding, the conception of the divine Word would not surpass reason as neither does the conception of the human word. We can, however, know what it is not and understand how it is not : and thus we are able to know the difference between the Word conceived by God and the word conceived by us. Thus first of all we know that in God there is but one act of understanding and not many as in us : for our act of understanding a stone is distinct from our act of understanding a plant : whereas God by one act understands himself and all else. Hence our intellect conceives many words, but the Word conceived by God is but one. Again our intellect frequently understands both itself and other things imperfectly ; whereas God's act of understanding cannot be imperfect. Hence God's Word is perfect, representing all things perfectly, while our word is often imperfect. Again, in our intellect, understanding and being are distinct, wherefore the word conceived in our intellect, since it proceeds from our intellect as such, is not united to it in nature but in the act of understanding. Whereas God's act of understanding is his being, so that the Word which proceeds from God as understanding proceeds from him as existing : and for this reason the conceived Word has the same essence and nature as the conceiving intellect. And because that which in living things is the recipient of nature, is said to be begotten and is called a son, the Word of God is said to be begotten and is called the Son. Whereas our word cannot be described as begotten of our intellect or as its son, except metaphorically.

Accordingly since the word of our intellect is distinct from our intellect in two respects, namely in that it proceeds from it, and is of a different nature, and seeing that difference of nature must be removed from the divine Word (Q. viii, A. 1), the only remaining distinction is that it proceeds from another. And whereas difference causes number it follows that the only number in God is that of relations. Now in God relations are not accidents, but each one is the divine essence in reality. Wherefore each of them like the divine essence is subsistent : and just as the Godhead is the same thing as God, so is Paternity the same thing as the Father, and therefore the Father is the same thing as God. Accordingly the number of relations is the number of things subsistent in the divine nature, and these are the three Persons as appears from the preceding Article. For this reason then we place a number of Persons in God.

Reply to the First Objection. By these words Boethius means to exclude number from the divine essence: for this is the point of his discussion.

Reply to the Second Objection. Although the Persons considered as subsistent do not detract from the idea of number, they do so considered as relations: because relative distinction is the least of all distinctions just as relation itself of all the genera has the least being.

Reply to the Third Objection. Unity and number are both attributed to God but not in the same respect: unity in respect of the essence, number in respect of the Persons: or unity in respect of absolutes, number in respect of relations.

Reply to the Fourth Objection. Since plurality of units is caused by a distinction, if this distinction be one of being the units must differ in being: but where the distinction is one of relation, the units that compose the number must differ only relatively from one another.

Reply to the Fifth Objection. Any kind of distinction suffices to cause a plurality of like kind. Wherefore as in God there is no distinction in that which is absolute (which distinction is inseparable from composition) but only a distinction of relations, even so in God there is not plurality in respect of what is absolute, but only in respect of relations, as already stated.

Reply to the Sixth Objection. The parts of a number are always units if we speak of absolute number whereby we count. But if we take number as it is in things, then the idea of whole and part does not apply to number itself but to the things numbered. Now the different relations in God are not parts: thus fatherhood and sonship are not parts of Socrates, although he is father of one and son of another. Wherefore neither are the units of the relations compared as parts to the number of relations.

Reply to the Seventh Objection. The creature differs from God in that it is produced in a number of essential principles. But this kind of number is not that of the Persons.

Reply to the Eighth Objection. The number which is a species of quantity is caused by a division of a continuous quantity : wherefore just as continuous quantity relates to mathematics, because it is separated from sensible matter logically and not in reality, so also number which is a species of quantity is the subject-matter of arithmetic the principle whereof is unity that is the first measure of quantity. Hence it is plain that number of this kind cannot be in immaterial things ; but in them is multitude that is opposed to the unity that is convertible with being : and this is caused by formal division which is into opposite forms whether absolute or relative : and such is number in God.

Reply to the Ninth Objection. Number that is a species of quantity is liable to such things : but this kind of number is not in God, as stated above.

Reply to the Tenth Objection. God is infinite in the perfection of greatness, wisdom and the like, wherefore it is written (Ps. cxlvi, 5) that *of his wisdom there is no number :* but procession in God, by reason of which there are several divine Persons, does not tend to the indefinite, for as Augustine says (*De Trin.*) the divine generation is not immoderate : therefore neither is the number of Persons infinite.

Reply to the Eleventh Objection. God is said to be finite to himself, not that he knows himself to be finite, but because he is compared to himself as we to finite things, in that he comprehends himself.

Reply to the Twelfth Objection. This is the definition of number as a kind of quantity to which the idea of measure is applicable.

Reply to the Thirteenth Objection. In created things the principles of individuality exercise two functions. The one is that they are the principle of subsistence (since the common nature does not subsist by itself except in the individual) : and the other is that they distinguish the supposits of the common nature from one another. But in God the personal properties only distinguish the supposits of the divine nature from one another, while they are not the principles of subsistence of the divine essence (since the divine essence is subsistent in itself) but on the contrary subsist by the essence; thus Paternity is a subsistent thing because the divine essence with which it is identical is a subsistent thing: so that it follows that as the divine essence is God, so is Paternity the Father. And hence it follows likewise that the divine essence is not numerically multiplied by reason of the multiplicity of its supposits, as happens here below. Because a thing is multiplied on account of that which gives it subsistence: and although the divine essence is so to speak individualized by itself as regards its self-subsistence, yet though it is itself one in number there are several supposits in God mutually distinct by subsistent relations.

Reply to the Fourteenth Objection. If the Father, Son and Holy Ghost differed from one another logically and not really, there would be no reason why one should not be predicated of the other: even so a shirt and an undergarment may be predicated of each other; and in like manner the Father would be the Son and vice versa: which is the heresy of Sabellius. Hence we must reply that Father, Son and Holy Ghost are three things, as Augustine says (*De Doctr. Christ.* i, 5), provided thing be taken for a relative thing: for if it be taken as absolute, then they are but one thing, as again Augustine says. In this sense we must take the words of Damascene where he says that they are really one. And when he says that they differ only logically, this is generally understood to mean relatively. For although a relation as compared with the opposite relation makes a real distinction in God, it does not differ save logically from the divine essence. Moreover relation of all the genera is the least stable in point of reality.

Reply to the Fifteenth Objection. In God plurality of things is plurality of subsistent opposite relations, and this does not cause composition in God: because relation as compared to the divine essence differs not really but only logically. Hence it does not enter into composition with it, as neither does goodness nor any other of the essential attributes : whereas if we compare it with the opposite relation there are several things, but not composition ; because opposite relations as such are distinct from each other : and composition is not of distinct things as such.

Reply to the Sixteenth Objection. The essential attributes are in no way opposed to one another as the relations are : wherefore although like the relations they subsist, they do not constitute a plurality of mutually distinct supposits, since plurality follows distinction : and formal distinction arises from opposition.

Reply to the Seventeenth Objection. In God there is no difference between what is signified as a form and what is signified as a supposit : for instance, Godhead and God, Paternity and Father. Hence although the relative properties are by way of constituent differences of the Persons, it does not follow that they enter into composition with the Persons thus constituted.

Reply to the Eighteenth Objection. Although the Father and the Son are not distinct from each other except by paternity and filiation, it does not follow that because paternity and filiation are specifically different relations in God there is therefore a kind of specific difference between Father and Son : for these relations do not specify the divine Persons, but rather distinguish and constitute the supposits. That which specifies the divine Persons is the divine nature wherein the Son is like the Father. Because the begetter begets his like in species and not in individual properties. Accordingly just as Socrates and Plato, even if the only difference between them as individuals were that one is black and the other white (which are specifically different qualities) would not differ themselves specifically ; since that which is a species to white and black is not a species to Socrates and Plato : even so the specific difference between paternity and filiation does not cause a specific difference between Father and Son. And yet in God it cannot be said properly that anything differs specifically, inasmuch as species and genus are not in him.

Reply to the Nineteenth Objection. It must by no means be granted that there is more than one being in God : seeing that being always refers to essence and especially in God whose being is his essence. But the relations which distinguish the supposits in God do not add another being to the being of the essence, because they do not enter into composition with the essence, as already stated. And every form that adds being to the substantial being enters into composition with the substance, and its being is accidental, for instance, the being of white and black. Accordingly difference in respect of being follows plurality of supposits, just as difference of essence in creatures : but neither of these obtains in God.

Reply to the Twentieth Objection. Operation issues from the agent in ratio to the form or power that is the principle of the operation : wherefore there is no reason why the one creation should not proceed from the three Persons since they are of one nature and power : thus if three hot things had the same identical heat, one identical heating would issue from them.

Reply to the Twenty-first Objection. The individualizing forms in creatures are not subsistent as in God : hence the comparison fails.

Reply to the Twenty-second Objection. In creatures multiplication of essence entails multiplication of supposits : but this is not the case in God ; wherefore the conclusion does not follow.

Reply to the Twenty-third Objection. Although the Godhead is wholly and perfectly in each of the three Persons according to its proper mode of existence, yet it belongs to the perfection of the Godhead that there be several modes of existence in God, namely that there be one from whom another proceeds yet proceeds from no other, and one proceeding from another. For there would not be absolute perfection in God unless there were in him procession of word and love.

Reply to the Twenty-fourth Objection. This argument takes it for granted that the divine Persons differ in essence. For thus the fullness of delight that the Father has in the Son would be in something extrinsic and the Father would not have it in himself ; but because the Son is in the Father as his Word, the Father could not have perfect joy in himself except in the Son; even so a man does not delight in himself except through the concept he has of himself.

ARTICLE VI

IN SPEAKING OF GOD CAN THE WORD 'PERSON' BE RIGHTLY PREDICATED IN THE PLURAL?

Sum. Th. I, Q. xxx, A. 4

THE sixth point of inquiry is whether when we speak of God we may rightly use the word *person* in the plural: and seemingly not.

1. A person is a substance, as appears from the definition of Boethius. But substance in God is not predicated in the plural. Neither therefore is *person*.

2. Other absolute names in God are only predicated in the singular, for instance *wise, good* and so forth. Now the word *person* is an absolute term. Therefore in God it should not be predicated in the plural.

3. The word *person* apparently is taken from subsistence, inasmuch as it denotes an individual in the genus *substance*, and is so to speak one by itself (*per se una*). Now subsistence would seem to pertain to the essence, and this is not multiplied in God. Therefore the word *person* should not be predicated in the plural.

4. To this it will be replied that even if subsistence be derived from essence, we can still say that there are three subsistents in God, and likewise three persons.

On the contrary terms that signify the divine essence cannot be predicated in the plural unless they be adjectives which do not take their number from the form signified but from the supposits, whereas the contrary obtains in substantives. Hence we may say that in God there are three eternal, if *eternal* be an adjective, whereas if it be a substantive then the words of Athanasius are true: *Not three eternals but one eternal*. Now *person* is a substantive and not an adjective. Therefore it should not be predicated in the plural.

5. Although essential adjectives are predicated of God in the plural, the forms signified by them are not predicated in the plural but only in the singular. Thus although in a certain sense we may use the plural in predicating *eternal* of God, in no way do we speak of three eternities. Therefore although in a sense we may speak of three persons in God, by no means may we say that there are three personalities.

6. Just as *God* signifies one who has Godhead, so a divine Person denotes one who subsists in the Godhead. Now just as we speak of three subsisting in the Godhead so do we speak of three having the Godhead. If then this suffices for us to say that there are three Persons in God, we may also say that there are three Gods, which is heretical.

7. Boethius (*De Trin.*) says that there are not three Gods because God does not differ from God in the Godhead. But in like manner seemingly one divine Person does not differ from another by a personal difference, since it is common to them to be a person. Therefore *person* cannot be predicated of God in the plural.

On the contrary Augustine says (*De Trin.* vii. 4) that when we ask, *what are these three, Father, Son and Holy Ghost?* the reply is: *Three persons.* Therefore person is predicated of God in the plural.

Again Athanasius says (*loc. cit.*) that *one is the person of the Father, another that of the Son, another of the Holy Ghost.* Now otherness is the cause of number, therefore *person* must be predicated of God in the plural.

I answer that substantives, as stated above, take their number from the form signified, and adjectives from the supposits: and the reason of this is that substantives signify after the manner of a substance, while adjectives signify after the manner of an accident which is individualized and multiplied by its subject, but a substance by itself. Accordingly seeing that *person* is a substantive the possibility of its being predicated in the plural depends on the form signified thereby. Now the form signified by the word *person* is not the nature absolutely, for in that case man and human person would mean the same thing which is clearly false: but person formally signifies incommunicability or individuality of one subsisting in a nature, as we have clearly explained. Since then there are several properties which cause a distinct and incommunicable being in God, it follows that *person* is predicated of God in the plural, even as it is predicated of man on account of the manifold individualizing principles.

Reply to the First Objection. A person is an individual substance which is a hypostasis: and this is predicated in the plural as is evident from its use in Greek.

Reply to the Second Objection. Person is an absolute term from its mode of signification: and yet it signifies a relation, as stated above.

Reply to the Third Objection. The word *person* indicates not only subsistence which apparently belongs to the essence, but also distinction and incommunicability, which are due to the relative properties in God.

Reply to the Fourth Objection. The form signified by the word *person* is not the essence taken absolutely, but is that which is the principle of incommunicability or individuation. For this reason is it predicated in the plural, although it is a substantive. And for this reason also, since there are several distinctive properties in God there are said to be several personalities. Wherefore the *Reply to the Fifth Objection* is clear.

Reply to the Sixth Objection. The word *person* signifies one that subsists in the divine nature distinctly and incommunicably: whereas the word *God* signifies one who has the divine nature without reference to distinction or incommunicability: hence the comparison fails.

Reply to the Seventh Objection. Although God differs not from God by a difference in the Godhead, for there is only one Godhead: yet divine Person differs from divine Person by a difference of personality, since in God personality includes also the property that distinguishes the persons.

ARTICLE VII

ARE NUMERAL TERMS PREDICATED OF THE DIVINE PERSONS ?

Sum. Th. I, Q. xxx, A. 3

THE seventh point of inquiry is as to how numeral terms are predicated of the divine Persons, whether positively or only negatively : and it would seem that they are predicated positively.

1. If they signify nothing positive in God, then by affirming three Persons we do not speak of something that is in God. Therefore by denying three Persons one would not deny anything that is in God : and consequently one would not say that which is untrue nor would one be a heretic.

2. According to Dionysius (*Div. Nom.*)[1] things are predicated of God in three ways : negatively, eminently and causally. Now in whichever of these three senses numeral terms are predicated of God they must needs have a positive signification. This is evident if they be predicated eminently or causally : and likewise if they be predicated negatively. For as the same Dionysius says (*Cœl. Hier.* ii ; *Div. Nom.* iv, xi) we do not deny things of God as though he lacked them altogether, but because they are not appropriate to him in the same way as they are to us. Therefore in any way numeral terms must have a positive meaning as applied to God.

3. Whatsoever is predicated of God and creatures is affirmed in a more eminent sense of God than of creatures. Now numeral terms are predicated of creatures positively. Therefore with much more reason are they thus predicated of God.

4. Plurality and unity as implied by the numeral terms when predicated of God are not mere mental concepts, for thus there would not be three Persons in God save logically, which belongs to the heresy of Sabellius. Therefore they must be something really in God, and consequently predicated of him positively.

[1] *Myst. Theol.* i.

5. As unity is in the genus of quantity, so is good in the genus of quality. Now in God there is neither quantity nor quality nor any accident, and yet goodness is predicated of God not negatively but positively. Therefore unity is predicated of him in the same way, and consequently plurality which is based on unity.

6. There are four transcendentals, namely being, unity, truth and goodness. Now three of these, to wit being, truth and goodness, are predicated of God positively. Therefore unity is also and consequently plurality.

7. Number and magnitude are two species of quantity, namely discrete and continuous quantity. Now magnitude is predicated of God positively (Ps. cxlvi, 5): *Great is our Lord and great is his power*. Therefore multitude and unity are also.

8. Creatures are like God inasmuch as they bear a trace of the Godhead. Now according to Augustine (*De Trin.* vi, 10) every creature bears a trace of the divine Trinity, inasmuch as it is *one particular thing, informed by a species*, and *has a certain order*. Therefore the creature is one in its likeness to God. Now *one* is predicated of a creature positively: and therefore of God also.

9. If *one* be predicated of God in a privative sense, it follows that it removes something, and this can only be plurality. Now it does not remove plurality, since if there be one *Person* it does not follow that there are not more. Therefore *one* is not said of God by way of remotion: and consequently neither is number.

10. Privation constitutes nothing: whereas unity constitutes number. Therefore the latter is not predicated in a privative sense.

11. There is no privation in God, since all privation is a defect. Now *one* is predicated of God. Therefore it does not denote a privation.

12. Augustine says (*De Trin.* v, 5) that whatsoever is predicated of God indicates either substance or relation. And Boethius (*De Trin.* iv) says that *whatsoever is predicated of God refers to the substance* except relative terms. If then numeral terms are predicated of God they must denote

either the substance or a relation, and consequently must be predicated positively.

13. One and being are convertible terms and are apparently synonymous. Now being is predicated of God positively. Therefore one is also and consequently number.

14. If *one* be predicated of God by way of remotion, it must remove number as being contrary thereto. But this cannot be the case, since number is constituted by units: and one contrary is not made up of the other. Therefore *one* is not predicated of God by way of remotion.

15. If *one* indicate the removal of number, it follows that *one* is opposed to number as privation to habit. Now habit is naturally prior to privation: as well as logically, since privation cannot be defined except in reference to habit. Therefore number will precede unity both naturally and logically: which is apparently absurd.

16. If one and number are predicated of God by way of remotion, then *one* removes *number* and *number* removes *unity*. But this cannot be admitted, since it would lead to a vicious circle, namely that unity is where there is not number, and number where there is not unity, and we should be none the wiser. Therefore we must not say that *one* and *number* are said of God privatively.

17. Since *one* and *many* are as measure and measured it would seem that they are opposed to each other relatively. Now when terms are relatively opposite both are predicated positively. Therefore both *unity* and *number* are predicated of God positively.

1. *On the contrary,* Dionysius says (*Div. Nom.* iv, 13): *That Unity with Trinity in which we worship the supreme Godhead is not the same unity or trinity with which we or any other living being are acquainted.* Therefore seemingly numeral terms are predicated of God by way of remotion.

2. Augustine says (*De Trin.* viii, 4): *The poor human tongue sought how to express the Three, and it called them substances or persons: not intending to imply that they are different, yet desirous to avoid saying that there is only one.* Hence in speaking of God these numeral terms are employed negatively rather than positively.

3. *One* and *many*, i.e. *number* are in the genus of quantity. Now there is no quantity in God, seeing that quantity is an accident and a disposition of matter. Therefore numeral terms indicate nothing positive in God.

4. To this it will be replied that although quantity as to its generic nature or considered as an accident cannot be in God, yet in its specific nature a certain kind of quantity may be predicated of God, even as a certain kind of quality such as knowledge or justice.

On the contrary only those species of quality can be predicated of God which in their specific nature contain no imperfection, such as knowledge, justice, equity, but not ignorance or whiteness. But all quantity by its specific nature implies imperfection: because since a thing that has quantity is divisible, the various species of quantity are distinguished according to various kinds of division: thus plurality is quantity divisible into non-continuous parts: a line is quantity divisible as to one dimension: while a surface is divisible as to two, and a body as to three. Now division is incompatible with the perfection of divine simplicity. Therefore no quantity as to its specific nature can be predicated of God.

5. But it will be argued that distinction according to the relations which causes the number of Persons in God, does not imply perfection in him.

On the contrary every division or distinction causes plurality of some kind. Now not every kind of plurality is that number which is a species of quantity, inasmuch as *many* and *one* pervade all the genera. Hence not any division or distinction suffices to set up number which is a species of quantity, but only quantitative division, and such is not relative division.

6. But it will be objected that every plurality is a species of quantity, and every division suffices to cause a species of quantity.

On the contrary given substance, quantity does not necessarily follow, inasmuch as substance can be without accident. Now given substantial forms only, there follows distinction in substances. Therefore not every distinction causes number, which is an accident and a species of quantity.

7. Discreteness that causes number which is a species of

quantity is opposed to continuity. Now discreteness is opposed to continuity because it consists in division of the continuous. Therefore only division of the continuous, which division is impossible in God, causes number that is a species of quantity : so that such a number cannot be predicated of God.

8. Every substance is one. Either then it is one by its essence, or by something else. If by something else, since this again must be one, it must be one either of itself or by something else, and this again by something else. But this cannot go on indefinitely : and hence we must stop somewhere. And it were better to stop at the beginning, so that substance be one of itself. Therefore unity is not something added to substance : and thus seemingly it does not signify anything positively.

9. But it will be argued that a substance is one not by itself but by accidental unity : and unity is one essentially, since the primary notions are named after themselves : thus goodness is good, truth is true and likewise unity is one. —On the contrary these are named after themselves because they are primary forms ; whereas second forms are not named after themselves : thus whiteness is not white. Now things which result from addition to others are not primary. Therefore unity and goodness are not additional to substance.

10. According to the Philosopher (*Metaph.* v) a thing is one in so far as it is undivided. Now to be undivided is nothing positive but only removes something. Therefore unity is predicated of God not positively but negatively : and the same applies to number which is composed of units.

I answer that about unity and number there are various points which have given rise to various opinions among philosophers. As regards unity it is to be observed that it is the principle of number and that it is convertible with being : and as regards plurality it belongs to a species of quantity called number ; moreover, it pervades all the genera like unity, which apparently is opposed to number.

Accordingly some philosophers failed to distinguish between unity which is convertible with being, and unity which is the principle of number, and thought that in neither sense does unity add anything to substance, and that in either sense it denotes the substance of a thing. From this it followed that number which is composed of unities is the substance of all things : and this was the opinion of Pythagoras and Plato.

On the other hand others who failed to distinguish between unity that is convertible with being and unity that is the principle of number held the contrary opinion that in any sense unity adds a certain accidental being to substance : and that in consequence all number is an accident pertaining to the genus of quantity. This was the opinion of Avicenna : and apparently all the teachers of old followed him : for they did not understand by one and many anything else but something pertaining to discrete quantity.

There were others who, considering that there cannot be quantity of any kind in God, maintained that words signifying one or many have no positive signification when attributed to God, but only remove something from him. For they cannot ascribe to him save what they signify, to wit discrete quantity, and this can nowise be in God. Hence according to these *one* is predicated of God in order to remove the plurality of discrete quantity ; and terms signifying plurality are said of God in order to remove that unity which is the principle of discrete quantity. Apparently this was the view of the Master (I., D. xxiv) : and granted the principle on which his opinion is based, namely that all multitude signifies discrete quantity, and all unity is the principle of such quantity, this opinion would seem of all the most reasonable. For Dionysius (*Cæl. Hier.* ii) says that we are nearer the truth when we speak of God in the negative, and that all our affirmations about him are figurative. For we know not what God is, but rather what he is not, as Damascene says (*De Fid. Orth.* i, 4). Hence Rabbi Moses says that whatever we affirm about God is to be taken as removing something from him rather than as placing something in him. Thus we say that God is a living being in order to remove from him that mode of being which inanimate beings have, and not in order to ascribe life to him ; since life and all such terms are employed to denote certain forms and perfections of creatures which are far distant from God. And yet this is not altogether true, for as Dionysius says (*Div. Nom.* xii) wisdom and life and the like are not removed from God as though they were not in him ; but because he has them in a higher degree than mind can conceive or words express : and from that divine perfection created perfections come down in an imperfect likeness to it. Wherefore things are said of God according to Dionysius (*Myst. Theol.* i : *Cœl. Hier.* ii : *Div. Nom.* ii) not only negatively and causally but also eminently. Still whatever the truth may be with regard to spiritual perfections it is certain that material dispositions are altogether to be removed from God. Wherefore since quantity is a disposition of matter, if numeral terms signify nothing outside the genus of quantity it follows that they are not to be said of God except as removing what they signify, according to the Master's opinion (*loc. cit.*), and although in his opinion unity removes plurality and plurality unity, this does not involve a vicious circle, because the unity and plurality removed from God are in the genus of quantity, neither of which can be ascribed to God. So that the unity ascribed to God which removes plurality is not removed, but that other unity which cannot be said of God.

Some, however, through not understanding how affirmative expressions can be predicated of God for the purpose of negation, and not conceiving unity and plurality except as included in the genus of discrete quantity, which they dared not ascribe to God, said that numeral terms are not predicated of God as though they expressed an idea with an objective reality, but as official expressions positing something in God, namely a kind of syncategorematic distinction, all of which is clearly absurd, since nothing of the kind can be had from the meaning of these terms.

Wherefore others, though holding that unity and multitude are only in the genus of quantity, said that these terms denote something positive in God. They say in effect that it is not unreasonable to ascribe some kind of quantity to God, although the genus is not to be attributed to him : even as certain species of quality, as wisdom and justice are predicated of God, although there cannot be quality in God. But as indicated in an objection (5) there is no comparison: because all the species of quantity from their specific nature are imperfect, but not all the species of quality. Moreover quantity properly speaking is a disposition of matter: so that all the species of quantity are mathematical entities which cannot exist apart from sensible matter, except time and place which are natural entities and which are better described as adjuncts of sensible matter. It is evident then that no species of quantity can be attributed to spiritual things otherwise than metaphorically. Whereas quality follows the form, wherefore certain qualities are altogether immaterial and can be ascribed to spiritual things. Accordingly the above opinions were based on the supposition that the *one* which is convertible with *being* is the same with that which is the principle of number, and that there is no plurality but number that is a species of quantity. Now this is clearly false. For since division causes plurality and indivision unity, we must judge of *one* and *many* according to the various kinds of division. Now there is a kind of division which altogether transcends the genus of quantity, and this is division according to formal opposition which has nothing to do with quantity. Hence the plurality resulting from such a division, and the unity which excludes such a division, must needs be more universal and comprehensive than the genus of quantity. Again there is a division of quantity which does not transcend the genus of quantity. Wherefore the plurality consequent to this division and the unity which excludes it are in the genus of quantity. This latter unity is an accidental addition to the thing of which it is predicated, in that it measures it: otherwise the number arising from this unity would not be an accident nor the species of a genus. Whereas the unity that is convertible with being, adds nothing to being except the negation of division, not that it signifies indivision only, but substance with indivision: for *one* is the same as individual being. In like manner the plurality that corresponds to this unity adds nothing to the *many things* except distinction, which consists in each one not being the other: and this they have not from anything added to them but from their proper forms. It is clear then that *one* which is convertible with *being*, posits *being* but adds nothing except the negation of division. And the *number* corresponding to it adds this to the things described as *many*, that each of them is *one*, and that each of them is not the other, wherein is the essence of distinction. Accordingly then, while *one* adds to *being* one negation inasmuch as a thing is undivided in itself; *plurality* adds two negations, inasmuch as a certain thing is undivided in itself, and distinct from another; i.e. one of them is not the other.

I say then that in speaking of God we do not predicate the unity and plurality which belong to the genus of quantity, but *one* that is convertible with being and the corresponding plurality. Wherefore *one* and *many* predicate in God that which they signify: but they add nothing besides distinction and indistinction, which is the same as to add negations as explained above. Hence we grant that as regards what they add to the things of which they are predicated, they are attributed to God by way of removal; but in so far as in their signification they include the things of which they are said they are predicated of God positively. We must now reply to the objections on both sides.

Reply to the First Objection. To speak of three Persons in God is to indicate a distinction of Persons: and to deny this is heresy. But this distinction adds nothing to the distinct Persons.

Reply to the Second Objection. It is true that while we remove certain things from God we understand at the same time that these things are predicated of God eminently and causally: but some things are denied of God absolutely and in no way predicated of him; as for instance, *God is not a body.* In this way according to the Master's opinion it might be said that numeral quantity is altogether denied of God: and in like manner according to our own opinion when we say: *The divine essence is one*, we altogether deny that God's essence is divided.

Reply to the Third Objection. In created things numeral terms posit nothing in addition to the things to which they are affixed, except in so far as they signify something in the genus of discrete quantity : in this way they are not predicated of God, and this pertains to his perfection.

Reply to the Fourth Objection. It is true that the unity and plurality signified by numeral terms predicated of God are not purely subjective but are really in God : and yet it does not follow that they signify something positive besides the things to which they are attributed.

Reply to the Fifth Objection. The good that is a kind of quality is not the good that is convertible with being. The latter adds nothing real to being, whereas the former adds a quality in respect of which a man is said to be good. The same applies to unity, as already explained ; yet there is this difference that good in either sense can be predicated of God, whereas unity cannot : because as already explained the comparison between quantity and quality fails.

Reply to the Sixth Objection. Of these primary notions being is the first, wherefore it must be predicated positively : because negation or privation cannot be the first thing conceived by the intellect, since we cannot understand a negation or privation unless we first understand what is denied or lacking. But the other three must add something that is not a contraction of being : for if they contracted being they would no longer be primary notions. Now this is impossible unless that which they add were purely logical, and this is either a negation which is added by unity as already stated, or relation or something which by its very nature is universally referable to being : and this is either the intellect to which the true bears a relation, or the appetite to which the good bears a relation, for the good is what all things seek (*Ethic.* i, 1).

Reply to the Seventh Objection. According to the Philosopher (*Metaph.* x) we speak of a *number* of things in two senses : first absolutely, and then *number* is the opposite of *one :* secondly comparatively, as denoting excess in relation to a smaller number, and then *number* is opposed to a *few.* In like manner magnitude may be taken in two ways : first absolutely, in the sense of a continuous quantity which is called a magnitude : secondly comparatively, as denoting excess in relation to a smaller quantity. In the first sense magnitude is not predicated of God but in the second, and denotes his eminence over all creatures.

Reply to the Eighth Objection. The unity that pertains to the trace of God in his creatures is the *one* that is convertible with being. As we have already stated this posits something, namely *being*, to which it adds nothing but a negation.

Reply to the Ninth Objection. One opposite does not exclude the other except from the subject of which it is predicated. For supposing that Socrates is white it does not follow that nothing is black, but that he is not black. Wherefore if the person of the Father is one it follows that there are not several persons of the Father, but not that there are not more than one Person in God.

Reply to the Tenth Objection. One is not a constituent of a number, on the side of privation, but inasmuch as it posits *being.*

Reply to the Eleventh Objection. Privation may be taken in three ways (*Metaph.* v, text. 27). First strictly, when a thing lacks that which by nature it should have, and when by nature it should have it : thus to lack sight is in a man privation of sight. Secondly in an extended sense, when a thing lacks that which is due not to its specific but to its generic nature : thus lack of sight may be called a privation of sight in a mole. Thirdly in a very broad sense, when a thing lacks that which may be naturally due to anything else but not to it, nor to any other member of its genus : thus lack of sight may be called a privation in a plant. This last kind of privation is a mean between real privation and simple negation, and has something in common with both. With real privation in that it is the negation of something in a subject, so that it cannot be predicated simply of non-being : and with simple negation, in that it does not require aptitude in the subject. It is in this way that *one* denotes privation, and in this sense it can be predicated of God, like other things that can be predicated of God in the same way, as, for instance, *invisible, immense* and so forth.

Reply to the Twelfth Objection. Numerical terms add nothing to God besides the subject of which they are predicated. Hence when they are predicated of essentials they signify the essence, and when they are predicated of personal properties they signify the relations.

Reply to the Thirteenth Objection. *One* and *being* are convertible as to their supposits: yet *one* adds logically the privation of division and thus they are not synonymous, because synonyms are words which signify the same thing from the same point of view.

Reply to the Fourteenth Objection. *One* may be considered in two ways. First as to what it posits, and thus it is a constituent of number: secondly as to the negation which it adds, and thus it is opposed to number privatively.

Reply to the Fifteenth Objection. According to the Philosopher (*Metaph.* x), number precedes unity objectively, as the whole precedes its parts and the composite precedes the simple: but unity precedes number naturally and logically. But this seemingly is not sufficient in order that unity be opposed to number privatively. For privation logically is an afterthought, since in order to understand a privation we must first understand its opposite whence its definition is taken: unless perhaps this refer, merely to the definition of the term, in so far as *one* has a privative signification, while *number* has a positive meaning: since we name things according as we know them. Wherefore in order that a term have a privative signification it suffices that the thing signified come in any way whatsoever to our knowledge as an afterthought: although this is not enough to make the thing itself privative, unless it come afterwards logically. It would be better then to say that division is the cause of number and precedes it logically; and that *one* since it is undivided being is predicated privatively in relation to division, but not in relation to multitude. Hence division logically precedes being but number follows it: and this is proved as follows. The first object of the intellect is *being;* the second is the negation of being. From these two there follows thirdly the understanding of distinction (since from the fact that we understand that this thing is and that it is not that thing we realize that these two are distinct): and it follows fourthly that the intellect apprehends the idea of unity, in that it understands that this thing is not divided in itself; and fifthly the intellect apprehends number, in that it understands this as distinct from that and each as one in itself. For however much things are conceived as distinct from one another, there is no idea of number unless each be conceived as one. Wherefore there is not a vicious circle in the definitions of unity and number. And this suffices for the *Reply to the Sixteenth Objection.*

Reply to the Seventeenth Objection. The *one* which is a principle of number is compared to *many* as measure to the thing measured: and unity in this sense adds something positive to substance, as stated in the Article.

After what we have said the arguments on the other side present no difficulty to those who realize that they contain a certain amount of truth. We must, however, take notice of one point advanced in these objections, namely that these primary notions, essence, unity, truth and goodness denominate themselves inasmuch as one, true and good are consequent to being. Now seeing that *being* is the first object of the intellect, it follows that every other object of the intellect is conceived as a being, and therefore as one, true and good. Wherefore since the intellect apprehends essence, unity, truth and goodness in the abstract, it follows that being and the other three concretes must be predicated of them. Thus it is that they denominate themselves, whereas things that are not convertible with being, do not.

ARTICLE VIII

IS THERE ANY DIVERSITY IN GOD?

Sum. Th. I, Q. xxxi, A. 2

THE eighth point of inquiry is whether there is diversity in God: and seemingly there is.

1. According to the Philosopher (*Metaph.* v) unity of substance makes things the same, multitude in substance makes things diverse. Now in God there is multitude of substance: thus Hilary says (*De Synod.*) that Father, Son

and Holy Ghost *are three in substance, one in harmony.* Therefore there is diversity in God.

2. According to the Philosopher (*Metaph.* x) diversity is absolute, but difference is relative: wherefore all that differs is diverse, but not everything that is diverse is different. Now it is granted that there is difference in God, since Damascene (*De Fid. Orth.* iii) says: *We acknowledge a difference between the Persons arising from the three properties, namely paternity, filiation and procession.* Therefore there is diversity in God.

3. Accidental difference only makes a thing other, but substantial difference makes another, i.e. a diverse, thing. Since then in God there is a difference, which must be substantial, seeing that it cannot be accidental, there must be diversity in him.

4. Number results from division, as stated above (A. 7, ad 15). Now where there is division there must be diversity. Therefore in God, since there is number, there must be diversity.

5. Identical and diverse are an adequate division of being. Now the Father is not the same as the Son, for it is not granted that in begetting the Son he begets God who is himself.[1] Therefore the Son is diverse from the Father.

On the contrary Hilary says (*De Trin.* vii): *In God nothing is new, nothing diverse, nothing foreign, nothing separable.*

Again Ambrose says (*De Trin.*): *Father and Son are one in Godhead, nor is there any substantial difference in them, nor any diversity whatsoever.*

I answer that, as Jerome says, the careless use of terms leads to heresy: wherefore in speaking of God we must choose our words so as to avoid any occasion of error. Now about the divine nature there are two errors especially to be avoided by those who would discuss the unity and trinity of the Godhead: namely the error of Arius who denied the unity of the essence, and asserted a difference between the essence of the Father and that of the Son: and the error of Sabellius who denied the distinction of the Persons and asserted that the Father is the same as the Son. Accordingly

---

[1] See *Sum. Th.* I, Q. xxxix, A. 4, obj. 4.

to guard against the error of Arius there are four points on which we must be wary in confessing our belief. First, *diversity* which is incompatible with that unity of essence which we acknowledge when we profess our belief in one God; secondly, *division* which is incompatible with the divine simplicity; thirdly, *inequality* which is incompatible with the equality of the divine Persons; fourthly, that we do not believe the Son to be *alien* to the Father, whereby we would deny their likeness. Again against the error of Sabellius four points call for caution. First, *singularity* which excludes communicability of the divine nature; secondly, the word *only* which excludes the real distinction of the Persons; thirdly, *confusion* which excludes the order existing between the divine Persons; fourthly, *dissociation* (*solitudo*) which excludes the fellowship of the divine Persons. Accordingly against diversity we acknowledge unity of essence; against division simplicity; against inequality equality; against difference likeness; not one only but several Persons; distinction against identity; order against confusion; and against dissociation the harmony and bond of love.

Reply to the First Objection. In the words quoted substance stands for hypostasis, not for essence, multiplication of which causes diversity.

Reply to the Second Objection. Although some doctors of the Church use the term difference in reference to God, it should not be employed as a general rule, or enlarged upon: because difference denotes a distinction of form, and this is impossible in God since God's form is his nature according to Augustine. But we must explain the term *difference* as standing for a *distinction* of the slightest kind: since some things are described as distinct in respect of a mere relation or even only logically. Again if we meet with the term diversity in connexion with God, we must explain it in the same way: for instance, if we find it stated that the Person of the Father is diverse from that of the Son, we must take *diverse* to denote *distinct.* Yet in speaking of God we must be more wary of using the word *diverse* than the word *different*, because diversity refers more to an essential division : inasmuch as any multiplication whatsoever of forms causes a difference, whereas diversity arises only from substantial forms.

Reply to the Third Objection. Though there is no accident in God there is relation ; and relative opposition causes distinction but not diversity in God.

Reply to the Fourth Objection. Though properly speaking there is not division in God, there is relative distinction, and this suffices to make a number of Persons.

Reply to the Fifth Objection. The Son is the same God as the Father, yet it cannot be said that the Father in begetting the Son begot God who was himself ; because *himself* being reciprocal indicates identity in the supposit : whereas in God Father and Son are two supposits.

ARTICLE IX

ARE THERE ONLY THREE PERSONS IN GOD : OR ARE THERE MORE OR FEWER THAN THREE ?[1]

Sum. Th. I, Q. xxxi, A. 1

THE ninth point of inquiry is whether in God there are only three Persons, or more or fewer than three. It would seem that there are more than three.

1. Augustine says (*Con. Maxim.* iii, 12) : *The Son did not beget a creator, not that he could not but because it was unfitting.* Now in God, just as in all perpetual things, there is no difference between the actual and the possible (*Phys.* iii, text. 32). Therefore the Son begot another Son : and thus there are two Sons in God, and consequently more than three Persons.

2. To this it may be replied that the words *he could not* mean that it was not due to his inability.

On the contrary the acts belonging to a particular nature are appropriate to every supposit of that nature, except through inability to execute them. Now generation is an act pertaining to the perfection of the divine nature, otherwise it would not be appropriate to the Father, in whom there is

[1] See above, Q. ii, A. 4.

nothing that is not perfect. If then the Son begets not another Son, this will be because he is unable to do so.

3. If the Son cannot beget he can be begotten: and therefore he has the power to be begotten but not the power to beget. Since then to beget differs from being begotten; and since powers are distinguished in reference to their objects, the Father's power will not be the same as the Son's: and this is heretical.

4. In things active and passive action and passion are reduced to different principles, since in creatures a thing acts by reason of its form and is patient by reason of its matter. Now to beget and to be begotten express action and passion. Therefore they must be referred to different principles: so that it cannot be the same power whereby the Father begets and the Son is begotten.

5. But to this it might be replied that it is the same power inasmuch as on either hand it is rooted in the divine essence which is one in Father and Son.

On the contrary the power to heat and the power to dry are rooted in one subject, namely fire: and yet they are not one and the same power, since heat which is the principle of calefaction is a distinct quality from dryness which is the principle of desiccation. Wherefore the unity of the divine essence does not suffice to make one the Father's power to beget and the Son's power to be begotten.

6. Every wise and intelligent subject forms a concept by his wisdom. Now the Son is wise and intelligent even as the Father. Therefore he has a concept. But the Father's concept is the Word which is the Son. Therefore the Son also has a Son.

7. To this it may be replied that *word* is predicated of God not only personally but also essentially, and thus the *Word* predicated essentially may be the concept of the Son.

On the contrary *word* denotes the species conceived and ordered for the purpose of manifestation, and thus it implies origin. Now those terms which indicate origin in God are predicated personally and not essentially. Therefore *word* cannot be predicated essentially.

8. Anselm (*Monolog.*) says that *as the Father utters* (*dicit*)

himself, so do the Son and the Holy Ghost. Now, as he says (*ibid.*), for the Father to utter himself is the same as to beget a Son. Therefore the Son begets another Son : and thus the same conclusion follows.

9. God is proved to beget from the fact that he bestows on others the faculty of begetting (Isa. lxvi, 9) : *Shall I that give generation to others be barren ? saith the Lord.* Now as the Father gives generation, even so does the Son : because the works of the Trinity are undivided. Therefore the Son begets a Son.

10. Augustine (*Dial. ad Oros.* lxv, 7) says that the Father begets the Son naturally : and Damascene (*De Fide Orth.* xxvii, 2) says that generation is a work of nature. Now the Father and the Son have the same nature. Therefore as the Father begets, so also does the Son : and consequently in God there are several Sons and more than three Persons.

11. But someone will reply that there cannot be more than one Son in God since there can be but one filiation : because the form of one species is not multiplied otherwise than by division of matter, and there is no such thing in God.

On the contrary any difference whatsoever must naturally connote number. Now there can be more than one filiation, not only by reason of the matter but also because this filiation is thiswise and that filiation is thatwise. Therefore nothing prevents several filiations being in God, although there is no matter in him.

12. The Son proceeds from the Father as brightness from the sun, according to Hebrews i, 3, *being the brightness of his glory.* Now one brightness can produce another brightness. Therefore the Son can beget another Son : and thus there would be several Sons in God and more than three Persons.

13. The Holy Ghost is the Father's love of the Son. Now the Father also loves the Holy Ghost. Therefore there must be another Spirit whereby the Father loves the Holy Ghost : and thus there will be four Persons in God.

14. According to Dionysius (*Div. Nom.* iv) the good is self-communicative. Now goodness is appropriated to the Holy Ghost, as power to the Father and wisdom to the Son.

Therefore one would think it most appropriate to the Holy Ghost that he should communicate the divine nature to another person: and thus there will be more than three Persons in God.

15. According to the Philosopher (*Meteor.* iv)[1] a thing is perfect when it can of itself produce its like. Now the Holy Ghost is perfect God. Therefore he can produce another Person: and consequently . . . etc.

16. The Son does not receive the divine nature from the Father more perfectly than the Holy Ghost. Now the Son receives from the Father the divine nature not only passively (so to speak) as being begotten of him, but also actively, because he can communicate the same nature to another. Therefore the Holy Ghost also can communicate the divine nature to another Person.

17. Whatsoever belongs to perfection in creatures must be attributed to God. Now it belongs to perfection in creatures to communicate nature, although the mode of communication has a certain imperfection in that it involves division or change in the generator. Therefore to communicate the divine nature belongs to perfection in God, and consequently it must be attributed to the Holy Ghost. Therefore a Person proceeds from the Holy Ghost, and thus it follows that there are more than three Persons in God.

18. Just as the Godhead is a good in the Father, so also is paternity. Now from the fact that no good is possessed with pleasure without others sharing in it, some prove that in God there are several Persons having the divine nature. Therefore for the same reason there are several Fathers, and several Sons and several Holy Ghosts in God: and consequently more than three Persons.

19. The Son and the Holy Ghost are seemingly distinguished from each other in that the Son proceeds from the Father by way of the intellect as his *word*, while the Holy Ghost proceeds by way of the will as his *love*. But there are other essential attributes besides the intellect and will, such as goodness, power and so forth. Therefore other Persons proceed from the Father besides the Son and Holy Ghost.

[1] *De Anima* ii.

20. Apparently the process of nature differs from the process of the intellect more than does the process of the will : inasmuch as in creatures the process of the intellect is always accompanied by that of the will, since whatever understands something also wills something : whereas the process of nature is not always accompanied by the process of intellect, thus not everything that can generate can understand. If then in God the Person who proceeds by way of the will as *love* is distinct from the Person who proceeds by way of the intellect as *word*, there will also be a Person who proceeds by way of the intellect distinct from the Person who proceeds by way of nature as Son. Hence there will be three Persons proceeding in God and one who does not proceed : and thus there are four Persons.

21. In God the Persons are multiplied on account of the subsistent relations. Now in God there are five relative notions, viz. paternity, filiation, procession, innascibility and common spiration. Therefore there are five Persons in God.

22. The relations which are attributed to God from eternity are not in creatures but in God. Now whatsoever is in God is subsistent, since in him there is no accident. Therefore any relation that belongs to God from eternity is subsistent and consequently is a Person. Now such relations are infinite in number : thus the ideas of creatures are in God from eternity, and they are not mutually distinct except by their relation to creatures. Therefore the Persons in God are infinite in number.

On the other hand it would seem that there are fewer than three.

1. In one nature there is but one mode of communication of that nature : wherefore, according to the Commentator (*Phys.* viii), animals generated from seed are not of the same species as those engendered from corrupt matter. Now the divine nature is supremely one : wherefore it can be communicated in one way only. Therefore there cannot be more than two Persons, one that communicates the Godhead in some particular way, and another that receives the Godhead in that same way.

2. Hilary (*De Synod.*) shows that the Son proceeds from

the Father naturally because he is such as God is, but that creatures proceed from God according to his will, because they are such as he wishes them to be, not such as he is. Now the Holy Ghost, like the Son, is such as God the Father is. Therefore the Holy Ghost, like the Son, proceeds from the Father naturally ; and consequently there is no distinction between the Holy Ghost and the Son through the Son proceeding naturally and the Holy Ghost not.

3. In God will and intellect differ not in nature but only logically : and consequently procession by nature, by intellect and by will differ but logically in God. Therefore if the Son and the Holy Ghost are distinguished through the one proceeding naturally and the other by the will, they will be but logically distinct : and they will not be two Persons, since plurality of persons implies a real distinction.

4. The Persons in God are distinct by relations of origin only. Now two relations suffice to indicate origin, namely one from whom is another, and one who is from another. Therefore there are but two Persons in God.

5. Every relation requires two extremes. Since then in God the Persons are not distinct save by the relations ; it follows that in God there are either two relations, and consequently four Persons ; or one relation, and therefore only two Persons.

On the contrary it is manifest that there are but three Persons in God from 1 Jo. v, 7, *There are three who bear witness in heaven :* and if we ask, *Three what ?* the Church replies : *Three Persons,* as Augustine says (*De Trin.* vii, 4). Therefore there are three Persons in God.

Moreover for the perfection of divine goodness, happiness and glory there must be true and perfect charity in God : for nothing is better or more perfect than charity, as Richard says (*De Trin.* iii, 2). Now there is no happiness without enjoyment, and this arises chiefly from charity : for as we read (*ibid.* 5), *Nothing is sweeter than charity, nothing more enjoyable, the intellectual life affords no sweeter experience, or delight more exquisite.* And the perfection of glory consists in the splendour of perfect communication, which is effected by charity. And true and perfect charity requires the trinity of Persons in God. For the love whereby a person loves himself is selfish love and is not true charity. But God cannot love supremely another who is not supremely lovable ; and none is supremely lovable that is not supremely good. Hence it is evident that true charity cannot be supreme in God if there be but one Person in him. Nor can it be perfect if there be but two Persons : since perfect charity demands that the lover wish that what he loves himself be equally loved by another. For it is a sign of great imperfection to be unwilling to share one's love, whereas to be willing to share it is a sign of great perfection : *The more one is pleased to receive a thing the greater our longing in seeking for it*, as Richard says (*ibid.*). In God therefore, since there is perfection of goodness, happiness and glory, there must be a trinity of Persons.

Again, as goodness is self-communicative, the perfection of divine goodness requires that he communicate his perfections supremely. But if there were only one Person in God he would not communicate his goodness supremely : for he does not communicate himself supremely to creatures : and if there were but two Persons, the delights of mutual charity would not be communicated perfectly. Hence there must be a second Person to whom the divine goodness is perfectly communicated, and a third to whom the delights of divine charity are perfectly communicated.

Further, according to Augustine (*De Trin.* ix, 1, 2), three things are required for love, the lover, the beloved and love itself. Now the two who love each other are the Father and the Son : and the love that is their mutual bond is the Holy Ghost. Therefore there are three Persons in God.

Again, as Richard remarks (*De Trin.* v, 6), in mankind it is to be observed that a person proceeds from persons in three ways : first, immediately only, as Eve from Adam : secondly, mediately only, as Enoch from Adam : thirdly, both immediately and mediately, as Seth from Adam, immediately as his son, mediately as the son of Eve who proceeded from Adam. Now in God one Person cannot proceed from another mediately only, since there would not be perfect equality. Hence we must conclude that in God there is one

Person that does not proceed from another, i.e. the Father from whom two other Persons proceed; one immediately only, i.e. the Son; and the other both mediately and immediately, i.e. the Holy Ghost, who proceeds from the Father and the Son. Therefore there are three Persons in God.

Again, to both give and receive the fulness of the Godhead comes between giving and not receiving it, and receiving without giving it. Now it belongs to the Person of the Father to give the fulness of the Godhead without receiving it: and to receive the fulness of the Godhead without giving it belongs to the Person of the Holy Ghost. Therefore there must be a third Person who both gives and receives the fulness of the Godhead: and this is the Person of the Son: and thus there are three Persons in God.

I answer that according to the opinions of heretics it is impossible to assign a definite number of Persons in God. Arius took the trinity of Persons to mean that the Son and Holy Ghost are creatures: and Macedonius was of the same opinion in regard to the Holy Ghost. Now the procession of creatures from God is not necessarily limited to a certain number, seeing that the divine power being infinite surpasses all mode, species and number of the creature. Wherefore if God the Father almighty created two super-excellent creatures, whom Arius stated to be the Son and Holy Ghost, there is no reason why he should not create others equal to them or even greater than they. Sabellius contended that the Father, Son and Holy Ghost are only nominally and logically distinct: and here again it is evident that there would be an indefinite multiplication, inasmuch as our reason can consider God in an infinite number of ways in respect of his various effects, and give him various names. The Catholic faith alone which acknowledges unity of the divine nature in Persons really distinct, can assign a reason for the trinity in God. For it is impossible that one simple nature be in more than one as principle: wherefore Hilary says (*De Synod.*) that whosoever acknowledges two innascibles in God must acknowledge two gods. Now the nature of one innascible God demands that we should acknowledge but one God. Hence certain philosophers asserted that in immaterial things there cannot be plurality except in respect of origin. For one nature can be equally in several subjects on account of the division of matter, which does not apply to God. Wherefore there cannot be in God more than one innascible Person that does not proceed from another. Now if other Persons proceed from him this must be by some action. Not, however, by an action passing into a subject outside the agent, as heating and cutting are the actions of fire and saw, and as creation is the act of God himself: since then the proceeding Persons would be outside the divine nature. It follows then that the procession of Persons into the one divine nature is by reason of an action that does not pass into an extraneous subject but remains in the agent: and in the intellectual nature such actions are but two, to understand and to will. In each of these actions something is found to proceed when the action is performed. The action of understanding is not exercised without something being conceived in the mind of the one who understands, and this is called the word: since before a concept of some kind is fixed in the mind we are not said to understand but to think about a thing in order to understand it. In like manner the act of willing is exercised by love proceeding from the lover through his will, for love is simply the fixation of the will in the good that is willed. In creatures word and love are not subsistent persons in the nature that is endowed with intelligence and will: for a creature's acts of understanding and will are not its very being. Hence its word and love are accessories of and accidental to the understanding and willing creature. But seeing that in God, being, intelligence and will are one and the same, it follows of necessity that word and love in God are not accidents but subsist in the divine nature For in God there is but one simple act of intelligence and one simple act of will, since by understanding his essence he understands all things, and by willing his goodness, he wills whatsoever he wills. Hence there is but one Word and one Love in God. Now the order of understanding and willing is not the same in God as in us. We receive our intellective knowledge from external things: and by our will we tend to something external as an end. Wherefore our act of intelligence is according to a movement from things to the soul: but our act of will is according to a movement from the soul to things. On the other hand God does not acquire knowledge from things, but by his knowledge is the cause of things: nor by his will does he tend to anything external as his end, but he directs all external things to himself as their end. Accordingly both in us and in God there is a certain rotation in the acts of the intellect and will: for the will returns to that whence came the beginning of understanding: but whereas in us the circle ends in that which is external, the external good moving the intellect and the intellect moving the will, and the will by appetite and love tending to the external good; in God, on the other hand, the circle ends in him. For God, by understanding himself, conceives his word which is the type of all things understood by him, inasmuch as he understands all things by understanding himself, and from this word he proceeds to love of all things and of himself. Thus someone[1] has said that *a monad engendered an atom and reflected its own heat upon itself*. And the circle being closed nothing more can be added, so that a third procession within the divine nature is impossible, although there follows a procession towards external nature. Hence in God there must be but one Person that does not proceed, and only two Persons that proceed, one of whom proceeds as love, the other as word: and thus the Persons in God are three in number.

In creatures a likeness to this trinity appears in three ways. First as an effect reflects its cause; and in this way the principle of the whole Godhead, i.e. the Father, is represented by that which holds the first place in the creature, namely by being in itself one subsistent thing. The Word is represented by the form of each creature; because in those things which are done by an intellectual agent the form of the effect derives from the concept of his intelligence. Love is represented in the order of creatures: because from the fact that God loves himself, he directs all things to himself in a certain order. Wherefore this likeness is called a

---

[1] Trismegistus, *Poemand.* iv.

vestigiary likeness in that this bears the trace of the foot as an effect bears a trace of its cause. Secondly, by reason of a similar kind of operation : and thus it is represented in the rational creature alone who like God can understand and love himself, and consequently produces his own word and love : and this is called the likeness of the natural image ; because in order that one thing be the image of another it must present a like species.[1] Thirdly, on account of the unity of object, inasmuch as the rational creature understands and loves God : this is a kind of conformity of union that is found in the saints alone who understand and love the same thing as God understands and loves.

Of the first kind of likeness it is written (Job xi, 7) : *Peradventure thou wilt understand the steps of God ?* Of the second (Gen. i, 26) : *Let us make man to our own image and likeness :* and this is called the image of creation. Of the third it is written (2 Cor. iii, 18) : *But we beholding the glory of the Lord with open face are transformed into the same image :* and this is called the image of re-creation.

Reply to the First Objection. The reason why Augustine says that it is not true that the Son was unable to beget, but that it was not fitting for him to beget, is that it was not through inability that the Son does not beget : so that the words *was unable* must be taken privatively and not simply negatively, and the words *it was not fitting* indicate that the consequence would be unfitting if in God the Son were to beget another Son. How true this is may be considered in four ways. First, seeing that in God the Son proceeds as word, if the Son begot a Son it would follow that in God word proceeds from word : and this is impossible except in an inquiring and discursive intellect, wherein word proceeds from word when the mind proceeds from the consideration of one truth to the consideration of another : whereas this is nowise consistent with the perfection and simplicity of the divine intellect which at one glance sees all things at the same time. Secondly, because that which renders a thing individual and incommunicable cannot possibly be common to several : thus that which makes Socrates to be

[1] *Sum. Th.* I, Q. xciii, A. 8.

this particular thing cannot even be conceived as being in others besides. Hence if in God filiation were common to several (Persons) it would not make the personality of the Son incommunicable, and thus the Son would have to be made an individual Person by something absolute, and this is incompatible with the unity of the divine essence. Thirdly, because nothing that is one in species can be more than one except by reason of matter : for which reason there can be but one essence in God, because the divine essence is utterly immaterial. Now if there were several Sons in God there would also be several filiations, and consequently they would have to be multiplied according to matter subjected to them : and this is incompatible with the divine immateriality. Fourthly, because a man is a son as resulting from a process of nature. Now nature is confined definitely to one effect : except when by accident several effects are produced on account of the matter being divided : and consequently where nature is uttely devoid of matter, there can be but one son.

Reply to the Second Objection. A thing may be of this or that nature in two ways. First, as considered absolutely : and thus whatsoever belongs to a particular nature must be appropriate to every supposit of that nature : in this sense it is competent to the divine nature to be almighty, creator and other similar attributes that are common to the three Persons. Secondly, a thing belongs to a particular nature as considered in one particular supposit : and then whatsoever belongs to the nature does not necessarily belong to every supposit of that nature. Thus just as the generic nature includes something in one species which does not belong to another species (for instance, the sensible nature endows man with certain qualities with which it does not endow dumb animals, such as a delicate sense of touch and memory and so forth) ; even so certain things belong to the specific nature in one individual, and not to another individual of the same species. For instance, it was peculiar to human nature considered as in Adam that it was not received by him through the natural process of generation, which does not apply to other individuals of human nature. In this way then the ability to beget belongs to the divine nature as in the Person of the Father, precisely because the Father is not constituted an incommunicable Person otherwise than by paternity which belongs to him as begetting: hence though the Son is a perfect supposit of the divine nature it does not follow that he can beget.

Reply to the Third Objection. Although the Father can beget whereas the Son cannot, it does not follow that the Father has a power which the Son has not: because in the Father and the Son it is the same power whereby the Father begets and the Son is begotten. For power is something absolute, wherefore it is not distinguished in God as neither is goodness nor anything else of the kind. On the other hand in God *to beget* and *to be begotten* do not denote something absolute, but merely a relation. Now opposite relations in God meet together in the one same absolute and do not divide it; thus it is clear that the one essence is in Father and Son; wherefore neither is power divided in God through being referred to begetting and being begotten. In fact not even in creatures does every difference of objects necessarily differentiate powers, but only when the objects differ formally within the same genus: thus the power of sight is not differentiated by seeing a man and seeing a horse, because these sensible objects do not differ *quâ* sensible: and in like manner the absolute is not divided by the relative in God.

Reply to the Fourth Objection. In every action that passes from the agent into an extraneous thing there must be a principle in the agent whereby it is agent, and another principle in the patient whereby it is patient. But in the operation which does not pass into anything extraneous, but remains in the agent, only one principle is required: thus in order to will a principle is necessary on the part of the willer that enables him to will. Now in creatures generation is an operation passing into something extraneous, wherefore the active power in the generator must be distinct from the passive power in the generated. Whereas the divine generation is an operation that does not pass into anything extraneous but remains within; consisting as it does in the conception of the Word. Wherefore there is no need for distinct powers, active in the Father and passive in the Son.

Reply to the Fifth Objection. Heat and dryness considered in themselves are qualities; however, we may call them powers, inasmuch as they are principles of certain actions. Hence it is clear that although the primary and remote root, i.e. the subject, is but one, the proximate root which is the quality is not one.

Reply to the Sixth Objection. As the Father is God begetting and the Son God begotten, so must we say that the Father is wise and conceiving, while the Son is wise and conceived. Because the Son in that he is the Word is a conception of a wise being. But since whatsoever is in God is God it follows that the very conception of a wise God is God, is wise, is powerful and whatsoever is appropriate to God.

Reply to the Seventh Objection. Taken in its proper sense *word* cannot be attributed to God otherwise than personally: because in God there cannot be any origination but what is immaterial and consistent with an intellectual nature, such as the origination of word and love: wherefore if the procession of word and love is not enough to indicate a personal distinction, no distinction of Persons will be possible in God. Thus John both in the beginning of his gospel and in his first epistle employs the term *Word* instead of *Son,* nor may we in speaking of God express ourselves in terms other than those of Holy Writ.

Reply to the Eighth Objection. Dicere may be taken in two senses. First strictly and then it means to utter a word: and in this sense Augustine (*De Trin.* vii) says that *in God each Person does not ' speak,'* but the Father *alone.* Secondly, in a broad sense in which to speak denotes intelligence: and thus Anselm (*loc. cit.*) says that not only the Father speaks but also the Son and the Holy Ghost: and though there are three who speak there is but one Word which is the Son: because the Son alone is the concept of the Father who understands and conceives the Word.

Reply to the Ninth Objection. That there is generation in God is not proved from the mere fact that God gives generation to others as efficient cause, since it would follow in like manner that there is motion in God because he gives motion to others. Generation is proved to be in God from the fact that he gives generation to others as both efficient and exemplary cause: and the Father is the exemplar of generation as begetting, while the Son is the exemplar as begotten: wherefore it does not follow that he begets.

Reply to the Tenth Objection. Generation is an operation of the divine nature as residing in the Person of the Father, as we have already stated, hence it does not follow that it is appropriate to the Son.

Reply to the Eleventh Objection. Since filiation is a relation arising from a determinate mode of origin, i.e. according to nature, it is impossible that filiation differ from filiation formally; unless perhaps by reason of a difference of natures communicated by generation: thus we might say that the species of filiation whereby a particular man is a son differs from the species of filiation whereby a particular horse is a son. But in God there is but one nature, wherefore there cannot be several formally different filiations: and it is evident that there cannot be several filiations differing in matter. Consequently in God there is but one filiation and one Son.

Reply to the Twelfth Objection. One brightness proceeds from another by the diffusion of light on to another subject: wherefore this is clearly due to a division of matter, which is impossible in God.

Reply to the Thirteenth Objection. A thing is loved in so far as it is good: hence since one and the same goodness is that of the Father, Son and Holy Ghost, the Father with the same love, which is the Holy Ghost, loves himself, the Son, the Holy Ghost and all creatures. Even so by the same Word, which is the Son, he utters himself, the Son, the Holy Ghost and all creatures.

Reply to the Fourteenth Objection. Goodness is something in which terminates the living being's operation that abides in the operator. First a thing is understood as true, and then is desired as good: and there the internal operation stops and rests as in its end. But from this point begins the process of external operation : because through the intellect's desire and love for that which it has already considered as good there follows an external operation towards that good. Wherefore from the very fact that goodness is appropriated to the Holy Ghost it is reasonable for us to conclude that the procession of the divine Persons goes no further. What does follow, however, is the procession of creatures, which is outside the divine nature.

Reply to the Fifteenth Objection. Of all lines the circle is the most perfect, because it admits of no addition. Hence this belongs to the perfection of the Holy Ghost that as it were he closes the circle of the divine origin, so that no addition is possible, as we have shown above.

Reply to the Sixteenth Objection. In the reception or communication of the divine nature there is no other difference but that arising from the relations : and this difference cannot cause inequality of perfection : because as Augustine says (*Cont. Maxim.* iii, 18), *when we ask who proceeds from whom, it is a question of origin, not of equality or inequality.*

Reply to the Seventeenth Objection. Just as the communication of the divine nature by the Father to the Son belongs to their perfection, so the perfect reception of the communicated nature belongs to the perfection of the Holy Ghost : and both perfections differ not in quantity but only in respect of relation which does not constitute imperfection, as already stated.

Reply to the Eighteenth Objection. As we have already observed, that which makes a person incommunicable cannot be common to many. Hence the result of sharing therein would be not enjoyment but the destruction of the distinction of the persons. Thus were the Father to have a companion in the Godhead to share his paternity there would be a confusion of Persons : and the same applies to filiation and procession.

Reply to the Nineteenth Objection. The other attributes have no intrinsic operation as the intellect and will have, whence could arise the procession of a divine Person.

Reply to the Twentieth Objection. The process of nature and the process of the intellect have this in common that in either case one thing proceeds from one thing in likeness to that whence it proceeds. But love which proceeds from the will, proceeds from two who love each other mutually : nor can we infer that because there is love there is a likeness of the lover. Wherefore in God the same (Person) proceeds by way of nature and by way of the intellect, i.e. as Son and as Word : whereas it is another Person that proceeds by way of the will as love.

Reply to the Twenty-first Objection. Although there are five notions in God there are but three personal properties constituting the Persons : and therefore there are but three Persons.

Reply to the Twenty-second Objection. The ideal relations in God refer to things outside, i.e. to creatures : and consequently they do not cause a distinction of Persons in him.

We must also reply to the other arguments which would prove that there are fewer than three Persons in God.

1. In every created nature there are many modes of procession, yet the specific nature is not communicated in each of them : and the reason of this is to be found in the imperfection of created nature, inasmuch as not everything of a created nature subsists in itself : thus the word that proceeds from a man's intellect is not subsistent, nor is the love that proceeds from his will : whereas the son who is begotten by an operation of nature subsists in human nature : wherefore this is the only way in which human nature is communicated, although there are several modes of procession. On the other hand whatsoever is in God is subsistent, wherefore in God the divine nature is communicated in every mode of procession.

2. There is no reason why something should proceed even naturally from the will : for the will naturally wills and loves something, viz. happiness and the knowledge of the truth. Hence there is no reason why the Holy Ghost should not proceed from the Father and the Son, although he proceeds by way of the will.

3. Although will and intellect do not differ in God except logically, he that proceeds by way of the intellect must be really distinct from him who proceeds by way of the will :

because the Word which proceeds by way of the intellect proceeds from one only as from the speaker: while the Holy Ghost who proceeds by way of the will as love, must needs proceed from two who love each other mutually, or from one who speaks and his word. For nothing can be loved unless the intellect has first conceived it by its word. Hence he who proceeds by way of the will must proceed from him who proceeds by way of the intellect, and consequently must be distinct from him.

4. He that proceeds from another in God may do so in two ways, namely by way of word and by way of love. Hence to be from another in a general way is not enough to constitute an incommunicable person, and must be defined in reference to that which is proper.

5. In God there are four relations and not only two: yet only three of them are personal, for one, namely common spiration, is not a personal property, seeing that it is common to two Persons: and for this reason there are only three Persons in God.

We grant the remaining arguments.

QUESTION X

THE PROCESSION OF THE DIVINE PERSONS

THERE are five points of inquiry : (1) Is there procession in God ? (2) Is there only one procession in God ? (3) What is the order between procession and relation in God ? (4) Does the Holy Ghost proceed from the Son ? (5) Would the Holy Ghost still be distinct from the Son if he did not proceed from him ?

ARTICLE I

IS THERE PROCESSION IN GOD ?
Sum. Th. I, Q. xxvii : *C.G.* IV, ii

THE first point of inquiry is whether there be processions in the divine Persons : and seemingly there are not.

1. Whatsoever proceeds from a thing is separated from it. But the divine Persons are not separated from one another : thus the Son says (Jo. xiv, 10) : *I am in the Father and the Father in me :* and the same applies to the Holy Ghost, namely that he is in the Father and the Son and vice versa. Therefore in God one Person proceeds not from another.

2. Nothing savouring of motion, even as nothing pertaining to matter should be attributed to God in its proper sense. Now procession denotes motion. Therefore it cannot be attributed to God in its proper sense.

3. Whatsoever proceeds is logically prior to its procession, since it is the subject thereof. Now in God nothing that proceeds can be prior to its procession : for the divine essence does not proceed as neither is it begotten ; and relation is not prior to procession, but contrariwise as we have already stated (Q. viii, A. 3). Therefore procession is impossible in God.

4. Even as that which proceeds is *from* something so also is it *to* something. But that which proceeds to something is not self-subsistent. Therefore seeing that the divine Persons are self-subsistent it would seem incompetent for them to proceed.

5. Inasmuch as the more excellent creatures are more like to God, that which is found in the lower creatures and not in the higher is not found in God: for instance, dimensive quantity, matter and so forth. Now procession is to be found in the lower creatures, where one individual engenders another of the same species: whereas this does not obtain in the higher creatures. Neither therefore in God is procession to be found.

6. We should by no means attribute to God anything that is derogatory to his dignity. Now God's dignity consists chiefly in his being the first cause of existence, and not deriving existence from anything else: which would seem incompatible with procession, since whatsoever proceeds derives its existence in some way from another. Therefore it must not be said that anything proceeds in God.

7. A person is *a hypostasis distinguished by a property pertaining to dignity.*[1] But it does not savour of dignity that one receive from another (which is implied by procession). Therefore procession should not be ascribed to the divine persons as though it were a personal property.

8. A thing is in some way the cause of that which proceeds from it. But one divine Person cannot be the cause of another: not an intrinsic cause, i.e. formal or material, since in God there is no composition of form and matter; nor extrinsic, since one Person dwells within the other. Hence there is no procession in God.

9. Whatsoever proceeds issues from another as from its *principium.* Now one (divine) Person cannot be described as the *principium* of another: for seeing that *principium* connotes that which is *principiated,* we should have to say that some divine Person is principiated, and this seemingly is peculiar to creatures. Hence there is no procession in God.

10. The word *principium* would seem to indicate priority:

---

[1] *Supra* Q. ix, A. 2: *Sum. Th.* I, Q. xxix, A. 3, ad 2.

whereas according to Athanasius there is no priority or posteriority in God. Therefore one Person is not the *principium* of another, and one should not be described as proceeding from the other.

11. Every *principium* is operative or productive. Now one Person is not productive or operative of another, else in God there would be something made or created. Therefore a divine Person has no *principium* and does not proceed.

12. If B proceeds from A, B must have something in common with A and communicated to it by A ; and also something proper whereby it is distinguished from A ; since nothing proceeds from itself. Now wherever there is something and something else there is composition. Therefore wherever there is procession there is composition. But there is no composition in God: and consequently neither is there procession.

13. That which proceeds from another receives something from it : and whatsoever receives something is of a needy nature : for if it needed not it would not receive : for which reason in natural things receptivity is ascribed to matter. Therefore whatsoever proceeds is by nature needy. But in God there is no such thing as need for he is supremely perfect. Therefore there is no procession in God.

14. To this it will be replied that the recipient is imperfect when it exists before receiving, and when having received it is in possession and no longer needy. Now the Son and the Holy Ghost receive indeed from the Father, but they do not exist before receiving : and thus they are not in need.

On the contrary every creature is needy by nature, and yet it does not exist before receiving existence from God. Therefore the fact of not existing before receiving does not disprove need.

15. Whatsoever has a thing only by receiving it from another, considered in itself lacks that thing : thus air considered in itself lacks light which it receives from something else. If then the Son and the Holy Ghost have being only through receiving it from the Father (which must be the case if they proceed from the Father) it follows of necessity that considered in themselves they do not exist. Now that which considered in itself is nothing, if it receive being from

another, must necessarily come from nothing and consequently must be a creature. If then the Son and the Holy Ghost proceed from the Father they must be creatures; and this is the blasphemy of Arius. Therefore there is no procession in God.

16. That which proceeds from another proceeds that it may come into existence: and that which proceeds that it may exist did not always exist: thus if a thing proceeds to a place it was not always in that place. But the divine Persons are eternal. Therefore no divine Person proceeds.

17. The principle whence a thing proceeds exercises a certain authority over that which proceeds from it as from a principle. If then one divine Person proceeds from another, for instance, the Son and the Holy Ghost from the Father, there must be in the Father some authority over the Son and the Holy Ghost: and thus, since authority is a kind of dignity there will be a dignity in the Father that is not in the Son and the Holy Ghost, and consequently there will be inequality in the divine Persons: and this is contrary to the saying of Athanasius (*Symb.*) that in the Trinity *there is neither priority nor posteriority, neither greater nor lesser: but all three Persons are co-eternal and co-equal with one another.* Therefore there is no procession in the divine Persons.

On the contrary the Son says (Jo. viii, 42): *From God I proceeded and came.*

Again it is stated (Jo. xv, 26) that *the Spirit of truth proceedeth from the Father.* Therefore there is procession in the divine Persons.

I answer that in us intellectual knowledge originates in the imagination and senses which do not transcend continuous matter. For this reason we take the terms that apply to continuous matter and transfer them to whatsoever we grasp with the intellect. Take, for instance, the word *distance* which is applied first to place and is afterwards transferred to any difference of forms: wherefore all contraries of any genus whatsoever are said to be the most distant, although distance is applied first of all to ubiety, as the Philosopher says (*Metaph.* x). In like manner the term *procession* was first employed to signify that local movement whereby a thing passes from one place through intermediate places to an extreme place in an ordinate manner: and thence it is transferred to denote the order between any two things one of which issues from or succeeds the other. Hence we apply the word procession to all kinds of movement: for instance, we say that a body proceeds from whiteness to blackness, or from a great to a small quantity or from non-being to being, and vice versa: and in like manner we use the word procession to indicate the emanation of one thing from another; thus we say that the ray proceeds from the sun, and the operation or even the thing produced from the operator; thus the thing made by a craftsman is said to proceed from him, and the thing generated from the generator, and in a general way we designate any such order as a procession. Now operation is twofold. There is an operation that passes from the operator into something extrinsic, as heating passes from fire into wood: this operation is not a perfection of the operator but of the thing operated, since the fire gains nothing by heating, whereas the thing heated acquires heat. Another operation does not pass into something outside but remains in the operator, such as understanding, sensation, willing and the like. These operations are perfections of the operator: for the intellect is not perfect except by understanding actually, and the senses except by sensing actually. The first kind of operation is common to animate and inanimate beings: whereas the second is proper to animate beings: wherefore, if we take movement in a wide sense for any kind of operation—as the Philosopher takes it (*De Anima* iii), where it is stated that sensation and understanding are a kind of movement—not indeed the movement which is the act of an imperfect thing (*Phys.* iii, 1) but that which is the act of a perfect thing—it would seem proper to animate beings; and this is what is meant when we speak of a thing being the cause of its own movement. Because whenever we observe that a thing operates of itself and in itself in any way whatever we say that it lives: and in this sense Plato (*Tim.*) says that the first mover moves itself. In respect of both kinds of operation procession is found in creatures. In regard to the first kind we say that the thing generated proceeds from the generator and the thing made from the maker. With regard to the second kind we say that words proceed from the speaker, and love from the lover. And we attribute both kinds of operation to God, when we say that he creates, preserves and governs all things. Nor by this do we signify that any perfection accrues to God by such operation, but rather that the creature acquires perfection from the divine perfection. We attribute the other kind of operation to God when we describe him as understanding and willing whereby we indicate his perfection. For he were not perfect did he not understand and will actually : and for this reason we acknowledge him to be living. In respect of either operation we attribute procession to God. As regards the first we speak of divine wisdom or goodness as proceeding to creatures, as Dionysius says (*Div. Nom.* ix), and of creatures as proceeding from God. As regards the second we acknowledge in God a procession of word and love ; and this is the procession of the Son from the Father (for the Son is the Father's word) and of the Holy Ghost who is his love and life-giving breath (*spiritus*). Hence Athanasius in a discourse pronounced in the Council of Nicea[1] says that the Arians through maintaining that the Son and Holy Ghost are not consubstantial with the Father, seemed in consequence to say that God is not a living and intelligent being, but dead and unintelligent.

Reply to the First Objection. This argument considers the procession that is an operation passing into something extrinsic. But the divine Persons do not proceed thus ; and their procession partakes rather of the nature of an immanent operation : since that which proceeds in this way is not distant from that whence it proceeds : even so the human word is in the mind of the speaker and not distant from him.

Reply to the Second Objection. The procession attributed to the divine Persons is not a local movement, but one that indicates order of emanation.

[1] Epist. *Contra eos qui dicunt Sp. S. esse creatum.*

Reply to the Third Objection. That which proceeds by local movement must precede its procession since it is the subject thereof: but that which proceeds in the order of origin is the term of the procession. Hence if it be composed of matter and form and comes into being by generation, the matter precedes the procession as subject, while the form or even the composite follows logically the procession as term: as when fire proceeds from fire by generation. But when that which proceeds is not composite but a pure form; or again if it come into being by creation the term of which is the whole substance, then that which proceeds in no way precedes the procession but on the contrary: thus the creature is not conceived as existing before creation, nor brightness as preceding its emission from the sun, nor the Word as preceding his procession from the Father.

Reply to the Fourth Objection. In so far as procession may denote order of origin, a thing may proceed as self-subsistent and without relation to another thing: although by local movement a thing does not proceed so as to subsist in itself simply, but so as to be in a place. Such procession, however, is not in God.

Reply to the Fifth Objection. In intellectual substances which are the most noble creatures there is also procession according to the operations of the intellect and will: and in this respect the image of the Trinity is in them. In them, however, word and love are not subsistent persons, because their understanding and willing are not their substance, and this is proper to God: hence in God word and love proceed as subsistent Persons, but not in intellectual creatures.

Reply to the Sixth Objection. It would be derogatory to God's dignity to originate from something essentially diverse, for this is proper to the creature: but to originate from that which is consubstantial pertains to the divine perfection. For there would not be perfection in the Godhead unless its understanding and willing were actual: and this being the case we must acknowledge in God the procession of word and love.

Reply to the Seventh Objection. Although receiving does not in itself connote perfection, it does imply perfection on the part of the one from whom something is received : and especially in the divine Persons who receive the fulness of the Godhead.

Reply to the Eighth Objection. Seldom or never do the Latin doctors employ the word *cause* to indicate the origin of the divine Persons ; both because with us cause connotes effect, wherefore lest we be forced to say that the Son and Holy Ghost are made, we do not say that the Father is their cause ; and because with us the word *cause* signifies something essentially diverse, for we describe as a cause that whence something different follows ; and again because the pagan philosophers apply the word *cause* to God to denote his relation to creatures : for they say that God is the first cause and that creatures are caused by him. Hence lest anyone think that the Son and the Holy Ghost should be reckoned among creatures differing essentially from God, we avoid the word *cause* when we speak of God. On the other hand the Greeks employ the word *cause* more absolutely when speaking of God, and indicate origin only thereby : wherefore they apply the word *cause* to the divine Persons. For an expression may be objectionable in Latin whereas in Greek it is admissible on account of a peculiarity of idiom. And if in speaking of God we admit the use of the word *cause* in Greek it does not follow that it has the same sense as when applied to creatures, and as divided by philosophers into four kinds.

Reply to the Ninth Objection. Of all the terms relating to origin, the word *principle* is most appropriate to God. For since we are unable to comprehend the things of God it is better for us to indicate them by means of general terms which have an indefinite meaning, than to employ special words that have a definite signification. Wherefore the name *He who is* (Exod. iii, 13, 14) is said to be most appropriate, seeing that according to Damascene (*De Fide Orth.* i, 9) it signifies the *boundless sea of substance*. Now just as *cause* is a more general term than *element* which denotes something primary and simple in the genus of material cause, so is *principle* a more general term than *cause ;* thus the first part of movement or of a line is called a *principium* but not a *cause*. From this it is clear that a *principium* may be something that is not essentially distinct, as a point in relation to a line; whereas a cause cannot, especially if we speak of an originating, i.e. an efficient, cause. Now though the Father is called the *principium* of the Son and the Holy Ghost, it does not seem right to say without qualification that the Son or Holy Ghost is principiated, although the Greeks use the expression, which may be allowed to pass if understood aright. Nevertheless we must avoid using words that seem to imply subjection, lest they be attributed to the Son or the Holy Ghost and we fall into the error of the Arians. Thus Hilary (*De Trin.* vii) while granting that the Father is greater than the Son on account of his pre-eminence as origin, denies that the Son is less than the Father since he received equality of essence from him. Likewise we must not stress such terms as *subjection* and *principiation* in the Son, although we employ the words *authority* and *principium* in speaking of the Father.

Reply to the Tenth Objection. Although the word *principium* is derived from *priority*, it is employed to signify not priority but origin: even as the word *lapis* is not employed to denote the hurt done to the foot, although it is thought that this is its derivation. Thus although the Father is not prior to the Son he is his *principium*.

Reply to the Eleventh Objection. Not every *principium* is operative or productive: for in neither way is a point the *principium* of a line.

Reply to the Twelfth Objection. In the Son there is something common to the Father, namely the essence; and something whereby he is distinguished from the Father, namely the relation. Yet there is not composition, because the relation is really the essence, as we have explained in previous discussions (Q. viii, A. 2).

Reply to the Thirteenth Objection. The recipient before receiving is in need, since he receives in order to supply his need: but after receiving he no longer needs, since he has what he needed. If then there be something that does not exist before receiving, and is always in the state of having received, it is by no means in need. Now the Son receives not from the Father as though he previously lacked and afterwards received, but he receives his very being from the Father. Hence it does not follow that he is in need.

Reply to the Fourteenth Objection. The creature receives from God a certain existence which would not continue unless God preserved it : wherefore even after it has received existence, it needs the divine action to preserve it in being and consequently is of a needy nature. On the other hand the Son receives from the Father identically the same being and identically the same nature as that of the Father : wherefore he is not of a needy nature.

Reply to the Fifteenth Objection. The Son is considered in himself in reference to that which he has absolutely, and this is the essence of the Father : and in this respect he is not nothing, but one with the Father. And if we consider him in reference to the Father, we conceive him as receiving being from the Father : wherefore thus again he is not nothing. Consequently in no sense is the Son nothing. He would, however, be nothing considered in himself if there were anything absolute in him distinct from the Father, as is the case with creatures.

Reply to the Sixteenth Objection. The Son does indeed proceed that he may exist : but his procession is eternal (even as the procession of light from the sun is coeval with the sun) wherefore the Son also is eternal.

Reply to the Seventeenth Objection. Authority in the Father is nothing but the relation of principle. Now equality or inequality refer not to relation but to quantity, as Augustine says (*De Trin.* vi, 4 ; v, 6). Hence the Son is not unequal to the Father.

ARTICLE II

IS THERE BUT ONE PROCESSION IN GOD, OR ARE THERE MORE ?

Sum. Th. I, Q. xxvii, A. 3

THE second point of inquiry is whether there is only one procession in God, or more than one : and seemingly there is but one.

1. Boethius (*De Trin.*) says that in God procession is substantial. Now in God what is substantial is not multiplied. Therefore there are not several processions in God.

2. To this it will be replied that the processions in God do not differ in respect of the substance which is communicated by procession and by reason of which the processions are said to be substantial, but by themselves.—On the contrary whenever a number of things are distinct from one another, their difference is either one of matter, as, for instance, individuals of the same species, or of form, as for example things of different genus or species. Now the processions in God are not distinguished in the same way as things that differ in matter, since God is altogether immaterial. Wherefore it follows that all distinction in God is after the manner of a formal distinction. Now all formal distinction is by reason of some opposition, especially in things of the same genus: because a genus is divided by contrary differences which differentiate the species (*Metaph.* x). Accordingly if there be a distinction between the divine processions, this must be by reason of some opposition. But processions, actions and movements are not mutually opposed except by reason either of their principles or of their terms; as, for example, heating and chilling, ascent and descent. Therefore the divine processions cannot be distinguished by themselves: but if they be distinguished at all, this must be either on the part of the principle of the procession, or on the part of the term, i.e. the Person in whom the procession terminates.

3. Things that can exist side by side cannot constitute a difference (thus white and sweet do not differentiate two substances, since they can be together in the same subject): because the reason why one thing is distinct from another is that the one cannot be the other. Now that certain things cannot be together in the same subject is due to some kind of opposition: for things are said to be opposite when they cannot coexist in the same subject. Hence there can be no distinction without opposition: thus even when things differ by reason of matter, there is opposition in regard to situation, since such a division is one of quantity. If then

there cannot be opposite processions otherwise than by reason of the terms or principles, as stated above (*Obj.* 2), it is impossible that the processions be distinguished by themselves.

4. But it will be replied that the divine processions are distinguished in that one is by way of nature, i.e. the procession of the Son, and the other by way of will, i.e. the procession of the Holy Ghost.—On the contrary, that which proceeds naturally proceeds by way of nature : and the Holy Ghost proceeds from the Father naturally : for Athanasius says[1] that he is the natural Spirit of the Father. Therefore he proceeds by way of nature.

5. The will is free : and consequently that which proceeds by way of will proceeds by way of liberty. If then the Holy Ghost proceeds by way of will he must proceed by way of liberty. Now that which proceeds by way of liberty may or may not proceed, and may proceed in this or that degree, since what is done freely is not confined to this or that. Therefore the Father could produce the Holy Ghost or not, and could give him whatsoever degree of greatness he wished. Hence it follows that the Holy Ghost was a potential being and not an essentially necessary being, and thus he would not be of divine nature, which is the heresy of Macedonius.

6. Hilary (*De Synod.*) in assigning the difference between creatures and the Son, says that *the will of God gave all creatures their substance, while the Son received his substance from the Father by a natural birth.* Therefore if the Holy Ghost proceeds by way of will it follows that he proceeds in the same way as creatures.

7. In God nature and will differ but logically. If then the processions of the Son and the Holy Ghost differ in that one is by way of nature and the other by way of will, it follows that these processions differ but logically : and thus the Son and the Holy Ghost are not distinct Persons.

8. But it will be replied that the spirative and generative powers in the Father differ but logically, and yet there is a real distinction between the Son and the Holy Ghost : and

[1] Epist. *Contra eos qui Spiritum Sanctum dicunt creaturam.*

likewise nature and will can cause a real distinction in processions and proceeding persons, although they differ but logically.—On the contrary, the Son and the Holy Ghost are distinguished by things that are in them. But the generative power is not in the Son, nor is the spirative power in the Holy Ghost. Therefore the Son and the Holy Ghost are not distinguished by these things.

9. Generation which is procession by way of nature is proved to be in God by the fact that its likeness is communicated to the creature according to Isaiah lxvi, 9, *Shall I that give generation to others be barren?* But procession by way of will is not communicated to the creature, since nothing created receives its nature otherwise than by generation. Therefore in God there is no procession by way of will.

10. Mode adds somewhat to a thing and consequently induces composition, especially if there be a number of modes. Now in God there is utter simplicity: and consequently there are not a number of modes in him to justify one's saying that the Son has one mode of procession, i.e. the mode of nature, and the Holy Ghost another, i.e. the mode of the will.

11. In God will differs from nature no more than does the intellect. But there is not in God a procession by way of the intellect other than that by way of nature. Therefore neither is there another procession by way of the will besides that which is by way of nature.

12. It will be replied that the procession of the Holy Ghost differs from that of the Son in that the procession of the Son is solely from one who does not proceed, i.e. the Father, whereas the procession of the Holy Ghost is both from one who proceeds not and from one who proceeds, and simultaneously, namely from the Father and the Son.—On the contrary, if we allow that there are two processions in God, they must differ either numerically only, or specifically. If only numerically, it follows that both must be called generation or birth, and each of the proceeding Persons must be called a Son: and if they differ specifically, the nature communicated by the procession must differ

specifically : for thus the procession of a man and that of a horse from their respective principles differ specifically, whereas the procession of Socrates and that of Plato do not. Since then there is but one divine nature there cannot be several specifically different processions, although one is from one who proceeds and the other not.

13. The Son and the Holy Ghost are not distinct in the same way as creatures that differ specifically, for they are hypostases of one nature. Now processions whereby things proceed that are of the same species but are distinct numerically, do not themselves differ specifically, as, for instance, the generation of Socrates and the generation of Plato. Therefore the procession of the Son and that of the Holy Ghost are not specifically distinct processions.

14. Just as it is possible for one to proceed from one who proceeds so is it possible for one to be born of one who was born : for instance, A who is the son of B may himself have a son C. If then there are two processions in God through another Person proceeding from one who proceeds, there will likewise be two generations through another Person being begotten of one who is begotten.

15. If the procession of the Holy Ghost differs from the procession of the Son, in that the Holy Ghost proceeds from one who does not proceed and from one who does, i.e. from Father and Son, then either he proceeds from them inasmuch as they are one or inasmuch as they are several. If inasmuch as they are several it follows that the Holy Ghost is composite, since one simple thing cannot proceed otherwise than from one as principle : and if he proceeds from them inasmuch as they are one, it matters not whether he proceed from both or from one only. Consequently the procession of the Holy Ghost cannot differ from that of the Son by the fact that the Son proceeds from one only and the Holy Ghost from two.

16. Procession is condivided with paternity and filiation ; for these are called the three personal properties. Now in God there is but one paternity and one filiation. Therefore there is likewise but one procession.

17. In creatures there is but one kind of procession

whereby the nature is communicated, for which reason the Commentator (*Phys.* vii) says that animals generated by seed are not of the same species as those which are engendered by corrupt matter and without seed. Now the divine nature is one only. Therefore it cannot be communicated by more than one kind of procession. Therefore there are not several processions in God.

18. The Son proceeds from the Father as *brightness* according to Hebrews i, 3, *Who being the brightness of his glory*: and this because he proceeds from the Father as co-eternal with him, as brightness from the sun or fire. But the Holy Ghost likewise proceeds from the Father as co-eternal with him. Therefore he proceeds from him in the same way as the Son, and thus there are not several processions in God.

19. The eternal procession of the divine Person is the type and cause of the temporal procession of the creature and of whatsoever is in the creature. Hence Augustine (*Gen. ad lit.* ii, 6) expounds the words of Genesis i, *He spoke . . . and it was made,* thus: *He begot the Word in whom* (the creature) *was that it might be made.* Now the Son is the perfect type and cause of the creature's production. Therefore there is no need of another procession of a divine Person besides that of the Son.

20. The more perfect a nature the fewer the things through which it works. Now the divine nature is most perfect. Since then one created nature is communicated by only one kind of procession, neither can the divine nature be communicated by more than one kind of procession.

21. From one simple thing only one thing can proceed. Now the Father is one simple thing. Therefore there can be but one procession from him: and thus there are not several processions in God.

22. A thing is said to be generated inasmuch as it receives a form: since in creatures generation is change terminating in a form. Now the Holy Ghost by proceeding receives a form, i.e. the divine essence, of which it is said (Phil. ii, 6): *Who being in the form of God thought it not robbery to be equal with God.* Therefore the procession of the Holy Ghost is

generation ; and thus it differs not from the generation of the Son.

23. Nativity is the way to nature as the very word implies. Now the divine nature is communicated to the Holy Ghost through his procession. Therefore the procession of the Holy Ghost is nativity : thus it differs not from the procession of the Son, and consequently there are not two processions in God.

On the other hand it would seem that there are more than two processions in God.

1. There is a procession by way of nature in respect of which the Son is named, and a procession by way of intellect, in respect of which the Word is named, and a procession by way of will in respect of which the proceeding Love is named. Therefore there are three processions in God.

2. It will be replied that in God the procession by way of nature is one and the same as the procession by way of intellect : since the Son is the same Person as the Word.—On the contrary processions in creatures are a representation of the processions of the divine Persons ; wherefore it is said of God the Father that of him *all paternity in heaven and earth is named* (Eph. iii, 15). Now in creatures the procession of nature whereby man begets man is distinct from the processions of the intellect whereby it produces its word. Therefore neither in God is there a distinction between procession by way of intellect and procession by way of nature.

3. According to Dionysius (*Div. Nom.* iii) it belongs to the divine goodness that it proceed. Now the Father is supremely good. Therefore he proceeds. Hence in God there are three processions, one whereby the Father proceeds, another whereby the Son proceeds, and a third whereby the Holy Ghost proceeds.

On the contrary it would seem that in God there are but two processions. For Augustine says (*De Trin.* v) that the procession of the Son is *a begetting or nativity, the procession of the Holy Ghost is not a nativity, yet both are ineffable.* Therefore in God there are but two distinct processions.

I answer that the early doctors of the faith were compelled to discuss matters of faith on account of the insistence of heretics. Thus Arius thought that existence from another is incompatible with the divine nature, wherefore he maintained that the Son and the Holy Ghost, whom Holy Writ describes as being from another, are creatures. In order to refute this error the holy fathers had to show that it is not impossible for someone to proceed from God the Father and yet be consubstantial with him, inasmuch as he receives from him the same nature as the Father has. Since, however, the Son in that he receives from the Father the nature of the Father is said to be born or begotten of the Father; whereas the Holy Ghost is not said in the Scriptures to be born or begotten while he is said to be from God, Macedonius thought that the Holy Ghost is not consubstantial with the Father but his creature : for he did not believe it possible for anyone to receive from another the latter's nature unless he were born of him and were his son. Hence he thought that if the Holy Ghost receives from the Father the latter's nature and essence it must infallibly follow that he is begotten and a Son. Wherefore to refute this error it was necessary for our doctors to show that the divine nature can be communicated by a twofold procession, one being a begetting or nativity, and the other not : and this is the same as to seek the difference between the divine processions. Accordingly some have maintained that the processions in God are distinct by themselves. The reason for this view was because they held that the relations do not differentiate the divine hypostases but only manifest their distinction : for they thought relations in God were like individual properties in creatures, which properties do not cause but only manifest the distinction between individuals. They say then that in God the hypostases are distinct only by their origin. And seeing that those things whereby certain things are distinguished primarily must be distinguished by themselves—thus opposite differences, whereby species differ, differ by themselves, otherwise we should go on for ever—they maintain that the divine processions are distinct by themselves. But this cannot be true : because one thing is distinguished from another specifically by that which gives it its species, and numerically by that which gives it individuality. Now the difference between the divine processions must not be merely like that which distinguishes things numerically; it must be like that which differentiates things specifically, since one is generation and the other not. Consequently the divine processions are distinguished by that which gives them their species. But no procession, operation or movement has its species from itself, but from its term or principle. Hence it is futile to say that any processions are distinguished by themselves: and they must differ in relation either to their principles or to their terms.

Wherefore some said that in God the processions are distinguished in relation to their principles: inasmuch as one procession is by way of nature or intellect, and the other by way of will, since the terms intellect and will would seem to indicate principles of operations and processions. But if we consider the matter carefully we shall easily see that this does not suffice for the distinction of the divine Persons unless something else be added. For since that which proceeds must bear a resemblance to the principle of the procession, just as in creatures a likeness to the form of the generator must be in the thing generated; it follows—if processions in God are distinguished by the fact that the principle of one is the nature or intellect, while the principle of the other is the will—that in the Person proceeding by the one procession there will be something pertaining only to nature or intellect, and in the other something that pertains only to the will: which is evidently false. Because by the one procession, i.e. of the Son from the Father, the latter communicates to the Son all that he has, nature, intelligence, power and will, and whatsoever is attributed to him absolutely; wherefore as the Son is the Word, i.e. Wisdom Begotten, so may he be called Begotten Nature, Will, or Power Begotten, i.e. received by generation, or rather the recipient of these by generation. Hence it is plain that since all the essential attributes concur towards the one procession of the Son, the difference between the processions cannot be ascribed to the different concepts of the attributes; as though one attribute were communicated by one procession, and another attribute by another procession. Now whereas the term of a procession is to have (since a divine Person proceeds so as to have what he receives by proceeding), and whereas processions are distinguished by their terms, it follows of necessity that in God he who proceeds is distinguished in the same way as he who has. Now in God haver is not distinguished from haver by the fact that the one has these attributes, and the other has those; but by the fact that the one has the same things from the other. For the Son has all that the Father has: yet in this is he distinguished from the Father, that he has them from the Father. Accordingly one proceeding Person is distinguished from the other proceeding Person, not as though the one by proceeding receives some things, while the other receives other things, but because one of them receives from the other. Hence whatever is in a divine procession that can at once be conceived as being in one procession without any other procession being presupposed, belongs to one procession only: but there will be at once another procession if those same things that were received by the first procession are again received by another procession. Thus it is only the order of processions, which arises from their origin, that multiplies processions in God.

Hence not without reason some held that one procession being by way of intelligence and nature, and the other by way of will, the former procession does not presuppose another procession, whereas the latter does: because love of a thing cannot proceed from the will except on the presupposition that the conceived word of that thing has already proceeded: since good understood is the object of the will.

Reply to the First Objection. Procession in God is said to be substantial because it does not arise from an accident: nevertheless thereby the proceeding Person receives substance.

We grant the *Second and Third Objections.*

Reply to the Fourth Objection. There is nothing to prevent something proceeding from the will naturally. For the will naturally tends to the ultimate end, just as every other power naturally works to attain its object. Hence it is that man naturally desires happiness, and in like manner God naturally loves his own goodness, just as he naturally understands his own truth. Accordingly just as the Son as Word naturally proceeds from the Father, so the Holy Ghost naturally proceeds from him as Love. The Holy Ghost does not, however, proceed by way of nature, because in God to proceed by way of nature is to proceed in the same way as in creatures things are produced by nature and not by the will. Wherefore to be produced naturally and to be produced by way of nature differ inasmuch as a thing is said to be produced naturally on account of its natural connexion with its principle, whereas it is said to be produced by way of nature if it be produced by a principle in the same way as nature produces.

Reply to the Fifth Objection. As Augustine teaches (*De Civ. Dei*, v, 10) the natural necessity under which the will is said to will a thing of necessity—happiness, for instance—is not incompatible with free-will: but free-will is opposed to violence or compulsion. Now there is no violence or compulsion when a thing is moved in accordance with the order of its nature, but there is if its natural movement be hindered, as when a heavy body is prevented from moving down towards the centre. Hence the will naturally desires happiness, although it desires it necessarily: and thus also God by his will loves himself freely, although he loves himself of necessity. Moreover it is necessary that he love himself as much as he is good, even as he understands himself as much as he is.[1] Therefore the Holy Ghost proceeds from the Father freely, not however potentially but necessarily. Nor was it possible for him to proceed so as to be less than the Father: but it was necessary for him to be equal to the Father, even as the Son who is the Father's Word.

Reply to the Sixth Objection. The creature does not proceed naturally or necessarily from the divine will: for though God by his will naturally and necessarily loves his goodness, and the love thus proceeding is the Holy Ghost, yet neither

[1] See *Sum. Th.* I, Q. xiv, A. 3.

naturally nor necessarily does he will creatures to be produced, but gratuitously. For creatures are not the last end of the divine will, nor does God's goodness depend on them (which goodness is his last end), since it gains nothing from creatures : even so man of necessity desires happiness, but not the things ordained thereto.

Reply to the Seventh Objection. Although nature and will in God differ not in reality but logically, nevertheless he who proceeds by way of will must be distinct from him who proceeds by way of nature, and the one procession must differ from the other. For we have already stated that to proceed by way of nature means to proceed in the same way as that which proceeds from nature, and that to proceed by way of will means to proceed as that which proceeds from the will. Now the will does not proceed without a previous procession ; for it does tend to a thing without the previous procession of the intellect in forming its concept of that thing, since the good understood moves the will. Now the procession from a natural agent does not presuppose another procession unless accidentally, inasmuch as one natural agent depends on another natural agent : but this is not essential to nature *quâ* nature. Therefore in God this procession by way of nature is one that presupposes no other : while the procession by way of will has its beginning from a procession that is presupposed. Hence there must needs be procession from procession, and proceeding Person from a proceeding Person : and this causes a real distinction in God.

We grant the Eighth Objection.

Reply to the Ninth Objection. God has implanted in the creature a likeness to both processions. By the procession that is by way of nature it is possible in created things for the nature to be communicated, since the effect is like the agent as such : wherefore by an action whereof nature is the principle, the effect can receive the nature : whereas by an action whereof the will is the principle, the effect can receive the likeness of that alone which is in the will, for instance, a likeness of the end in view ; or of the form, as in the products of art. But whatsoever is in God is the divine nature : and consequently the nature must be communicated by either procession.

Reply to the Tenth Objection. When we speak of procession in God by way of nature or will, we do not ascribe to God a mode as though it were a quality added to the divine substance, but we indicate a comparative likeness between the divine processions and the processions to be observed in creatures.

Reply to the Eleventh Objection. In God there is no distinction between procession by way of intelligence and procession by way of nature : but there is a distinction between both of these and the procession by way of will : and this for three reasons.—First, because just as procession by way of nature does not presuppose another procession, so neither does procession by way of intelligence : whereas procession by way of will necessarily presupposes procession by way of intelligence.—Secondly, because just as nature produces something in likeness to itself, so also does the intellect both within and without : within, since the word is the likeness of the thing understood, and of the intellect understanding itself : without, as when the form understood is introduced into the product of art. On the other hand the will does not produce its likeness either within or without. Not within, since love which is the intimate procession of the will is not a likeness of the will or the thing willed, but a kind of impression made on the will by the thing willed,[1] or a kind of union between these two.[2] Nor without, because the will imprints on the artifact the form which in the logical order was understood before it was willed, wherefore it is a likeness first of the intellect, though secondly of the will.—Thirdly, because the procession of nature is from only one agent, if the agent be perfect. Nor does it matter that in animals one is generated of two, namely the father and mother ; since the father alone is agent in generation while the mother is patient. Likewise the procession of the intellect is from one only ; whereas friendship or mutual love proceeds from two loving each other.

[1] *Sum. Th.* I-II, Q. xxvi, A. 2, ad 3.
[2] *Ibid.*, Q. xxviii, A. 1.

Reply to the Twelfth Objection. Although strictly speaking genus and species, universal and particular, are not predicated of God, nevertheless as far as it is possible to compare God to creatures, the Father, Son and Holy Ghost are distinguished from one another like several individuals of one species, as Damascene says (*De Fide Orth.* iii, 4). It must be observed, however, that there are two ways of considering the species in a particular individual of the genus of substance: we may consider the species of its hypostasis, or we may consider the species of its individual property. Thus given that Socrates is white and Plato black, and granted that white and black are properties individualising Socrates and Plato, it will be true to say that Socrates and Plato are one in species, in which their hypostases are contained. For they agree in humanity, but differ in the species of their property; since white and black differ specifically. It is the same with the Father and the Son. For they are considered as one in the species of which their hypostases are supposits, in that they agree in the nature of the Godhead: but they differ in the species of a personal property: since paternity and filiation are relations of different species. It must also be observed that in creatures generation is *per se* directed to the species, for nature intends to generate a man; wherefore the specific nature is multiplied by generation in created things. But in God procession is directed to the multiplication of hypostases in which the divine nature is numerically one: wherefore in God the processions are quasi-specifically different by reason of the difference between the personal properties, although in the proceeding Persons there is one common nature.

This suffices for the *Replies to the Thirteenth and Fourteenth Objections.*

Reply to the Fifteenth Objection. The Holy Ghost proceeds from the Father and the Son as from two Persons if we consider the spirating supposits: because since the Holy Ghost is the mutual love and bond of two he must needs be spirated by two. But if we consider that whereby they spirate, thus he proceeds from them as one in the divine nature: since from none but God can God proceed.

Reply to the Sixteenth Objection. Procession as condivided with paternity and filiation is the personal property of the Holy Ghost: and although it is a relation, yet since it has not a special name as paternity and filiation have, it is indicated by the name procession, just as if filiation were unnamed, and signified under the name of nativity, which is the special name of the Son's procession. The procession of the Holy Ghost has no special name because, as already stated, in creatures a nature is not communicated in this way: and we transfer names from creatures in speaking of God. Hence it does not follow that in God there is but one common procession.

Reply to the Seventeenth Objection. In a creature which is susceptive of accidents there can be something in a thing besides its nature: but not in God. For this reason in God the nature is communicated by any mode of procession, but not in creatures: because although there are various processions in creatures, the nature is communicated in one way only.

Reply to the Eighteenth Objection. The procession of the Son is co-eternal with the Father inasmuch as it is a divine procession, wherefore this applies also to the procession of the Holy Ghost: but it does not apply to the procession of the Son as distinct from that of the Holy Ghost.

Reply to the Nineteenth Objection. The Son is a sufficient type of the temporal procession of the creature, if we consider him as Word and exemplar: but the Holy Ghost must needs be the type of that procession inasmuch as he is Love. For just as it is said (Wis. ix, 1) that God *made all things by his Word*, so is it stated (*ibid.* xi, 23) that he loves all things that are and hates none of the things which he has made: and Dionysius says (*Div. Nom.* iv) that *God's love did not permit him to be barren.*

Reply to the Twentieth Objection. Perfect nature is capable of many works although few things suffice it for each one.

Reply to the Twenty-first Objection. From the one Father alone there is only one procession, namely of the Son: but from the Father and Son together, there is another procession, that of the Holy Ghost.

Reply to the Twenty-second Objection. The procession of the Holy Ghost is a procession of love. Now by a procession of love nothing is produced as a recipient of the form or nature of that whence it proceeds : and consequently it is not a generation or nativity. That the Holy Ghost receives by his procession the nature and form of God the Father is owing to the fact that he is God's love, wherein there is nothing that is not the divine nature.

This suffices for the *Reply to the Twenty-third Objection.*

We must also reply to the arguments which concluded that there are more than two processions in God.

1. As stated above (replies to seventh and eleventh objections) in God it is but one and the same procession by way of intelligence and by way of nature.

2. Human nature is material, that is to say composed of matter and form : wherefore in man there cannot be procession by way of nature save in respect of a natural transmutation. But procession by way of intelligence is always immaterial, wherefore in man procession by way of nature and procession by way of intelligence cannot be one and the same, whereas in God it is one and the same because the divine nature is immaterial.

3. Procession *into* differs from procession *from.* To proceed *into* something is to communicate one's likeness to something, and in this sense Dionysius means that the divine goodness proceeds into creatures. To proceed *from* a thing is to receive one's being from another, and as in this sense we are speaking of procession now, it is clear that procession is not to be attributed to the Father.

ARTICLE III

OF THE ORDER BETWEEN PROCESSION AND RELATION IN GOD
Sum. Th. I, Q. xlii, A. 3.

THE third point of inquiry concerns the order between procession and relation in God : and it would seem that in God procession logically precedes relation.

1. The Master (I., D. 27) says that the Father is Father

from eternity because from eternity he begot the Son. Now *begot* indicates procession and *Father* indicates relation. Therefore logically procession precedes relation in God.

2. The Philosopher (*Metaph.* v) says that relations result from action or quantity. But it is plain that the divine relations do not arise from quantity: therefore in our way of thinking they arise from action. Now processions in the divine Persons are designated after the manner of divine actions. Therefore the divine processions logically precede the relations.

3. The absolute precedes the relative, even as unity precedes number. Now actions are more akin to the absolute than relations are. Therefore logically they precede.

4. A thing is said to be relative in relation to something else. Now there cannot be something else where there is no distinction. Therefore relation presupposes distinction. But in God distinction in the divine Persons is according to origin, inasmuch as one Person proceeds from another. Therefore in God the processions precede logically the relations.

5. Logically every procession precedes its term. Now filiation which is the relation of the Son is the term of nativity which is his procession. Therefore the Son's procession precedes filiation. But filiation and paternity not only in nature and time but also logically are simultaneous: because the one relative cannot be understood without the other. Therefore the Son's nativity and *a fortiori* generation which is the act of the Father logically precede paternity: and consequently the processions in God simply precede the relations logically.

On the contrary logically person precedes personal action. Now the divine relations constitute the Persons, while the processions are personal actions as it were. Therefore the relations precede the processions logically.

Again procession must needs be from one thing to another, for just as nothing brings itself into being according to Augustine (*De Trin.* i, 1) so nothing proceeds from itself: wherefore in God procession postulates distinction. But there is no distinction in God except by the relations. Therefore in God procession presupposes relation.

I answer that there is no order without distinction : hence where there is no real but only logical distinction there can be only a logical order. Now in God there is no real distinction except between the Persons and opposite relations : wherefore in God there is not real order except as regards the Persons between whom, according to Augustine (*Contra Maxim.* iv), *there is order of nature inasmuch as one is from another, not one before another.* Now in God processions and relations are not really but only logically distinct. Wherefore Augustine[1] says that it is proper to the Father to beget the Son : whereby he gives us to understand that to beget the Son is the personal property of the Father ; nor is there any other property besides paternity that is the personal property of the Father. Consequently we are not to look for real order but only for logical order between the divine processions and relations. Now just as in God relation and procession are in reality the same thing and do not differ except logically ; even so relation itself, although but one in reality is in our way of thinking manifold. For we consider relation as constituting the Person : and yet it does not do this *quâ* relation : which is clear from the fact that in man relations do not constitute persons, since relations are accidents, while person is something subsistent in the genus of substance ; and substance cannot be constituted by an accident. But in God relation constitutes a Person inasmuch as it is a divine relation : because it is identical with the divine essence, since in God there cannot be any accidents : wherefore relation being in reality the divine essence can constitute a divine hypostasis. Consequently the consideration of a relation as constituting a divine Person differs from the consideration of a relation *quâ* relation. Wherefore there is nothing to prevent relation from presupposing procession if we consider relation from the one point of view, whereas the contrary obtains if we consider it from the other point of view. Accordingly we conclude that if we consider relation as such it presupposes procession logically, whereas if we consider it as constituting a Person, the relation that constitutes the Person from whom there

[1] Fulgentius, *De Fide ad Petrum* ii.

is a procession precedes that procession logically: thus paternity as constituting the Person of the Father logically precedes generation. On the other hand the relation that constitutes the proceeding Person, even considered as constituting that Person, is logically posterior to the procession, as filiation is posterior to nativity: and this because the proceeding Person is considered as the term of the procession.

Reply to the First Objection. The Master is speaking of paternity considered as a relation: and the same answer applies to the *Second and Third Objections*.

Reply to the Fourth Objection. In things where relations are accidents relation must presuppose distinction: but in God the relations constitute three distinct Persons.

Reply to the Fifth Objection. If we consider paternity and filiation as relations the one cannot be understood without the other: and in this sense we say that relations follow the processions in the logical order.

The remaining two objections consider the relations as constituting the Persons.

ARTICLE IV

DOES THE HOLY GHOST PROCEED FROM THE SON?

Sum. Th. I, Q. xxxvi, A. 2: *C.G.* IV, xxiv, xxv

THE fourth point of inquiry is whether the Holy Ghost proceeds from the Son: and it would seem that he does not.

1. Dionysius (*Div. Nom.* iii) says that *the Son and the Holy Ghost are as it were flowers of the God-bearing divinity*. Now flower does not proceed from flower. Therefore the Holy Ghost is not from the Son.

2. If the Son is the principle of the Holy Ghost he has this either from himself or from another. He has it not from himself, since it belongs to the Son, as Son, to be from another rather than to be a principle. And if he has this from the Father he must needs be a principle in the same way as the Father. But the Father is a principle by generation. Therefore the Son must be the principle of the

Holy Ghost by generation, and thus the Holy Ghost will be the Son of the Son.

3. Whatsoever is common to the Father and the Son belongs to each in the same way. If then it is common to the Father and Son to be a principle, the Son will be a principle in the same way as the Father: and since the Father is a principle by generation the Son will be so also: and thus the same conclusion follows as above.

4. The Son is Son because he proceeds from the Father and is his Word. Now the Holy Ghost is the word of the Son, according to Basil *(Contra Eunom.* v), who gathers this from the statement of the Apostle (Heb. i, 3) that the Son *upholds all things by the word of his power.* Therefore if the Holy Ghost proceeds from the Son he must be the Son of the Son.

5. Although in reality paternity and filiation are in God before being in us, according to the saying of the Apostle (Eph. iii, 15): *Of whom,* i.e. God the Father, *all paternity in heaven and earth is named:* yet as regards the use of the terms they were transferred from human things to divine. Now among men the offspring of a son is a grandson: so that if the Holy Ghost proceeds from the Son he will be the Father's grandson, which is absurd.

6. The property of the Son consists in his receiving: for he is called Son because he receives the Father's nature by generation. If then the Son sends forth the Holy Ghost from himself there will be two contrary properties in the Son, which is inadmissible.

7. Whatsoever is in God is either common or proper. Now the emission of the Holy Ghost is not common to all the Trinity, since it does not apply to the Holy Ghost. Therefore it is proper to the Father and does not apply to the Son.

8. Augustine proves *(De Trin.* vi) that the Holy Ghost is love. Now the Father's love of the Son is gratuitous, since he loves the Son not as though he received something from him but only as giving him something: whereas the Son's love of the Father is a love that is due; because he loves the Father in that he receives from him. Now the love

which is due is distinct from the love that is gratuitous. Hence if the Holy Ghost is love proceeding from the Father and Son it follows that he is distinct from himself.

9. The Holy Ghost is gratuitous love : wherefore from him flow the diversities of graces according to 1 Cor. xii, 4 : *There are diversities of graces, but the same spirit.* If then the Son's love of the Father is not gratuitous, the Holy Ghost will not be the Son's love, and thus he does not proceed from him.

10. If the Holy Ghost proceeds from the Son as love, since the Son loves the Father as the Father loves the Son, it will follow that the Holy Ghost proceeds from the Son to the Father just as he proceeds from the Father to the Son. But this is apparently impossible : for it would follow that the Father receives from the Son, which is utterly inadmissible.

11. As the Father and Son love each other, so also do the Son and the Holy Ghost, or the Father and the Holy Ghost. If then the Holy Ghost proceeds from Father and Son because Father and Son love each other, in like manner because Father and Holy Ghost love each other, the Holy Ghost proceeds from himself : and this is impossible.

12. Dionysius (*Div. Nom.* i) says : *We must not dare to say or even think anything concerning the supersubstantial and hidden Godhead except what has been divinely revealed to us by the sacred oracles.* Now Scripture does not assert that the Holy Ghost proceeds from the Son, but only that he proceeds from the Father, according to Jo. xv, 26 : *When the Paraclete cometh whom I will send you from the Father, the Spirit of truth, who proceedeth from the Father.* Therefore we must neither say nor think that the Holy Ghost proceeds from the Son.

13. In the Acts of the Council of Ephesus it is stated that after the reading of the Creed of the Council of Nicæa the holy synod decreed that *no one might profess, write or devise any other faith other than that which was defined by the holy fathers assembled at Nicæa together with the Holy Ghost, and whosoever shall either presume to devise or teach or suggest another faith to such pagans, Jews or heretics as are desirous*

of being converted to a knowledge of the truth, let them be deprived of their bishopric if they be bishops, and banished from the clergy if they be clerks : if they be laymen let them be excommunicated. In like terms the Council of Chalcedon, after setting forth the decisions of other councils, continues : *Whosoever shall dare to devise another faith, or pronounce, teach or deliver another Creed to pagans, Jews or heretics wishing to be converted, such, if they be bishops or clerks, shall be deprived of their sees in the case of bishops, and unfrocked if they be clerks ; and if they be monks or laymen they shall be excommunicated.*

Now in the definitions of the foregoing councils it is not stated that the Holy Ghost proceeds from the Son, but only that he proceeds from the Father. Moreover we read in the profession of faith of the Council of Constantinople : *We believe in the Holy Ghost, Lord and Lifegiver, who proceedeth from the Father ; with the Father and Son to be adored and glorified.* Therefore by no means should it have been added in the Creed that the Holy Ghost proceeds from the Son.

14. If it be asserted that the Holy Ghost proceeds from the Son, this statement is made either on the authority of Scripture or on account of some proof. But seemingly Scripture nowhere affords sufficient authority for this statement. It is true that Holy Writ speaks of the Holy Ghost as being of the Son, thus (Gal. iv, 6) it is said : *God sent the Spirit of his Son into your hearts,* and (Rom. viii, 9) : *If any man have not the Spirit of Christ, he is none of his.* Again we read that the Holy Ghost was sent by the Son ; thus Christ said (Jo. xvi, 7) : *For if I go not, the Paraclete will not come to you, but if I go, I will send him to you.* Now it does not follow that the Holy Ghost proceeds from the Son, from the fact that he is the Spirit of the Son, because according to the Philosopher the genitive case has many significations. Again it does not follow from the fact that the Holy Ghost is stated to be sent by the Son ; since although the Son does not proceed from the Holy Ghost, he is said to be sent by the Holy Ghost, according to the words (Isa. xlviii, 16) spoken in Christ's person : *And now*

the Lord God and his Spirit hath sent me, and (Isa. lxi, 1) : *The Spirit of the Lord is upon me . . . he hath sent me to preach to the meek :* which words Christ declared to have been fulfilled in himself.[1] Furthermore the statement cannot be upheld by any satisfactory argument. Thus even if the Holy Ghost did not proceed from the Son they would still remain distinct from each other, since they differ by their personal properties. Nothing therefore compels us to say that the Holy Ghost proceeds from the Son.

15. Whatsoever proceeds from another derives something from that other. If then the Holy Ghost proceeds from two, namely the Father and the Son, it follows that he receives from two, and thus apparently that he is composite.

16. It is essential to a principle that it derive not from another, according to the Philosopher (*Phys.* i, 6). Now the Son proceeds from another, namely the Father. Therefore the Son is not a principle of the Holy Ghost.

17. The will moves the intellect to its act, since a man understands when he wills. But the Holy Ghost proceeds by way of will as love : and the Son proceeds by way of intellect as word. Therefore seemingly the Holy Ghost does not proceed from the Son but contrariwise.

18. Nothing proceeds from that wherein it abides. Now the Holy Ghost proceeds from the Father and abides in the Son, as stated in the Acts of the Blessed Andrew.[2] Therefore the Holy Ghost does not proceed from the Son.

19. A simple thing cannot proceed from two, since then the effect would be more simple than and prior to the cause. But the Holy Ghost is simple. Therefore he does not proceed from two, namely the Father and the Son.

20. If a thing proceeds perfectly from one it is superfluous for it to proceed from two. Now the Holy Ghost proceeds perfectly from the Father. Therefore it would be superfluous for him to proceed from the Father and Son together.

21. As the Father and the Son are one in substance and nature, so also are the Father and the Holy Ghost. Now the Holy Ghost does not concur with the Father in the

---
[1] Luke iv, 18.
[2] For the text of the Acts see *Sum. Th.* I, Q. xxxvi, A. 2, obj. 4.

generation of the Son. Neither therefore does the Son concur with the Father in sending forth the Holy Ghost.

22. As Dionysius expresses it (*Coelest. Hier.* 1) the Son is the ray of the Father. Now the Holy Ghost is brightness: and brightness does not issue from the ray. Therefore neither does the Holy Ghost proceed from the Son.

23. The Son is a kind of light of the Father, since he is his word : and the Holy Ghost is like heat, for he is love : wherefore he appeared over the Apostles under the form of fire (Acts xi). But heat does not come from light. Neither then does the Holy Ghost proceed from the Son.

24. Damascene (*De Fide Orth.* i) says that the Holy Ghost is said to be of the Son but not from the Son.

On the contrary Athanasius says (*Symb.*) : *The Holy Ghost is from the Father and the Son ; not made, nor created, but proceeding.*

Again, the Holy Ghost is said to the third Person in the Trinity, the Son the second, the Father the first. Now the number three proceeds from unity through the number two. Therefore the Holy Ghost proceeds from the Father through the Son.

Again, since there is supreme agreement between the divine Persons, each of them is immediately akin with the others. But this would not be the case if the Holy Ghost were not from the Son, for then the Son and the Holy Ghost would not be immediately akin with each other, but only through the Father, inasmuch as both are from one. Therefore the Holy Ghost is from the Son.

Again, the divine Persons are not distinct from one another otherwise than according to origin : so that if the Holy Ghost were not from the Son he would not be distinguished from him ; which is inadmissible.

I answer that according to what has already been concluded it is necessary that the Holy Ghost proceed from the Son. For since the Son and the Holy Ghost are two Persons the procession of one must be distinct from the procession of the other. Now it has been proved (A. 2) that there cannot be two processions in God except by reason of order between processions, namely that there be a second procession from one who proceeds. It follows then of necessity that the Holy Ghost must be from the Son.

Besides this argument, however, there are other reasons which prove that the Holy Ghost is from the Son. All differences between any two things must arise from the original root of their distinction (except in the case of an accidental difference, as that between one who walks and one who sits) and this because whatsoever is in a thing *per se*, is either essential to it or results from its essential principles, and these things are the original root of distinction between things. In God, however, nothing can be accidental: because whatsoever is in a thing accidentally, since it is outside the nature of that thing, must come to it from some external cause, and this cannot be said of God. Accordingly any difference between the divine Persons must follow from the original root of their distinction. Now the original root of the distinction between the Father and the Son is paternity and filiation. Wherefore any difference between the Father and the Son must follow from the fact that this one is the Father and that one the Son. But it does not belong to the Father as Father by reason of paternity to be the principle of the Holy Ghost, since thus he is related to the Son only, and it would follow that the Holy Ghost is the Son. In like manner this is not repugnant to the notion of filiation, since filiation implies relation to none but the Father. Consequently the difference between the Father and the Son cannot arise from the fact that the Father is the principle of the Holy Ghost and the Son not.

Again, as stated in *De Synod.*, it is proper to the creature that God produced it by his will: and Hilary proves this from the fact that the creature is not as God is but as God wills it to be. Now because the Son is as the Father it is said that the Father begot him naturally. For the same reason the Holy Ghost is from the Father naturally because he is like and equal to the Father, since nature produces its like. Now the creature which proceeds from the Father according to his will must also proceed from the Son, since the Father and the Son have the same will. Likewise they both have the same nature. Consequently as the

THE DIVINE PERSONS

Holy Ghost is from the Father so also must he be from the Son. And yet it does not follow that the Son or the Holy Ghost is from the Holy Ghost, although he also has the same nature with the Father (whereas it does follow that the creature is from him inasmuch as he also has the same will with the Father) on account of the absurdity that would follow if one were to say that the Holy Ghost proceeds from himself, or that the Son, who is his principle, proceeds from him.

The same conclusion may be proved in yet another way. No distinction is possible between the divine Persons except according to the relations, since in God whatsoever is ascribed absolutely signifies the essence and is common, such as goodness, wisdom and so forth. But diverse relations cannot cause distinction except by reason of their opposition: since one and the same thing can have diverse relations to the same thing. Thus A may stand to B in the relation of son, disciple, equal or any other relation that does not imply opposition. Now it is plain that the Son is distinguished from the Father in that he stands in a certain relation to him, and likewise the Holy Ghost is distinguished from the Father by reason of a relation. Wherefore, their relations, however diverse they may appear to be by no means distinguish the Holy Ghost from the Son unless they be opposed to each other. But there can be no opposition in God other than that which is by reason of origin, in that one Person is from another. Therefore the Son and the Holy Ghost can by no means be distinguished from each other simply because each is differently related to the Father, unless one of them be related to the other as proceeding from him. Now it is evident that the Son does not proceed from the Holy Ghost, since the notion of son consists in being related to father by receiving existence from him. It remains then of necessity that the Holy Ghost is from the Son.

Since, however, someone might say that articles of faith should be confirmed not only by reasons but also by authorities, it remains for us to show by the authority of Holy Writ, that the Holy Ghost proceeds from the Son. In several passages of Scripture the Holy Ghost is mentioned as (the Spirit) of the Son. Thus (Rom. viii, 9) *He that hath not the Spirit of Christ is none of his;* (Gal. iv, 6) *God hath sent the Spirit of his Son into your hearts*; and (Acts xvi, 7) *They attempted to go into Bithynia, and the Spirit of Jesus suffered them not.* For we cannot take this as meaning that the Holy Ghost is the Spirit of Christ as to his humanity, filling him as it were, because the Holy Ghost is the Spirit of a man as haver and not giver : whereas the Holy Ghost is the Spirit of the Son as giver, according to 1 Jo. iv, 13, *In this we know that we abide in him and he in us, because he hath given us of his Spirit :* and (Acts v, 32) it is said that *God hath given his Spirit to them that obey him.* Accordingly the Holy Ghost must be called the Spirit of the Son inasmuch as he is a divine Person. Either then he is said to be *his* absolutely, or *his* as his spirit. If absolutely, then the Son must exercise authority over the Holy Ghost. Thus with us one may be said to be another's in a restricted sense, as, for instance, *Peter is John's companion,* but we cannot say that *Peter is John's* absolutely, unless there be some kind of possession, thus a slave as to all that he is is his master's. Now in God there is no slavery or subjection, and authority in him is only in respect of origin. Consequently the Holy Ghost must originate from the Son. The same conclusion follows if it be said that the Holy Ghost is the Son's as his spirit : because Spirit as a personal name, implies the relation of origin to the Spirator, as the Son to the Begetter.

Moreover we find it stated in the Scriptures that the Son sends the Holy Ghost, as stated above. For the sender apparently always exercises authority over the one sent. Now as already stated authority in God is only in respect of origin. Hence it follows that the Holy Ghost originates from the Son. Now we have it from Holy Writ that by the Holy Ghost we are conformed to the Son, according to Rom. viii, 15, *You have received the Spirit of adoption of sons;* and Gal. iv, 6, *Because you are sons God hath sent the Spirit of his Son into your hearts.* But nothing is conformed to a thing except in its proper characteristics.

And in creatures that which conforms A to B is from B, thus the seed of man produces the like not of a horse but of a man whence it is. Now the Holy Ghost is from the Son as his proper characteristic, wherefore it is said of Christ (2 Cor. i, 22): *Who hath sealed us and given the pledge of the Spirit in our hearts.* More explicit still are the words spoken by Christ of the Holy Ghost (Jo. xvi, 14): *He shall glorify me because he shall receive of mine.* Now it is plain that the Holy Ghost does not receive from the Son as though he had not before, since thus he would be of a changeable and indigent nature. It is evident then that he received from the Son from eternity; nor could he receive anything that was not his from eternity. Therefore the Holy Ghost received the essence from the Son. The reason why the Holy Ghost received from the Son, is stated by the Son himself when he says (*ibid.* 15): *All things whatsoever the Father hath are mine : therefore I said that he shall receive of mine :* as though to say : ' Since mine and the Father's is the same essence, the Holy Ghost cannot have the same essence as the Father without having mine.'

Holy Scripture also states that the Son works through the Spirit: for instance (Rom. xv, 18, 19): *Which,* i.e. miracles and other blessings, *Christ worketh by me,* says the Apostle, *in . . . the Holy Ghost,* i.e. through the Holy Ghost: and (Heb. ix, 14) it is stated that Christ *offered himself by the Holy Ghost.* Now whenever one person is said to work through another, either it is he who gives active power to the one through whom he works, as a king is said to work through a provost or bailiff, or contrariwise as when the bailiff is said to work by virtue of the king. Accordingly if the Son works through the Holy Ghost, either the Holy Ghost gives operative power to the Son, or the Son to the Holy Ghost : and consequently one gives the essence to the other, since the operative power in each is not distinct from the essence. Now it is plain that the Holy Ghost does not give the essence to the Son, since the Son is Son of none but the Father. It follows therefore that the Holy Ghost is from the Son.

Yet another argument in support of the same conclusion

may be taken from the points acknowledged by the Greeks. They believe that the Holy Ghost is from the Father through the Son, and that the Father spirates the Holy Ghost through the Son. Now that through which a thing is produced is always a principle thereof. Wherefore it follows that the Son is a principle of the Holy Ghost. If, however, they refuse to acknowledge that the Holy Ghost is from the Son because the Son is from another and consequently is not the first root of the Holy Ghost's origin, it is plain that this motive is unreasonable : since no one declines to allow that the stone is moved by the stick, although the stick is moved by the hand : or that Jacob was of Isaac, although Isaac was of Abraham. In fact in the point at issue still less reason is there for this refusal : since Father and Son have one and the same productive power, which is not the case in created movements and agents. Therefore just as we must acknowledge that creatures are from the Son though the Son is from the Father, even so must we acknowledge that the Holy Ghost is from the Son, though the Son is from the Father. It is evident then that those who assert that the Holy Ghost is from the Father through the Son, but not from the Son, know not what they are talking about, as Aristotle said of Anaxagoras : and it is written : *Desiring to be teachers of the law, understanding neither the things they say nor whereof they affirm* (1 Tim. i, 7).

Reply to the First Objection. The Son and the Holy Ghost are said to be flowers of the *Godbearing*, i.e. paternal *Divinity*, inasmuch as both are from the Father. But inasmuch as the Holy Ghost is from the Son, the Son may be called the root and the Holy Ghost the flower : for comparisons with corporeal things must not be extended to all things in God.

Reply to the Second Objection. The Son has this from the Father that of himself he sends forth the Holy Ghost : wherefore it belongs to him in the same way as to the Father. Now the Father is the principle of a divine Person not in one way only, but in two ways, namely by generation and spiration. Wherefore we cannot conclude that the Son is the principle of the Holy Ghost by generation : this is a fallacy of the consequent, and so much the more so, seeing that the Father is not the principle of the Holy Ghost by generation.

The same answer *applies to the Third Objection.*

Reply to the Fourth Objection. The Holy Ghost cannot be called the Word strictly speaking, but in a loose manner of speaking, for as much as anything that makes a thing known is the word of that thing. Thus the Holy Ghost makes the Son known as stated by this same Son concerning the Holy Ghost (Jo. xvi, 14): *He shall glorify me because he will receive of mine.* But the Son is called the Word in the strict sense, because he is the concept of the divine Intellect.

Reply to the Fifth Objection. In a human genealogy a grandson is one who proceeds from the son in the same way as the son from his father : whereas in God the Holy Ghost does not proceed from the Son in the same way as the Son from the Father : hence the objection fails.

Reply to the Sixth Objection. There is no opposition between being a principle and being from a principle except in respect of the same thing ; thus A cannot be a principle of B if B is a principle of A. Hence it does not follow that there are contrary properties in the Son if he proceeds from the Father as his principle and is himself the principle of the Holy Ghost.

Reply to the Seventh Objection. Whatsoever is in God is indeed either proper or common. *Proper,* however, admits of a twofold application : it is said simply and absolutely of a thing to which it applies exclusively, thus risibility is proper to man : and it is said of a thing not simply but relatively, as, for instance, one might say that rationality is proper to a man in relation to a horse, although it applies to another, viz. an angel. Accordingly in God there is something common that applies to the three Persons, for instance ' to be God ' and so forth : something that is proper simply and applies to one Person only : and something that is proper relatively, as, for instance, to spirate the Holy Ghost is proper to the Father and the Son with respect to the Holy Ghost : since we must needs acknowledge this kind of property in God even if the Holy Ghost were not from the Son, because ' to be from another ' still remains proper to the Son and Holy Ghost as compared with the Father.

Reply to the Eighth Objection. If we are to come to a right decision on this point it seems hardly correct to speak of anything being due in the divine Persons, since this word *due* implies subjection and obligation of a kind, and such things cannot be in God. Richard of St Victor, however (*De Trin.* iii, 3 ; v. 17, 18), distinguishes between due and gratuitous love : but by gratuitous love he means love not received from another, and by due love, that which is received from another. In this sense there is nothing to hinder the same love from being gratuitous as the Father's, and due as the Son's : since it is the same love whereby the Father loves and whereby the Son loves : yet this love the Son has from the Father, but the Father from none.

Reply to the Ninth Objection. The Holy Ghost is gratuitous love, only inasmuch as it is opposed to mercenary love whereby a thing is loved not for itself but for the sake of some benefit extrinsic to it. But if by gratuitous love we understand the love that originates from another, it is not incompatible with the Holy Ghost that he be gratuitous love, since the love whereby we love God through the Holy Ghost originates in God's benefits bestowed on us: and thus nothing prevents even the love of the Son who derives this love from another, from being the Holy Ghost.

Reply to the Tenth Objection. The Holy Ghost proceeds both from the Father to the Son and from the Son to the Father, not as recipients but as objects of love. For the Holy Ghost is said to proceed from the Father to the Son inasmuch as he is the love whereby the Father loves the Son ; and in the same way it may be said that the Holy Ghost proceeds from the son to the Father inasmuch as he is the love whereby the Son loves the Father. He may be understood, however, to proceed from the Father to the Son inasmuch as the Son receives from the Father the power to spirate the Holy Ghost, and in this sense he cannot be said to proceed from the Son to the Father, seeing that the Father receives nothing from the Son.

Reply to the Eleventh Objection. This word *love* signifies not only the outpouring of love, but also a certain affection or disposition according to love. Now in God whatsoever is significative of outpouring must be taken as referring to the Person only, as, for instance, begetting, spirating and so forth : while terms that do not denote outpouring but pertain rather to the information of the subject whereof they are predicated, must be taken as referring to the essence, as, for instance, being good, intelligent, and the like. For this reason the Holy Ghost is said to love not as emitting love—for thus it applies to the Father and the Son—but for as much as *to love* is an essential property in God.

Reply to the Twelfth Objection. In Holy Writ it must be regarded as a constant rule that what is said of the Father must be understood as applicable to the Son, and what is said of both or either of them must be taken as applicable to the Holy Ghost, even though the expression should contain an exclusive term, except when reference is made to the distinction between the divine Persons. Take, for instance, the following : *This is eternal life that they know thee the only true God, and Jesus Christ whom thou hast sent* (Jo. xvii, 3) : for it cannot be denied that the Son is true God, although the Son himself affirms this of the Father alone, because since the Father and Son are one thing though not one Person, it follows that what is said of the Father must be understood of the Son also. Nor again may we deny (seeing that no mention is made there of the Holy Ghost) that eternal life is in knowing the Holy Ghost, since there is but one knowledge of the Three. In like manner we are not to deny that the Holy Ghost knows the Father and the Son, although it is said (Mt. xi, 27) : *No one knoweth the Son but the Father, neither doth any one know the Father but the Son.* Wherefore since to have the Holy Ghost proceeding from oneself does not enter into the notion of Paternity or Filiation whereby the Father and the Son are distinguished from each other, it follows that from the very fact that it is said in the Gospel that the Holy Ghost proceeds from the Father we must gather that he proceeds from the Son.

Reply to the Thirteenth Objection. The doctrine of the Catholic Faith was sufficiently laid down by the Council of Nicæa : wherefore in the subsequent councils the fathers had no mind to make any additions. Yet on account of the heresies that arose they were at pains to declare explicitly what had already been implicitly asserted. Thus in the definition of the Council of Chalcedon it is said : *This holy, great and universal synod teaches this doctrine which has been constantly held from the beginning, the same which* 318 *holy fathers assembled at Nicæa defined to be the unalterable faith. On account of those who contend against the Holy Ghost, we confirm the doctrine delivered afterwards by the* 150 *fathers assembled at Constantinople concerning the substance of the Holy Ghost, which doctrine they made known to all, not indeed as though something were lacking in previous definitions, but by appealing to the authority of the Scriptures to explain what had already been defined against those who endeavoured to belittle the Holy Ghost.* Accordingly we must acknowledge that the procession of the Holy Ghost from the Son was contained implicitly in the definition of the Council of Constantinople inasmuch as it is declared there that he proceeds from the Father : because what is said of the Father must be understood to be true of the Son, since they differ in nothing except in that one Person is the Son and another the Father. However, on account of errors arising of those who denied that the Holy Ghost proceeds from the Son, it was becoming that in the Creed should be made an insertion not by way of addition but by way of explicit interpretation of what it already contained implicitly. Thus were a heresy to arise denying the Holy Ghost to be the Maker of heaven and earth, it would be necessary to mention this explicitly, since in the Creed this is attested explicitly of the Father only. Now just as a subsequent Council has the power to interpret the Creed of a previous Council, and to insert an explanation of what that Creed contains, as appears from what has been said above ; even so the Roman Pontiff can do this of his own authority, since by his authority alone can a council be convoked, and by him are its decisions confirmed, and since from the Council appeals can be made to him : all of which is clear from the Acts of the Council of Chalcedon. Nor does such an explanation require the assembling of an ecumenical council, since sometimes this is impossible on account of war : thus we read of the sixth Council[1] that the Emperor Constantine found that he was prevented by the imminence of war from summoning all the bishops together : and yet those who met decided certain doubtful points of faith in accordance with the mind of Pope Agatho, to wit that in Christ there are two wills and two operations. In like manner the fathers assembled in the Council of Chalcedon adopted the view of Pope Leo who defined that after the Incarnation there were two natures in Christ.

We must observe, however, that we may gather from the definitions of the principal councils that the Holy Ghost proceeds from the Son. Thus as stated in its decree the Council of Chalcedon received the synodal letters of the Blessed Cyril, bishop of Alexandria, addressed to Nestorius and others in the East. In one of these we read : *Seeing that Christ in proof of his Godhead used his Spirit to perform great works, asserted that he was glorified by him, even as a man might say of his own strength, knowledge or any other gift that they glorify him : even so is this true of the subsistent Spirit considered as a distinct Person from the Son ; although he is not of a different nature, for he is called and is the Spirit of truth and flows from him, as also from God the Father.* It does not signify that he says *flows* and not *proceeds*, because as we have already clearly stated this word *proceed* is the most general of all the terms denoting origin. Wherefore anything that is emitted or flows forth or in any way originates may be said for this very reason to proceed. Again in the definition of the fifth Council held at Constantinople it is said : *In all things we follow the holy doctors of the Church, Athanasius, Hilary, Basil, Gregory the Theologian, Gregory of Nyssa, Ambrose, Augustine, Theophilus, John of Constantinople, Leo Cyril Proclus, and we receive all that they have taught in the true faith for the refutation of heretics.* Now it is plain that many of these taught that the Holy Ghost proceeds from the Son, and that this has not been denied

[1] Third Council of Constantinople, A.D. 680–1.

by any one of them. Wherefore it is not contrary to but in harmony with the Councils to say that the Holy Ghost proceeds from the Son.

Reply to the Fourteenth Objection. It is true that the genitive case of the personal pronoun has many significations, but in God it has no other signification than that of origin. As regards mission it must be observed that all doctors are agreed that no Person is sent who does not proceed from another : wherefore it is altogether inappropriate to the Father to be sent since he proceeds not from another. But as regards the Person sending doctors are divided in opinion. Athanasius (in his epistle against those who said that the Holy Ghost is a creature : and beginning *Literae tui sanctissimi*) and others say that no Person is sent temporally save by the Person from whom he proceeds eternally : thus the Son is sent temporally by the Father from whom he proceeds eternally : and in accordance with this view it may be inferred without fear of error that if the Holy Ghost is sent by the Son, he proceeds from him eternally. And if the Son is said to be sent by the Holy Ghost this must be understood in reference to the Son in his human nature being sent to preach by the Holy Ghost. Wherefore it is said explicitly (Isa. lxi, 1) : *He hath sent me to preach to the meek !*[1] This is the interpretation given by Ambrose (*De Spir. Sanct.* iii, 1) : but Hilary (*De Trin.* viii) expounds the words as referring to the Father inasmuch as in God the word spirit may be taken essentially. On the other hand Augustine (*De Trin. et Unit.* x) holds that a Person who proceeds may be sent temporally even by one from whom he does not proceed eternally. For since the mission of a divine Person is understood in reference to some effect in creatures who proceed from the whole Trinity, the Person sent is sent by the whole Trinity : so that mission does not imply authority of the sender over the Person sent, but causality in reference to the effect, and with regard to this effect the Person is said to be sent.

The argument proving that the Holy Ghost proceeds from

---

[1] The full text is : *The Spirit of the Lord is upon me . . . he hath sent me*, etc.

the Son because they are distinct from each other is not refuted by saying that they are distinct by their properties, since these properties are relative and cannot cause distinction unless they be mutually opposed, as already stated (Q. viii, AA. 3, 4).

Reply to the Fifteenth Objection. Although the Holy Ghost proceeds from two he is not composite : because those two, namely the Father and the Son, are one in essence.

Reply to the Sixteenth Objection. The Philosopher (*Phys.* 1) says that principles derive from nothing else in so far as they are first principles : and the First Principle (so to say) is a Principle proceeding from no other, and that is the Father.

Reply to the Seventeenth Objection. Although the will moves the intellect to the act of understanding, it cannot will but what is already understood : wherefore since it is impossible to go on indefinitely, one must come at length to an act whereby the intellect understands something naturally and not at the will's command. Now the Son proceeds from the Father naturally, so that although he proceeds by way of intelligence, it does not follow that he proceeds from the Holy Ghost but vice versa.

Reply to the Eighteenth Objection. The Holy Ghost may be said to abide in the Son in three ways. In one way in respect of the human nature, according to Isaiah xi, 1 : *There shall come forth a rod out of the root of Jesse, and a flower shall rise up out of his root, and the Spirit of the Lord shall rest upon him.* In another way the Holy Ghost is said to rest in the Son, since the spirative power is given to the Son by the Father and extends no further. Thirdly, according as love is said to rest in the beloved, thereby staying the emotion of the lover. In none of these ways is the procession of the Holy Ghost excluded from the Son.

Reply to the Nineteenth Objection. It is not incompatible with the simplicity of the Holy Ghost that he proceeds from two, namely the Father and the Son, inasmuch they are of one essence.

Reply to the Twentieth Objection. The same perfection is that of Father and Son : wherefore the fact that the Holy

Ghost proceeds from the Father perfectly does not exclude his proceeding from the Son : else it would follow that the creature is not created by the Son, since it is created perfectly by the Father.

Reply to the Twenty-first Objection. Unity of essence does not involve confusion of Persons : wherefore from unity of essence we cannot draw conclusions that are incompatible with relative distinction : thus from the fact that Father and Son are one thing, we cannot infer that the Son proceeds from the Holy Ghost although he proceeds from the Father, because the Holy Ghost proceeds from him : and again because it would follow that the Holy Ghost is the Father, seeing that to be the Father is nothing but to have the Son proceeding from him.

Reply to the Twenty-second Objection. Brightness comes indeed from the ray, since it is nothing else than the reflection of light shining on a clear body. Moreover brightness is attributed to the Son (Heb. i, 3), *Who being the brightness of glory.*

Reply to the Twenty-third Objection. Heat proceeds from brightness : for the heavenly bodies by their rays cause heat in the lower world.

Reply to the Twenty-fourth Objection. It was the contention of the Nestorians that the Holy Ghost does not proceed from the Son : hence in one of their synods condemned by the Council of Ephesus it is said thus : *We hold that the Holy Ghost neither is the Son nor receives his essence from the Son.* For this reason Cyril in the epistle already quoted, affirmed against Nestorius that the Holy Ghost proceeds from the Son. Again Theodore in an epistle to John of Antioch expresses himself as follows : *The Holy Ghost does not come from the Son nor has he his substance from the Son, but he proceeds from the Father : he is called the Spirit of the Son because he is consubstantial with him.* Now the above words were attributed by this Theodore to Cyril, as though he had written them in a letter which he wrote to John of Antioch, and yet they are not to be found there : but he expresses himself thus : *The Spirit of God the Father proceeds indeed from him, but he proceeds also from the Son, being one with him in essence.* Later on Damascene followed this opinion of Theodore, although the latter theologian's teaching was condemned in the fifth Council. Wherefore in this we must not agree with Damascene.

ARTICLE V

WOULD THE HOLY GHOST STILL BE DISTINGUISHED FROM THE SON IF HE DID NOT PROCEED FROM HIM?

THE fifth point of inquiry is whether the Holy Ghost would still be distinguished from the Son if he did not proceed from him : and seemingly he would.

1. Richard of S. Victor (*De Trin.* iv, 13, 15) says that the Persons differ in origin in that one has an origin and the other not : or if they have an origin, in that the origin of the one differs from the origin of the other. Now the origin of the Holy Ghost differs from that of the Son, since the Holy Ghost proceeds as spirated, but the Son as begotten. Therefore the Holy Ghost would differ personally from the Son even if he did not proceed from him, on account of the difference of origin.

2. Anselm says (*De Process. Sp. S.* ii) : *The Son and the Holy Ghost have their being from the Father, but each in a different way ; one by birth, the other by procession, so that thus they are distinct from each other*, and afterwards he adds : *For even if for no other reason were the Son and Holy Ghost distinct, this alone would distinguish them.* Therefore even if the Holy Ghost did not proceed from the Son, he would be a distinct Person from the Son on account of the different manner of origin.

3. The divine Persons are distinct from one another for the reason that one is from another according to a particular manner of origin. Now in God one Person proceeds according to one manner of origin : and consequently if there be two manners of origin there will be two proceeding Persons, even though one proceed not from the other. Now it is agreed that the Son and the Holy Ghost proceed from the Father according to different ways of origin. Therefore the

Son and the Holy Ghost are distinct Persons even if we suppose that one does not proceed from the other.

4. No hypostasis can possibly proceed in respect of one nature by more than one procession, since a hypostasis receives its nature by proceeding: thus the Son has two nativities corresponding to his two natures. Now in God there are two processions, one in respect of nativity, the other in respect of spiration. Consequently it is impossible that one and the same Person proceed according to these two modes of procession. Therefore the Persons who proceed by these two processions must needs be distinct. Therefore the Holy Ghost would still be personally distinct from the Son even if he did not proceed from him.

5. The eternal relations in God are neither accidental nor assistant,[1] but are subsistent Persons. Consequently whatever causes plurality of relations in God suffices for a distinction of Persons. Now specific diversity of actions suffices for a diversity of relations. Thus from the action of governing follows the relation of Lordship, while from the action of begetting follows another relation which is Paternity. Even so different relations follow from specifically different quantities: thus the relation *double* results from the number *two* and *treble* from the number *three*. Now in God processions are indicated as actions: wherefore if there are two processions there must be two relations resulting from the processions and consequently two Persons: so that we come to the same conclusion as before.

6. Procession is more perfect in God than in creatures: therefore the Apostle says (Eph. iii, 15) that of the heavenly Father *all paternity in heaven and earth is named*. Now in creatures procession suffices to distinguish the proceeding supposits: thus distinct men are born by distinct processions or births. Therefore in God a difference of procession suffices to distinguish the divine Persons, namely the Son and the Holy Ghost.

7. Procession by way of nature is not the same as procession by way of love. Now the name *Son* designates a Person proceeding by way of nature, while the name Holy

---

[1] See above, Q. viii, A. 1.

Ghost indicates a Person proceeding by way of love. Therefore even if the Holy Ghost did not proceed from the Son he would be distinct from him for the sole reason that their processions are different.

8. In the Father there are active generation and active spiration. Now generation and spiration distinguish the Persons in God. Therefore as the Son proceeds from the Father as a distinct Person by the fact that he is begotten of the Father; even so the Holy Ghost by the fact that he is spirated by the Father proceeds, as a distinct Person, from the Father. Thus then there are three Persons in God even if the Holy Ghost proceed not from the Son.

9. Anselm (*De Process. Sp. S.*) says that the Holy Ghost is as perfectly from the Father as from the Father and the Son. Now he proceeds from the Father and the Son as distinct from both. Therefore he would still be distinct from both even if he proceeded from the Father alone.

10. The Father is an adequate and perfect principle. Now the perfect principle of a thing needs not another in order to produce perfectly that whereof it is the principle. Consequently the Father needs not the Son in order to produce a third Person, namely the Holy Ghost. Therefore granted that the Holy Ghost does not proceed from the Son, there would still be three distinct Persons in God.

11. The removal of that which follows does not of necessity involve the removal of what proceeds: thus if we remove *man* we do not thereby remove *animal*. Now three things are predicated of the divine Persons, to wit procession, communion and kinship. The notion of procession precedes the notion of community as also the notion of kinship. But there would be neither communion nor kinship in God without plurality of Persons multiplied by procession. Consequently if we remove communion and kinship from God procession still remains. Hence even if there were not community of Father and Son in spirating the Holy Ghost, nor kinship of the Holy Ghost to the Son resulting from his proceeding from him: there would still remain procession of the Holy Ghost from the Father, and

thus there would still be three distinct Persons, namely two proceeding and one from whom they proceed.

12. We speak of properties, relations and notions as being in God. Now property logically precedes relation or notion, since the Persons are first understood as constituted with their personal properties and afterwards as related to one another and beknown. Moreover apart from the relations the properties still remain which constitute the Persons. Therefore even if the Holy Ghost were not related to the Son as having existence from him, the Son and Holy Ghost would still be distinct Persons by reason of their properties.

13. Filiation is the property of the Son constituting his Person : and procession is the property of the Holy Ghost constituting his Person. But Filiation is not procession nor is it opposed thereto relatively. Therefore even if we entirely remove relation of the Holy Ghost to the Son, the Son and Holy Ghost will still be distinct Persons.

14. Many, the Greeks for instance, have denied that the Holy Ghost proceeds from the Son, and yet acknowledged three Persons in God. Therefore even if the Holy Ghost did not proceed from the Son, he would still be distinct from him.

15. Damascene (*De Fide Orth.* i, 11) says : *We assert that the Holy Ghost proceeds from the Father but not from the Son : but we call him the Spirit of the Son.* Consequently even if he proceed not from the Son he is still the Spirit of the Son and therefore distinct from him.

16. The Greek saints in speaking of the Son and Holy Ghost in comparison with the material world, say that they are like two rays of the Father's splendour ; as two streams of the Godhead that is in the Father ; and as two flowers of the Father's nature. Now rays, streams and flowers are mutually distinct even if one does not proceed from the other. Therefore the Son and the Holy Ghost are in like manner distinct from each other.

On the contrary, Boethius (*De Trin.* vi) says that in God *relation alone multiplies the Trinity.* But if the Holy Ghost proceed not from the Son there will not be a relation of the Holy Ghost to the Son. Therefore he would not be personally distinct from him.

Again, Anselm (*De Process. Sp. S.* ii) says that *the Father and Son are in every respect one except in so far as they are distinguished by relative opposition:* and this by reason of the unity of essence. Now the Son and Holy Ghost are likewise one in essence. Therefore they are one in every respect, except in those things wherein relative opposition makes them distinct. But if the Holy Ghost proceed not from the Son they would nowise be distinct by reason of relative opposition: and consequently they would in no way be distinct from each other.

Again, Richard of S. Victor (*De Trin.* v, 14) says that in the Trinity there can be but one Person who proceeds from only one. Now if the Holy Ghost be not from the Son: then like the Son he will be from one Person only, namely the Father: and consequently the Son and Holy Ghost will be but one Person.

Again (*ibid.*) he says that in God there can be but one Person from whom no other Person proceeds. But if the Holy Ghost proceed not from the Son, just as he has no Person proceeding from him, so neither has the Son: and thus the Son and the Holy Ghost will be only one Person.

Again, wherever persons are distinguished by relations the persons thus distinct must be related to each other. Now in God the Persons are distinguished by relations: since they cannot be distinguished by anything absolute. Therefore in God there is no distinction where there is no relation. But if the Holy Ghost proceed not from the Son he is not related to him: and consequently is not personally distinct from him.

Again, of two opposites the one does not differentiate its subject otherwise than from the subject of the other: thus whiteness does not differentiate a thing except from that which is black. Therefore a relation does not distinguish its subject except from the subject of the opposite relation. Now the relation proper to the Holy Ghost and whereby he is a distinct Person is procession. Consequently he is not personally distinct save from the Person in whom is the opposite relation which is active spiration: and this is not in the Son unless the Holy Ghost proceeds from him. Therefore if the Holy Ghost be not from the Son, he is not personally distinct from him.

Again, in God two things belong in common to relation, *one from whom another is* and *one who is from another*. Now *he from whom another is* is not personally distinct by reason of a different mode of origin, since from the same person of the Father is the Son by generation, and the Holy Ghost by procession. Neither then is he who is from another by spiration (i.e. the Holy Ghost) distinct from him who is from another by generation (i.e. from the Son).

Again, Richard (*De Trin.* vi) states the difference between the two processions of the Son and of the Holy Ghost in the following terms: *Communion of majesty, so to speak, was the cause of the one's origin,* namely the Son's; *communion of love was the cause of the other's origin,* namely the Holy Ghost's. Now the procession of the Holy Ghost would not be caused by communion of love, unless the Father and the Son loved each other, and thus the Holy Ghost would proceed from them. Therefore if the Holy Ghost proceeded not from the Son there would be no difference between the procession of the Holy Ghost and the generation of the Son, and consequently neither would the Holy Ghost be personally distinct from the Son.

I answer that if we take careful note of the statements of the Greeks we shall find that they differ from us in words rather than in thought. Thus they will not grant that the Holy Ghost proceeds from the Son, either through ignorance, obstinacy or sophistry or some other cause, no matter what, and yet they acknowledge that the Holy Ghost is the Spirit of the Son, and that he is of the Father through the Son, which would not be true if the procession of the Holy Ghost were entirely independent of the Son. Hence we may infer that even the Greeks themselves understand that the procession of the Holy Ghost has some connection with the Son. But I say that if the Holy Ghost be not from the Son, and if the Son be in no way a principle of the Holy Ghost's procession, then it is impossible that the Holy Ghost be a distinct Person from the Son, and further that the procession of the Holy Ghost cannot possibly differ from the generation of the Son.

This will be evident if we consider those things in reference to which various writers explain the distinction between the divine Persons. Thus some refer the distinction of the Persons to the relations; others, to the mode of origin; others, to the essential attributes. If then we consider the manner of distinguishing the Persons by the relations, it is evident that the Holy Ghost cannot be personally distinct from the Son if he does not proceed from him. First, because things cannot be properly distinct from one another otherwise than either by reason of matter, i.e. by a difference of quantity, or by reason of form. Now distinction in respect of material and quantitative division is to be found in corporeal things wherein there are several individuals of the same species by reason of the specific form being in various parts of matter according as it is divided quantitatively: wherefore if there be an individual consisting of all the matter wherein the specific form can be, there cannot be more than one individual of that species, as Aristotle proves (*De Cœlo et Mundo* i). Now this kind of distinction is utterly foreign to God, seeing that in him there is neither matter nor corporeal quantity. Things that have a common, and at least generic, nature, cannot be distinct from one another by reason of a difference of forms except on account of some kind of opposition. Hence we find that the differences of any genus are in opposition to one another: and consequently it is impossible and even inconceivable that there be any distinction save one of opposition in the divine nature, seeing that it is one not only in genus but also in number. Wherefore since the divine Persons are distinct from one another, this must be on account of a relative opposition, in that no other opposition is possible in God. This is sufficiently evident, since no matter how much certain things may differ in definition, for instance the essential attributes, they do not distinguish the Persons, since they are not mutually opposed to one another. Thus again several notions are to be found in one divine Person, for the reason that they are not opposed to one another: for instance, in the

Father there are innascibility, paternity and active spiration. For there do we first find distinction where first there is relative opposition : for instance, in this that there are Father and Son. Accordingly in God where there is no relative opposition there can be no real distinction and this is a distinction of Persons. Now if the Holy Ghost does not proceed from the Son, there will be no opposition between them and the Holy Ghost will not be a distinct Person from the Son. Nor can it be said that for this distinction opposition of affirmation and negation is enough : because this kind of opposition follows and does not cause distinction, since that which already exists is distinct from another by something inherent either substantial or accidental : whereas that *this* is not *that*, is a result of their being distinct. Likewise it is evident that the truth of a negative statement about things in existence is based on the truth of a positive statement : thus the truth of this negation, *An African is not white* is based on the truth of this affirmation, *An African is black :* wherefore all differences in respect of affirmation and negation must be reducible to a difference of positive opposition. Consequently the primary reason for the distinction between the Son and Holy Ghost cannot be that the one is begotten and not spirated, the other spirated and not begotten, unless we presuppose the distinction between begetting and spirating and between Son and Holy Ghost by reason of an opposition between two affirmations.

Secondly, because according to Augustine (*De Trin.* vi, 2) whatsoever is said of God absolutely is common to the three Persons. Whence it follows that distinction between the divine Persons can only be in respect of what is said relatively : for these two predicaments are applicable to God. Now the primary relative distinction to be found in God is that between *one from whom is another* and *one who is from another*. And if one of these must be subdivided, namely *one that is from another*, it must be subdivided by something that belongs to it *per se*. For as the Philosopher teaches (*Metaph.* viii) it is against the rules of subdivision to subdivide a thing in reference to that which is accidental to it and does not belong to it *per se :* thus, if one were to say animals are divided into rational and irrational, and irrational animals are divided into white and black, the division would not be right, because since things that are accidental do not combine to make that which is simply one, the ultimate species resulting from many differences would not be one simply. Accordingly, if in God *he who is from another* be distinguished or subdivided, this must be in reference to differences *per se*, namely that one of those who is from another be from the other : and this involves a difference of processions, which is indicated when we say that one proceeds by generation, the other by spiration. Hence Richard of S. Victor (*De Trin.* v, 10) distinguishes the Person proceeding from another thus—one who has another proceeding from him and one who has not.

Thirdly, because whereas in the Father there are two relations, paternity and active spiration, paternity alone constitutes the Person of the Father : wherefore it is said to be a personal property or relation : while active spiration, being adventitious, so to speak, to the already constituted Person, is the relation of a Person but not a personal relation. Hence it is plain that active generation or paternity, in the logical order, precedes active spiration. Consequently in like manner filiation which corresponds to paternity as its opposite must in some order be presupposed to passive spiration which is the procession of the Holy Ghost : and this must mean—either that passive spiration is understood as supervening to filiation in the same Person, just as active spiration supervenes to paternity, and thus the same Person will be spirated and begotten just as the same Person begets and spirates—or that there is some other order between filiation and passive spiration. But there is no order in God other than that of nature, in respect of which one is from another, as Augustine says (*De Trin. et Unit.* xiii). It follows then that either the Son and the Holy Ghost are one Person, or the Holy Ghost is from the Son.

We shall come to the same conclusion if we consider the distinction of the divine Persons in reference to their origin, but not to their relations of origin. This is evident for the following reasons. First, if we consider a property of the divine nature, we shall see how impossible it is that there be distinction between the divine Persons unless one originate from another, and that the fact that two originate from one does not cause a personal distinction. This is made plain if we observe how various things are distinguished from one another. In the material world where, as stated above, it is possible for things to be multiplied by a division of matter and quantity, two individuals of the same species can be on an equal footing, thus two quantitative parts may be equal: but where the primary difference is one of form it is impossible for two individuals to be on a par with each other. For as the Philosopher says (*Metaph.* viii) forms are like numbers in which the species vary by the addition or subtraction of unity: and formal differences consist in a certain order of perfection. Thus the species of the plant differs from that of the stone in that it has life in addition: and the species of the dumb animal from that of the plant in that it has sensation, and the species of man from that of the dumb animal in that reason is added to it. Wherefore in immaterial things which cannot be multiplied by a division of matter, there cannot be plurality without some kind of order. Thus in created immaterial substances there is order of perfection according as one angel is in nature more perfect than another. And as some philosophers thought that every imperfect nature is created by a more perfect one, they therefore contended that in separate substances there cannot be multiplication otherwise than by reason of cause and effect. The true Faith, however, does not hold this, since we believe that the various orders of immaterial substances were produced according to the disposition of divine wisdom. Now whereas in God there cannot be order of perfection, as the Arians contended, saying that the Father is greater than the Son, and each of them greater than the Holy Ghost, we must conclude that plurality in the divine Persons cannot even be conceived otherwise than according to the sole order of origin: so that, to wit, the Son be from the Father, and the Holy Ghost from the Son. For if the Holy Ghost were not from the Son, they would be equally referred to the Father in point of origin: wherefore either they would not be two Persons, or there would be order of perfection between them as the Arians pretended, or there would be a distinction of matter between them : which is impossible. Hilary follows this line of argument (*De Synod.*) when he says that to assert that in God there are two who are unbegotten, i.e. who do not derive existence from another, is to posit two Gods : since if multiplication be not by the order of origin, it must be by the order of nature : so that the same argument avails if we do not acknowledge order of origin between the Son and Holy Ghost.

Secondly, because that which proceeds naturally from one must itself be one : since nature is always confined to one effect : whereas things which proceed from the operation of the will may be many, although they proceed from one : thus from one God a diversity of creatures proceeded according to his will. Now it is certain that the Son proceeds from the Father naturally, and not through his will as the Arians maintained : and this because, as Hilary says (*De Synod.*), *that which proceeds from its source naturally is of the same nature as its source, but that which proceeds according to the direction of a will, is not of the same nature as he from whom it proceeds, but such as he wishes it to be.* Now the Son is of the same nature as the Father : while creatures are such as God wished them to be. Hence the Son is from the Father naturally, and creatures proceed from him according to his will. In like manner the Holy Ghost is of the same nature as the Father, for he is not a creature as Arius and Macedonius asserted. Wherefore he must proceed from the Father naturally : for which reason he is said by Athanasius and other holy men to be the natural spirit of the Father and the Son. Consequently it is impossible that the Son and Holy Ghost proceed from the Father except in suchwise that from the Father alone one alone, i.e. the Son, proceeds, and from the Father and Son inasmuch as they are one the one Holy Ghost proceeds.

Thirdly, because as Richard (*De Trin.* v, 9) proves, there cannot be an indirect procession in God. Because since each divine Person dwells in the other, each must be ordered immediately to the other. But if the Son and Holy Ghost were from the Father without the Holy Ghost being from the Son, there would not be immediate order between the Son and the Holy Ghost, since they would not be ordered to each other except through the one from whom they proceed; like two brothers begotten of the same father. Hence it is impossible that the Son and the Holy Ghost proceed from the Father as distinct Persons, unless one proceed from the other.

Again, if we consider the distinction of the Persons in reference to the essential attributes we shall come to the same conclusion. First, because in this respect we say that the Son proceeds by way of the nature, and the Holy Ghost by way of the will: and the procession of nature is the source and origin of every other kind of procession, for whatsoever things have their being through art and the will or the intellect, proceed from things that are according to nature. Hence Richard (*De Trin*. vi, 17) says that without doubt of all modes of procession the first and chief place belongs to the way in which the Son proceeds from the Father: since unless the Father had preceded neither of the other Persons would have had any foundation for his existence. Secondly, this is evident if we realise that the Son proceeds by an intellectual procession as the Word, and the Holy Ghost by a procession of the will as Love. For it is both impossible and inconceivable that an object can be loved that has not first been understood by the intellect, wherefore in the intellectual nature all love proceeds from a word. Thirdly, it is evident, if we say with Athanasius that the Holy Ghost is *the life-giving breath of the Godhead*. Because all vital movement and action is directed by an intelligence, unless the contrary occur on account of an imperfection of nature. Hence from all that has been said we infer that the Holy Ghost would not be a distinct Person from the Son if he proceeded not from him, nor would spiration be distinct from generation.

Reply to the First Objection. The Holy Ghost is personally distinct from the Son in that the origin of the one differs from the origin of the other: but this very difference **of** origin is due to the Son being from the Father alone, whereas the Holy Ghost is from both the Father and the Son. Richard of S. Victor makes this plain when he says (*De Trin.* v, 20): *Observe that this difference of properties consists merely in the number of persons producing, in that the first has being from no other, the second from one only, the third from two.*

Reply to the Second Objection. Anselm is quite correct in saying that the Son and the Holy Ghost are distinct from each other by this alone that they proceed in different ways: but as we have already shown, they cannot proceed in different ways unless the Holy Ghost proceed from the Son: wherefore if it be denied that the Holy Ghost is from the Son, it must likewise be denied that he is distinct from the Son. However, it is Anselm's intention (in his work on the Procession of the Holy Ghost) first to indicate the points in which we agree with those who deny that the Holy Ghost proceeds from the Son and yet assert that he is a distinct Person from him. Wherefore the words quoted from Anselm are in the nature of an argumentative hypothesis rather than a statement of the truth.

Reply to the Third Objection. If there are two modes of origin in God it is right to infer that there are two Persons who proceed: but as we have shown there cannot be two modes of origin except by reason of the Holy Ghost proceeding from the Son.

The same answer applies to the *Fourth Objection.*

Reply to the Fifth Objection. There need not be as many subsistent Persons in God as there are relations: since in the one Person of the Father there are two relations, namely paternity whereby he is referred to the Son, and common spiration whereby he is referred to the Holy Ghost. For the relation of paternity constitutes a subsistent person; whereas the relation of common spiration is not a property constituting a Person, but a relation inherent to a subsistent Person. Thus if two relations result from generation and procession it does not follow that therefore there are only two subsistent Persons: since one might reply that there are not two processions unless one of the proceeding Persons proceed from the other, as we have already stated.

From this may be gathered the *Reply to the Sixth Objection*.

Reply to the Seventh Objection. As already explained, that which proceeds as love must proceed from that which proceeds by way of nature.

Reply to the Eighth Objection. Spiration distinguishes the Holy Ghost from the Spirator, just as generation distinguishes the Begotten from the Begetter : but it does not follow that the Spirated is distinct from the Begotten, since both Spirator and Begetter are the same Person. Nor does it follow from the fact that the same thing can proceed by two processions, that processions in God cannot differ except by reason of one proceeding Person being from another, as proved above (A. 4).

Reply to the Ninth Objection. The Holy Ghost proceeds from the Father as perfectly as from the Father and Son : yet he is distinct from the Son, not because he proceeds from the Father, but because he proceeds from the Son.

Reply to the Tenth Objection. The Father is the sufficient principle of the Holy Ghost, nor does he need another principle for the Holy Ghost's spiration : because in spirating the Holy Ghost the Son is not a distinct principle from the Father, but is one principle with him.

Reply to the Eleventh Objection. Although procession is logically prior to communion, as communion is to property : nevertheless in this particular kind of procession, namely that of the Holy Ghost who proceeds as love, communion and kinship of Father and Son is not logically prior to communion : wherefore it does not follow that if we remove communion procession remains : thus animal is prior to man logically, whereas rational animal is not.

Reply to the Twelfth Objection. In God property, relation and notion are one and the same in reality : except that there are but three properties, to wit paternity, filiation and procession, while there are four relations, common spiration being added to the three aforesaid relations, since it is a relation but not a property, inasmuch as it belongs not to one Person but to two. The notions are five in number, since they include innascibility which is not a relation but a notion, inasmuch as by it the Father is known : besides which it is a property since it belongs to the Father alone, but not a personal property, since it does not constitute the Person of the Father. Accordingly there can be no real order between the properties, relations and notions since the same thing is identified with all three. But if we consider their order in the light of their respective definitions, then notion precedes relation logically in the same way as one thing is prior to another from our point of view : while relation and property precede in the order of real priority. If, however, we seek the order between relation and property, we can find no such order in creatures : because some properties are relations, but not all, and in like manner some relations are properties, but not all. If, however, we consider property in something absolute, then property precedes in the order whereby the absolute precedes the relative. In the divine Persons relation precedes property logically : because as the property is that which belongs to one alone, property logically presupposes distinction : and in God nothing is distinct otherwise than by reason of a relation. Wherefore relation which is the principle of distinction in God is logically prior to property. It must be observed, however, that neither property nor relation as such are defined as constituting a Person. Because since a Person is an individual substance of rational nature, that which is outside substance cannot constitute a Person : wherefore in created things properties and relations are not constituent of, but are incidental to the persons already constituted : whereas in God the relation itself which is also a property is the divine essence : so that by this very fact that which is constituted thereby is a Person : inasmuch as unless paternity were the divine essence, the name *Father* could by no means signify a Person, but only a relative accident of a Person, as in the case of human persons. Hence paternity inasmuch as it is the divine essence constitutes a hypostasis subsisting in the divine nature ; inasmuch as it is a relation it distinguishes ; inasmuch as it is a property it belongs to one Person only, and not to another ; inasmuch as it is a notion it is the principle whereby that Person is known. Accordingly in the logical order, the first is that which constitutes the

Person, the second is that which distinguishes it, the third is the property, and the fourth is the notion.

Reply to the Thirteenth Objection. Although filiation is not opposed relatively to procession, nevertheless the Person proceeding is opposed relatively to the Son ; and this is the reason why procession is distinguished from filiation.

Reply to the Fourteenth Objection. Though the Greeks do not acknowledge that the Holy Ghost proceeds from the Son, they believe that the Son in some way is the principle whence the Holy Ghost originates. This is plain from the fact that they state that the Holy Ghost proceeds from the Father through the Son, and that he is the Spirit of the Son. And yet a statement may imply a contradiction, whereas one who is ignorant may grant it explicitly : and thus an unintelligent person might say that the Holy Ghost does not proceed from the Son and yet is distinct from the Son.

Reply to the Fifteenth Objection. By acknowledging that the Holy Ghost is the Spirit of the Son Damascene implies that in some way the Holy Ghost originates from the Son.

Reply to the Sixteenth Objection. The Holy Ghost and the Son are said to be two streams inasmuch as both proceed from the Father. Yet the Greek doctors say that the Son is the fount of the Holy Ghost, but that the Holy Ghost does not proceed from him. The same applies to the other comparisons.

THE END